THE
ANTIOCH REVIEW
ANTHOLOGY

THE
ANTIOCH
REVIEW
ANTHOLOGY

Essays, fiction, poetry, and

reviews from

The Antioch Review.

Edited by PAUL BIXLER

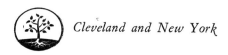 *Cleveland and New York*

THE WORLD PUBLISHING COMPANY

Library of Congress Catalog Card Number: 53-6635

FIRST EDITION

HC 1053

CONTENTS

MEN AND MACHINES

POETRY

REVIEWS

INTRODUCTION

At the time the first issue of *The Antioch Review* appeared, in March, 1941, the outlook for democracy was the darkest it had been for a hundred years. In the preceding twelvemonth, Hitler, with Poland already in his grasp, had accepted the gift of Norway from his quislings, had overrun Holland and Belgium, had knocked out France. Britain stood alone. On the continent of Europe, almost no island of democracy survived above ground.

Listening to the play-by-play account of Nazi conquest as reproduced over the radio, Americans looked to their weapons and re-examined their traditional ideas of democracy, of liberalism, of the values of Western civilization. The pages of journals of opinion rang with denunciation and self-criticism. Hitler could be right; democracy could be decadent. For such a state of affairs, according to one critic, much of the blame lay with the intellectuals on account of their "irresponsibility." Another berated liberals for surrendering in advance of conflict, for taking no steps because steps might be hazardous, and for pursuing an illusory perfection which in the end achieved only paralysis. Liberals, in summary, were "tired," and liberalism "corrupt." Among thoughtful men at this time there was a desperate reviewing of old errors and first efforts at a moral rearmament that had nothing to do with Frank Buchman.

In its first brief editorial, written by J. Donald Kingsley, then chairman of the Editorial Board (today UN chief of Korean reconstruction), *The Antioch Review* touched upon all these matters. It referred to the common man, to western values, to humanism. It called upon intellectuals to abandon their "objectivity" and get down to the problems at hand. It said, in short:

> *He who does not now speak out assists in the degradation of the democratic doctrine as surely as the outright exponent of totalitarianism . . .*
>
> *We believe in democracy so strongly that we think it should be enormously extended . . .*

We believe . . . in the application of scholarship to the solution of social problems . . . This is our purpose in founding a magazine.

These words still apply, and the parallel of their application is too plain for comfort. For today, quite as much as in 1941, democracy is under attack, this time from a totalitarian power fully as ruthless as Nazi Germany and for the long run probably far more powerful. Again, military force is necessary to check the enemy. But again, no victory is possible unless democracy is internationally deepened, extended and made more effective.

I would not suggest, of course, that the pattern of our publication is the same today as a decade ago. During the war years we emphasized political action and the extension of democracy by whatever means seemed most useful at the moment. In the postwar years we shifted our emphasis toward the long-term, more scholarly approach to the solution of social problems. In 1945 we introduced short fiction and a book review section, and three years later we began to publish an occasional poem. In twelve years we have become more flexible, less interested in complete unity and a self-contained program. But our aim is essentially the same.

We should have preferred to demonstrate continuity of editorial policy in the choice of material for this anthology. Our first impulse was to spread the selections with some evenness between the early and the later years. That plan, on examination, we had to reject: too many of the articles of the war years were dated by forgotten references, or simply by the passage of days and the disappearance of circumstance. We attempted, then, to make the collection representative of subject matter and of treatment. Here we were more successful. I note with a critical eye that the number of selections dealing with labor, foreign policy, and Soviet Russia do not represent the extent of the *Review*'s interest in these subjects as documented in its quarterly pages. (Since less than a twelfth of the available material could be included, something was bound to be slighted.) Yet the variety of the selected articles alone guarantees a certain representativeness.

We naturally sought also to choose the best. But what were to be the criteria? One measurement might have been the demands for reprint. There have been over three hundred reprintings of *Review* articles—almost as many reprintings as original articles—on requests from newspapers, magazines, the publishers of books, and the State Department. One of the articles included here, John Howard's "Democracy in City Planning," has been reprinted twenty-seven times. Yet two articles, reprinted and distributed in the greatest numbers, have been excluded from the anthology—were, in fact, never considered for inclusion. Reprinting history was only one criterion, and more important were the significance of the article's view, the depth and the quality of the author's treatment. The anthology stands (at least with one very heavy foot) upon our subjective judgment of these individual achievements.

The "we" and the "our" used above is no editorial convention. The original list of articles and short fiction was the result of the collective judgment of the Editorial Board, and later shifts, to give balance and to fit the space at our disposal, were accomplished with the Board's approval. The anthology, like the magazine, has been a co-operative enterprise. Members of the present Board are George R. Geiger; Louis Filler, Book Review Editor, who drew up the preliminary list of selections in poetry and reviews; Freeman Champney, Business Manager; Heinz Eulau (Book Review Editor, 1950-51); W. Boyd Alexander, Albert W. Liddle, Herman Schnurer, Albert B. Stewart, and Everett K. Wilson.

One further word needs to be said. *The Antioch Review* is sometimes thought, mistakenly, to be an official publication of Antioch College. Our editorial policy is independent of college policy although all editors are members of the faculty. It seems fitting, nevertheless, that this volume will appear as Antioch is celebrating its hundredth birthday. If there were a dedication, it would be to the officials of the college, administration and trustees, and to faculty and students for their considerable financial assistance over the years and for their steady interest.

PAUL BIXLER
Chairman of the Editorial Board

March 28, 1953

THE POLITICAL ANIMAL

WALTER LOCKE

George W. Norris, Independent

Nᴇʙʀᴀꜱᴋᴀ, when George W. Norris came up for Congress there, was a fief of the two chief railroads of the state. The Union Pacific and the Burlington divided the bi-partite state along the valley of the Platte. The north of the Platte senator was the property of the Union Pacific. The Burlington ruled the south. The McCook district, whence Norris went to Congress, was Burlington.

The Populists, combining with the Democrats under Bryan, were then contesting this railroad rule. The Republican party was still the agent of the railroad regime. Its delegates rode to the nominating conventions on free railroad passes. Each county seat had its politician, usually a lawyer, retained by the railroads to hold the county in line and see that only the right men went to the conventions and named the right candidates.

When Norris, in the '90's, became a district judge, we took for granted that he was a Burlington man or he could not be a judge. When, in 1902, Norris was elected to Congress, the assumption was the same. George W. Holdredge, general superintendent of the Burlington, must have approved him or he would not be a congressman.

Men in Nebraska newspaper offices, knowing their politics, put Norris in the Burlington pigeonhole and forgot him there. We knew without telling what his course in Congress would have to be. Whatever the Burlington and the interests allied with it, such as the grain and lumber "trusts" and the subsidized sugar industry required of him, he, a Republican from a Bur-

1

lington district, would have to do. He would do it or out of Congress he would promptly go.

We were long in discovering our mistake—and the Burlington's. The story of those years in the House and of the awakening of the Norris the nation later knew is familiar now. It was slow to reach us on his own western plains. Norris from the first was irked and disillusioned, as we later knew, by the ways of Congress under "King Caucus" and "King Cannon," then omnipotent there.

He had been born in Northern Ohio in the atmosphere of the Civil War. He had lost a brother in that war. He grew up among devoted Republicans, firm in the faith that the Republican Party was wholly good and that in politics and government that party was the only good there was. Now in Congress the things he saw done shook that faith. He saw a duty on oil for which there was no least excuse forced into a tariff bill against the will of the party majority by order of "Uncle Joe." It was a sale of legislation, a special privilege, in return for a large contribution by oil companies to the party campaign fund. Other honest Republican congressmen saw the crime and sighed. Norris saw it, went to war, and by hard, clever work prevented it.

In Nebraska we had written Norris off as a sheep for the Burlington fold. His rising rebellion, so quietly he worked and so poor a self advertiser he was, went all unknown to us. Then out of a clear sky burst the great thunderclap. Norris had bearded Joe Cannon and all he stood for in his den and won. We watched the dramatic battle in the House that day in 1910, with Norris in command, with surprise and joy.

When Norris emerged as the superb fighter who had taken the Cannon congressional autocracy to a fall, it was the answer to a Nebraska prayer. The state had been for years struggling to free itself from serfdom to its corporate controls. Revolting against a slavish legislature in 1905 it had won in 1907 the direct primary. Here now was a chance to put in the Senate a fighter reflecting the rising spirit of the state. At the first chance, in 1912, the thing was done. From that year to the end of his days George Norris kept the course then begun.

Some men who rise as he rose turn out to be men of one battle and no more. Unaffected by the lures and pressures of Washington, Norris remained to the end the same Norris who blocked the oil tariff purchase and knocked out Cannon before he became a senator.

The Senate, when Norris entered it, had in Aldrich of Rhode Island a Joe Cannon of its own. Norris was soon at grips with the Aldrich machine as he had been with the Cannon machine. The story is now a familiar one. He opposed his party's log-rolled tariff bills. The nation was amazed when a Nebraska senator refused to vote for a subsidy for a Nebraska industry.

That was Norris' vote against a tariff for his own beet sugar farms and factories. Even Democratic congressmen, as a party opposing the tariff, had a way of getting into the record with a vote for subsidies for their own local industries. Norris refused to vote for what he accounted a graft even for his own constituents.

His fight for the lame duck amendment, blocked year after year by Speaker Longworth in the House, is well-known history. The level of the politics of that day is reflected in the fact that it was not the lame duck amendment which Longworth and his fellows primarily opposed but the author—any measure which Norris, the party outlaw, might propose. His almost single-handed fight to save Muscle Shoals, the germ of the TVA, is one of the dramatic incidents of our history. How Norris saved here by a brilliant parliamentary stroke a battle that seemed lost is a little known incident of that long fight. His triumph over the "yellow dog" contract; his single-handed and almost successful effort as a Nebraska senator to carry the state of Pennsylvania against an unfit candidate of his own party for the Senate; his return to his home state to win for it America's first unicameral state legislature—the record is reminiscent of the labors of Hercules.

He looked no Hercules! Norris' friends, to say nothing of his crowding enemies, disputed whether he was even great. We found him, when we came at last to know him, a man without a front. He was plain George Norris, taking the back seat in any crowd with a modesty not put on. Not till, in his talk, he came to some wrong weighing upon his mind, did the power that was in him show itself. Then would come a certain outward thrust of the jaw which told you this man, for all his mildness, was dangerous. His words were soft. Seldom did anger rule his tongue. He spoke kindly of the men he had to fight, and he felt as kindly as he spoke. But of the fighting man that unconscious thrust of jaw spoke louder than his words.

Norris had devoted friends, but not a "cabinet." No man ever needed advice less or took it less. He waited and studied till the justice in a cause came clear to him. Then, regardless of consequences, or advice of friends, he took his stand and could not be moved.

When he packed his handbag and set forth single-handed to wrest the state of Pennsylvania from the powers devouring it the whole country showered its advice. It was an absurd venture, as any man could see. Don Quixote had never been crazier. From his home state, from Washington, from everywhere came letters, telegrams, telephone calls begging him to return to his senses and leave Pennsylvania politics, which was none of his business, alone. It was water on a duck's back. Vare had bought a Senate nomination. It was a disgrace to American politics and a menace to America. That was all Norris cared to know. Vare should not pass.

Vare was elected, but the fight Norris made had so aroused the country that the Republican Senate did not dare seat him. Vare, thanks to Norris, was turned back at the Senate door, a triumph for political decency.

Among the friends of Norris in Washington and in his home state alike, newspapermen were most numerous. They found in him one senator in whom there was no guile, and to such a rare jewel they clung with delight. The part of Paul Anderson, a Washington correspondent devoted to the senator, in frustrating in 1924 the senator's determination to retire is a tale which reflects the feeling of many a journalist.

Anderson entered Norris' office one day as a messenger boy came out. The messenger, a clerk told him, carried a telegram from the senator to his representative in Lincoln instructing him to refuse a filing for renomination. Anderson overtook the messenger, said he was from Norris who wanted the message back. Receiving it, Anderson put it in his pocket and kept it there. The senator had written the telegram in a moment of discouragement and was later induced to change his mind. But for that intercepted telegram would there have been a lame duck amendment, a TVA, an end to the Yellow Dog contract, an REA?

In 1922, Robert B. Howell, who had led the long battle for municipal water in Omaha, was elected to the Senate as Norris' colleague. Before he had been long in Washington a capital reporter broke into a press club gathering with sensational news. It was not unknown or even uncommon, the hard-boiled reporter said, for a state to have one honest senator. He was now to report, that for the first time in history a state had two honest senators simultaneously.

The friends with whom Norris' career in the Senate began remained his friends to the end. They became his friends for what he was at the beginning. They remained his friends because he never swerved. Politicians in this group were few. Norris, disgusted with spoils politics, distributed no gifts to buy an organization of his own. Insofar as he needed to be represented in politics such of his friends as C. A. Sorensen, attorney general for a time, and James E. Lawrence, collaborator in the Norris autobiography,[1] who had no private ends to serve, sufficed. The appeal of his record to the unorganized multitude did the rest.

From first to last he had the unyielding enmity of his party organization, both state and national. The bitterness of the party managers and the desperation to which it led them appeared in the famous "Grocer Norris" case. An obscure man in a western Nebraska town, of the same name as the senator, was induced by Republican leaders, with the knowledge of officers of the national organization, to file as a candidate for the nomination against the senator. This would have made the nomination

---

[1]George W. Norris. *Fighting Liberal*. Macmillan.

of the senator impossible, since there would be no way to tell which Norris had been voted for. The plot was foiled only on a technicality sustained by the courts. One Republican leader went to prison for perjury in connection with the case.

Norris sinned, his whole life through, against party regularity. That, to the party machine, was treason to the party name. A Democratic regular the Republican regular could respect and even sometimes embrace as an ally. An independent was beyond the pale. The rage of the party regulars as Norris, with only the people for him, held his place, term after term, grew fiercer with the years, to be sated finally by his defeat in 1942.

That final defeat raises the omnipresent question: How could Norris, always opposed by his party machine, have remained in Congress without a break for 40 years? And why, then, was he finally beaten while at the height of national admiration and approval, by his own Nebraska folk?

His greatest service to his state, as well as to the nation, had been done in his final years. He had succeeded at last in harnessing the streams of his state for irrigation and for power. The agricultural measures which he had fostered had saved the farmers of his state from bankruptcy. The business interests of the state had been saved from extreme disaster by the rescue of the agriculture on which Nebraska business thrives. Nebraska, from 1920 till after 1929, had been sickest of the states. The droughts of the 1930's would hardly have been survived without a wholesale exodus of population but for the measures which Norris helped to provide. Now in the flush of prosperity, at the first opportunity to pass judgment on its rescuer, Nebraska voted Norris out.

The nation, through an almost unanimous press, had praised his state for its gift of Norris to his country. He had been of immeasurable value to the nation as well as to his state. He had been truly a national senator (one thing for which he was attacked by his enemies at home). Now, at the height of the nation's praise for his extraordinary services, his state had turned him down. It had the look of crass ingratitude, of wanton cruelty. How is that explained?

It does no good to deceive ourselves concerning the stern and often bitter realities of the democratic process which we call politics. It would be pleasant to suppose that a large majority of the voters of Nebraska were so single-mindedly and intelligently attached to sheer honesty and capacity in a senator that for no other reason they put George Norris in the Senate and kept him there. In some degree this happy view holds true. But why, then, was there in the Senate only one George W. Norris? Honest men in any state are not rare; no more are honest and intelligent voters rare. Nebraska had no monopoly on either; yet it alone gave us a Norris; then took him away again.

The answer, unpleasant as it may be, is: it takes more than the honest man and the honest voter to put a Norris in Congress and keep him there.

That more is favoring time and circumstance. To recognize the part played by time and circumstance in the course of politics and the course of government is the beginning, not of spiteful cynicism, but of competent democracy. There is a time for everything. George Norris, incorrigibly independent, instinctively honest, would have been independent and honest at any time in any place. He might not, in a different time and place, have had much chance to be forty years a congressman and nationally beloved senator.

To make the opportunity which Norris so notably employed required a rare combination of circumstances. The origins of the people of Nebraska made one circumstance. The general course of the times within and without the state made another circumstance. The particular economy of Nebraska made yet another.

Nebraska, as we have said, was at the beginning of Norris' career, largely a pawn of the railroads which the state was compelled to serve and of the corporate interests which the railroads served. The railroads, making rates at their own free will, distributing privileges to serve their pleasure, held the state politically and economically in the hollow of their hands. They designated governors, legislatures, and congressmen. They made or unmade cities at their will. They decided which industries and businesses might thrive and which decay. It was a potent private totalitarianism with its privileged political and business hierarchies doing their master's will and supervising the destinies of the rest. It was through Norris' Republican party, the party of Lincoln which he was brought up to trust, that this power ruled the Nebraska of that day.

But even while the young Norris was a judge a revolt against this rule was getting under way. The Populist Party had begun a decade before to wean Republican farmers away from their party allegiance. When Norris went to Congress in 1902 the Populists had already elected governors and congressmen. He fought them as foes of "the only party fit to govern." Not till he was in Congress, a cog in the Cannon machine in power there, and saw at first hand the power of special privilege there, were his eyes opened, his illusions dispelled.

By that time the tide of revolt which was to land him in the Senate had begun to rise in his own party. The party was dominated and its courses controlled by eastern interests. Thence came its campaign funds and the free railroad tickets on which the party leaders, state and county, rode. The organization submitted to this control. The rank-and-file Republicans, to defend their own obvious interests, had to oppose these controls. That meant revolt within the party. To the free-pass-riding Republican this was treason, but to the mass of Nebraska voters it was common sense. They revolted to such effect that in 1907 a Republican state convention routed the party machine, wrote its own platform, and smashed the machine slate of candidates.

The defiance by Senator Norris of the party machine was thus popular with the Nebraska people, though never with the party bosses. This continued long to be the fact. The farm depression following the first World War did not wait for '29. While the business boom of the Harding-Coolidge days swept up and on, the farmers slid steadily into insolvency. Republican Presidents vetoed the farm relief bills which Norris helped push through Congress. His opposition to these Republican Presidents was pleasing to suffering Nebraskan Republicans, save only the professional party regulars. Norris became the symbol of bold and able resistance to the powers which had so long exploited the state. Farmers began at last to see how the tariffs imposed by the party for which they had voted had bled them. They applauded Norris' tariff insurgency. They approved him so decidedly that they did in 1936 the amazing, unprecedented thing of electing him, though unsupported by any party organization, as an independent candidate. The interests of the masses of the people were served by the independence of Norris from the first. In supporting the insurgent Norris the people of Nebraska had served their own proper economic needs and interests. And the people, with their direct primary, ruled.

Why, then, did they desert him finally in 1942?

Here enters a circumstance unrelated to Nebraska economic interests or party lines. The people, partly because of the help of such as Norris, partly by reason of the war, had become prosperous enough to be content awhile, to forget old favors and old friends. Norris' age argued against him. He was slow in deciding to run. He had no party support to bring him a "pigeonhole" block of votes and had made no great campaign. But the decisive force, without which the others would not have ruled, was one not often noted abroad or understood. To illustrate its potency, consider Norris' second election in 1918 as senator.

In 1917 Norris voted against the declaration of war with Germany. He filibustered successfully against the proposal to arm the merchant fleet against Germany. He was one of Woodrow Wilson's excoriated "twelve wilful men." For this he was the most loudly execrated senator in all Nebraska's history. Clearly, he had committed political suicide. In the dark days of the following early winter, he came to Lincoln to visit his daughter, then in the University there. All day he sat in his Lindell Hotel room. A United States senator back from Washington was regularly sought by crowds. Only one person, a newspaperman,[2] ventured, in fact, to call then on the detested senator. One year later he was re-elected by an ample majority!

Had the people so respected his courage they swallowed their disapproval of his act and re-elected him? It would be pleasant so to think. A sense of reality forbids.

Nebraska, an almost empty territory until the Civil War, was settled by two chief elements. First came the Union soldiers to their free land with their unyielding Republican sympathies. The independent Republican revolt could get nowhere till their number had declined. Then came those scores of thousands of industrious immigrant Germans to whom Nebraska is most indebted for its quick rural development. They were hard-working, good citizens and with few exceptions loyal Americans. More than a third of the voters of Nebraska in 1918 were these Germans and their sons. Who can forget his fatherland? Norris had voted to keep America out of war with their old home country. A glance at the senatorial vote in the German counties told the tale. The reversal which returned in 1918 the bitterly reviled senator of the year before was no miracle, no mystery. Norris, the independent, antiwar senator had been saved by a circumstance, the "German vote."

The years rolled on and the bitterness of the war years was forgot. Muscle Shoals was saved. The lame duck was destroyed. The TVA, the unicameral legislature, "farm relief" emerged. Norris was America's most loved and approved senator. Then Hitler came.

Norris, like many who were of his antiwar mind 20 years before, was among the first to feel the portent. Promptly, strongly, he took his stand. The Nazi must be repelled. He voted and spoke for the measures to curb the German drive. He voted willingly, in 1941, to go to war—war with the fatherland of the Germans, still of their old strength at the Nebraska polls, still unable to think ill of the fatherland! He voted thus in 1941 to affront the element that saved him after 1917.

As in 1918, so in 1942, he came up for re-election the year after his vote on the declaration of war. Now he had offended, not pleased, those voters who could not forget their fatherland. The returns from strongly German counties tells the tale. The lifetime of brave service to state and nation no more availed. Circumstance, so long his aid and ally, had turned the other way. Now he was done.

The "fell clutch of circumstance" had spared him far longer than it spares most public men who stand out against the power and privilege

---

[2]*Editor's Note:* That man was Walter Locke.

of their time. The old senator was for a moment stunned, then he smiled. After all, his work had been its own reward.

Yet other rewards of a most heart-healing sort came pouring in. From every nook and corner of America came letters, thousands of them, glorying in the life the senator had lived. From the humblest and from the greatest the tributes poured in. There were enough to make a great volume, could they be printed, revealing what the best of Americans desire and approve in the best of their spokesmen in the best of governments. Some of these spoke of the ingratitude of republics. The senator did not. He had done a job to please himself. He did not ask for gratitude. A shower of calls for his services, something to keep him still on guard for the people, poured in. He turned away. He had been the nemesis of the "lame duck." It was not for him, he said, to be a lame duck now.

A man who did not love people, the people as they are, could never have walked as straight before them as did he. When he thought, as he was often urged to do, of the autobiography which he might write, his mind turned from the times and events in which he had played so great a part to the boyhood and youth out of which this career of his had grown. That, to him, was the decisive thing. The Norris of the war in the Senate on graft and privilege was born, he saw, of the struggle of the half-orphan on that old Ohio farm. The parliamentary point of order in the Senate that saved Muscle Shoals was born in the country debating society of his youthful days. Norris, to the end, was what he was there on that farm, the common man, a lover and defender of the common man.

The secret of his power is not far to seek. His judgment of measures and of men, so unerring that senators hesitated long before taking sides against him, is no mystery. He was possessed, as a lover of men must be, by an abhorrence of injustice, of oppression, which he could not repress. His strength, by reason of this passion, was as the strength of ten. Wherever he saw men suffering wrong, there in the thick of the fighting was he to be found. A Pennsylvania small business man facing ruin by collusion of powerful business interests with a federal judge won his help no less readily than a constituent of his own. No Pennsylvania congressman dared listen to the complaint. It was the Nebraska congressman who could not suffer wrong who saved the little Pennsylvania man and impeached the recreant judge. To him a West Virginia coal miner, writhing under a "yellow dog" contract and an overcharged Nebraska farmer were the same. So simple is honesty, so easy is virtue to one who does justly and loves mercy and walks humbly as George Norris did.

The prophet was at last without honor in his own country, in his own house. The people had given; the people had taken away. Blessed be the name of the people, George Norris meekly said. Refusing all calls elsewhere, he turned his face homeward to the people who had at last rejected him. To his own Nebraska village whence he had come just forty years before, he returned to wait and die among the people he had loved and served so well and still loved, even though their love for him had cooled.

He vanished into his own west, carrying with him such confidence, admiration and love from the whole nation as no other senator in a century had earned; such a record of achievement, perhaps, as no other member of Congress in all history had made. Grant that circumstance gave him his opportunity and took it away again. Washington, but for the times which brought his chance, would be a forgotten Virginia squire, Lincoln a never known country lawyer. President Franklin Roosevelt, reproached for trying to do so much so fast, replied that the chance to make progress comes only three or four times in a century. He must work fast while circumstances made work possible.

These met their opportunity and had the greatness to make the most of it. The homespun senator from Nebraska, too.   —*Summer* 1945

LOUIS FILLER

The Dilemma, So-Called, of the American Liberal

THE intention here is not to bury liberalism or to praise it. It is, rather, to inquire into its elements, and to ask which, if any, retain vitality for purposeful men. I assume that we are living in crisis times, and that this is not the last such inquiry. It is certainly not the first. These have, unfortunately, too often been informed by the spirit of cant and sentimentality, and especially so in dealing with the famous "dilemma" of the liberal. This has never been a particularly suggestive concept. It has generally been a vehicle for self-flattery, and not serious investigation. Here we are, it seems to say, earnest, eager, honest men seeking nothing but the world's good. If only others were like us. . . . Broad-minded and intelligent, we probe deeply into all programs. But we are also feeling people; we look beyond mere programs to man himself. We don't forget the past, but we keep our faces to the future. We hail nobility and courage wherever we can find it; willingly work—more or less—with anybody having a reasonable idea to contribute; and will fight—in moderation— with those who are in the vanguard of human progress. If only those we admire, or, at least, respect, would not take extreme positions which leave no room for dissent! But they will, and we shy of being too critical of them, the genuine doers, the authentic spokesmen of the time. And so here we stand, or, more comfortably, sit, not sure just what we can do. We are in a dilemma.

There are implications here which can be challenged: for example, just how much good will, courage, and even intelligence specific liberals have manifested at any given time, and how their significant qualities have compared with those of others who would not insist on being called liberals. But aside from that, there are other questions which have to be faced. In the very first place, there is the question of definition: what is a liberal? Nicholas Murray Butler deemed himself one, apparently of a different stripe from that of Charles Beard, who found Columbia University an unenthusiastic host during World War I. Liberals were often equated with communists during the 1920's and since. There is some evidence that communists have sometimes equated themselves with liberals. And what of the socialists: liberals or radicals?

Secondly, there is the problem of results. A person may indeed convince us that he is an authentic liberal: and so what? If he is programmatically weak; if he is like Stephen Leacock's horseman, dashing madly off in all directions at once; if, in practice, he seems to be able to organize nothing but defeats, we might begin to wonder what he is good for. Liberalism tends to be a soothing concept, to suggest honor, decency, reasonableness, free creativity. But if it is actually a depressant, if it is vain, ineffectual, and futile, the uncongenital optimist might well consider whether he ought not to be out shopping for something better.

I am reminded of a meeting which was convened in 1940 to inaugurate a "new approach" to liberalism—a meeting presumed to be attended by liberals. It included some very well-known characters in journalism, education, and other businesses. The meeting highly resolved to examine the current situation, involving, it will be remembered, such matters as the Nazi-Soviet Pact, the European War, the failure of the Spanish Republic, what was held in some quarters to be a "conservative reaction" in the United States, among other matters of more than academic interest.

An outsider found it a real experience to listen to the conversation of some of the participants in the conference. One of them seemed to feel that something had definitely to be done, but he was a little concerned about what the conference ought to commit itself upon. Another complained that she had tried again and again to work with the communists, and always been betrayed by them, always. Since she looked anything but gullible, one had the impression that she had endured an enormous amount of nonco-operation—in just what interest was not clear; perhaps liberalism. All those present agreed on the need for throwing light on the immediate situation. If only the truth could be ferreted out, it would make us free—us, and all our fellow-Americans. And so the meeting set itself to drawing up elaborate plans for studying and reporting on every conceivable aspect of the domestic situation, and for becoming a rallying point to liberal forces in the entire country.

The subsequent history of this group can be shortly stated. The reports did not come in. The meetings dribbled to nothing. The whole business was mercifully forgotten. In the course of events, one of the mighty figures of the conference evolved into a violent defender of freedom, which he unmistakably identified with free enterprise. Another was cited by the Dies Committee about matters I do not recall being discussed at the conference. Still another went on talking, and to larger and larger audiences, in the somewhat banal way he had talked in '40. So it went. None of my colleagues, so far as I know, departed entirely from our economic and cultural and social life. But one thing is clear: as liberals, as people who were apparently aware that liberalism had been impugned, challenged, depreciated, they lacked what it took to float a standard which would be equally challenging and which could command the respect of the public.

Liberalism has so long been a subordinate part of the procession, a kind of J. Alfred Prufrock "that will do/ To swell a progress, start a scene or two"—to complete the quotation from T. S. Eliot:

> Advise the prince; no doubt, an easy tool,
> Deferential, glad to be of use,
> Politic, cautious, and meticulous;
> Full of high sentence, but a bit obtuse;
> At times, indeed, almost ridiculous—
> Almost, at times, the Fool

that it is an effort to remember that liberalism was once the very voice of the country, in excellent repute, and with a long list of achievements to its credit. To be sure, there are those who would maintain that the Franklin D. Roosevelt administrations were liberal administrations, in which case there would be some question as to why there had to be any meeting at all by my honorable friends of 1940. But this brings us back again to the question of what a liberal is or has been held to be.

II

Liberalism, historically speaking (and here we can understand why Dr. Butler entitled one of his books *The Faith of a Liberal*), referred to free enterprise, an unleashing of social and economic forces in the interests of natural selection. Manchester Liberals could sincerely claim humanitarian aims; Cobden and Bright spoke in moving tones about the effect of the Corn Laws on the poorer classes. But dearer to them was the principle of freedom and individual rights, and they fought factory legislation as a cardinal sin. They and their followers gave way slowly to workers' demands, and only under the pressure of a new type of liberal, who was also interested in liberty, but who better appreciated the need for seeing to it that the machine was to some degree controlled, and its negative effects kept at a minimum. To turn directly to the Post-Civil War era, and to America, now wholly in the toils of the Industrial Revolution, the Society for the Prevention of Cruelty to Animals was founded by the picturesque Henry Bergh, who, as an afterthought, then founded the Society for the Prevention of Cruelty to Children. Henry George mixed religion with economics to evolve what he thought was the answer to all human trouble. Suppressed classes made various attempts to raise their social status, sometimes using methods which could hardly be termed liberal, but which had some possible defense in the theory that organized society offered them too little, and that their efforts would help to right the balance. If the person who threw the bomb at the Haymarket in Chicago in 1886 as a protest against police brutality and suffering brought on by economic depression was no liberal, certainly William Dean Howells was, for protesting publicly the railroading of various labor leaders and anarchists to the gallows or prison with only the travesty of a trial.

Here we seem to come closer to the idea of what liberalism, modernly conceived, involves: the seeking of a solution to social problems which will freely express the best interests of the general public—*all classes*—in a reasonable and candid fashion. Henry Bergh, so far as his social thinking went—it didn't travel far—was a liberal; but his societies dealt with effects, not causes. William Dean Howells acknowledged the existence of more fundamental questions, in denouncing the Haymarket executions, but in no penetrating way. Henry George called attention to social distress and offered a vigorous solution. The Single Tax theory has been challenged, but the liberal is no more bound to produce air-tight panaceas than is anyone else. What is important is that George had displayed a social conscience, had offered a reasoned solution to social and economic difficulties, and had made a democratic appeal. Note these characteristics of liberalism. E. L. Godkin of the *Nation* was one of the most brilliant minds in the journalism of the post-Civil War decades. He was a free-trader, antiwar, and antigraft. But he despised the lower classes, feared democracy and democratic government, and though he had only a limited respect for the robber barons of his time, preferred anything they might do to what an unleashed rabble might. Godkin dreamed of government by an élite, but in effect supported unbridled free—one might say free-booting—enterprise. He was a Manchester Liberal, and, in his time, did not add up to liberty.

It is a striking fact that the developing liberalism of the latter part of the nineteenth century was middle-class in essence. It sought solutions to social ills which would take unwarranted power out of the hands of economic or social royalists, but would not transfer it entirely to any other one group, whether it be farmers, workers, or "intellectuals." Even William Jennings Bryan, a spokesman for the agrarians, remembered, in his Cross of Gold speech, to speak for "a broader class of businessman," and cited the attorney and the worker, as well as the farmer, as deserving consideration. To be sure, the industrial worker nevertheless voted for McKinley in 1896. But that fact reminds us that liberalism in that year had not yet permeated the fabric of American life, that classes were fighting their separate battles as best they could, and were not united on a minimum program which would galvanize liberals in behalf of a *national* drive toward reform.

Furthermore, there is a legitimate question about what kind of future for America our Populists and workers, and the liberals who sought to mediate between them, had in mind. They denounced monopoly and monopoly government, yet none of them was, in practice, willing to give up the high production made possible by industrial combinations. The effect of the Sherman Anti-Trust Act of 1890, if taken seriously, would have been to frustrate the powers of business for good, as well as for ill —in other words, to prevent it from achieving greater efficiency, greater stability, greater productive capacity. This was a Jeffersonian implication which the Populists never faced frankly. As for the working-class groups, they were less interested in what the Sherman Act might or might not do to big business than with the fact that it might be used—as it was used —to prevent their own growth and the militant operation of their own unions.

What could satisfy both farmers and workers? Logically, the answer was government ownership of basic industries. But this meant central-izing enormous power in government. The American tradition had always been to attempt to strike a balance between weak government, as theoretically represented by Jeffersonianism, and strong government, as represented by the Hamiltonian ideal. If the liberal-agrarian theory of

Jefferson was to be repudiated, who would guarantee the democratic operation of centralized government? It was all well and good to speak of curbing trusts, but who would curb the enormously strengthened government? Suppose it should stop suppressing trusts and begin suppressing people? Here were questions which late nineteenth-century liberals found it expedient to avoid. Their emphasis was upon humanitarianism and the danger to society because of the growth of businesses which added up to a state within a state. This is their justification and their strength. But it is evident, at least today, that the liberals were storing up a great deal of ideological trouble for the future.

From the practical point of view, they proceeded to establish a record which has become historical. It is well known that the lid blew off the top of the country in the 1900's. Liberal reformers broke loose in every part of the country and scattered old politicians, old laws, old traditions to the winds. They created the city-manager plan, they initiated movements which brought about the passage of laws controlling food standards, forest conservation, working conditions, housing regulations, and other necessary social operations. The long list of achievements of the Reform Era makes impressive reading, and is, in fact, impressive. It should be observed, however, that to some extent there was nothing especially liberal in the ultimate workings of the new laws and institutions. Much of the Square Deal legislation did no more than *modernize* outmoded and intolerable conditions. Frank Hague became mayor of Jersey City, proud of its up-to-date commission form of city government. The battle for pure food simply continued. Housing legislation, again, did little more than provide rules within which conservatives as well as humanitarians could fight their battles.

Above all, it should be noted that the question of the role of government in a business civilization was carefully avoided throughout this earlier reform period. The two major parties continued much as they had before, despite reforms which could be recorded. And the crucial battle against trusts lagged.

If liberalism which stands up as strong and as generally desirable today as yesterday is to be found in the panorama of reform history, it has to be found in the career of the journalism of the time. This created a host of investigators, analysts, and organizers who brought basic issues of American life into focus and mobilized mass opinion sensationally for social action. The exposés of *Frenzied Finance*, provided by Thomas W. Lawson, an insider, startled the country with their revelations of business practices. David Graham Phillips' blast against the Senate as a treasonable body set the ball rolling which culminated in the passage of the Seventeenth Amendment to the Constitution, providing for the direct election of senators. The struggle against Secretary of the Interior Richard A. Ballinger, led by *Collier's* magazine, not only saved valuable Alaskan holdings of the government from falling into the hands of private interests, but turned a glaring light on organized bureaucracy. In addition, the concerted search for facts useful to the general public created a certain tone of disinterestedness in public discussion which allowed candid reviews of the socialist position, the I. W. W. position, even the anarchist position—not, of course, in ways which always satisfied the groups involved, but in ways which opened the door to their own publications and organizations. These were relatively large, vital, and run by capable leaders. Ray Stannard Baker, who was no socialist, foresaw the dissolution of the old parties. Upton Sinclair was a socialist, and Charles Edward Russell joined the socialists. A magazine like the *American*, which had on its editorial board a skeptic like Lincoln Steffens, a man of the people like Finley Peter Dunne, an aristocrat like A. J. Nock, and such other figures as Ida M. Tarbell, William Allen White, and Ray Stannard Baker, could claim breadth and vitality. The point about liberalism in the age of reform was not that all liberals thought alike, or that there was harmony between liberals, socialists, and syndicalists, to say nothing of conservatives—but that the several social components challenged each other on the basis of their own strength, rather than their opponents' presumed weaknesses; and that the spirit of the times demanded at least the appearance of candor and a willingness to learn on the part of those responsible for public opinion—especially those within the spectrum of liberalism.

III

So far, so good. As historic a phenomenon, however, if less known to history, is the collapse, or, better still, the disintegration of liberal strength in the pre-World War I era. The destruction of the muckraking magazines was effected mainly between 1910 and 1912. In part, the reason for this dramatic demise lay in the actions of private interests which, to put it mildly, resented being treated too familiarly by independent journalists. A good example is furnished by *Success* magazine, which died in a matter of several months despite its half-million readers. In part, however, the cause must be sought elsewhere. The journalists had not created the reform movement out of themselves alone. They had been supported by the public, lifted to eminence, in some instances, almost despite themselves. If the public did not rally to their support in the dark hours when banks refused them credit, when distributing agencies refused to handle their publications, when organized concerns acted to discredit them, confuse their stockholders, infiltrate their business offices, or simply buy them up and transform their editorial policies, it was because their program of enlightenment and reform had lost its hold on the public imagination. It was, in fact, because the magazines stood at crossroads and were required to define their position, to determine where they were going and why, and because they were unable to do so, that they died.

They had consolidated America around the question of domestic reform, but the core of that question they had not touched. What was the meaning of the trust, internationally as well as nationally? What did expanding democracy demand of Americans, at home as well as abroad? Intellectual compromises prevented a deepening of our understanding of these questions. Americans who could calmly accept our Caribbean policy were hardly in position to come to sincere grips with our domestic Negro and immigrant policies. Americans who accepted John Hay as a great statesman, and approved Theodore Roosevelt's boast that he had taken the Panama Canal were not in position to judge the morals of European Foreign Offices.

The support for which the besieged magazines appealed in their distress presupposed a keener sense of wrong in general than Americans were able to sustain. Although muckraking died unnaturally, one can understand why the public should have been satisfied with its national affairs in 1912. The current "Money Trust" investigation gave apparent evidence that no economic interest was above inspection. Ambitious trust prosecutions portended a growing control over private business operations. The candidates for President were competing with one another in their promises of further and more intensive reforms. Of what special use were the magazines? A slick and upholstered *Collier's*, a senile *Everybody's* (which ultimately became *Romance Magazine*), a deflated *McClure's* did not inspire storm signals, certainly not from the socialists, who had little faith in the traditional American promise and were perfectly willing to let the muckrakers pass into the shadows.[1]

It is a remarkable fact that the great magazines passed under the halter *before* the Wilsonian reform program got under way. What, then, if anything, distinguished reform before 1912, in the time of Theodore Roosevelt and Taft, from that practiced by Woodrow Wilson? It is significant that Theodore Roosevelt was now preaching a "New Nationalism" and Wilson a "New Freedom," for something new was being added to the national scene which was evolving a new liberalism. Reform itself was still going on, on the momentum whipped up during the earlier reform period; but the heart of reform—the candid, aggressive, democratic inquiries of the unaffiliated liberals—was gone. Something had

---

[1]For details respecting these and related events, see Louis Filler, *Crusaders for American Liberalism*, New York, 1939, in particular chapter 28, "The End of Muckraking."

been put in its place. The turmoil of the old liberalism had precipitated to the surface the problem of *what to do about the economic and social structure of the country*; and more sophisticated liberals than Steffens, Tarbell, and Lawson rose to meet the challenge.

Herbert Croly, in his influential and highly significant study, *The Promise of American Life* (1909), minimized the efforts of the muckrakers. They dealt, he believed, with effects, not causes. Crime, graft, social mayhem in general stemmed from a disorganized society, he believed. The great need of the time was to organize it about a spirit and a system which would attract the best elements of society as administrators. The fault in the American system lay deep; it was Jeffersonian. "Jefferson's policy," Croly asserted, "was at bottom the old fatal policy of drift, whose distorted body was concealed by fair-seeming clothes, and whose ugly face was covered by a mask of good intentions." Enough of this! America had to be reorganized about another policy: one of "energetic and intelligent assertion of the national good." Hamilton, after all, had the answer. "He knew that the only method whereby the good could prevail either in individual or social life was by persistently willing that it should prevail and by the adoption of intelligent means to that end. His vision of the national good was limited; but he was absolutely right about the way in which it was to be achieved."

It was, therefore, absurd to denounce trusts; trusts were here to stay. Only, they had to be intelligently regulated. All classes and interests of society had to be intelligently regulated. The key word is "intelligently." What, for example, such regulation would mean in practice to the Negroes, whom Croly believed to be "a race possessed of moral and intellectual qualities inferior to those of the white men," was not specified. At any rate, there was an obvious need for a strong and intelligent government, if Croly's program was to be given skin and bones.

This, in turn, meant that there had to be a strong and intelligent Executive. There had to be an end to the vulgar denunciation of bosses. Mark Hanna—whose biography Croly later wrote—had not been subverting democracy with his iron organization of the Republican party. He had been a statesman responding to general social needs, and directing democratic processes. There was too much cant talked in the name of democracy, anyhow. The fact was, Croly insisted, that liberty helps the minority. The masses needed protection from their own inadequacies; and what could protect them but a common ideal which would control all classes? Pride in America, patriotism, a dedication to national interests needed to be augmented—what else could bind the unthinking classes dynamically to the state? Mere humanitarianism signified nothing in contrast to the national destiny.

Croly's thoughts on patriotism and justice were interesting. He sought "a democratic social ideal, which shall give consistency to American social life, without entailing any essential sacrifice of desirable individual and class distinctions." But, to be specific, William Jennings Bryan had disqualified himself by his antinationalism "for effective leadership of the party of reform." How would one recognize the effective reformer? Presumably he would, like Croly, view with grave concern "the recent outbreak of anti-militarism" in France. He would doubtless believe that England had acquired her latest batch of colonies in Africa at "excessive cost." He would surely approve the wars "deliberately provoked by Bismarck at a favorable moment, because they were necessary to the unification of the German people under Prussian leadership." He would certainly be skeptical about unifying Europe "by congresses and amicable resolutions," and would hold that this could be attained "only by the same old means of blood and iron." And with Croly he would plan, in the bloodless language of diplomacy, a persistent and unappeasable expansionist program, giving not the slightest thought to the feelings and ideas of the colonial peoples involved. What type of *domestic* reform program he would institute while these interesting events were taking place, one could well imagine.

In any event, such perspectives were obviously not for the man in the street, still bemused by humanitarianism. They were for an élite. Croly could observe the disappearance of the muckraking magazines without alarm; and several years after they had died for lack of money could obtain the support of the wealthy Willard Straight for a magazine of his own.[2] The *New Republic*, which he founded in 1914, was content to appeal to the "thinking" minority of liberals, who were less interested in carrying light to the masses than in engineering a plan for America which was essentially Hamiltonian and, it can now be told, had totalitarian implications.

Theodore Roosevelt himself was, of course, more directly interested in the masses, or, at least, their votes, than was Croly, who was content to affirm his convictions and wait for time to vindicate them. Roosevelt embraced Croly's plan with ardor. No wonder he could toss aside his old scruples against moving too fast in the direction of socialization, and borrow generously from socialist and old Populist platforms. Roosevelt was no socialist or Populist. He had no intention of destroying monopo-

---

[2] It would be instructive to ask why so many wealthy patrons were found to support the new liberal, and even radical, periodicals in the 1910's, who would not have put their money into muckraking publications, and who, indeed, opposed them in specific cases. It would also be interesting to determine who, precisely, paid the bills for the *Masses*, the *Metropolitan*, the *Seven Arts*, and other magazines.

lies. His aim was to direct their operation. He was an élitist, who esteemed himself better than Americans from most classes of the population. So, less crudely, more intelligently, perhaps more idealistically, was Woodrow Wilson. "It will be understood," Wilson emphasized in 1914, "that our object is *not* to unsettle business or anywhere seriously to break its established courses athwart. On the contrary, we desire laws we are now about to pass to be the bulwarks and safeguards of industry against the forces that have disturbed it. What we have to do can be done in a new spirit, in thoughtful moderation, without revolution of any untoward kind."

The reform legislation of Wilson's first administration was legislation handed down from *above*. It did not challenge monopoly; monopolistic combinations remained, substantially, masters in their own houses. It made their operations more efficient, it sought to lance their more obvious bad spots, and cleanse them—in other words, to make them more modern, more readily acceptable, and note, please, without any of the disturbing emphasis upon details and specific individuals which had attended muckraking. Wilsonian reform corresponded, in government, to Taylorization in industry. Though labor-capitalist relations became temporarily somewhat more smooth as a result of the reform legislation, it did not strike at fundamentals. It did not construct an adequate machinery for expressing the changing needs of the several economic classes involved.

The reformers, old and new, responded to the Wilson "revolution" in no very complicated way. A few, a very few of the old guard, like Lincoln Steffens and Charles Edward Russell, perversely refused to notice that the millennium had arrived. Many more, like Ray Stannard Baker, brought the glad news that it had. The less said of individuals like the latter the better. The *New Republic* intellectuals were somewhat more vigorous and alive, their attitude toward the Master of the White House varying from critical to enthusiastic, but in effect they supported the administration. The new liberalism enjoyed its taste of élitism, of being In the Know, of making and, to some extent, even breaking. But if it sounded more modern than did the old, it had a less intimate knowledge of American realities than the latter, and less power to influence the direction American life might take.

Is it so surprising, therefore, that many young and eager intellectuals should have been disillusioned with reform, with liberalism, and should have looked about for programs which had greater apparent vitality and more persuasively promised the better life? Notice that the new liberals, despite their pretensions, were repeating the errors of the old, without even being able to bring the questions which interested them to the general public. The muckrakers had concentrated upon domestic affairs almost to the exclusion of foreign affairs. The Croly liberals made a fetish of a national program. The crisis of World War I, when it came, found neither of them adequate. Of the old muckrakers, many joined George Creel, also an ex-reformer, in his famous wartime committee, to create the kind of intellectual conformity which characterized the war years. Croly liberals like Walter Lippmann contributed more cerebration to the war effort, but, in effect, directed what little thought there was left into the thin idealism which accompanied power politics. They could ill complain that the masses had not followed Wilson's plans for a post-war world with sufficient care. They had not asked the masses to think. The masses, it soon appeared, could be as opportunistic as they were themselves, as cynical, as tired. If the masses had failed them, they, in turn, had failed the masses.

I V

Hence, one can appreciate the persuasive power which the new Soviet state exercised over the imagination of fresher and less contented elements of the intellectuals. Capitalism, it seemed, had failed to cleanse itself. It had found no way out of its contradictions but war. Free enterprise was a joke when conceived in terms of the gigantic monopolies. Government was fundamentally business, and business was government. Centralization of power was apparently inevitable in modern life; why not, then, establish it in the interests of the toiling classes? The Bolsheviks were no doubt acting ruthlessly, but they were acting at the command of "workers' soviets," they were directed by "democratic centralism," and they were defending themselves against intervention and lies. They were expropriating private property, true, but they were administering it in the interests of the working classes. Was the principle of freedom being compromised, in Russia? Perhaps; but only in the interests of a really new freedom—the right to work in the general interests of the community. Let the U.S.S.R. throw off its enemies, carry its principles beyond its borders, and a world of peace and plenty could be constructed such as the League of Nations did not even dare to offer. Some of the younger intellectuals threw over liberalism entirely to join the new crusade for the final emancipation of mankind; but more of them merely emptied themselves of their old, discredited American content, and began to evaluate the world crisis in terms of what seemed (after Mussolini's march on Rome) the great alternative of communism versus fascism.

That America had something to contribute to the world situation seemed less and less likely as the 1920's progressed. Ray Stannard Baker, in his autobiography, was to complain that his analysis of the postwar industrial situation, *The New Industrial Unrest* (1920), was not discussed with the seriousness to which he had become accustomed during his muckraking days. But the world had widened since then. Baker wrote as though a bloody war had not taken place, as though there was no connection between industrial unrest and international relations. The public was right in sensing that Baker had nothing to contribute to its understanding. So far as it could see, it had been taken for an idealistic ride by Wilson and his educated scribes. It preferred its boozy prosperity jag to Baker's documented drivel. To hell with reform! And reformers, too.

However, America had been historically more than a machine for the production of high-grade bathtubs, automobiles, and slick magazines. It had been an arena for political revolutions, social experiments, and libertarian thought, and could, conceivably, be so again. The liberal found it hard to concentrate on the possibility. His faith in liberalism had been shaken. In the postwar period, which placed a premium on a type of "Americanism" which was made a synonym for smugness, even liberalism came under general suspicion. The time was highlighted by anti-Red raids, antiunionism, antifree speech—Upton Sinclair was arrested for reading the Bill of Rights—and such affairs as that involving Sacco and Vanzetti. The distinguished history of American liberalism was forgotten not only by the communists, but by the conservatives as well. Small wonder that even the liberal who might have been willing to exercise his historic function tended to turn toward the lively radical forces and away from the blank wall of servile intellectual obeisance. To some extent, America was back in the 1890's again, with society atomized, with government legislating frankly in behalf of big business—but without a strong, native opposition, such as Populism had been.

Here was the central difference between the 1890's and the 1920's: *the liberal's belief in liberty, in his own democratic energies and those of the American middle-class, had been compromised.* Babbitt, as seen by Sinclair Lewis, impressed him as hideously real. Walter Lippmann's liberalism seemed as far from the scene of fundamental issues as that of Al Smith. He himself was as far removed from the masses as either. The LaFollette bid for the presidency in 1924, which might well have furnished him with a new beginning, was, in fact, an end. Not only did the liberal lack political power; he lacked humanitarian strength. Felix Frankfurter wrote the most cogent analysis of the Sacco-Vanzetti case, but he, and men like him, were unable to save them. Is it surprising that other, more frustrated liberals should have begun to despise themselves, and feel that they had nothing original to contribute; that others better understood than they did the fundamental forces of society, that they were the "unpossessed," as the novelist Tess Slesinger was to call them, who needed a master?

V

So we come to the 1930's, when social need once more waylaid the masses of Americans. The first Franklin D. Roosevelt administrations resulted from a general upheaval. The question is whether one can find in them the kind of liberal direction which can be distinguished in the pre-World War I era. To be sure, Republicans saw in the New Deal a grave for the American way. Old Progressives and Wilsonians served in official capacities. A large network of reforms was erected, and the administration undertook to see that no one starved—or, at least, that relatively few people starved completely. However, since 1900, perspectives had changed. In 1932, the problem of Whither America? stared Americans directly in the face. The spirit in which the New Deal as a whole attempted to meet it is well expressed by Ed Flynn of the Bronx, in his book, entitled without irony, *You're the Boss*:

> The fundamental idea insofar as the New Deal was concerned was the President's own. . . . He believed the entire world was trending to the Left, and subsequent events proved he was right. This was a world-wide trend that few people saw as early as he did. But he felt that in order to preserve the capitalist system much legislation had to be put on the books that was Left of Center.

It is absurd to call Flynn a Democratic wheelhorse whom Franklin D. Roosevelt endured for the sake of the higher good. Flynn was an integral part of the New Deal. The Administration was an uneasy pilot working its way between aggressive elements of the Right and the Left. It was liberal in the sense that it struggled for a middle way, but the pressures to which it responded, and which helped define it, were not liberal. All of them were overshadowed by the gigantic, world-wide struggle between communism and fascism. At best, the New Dealers were Croly liberals, accepting the need for strong government regulation and trying to meet the needs of modern life. They were in positions of power, but not in position to criticize themselves adequately, even if they had felt like it. At worst, they played a ruthless game of domestic power politics with nonliberal elements. Judge Gary, of United States Steel, had, a generation before, had the temerity to say, "We are all socialists today." A contemporary cynic might as justly have said—one was reported to have done so—"We are all communists today."

What did the New Deal accomplish? It rescued free enterprise, but at a cost. It was no small achievement for it to have welded our cynical, absent-minded, indifferent, and uninformed post-World War I classes together for the crisis of 1939-1941; but was that the best it could have done? Had we no right to hope for anything better? It concentrated on domestic problems, and in this way repeated the old errors of reform. The record is clear. Was the meaning of the London Economic Conference hammered out in open democratic debate? Was the Japanese movement upon the Chinese mainland? What was the role of the United States in the Italian Ethiopian adventure? How did we respond to the Spanish Civil War and to the complex questions posed by the Madrid Republican government?

Here was the liberal's opportunity. The New Dealers were busy with their nationalistic enterprise. The harassed economic and social interests, the socialists, fascists, communists, and Republicans were absorbed in partisan concerns. Here was the time for the liberal to make himself heard, to speak in the name of liberty, reason, and all the other household gods he carried around with him. How did the liberal stand on the questions which pressed upon him?

I think we can generalize. I think it can be said that the liberal— lost in the ramifications of the *New York Times, Today, Life,* the *Daily Worker,* and the *New Leader,* not to mention the numerous governmental and quasi-governmental agencies tossed up by the economic crisis —was not a thing of beauty. I believe it can be said that too often the liberal acquiesced in formal government operation, permitting, as someone has said, the nation to function in behalf of the diplomatic service, rather than the other way around. Nor was his inability to affect fundamental government policy accidental. He had alienated himself from mere Americans, and could not influence them on basic matters.

Too often the liberal let himself be led by the nose by radical elements, and to accept party lines without question. "We all worked with the communists," one of the Washington livestock told me with a deprecating smile. The liberal, in other words, continued in abdication, his function as a mediator, as a bringer of light, as a challenger of pretensions remaining where he had put it after the fiascos of the 1910's. Radicalism had become a vested interest, much as were industry and labor. The liberal continued to conform, only, now, he broadened the field in which he conformed. The liberal in the State Department, for instance, who drew his stipend and went home to read his copy of the *Daily Worker,* now conformed to radical protocol as well as conservative. The same was true in unions, colleges, on magazines, and elsewhere.

Hence, it had to be Westbrook Pegler—no liberal, in my opinion— who denounced labor racketeers, naming names and stimulating action. It had to be Martin Dies—again, no liberal—who conducted more or less open forums on the nature of radicalism in America, the liberal's contribution being to click his heels and come to attention, to shout Amen and Halleluiah whenever his masters peremptorily reminded him that "Dies lies!" Marx and Engels, in the *Communist Manifesto*, had written, "The Communists disdain to conceal their views and aims. They openly declare that their ends can be attained only by the forcible overthrow of all existing social conditions." But now communists less and less disdained to conceal their views and aims. They emerged as, and, in cases became indistinguishable from, misunderstood liberals who were being persecuted because of their attachment to what was called "Twentieth Century Americanism." They must have had support. A distinguished educator, later himself actually accused of fascistic tendencies, informed me that it was not good policy to discuss the right and wrong of communism; it suggested, of all things, demagogy.

The present writer witnessed the browbeating, as it seemed to him, at a public forum, of Scott Nearing by some permutation of communist or fellow-traveler—Nearing, who had made his reputation as a fighter for academic freedom. Picket lines kept the liberal out of motion-picture houses; he had to console his curiosity with newspaper reports that the films in question were unhealthy for his tender mind. Money baskets rattled before him at meetings, and it was the brave man who refused to save his soul by putting his nickel on the drum for the Abraham Lincoln Brigade, workers defense organizations, strike committees, dance groups, and the support of militant publications. At his office there were perhaps petitions to conjure with, undercover or otherwise, and other worthy causes that only suspicious characters would have the boldness to question. Liberals signed and mailed form postcards protesting (presumably they did not have the brains to construct protests of their own manufacture) the meagerness of relief appropriations, the curtailment of work projects, the increase in the War Department budget, and the like. All these cards were neatly collected according to subject by Government officeworkers, and consigned by them to the Gripe Department files.

It is too easy to blame the communists for such antics. Were they so numerous that they could intimidate hardy noncommunists? What prevented the liberal—if he was a liberal—from crossing the picket line and seeing the movie for himself? Who forced him to go to meetings and imbibe the party line? Is there any escape from the conclusion that there was a little piece of totalitarianism in the liberal himself? That he was torn two ways—by his Croly thinking, on the one hand, his "worker's fatherland" feelings, on the other—and so was adrift from liberalism?

One looks not too happily back to the *Nation* of E. L. Godkin's time and compares it with a more contemporary *Nation*. Godkin was no great shakes as a liberal, as we have seen, and his journal ignored whole universes of living affairs. No doubt he could afford to ignore those who resented his aristocratic contempt for the masses. But his point of view emerges clearly and unequivocally from the pages of his magazine. Can one say the same for the modern *Nation?* Or the *New Republic?* Can one trace a straight line of inquiry and analysis in their pages? Compare their recent past and present with profit?

One recalls an article in the latter publication written by Carey Mc-Williams in appreciation of the late Humphrey Cobb, whose novel, *Paths of Glory,* etched a bitter and moving picture of World War I. Mr. Mc-Williams praised Cobb's unadulterated courage and honesty—which, by the way, found no better vehicle of expression than service to Hollywood —as being almost unique in modern times—unique, presumably, also in the pages of the *New Republic.* Are courage and honesty outmoded? Mr. McWilliams did not seem to imply as much. But where he expected to find it, he did not indicate.

For the liberal has now sprouted a new characteristic: scratch the liberal to find a cynic. He has seen too many vital energies poured into purportedly altruistic causes and reappear in the form of private ambitions. He has witnessed too many defeats. He has participated in too many barbecues which were supposed to be prepared for society in general. He has caught himself too many times still talking long after his conviction has seeped out of his shoes. He goes on talking—what else can he do? He continues to take additional helpings when he gets close enough to the spit. He continues to complain about the really bad men who are responsible for the world's troubles. But he can hardly help noticing that he himself is not hanging from a cross on Calvary, and that his programs have less and less likelihood of being fulfilled.

Perhaps some of the most depressing memories which the liberal has inherited from the 1930's relate to his capacity for loyalty and steadfastness and that of others of what he liked to term "the forces of progress." German Communists, Socialists, and Republicans died as the dog dieth in the Nazi bloodbath of 1933—who remembers their names, and what they stood for? Have Americans better memories for their own? To escape briefly into literature, who will find dignity and significance in the life and death of John Dos Passos' hero in *Adventures of a Young Man?* More specifically, who, here in America, cares to remember the Friends of the Soviet Union? Who will recite the anticlimax to the Scottsboro case? V. F. Calverton wrote of *The Liberation of American Literature;* many of the liberators are still alive. Who will review their services to American culture?

The extreme thinness of contemporary liberal history has not been entirely due to the rush of events. Too often the liberal has found it unprofitable to remember old issues and campaigns. In fact, he has sometimes found it expedient to hasten the process of forgetting, even to the point of suppressing would-be troubadours. J. B. Matthews, in 1938, wrote a wretched volume entitled *Odyssey of a Fellow Traveler,* but one which was filled with reproductions of letterheads of organizations, telegrams, leaflets, and other material referring directly to all manner of people who called themselves liberals. Who ever saw a review of this book which even denounced it as the whining apologia of a renegade? Who ever saw the book?

I am not sure that the liberal's repudiation of his radical, or otherwise ineffectual, past was entirely contemptible. Can it not be that he permitted himself to be led a considerable distance from his own people and his own integrity—using the word in a scientific sense—only to find, at the end, that he could not take the final step of severing himself from his roots? Perhaps it speaks well for the liberal, for his human, if not heroic, qualities, that, after he had burnt up old magazines and pamphlets in fright, and made a habit of ignoring old acquaintances, he began to find his way back, to "rediscover America," as the phrase went, to begin to look for positive qualities in the American way.

The liberal was no decisive force during the late war. Too often, he was merely glib, in the style of Archibald MacLeish, among others, or merely one of the help in the OSS, the OWI, and other government agencies. Some of the most serious statements about what America was, or ought to be, came from individuals who had no special fame as liberals. In any event, the war effectively internationalized, finally, the problem of business and government, and the atom bomb made its solution more drastically urgent. This situation has offered the liberal, so to speak, another chance. He, like others, has a sense of vast forces having been let loose which can play with merely human efforts and aspirations. Like others, he has his impulses to give up the ideal of human dignity, and seize on some consoling philosophy which will prepare him for anything. Yet, if he is truly a liberal, he must know that a world in which men cannot respect themselves would hardly be worth the powder to blow it up. He must, if he has regained his self-respect, insist on a solution to social problems which does not insult his heart and mind.

Here, it seems to me, one comes upon the genuine dilemma of the liberal, if it can be called that. In a world which tends more and more to march in lockstep, to put a premium on special interests rather than mutual interests, to discount the human impulse to link itself to old experience, he is required to forge a program which will bring the major contestants to terms. How much free enterprise offers the future, how much the methods of socialization, who can say precisely? It is no negation of liberalism to keep the mind open to the possibility that more socialization than one might offhand think will be necessary to a working society. Even L. T. Hobhouse's old book on liberalism, emphasizing Manchester traits rather than humanitarian, recognized that liberalism would have to adapt itself to many features of socialism. England accepted factory regulation, old-age insurance, unemployment insurance, minimum hours and wages, and she is now struggling with broader socialist measures. But whatever form of society the future may demand, surely it requires organization and methods which will respond to the needs of special social groups. Can the liberal serve his fellow-citizens better by following special party "lines" (radical or conservative) or by—in the time of atom bombs— candidly investigating the reality of various points of view, and insisting upon candor?

The liberal is first of all a person; he might well begin by insisting upon that fact. He is a citizen. He must see that he is a part of the scene, as unmistakably as the courthouse, the ward heeler, the Civil War cannon in the public square, the ramshackle house where a Negro lives. Liberalism as a weak, ineffectual instrument, eager to understand all sides of all questions for fear of subscribing to any, properly deserves contempt. A liberalism which does not require courage, conviction, social-mindedness, and also the will to make a positive contribution ought hardly to be taken seriously. But the liberal, conscious of the degraded position into which he has sunk, aware that his freedom to weigh and decide has too often been taken away from him with the excuse that there is an emergency, and not a second to lose, might well rebuff attempts to push him in any direction before his inquiries have been satisfactorily answered.

If the liberal cannot speak out, in one way or another, what is truly on his mind and the minds of his fellow-citizens, he deserves to be despised and ignored. He will, in that case, be everything he was once so scornfully called, before it became fashionable to be called a liberal: petty bourgeois, deviating, vacillating, opportunistic, ultraright, ultraleft, objectively counterrevolutionary . . . and above all, that thing of special scorn, an "intellectual."

Whether the liberal can save the world is not certain. It's not certain just who, if anyone, can save the world. But the liberal has a function to perform, and he must perform it effectively. The question is not, merely, whether he can satisfy himself that he is correct; "the question is," as Humpty Dumpty wisely remarked, "which is to be the master—that's all." And if liberalism cannot serve society in general any better than it has served it in recent decades, then the future is not likely to be any brighter, the promise of American life closer to fulfillment than it has been—at least for liberals.   —*Summer* 1948

BEN W. LEWIS

It's Political (Repeat Political) Economy

In the early spring of 1933, Washington, D.C. broke out with a rash of economists. The symptoms occurred suddenly and developed with epidemic sweep and swiftness. A couple of economists came to town in the company of the new President. These economists asked for more economists —and they came; and these for still more and they came. Then, the colleges and universities in a great burst of patriotic sacrifice sent practically *all* of their economists down to Washington. This was the golden age for economists; there have been those unkind enough to say that it was, as well, the golden age for the colleges and universities. You couldn't see the economics for the economists. Committees became seminars; term papers took the place of state papers; floor-leaders became cheer-leaders, and sessions opened with "alma mater" instead of prayer. The praying was done by the rest of the country—in volume.

It all came about in this fashion: economists are students of the economic system—the economy—the set of arrangements, institutions, and processes by which society's limited stock of natural and human resources is put continuously to its fullest and most productive use, and the resulting goods so divided as to satisfy in the most gratifying manner the unlimited wants of society's members. As scientists, that is when we put on our eye shades and gowns and rubber gloves, we examine and analyze these phenomena and seek to derive universal laws and principles of production, distribution and consumption—and thus keep our textbooks in a continual state of profitable revision.

In the late twenties and early thirties we did not like what we saw. An economy—allegedly a system—which permitted factories and firms and men—thirteen million men, good men, honest and eager and confused and hungry and ashamed—to be idle against their will, while soup-lines formed and the nation's flow of food and goods dried up by nearly fifty per cent, was not a pretty sight. But it was a tempting sight—a "challenge" I believe it is called. So we threw off our mortar boards, put on our homburgs, and became practitioners—and we have been practicing (I use the word advisedly) ever since. Of late our practice has been directed not

29

against debility in the economic body, but against a quite different disorder —inflation—a kind of economic high blood pressure—a feverish condition which turns out goods in unprecedented quantities, but under circumstances and at prices which make them quite unavailable to large sections of our population—a disorder that could run easily into uncontrolled catastrophe and disintegration.

Now, at the *very* present moment, as the patient rolls his eyes and exhibits a new array of symptoms, we are pondering the advisability of changing the prescription once more—from sedatives to stimulants.

One hundred and seventy-five years or so ago, when the Un-English Activities Committee was investigating Adam Smith for his leftish tendencies, the discipline now known as economics was called political economy. The title of Smith's best seller, the first systematic treatise of its kind, was, significantly, *The Wealth of Nations*, and it undertook to spell out the economic policies which nations should follow in order to increase their wealth and economic power. Smith's heresy consisted in the proposition that if a king really wanted to rule over an economically strong nation he should take up badminton and let the economy run itself. The economic system, according to Adam Smith, was so marvelously and delicately contrived that even though each person among the vast multitudes of the civilized world pursued without guidance or restriction the goal solely of his own economic gain, the net effect of the combined interaction of this mass of separate endeavors would be the complete and continuing economic salvation and happiness of all. Individual selfishness would be transmuted by an invisible hand into social benefit. To put the matter in a contemporary setting, Adam Smith broke the ground now being cultivated and enriched by the National Association of Manufacturers.

Until Smith's time, the State—the government—had played a leading part in economic affairs; the business of statecraft was pretty much the running of the economy. The effect of *The Wealth of Nations* together with a few dozen other contributing factors was to transform the art of political economy into the dismal science of economics. For one hundred and fifty years it slumbered fitfully in a network of brambles. And then, one cold day in the early spring of 1933, young Prince Franklin and young Lord Keynes cut their way through the brambles and dropped twin caresses on the creamy brow of the sleeping beauty—and ever since—insomnia! Plenty of brambles, but definitely no sleep!

Of course, this is the Hollywood version. As a matter of fact government and economics never stopped holding hands throughout the entire nineteenth century; and their interest in each other showed clear signs of picking up for forty years prior to the pealing of the bells for the New Deal and the New Economics. Today we study the problems of production, distribution and consumption not in terms of abstract economic units operating surely and predictably in space; we talk of corporations (and the Securities Exchange Commission); labor and management (and the National Labor Relations Board and the Taft-Hartley Act); money and banking (and Treasury policy and the Federal Reserve Board); inequality of wealth and income (and Federal and State taxes, and public debt policy); pricing (and the OPA and the FPC and the ICC and the FCC and 48 State Utilities Commissions); international trade (and the State Department and ECA and the Tariff Commission); the farmer (and, God forgive us, the Department of Agriculture).

And there's nothing temporary about it. You may think of these as emergency phenomena, but let me remind you that the world has been in a state of emergency most of the time since 1914. The generations now extant have known practically nothing but first and second degree depressions and inflations and hot and cold wars since they came on the scene, and the future, as far as we can now divine it, appears to be something other than a bountiful picnic spread beside cool waters in a shady glade. Oh no! However we may prefer to characterize the November groundswell that brought Harry Truman and his merry men back from the suburbs for four more years of temple cleaning, it was most certainly no aberration. The people of this country want big government and they are going to have it. And that means that, as far as the relation of economics to everyday life is concerned, when we study economics today we are studying political economy—the economic life of the nation and what we can do about it—*collectively*.

Government today is *big* government and it is getting bigger—and it is up to its neck in economic issues and processes. A forty billion dollar budget—forty *billion* dollars—that's *nine* zeros following the forty—to be collected from and spent among us every 365 days is a *big* budget; and a federal government which in its ordinary, everyday, non-emergency course of conduct undertakes to affect and assume a measure of responsibility for our food, clothing, shelter, jobs, income, savings, morals, health, happiness and hereafter, is a far cry from the federal government which within the memory of many here nodding, whipped itself into a fury over the projected dredging of Swizzle Creek and scandals in the Congressional distribution of nasturtium seeds.

But our government activities have changed even more markedly and more significantly in their direction than in their volume and extent. Since the turn of the century the federal government has been doing more things, dealing with more problems, providing more services. There is nothing peculiar in this fact; as population expands and our modern urban, industrial, corporate life grows more complex, there are inevitably more matters that demand collective action. Growth of this sort does not take place evenly, of course—government budgets respond to events and personalities—but there is certainly nothing startling in the fact of growth alone. The feature of our increasingly pervasive government that should arrest attention is its gradual acceptance of a responsibility broader than any one or any combination of its other burdens—*responsibility for the full and successful over-all operation, no less, of the entire economic system.*

This is something quite different from the "full dinnerpail," "two cars in every garage" platitudes with which we are regaled at regular four-year intervals; this is far beyond the promised "prosperity" of party platforms; this is a cold recognition that our economic system, left to its own devices, has failed and will fail again to do its job, and that no government which wants to survive can afford to be indifferent to the prospect, or inactive in the presence of a collapsing economy. We are not happy with *inflation*—it is quite possible that free America cannot stand the onslaught of another full-blown *depression.* Such an economic system needs shoring, and shoring is what it has been getting for the past fifteen years. Whether it needs more than shoring—whether it needs replacement rather than remodeling—is for the future to determine. But that business fluctuations are a matter of legitimate, of *necessary* government concern is beyond question. In a democracy this means that it is *our* collective concern.

We believe that booms and depressions are not inevitable; we believe that our economic system is our servant rather than our master; we believe that if we are engulfed again we have only ourselves to blame. These things we must believe. Political parties will differ on façades and trimmings, but no party henceforth will dream of denying government responsibility in this area.

I should like now to bare the workings of economic analysis to the test of your cold and skeptical scrutiny—to demonstrate its potentialities for the handling of a task that we are all agreed must be handled. We must stabilize our economy; how shall we proceed? The instruments are at hand: federal taxes, federal expenditures, federal debts—the federal "budget"—together with the federal credit and banking machinery and the federal monetary system. And we have a new philosophy to match, thoughtfully supplied by Lord Keynes in our hour of greatest need.

The first thing to note is that the government cannot possibly refrain from influencing the ups and downs of business. A forty billion dollar budget, banks, credit, money and debts—these are the very stuff of business cycles. We may use them unwittingly, but use them we must. We may prefer to pretend that they are neutral in their effects, but we know that they cannot be neutral. It is our task, then, to use them positively and purposefully.

First, let us consider taxes, assuming for purposes of the discussion that we want at this time to check the rise in prices and temper the business boom which we feel is swelling to dangerous proportions. Shall we increase taxes in order to draw money out of circulation and thus reduce the excessive demand for goods and so retard the rise in prices? Of course, our move may have the result of taking money from hoarding rather than from funds which would be devoted to spending—thus putting more money into the income stream and raising prices and stimulating the boom. Or would higher taxes increase business costs and for this reason raise prices? Or would increased taxes reduce business profits and so soften the demands of labor for another round of wage increases—thus holding costs and prices constant? Or would higher taxes reduce the amount of labor's take-home pay so that higher wages must be forthcoming from industry in order to compensate, with resulting higher costs and higher prices? Or will laborers, with less income due to higher taxes, lessen their demands for goods in the marketplace and so reduce the upward pressure on prices and keep them down? Would higher taxes make business ventures so much less profitable that businessmen will slow down production, thus diminishing the supply of goods and causing prices to rise? And, on the same reasoning, might prosperity be dealt such a blow by a tax increase that we would be plunged precipitously into another depression? That is, can we ever be sure that measures designed to temper will not, once they are in operation, result in destruction? Of course, by reducing business incomes, such taxes might operate to induce greater effort on the part of businessmen in order that their net incomes after taxes might remain unchanged—and so stimulate rather than retard the production of goods and services, increase supply and hold prices unchanged. Then too, there is a chance that higher taxes by lessening the stimulus for risk investment will enhance the volume of saving, and so slow up the tempo of business activity. Or, because increased taxes seem to presage the coming of the fully Collective State, will people of large wealth fly from dollars to goods, and by their increased spending send prices skyrocketing even higher? Or, because the wealthy fear the Revolution, will they hoard their money, with opposite effect?

Now that we have settled our tax program, let us turn to government expenditures. This device is reputedly suitable for use during periods of slackened employment. Will such spending start the ball of private enterprise rolling again or will it, by frightening private enterprisers, or by invading what private enterprisers regard as their personal domain, cause individual economic activity to shrivel on the vine? Or, conversely, shall we refrain from large government expenditures during times such as the present when private business is really rolling? The answer is "yes" if we look alone to the effect of government spending on the business cycle. But can we look to this alone, when the whole future of our civilization may depend on our spending vast sums to rehabilitate Europe— or when great sections of our own population stand in the direst need of such a gigantic program of housing construction as only our government can provide?

Let us review the possibilities of public debt policy and credit controls. Shall we pay off the public debt and lighten the debt-carrying load which now burdens the taxpayer? Surely this is a defensible measure of economy. But will this not put more money into circulation and aggravate the very ills of inflation which now plague us? Or, by a careful selection of those portions of the public debt which we retire, shall we reduce materially the excessive purchasing power of the nation and so ease the pressure of inflationary forces—at a high present cost to our taxpayers and to the dismay of our debt-holding banks? Shall the government support low-interest bearing government bonds in the financial markets, thus encouraging borrowing and consequent bidding up of prices and a dangerous expansion of credit; or shall the government permit low-interest government bonds to find their own level in the market, permit interest rates to rise as dictated by regular market forces and hence to retard the processes of expansion—possibly so greatly as to induce the onset of depression? And when shall we borrow rather than tax, and from whom and at what rates of interest—and with what uncertain effects?

Should the government, through the Federal Reserve System, seek by raising the re-discount rate and the reserve requirements of member banks to lessen the demand for credit in the interest of curbing the boom and the rise of prices; in the meantime trying frantically to predict whether its action will, on the one hand, be wholly ineffective or, on the other, be so dramatically effective as to bring a halt to such prosperity as we now enjoy? Again, conversely, in the trough of a prolonged depression, can the government expect that action designed to loosen credit will operate positively to induce businessmen to borrow, when business prospects still are dim? How shall we manipulate higher produce prices for farmers so that they will emerge as lower food prices for consumers?

And by the way, do we ever know until months after the event just which stage of which phase of the business cycle we are currently occupying, and just when the turning points of the cycle are at hand? Can we ever know the differences between just enough anticipatory governmental action and just too little and just too much, bearing in mind that this delicate difference can mean the whole vast difference between misery and happiness for millions of people? Just when does a rising price level rise too high, or a falling level drop too low, bearing in mind again that a moving price level produces gains for some people and losses for others at the same moment? When should the movement be stopped? When should we shift our policies and reverse the field?

I do not offer the foregoing as an example of economic analysis at its unexcelled best. But what I am saying is that the problem of economic stabilization is confusing and baffling in the extreme. The processes of stabilization are not mechanical. We can select the instruments of control and we can put them to work, but we can govern their operation only imperfectly, and even the direction, to say nothing of the extent and the incidence of their effects are quite as likely as not to be unpredictable. These instruments and controls must work through human beings engaged in living their own individual economic lives, and in a democracy (as the *Literary Digest* told us many years ago and as Mr. Gallup has recently confirmed), human beings are simply not predictable. They just aren't reasonable. They won't stay put, and no one knows which way they will jump! It is all very confusing and discouraging. We live in a mechanical age, but we have no mechanical answers.

Economists, to be sure, have a fascinating array of technical tools and terms to bring to bear—diminishing returns, Say's Law, Gresham's Law, marginal propensity to save, multipliers and accelerations, marginal revenue and marginal costs, all kinds of elasticities, indifference curves, liquidity preference, equilibria—the works. These are useful, possibly increasingly useful, but when we pull all the stops and throw everything we have into the breach, we are still not free from abject dependence upon our very personal value judgments.

It occurs to me, in this discouraging situation, that if we were to take brief stock of our problems and our tools we might be less discouraged—that if we were to appreciate the nature of our over-all economic task and to recognize and accept quite openly the limitations of our tools, we might find our problems reasonably soluble and our technical equipment altogether helpful.

First, a confession of faith. It is probably not true that the World is going to Hell in a wheelbarrow. Our generation ought by now to be pretty well inured to wolf cries. F.D.R. was elected for four terms but we still have elections so free that many of our more enthusiastic and better paid voters find it possible to cast several ballots in the same box. The SEC has been blighting the investment market for fifteen years, but stocks and bonds still constitute one of our most abundant crops. The depression of 1929 and World War II were both pressagented as the final destroyers of our way of life but, somehow, we still live, breathe and have our dividends. Our society is pretty tough. It thrives on problems that threaten its destruction; its staying power is *almost* beyond belief, but *certainly* beyond question. In *any* age, problems are new in their current setting; just possibly that's why they are problems. The world, its problems and its economists will be around for a long, long time.

We need to face up to the fact that the great issues of economic policy which concern us are *inherently* incapable of firm, precise, lasting answers. We deal here not only with humans, but with human *relationships*. Higher wages for you are quite likely to mean lower profits for me; tax reduction means less in the way of social services and an extension of the debt burden for everyone, and more net income for those released from taxes; public responsibility and a public program for forestalling and alleviating the devastation of depressions may mean the difference between economic life and death to millions, and the end of desirable freedoms to others—if the program works and an unholy mess for everyone if it doesn't. What we are seeking, and what we and our children will always be seeking are *satisfactory working arrangements*— acceptable adjustments of shifting and conflicting claims in a complex and constantly changing environment. At times it is easier to effect workable adjustments than at other times, but the settlement of your continuing claims against mine, our claims against those of others and the claims of all of us against those of posterity can, in the very nature of the case, never be made with finality or with the certainty of right. There are no single answers to great public problems that are "right" as distinct from all others that are, perforce, "wrong."

Somehow we must learn to take and expect to take something less than absolutes as answers. We need not seek compromises, but it will be a mistake to shun compromises that advance our causes materially in the direction we want our causes to go. We should shoot for the moon, but we should be willing to settle for a good light bulb (unused, made in U.S.)—and then shoot for the moon again! This is no "mess of pottage" philosophy; it is a working doctrine that emerges surely and coldly from (1) a recognition of the honest and sincere claims of all of us to the enjoyment of the limited opportunities and satisfactions which the world, at its very best, can make available, and (2) the fact that *decisions* have to be made, chances have to be taken. Public policy demands action as well as debate. We need principles and standards and techniques, and we need to work for their recognition and use, because good solutions short of the "best" are still better than poor solutions. But we must live today in order to live tomorrow.

The *processes* by which livable working arrangements are developed and operated are the important phenomena—the planning, the give-and-take, the conflict of interests and efforts—because this is life itself. The constant, constant working out of feasible solutions is the very business of life; that's all there is to it, both for the individual and for our "way of life." When a man is through seeking solutions for the problems that arise from living with other people, he is through living. We needn't worry about the existence of our uncertainties or the fact that we are groping for answers. There would be cause for worry only if we didn't seek, didn't grope, either because we didn't care or because we thought we had the answers. (God save us from people who have the answers!) It is important only that our seeking be purposive; and that our natural healthy concern for the results not degenerate into enervating anxiety.

A large part of what goes on in public affairs today seems to us to be characterized by greed, pressure, confusion and messy half-answers. That this is bound to be the case as long as public affairs deal with conflicting human desires and aspirations and as long as the disposition of public affairs is the legitimate active concern of all of us rather than solely of a governing group, is not always recognized. If this fact and its significance were generally understood we would hear less than we do about the failure of democracy. It is no excuse for cheap objectives and shoddy performance; democracy can be made much tighter and more efficient than its current practice might indicate. But it does give us a background against which we can reasonably appraise the performance of democratic ways; it enables us to fix our sights on attainable goals. I will venture the conclusion that the goals which we can attain under democracy are high enough for all human purposes and that the process of striving for their attainment, with responsibility in all of us for the outcome, is in itself the highest goal of all.   —*Fall* 1949

DAVID SPITZ

Why Communists Are Not of the Left

Oɴᴇ of the depressing facts of history is the tenacity with which men cling to labels long after the meaning has changed. The liberalism of John Stuart Mill is not that of Bertrand Russell and Morris Cohen. The communism of Karl Marx is in important respects different from that of Stalin. Yet a proclivity for loose thinking and heated argumentation leads men to blur the distinctions for the sake of a common identification. This is bad logic and bad history. It also ensures bad results.

One such result is the confused notion that communists belong to the left. Why this should be so is not difficult to understand, for when Marx and his disciples attacked the injustices of the economic and, more broadly, the social order, they aligned themselves with those rebellious souls who were championing the cause of human decency and human rights. And whatever the factors that kept communists and Trotskyites, socialists and anarchists, Fabians and syndicalists, apart, they were as one in their insistence that the servant has as much claim to freedom and security as his master, that the ordinary man is not designed to move eternally at the base of a pyramid which he has not constructed but which he is commanded to maintain.

In their adherence to this cause communists have been both loud and vigorous. By word and by deed they have set themselves forth as the assailants of the rich and the defenders of the poor. They have sought to lay bare the intricacies of the economic system, so as to account for the causes, and make plain the correctives, of poverty and insecurity. They have noted, with much insight, the paradox of certain Western countries that possess undemocratic institutions and permit undemocratic practices yet profess democratic ideals. They have pleaded, in those same countries, for an educational system divorced from the injustices of minority discrimination and bigoted controls. Through these and other approaches they have endeavored to justify their inclusion among the forces of the left.

But if any one thing is clear, it is that communists today are in spirit, thought, and action alien to the tenets of the left. This raises the questions: What is a communist? And what is meant by "the left"?

I I

At the outset, let us be clear that there are many things that a communist is not. He is *not* simply a radical, nor is a radical necessarily a communist. This is a common but dangerous confusion. If by radical we mean one who would do away with the existing order for some conception of what ought to be, one who seeks drastic, all-encompassing change, then socialists, anarchists, and indeed fascists, are radical; but they are not communists.

Nor are communists always radical. In the Soviet Union a communist is a conformist, a defender rather than an attacker of the *status quo,* which in its authoritarian practices and denial of political and intellectual freedoms bears little resemblance to the historical aspirations of the left. Outside the Soviet Union a communist is a radical only with respect to the policies of noncommunist governments, and then only when these policies are not in harmony with the interests of the USSR.

In Britain and the United States during the war, for example, communists sought to suppress criticism of the "capitalist democracies" on policies they themselves attacked prior to Soviet participation on the side of these countries and since the end of the war. More recently, in postwar Austria, local Communist Party officials joined Soviet commanders in opposing the nationalization of Austrian industries, because control of those industries would then go to the Austrian government rather than to the USSR, which has been claiming them for itself. In Italy the communist leader Palmiro Togliatti supported the union of Roman Catholic church and state in the new constitution; while in Czechoslovakia the Communist Party denounced the "bourgeois" five-day work week and instituted a six-day work week, reverting, in justification of this act, to very much the same arguments advanced by capitalists in early nineteenth-century England against higher wage rates and fewer hours.

To equate communism with radicalism, therefore, is to ignore the profound sense in which communists are conservative. More important, labeling as communists those noncommunists who seek substantial change is to pave the way for reactionary attacks on liberals and socialists; for a radical may be many things, including a communist.

It is equally misleading to identify a communist as one who advocates the overthrow of the government by force. Many non-Stalinists—Trotskyites, some anarchists, some fascists—fall into this category. More important, except where they are a substantial minority with a real chance of achieving power through revolution, communists as a matter of strategy rarely, today, advocate the overthrow of the government by force. What they contend is that a communist victory at the polls will lead to opposition by reactionary groups which will refuse to surrender control of the state machine, in which case the then constitutionally elected (communist) government will be compelled to seize power and suppress the rebellion by force. This, they note, is the business of any government that is properly elected and desires to survive.

A communist, again, cannot be defined simply as a Marxist. It is possible to claim adherence to a substantial part if not all of Marx's thought without accepting the interpretations of Lenin, just as one may subscribe to Marxism-Leninism without rendering obeisance to Stalin's several versions. Marxism and Marxism-Leninism are part of the baggage of a communist, but in some degree they also make up the intellectual inheritance of Trotsky, the social democrats of pre-Hitler Germany, and the Socialist Labor Party of Daniel de Leon, not to mention the numerous individuals and splinter groups that everywhere profess varying degrees of allegiance to Marx.

A communist is not simply a member of the Communist Party. Many who are communists do not hold membership cards: the party may think it more strategic that they not be known as party members; they may be communists who fear to avow it; or they may be communists without realizing it. In addition, some who hold membership cards are not communists. This is a delicate distinction and one that is not always easy to establish. Ordinarily, one who holds a membership card is a communist. But there are exceptions. It is too obvious and inconsequential, perhaps, to call attention to the espionage agent who joins the party for anticommunist purposes. It is less obvious but more common, however, that some are members only temporarily because of the party's stand on a particular issue. Thus for many Negroes the Communist Party is like a sieve: they join in the belief that the party stands for the betterment of their race and in the hope that by joining they will help the party to improve their condition; but after a short while they learn that the party is more interested in using them to achieve its special goals, which may not coincide with the purpose for which they have joined, and they get out. Similarly, there are at all times within the party men who, for one reason or another, do not go along with the Politburo on all policies or details. These "deviationists" periodically become the subjects of the mass purges whereby the party seeks to cleanse itself of all recalcitrants and ensure absolute conformity.

A communist, finally, is not one who occasionally or even frequently speaks with admiration for the achievements of the USSR, or more commonly for certain features of the USSR, or who stands for certain policies with which the Communist Party may at any one time happen to agree. It is possible to commend certain economic and judicial reforms instituted by the Soviet Union, or to applaud the great strides that have been made in that country in the conquest of illiteracy, without being a communist. And it is possible to support legislation designed to promote equality of citizenship and of opportunity for all the people, without being a communist, even if the Communist Party should commit itself to the same measure. A cause does not cease to be just because the wrong people affiliate themselves with it.

Who, then, is a communist? He is one who accepts *and consistently follows* the policies and tactics set forth by the Cominform, or, in the formal absence of a Cominform, by the rulers of the Soviet Union. This definition draws no sharp distinction between fellow-travelers and members of the party. They are cut from the same cloth though they display slightly different garb; a membership card hidden in the pocket is no real mark of distinction. On the other hand, this does permit a distinction to be drawn between those party members who are communists and those who are temporarily there because of error or misunderstanding. It includes communists who advocate the overthrow of the government by force when the Kremlin desires to avow this policy, and those who dissemble by advancing the same thesis under the guise that they are preparing to defend the government (when it is *their* government) from those who would use violence to overthrow it. It includes communists who are conservatives and communists who are radical, depending on whether it is loyalty to the USSR or rebellion against noncommunist states that is the standard by which they are to be judged.

In every case, what is central in the delineation of a communist is that he accepts not simply Marx but Marx as amended by Lenin; and not simply these but both as revised by Stalin, even and indeed especially where Stalin chooses to reverse his policy and his direction. Fidelity to the Kremlin, in a word, is the crucial determinant.

III

When we turn to the problem of left and right we move to more difficult ground. This is because the passion for simplicity has led men to draw a dichotomy between left and right on the basis of a single standard. Most commonly, this standard has been acceptance of or opposition to the established order. The right has been identified with those who wished to preserve the established order and the left with those who wished to change it. This simple division, however, does not correspond to historical reality; nor is it logically sound.

This becomes evident when we reflect that opposition to the established order merely indicates a desire for change; it does not indicate the direction of the change. Reactionaries are opposed to the *status quo,* but their desire to return to the *status quo ante* scarcely warrants their inclusion in the forces of the left. Fascists, too, are opposed to the established order, but their revolutionary appeal is to an authoritarianism that can in no way be identified with the methods and objectives of the left. Moreover, if we identify the right with the existing order and the left with the attack on it, we produce a paradoxical situation in which, after a political revolution, left and right assume reverse roles. On the other hand, where the left achieves power and pursues the policies it had formerly espoused, as is the case with the Labor government in England today, support of the established political order is in no sense a deviation from the precepts of the left.

Can we then define the right as the group which favors private property and individual enterprise, in contradistinction to the left which opposes private property and urges collectivist controls? If we do, we are embarrassed by the fact that the fascist right is quick to adopt collectivist measures and to do away with private property when it is deemed expedient or necessary; while the concept of individual enterprise held by the reactionary and even conservative right is increasingly one which restricts that enterprise to those few who share in the ownership or management of the huge concentrations of capital and industry. The allegedly communist left, on the other hand, does away with the system of private property, but in doing so it creates a new economic élite based on the control rather than the ownership of property, and abrogates those political and cultural freedoms that the liberal and radical left have historically cherished.

Is the left, then, the home of those who would increase the area of freedom, and the right the refuge of those who would destroy it? Historically, there is much substance to this view, for one of the hallmarks of the left has always been its refusal to conform to customary ways and traditional beliefs. But here again we are confronted with the paradox that undemocratic practices and authoritarian programs are common to communists and Trotskyites as well as to some political parties of both the left and the right, while the espousal of civil liberties frequently cuts across the left-right dichotomy.

These considerations make plain the difficulty of a linear conception in which left and right represent the polar extremes. If we take property as our line of division, communists are indeed in the left but so too are the fascists of Nazi Germany, even if in varying speed and degree. If we use liberty as our point of departure, elements of the conservative right assume some of the attributes of the left while the communists join the fascists on the right.

A solution to this dilemma has been suggested by some writers who urge the substitution of a circle in place of a line, with the extreme (fascist) right and the extreme (communist) left meeting at the bottom. Then the circle can be viewed in two ways: from the standpoint of property, fascism and the moderate right are aligned against communism and the moderate left; from the standpoint of liberty, fascism and communism stand together against the moderate right and the moderate left.

This conception has the virtue of joining the two authoritarian systems on the basis of their common opposition to liberty. But it overlooks the fact that in Nazi Germany and increasingly in Mussolini's Italy, the demands of the state took priority over the perquisites of private property. Moreover, the position of some sectors of the moderate right on questions of freedom of speech for dissenters, or of civil liberties for Negroes and other minority groups, is hardly calculated to unite them with the noncommunist left.

Once again, therefore, we must reject the attempt to reduce complex social phenomena to a simple mathematical symbol, whether it be a line or a circle. In both cases the kind of distinction that is offered fails to give us the precision we seek: a category that will enable us somehow to distinguish left from right with some semblance of consistency.

The basis for such a category appears if we abandon the idea of a single standard and think instead in multidimensional terms. We must take not liberty *or* property but *both*, and on three levels at least—the political, the economic, and the intellectual.

On the political level, the tradition of the left is clear. It has always been associated with the fight against authoritarianism in government, with the attack on limited suffrage and oligarchical rule. Apart from the anarchists who reject all forms of organized coercion and thus government itself, the left has been the party of democracy, the sector of the population that has denied the claim of any special group permanently to control the government and to determine public policy. Where elements of the right have sought to restrict the exercise of political power to the allegedly superior few, the left has denied that racial composition, or economic or physical advantage, is a rational criterion of political competence. The fallibility of men in power, and the tendency they demonstrate to abuse that power, has convinced the left that whatever else a proper political system requires, the mechanism for the correction of error must always be present. Only democracy offers such a constitutional mechanism for the correction of error, for only democracy provides for the periodic election *and removal* of the rulers by the ruled.

Economically, the left has always represented the interests of the lower classes, while the right—revolutionary fascists apart—has tended to defend the interests of the upper or ruling classes. The left has been opposed to private property because it has believed that private ownership gives power without responsibility; he who owns property has the legal right to use it for his own interests, even at the sacrifice of the welfare of others. Accordingly the left has supported the efforts of labor unions, through collective bargaining, to curb the great economic powers of the owners and managers, and to give workers a voice in the formulation of the conditions under which they labor. It has sought the intervention of government, both to curtail the growth of monopoly, which dooms individual enterprise and economic freedom, and to prevent the use of discriminatory practices in employment. More, it has encouraged government to move directly into the economic sphere through the public ownership and operation of industry. Through all these devices, the left has endeavored to equalize opportunity and to eliminate what it regards as unmerited privilege and advantage. It has tried to establish in the economic, as in the political sphere, those conditions that free men can respect and find adequate to the fulfillment of their capacities and their dreams. In this the left, unlike the right, has fought for man's emancipation from arbitrary command.

On the intellectual level, the left has consistently stood for intellectual freedom and the right of all men to pursue their chosen ways of life. It has attacked the dictates of authority and the theory of the closed mind, arguing instead that only where men are free to examine the pronouncements of others can reason emerge to lead the way. The left does not claim that the opinions of those in authority are inevitably wrong; it insists only on the freedom to examine them. Since it denies that any one system or group of men embodies final truth, it refuses to accept the principle of conformity but defends the principle of free inquiry and free expression—in art, in music, in scholarship, in religion. The left is rebellious, not against everything, but against authoritarianism of the mind.

In brief, the left—liberals, socialists, and anarchists alike—is that group which stands for emancipation from authoritarian government and arbitrary command, for equality of opportunity and the elimination of artificial privilege, for freedom of the mind to pursue truth and even error as one's reason, capacities, and interests may indicate. The left has always been, and still remains, that sector associated with the fight for political and intellectual freedom, and for economic change, where necessary or desirable, in the interests of the many rather than the few, of the lower rather than the upper classes.

I V

How do the communists meet this threefold criterion of the left? At first blush, there is no simple answer to this question. It depends on whether the communists are in power or out of power, and if out of power on the position currently held by the Soviet Union. But closer examination will reveal that underlying all the shifts in policy there is a common purpose and a common theme. If we look at the political, economic, and intellectual phases of communist philosophy and tactics, we may find our answer.

On the political side, wherever the communists are in power, as in the Soviet Union and its satellite countries, they deny the principle of democracy and affirm the right of the party élite to rule. Stalin, to be sure, contends that the Soviet constitution and political system are the most democratic in the world. He bases this claim on the fact that electoral results regularly show the people to be almost unanimously agreed in support of the government, as in the 1946 elections to the Supreme Soviet, where 96.8 per cent of those eligible to vote actually voted, and of those voting 99.7 per cent voted for the "bloc" of party and nonparty Bolsheviks.

Apart from the dubious validity of these figures, this is clearly a spurious argument. In the absence of free elections, of a choice of alternatives, of a legal opposition, there can be no democracy. And when we look carefully at the institutions and practices of the USSR the lack of democracy is precisely what we find. Instead of rule by a popularly elected legislature, the Soviets employ rule by the Politburo, by executive decree. For a political party system in which, in England at least, the parties represent different conceptions of public policy, the Soviets have instituted a single party, the Communist Party, whose role it is to execute the will of the Politburo. For the free play of conflicting ideas, the Soviets have substituted a single creed, Marxism-Leninism-Stalinism, under which criticism of the government is construed as treason. In place of a responsible executive, there is a Leader, Stalin, whose will, unchallengeable, is law. These, however else we may regard them, do not add up to democracy.

Where the communists are out of power, as in the United States, their position is greatly confused. They are quick to defend the political institutions of the USSR and to insist that these are democratic. More than that, they maintain within their own communist party organizations the same rigid controls, the same hierarchy of authority, the same intolerance of dissent. Nevertheless, they do not hesitate to condemn these principles when practiced by others. Thus they point to the denial in certain communities of the right to freedom of speech for dissenting groups, to the perversion of democracy embodied in boss-rule, to the restriction of suffrage in southern states, and the like. If any conclusion from this double system of bookkeeping is possible, it can only be that communists, when seeking power, represent themselves as the champions of democracy; but once in power they pursue the very authoritarian practices they applaud in Georgia, USSR, but denounce in Georgia, USA. In this they remain true to Lenin who said: "There are no morals in politics; there is only expediency." But they are not thereby true to the left.

The position of the communists in the economic sphere is less clear. In the Soviet Union much has been done, through a broad system of social services, to establish certain minimum standards for the great masses of the people. Much also has been done to eliminate the class of the idle rich and, in lesser degree, to seek to narrow the gap between the economically favored and the lower social classes. Everybody not only has a right to a job, everybody works; and this includes both the powerful and the privileged.

But the system of disproportionate rewards remains. The new upper classes of party officials, bureaucrats, managers, and technicians, scientists and artists, army and navy officers and the chieftains of the secret police, enjoy a standard of living far greater than that of the people over whom they rule. Between manager and worker there is a chasm of privilege exceeded only by that of power. The Russian worker who in any way expresses dissent on questions of political or economic policy finds his opportunity to rise severely limited; and there are no alternatives to government employment. His wage rates are set by the agencies of the government, and the leaders of his trade unions are responsible not to him but to the Communist Party. Since the abortive attempt of the Kronstadt sailors in 1921, there have been no strikes on wages and related matters in state industries; the Russian worker knows that a strike is liable to prosecution as a counter-revolutionary measure or an act of sabotage. He carries a card or "labor passport" which bears much of his life and occupational history and without which he cannot be employed. He can change his job only with permission of the manager of his industry, and if he is frequently late or absents himself from his place of employment he is guilty of a crime punishable by imprisonment. The economic freedoms and opportunities traditionally defended by the left are not, it would appear, defended by the communists in the USSR.

What of communists outside the Soviet orbit? Do they not speak for the interests of the many rather than the few? Here the record is equally blurred. The Communist Party in the United States, for example, has a long history of opposition to economic privilege, to big business and monopoly; it has a long history too in support of the economic struggles of the wage-earners, the unemployed, the consumers. Indeed, communists have sacrificed their very lives as they have fought in the forefront of many struggles for more humane treatment and a greater share of economic wealth for the underprivileged.

However, a study of the history and functioning of communists in such struggles reveals that their underlying policy is always that of rule-or-ruin. They have become active in labor organizations, unemployed leagues, farm groups, consumer councils, and the like, in an effort to secure positions of leadership in them. Once in control, they use these organizations not simply for the avowed purposes for which these organizations were designed but as a springboard from which to proclaim communist doctrine on all subjects, and especially to propagandize for the Soviet Union and its policies. After the disruption of the Nazi-Soviet Pact, for example, and the entrance of the Soviet Union into the war, communist-dominated unions vigorously promoted the institution of industry wage incentives to increase production, a program they bitterly opposed during the pact and since the end of the war. Communist-dominated unions in France and Italy currently oppose Marshall Plan aid which would give their members jobs and aid their countries economically, thereby demonstrating that communists will not hesitate to sacrifice the economic ends of organizations they control for the political ends of the USSR.

Where communists have not been able to control the economic organizations of the lower income groups, they have followed, in the main, two alternative patterns of strategy. One has been to promote internal dissension and thus prevent the organization from effectively pursuing its avowed purposes, while at the same time calling for "internal democracy" so as to maintain the conditions that will enable them to continue their activities and eventually to achieve control. Along with this there is generally involved the most extreme type of personal vilification of noncommunist leaders, in an effort to discredit them and alienate their following. The other pattern has been to sabotage the organization by setting up a rival group under their control to combat it, or to prevent it from functioning by attack from without. This takes the form of name-calling, of labeling the organization a fascist tool, of denying it any assistance and urging those whom it influences not to support it, and so on. In every case, from the communist standpoint, either it shall be communist-ruled or it shall be communist-ruined.

Communist abdication from the principles of the left is nowhere more clear than in the intellectual sphere. In the Soviet Union the body of thought we call communism has become a theology, to be accepted in all its details and to be removed from the area of scrutiny. There is the bible, containing the old testament of Marx and Engels and the new testament of Lenin. There are the high priests—Stalin and the Politburo —to interpret the bible. And there are the inquisitors, swift to castigate those who deviate from the true path and to place their books and their theories on the Soviet Index. Whether it is political doctrine or economic analysis, architecture or biology, musical composition or the drama, mathematics or statistics, history or literature, conformity to the Communist Party position is the necessary prerequisite to survival.

It is not important to ask whether the particular position of the Soviets on a question of art or genetics is the right one. What is important to note is that, whether right or wrong, it is a *political* decision and must be obeyed, even if one's knowledge and reason were to dictate otherwise. Consider, for example, the revealing remark of Professor Anton Zhebrak, a distinguished Soviet geneticist: "I, as a party member, do not consider it possible for me to retain the views [on genetics] which have been recognized as erroneous by the Central Committee of our party." Were a scientist in England or the United States to utter such a statement with reference to the noncommunist political parties of his country, he would almost certainly be regarded as ready for incarceration in a home for the mentally deranged.

It is interesting to note that this intellectual authoritarianism—what the communists call "democratic centralism"—is not a new but a very old article in the communist theology. Lenin "proves" many of his arguments by quotation from Marx and Engels; Stalin "proves" his theses in the same way. Thus, with reference to the once controversial issue of equalitarianism, Stalin observed that Marx and Lenin had said one thing, their critics another. "Who is right," Stalin then asked, "Marx and Lenin, or our equalitarians? We may take it that Marx and Lenin are right."

What emerges from this pattern of faith is a slavish obedience to presumed first principles. In place of scientific method, experimentation, and the inductive process, we have a closed system in which one reasons by simple deduction from truths already established or newly proclaimed by those who have the power to do so. That these truths are altered or reversed as the contingencies of the moment seem to dictate, only to be restored again, is no cause for concern to the faithful. The truth is always true, even if it had once been false.

This applies equally to communists outside the USSR. Nothing in modern history is so striking as the consistency with which communists in England, the United States, France, and other noncommunist states, have changed their ideas and their positions at the dictates of the Soviet Union. Before the Nazi-Soviet Pact, the fascists were "beasts" who had to be crushed. After the pact, in accordance with Molotov's declaration, a war against fascism was held to be a crime against humanity, a barbaric medieval crusade; for fascism, Molotov said, was only "a matter of political views." When the Soviets were invaded by Germany, the war changed into a people's struggle for democracy and freedom. And now that the war is over, only the Soviet Union is pursuing the right foreign policy, and only the "capitalist democracies" are imperialist aggressors. These intellectual gyrations have recently been displayed on questions of Zionism, the acceptance or rejection of Western culture, nationalism versus internationalism, cooperation with liberal forces in politics, and the like, *ad infinitum*.

What is fascinating in this process to the noncommunist observer is the way in which all but a very few communists—who are promptly vilified as renegades—change their minds concurrently. In all countries and within a few days, the new "line" is adopted and the old "line" cast aside. The rapid succession with which Togliatti in Italy, Pollitt in England, and Foster and Dennis in the United States parroted Maurice Thorez's declarations of allegiance to the Soviet Union in the event of war between the USSR and his own country, is only one of the more recent of many cases in point. In a habitat of intellectual freedom and intellectual respect, would not some express skepticism that what had been true on Monday should be false on Tuesday?

But what we have here is an authoritarianism of the mind based on a conviction that the leaders of the party are both omniscient and unerring. If communists ceased to have this conviction, they would be compelled to say, with Rubashov, the tragic hero of Koestler's *Darkness at Noon*: "The fact is: I no longer believe in my infallibility. That is why I am lost."

V

The conclusion is inescapable: communists are not of the left. They are not democrats but totalitarians, not radicals but conformists, not fighters for freedom and the economic welfare of the ordinary man but harbingers of a new slavery and a new privileged class. For the liberal who cherishes individual judgment and the freedom to choose between alternative possibilities, for the democratic socialist who seeks more quickly to alter the economic foundations of the social order so as to effect a more desirable distribution in economic power and economic goods, for the anarchist who rejects political and economic coercion so as to establish the conditions for the free flowering of the individual personality, there is no kinship with communism.

The myth of communist leftism cannot long survive contradictions. Until it is completely dead, liberals and their brethren of the left must guard against those who would stand in disguise alongside them.

—*Winter* 1949-50

BERTRAM D. WOLFE

Science Joins the Party

IF THE Man-from-Mars, or from that scarcely less remote planet, the Western World, had wandered into the 1948 Summer Congress of the Lenin All-Russian Academy of Agricultural Sciences to listen to the "discussion" on genetics, he would never have imagined that he was at a scientific congress at all. There was only one report, "On the Situation in Biological Science,"[1] and only one reporter, who chaired the sessions, had the first word and the last. The "sessions" had the air of a political mass meeting with a touch of Roman gladiatorial circus. The forty-six members of the Academy present were drowned in a turbulent sea of over "700 practical workers from the agricultural research institutes, biology teachers, agronomists, zootechnicians, economists," political commissars and "dialectical materialist philosophers." The members of the Academy were not there to discuss their experiments, present their papers, submit their difficult and subtle specialties to the judgment of their peers. Indeed, there were no papers presented, no breaking up of the general sessions into special subsections for the consideration of specialties—only eight days of target practice with Trofim D. Lysenko as the number one sharpshooter, and all of Russia's most distinguished geneticists as targets.

Throughout this singular "genetics discussion" there were outbursts of stormy applause, raucous laughter, hoots, catcalls, sinister threats, and a constant hail of abuse for the more important members of the Academy. Geneticists who tried to remain silent were provoked and taunted for their "cowardice." Those who sought to speak on their difficult technical specialties, genes, chromosomes, diploids, polyploids, pure strains, and hybrids, before an unprepared audience, were heckled, interrupted, silenced by a storm of ignorant jests and coarse epithets. Those who, faces white with fear, sought to "confess their errors," were mocked for the "belated" and "inadequate" nature of their confessions. As they heard the work of a lifetime ridiculed and called into question, a few tried to explain some fragment or save some remnant. They were heckled more cruelly than the others. The epithets might not all seem like insults to the Man-from-Mars, but they were genuine cusswords in the murky twilight-world in which Soviet science is now fighting its last, dim, losing battle for scientific freedom. These scientists, themselves convinced communists and dialectical materialists whose only ambition had been to excel in their field, to serve science and their people, heard themselves called "idealists" (which, in the land of dialectical materialism made the State Faith, is not a compliment but the master cussword). They were called "metaphysicians," "adherents of clerical reaction,"[2] "Mendelist-Weismannist-Morganist scholastics," "men alien to the world outlook of the Soviet people," "unpatriotic fly-breeders," "formal geneticists, cog-

---

[1] *The Situation in Biological Science: Proceedings of the Lenin Academy of Agricultural Sciences of the U.S.S.R. Complete Stenographic Report.* International Publishers, 1949.
[2] "Unfortunately for the reputation of genetics in the Soviet Union, there have been two clerics, Malthus and Mendel, who have played important parts in developing its theoretical ideas." Hudson and Richens: *The New Genetics in the Soviet Union,* published by the Imperial Bureau of Plant Breeding of Cambridge University, 1946.

nitively effete and practically sterile," "wagers of an unseemly struggle against Soviet science," "Menshevik idealists in philosophy and science," "rotten liberals," "corrupters of the scientific student youth," "adherents of reactionary-bourgeois racist theories," "debasers of Darwinism," "propagators of the harmful, hostile myth of the international unity of science," "servile worshippers of alien, hostile, enemy, reactionary bourgeois science," "enemies of the progress of Soviet science and the Soviet people."

II

The director of this orchestration of abuse was Trofim D. Lysenko, a thin, broad-shouldered man of peasant origin, with the Order of Lenin on his breast, a protruding, active "Adam's apple," blazing, slightly asymmetrical eyes lit with a fanatical gleam of triumph. He stood there supremely confident, for as he repeatedly hinted to his appreciative claque and to the cringing veteran scientists, behind his assault stood "the Party of Lenin-Stalin and Comrade Stalin personally." If they doubted it, there was the Order of Lenin on his breast, the two Stalin First Prizes for Achievement in Science, and the pages of *Pravda*, which reported these speeches and epithets as if genetics had become a popular sporting event, or *Pravda* a scientific journal for genetical specialists.

Moreover, the Party had been moving Lysenko steadily upward into positions of power: Vice Chairman of the Supreme Soviet; since 1938 President of the Lenin Academy of Agricultural Sciences; since 1940, Director of the Institute of Genetics of the Academy of Sciences; and henceforth, wielder of the unseeing shears that can cut a lifetime scientist off from scientific work, or even cut the thread of life itself.

This singular figure first appeared in Soviet biology in the early '30's. We get revealing close-ups of Lysenko in that stage of his career from the fact that he was interviewed and his work investigated by two foreign scientists, both so sympathetic to the Soviet Union and so impressed by its work in the field of genetics that one visited its laboratories and the other went to live and work in them.

Dr. S. C. Harland, aging and highly esteemed British geneticist, has this to say of his interview:

> I found him completely ignorant of the elementary principles of genetics and plant physiology. Having worked on genetics and plant-breeding for some thirty-five years, I can honestly say that to talk to Lysenko was like trying to explain the differential calculus to a man who did not know his twelve times table.[3]

---

[3]*Russia Puts the Clock Back*, by John Langdon-Davies, with a foreword by Sir Henry Dale. Gollancz, 1949.

Dr. H. J. Muller, Nobel Prize winner in genetics for his ground-breaking work in producing mutations in the genes of fruit-flies by X-ray irradiation, honored by the Soviet Union by an appointment as Senior Geneticist at the Institute of Genetics of Moscow for four years (1933-37) and by membership in the Soviet Academy of Sciences, has this to say of Lysenko:

> In 1935 genetics had reached a very high state of advancement in the U.S.S.R., and many eminent scientists were working in it. The Soviet Communist Party, unable to find a single reputable scientist willing to take part in its attack on genetics, began systematically to build up in that year the reputation of an alleged "geneticist," a peasant-turned-plant-breeder named Trofim Lysenko, who had achieved some dubious success in applying, by trial-and-error proceedings an early American discovery about pre-treating of seeds in order to influence the time of maturation of certain crops. Lysenko's writings on theoretical lines are the merest drivel. He obviously fails to comprehend either what a controlled experiment is, or the established principle of genetics.[4]

The interpreter at the interview between Dr. Harland and the future dictator in Russian biology, was Nikolai Ivanovich Vavilov, at that time head of the Academy of Agricultural Sciences and of the Genetics Institute, and famous throughout the world for his researches on the geographical centers of origin and the genetical evolution of the most important cultivated grains. Dr. Harland, finally throwing up his hands in despair, said to Vavilov: "Will you ask Citizen Lysenko to answer my question with a 'yes' or a 'no,' if such a fine distinction is possible in the language he speaks." Vavilov smiled protectively and shook his head:

"Lysenko is one of the 'angry species.' All progress in this world has been made by angry men, so let him go on working. He may find out how to grow bananas in Moscow. He does no harm, and some day may do some good."

There are still no bananas growing in Moscow, but Lysenko has hounded Vavilov out of genetics. He has displaced Vavilov as Director of the Genetics Institute and as President of the Academy of Agricultural Sciences. In 1939 he made Vavilov chief target of his attacks. In answer, Vavilov praised, as well he might, the practical and theoretical achievements of Soviet experimental biology; but he urged also the international interdependence and unity of world science, and pleaded that Soviet biology should not deny itself the privilege of learning from other lands. This brave defense of the internationalism of science (once a basic belief of communism, and indeed of all civilized men), sealed Vavilov's fate. He was befouled in the press.

---

[4]"The Destruction of Science in the U.S.S.R." By H. J. Muller. *Saturday Review of Literature,* Dec. 4 and 11, 1948; *Bulletin of Atomic Scientists,* December, 1948.

His posts were taken from him. Before the Nazi-Soviet Pact he was pronounced a "propagator of Nazi racist theories," and after the Stalin-Hitler Pact he was sent to the Siberian Arctic as a "British spy" (he was an honorary member of the British Royal Academy of Sciences), where he died under circumstances which the Soviet government refuses to clarify on inquiry from his foreign colleagues. To Vavilov's own brother, Sergei, has been given the painful and shameful task of delivering lyrical public addresses praising the "thoughtful care which the Soviet government and Comrade Stalin personally show for Soviet science and Soviet scientists." No less interesting is it to note that Lysenko's own brother, Pavel D. Lysenko, leading fuel and coke chemist, has fled from the "sheltering care of the Soviet government and Comrade Stalin personally," and now resides (since the summer of 1949) in America.

III

The purpose of Lysenko's address at the 1948 Summer Congress was to put an end to a theoretical controversy that had been raging for more than a decade, and to consummate a purge of all remaining experimental geneticists. Ever since 1931, when scientists had been ordered to give up their long-range investigations in favor of "work of immediate practical application," and to coordinate all their work into the framework of the five-year plans, all of Russia's leading geneticists, and they were among the world's best, have been under steadily increasing fire. In 1933, geneticists Chetverikov, Ferry, Ephroimson, and Levitsky had disappeared from their laboratories to turn up later in forced labor camps. In 1936, Agol followed, and the impressive Medico-Genetical Institute was dissolved. All through the following decade, the casualty rate among Russian geneticists, and, along with that, the moral casualty rate (renunciation of doctrines, abandonment of experiments, forced confessions of "scientific and philosophical guilt") remained high. Yet, as a body, these devoted scientists continued their dedication to their difficult and complicated experiments and to scientific truth as they found it in their laboratories. And the Soviet government, a little distrustful of anything which could not readily be comprehended by the "greatest genius, scholar-scientist of all lands and all times" and could not readily be settled by ukase or Politburo resolution, nevertheless, saw how much the world esteemed these men and their work, and continued to "tolerate" it, and to recognize by that tolerance that truth is a modest and elusive maiden that cannot always be taken by shock troops or storm attacks.

Not until 1939 did the geneticists of the entire world become aware of the fateful drama that was being enacted in Soviet science. In 1936, they had chosen Vavilov to preside over a congress of the geneticists of the world, which was to have been held in Moscow. But Moscow had suddenly cancelled the invitations, without explanation. After repeated postponements, it was set at last for Edinburgh for the summer of 1939. Papers by Vavilov and fifty other Russian scientists were received, yet, at the last moment, they did not appear. Vavilov's chair, as president, remained dramatically vacant throughout the sessions. Along with the fifty Russians, six out of twelve German experts had been "unable to attend."

IV

Even from his new vantage point as President of the Academy of Agricultural Sciences, Lysenko proved unable to convince the serious scientists who made up the majority of the Academy members. The Party began to pack the Academy with a whole detachment of new members to outvote the old, if they could not outtalk them. Yet the real leaders of Soviet genetical experiment, though they could be bullied and outvoted, still felt that no quotation from Marx or Engels or Michurin or Stalin, could quite take the place of experimental evidence and theoretical reasoning. No mere vote could convince them that Lysenko understood the genetical experiments he so brashly attacked. Nor convince them that, in experiments involving artificial pollenization of a castrated plant (to cite one instance), for their careful conveying of a single pollen grain of a single pure strain, and their washing of hand and glove and apparatus with alcohol before the next pollen grain was handled, one could substitute a mass of mixed and un-pedigreed pollen grains, letting the female organ of the plant or its ovule "select" by "love marriage" (*brak po lyubvi*) "the best spermatazoid from the mixture which will produce the best adapted offspring." Nor that heredity could be usefully or scientifically defined as "the property of a living body to require definite conditions for its life and development and to respond in a definite way to definite conditions." Or that variation or mutation could be induced in offspring of a plant or animal at will by subjecting it "to external conditions which, to one extent or another, do not correspond to the natural requirements of the given organic form."[5]

The science of genetics, they knew, was very young, no older than the years of the present century. But they were not disposed to deprive their laboratories or their land of its growing body of important, ever more exact and refined, and overwhelmingly verified and verifiable conclusions concerning the chromosome and gene as the specialized substance that decisively determines hereditary characters, and mutations in the genes and chromosomes as the primary cause of variation from heredity. Nor to accept the dogma that the will of a fanatical plant-breeder, or the enactment of laws of Nature by an ignorant Politburo, could automatically make it

---

[5]*The Situation in Biological Science.* T. D. Lysenko and Others. pp. 35-37 and 122.

possible to control heredity by ukase and "Bolshevik-tempo plan" in any desired direction, by some uncontrolled, undefined, and scientifically unverifiable changes in the environment, or random mixtures of impure strains, depending on the passion and wisdom of the ovum or spermatazoon to take the place of the intelligence and planful care of the experimenter.

V

It is impossible in a single article to do more than suggest some of the differences that have arisen in a field as technical as that of genetics, but the above examples, crude and strange as they sound, are actually taken from Lysenko's propositions and are not unrepresentative of the "theories" and methods which Lysenko has been advancing to replace the whole body of careful experiment and close reasoning by the geneticists of many lands, including those of the Soviet Union, a body of experiment and reasoning which has been growing steadily since Darwin first tried to put the rule-of-thumb methods and superstitions of plant and animal breeders on a scientific basis, since Mendel first made his experiments with the hereditary results of mating round and wrinkled peas, since Weismann first postulated the useful division into soma and chromosome, and since Morgan and others first began their famous experiments on the heredity of such easily and swiftly reproducing organisms as fruit flies.

Some others of Lysenko's views which are rejected by the geneticists of all lands may be schematically stated as follows:

1. Lamarck was right as against Darwin.

2. There is no special hereditary substance (chromosomes with their genes), but the whole plant or animal, by "assimilation and dissimilation" of its "external and internal environment" determines the character of the offspring. The breeder has only to change the environment or assimilation slightly and he can produce variations or new species at will.

3. Hereditary changes in plants can be determined at will by grafting, the graft being able to change the heredity of the stock or the stock of the graft, according to which is made the "mentor."

4. At the present stage of genetical knowledge, "chance" and "fortuity" can be completely expelled from mutation or variation, and hereditary changes can be introduced, decreed, "planned" or "directed" in any direction desired by the breeder. Whoever does not recognize this is "asking favors from nature" instead of giving her orders. He is a bourgeois, reactionary, fascist, metaphysical, scholastic, foreign-minded element, agent of the enemies of the Soviet Union, saboteur and wrecker of Soviet agriculture. Whoever wants to work on these slow

and difficult and painstaking genetical experiments is by that fact committing treason to Soviet agriculture and the Soviet people.

5. Statistics and mathematical reasoning are inapplicable in biological problems. (This last is particularly interesting since England's leading mathematical genetical expert, J. B. S. Haldane, as a scientist has helped develop the refining techniques of mathematics for the analysis of genetical experiments; but as Chairman of the Editorial Board of the *Daily Worker* he tries to defend Lysenko and deceive the British public as to the issues in the pogrom against Soviet science. In England he can still thus serve the Communist Party and the *Daily Worker* without giving up his mathematical genetics, but in Russia he would long ago have disappeared in the purges.)

6. The heredity of a plant or animal is but the accumulated assimilation of its past environment through many generations. The "conservatism" of the plant or animal (Lysenko's word for the tendency of offspring to resemble their parents) can easily be "shattered" by changes in the environment, and the new characters thus inculcated will breed true. "It is possible to *force* any form of plant or animal *to change more quickly* and in the *direction desirable to man.*" (Emphasis by Lysenko.)

There is not one of the above assumptions, and Lysenko makes many more like them, which would be accepted by the geneticists of other lands, or was freely accepted by those of Russia. All of them require precise definition, and could easily be tested under conditions of scientific freedom, by the devising of a critical or crucial experiment with proper controls, and all of them could easily be proved, indeed have been proved, to be: a) too sweeping; b) meaningless for both theory and practice; or c) arrant nonsense— or all three at once. The interested reader can further study the issues involved, insofar as they are biological and not political, by reading the balanced scientific summary of Lysenko's views in Hudson and Rich: *The New Genetics in the Soviet Union*, or more polemical statements of the controversy for laymen in Langdon-Davis: *Russia Puts the Clock Back*; Julian Huxley: *Heredity East and West*; Conway Zirkle (Editor): *The Death of a Science in Russia*. The latest bibliography on the subject is Morris C. Leikind: *The Genetics Controversy in the U.S.S.R.* (American Genetic Association.)

VI

The Summer Congress of 1948 was the hour of Lysenko's triumph. For in his possession that July day was a secret weapon, more powerful in Russia than the atomic bomb. In his opening address he hinted at it ominously:

So far I as President of the Lenin Academy of Agricultural Sciences have been wanting in the strength and ability to make proper use of my official position to create the conditions for the more extensive development of the Michurinite trend . . . and to restrict the scholastics and metaphysics of the opposite trend. . . . We Michurinites must frankly admit that we have hitherto proved unable to make the most of the splendid possibilities created in our country by our party and the government for the complete exposure of Morganist metaphysics in its entirety, an importation from foreign reactionary enemy biology. It is now up to the Academy, to which a large number of Michurinites have just been appointed, to tackle this task. . . .

Now that genetics had joined the Party, as the reader will note, it had developed its "ites" and its "isms," its unexaminable dogmas, its orthodoxy and its heresy, its loyalties and its treasons, its political promotions and purges. Even as Stalin professed to inherit the mantle of Marx, Engels and Lenin, so Lysenko professes an apostolic succession from Timiryazev, Williams, and Michurin, hence the term, Michurinites. (Michurin was the "Soviet Luther Burbank," another man with a "green thumb," an ardent plant-breeder who, like our Burbank had his hits and misses without ever getting to understand very much of the theoretical problems of the new science of genetics which is just beginning to reduce the thousand-years-old rule-of-thumb plant and animal breeding to a systematic, experimental science.) And just as Stalin has made a hate-word out of the names of his opponents—"Trotskyite-Zinovievite-Bukharinite-diversionist-wrecker-agent-spy"—so the Michurinite-Lysenkoites now speak with "class hatred" and "nationalistic indignation" of the "unpatriotic fly-breeder, hostile, alien, reactionary, capitalist, Mendelite-Morganite-Weismannite genetics."

But it was not this abuse which was new or sent the chill of fear down the spines of the Russian scientists. It was the dread hint contained in the words, "Party, Government, and Comrade Stalin personally." Yet the majority of the geneticists still held their tongues or tried to avoid head-on collision or moral suicide, still believing that surely the government which they had served so loyally would not altogether abandon its uneasy neutrality before the issues of the laboratory.

Still cheated of his public triumph, Lysenko began his closing speech by hurling his secret weapon:

Before I pass to my concluding remarks, I consider it my duty to state the following. The question is asked in one of the notes handed up to me, What is the attitude of the Central Committee of the Party towards my report? I answer: *The Central Committee of the Party has examined my report and approved it.*

At this point, *Pravda* reports:

> With one impulse, all present rose to their feet and gave a stormy, prolonged ovation in honor of the Central Committee of the Party of Lenin-Stalin, in honor of the wise leader and teacher of the Soviet people, the greatest scientist of our epoch, Comrade Stalin.

And among those who had perforce to rise to their feet and cheer with all their might were those who had just heard the sentence of doom and knew that their work had ended and all the issues of all the genetics experiments in all the laboratories of the world had been settled by a simple vote of a group of tough, ignorant politicians.

Now began the surrenders and desertions and self-humiliations, for now there was no longer any crevice in which science might hide in this totally coordinated society. Yet, as sometimes a dying bull rises to its forelegs and makes one more desperate thrust at the triumphant matador, so there was one more thrill reserved for these spectators of the gladiatorial death pangs. Old Nemchinov, Director of the Timiryazev Agricultural Academy, rose to his feet:

> "Comrades, not being a biologist, I did not intend to speak. . . . I observe that there is no unity among our scientists on certain questions and I personally as director of the Timiryazev Academy see nothing bad in this. (*Commotion in the hall.*)

> "Both tendencies are allowed to teach at my Academy. . . . I have said, and I repeat it now that the chromosome theory of heredity has become part of the golden treasury of human knowledge, and I continue to hold that view."

> *A voice:* "But you are not a biologist, how can you judge?"

> "I am not a biologist, but I am in a position to verify this theory from the viewpoint of the science in which I do my research, namely, statistics. (*Commotion.*)

> "And it also conforms to my ideas, but that is not the point."

> *Voice:* "How is it not the point?"

> "Let it be the point. I must then declare that I do not share the viewpoint of the comrades who assert that chromosomes have nothing to do with the mechanisms of heredity." (*Commotion.*)

> *Voice:* "There are no such mechanisms."

> "You think there are no mechanisms. But this mechanism can not only be seen, it can be stained and defined."

> *Voice:* "Stains and statistics!"

> ". . . I bear the moral and political responsibility for the line of the Timiryazev Academy. . . . I consider it right, and as long as I am director I will continue to pursue it. . . . It is impermissible, in my

opinion, to dismiss Professor Zhebrak who is a serious scientist. . . . The course on genetics should present the views of Academician Lysenko, *and* the principles of the chromosome theory of heredity should likewise not be kept from the students. . . ."

Thus in the nine pages of the stenogram devoted to the remarks of the venerable Nemchinov, every other paragraph is devoted to taunts, commotion, laughter, "a voice," known or unknown, of bullies sure they are playing the winning side. *Pravda* grimly commented:

> The declarations of Comrades Zhukovsky, Alikhanyan and Polyakov [three who "repented"] showed that in the minds of a number of yesterday's adherents of the Mendelite-Morganite tendency, a deep transformation was beginning. . . . On such a background the position of such participants as V. S. Nemchinov exhibited themselves as especially unseemly (*nepriglyadni*).

It is not hard to conjecture what this brave man's fate will be.

VII

Purges in the Soviet Union invariably have the character of a chain reaction. Slowly the purge has been spreading in an ever widening wave, to the Institute of Cytology, Histology and Embryology, the Institute of Evolutionary Morphology, the Institute of Plant Physiology, the Direction of the Botanical Gardens . . . next to medicine. Then to the general Academy of Sciences, and each of the national academies. Next physicists went under fire, then economists, statisticians, mathematicians. Then the purge widened into a general onslaught on the very idea that there is an international community of science, until this land of erstwhile internationalism proclaimed the parochial nationalism of the human spirit and a mad isolationist chauvinism in every field: in culture and thought, in music and art, in drama and movies and circus and criticism and philology. . . .

And each field, each group, each academy, as it began to suffer a purge, was forced at that very moment to write a hymn of thanksgiving and praise to the source of the evil, such as is unparalleled in the whole history of sycophancy, whether in the Tsarist empire or that of the mad Emperor Caligula.

> The Academy of Sciences turns to You, our beloved Leader [*You* is capitalized as if they were referring to a deity, and the word for Leader is *Vozhd*, correlate of *Fuehrer* and *Duce*] with heartfelt gratitude for the attention and help which you are daily showing to Soviet science and the Soviet scientist. . . .

Glory to the leader of the Soviet People, the coryphaeus of Advanced science, the Great Stalin! . . .

We promise You, our beloved Leader, to correct in the shortest time the errors we have permitted, to reconstruct the whole of our scientific work . . . to struggle for Bolshevik partyness (*partinost*) in medicine, to root out the enemy, bourgeois ideology and blind servility before foreignness (*inostranshchina*) in our midst. . . .[6]

These two strange words, "partyness" and "foreignness," bring us to the heart of the attack by Soviet politicians on Soviet and on human thought. Modern science has been made possible by 1) freedom of inquiry; 2) the agreed use of terms and of a general logical language capable of being tested anywhere by critical experiment, rather than being settled by appeal to authority, *argumentum ad hominem* or *opinionem* or *creditum* or nonlogical emotion; 3) the unity of science as a worldwide body of knowledge, based on international interchange and the recognition that every achievement is a cumulative growth built upon countless contributions by men in many lands. All three foundations have here been dynamited. Even if Lysenko were correct in all his biological claims and fantasies, still the decision of the issues by the Politburo or "Comrade Stalin personally" would be fatal to the further flourishing of science, for the dispute does not concern genes and chromosomes but the very functioning of the human spirit.

Twice in our generation have we watched an authoritarian state making this effort to "coordinate" all science into its totalitarian politics. In both cases there was a demand that science abandon its objectivity and specialized methods and "join the party," suiting methods, investigations, and conclusions to the requirements and dogmas of a police state. Both states set party commissars over scientists, or made cranks and pliable scientific politicians into the directors of scientific institutions. Both showed a profound incomprehension and suspicion of pure theoretical science, of the pursuit of truth for its own sake, wherever it might lead. Genetics, too, was a particular target of the Nazis because its free pursuit was incompatible with the state dogma of the master race. In Russia it became a target because a Lysenko had convinced the all-powerful, all-directing and all-meddling, but not all-wise Politburo, and Comrade Stalin personally, that the "conservatism" of plant and animal heredity could be "shattered" according to plan or command, by quick, easy, simple, and carelessly random changes in the environment.

Both Hitler and Stalin have made the mistake of believing that pure

---

[6]The three paragraphs above are taken respectively from the addresses of the All-Union Academy, the Lithuanian Academy and the All-Union Academy of Medical Sciences.

theoretical science has no great practical significance in the immediate power struggles that are their central preoccupation. Yet even this scientific pursuit of truth for its own sake and not for the state's or the Leader's, often has startling practical results. It was the banished Einstein with his mass-energy conversion formula who called the attention of Roosevelt to what had been done in Germany and elsewhere in atomic research. And this country "happened" at the moment to have most of the world's best theoretical physicists in that remote and speculative field, among them Bohr, Fermi, Bethe, Szilard, von Neumann, victims of totalitarian persecution. Thus did the most "pure and remote," the most lonely "metaphysical and alien-Jewish" pursuit of truth for its own sake prove to have the most decisive "practical results."

So, too, when the Politburo and Stalin personally discovered "alien, hostile, diversionist wrecking in astronomy," (*Izvestia,* December 16, 1937), the galactic systems may have seemed infinitely remote from practical consequences for the total state and its power plans. Yet science itself was delivered a staggering blow in those purges.

Biology, because its by-products are vegetable and animal and industrial materials, obviously touches practical matters more closely. Stalin, who is now an authority on all things and whose authority in all things is unlimited, is convinced that Lysenko's get-rich-quick methods will deliver the goods. In vain did Vavilov, in 1939, warn that American genetics had produced a superior corn hybrid which enabled the American corn farmer to lead the world and which the Soviet Union would do well to imitate. That patriotic defense of American genetics for Russia's sake was the very heart of his crime.

Under such circumstances, the talents of the thinker must yield to those of the parrot, science wither into dogma and die of lack of intellectual freedom and theoretical courage. The new authoritarian religion of untouchable dogmas which are prior to investigation; the official state philosophy-religion to which all research must conform; the intuitive infallibility in all fields he cares to turn to on the part of *Vozhd* or Leader; the decision of subtle and difficult questions by a group of bureaucrat-politicians or a single absolute ruler; the purge of all those who would learn from, teach to, communicate with the scientists of other lands—these things in the long run must corrode the giant of brass until its feet crumble into dust. For in our modern world, even the power-purposes of great states can not in the long run be served except where the state knows enough to limit its interference and leave the human spirit free to seek the truth.   —*Spring* 1950

DANIEL BELL

Socialism: The Dream and the Reality

Socialism was once an unbounded dream. Fourier promised that under socialism people would be at least "ten feet tall." Karl Kautsky proclaimed that the average citizen of a socialist society would be a superman. The flamboyant Antonio Labriola told his Italian followers that their socialist-bred children would each be Galileos and Giordano Brunos. And the grandiloquent Trotsky described the socialist millennium as one in which "man would become immeasurably stronger, wiser, freer, his body more harmoniously proportioned, his movements more rhythmic, his voice more musical, and the forms of his existence permeated with dramatic dynamism."

America, too, was an unbounded dream. The utopians gamboled in the virgin wilderness. Some immigrants called it the *golden medinah*, the golden land. Here it seemed as if socialism would have its finest hour. Both Marx and Engels felt a boundless optimism. In 1879 Marx wrote, ". . . the United States have at present overtaken England in the rapidity of economical progress, though they lag still behind in the extent of acquired wealth; but at the same time, the masses are quicker, and have greater political means in their hands, to resent the form of a progress accomplished at their expense." Engels, who wrote a score of letters on the American scene in the late 1880's and early '90's, repeated this prediction time and again. In his introduction to the American edition of *The Conditions of the Working Class in England,* written at the height of enthusiasm over the events of 1886—notably the spectacular rise of the Knights of Labor and the Henry George campaign—he exulted: "On the more favored soil of America, where no medieval ruins bar the way, where history begins with the elements of modern bourgeois society, as evolved in the seventeenth century, the working class passed through these two stages of its development [i.e., a national trade-union movement and an independent labor party] within ten months." And five years later, his optimism undiminished by the sorry turn of events, Engels wrote to Schlüter: ". . . continually renewed waves of advance, followed by equally certain set-backs, are inevitable. Only the advancing waves are

This article also appeared as a chapter in *Socialism and American Life*, edited by Donald Drew Egbert and Stow Persons, Princeton University Press. Copyright by Princeton University Press, 1952.

becoming more powerful, the set-backs less paralyzing. . . . Once the Americans get started it will be with an energy and violence compared with which we in Europe shall be mere children."

But there still hovers the melancholy question, posed by Werner Sombart at the turn of the century in the title of a book, *Why Is There No Socialism in the United States?* To this Sombart supplied one set of answers. He pointed to the open frontiers, the many opportunities for social ascent through individual effort, and the rising standard of living of the country as factors. Other writers have expanded these considerations. Selig Perlman, in his *Theory of the Labor Movement,* advanced three reasons for the lack of class consciousness in the United States: the absence of a "settled" wage-earner class; the "free gift" of the ballot (workers in other countries, denied such rights—for example, the Chartists —developed political rather than economic motivations); and third, the impact of succeeding waves of immigration. It was immigration, said Perlman, which gave rise to the ethnic, linguistic, religious, and cultural heterogeneity of American labor, and to the heightened ambitions of immigrants' sons to escape their inferior status.

In the end, all such explanations fall back on the naturally-endowed resources and material vastness of America. Other explanations have indicated equally general, and relevant, facts. Some have stressed the agrarian basis of American life, with the farmer seesawing to radicalism and conservatism in tune to the business cycle. Others have pointed to the basically geographic, rather than functional, organization of the two-party system, with its emphasis on opportunism, rhetoric, and patronage as the mode of political discourse; hence, compromise, rather than rigid principle, becomes the prime concern of the interest-seeking political bloc.

Implicit in many of these analyses, however, was the notion that such conditions were but temporary. Capitalism as an evolving social system would of necessity "mature." Crises would follow, and at that time a large, self-conscious wage-earner class and a socialist movement, perhaps on the European pattern, would probably emerge. The great depression was such a crisis—an emotional shock which shook the self-confidence of the entire society. It left permanent scar tissue in the minds of the American workers. It spurred the organization of a giant trade-union movement which in ten years grew from less than three million to over fifteen million workers, or one-fourth of the total labor force of the country.[1] It brought in its train the smoking-hot organizing drives and

---

[1]Actually such a statistic slights the real magnitude of labor's swift rise. The nonagricultural labor force is approximately forty-five million, so that unionization touches one in three. Even here a further breakdown is revealing. Nearly every major manufacturing industry (except chemicals and textiles) is more than 80 per cent unionized.

sit-downs in the Ohio industrial valley which gave the country a whiff of class warfare. In the 1940's labor entered national politics with a vigor —in order to safeguard its economic gains. Here at last was the fertile soil which socialist theorists had long awaited. Yet no socialist movement emerged, nor has a coherent socialist ideology taken seed either in the labor movement or in government. So Sombart's question still remains unanswered.

Most of the attempted answers have discussed not *causes* but *conditions*, and these in but general terms. An inquiry into the fate of a social movement has to be pinned in the specific questions of time, place, and opportunity, and framed within a general hypothesis regarding the "why" of its success or failure. The "why" which this essay proposes (with the usual genuflections to *ceteris paribus*), is that the failure of the socialist movement in the United States is rooted in its inability to resolve a basic dilemma of ethics and politics. The socialist movement, by its very statement of goal and in its rejection of the capitalist order as a whole, could not relate itself to the specific problems of social action in the here-and-now, give-and-take political world. It was trapped by the unhappy problem of living "*in* but not *of* the world," so it could only act, and then inadequately, as the moral, but not political, man in immoral society. It could never resolve but only straddle the basic issue of either accepting capitalist society, and seeking to transform it from within as the labor movement did, or becoming the sworn enemy of that society, like the communists. A religious movement can split its allegiances and live *in* but not *of* the world (like Lutheranism); a political movement can not.

In social action there is an irreconcilable tension between ethics and politics. Lord Acton posed the dilemma in a note: "Are politics an attempt to realize ideals, or an endeavor to get advantages, within the limits of ethics?" More succinctly, "are ethics a purpose or a limit?" In the largest sense, society is an organized system for the distribution of tangible rewards and privileges, obligations and duties. Within that frame, ethics deals with the *ought* of distribution, implying a theory of justice. Politics is the concrete *mode* of distribution, involving a power struggle between organized groups to determine the allocation of privilege. In some periods of history, generally in closed societies, ethics and politics have gone hand in hand. But a distinguishing feature of modern society is the separation of the two; and ideology—the façade of general interest and universal values which masks a specific self-interest—replaces ethics. The redivision of the rewards and privileges of society can only be accomplished in the political arena. But in that fateful commitment to politics, an ethical goal, stated as purpose rather than limit, becomes a far-reaching goal before which lies a yawning abyss that can be spanned only by a "leap." The alternatives were forcefully posed by Max Weber in his contrast between the "ethics of responsibility" (or the acceptance of limits) and the "ethics of conscience" (or the dedication to absolute ends). Weber, arguing that only the former is applicable in politics, writes: "The matter does not appear to me so desperate if one does not ask exclusively who is morally right and who is morally wrong? But if one rather asks: Given the existing conflict how can I solve it with the least internal and external danger for all concerned?" Such a pragmatic compromise rather than dedication to an absolute (like bolshevism or religious pacifism) is possible, however, only when there is a basic consensus among contending groups about the rules of the game. But this consensus the socialist movement, because of its original rejection of capitalist society, while operating within it, could never fully accept.

The distinctive character of "modern" politics is the involvement of *all* strata of society in movements of social change, rather than the fatalistic acceptance of events as they are. Its starting point was, as Karl Mannheim elegantly put it, the "orgiastic chiliasm" of the Anabaptists, their messianic hope, their ecstatic faith in the millennium to come. For, as Mannheim and others have pointed out, the Anabaptism of the sixteenth century, of Thomas Münzer and those who sought to establish at Münster the Kingdom of God on earth, proclaimed not merely that equality of souls stressed by Luther, but also equality of property. Other-worldly religious quietism became transformed into a revolutionary activism in order to realize the millennium in the here and now. Thus the religious frenzy of the chiliasts which burst the bonds of the old religious order threatened to buckle the social order as well; for unlike previous revolutions, chiliasm did not aim against a single oppression, but at the entire existing social order.

The characteristic psychological fact about the chiliast is that for him "there is no inner articulation of time." There is only the "absolute presentness." "Orgiastic energies and ecstatic outbursts began to operate in a worldly setting and tensions previously transcending day to day life became explosive agents within it." The chiliast is neither "in the world nor of it." He stands outside of it and against it because salvation, the millennium, is immediately at hand. Where such a hope is possible, where such a social movement can transform society in a cataclysmic flash, the "leap" is made, and in the pillar of fire the fusion of ethics and politics is possible. But where societies are stable, and social change can only come piecemeal, the pure chiliast in despair turns nihilist, rather than make the bitter-tasting compromises with the established hierarchical order. "When this spirit ebbs and deserts these movements," writes Mannheim, "there remains behind in the world a naked mass-frenzy and despiritualized fury." In a later and secularized form, this attitude found its expression in Russian anarchism. So Bakunin could write: "The desire for destruction is at the same time a creative desire."

Yet not only the anarchist, but every socialist, every convert to political messianism, is in the beginning something of a chiliast. In the newly-found enthusiasms, in the identification with an oppressed group, hope flares that the "final conflict" will not be far ahead. ("Socialism in our time," was the affirmative voice of Norman Thomas in the 1930's.) But the "revolution" is not always immediately in sight, and the question of how to discipline this chiliastic zeal and hold it in readiness has been the basic problem of socialist strategy.

The most radical approach was that of Georges Sorel with his concept of the revolutionary myth (*"images de batailles"*), a myth which functions as a bastardized version of the doctrine of salvation. These unifying images, Sorel wrote, can neither be proved nor disproved; thus they are "capable of evoking as an undivided whole" the mass of diverse sentiments which exist in society. "The syndicalists solve this problem perfectly, by concentrating the whole of socialism in the drama of the general strike; thus there is no longer any place for the reconciliation of contraries in the equivocations of the professors; everything is clearly mapped out so that only one interpretation of Socialism is possible." In this "catastrophic conception" of socialism, as Sorel called it, *"it is the myth in its entirety which is alone important."*

But in the here and now, people live "in parts." "History does not work with bottled essences," wrote Acton, "but with active combinations; compromise is the soul if not the whole of politics. Occasional conformity is the nearest practical approach to orthodoxy and progress is along diagonals. . . . Pure dialectics and bilateral dogmas have less control than custom and interest and prejudice." And for the socialist movements, operating on "partial" day-to-day problems, the dilemma remained.

II

Neither nineteenth-century American radicals nor the American socialists faced up to this problem of social compromise. The utopias that were spun so profusely in the nineteenth century assumed that in the course of evolution "reason" would find its way and the perfect society would emerge. But so mechanical were the mannikin visions of human delights in such utopias that a modern reading of Bellamy, for example, with its plan for conscript armies of labor ("a horrible cockney dream," William Morris called *Looking Backward*) only arouses revulsion.

The "scientific socialist" movement that emerged at the turn of the century mocked these utopian unrealities. Only the organization of the proletariat could bring a better world. But this apparent relatedness to the world was itself a delusion. The socialist dilemma was still how to face the problem of "in the world and of it," and in practice the early socialist movement "rejected" the world; it simply waited for the new. Although the American Socialist Party sought to function politically by raising "immediate demands" and pressing for needed social reforms, it rarely took a stand on the actual political problems that emerged from the on-going functioning of the society. "What but meaningless phrases are 'imperialism,' 'expansion,' 'free silver,' 'gold standard,' etc., to the wage worker?" asked Eugene V. Debs in 1900. "The large capitalists represented by Mr. McKinley and the small capitalists represented by Mr. Bryan are interested in these 'issues' but they do not concern the working class." These "issues" were beside the point, said Debs, because the worker stood outside society. Thus Debs and the socialist movement as a whole would have no traffic with the capitalist parties. Even on local municipal issues the party would not compromise. The socialist movement could "afford" this purity because of its supreme confidence about the future. "The socialist program is not a theory imposed upon society for its acceptance or rejection. It is but the interpretation of what is, sooner or later, inevitable. Capitalism is already struggling to its destruction," proclaimed the Socialist national platform of 1904, the first issued by the Socialist Party.

But unlike the other-worldly movements toward salvation, which can always postpone the date of the resurrection, the Socialist Party, living in the here and now, had to show results. It was a movement based on a belief in "history"; but it found itself outside of "time." World War I finally broke through the façade. For the first time the party had to face a stand on a realistic issue of the day. And on that issue almost the entire intellectual leadership of the party deserted, and the back of American socialism was broken.

The socialist movement of the 1930's, the socialism of Norman Thomas, could not afford the luxury of the earlier belief in the inevitable course of history. It was forced to take stands on the particular issues of the day. But it too rejected completely the premises of the society which shaped these issues. In effect, the Socialist Party acknowledged the fact that it lived "in" the world, but refused the responsibility of becoming a part "of" it. But such a straddle is impossible for a *political* movement. It was as if it consented to a duel, with no choice as to weapons, place, amount of preparation, etc. Politically, the consequences were disastrous. Each issue could only be met by an ambiguous political formula which would satisfy neither the purists, nor the activist who lived with the daily problem of choice. When the Loyalists in Spain demanded arms, for example, the Socialist Party could only respond with a feeble policy of "workers aid," not (capitalist) government aid; but to the Spaniard, arms, not theoretical niceties, were the need of the moment. When the young trade unionists, whom the socialists seeded into the labor movement, faced the necessity of going along politically with Roosevelt and the New Deal in order to safeguard progressive legislative gains, the socialists proposed a "labor party" rather than work with the Democrats, and so the Socialist Party lost almost its entire trade-union base. The threat of fascism and World War II finally proved to be the clashing rocks through which the socialist argonauts could not row safely. How to defeat Hitler without supporting capitalist society? Some socialists raised the slogan of a "third force." The Socialist Party, however, realized the futility of that effort; in characteristic form, it chose abnegation. The best way to stem fascism, it stated, "is to make democracy work at home." But could the issue be resolved other than militarily? The main concern of the antifascist movement had to be with the political center of fascist power, Hitler's Berlin, and any other concern was peripheral.

In still another way the religious, chiliastic origin of modern socialism revealed itself—the multiplication of splits, the constant formation of sectarian splinter groups each hotly disputing the other regarding the true road to power. Socialism is an eschatological movement; it is sure of its destiny, because "history" leads it to its goal. But though sure of its final ends, there is never a standard of testing the immediate means. The result is a constant factiousness in socialist life. Each position taken is always open to challenge by those who feel that it would only swerve the movement from its final goal and lead it up some blind alley. And because it is an ideological movement, embracing all the realm of the human polity, the Socialist Party is always challenged to take a stand on every problem from Viet Nam to Finland, from prohibition to pacifism. And, since for every two socialists there are always three political opinions, the consequence has been that in its inner life, the Socialist Party has never, *even for a single year,* been without some issue which threatened to split the party and which forced it to spend much of its time on the problem of reconciliation or rupture. In this fact lies the chief clue to the impotence of American socialism as a political movement, especially in the past twenty years.[2]

---

[2]Far beyond the reaches of this essay is the problem of the psychological types who are attracted by such a sectarian existence. Yet one might say here that certainly the illusions of settling the fate of history, the mimetic combat on the plains of destiny, and the vicarious sense of power in demolishing opponents all provide a sure sense of gratification which makes the continuance of sectarian life desirable. The many leadership complexes,

III

But what of the proletariat itself? What is its role in the socialist drama of history? How does the proletariat see through the veils of obscurity and come to self-awareness? Marx could say with Jesus, "I have come to end all mysteries, not to perpetuate them." His role, in his own self-image, was to lay bare the fetishes which enslave modern man and thus confute Hegel's claim that freedom and rationality had already been achieved. But like his old master he could only deal with the "immanent" forces of history, not the mechanics of social action.

All political movements, Marx wrote, have been slaves to the symbols of the past. But history is the process of progressive disenchantment: men are no longer bound to the river gods and anthropomorphic deities of the agricultural societies; nor need they be bound to the abstract impersonal deity of bourgeois Protestantism. Man himself was potential. But how to realize his potentiality? The intellectual was, in part, capable of self-emancipation because he possessed the imagination to transcend his origins. But the proletariat, as a class, could develop only to the extent that the social relations of society itself revealed to the slave the thongs that bound him. Man is no more free, said Marx in *Das Kapital,* because he can sell his labor power to whom he wishes. Exploitation is implicit in the very structure of capitalist society, which in order to live must constantly expand by extracting surplus value and thus accumulate new capital. In the process, the proletarian would be reduced to the barest minimum of human existence (the law of increasing misery) and thus robbed of any mark of distinction. In the agony of alienation and the deepening class struggle he would realize consciously a sense of identity which would unite him with others and create a cohesive social movement of revolution. In action he would no longer be manipulated but "make" himself.

Thus the scene is set for the grand drama. Out of the immanent, convulsive contradictions of capitalism, conflict would spread. The proletariat, neither in nor of the world, would inherit the world. But History (to use these personifications) confounded Marx's prophecy, at least in the West. The law of increasing misery was refuted by the tremendous advances of technology. The trade union began bettering the worker's lot. And, in the political struggles that followed, it found that

the intense aggressiveness through gossip, the strong clique group formations, all attest to a particular set of psychological needs and satisfactions which are fulfilled in these opaque, molecular worlds.

it could sustain itself not by becoming a revolutionary instrument against society, but by accepting a place within society.

In the America of the nineteenth century, almost every social movement had involved an effort by the worker to escape his lot as a worker. At times the solution was free land, or cheap money, or producers' cooperatives, or some other chimera from the gaudy bag of utopian dreams. The rise of the American Federation of Labor signaled the end of this drive for some new "northwest passage." Under Gompers, labor's single ambition was to achieve a status on a par with that of business and the church, as a "legitimate" social institution of American life. The socialists within and without the A.F.L. challenged this approach, and lost. As a result, before World War I they found themselves isolated from the labor movement which they regarded as necessary for the fulfillment of socialism. During the New Deal and after, however, the socialists in the unions, faced with a similar dilemma, chose the labor movement. When the Socialist Party refused to go along, it lost its strength as a tangible force in American political life.

But even apart from its presumed relation to socialism, perhaps the most significant fact regarding the "consciousness" of the American proletariat is that in the past thirty years American middle-class mass culture has triumphed over capitalist and worker alike. The America of 1890, the capstone of the Gilded Age, was a society of increasing differentiation in manners and morals, the area, that is, of *visible* distinction and the one that could give rise, as in Europe, to class resentment. It saw the emergence in baroque mansion, elaborate dress, and refined leisure activities of a new *haut* style of life. By the 1920's this style was already gone. Beneath this change was the transformation of entrepreneurial to corporate capitalism, with a corresponding shift in the social type from the self-made man to the smooth, faceless manager. But beyond that it was a change in the very character of society, symbolized in large measure by the adjective which qualified the phrases "mass production" and "mass consumption." Production—apart from war needs—was no longer geared *primarily*, as it had been in the late nineteenth and early twentieth centuries, to turning out capital goods (steel, railroad equipment, tools), but to the output of consumers' durable goods (autos, washing machines, radios, etc.). The mass market became the arbiter of taste, and the style of life was leveled. In another dimension of this vast social revolution that has been taking place during the past quarter of a century, professional skill has been replacing property as the chief means of acquiring and wielding power, and the educational system rather than inheritance has become the chief avenue for social ascent. In short, a new-type, bureaucratic, mass society has been emerging, and with it, new institutions, of which the modern trade union is one. If the worker was "absorbed" culturally into the social structure of this new, bureaucratic mass society, the trade union itself finally achieved its respectability. World War II brought a social truce and the beginnings of a social merger between the major power blocs in American life. "Labor" was living in and of the capitalist society. It was represented on government boards and was consulted on policy. The rise of totalitarianism demonstrated that all social groups had a common fate if democracy fell. In this respect all other values have become subordinate. And the emergence of a garrison economy as a response to the threat of a third world war illustrated the need for some defined national interest in the form of government decision to bring the particular self-interest groups to heel.

For the fast-dwindling Socialist Party the answer to this new dilemma was still a "third force," or a "neither-nor" position which sought to stand apart and outside the swirling sandstorm of conflict. Like the ostrich in the Slavic parable, they put their heads in the sand and thought no one was looking. By 1950, nobody was.

IV

For the twentieth-century communist, however, there are none of these agonizing problems of ethics and politics. He is the perpetual alien living in hostile enemy territory. Any gesture of support, any pressure for social reforms—all of these are simply tactics, a set of Potemkin villages, the façades to be torn down after the necessary moment for deception has passed. His is the ethic of "ultimate ends"; only the goal counts, the means are inconsequential. Bolshevism thus is neither in the world nor of it, but stands outside. It takes no responsibility for the consequences of any act within the society nor does it suffer the tension of acquiescence or rejection. But the socialist, unlike the communist, lacks that fanatical vision, and so faces the daily anguish of participating in and sharing responsibility for the day-to-day problems of the society.

It is this commitment to the "absolute" that gives bolshevism its religious strength. It is this commitment which sustains one of the great political myths of the century, the myth of the iron-willed Bolshevik. Selfless, devoted, resourceful, a man with a cause, he is the modern Hero. He alone, a man of action, a soldier for the future, continues the tradition of courage which is the aristocratic heritage bestowed on Western culture and which has been devitalized by the narrow, monetary calculus of the bourgeoisie. (Can the businessman be the Hero?) Such is the peculiar myth which has taken a deep hold among many intellectuals. It is a myth which is also responsible for a deep emotional hatred and almost pathologic resentment felt most keenly by the ex-communist intellectual, the "defrocked priest," toward the party. For the "Bolshevik," through the myth of absolute selflessness, claims to be the "extreme man," the man of no compromise, the man of purity. The intellectual, driven to be moral, fears the comparison and resents the claim. He thus bears either a sense of guilt or a psychological wound.

In addition to the myth of the Bolshevik as iron-willed Hero, twentieth-century communism has made several other distinctive contributions to the theory and practice of modern politics. Like so many other social doctrines, these were never put down systematically in a fully self-conscious fashion; yet over the years they have emerged as a coherent philosophy. Of these contributions some five can be linked schematically. These are central for understanding the history of the Communist Party in this country and are summarized here.

One of the major innovations of the Bolsheviks is their theory of power. Against the nineteenth-century liberal view which saw social decisions as a reconciliation of diverse interests through compromise and consensus—a theory which social democracy gradually began to accept after World War I when it was called upon to take responsibility for governments and enter coalitions—the Bolsheviks saw politics as a naked struggle for power, power being defined as a monopoly of the means of coercion. Power was thought of almost in the sense of physics, its equation being almost literally mass times force equals power. The individual, while central to a market society, was for the Bolshevik a helpless entity. Only the organized group counted, and only a mass base could exert social leverage in society.

But a mass requires leadership. The great unresolved dilemma of Marxian sociology was the question of how the proletariat achieves the consciousness of its role. To await the immanent development of history was to rely on the fallacy of misplaced abstraction. "Spontaneity" was not for Lenin a reality in mass politics; nor was the trade union an effective instrument. His answer, the most significant addition to revolutionary theory, was the vanguard role of the party.

Against "economism" which glorified the role of the trade union, Lenin argued that the mere organization of society on a trade-union basis could only lead to wage consciousness, not revolutionary consciousness; against the spontaneity theories of Rosa Luxemburg he argued that the masses, by nature, were backward. Only the vanguard party, aware of the precarious balance of social forces, could assess the play and correctly tip the scales in the revolutionary direction. The classic formulation of revolutionary avant-guardism Lenin outlined in his *What Is to Be Done*, published as early as 1903.

In it he wrote that without the "dozen" tried and talented leaders (and talented men are not born by the hundred), professionally trained, schooled by long experience and working in perfect harmony, no class in modern society is capable of conducting a determined struggle. "I assert," said Lenin, "(1) that no movement can be durable without a stable organization of leaders to maintain continuity; (2) that the more widely the masses are spontaneously drawn into the struggle and form the basis of the movement, the more necessary it is to have such an organization and the more stable must it be (for it is much easier for demagogues to sidetrack the more backward sections of the masses); (3) that the organization must consist chiefly of persons engaged in revolution as a profession."

If the party were to become a vanguard, it needed discipline in action, and thus there arose the principle of party hierarchy and "democratic centralism." In theory there was full discussion of policy before decision, and rigid adherence to policy once discussion had been closed. In practice a line was laid down by the leadership which was binding on all. Lenin's promulgation of these doctrines split Russian socialism in 1903 and brought about the emergence of the Bolshevik and Menshevik factions. In the beginning Trotsky opposed Lenin's ideas, but later he capitulated. As he reveals in his autobiography: ". . . there is no doubt that at that time I did not fully realize what an intense and imperious centralism the revolutionary party would need to lead millions of people in a war against the old order. . . . Revolutionary centralism is a harsh, imperative and exacting principle. It often takes the guise of absolute ruthlessness in its relation to individual members, to whole groups of former associates. It is not without significance that the words 'irreconcilable' and 'relentless' are among Lenin's favorites."

From the principle of power and the theory of party organization rose two other key tenets of bolshevism. One was the polarization of classes. Because it looked only toward the "final conflict," bolshevism split society into two classes, the proletariat and the bourgeoisie. But the proletariat could only be emancipated by the vanguard party; hence anyone resisting the party must belong to the enemy. For Lenin, the maxim of the absolute ethic meant that "those who are not for me are against me." Hence, too, a formulation of the theory of "social fascism," which in the early 1930's branded the social democrats rather than Hitler as the chief enemy, and led the communists to unite, in several instances, with the Nazis in order to overthrow the German Republic.

The second tenet, deriving from the backward nature of the masses, was the key psychological tactic of formulating all policy into forceful slogans. Slogans dramatize events, make issues simple, and wipe out the qualifications, nuances, and subtleties which accompany democratic political action. In his chapter on slogans, Lenin wrote one of the first manuals on modern mass psychology. During the revolution, the Bolsheviks achieved a flexibility of tactic by using such slogans as "All Power to the Soviets," "Land, Peace, and Bread," etc. The basic political tactic of all Communist parties everywhere is to formulate policy primarily through the use of key slogans which are transmitted first to the party rank and file and then to the masses.

The consequence of the theory of the vanguard party and its relation to the masses is a system of "two truths," the *consilia evangelica*, or a special ethic endowed for those whose lives are so dedicated to the revolutionary ends, and another truth for the masses. Out of this belief grew Lenin's famous admonition—one can lie, steal, or cheat, for the cause itself has a higher truth.

Communism as a social movement did not, with the brief exception of the late 1930's, achieve any sizable mass following in the United States. Its main appeal, then, was to the dispossessed intelligentsia of the depression generation and to the "engineers of the future" who were captivated by the type of elitist appeal just described. Within American life, its influence was oblique. It stirred many Americans to action against injustices, and left them with burnt fingers when, for reasons of expediency, the party line changed and the cause was dropped. It provided unmatched political sophistication to a generation that went through its ranks and gave to an easygoing, tolerant, sprawling America a lesson in organizational manipulation and hard-bitten ideological devotion which this country, because of tradition and temperament, found hard to understand. But most of all, through the seeds of distrust and anxiety it sowed, communism has spawned a reaction, an hysteria and bitterness that democratic America may find difficult to erase in the rugged years ahead.

Thus within the span of a century American socialism passed from those bright and unbounded dreams of social justice which possessed the utopians and early Marxians alike to—in the deeds of one bastard faction at least—a nightmare of distrust and bitterness.   —*Spring* 1952

JOHN P. ROCHE

The Crisis in British Socialism

British socialism is today in the throes of a profound internal crisis. If we are to believe what we read in the American newspapers, Aneurin Bevan's strength is growing daily among the British trade unions, and no less an authority than the *New York Times* highlighted the recent Labor Party Conference at Morecambe as a Bevan victory. Some "experts" on British socialism even tell us that Aneurin Bevan will be the next Labor Prime Minister. In short, we are led to believe that the extremists are virtually in command of the Labor Party.

It is the purpose of this analysis to demonstrate that these prophets of gloom are mistaken, that their analyses are based on inadequate knowledge of both the internal organization of the Labor Party and of the political process in general, and finally that the real nature of the Bevanite threat is quite different from that suggested above. In fact, it is here submitted that Aneurin Bevan can never capture the Labor Party as it is now constituted, but he can ruin it. To put the point precisely, the Bevanites may make it impossible for the British Labor Party to win another election, which in political terms is to condemn the party to death by slow strangulation. British socialism has not been an "ideology" in the Continental sense; it has been a concrete bid for political power. Thus, if the pragmatic and thoroughly nondialectical average British socialist decides that the Labor Party is destined to be a permanent minority, he may well take his political business elsewhere.

The leaders of British socialism are on the horns of a horrible dilemma. On one extreme stand the powerful trade union bureaucrats who would destroy the party sooner than have it fall into Bevan's hands, while on the other, stand Bevan and his associates who cripple the party's power to win elections. The major bone of contention is the British middle class. The facts are clear: in 1945, and to a lesser extent in 1950, the Labor Party victory was based on middle class support. In 1951, the party lost precisely because this *bourgeois* segment of the electorate was alienated. The Laborites did, indeed, win a "moral victory" over the Conservatives by polling a larger percentage of the total vote than did the victors, but this slight over-all advantage was more than offset by the fact that Labor piled up unnecessary majorities in safe constituencies. Under the British electoral system, as in the United States, a one-vote majority elects as surely as a majority of ten thousand. Thus, while the Labor Party can gain limited comfort from its popular plurality, it is also acutely aware that, in the words of a great Rugby coach, "moral victories are for the chaps who can't get the other kind."

To win the other kind of victory, Labor must regain the confidence of the middle-class voter. The working class of industrial Britain simply can not, at least under the present election system, go it alone. And, although Mr. Churchill has, in the course of his campaign to seduce the Liberal Party into the Conservative bed, grumbled some favorable comments about proportional representation, it may be assumed that the single-member constituency is a permanent feature of British political life. The implications of this electoral situation are tremendous and may be summarized in one sentence: If the Labor Party is to win any future elections, socialism must be given even more of a middle-class veneer. Or, to put it another way, British socialists, unless they are prepared to become permanent wilderness dwellers, must formulate a program acceptable to the middle class.

To many foreign socialists, this would appear to be unnecessary. British socialism has long been considered petty *bourgeois* reformism by the Continental comrades, and further adjustments in the program of the Labor Party would probably appear unimportant to the Sanhedrin of socialist orthodoxy—or at worst, as another step in the betrayal of socialism that began a half century ago. But at this particular time there happens to be a considerable opposition within the Labor Party to the further *embourgeoisement* of British socialism, and it may yet appear that the type of schismatic who gives an air of authenticity to a Continental socialist party will pop up in British socialism. Aneurin Bevan, although his chances of dominating either the British Labor Party or the British Trades Union Congress are virtually nonexistent, could serve as the catalyst and spearhead of a movement that would disrupt the Labor Party and weaken the bonds between the party and the Trades Union Congress.

In order to put Bevan in perspective, it is necessary to review briefly the internal history of the Labor Party. Initially formed by a reluctant marriage between the Trades Union Congress and socialist intellectuals (the majority at the T.U.C. Convention which in 1899 authorized independent political action was a scant 5-4), the Labor Party soon became the nesting place of every radical reformer in Great Britain. Pacifists, vegetarians, feminists, anti-bloodsporters, republicans, all joined the Independent Labor Party which served as the intellectual organization in the over-all federal party structure. (It was not until 1917 that the Labor Party accepted individual memberships except through intermediate constituent organizations.) In addition, a considerable body of Christian Socialist intellectuals—doctors, lawyers, dons, ministers—affiliated with the party on the ground that it was continuing the nonconformist tradition abandoned, in their view, by the Liberals.

The trade unionists, interested primarily in their own objectives, viewed the tremendous accretion of intellectuals with some alarm, but recognized that these "toffs" were helping them in their fight for industrial democracy. Furthermore, the unions had the situation in the party thoroughly under control. When all the shouting at party congresses was over, and the radical speeches at last subsided, the trade unionists with their bloc votes could decisively settle matters in a respectable fashion. In addition, it should be noted that the unionists were themselves in a radical frame of mind, and, if they were not particularly interested in socialist metaphysics, they were decidedly in favor of the immediate demands of the metaphysicians. Consequently the unions supplied the funds for socialist education and agitation while taking little direct leadership in the campaign.

The intellectuals who joined the party and led it throughout its early years were divided into roughly two camps. One group, which included a substantial number of Marxists, talked in traditional class-war terms. They looked upon capitalism as a foul cancer which should be cut from the British body-politic at the earliest possible date and by whatever means were necessary and expedient. This segment of the party was violently antimilitarist, as distinguished from pacifist, and frequently expressed its scorn for the reformist tactics of the trade unions. In the eyes of these intellectuals, and their few trade union allies such as young Ernie Bevin, real democracy could only develop under socialism and the "mere political democracy" that existed in Britain was a snare and a delusion. Capitalism, they insisted, could not be modified into socialism through the democratic process, for the latter was designed by capitalists for their own protection and would be abandoned in favor of suppression if any real threat to capitalism arose. Socialism would come first; democracy would come later.

The second segment of intellectuals took a different view of the matter. Strongly influenced by the nonconformist Christian tradition, these Laborites tended to look upon the capitalist as Christ looked upon the sinner: a man more to be pitied than hated. A strong pacifist contingent vigorously opposed class-war doctrines, and an even stronger admixture of Fabians eschewed radicalism in favor of the "inevitability of gradualness." To the members of this segment, socialism was a superstructure on democracy, and the way to achieve socialism was the democratic route of political victory in peaceful elections. Indeed, most Fabians were "state socialists" who unreservedly advocated the use of the capitalist state apparatus to attain socialist ends.

The trade union leaders who were, after all, dedicated to exploiting capitalism for the benefit of the wage earner rather than to overthrowing it, aligned themselves firmly with the moderate intellectuals and set out on the long tortuous road to political power. The extremist intellectuals, with a motley crew of unionists, mainly syndicalists, worked desperately to move the Labor Party to the "left," but events both internal and external worked against them. Internally they were confronted by the passionate solidarity of the trade unionist who viewed any attack on his union leaders as both an attack upon his judgment and a bonus for management. Externally, the Russian Revolution and the formation of the British Communist Party as a competitor with the Labor Party created additional difficulties. While the British workers had great sympathy for the Bolsheviks and the Soviet Revolution, they were completely merciless toward scissionists within their movement and party. Thus many of the extremists trickled off into the wilderness where they usually went through successive seizures of Leninist, Trotskyist, Syndicalist, Mosleyite, and other unnamed enthusiasms. The British workers would not even crucify these proletarian messiahs; they simply ignored them.

By about 1935, the pattern was firmly established and had survived several grave crises: The moderate intellectuals ran the Labor Party, supported by the great trade unions. Furthermore, two experiences with political power had whetted the appetites of the moderates and the unionists to the point where they would not let any niceties of socialist dogma interfere with the democratic process of getting votes. Socialism as theory became almost wholly identified with the victory of the Labor Party in a general election. What content there was to the Labor program consisted almost wholly of projects of public ownership which would alter the conditions of the industrial sector and advance the cause of industrial democracy. But it should again be emphasized that in the mind of the average Laborite socialism was the victory of his party, or, to use the expressive colloquialism, of "our people." Consequently throughout the Twenties and Thirties the Labor Party began to resemble its own ancestors less and less and its competitors for power more and more.

The genius behind this *embourgeoisement* was Herbert Morrison, Labor's apostle to the middle class. He saw the objective of the Labor Party clearly to be the collection of middle class votes so as to achieve a majority in Parliament, and, as his political talents began to mold the party, less and less was heard about class war and more about common destiny. There was indeed opposition to Morrison's "socialism without tears," but several factors combined to keep it subdued. First, the desertion of James Ramsay

MacDonald and his few followers in 1931 served as a convenient touchstone of socialism. Morrison could turn to his left-wing critics and say: "If we were not socialist, would we still be here?" This suggestion that all the untrue socialists had deserted was difficult to answer, for the immediate rewards for betrayal had been great and the reward for faithfulness had been the devastating Labor defeat in the election of 1931. Second, in spite of the debacle of 1931, or perhaps because of it, the average Laborite devoted even more of his efforts to the achievement of future victory and was prepared to be ruthless towards potential schismatics who might delay victory. The general feeling seemed to be that the definition of socialism in specific terms could await the morrow of a socialist victory. The Labor Party in opposition succeeded in channeling the industry and vigor of all sorts of diversified enthusiasts into one stream directed at overthrowing the Conservatives in the immediate future. The greatly enlarged Labor minority which resulted from the election of 1935 spurred them on to greater hopes. Socialism, real socialism, was in the offing, and this time the Labor government would not be at the mercy of a capitalist minority, but would have a majority in its own right.

The Labor victory in the General Election of 1945 came as a tremendous shock to all concerned. The Labor leadership, while publicly jubilant, were in private quite uneasy about the prospect before them. It is difficult to believe that the electorate voted for socialism; it would rather seem that several other factors played a more important role: reaction against the war and its restrictions, the feeling that the Tories were unprepared to face the problems of the postwar world, and last, but not least, a not inconsiderable body of sentiment to the effect that while Churchill was ideal to lead a parade, he was not the man to supervise the subsequent street cleaning. But in any case, and however motivated, the British people installed a socialist government, and the eager Laborites faced towards the dawn of a new England. The lean years were over, and the enthusiasts swarmed to the building of Jerusalem "in England's green and pleasant land."

This was indeed to be the pay off. The Labor Party had been given such a thumping majority in the House of Commons that there was no possibility of parliamentary sabotage. Nothing now stood in the way of implementing British socialism except defining it. At first this was easy, for the party had long stood for nationalization of coal, the Bank of England, and transport, and for socialized medicine, and it proceeded to put these promises into legislation. Foreign Secretary Ernest Bevin solemnized the end of the old colonial system by wishing India, Pakistan, Burma and Ceylon well as they began their ventures as independent nations. The Trades Disputes Act passed as a punitive measure after the General Strike of 1926 was repealed, and the trade union movement was consulted on matters of industrial policy as it had never been before. The Attlee government could face the British people with the assurance of men who have lived up to their promises; and seldom has a nation been fortunate enough to have a government with such a high level of competence.

But this was not enough. The election of the socialists, while it had led to the amelioration of the lot of the average Briton, had not transformed the spirit and face of Britain. The coal miners found that the National Coal Board was not greatly different from a private employer. The pacifists discovered that the Labor government had no intention of abolishing the army. The unions found "their government" coming to them and imploring wage restraint. The enthusiasts began to chafe and mutter that the voice was Attlee's voice, but the hands were the hands of capitalism. Some left wingers began to talk about "state capitalism." Something was wrong, and since it had been accepted that the transformation of Britain would result from a Labor victory, the fact that the world remained largely the same was taken as proof of the inadequacy of British socialism.

To those in positions of responsibility, it must have seemed as though there were a historical conspiracy against the Labor Party. In the first place, the nation which had been turned over to them in 1945 was on the edge of bankruptcy. The nationalization of coal and transport, far from being noble socialist experiments, were economic imperatives, for only if the resources of the government were thrown into these fields would reconstruction be possible. Private investors could not have supplied the capital needed, for example, to rebuild the bombed railway system. In the second place, the government was stuck with a world they never made; they had certainly never thought that a large portion of national output would have to be channeled into nonproductive armaments. To take another example, socialist enthusiasm was of little value in dealing with the dollar shortage. Obviously socialism was more useful as a slogan of opposition than it was as an operational code for responsible ministers. A new disorder known as "Socialist ulcers" began to trouble the leaders of the Labor Party.

So long as the disillusioned enthusiasts had no leadership, the party leaders did not have to take them too seriously. Indeed, Attlee and his top strategy advisors were remarkably successful in keeping the disgruntled leaderless for so long. The main problem in this respect was obviously Aneurin Bevan, a first-rate demagogue with compulsive proletarian tendencies, but Attlee dampened Bevan's powder by making him Minister of Health, a position with immense responsibilities in the fields of housing, socialized medicine, and public health generally. Bevan was, in effect, told to put up or shut up. He put up, and did a superb job. Nevertheless, Bevan was obviously chafing under the yoke of responsibility, and he did succeed in taking sufficient time off from his ministerial duties to make some speeches which, it is estimated, lost the Labor Party 150,000 votes each among the middle class. It was in one of these that he referred to the Tories as "vermin" with the obvious implication that they should be exterminated. Bevan needed a heavier yoke, so Attlee handed him the heaviest in the Cabinet—the Ministry of Labor and National Service.

This appointment really put Bevan on the spot. The trade unions were becoming more and more restive under the policy of wage restraint, and Bevan was told, in effect, to use his great reputation acquired as Minister of Health to hold them in line. Faced with the acute possibility that he would be required by the imperatives of his position to sacrifice his status as champion of the British worker, Bevan took the first plausible opportunity to resign. At once the leaderless enthusiasts had a leader, and one who could not be called a communist, and the leaders of the British Labor Party were brought face to face with a showdown that they wanted desperately to avoid.

Before discussing the future of Bevanism, it is important to analyze it. It is almost as difficult to answer the question, "What does Bevanism stand for?" as it is to describe precisely the views and program of the party leadership. But this much does seem clear: Bevanism is an amorphous body of complaints about a cruel world. It is, in a real sense, an attempt to recreate the childhood of the Labor Party when the lines between "socialists" and "capitalists" were clearly drawn and enthusiastic crusading was the order of the day. One observer of French politics has noted that the French Socialist Party is the prisoner of its childhood, and it may be suggested that Bevanism represents a similar manifestation in British socialism.

Practically speaking, Bevanism is characterized by a frenetic repudiation of the middle class, of middle-class virtues, of middle-class socialism, of gradualism. The defeat of Herbert Morrison for re-election to the Executive Committee of the Labor Party, which occurred at the party conference at Morecambe in October, 1952, was the symbolic vengeance of this group upon the man whom it feels is the incarnation of socialist Babbittry. The enthusiasts had their revenge on the Grand Inquisitor!

Thus around the standard of Aneurin Bevan have rallied all the social malcontents, the crusading enthusiasts, the crypto-communists, and others whose common bond is little more than their disillusionment with the democratic process. If there is any one thread that unites the Bevanites, it would seem to be faith in historical short-cuts.

Will Bevan split the party? Probably not, at least, not if he can avoid it. Bevan was on the verge of expulsion in the Thirties, at the time of the Socialist League incident, but while Stafford Cripps was then prepared to go into the wilderness with his principles, Bevan capitulated and remained in the party. But his very presence there constitutes a tremendous problem both for him and for the party leaders. Attlee will be very cautious lest he create a martyr; and Bevan will be careful not to give good grounds for expulsion, or to bolt, for he is well aware of the solidarity of the party in the face of schism. At the same time, Bevan makes it very difficult for the moderate leaders to gain the confidence of the middle class, while he cannot himself organize a faction or a new party without being expelled. In short, for the time being, an organizational stalemate exists.

How much support does Bevan have in the Labor Party? At the last party congress at Morecambe, the Bevanites won six seats on the party executive. This was a gain of two, since the Bevan group had four members on the last executive. But the significant aspect of this election was that all six were elected from the Constituency Labor Parties. (The twenty-seven-member Executive is elected in a peculiar fashion, growing out of the original federal design of the party: two hold *ex officio* membership, twelve are chosen by the trade unions, six by the whole party membership, and seven by the constituencies. In effect, eighteen are in the pocket of the trade union section.) Bevanite strength was greatest among the intellectuals, and least among the trade unionists. This last statement should be qualified somewhat since the trade-union custom of casting each union's vote *en bloc* may cover up significant minority strength. But at any rate, it appears as though Bevan is another proletarian messiah without a proletariat.

Some newspaper accounts tell us of wide-spread Bevanism in the trade union movement. However, these analyses fail to distinguish between trade-union agreement with one of Bevan's many complaints, and trade-union support for Bevanism as a political movement. Bevan has voiced so many objections to the present situation that it is virtually impossible for anybody, anywhere to complain about anything without agreeing with Bevan! But agreement with some of Bevan's views does not make a Bevanite. For example, one of the unions which has complained the loudest about the restraints of British life is the Chemical Workers. Objectively, it would seem to fall into the Bevanite category. But, subjectively, it is dominated by old Independent Labor Party men who consider Bevan to be a dishonest political operator, and would never support him. Consequently, while there is considerable discontent in trade-union circles, it can not be automatically registered as Bevanism. Moreover, at the T.U.C. Congress, held at Margate in September, 1952, the combined oppositions never rallied more than a quarter of the votes.

This does not, however, alleviate the crisis for the leaders of the Labor Party. They are not particularly worried about losing the trade unions to the Bevanites. Their major problem is the middle class whose fear of undemocratic extremism must be alleviated if another election is to be won for Labor. If the left-wing intellectuals can succeed in alienating the middle class from socialism over a period of years, the Labor Party may begin to disintegrate. British politics are quite similar to American in this respect: a political party keeps strong by delivering the goods to its supporters. The Labor Party has held the support of the British worker not so much because the latter is committed to "socialism," as through the worker's conviction that he will be better off with his friends in power. Indeed, it should be noted, the Labor Party's control of the "union vote" is far from complete; it has been estimated in Labor circles that one worker in four votes Conservative. However, if the Laborite workers ever decide that the party has lost its utility, that is, that it can win no more elections, he may very well switch his allegiance.

An additional factor deserves mention. Labor unions in despair take quite different attitudes from unions that are thriving. The Labor Party in the course of its struggle for industrial democracy may, by its very success, have weakened its hold over the workers. It should not be forgotten that the New Deal weakened its farm support largely by creating agricultural prosperity. If the Conservative Party, under the pressure of political imperatives, has really mended its antilabor ways, there is no reason to suspect that the British Trades Union Congress will engage in a quixotic defense of socialism. As the General Council of the T.U.C. recently pointed out to the Churchill government: "On our part we shall continue to examine every question solely in the light of its industrial and economic implications. The trade union movement must always be free to formulate and to advocate its own policies." Gompers himself could not have said it better.

In short, then, the problem the Laborites face is that of adjusting socialism to a middle-class, democratic society. To do this, they must face squarely up to the Bevanites, who represent a fundamentally undemocratic tendency. If the Labor Party cannot master this problem in a satisfactory manner, it may well become a permanent and progressively disintegrating minority. There is, however, no reason to suspect that democratic British socialists cannot overcome this barrier as they have solved the difficulties that faced them in the past. The heart of British socialism is a mature, humanistic approach to the problems of life and a dedication to the principle that men can, working together in a piecemeal, pragmatic fashion, master their destinies. In all probability, Bevanism will terminate on the scrap heap along with the Independent Labor Party, the Socialist League, and other Labor offshoots that rejected prosaic democratic maturity in favor of conspicuous proletarianism.   —*Winter* 1952-53

PATTERNS OF BELIEF

M. C. OTTO

Scientific Humanism

A_{LL} humanisms have one thing in common. It is the ideal of realizing mankind's completest development. From here on they diverge. The most far-reaching disagreement turns on the question whether man is or is not absolutely distinct from everything else in the hierarchy of earthly existences. It is at this point that the designation of one humanism as scientific takes on significance.

What does scientific mean in this connection? It means that human beings are viewed naturalistically. They are placed in the natural world along with the lower animals, plants, rocks, minerals, and star clusters. Their intellectual, moral, and aesthetic powers, their ideas of decency, their feelings of good will, all they are and aspire to be is looked upon as the consummation of a long evolution from the animal status. Scientific humanism is a form of naturalism.

This is part of the answer. The rest of it is that the scientific humanist is wholeheartedly committed to the use of scientific method. He favors its extension to moral and social problems of every kind, and he believes that a correct understanding of scientific procedure permits this to be done. As a rule this procedure is so narrowly defined that it cannot be applied to human beings in their actuality, to human interests as they are experienced, or even to the world of which human beings are aware. Take Sir Arthur Eddington's example of the elephant sliding down a grassy hillside. From

85

the viewpoint of physics the elephant fades out and is replaced by the reading of the pointer indicating a certain mass. The hillside disappears and its place is taken by the reading of a plumb line against the divisions of a protractor. In the same way the descent becomes a pointer-reading on the seconds' dial of a watch. The result is, says this professor of astronomical physics, that what really slides is a bundle of pointer-readings, and the sliding is a function of space and time measures. There is simply no elephant to slide down a hill and no hill for an elephant to slide down. "The whole subject matter of exact science," as thus conceived, "consists of pointer readings and similar indications."

Ordinarily, when we think of science, it is this kind of science we think of. Our notion of scientific method is our notion of what goes on in physical or chemical laboratories, including what we believe to be the special kind of subject matter dealt with in them. Consequently, we conclude that if man is to be studied scientifically he must be reduced to a mindless, indeed lifeless, concourse of material entities, to atoms, electrons, or even to more abstract elements. And a purely material assemblage or a pattern of abstract entities is certainly anything but human.

Suppose, however, that we broaden our idea of science, as in the end I think we must, to take in every field of knowledge where a sufficiently painstaking effort is made to establish conclusions on a thorough-going examination of relevant fact. In that case the word scientific takes on a meaning to correspond. We may then say that a method of investigation is scientific to the extent that it exemplifies the ideal of objective verification. Objective verification is of course a kind of technical shorthand. It has to be broken down into a statement of particulars, and I shall presently attempt to enumerate those particulars. But before undertaking to do this it may be well to note that a certain broadening in the meaning of scientific has taken place in the development of science itself.

There appears to be general agreement that for the most perfect exemplification of scientific method we must go to physics. From there on down through chemistry, physiology, biology, and the rest, factors are thought to intrude which render the investigation, from the standpoint of exactness, more and more impure. For that matter, even physics is impure when compared with mathematics. Shall we say then that, strictly speaking, there is but one science? Some have made just this claim. And many who do not say so, act as if they believed it, for they try their best to bring the material with which they deal into the closest possible resemblance to that of physical science, even though in the attempt they completely distort their proper subject matter.

This surely creates more problems than it solves. For one thing, if physics, chemistry, physiology, biology are not sciences, what are they? Yet if the meaning of "scientific" need not be limited to the exactest science, but may designate types of investigation which fall short of scientific methodology in its purest form, what ground is there for arbitrarily ruling out any type of inquiry that aims at objective verification? For another thing, if we insist upon holding to the conventional conception of scientific, in what terms shall we make a proper and much needed distinction between loose and rigorous thinking in the solution of problems not dealt with by the natural sciences?

In line with this revised conception, here are five requirements of objective verification:

1. Formulation of only such problems as can be solved by an appeal to facts in the external world. 2. Gathering of facts and, so far as possible, all obtainable facts pertinent to the problem. 3. The subjection of facts, inferences, hypotheses, generalizations, to a test admitted to be decisive, publicly applicable, open to the scrutiny of friend or foe. 4. Progressive building up of verification in which different investigators participate. 5. Recognition of the provisional result of even the most exacting demonstration, hence the relativity of all knowledge.

Of these requirements, the one of chief significance is the third. Probably all the others would follow from the appeal to a "publicly applicable" test, rigorously interpreted. Of course everybody who engages in an investigation worthy of the name appeals to facts and uses criteria to determine what knowledge his facts yield. Not everybody, however, appeals to the kind of facts or uses the kind of criteria of knowledge which can be judged by others than the investigator himself. On the contrary, certain claims to the possession of truth, regarded as the highest truth at that, are frankly declared to rely on criteria which are and must be strictly private. Moreover, there are so-called facts and truths which have logical force providing they can count on a "will to believe." They are powerless to convince a critic who demands to be "shown." In contrast with attitudes like these, scientific method calls for willingness to try conclusions by the application of a test that is recognized as definitive whatever may be the hopes or fears of investigator or critic.

A simple description of scientific procedure by a man of science will make all this clear. It occurs, as it were incidentally, in a discussion by Lewis G. Westgate of a geological problem, and seems to me admirably put:

> Science is a growth, a series of approximations; as it advances some old views are discarded, new views introduced. The discarded views are seen in the light of fuller knowledge to be in error. Inadequate approximations would be a better characterization; they were the best formulation the earlier science could make.

The individual worker

builds on the work of his predecessors, sometimes on their errors. By his own field work and thought he corrects some of these errors and adds new material. . . . His published results bring the matter out into the open for discussion and criticism by his fellow workers. His errors can be challenged by other facts unknown to him. His statements may suggest other studies, which may or may not corroborate his views. And so science advances by a process of trial and error, ever working toward a more truthful generalization.

There it is: the collection of data or facts in the outside world; the suggested solution brought out into the open to be tested by critical thinking and active field work; the development of a conclusion supported by cooperative examination and verification; the recognition of the approximate truth of the best established position. Now why should anyone doubt the feasibility of adapting this technique to every field where problems are to be solved? The difficulty of its application grows, to be sure, with the irreducible complexity of certain problems, and with the presence in men of prejudicial habits of thought or feeling which interfere with objective inquiry. But this in no way invalidates the claim that, properly understood, scientific method is applicable to areas from which it is conventionally thought to be barred.

Summarizing this phase of our study we may say that the scientific humanist sees no valid ground for believing men and women to be isolated or insulated creatures in nature. On the contrary, he regards them as strictly integrant to the great complexity of things, living and nonliving, which is commonly spoken of as the world. In conformity with this naturalistic interpretation the scientific humanist rejects both pure Reason and Revelation as sources of light for the understanding of human nature or the art of life. For his part he tries to emulate as best he can in his own field of interest the temper of mind and the workmanship of scientists.

II

We turn now to the other word in the title—humanism. I was just saying that the scientific humanist looks upon man as belonging altogether to the order of nature. I did not say that he thinks man identical with the lower animals, not to speak of lifeless matter. The fact is that no other humanist so consistently exalts man, or looks with equal generosity upon his *humanitas*, upon those attributes which differentiate man from all other living creatures. In a word, the scientific humanist does not lose any of his interest in the human aspect of human nature because he aspires to be scientific in his thinking.

Critics make short work of this avowed dual responsibility. Few of them think it worth while to examine the position. They simply rely upon derogatory names as if these had power to kill. The critics acknowledge that science has a large place in modern life. Sometimes they even advise that education should by all means introduce the student to some knowledge of science. But what do they expect from science? This is their answer: "From scientific investigation we may expect an understanding of scientific knowledge. We are confusing the issue and are demanding what we have no right to ask if we seek to learn from science the goals of human life and of organized society." Rarely do we find anything beyond this bare assertion. Any attempt to extend scientific method beyond the physical substance of things is dubbed "the cult of scientism," a "cult" that "does a disservice to both science and civilization." Perhaps that should kill scientific humanism on the spot, or even better, cause it to crawl off to die in some out-of-the-way corner.

It is, however, an interesting and happy fact that people will try to do, and sometimes succeed in doing, things they are told cannot be done. Either they do not know or do not believe that the things are impossible. The scientific humanist is one of those people. In spite of reiterated arguments purporting to show that the very attempt is irrational, he persists in trying to extend scientific thinking to every kind of individual and social problem. And what is more, he succeeds. Let us consider two or three great human goals or ends, observe how he reinterprets them, and then decide whether his view is as sterile culturally as the opponents charge.

III

Among the great goals of man's long endeavor is truth. In one of his poems Stephen Crane tells of two travelers. The first traveler calls truth a rock, a mighty fortress, and claims that he has often been to it, even to its highest towers. The second traveler likens truth to a phantom, which, though he has long pursued it, has always eluded his grasp. "And I believed the second traveler," says the poet.

This disjunctive proposition—that truth is either absolute or there is no truth at all—puts before us an article of popular theory as widely held, I believe, as any that could be mentioned. Now a little observation of people shows that they hold to this disjunction in a curious manner. If a man feels sure that a belief is true, and another feels as sure that the contrary is true, and neither of them knows of any way to adjudicate the disagreement, both of them will as a rule agree that a thing may be true for one person and untrue for another. In doing so each takes the position that truth is absolute and, at the same time, that there is no truth at all. For surely a type of truth which rests solely upon personal conviction is about as variable as you please.

Between such truth and truth as a shadow or a phantom there is nothing to choose.

The scientific humanist refuses to play fast and loose with truth in this manner. He places too high a value on it to let it go at that. Convinced that it is important for men to have *true* ideas, and that *un*true ideas do them harm, sometimes irreparable harm, he thinks it necessary to reach a better conception of the truth situation. And as he looks about he discovers that the truths men live by are not in either of the classes referred to by Stephen Crane. They are not true in any *absolute* sense, yet are not mere *fantasies*, either. They are as true as the tests by which they are established are reliable; no more true, but also no less true. This is what is meant by calling truth relative; it is dependent truth.

Many persons seem to think that relative truth means less than truth; a sort of truth; pseudo-truth. What it actually means is *related* truth; truth in the contexts of some kind of ongoing experience and in conformity with the kind of measure used in that context. For instance, there is no *absolute* quart, pound, or inch floated down from heaven to some receptive spirit, and no one thinks there is; yet no one takes the position that quarts, pounds, inches may be anything anyone pleases. We insist upon having true measures of value where quarts, pounds, inches are used in our dealings with one another. And if any dispute arises, we can go to the place where the master-standard is on exhibition.

That we have accurate weights and measures for meat, groceries, milk, potatoes, gasoline, cloth, boards, and such things, and not for what we call spiritual attainment or for measuring progress in the good life, is an accident of our history. We have done "field work" in the one case and not in the other; we have appreciated the advantage to all concerned of specific and common means of verification in buying and selling, while we have generally remained satisfied with abstract, individual, frequently purely verbal verification in ethics, religion, and philosophies of life. Possibly this proves that most of us think more highly of the business of buying and selling than we do of mental development and growth in character. Or the explanation may be that it is considerably easier to come to an agreement on tests of quantity than of quality.

At any rate, the scientific humanist takes the position that when something is spoken of as true it is presumed to measure up to the test by which the true is distinguished from the untrue in some field of operation. He therefore does not spend time trying to make contact with Truth as a spiritual essence which hovers above the earth and out of reach of human contamination. He labors to invent and put into practice better and better truth tests, especially in areas of human interest where the need to do this has received and still receives little attention. He does "field work" in the service of social idealism. In his effort to improve truth tests he shows his scientific bent; his humanistic bent is shown in the determination to extend the use of such improved truth tests to all the phases of individual and communal experience where the better potentialities of human beings may either turn out well or come to naught.

This buckling down to the task of furthering the true as against the false in the big and little affairs of every day, although it is not highly regarded by the devotee of absolute and abstract Truth, happens to be the kind of truth-concern upon which progress in the attainment of truer beliefs, attitudes, and ideas depends. Truth from this point of view is a collective name for a sum of particular truths, as true as they are and no truer. Since the scientific humanist consistently endeavors to improve the standard of the true precisely where there is greatest need that this be done, it should be obvious that truth has a place of unusual honor in scientific humanism.

IV

Another of the great human goals is moral character. In that impressive book, *The Dawn of Conscience,* J. E. Breasted undertakes to show how the idea of right, as distinguished from wrong in the ethical sense, had its origin in Egypt 4,000 or more years ago. Early in occidental history authority in the realm of moral ideas and ideals was taken over by church religion. In the course of time secular life took it away again. But long association with theology left its mark. The belief, not to say illusion, for which this association is responsible, that morality must be defined and vitalized "from on high," is still with us. Likewise the alleged antagonism between character and wants or desires. Innumerable people continue to believe that there is something shameful, if not pathological, about desires. What they spontaneously think of when they hear the word moral or immoral is sex. Sex desire, taken to be the most unruly, leaps to the foreground of the mind because the inherited conception of morality is essentially the mastery of desire by something in man higher than desire.

The scientific humanist does what he can to liberate himself from this prejudice against desires. He accepts with hope the fact that men and women have wants and desires. He believes that the human energies called desires are the only driving power we have to help us toward the good life— the happy life as well as the noble life. The good life involves more than desires: intelligence, knowledge, imagination, and at its best, creativeness of a high order. But desires are the life of the whole business. Not to recognize this openly and frankly has no end of unhappy results. Desires are made to work themselves out surreptitiously, abnormally. Maliciousness, coarseness, brutality can cloak themselves in sanctity. The fanatic gets the opportunity to step forth as moral dictator.

Does the scientific humanist then refuse to divide desires into good and bad? In one sense, yes; in another sense, no. Anything a person wants he wants because it appears good. That is why he wants it. I say "appears," rather than "is," for no better reason than to avoid immediate disagreement. Whether it is wants or needs or obligations he goes out for, he believes them good to have. If he believed them bad to have he would not want them. However, every one soon finds out, and finds out again and again, that the wanted, the good, can not be isolated from antecedents and consequences. These antecedents and consequences may in certain cases not be wanted at all. And sometimes upon reflection the not-wanted aspect so outweighs the wanted that the offering as a whole fails to appeal and so is not regarded as good. And every person soon finds out that his own wants and the wants of others overlap in ways to further or to thwart each other. It turns out, moreover, that every individual is interested in wants of other individuals, wanting some of them satisfied and some not. Thus the wanted and the not-wanted are frequently tied up in one package.

A desire is morally bad when the desirer insists on having what he wants in disregard of his want's unwanted concomitants. A desire is bad when the desirer insists upon having what he wants no matter what holes he tears in the fabric of human interdependence without which no life can approach all-over satisfactoriness.

This interpretation of character and the good life implies that everybody is desirous of finding life as livable as possible; that the goal of life, to put it in a word, is happiness. Is this a valid assumption? There are those who deny it. Alexander Meiklejohn, for example, contends that the objective is not happiness but a personal quality which he calls "excellence." His moral philosophy is socially conscious, clean and fine-spirited, free from the conceit of learning, high-minded and intentionally austere. I introduce a quotation from his book *What Does America Mean?* in order to sharpen the humanistic argument for the dignity of desires.

In Mr. Meiklejohn's view, "It is not imperative that any individual, or any nation, or even the race itself, should continue to be happy, should even continue to exist. It is imperative that so long as we live, we do so with taste and intelligence, with fineness and generosity." And the reason is this: "Many things are worse than unhappiness. But nothing is worse than being contemptible." The scientific humanist agrees with the college student who, having read Mr. Meiklejohn, made this comment: "Yes, let us include among our desires the desire for taste, intelligence, fineness, generosity, for they are helps in the production of happiness. Many things are worse than being contemptible. But nothing is worse than being unhappy. The worst thing about being contemptible is that it makes you so damn unhappy."

Looking back over this section, it is obvious that the analysis is over-simple. Possibly it is not too simple for the present purpose, which is to spotlight the distinctive element in the moral attitude from the standpoint under review. No desire liveth to itself or dieth to itself. At bottom the difference beween the moral and the immoral or nonmoral attitude is the presence in the former, and the absence from the latter, of scrutiny and appraisal of desires with regard to their effect upon what was just called all-over satisfactoriness. Satisfactoriness may of course be envisaged broadly or narrowly; may be restricted to pleasurable excitement, physical convenience, social prominence, the exercise of power, or include appreciation of art, music, literature, religion, philosophy. It may be bounded by the welfare of the self or the family, or be touched by interests as wide as the world. While the practical necessity of acting will inevitably impose limits, the measure of moral personality is sensitiveness to the consequences of desiring what is desired. Naturalistic in outlook as scientific humanism is, and thus at pains to vindicate desires, it is, being also humanistic in outlook, at equal pains to emphasize the need for criticism and discipline. The ideal is that desires shall spring up spontaneously, freely, and differently in response to the richest, most various goods, and that this dynamic exuberance shall be matched by well developed habits of critical appraisal and intelligent choice.

We conclude, then, that the moral ideal here outlined cannot fairly be described as a cheap, superficially conceived, or easily realized ideal. To commit oneself to it is to undertake a difficult, complicated, often elusive assignment. Even moderate success in it calls for thoughtful application and takes time. One may know at a given moment what it is one wants, but whether it would still be wanted were there a looking before and after, whether the wanted is also, when well considered, the wantable, that is not so easy to be clear about. Still, with some people it becomes second nature to seek a genuinely richer, worthier, happier life-experience, and they show remarkable expertness in discovering the right means and ends. It would be a long step in advance if public education naturally introduced the young to this way of life and prepared them for effectiveness in it. There are teachers who do just that, and some day they may be the majority. Some day, too, the world of affairs may encourage instead of discourage moral progress. And while in some respects each one must define and realize the good life for himself, no one can attain his moral growth except in reciprocal relationship with other human beings, so that there is the additional problem of making our way together toward a social arrangement which provides the indispensable opportunities.

All this is part of the scientific humanist's moral program. It is an ironical fact that the humanist who regards it as essential that all wants be related to disciplined taste, and who is everlastingly stressing the need for informed criticism of the self and of society, should be accused of working against moral idealism and moral integrity.

V

Now what of man's religious interest? Does this humanism unite the religious and the scientific outlooks? The answer depends, as answers so often do, on how the terms are defined. We have adopted a meaning for *scientific* and shall have to do likewise for *religious*.

No simple description can do justice to religion even as this has been formulated and practiced in the Occident. But a central feature of our whole religious tradition is its positive relation to the supernatural. To be religious has meant to seek companionship with a friendly being believed to abide behind or within the drift and waste of temporal events. Possibly there is actually a continuity between the "Friend behind phenomena" that men seek, to borrow Gilbert Murray's idea, and "the pack which a dog tries to smell his way back to all the time he is out walking." "It is a strange and touching thing," says Mr. Murray, "this eternal hunger of the gregarious animal for the herd of friends who are not there." "And it may be," he continues, "it may very possibly be," that our religious searchings are at bottom "the groping of a lonely-souled gregarious animal to find its herd or its herd leader in the great spaces between the stars."

Well, if this reliance upon a Cosmic Friend is what religion must be, because that is what religion in our region of the world has been, then scientific humanism can touch religion as a line can touch a circle, but the two cannot interpenetrate to form a blended philosophy. There are, however, other definitions of religion. One of these is readily seen to have close affinities with the humanism discussed in this paper. The world as described by science is accepted as such and this very description is made the ground for the highest human aspiration. It is surely an invitation to religion which W. Macneil Dixon extends to the reader in these words from his book, *Thoughts for the Times*:

> When I am told that throughout the realm of nature there is "no tendency that makes for righteousness," that justice is nowhere to be found there, that in her soil the tree of justice refuses to take root . . . I do not find nature ennobled and man humiliated. . . . Quite the reverse. To me it seems to exalt him to a plane immeasurably far above hers, and moreover to provide him with an aim, a purpose, a cause, an inspiration that fires the blood and hardens resolution. If justice be no concern either of nature or of the gods, it is the more preeminently ours. . . . If this world be without justice it is man's unique privilege to

place it there—a superb design, an enterprise the immortals might envy, yet have left to mortal hands.

A similar view of religion has been defended with eloquence and learning by A. E. Haydon for a quarter of a century. Essential religion, in his view, is and has always been the shared quest of a good life in a good world, made ever more possible by advancing knowledge and now especially by science. Says Mr. Haydon in his book, *The Quest of the Ages*:

> In contrast with the great believers who imposed their noblest dreams by faith upon the universe, there have been men in all cultures who clipped the wings of their hopes and built a more modest ideal in the everyday world of fact. Though life might not be altogether lovely, they made the best of life. With no hope of help from gods, and no faith in life immortal, the beauty of human comradeship became more precious.
>
> It is encouraging, therefore, and of deep significance to religion, that a common refrain runs through the writings of modern thinkers. The notes of the melody are freedom, democratic opportunity, cooperative individualism, meliorism, internationalism. The march of religions moves toward the Great Society in which all individuals will have a fair chance for the joy of living, and personal satisfactions will blend with social responsibility and creative power.

An inspired statement of this nontheistic, socially oriented religious attitude is condensed into a paragraph at the end of John Dewey's *Human Nature and Conduct*. These four sentences bring the paragraph and the book to end:

> Within the flickering inconsequential acts of separate selves dwells a sense of the whole which claims and dignifies them. In its presence we put off mortality and live in the universal. The life of the community in which we live and have our being is the fit symbol of this relationship. The acts in which we express our perception of the ties which bind us to others are its only rites and ceremonies.

Personally, I have never been willing to stop at this point in defining religion, not because of its naturalistic, nontheistic, socially dedicated aspect, but because something seems to me left out which is more profoundly characteristic of the religious mood than any kind of special knowledge, devotion, or service. This is a response to the awesome and mysterious in life and the world. A positive response to the awesome and mysterious has had a central place in the most various religions throughout religious history. Without it religion seems to me to lose its differentiating quality and to become identical with morality, differing from it, if at all, in emotional tone. In theistic religions and in religious mysticism the response is not so much to the awesome mystery itself as to the Being behind the mystery, even though what this Being is may only be statable in symbols or not at all. In the nontheistic religion with which we are concerned the response is to the mystery as mystery. The difference between these attitudes is deeply significant, but there is at the same time a relationship between them which justifies the application of the term religious to both. At any rate I believe it necessary to add another quotation to those preceding:

> I have not said and I have no intention of saying, that the nontheist must limit his interests to what can be weighed and measured, intellectually delineated, or presented in some embodied form with clear outlines; that he must never allow himself to stray into the land described by Virginia Woolf, where words "fold their wings and sit huddled like rooks on the tops of the trees in winter." . . . We need to keep a window open toward the uncharted.
>
> A conscious awareness of this mystery does healing work on the inward man. It is the healing work of acknowledged ignorance in the revered presence of that which eludes comprehension—the incomprehensible in each other, in the life we are called upon to live, in the great cosmic setting that reaches from our feet to the infinities.

At all events, whether this sense of mystery is a religious indispensable or not, humanists of the scientific persuasion reject the dualism which assigns to religion final authority in the realm of value and to science final authority in the realm of fact. They refuse to divide the experienced world into two realms, one of which is the locus of fact and the other the locus of value; and if they recognize any authority as final, which in a manner of speaking they may be said to do, it is not any religious or scientific interpretation of the cosmos; it is man's unremitting search for a livable life and the stubborn conditioning facts of human nature and the natural and social environment. Scientific humanists share in the "quest of a good life in a good world," and hold steadily to the conviction that progress toward this authoritative end is contingent upon the best kind of objective thinking whether the question is one of fact or of value. Which is another way of saying that in their philosophy the scientific and the religious spirit are united in a common enterprise. Matter and spirit may be enemies, but they may also be allies.

VI

We come to the end of this sketch with whole areas of important endeavor left untouched. Scientific humanistic principles and methods are

of course applicable to those omitted areas. Some persons will nevertheless remain unpersuaded. They are sure to complain that scientific humanism is not enough. And the complaint is understandable. Scientific
civilization, so widely extolled, still shows glaring faults. Innumerable
people get little indeed out of living, and all they are promised in the
scheme of life most prominently and alluringly set before them, even
could they attain it, is far less than the human spirit craves. Can we take
pride in the global strife which scientific civilization has made possible?
Are we to enjoy the spectacle of millions of human beings deliberately
engaged in killing each other? Is there anything reassuring in a colossal
waste of economic goods or in the destruction of the best that artistic
genius has achieved through centuries of labor? No, there is nothing un-
natural in the conclusion that any view which is allied to scientific civilization is not enough; that to be really adequate a way of life must transcend
life, must make good its shortcomings by laying hold upon the realities
of a promised experience that is to begin when the earthly experience is
over.

The complaint, I repeat, is understandable, but it is a pointless and
futile complaint unless a better philosophy can be shown to be available.
What if this is a vain hope? What if it is an unrealizable dream? What if
scientific humanism, although it does not set before us all that can be
imagined, does offer the best we can actually get? "Imposter for imposter," George Bernard Shaw flippantly declares, "I prefer the mystic to the
scientist—the man who at least has the decency to call his nonsense a
mystery, to him who pretends that it is ascertained, weighed, measured,
analyzed fact." Others assert, "There are no atheists in foxholes," as if this
were complimentary to God. A gull landing on the head of a man adrift
in a rubber boat is supposed to have established theistic cosmology. Well-
known theological philosophers urge a return to a time when men are
said to have preferred spiritual worth and inner peace to physical comfort and outer power. But Shaw's irresponsible witticism is not quite a
philosophy of life. Foxholes are at best temporary domiciles. Gulls are
not unfailingly responsive to prayer. The men on the raft with Seaman
Izzi called upon God in vain. Two of them finally died of exhaustion,
and the three who survived were not picked up in answer to prayer, so
far as one can tell. As for returning to the theism of the past, the clock of
experience cannot be turned back. It has never been done in human history.

If wishes could make universes we might have the one we want and
exactly as we want it. But we have learned a few things in the last three
hundred years, and it is just possible that in the light of what we have
learned scientific humanism will have to be enough. Superearthly ideal-

ism was once compatible with the best established knowledge of the day. For better, for worse, our ancestors ventured beyond the walls of that knowledge and the gates were shut upon their descendants forever. Truth, goodness, beauty, individual personality, these remain and must always remain among the primary objectives of a life in search of lasting happiness. All of them, however, have had to be sought in a vaster world because our forebears refused to stay at home. And every value of life must henceforth be sought in the strange new world that is shaping itself about us.

One of the foremost educators of our time, Boyd H. Bode, has long been telling college students, prospective teachers, that the supreme contemporary issue is whether the democratic way of life as a moral system can stand on its own feet. The choice, as he sees the situation, is between a naturalistically based democracy or something worse, not something better. Since he began life in Iowa I cannot believe that this is a prejudice to which he was conditioned as a boy. He could scarcely have picked it up during his college days in Michigan or as a graduate student at Cornell. I have not consulted him to find out, but the probabilities are that, trained as he had been in the traditional religious outlook, exposed as he then was to naturalistic modernity, and sensitive to both influences, he grew to appreciate the fact that nothing can in the end save the great ideals of the human spirit but their profound reinterpretation. In setting forth that reinterpretation he became a pioneer of scientific humanism. The persistent theme of his lectures and articles and books has been the many-sided problem of how to increase the meaning and joy of life on earth by making use of the best intellectual and moral tools. In the educational philosophy of this keen, most clear-headed and mature American we have a striking and happy illustration of the kind of high-mindedness and objective-mindedness that can work hand in hand in the world as it has now to be faced.

So it all comes to this. Scientific humanism is not a bleak materialism and it is not a superstitious or an intellectualized spiritualism. The scientific humanist does not pretend that every experience of life can be forced into a test tube or that every interest can be weighed on a scale. He knows that something in everything always escapes the technique of measurement. It must be directly appreciated or go unnoticed. And when he contemplates the whole of things he exclaims as Heraclitus did when philosophy was young: "Nature loves to hide." He says with Gilbert Murray who belongs to the present age: "The life of man can be divided, like the old maps of the world, into the charted and the uncharted. The charted is finite and the other infinite." But he knows also that there is no way of escaping the new world-order or the new moral and intellectual climate, and that man's aspirational life must adjust itself to these conditions or lose its redemptive power. Scientific humanism is the name for his determination to stand up to the task and the opportunity.

—Winter 1943

SIDNEY HOOK

Education for Vocation

The education of the future will in the case of every child over a certain age, combine productive labor with education and athletics not merely as one of the methods of raising social production but as the only method of producing fully developed human beings.—KARL MARX[1]

NOTHING is more familiar than the contrast drawn by modern educators between liberal education and vocational education. But as soon as we try to track down the specific differences between them we discover that no hard and fast lines can be drawn. Usually a liberal education is so defined that if it has any other end beyond itself, if it involves more than the joys of consummatory experience, it is illiberal. It thus automatically excludes any activity connected with "earning one's living." This conception reflects elements drawn from both the Greek and Hebraic traditions. In ancient Greek society most citizens did not have to earn their own living. The work of the world was performed by slaves, and concern with material *means* was the distinctive mark of the *menial* in spirit. According to the Hebraic legend, work in the sweat of his face is man's curse and punishment. With primitive tools or none at all it could hardly have been conceived differently. But it recognizes in a dim way that it is work which makes man human. The knowledge to which it is counterposed is not imperfect human knowledge, laboriously acquired

---

[1]*Das Kapital,* I, edited by Karl Kautsky, 8th ed. Berlin, 1928, p. 425. In the interest of the context, I have freely rendered *"Unterricht"* (literally "instruction") as "education," and *"Gymnastik"* as "athletics."

by a body of clay, but divine. Man is expelled from the Garden of Eden because he has sought to become like unto God: his earthly career begins with the quest through *work* of human knowledge and happiness.

In the modern world liberal education has always been a serious enterprise despite the existence of some students who did not take it seriously, who regarded it as a personal adornment or a badge of social superiority. It was always connected with earning one's living although the "livings" were of a highly selected sort. The notion that the opposite of the liberal arts was the useful arts and that therefore the liberal arts could be designated as useless, would have been dismissed as preposterous even by the most traditional of educators. For the curriculum of the liberal arts colleges of the past few centuries trained for vocations, too. The teachers, ministers, lawyers, physicians, and better-paid public servants were largely drawn from the ranks of the college educated. A liberal arts education was in fact a sufficient preparation for many kinds of careers. Like the great medieval universities, but in a lesser measure, they were really professional schools.

In the contemporary world this is still true. But it is often concealed by dubbing some careers "professions" and regarding the others as "vocations." Flatly to contrast the "professions," even when we prefix the adjective "liberal" to them, with "vocations," is to express an invidious distinction. It is derived from the scorn felt by those who imagine they use only their brain as an instrument in earning their living, toward those who seem to use only their hands. It is explained mainly by the fact that most "vocations"—in ordinary times—carry with them less power, less money, and less prestige in the eyes of the community, than most professions.

When does a "vocation" become a "profession"? Take the lowly street-cleaner on whom the health of our cities depends. Give him civil-service status after rigorous training and examinations, raise his income to that of college professors—the difference at present is not great—provide liberal pension and retirement allowances, give him the official title of "social physician," deck him out in a resplendent dress uniform, and before long his "vocation" will become a "profession," too.

A liberal education should do something more than prepare the student to earn his own living. But it should at least prepare him for it. The crucial question is *how* he should be prepared. No conception of liberal education is worth a second glance which professes to be unconcerned with the quality of the life a student will lead after he is through with his formal schooling—a life in which the fruits of his schooling first become apparent. All the great educators of the modern world, despite their differences as to what contitutes the best education, agree that it should be complete in the sense that it should fit men to grapple with their duties as citizens of the community. But a citizen of the community is not only a "political" entity. He is a producer, a consumer, a potential warrior, a critic, a teacher in some respects, a learner in others. He is sometimes more of one or another. But in the life of the citizen all are related. This thought was expressed long ago by John Milton whose conception of a "complete" education is a measure by which we may still judge what belongs to a desirable education and how it belongs. "A complete and generous education," he said, "is one that fits a man to perform skilfully, justly and magnanimously, all the acts, both public and private, of peace and war." Vocational education is part of a complete and generous education.

The fundamental problem of vocational education today is whether it should be considered as a form of vocational *training,* serving industry and government, or whether it should be considered as an aspect of liberal education in which preparation for careers in industry and government is justified *both* by the needs of a developing personality and the interests of the community. Here, as elsewhere, we can observe a meeting of extremes which in effect makes allies of the lily-pure academician and the tough-minded practical man. The first finds utterly distasteful the idea that vocational interests should obtrude on the course of study. In his heart he believes that students who study for any other reason save the sheer love of it degrade learning. They therewith prove themselves in his eyes to be no true students at all. The second regards liberal arts studies as initiating conventional preliminaries to useful subjects whose mastery has a cash value. Wherever possible, he seeks to give vocational courses a content that is directly relevent to the tasks that must be performed on the job. For all their opposition, both agree on sharply separating liberal from vocational study, although they differ in the grounds offered for the separation. Both are united in strong opposition to any plan to make vocational education integral to liberal education.

The type of education which today is specifically labeled "vocational" is largely job training. Despite the war of words raging against its narrowness, it is enjoying a mushroom growth, especially in the higher reaches of the educational process. It is easy to understand this growth. School is short, life is long, and no one enjoys an enforced leisure without comforts. The desire to prepare for a dignified and well remunerated calling is perfectly legitimate. Where it is absent, a society is in the last stages of decay. The greater are the immediate opportunities for employment, the greater is the demand for special training from industry, and the greater is the interest in vocational subjects among students, particularly among those who are unhappy with the traditional course of liberal education and, as they quaintly put it, want something more "serious." Educational administrators responding to the needs created by the war have looked with marked favor upon plans for extension of vocational education. Returning veterans have voiced their intentions of concentrating on an education which will qualify them for new jobs in new industries and better jobs in old ones.

Vocational education conceived as job training represents the greatest threat to democratic education in our time. It is a threat to democracy because it tends to make the job-trained individual conscious only of his technological responsibilities but not of his social and moral responsibilities. He becomes a specialist in "means" but is indifferent to "ends" which are considered the province of another specialist. The main concern becomes with "getting a job" and after that with "doing a job" no matter what the political direction and moral implications of the job are. Social programs are judged simply by whether they promise to provide the jobs for which the technician is trained. If a democratic community can supply the opportunity for work, well and good; if it can't, and a totalitarian party or government offers the opportunity, why not? Observers have noted that the technically trained students in institutions of higher education in Germany and Italy have in the mass been much more susceptible to totalitarian propaganda than students whose education has primarily been in the pure sciences. An education that is narrowly vocational, without cultural perspective or social orientation, unillumined by knowledge of large scientific principles considered in a large way, undisciplined by a critical method that sets the range of relevance for methods of technical thinking, is even worse for democratic purposes than a narrow and pure scientific training which, as a special kind of professionalism, is bad in its own way. For the problems on the job are *application* of scientific knowledge in contexts of social values and human relationships. And it is these which conventional education persistently ignores.

The high incidence of interest in vocational training among youth today reflects the expectation that our economy will have a place for them. The underlying assumption is that the seller's market for the vocationally trained will indefinitely continue in peace as well as in war. This is far from being a sure thing. The history of American capitalism does not provide grounds for great confidence. Vocationally trained talents rusted for almost a decade after the depression. Educators made desperate efforts to revamp curriculums so as to keep youth out of the labor market. We may witness the same thing again. Dearth of vocations may be the most powerful argument against vocational education of the present type. But it would be the weakest argument, and the wisdom it would enforce, besides being costly, would be limited. For even if prosperity were to continue unabated in years of peace, there is no reason why a truncated vocational education should be substituted for an integrated liberal one. We could well forego the difference in national wealth that would result from keeping young people out of the labor market for a few years, if it added to the immeasurable but more genuine wealth of a well informed, critically minded youth.

Such a critically minded youth would think not only about jobs but about the economy as a whole which provided the jobs and sometimes took them away. Such a youth would not be educated to "adjust" themselves to an economic and social order as if it were as perennial as the course of the stars. They would be encouraged to view it in its historical development. They would be taught to recognize its present-day problems as *occasions for choices* which they, among others, had to make. They would adjust not to the present but to the future as if it were present. To adjust to the future as if it were present is never an automatic reaction in human beings. For it is the essence of reflection.

There is a paradox connected with vocational training. The more vocational it is, the narrower it is; the narrower it is, the less likely it is to serve usefully in earning a living. Techniques, know-hows, operative skills change so rapidly in industry that the student who has been trained to perform certain specific tasks runs the risk of suffering from what Veblen called "trained incapacity." This is particularly true for manual crafts. For all their previous vocational training, those who are muscle-bound, either physically or intellectually, must unlearn and relearn if they are to continue to earn their living. Proper vocational education stresses doing, of course. Its skills are largely practical, not abstract. But at the same time it must nourish and strengthen powers of flexibility which will enable students to breast the waves of vocational changes intelligently. To a certain extent this is achieved in the kind of vocational education we call "professional" about which I shall have more to say later.

The indictment against vocational education summarized above would be signed with both hands by those who desire to keep liberal education uncontaminated by concern for earning a livelihood. They offer two distinct solutions to the problem. The first is a sharp separation between liberal arts education and vocational education. Liberal arts education above the elementary levels, is to be open to anyone who can qualify for it. After it is completed, it may be followed by vocational education. The second solution is much more radical. It has the great merit of making the problem disappear from view. It proposes that vocational education be left to apprentice experience on the job, and that the schools abandon all vocational instruction. I shall discuss this proposal first.

"The thing to do with vocational education," says Mr. Robert Hutchins, "is to forget it. As the war training programs in industry have shown, industry can train its hands if it has to, and can do it at lightning speed."[2] If one believes this and also holds, as Mr. Hutchins did a few years ago, that individuals may be divided into those who are "hand-minded" and those who are not and that the former cannot derive large benefits from a liberal education, the prospects of continued education beyond elementary levels for a large section of the population would appear bleak indeed. But even if we surrender to the view that individuals can be segregated into the "hand-minded" and the verbal-minded, the reason offered for abandoning vocational education is far from convincing.

It is one thing to train men and women in a national emergency for jobs that are temporary, and whose temporary character is emphasized in order to draw people away from other pursuits, not needed in war, for which they may have inclination and capacity. The human costs are justified by national need and much of the economic costs are under-written by the government. It is quite another thing to make the choice of a lifetime vocation dependent upon the happy chance that individuals who have completed their formal education without any conception of what they are qualified to do, will stumble upon just the right thing. After all, the better part of one's waking hours is spent on earning a living unless one is a man of leisure, a prizefighter, or a college president. The very fact that for many people life begins when work is over is a sign that they may have been miscast in their occupation. An intelligent person can hardly give too much thought to the problem of discovering the type of work which will afford him an opportunity to bring his best talents into play and therewith get the sense of significant achievement. Plato's insight is still valid: as a rule most people are happiest doing the work for which they are best qualified. That is why a good education is one which helps the individual discover what he is best qualified to do —no easy task. And that is why—and here we go beyond Plato—a just state strives to help its citizens to realize their voluntary and intelligent choice of vocations by equalizing relevant, educational opportunity.

Is it true that training-on-the-job and at "lightning speed," too, can be adequately substituted for vocational training? It would be hard to distinguish between skilled and unskilled work if this were so. There are two gross confusions in the recommendation that the main varieties of vocational activity should be learned on the job. The first is confusion between certain types of work which almost anyone can adequately do

---

[2]"Education for Freedom," *Christian Century,* November 15, 1944.

in two weeks of training or less like punching a machine or doing nurse's aid, and other types of work which require years of preparation like designing precision tools or medicine. Hazards to health and wealth would mount dangerously if all vocational education took place on the job.

The second confusion is between specific skills, knacks or tricks of the trade that are always learned best on the job because they change so rapidly, and basic principles whose mastery facilitates the acquisition of these skills. Professional education in medicine, engineering, and law is vocational, too. The schools cannot teach the things the physician learns at the bedside, the lawyer in court, the engineer when a particular dam gives way. But without an education in general principles, these practitioners would not know enough to learn from experience. Experience is the source of knowledge, not a guarantee of knowledge; not even total immersion in the stream of experience will fill an empty head.

Those who speak of vocational training on the job would never apply this piece of wisdom to the professions because professions, forsooth, are not vocations. But they owe us a justification of the distinction. Some vocations demand for their most effective performance more theoretical education than others. But this is only a matter of degree. And as we shall see, there is some kind of "theoretical" education which should be a *sine qua non* of all "vocational" education.

The more plausible solution presented by academic traditionalists who agree with our indictment of present-day vocational training is to recognize the legitimacy of education for a living but to separate it sharply from liberal education or "education for freedom." The individual is a citizen. He must therefore receive "education for freedom" which is identical for everyone. He is also a worker with a special job to do. He must therefore receive "training for a job" which will not be identical for all individuals. But the two kinds of education have nothing in common. As Alexander Meiklejohn puts it in answering the question how men can be free in modern industrial society:

> Now the American theory of freedom answers that question. It does so by distinguishing Education for Freedom from another kind of education. In a free society, we say, every citizen has two different parts to play. He must, therefore, have two different educations. *Unless we can sharply separate these two sets of learning, we cannot understand what the American doctrine of free institutions is.*[3]

To some extent this is a description of the way in which much of vocational education actually functions today. At various levels students

---

[3]"Equality and Education," radio address of February 14, 1944 (Mutual Broadcasting System). My italics.

are given instruction in certain liberal arts although the instruction lacks the content and uniformity Mr. Meiklejohn thinks desirable: and there then follows a purely vocational training.

But it is this very *separation* between the two kinds of education which is pedagogically defective. Vocational education is simply overlaid on liberal education. The bearings of the general ideas and philosophy acquired through liberal education are not integrated with the vocational subject matter at the points where they are the most important. Why a man works, the effects of his work, its relation to the tasks of the community are questions quite germane to his vocational activity. They are best studied in specific contexts. The worker remains a citizen while he is at his job. His knowledge of the fact ofttimes will make a difference to what he does and how he does it. What is called a liberal education should be a continuous process, and there is no reason except unfamiliarity with the idea why vocational education should not be liberalized to include the study of social, economic, historical, and ethical questions whenever relevant instead of assuming, as in the existing practice, that education in these matters is something already gone through and forever done with.

Should liberal arts courses be given in addition to the practical courses in vocational education? Or should practical courses be taught in such a way as to introduce an historical and social awareness, knowledge of scientific method and sensitiveness to persons and ethical principles into consideration of concrete problems? Neither procedure can be laid down as a fixed principle to be followed although the second is educationally preferable. It depends upon the type of course and the specific subject under study.

The greatest obstacle to this attempt to integrate vocational and liberal education flows from the suspicions of the specialist against introducing anything outside the narrow confines of his specialty. He regards cultural studies in professional schools as a kind of academic "boondoggling." It wastes time which in his eyes is already insufficient for the technical matters students should know. The specialist has a natural tendency to view the whole curriculum from the standpoint of his own professional concern. He recognizes how narrowing and educationally disastrous such a perspective is when it is drawn by *other* specialists. This recognition should serve as one of the checks upon his natural appetite. Even in liberal arts colleges, as we have already observed, many subjects, particularly the sciences, are taught from the specialist's point of view to the detriment of broader understanding and abiding interest on the part of students most of whom, if they become specialists, will be specialists in something else.

Recent tendencies in our best vocational schools, viz., our professional schools, show a growing realization that vocational and liberal education cannot be sharply separated. A dawning perception is now manifest that the best specialist is not necessarily the man who has received the most vocational training. The work of the physician, the work of the lawyer, the work of the engineer in different ways demands a *continuing* familiarity with subjects that would seem to the specialist to be utterly irrelevant to his proper vocational tasks. Yet as the *Report of the Commission on Medical Education* made clear years ago "the health" of the individual is as much a social concept as a biological one. It did not say this in so many words but it is unmistakably implied in the following key passage from its report:

> Medical education should emphasize to students the influence of urbanization, industrialization, and present-day conditions of living which are important in the causation, treatment, and prevention of disease. These factors must be appreciated if the physician is to perform his function of advising patients in regard to their health problems. The unit of practice, regardless of how medical services are organized or how social organization is changed, will continue to be the individual patient. If the individual is to obtain the most helpful counsel, it is important that the physician be acquainted with the social, economic, and other environmental factors which have an influence on the individual and his health.

These observations, unhappily not yet given force in the curriculum of most medical schools, apply in principle to other fields as well. The best illustrations of legal education today incorporate large bodies of psychological, sociological, and economic analysis into the course of study. The lawyer who knows nothing more than "the law books" is ill-equipped to practice law, handicapped in judging when he is elevated to the bench, and hopelessly at sea when he is called in to advise on, or participate in, the determination of public policy. Although there is a wide acceptance of this truth, actual curricular practices lag far behind.[4]

Whether it be business or journalism, government service or social work, engineering or communications, the subject matter of these fields cannot be properly mastered without including much more than vocational techniques. Sometimes the interrelation of studies flows outward, so to speak, from a consideration of problems *within* the technical field, for example, in the study of peptic ulcers in medicine or tax laws in

---

[4]Cf. the ambitious recommendations for the reform of legal education in "Legal Education and Public Policy: Professional Training in the Public Interest" by Lasswell and McDougal, 52 (*Yale Journal*) 203.

accountancy. Sometimes the integration of studies is achieved by considering the relation of the entire field to the social and political context, for example, the nature and limits of freedom of expression in radio, cinema, and newspaper. An apparently hackneyed theme like censorship in any one of these fields opens up fundamental philosophical and social questions of the most momentous practical importance. The merely trained, run-of-the-mill technician takes sides on such questions without understanding what it is all about.

Another obstacle to the program of integrating liberal and vocational studies is the almost willful misunderstanding of what the program recommends. Where vocational education is given, aside from the problems that open outward to other subjects, there are at least two fields in which the integration can take place. The first is the place of the calling within the social economy, and the relation of its professional ethics to the larger issues of social and ethical philosophy. The second is the study of the rationale of scientific method as exemplified in the industrial and technical processes, the inventions and leading ideas, which are used in the work of the special field. I say "exemplified" and "identified" because although the logic of scientific method is generally the same for all fields, the specific techniques of reaching warranted conclusions will reflect the differences between the subject matters thought about. This minimum program of interrelation, according to John Dewey, should contribute an essential part of modern liberal education:

> A truly liberal, and liberating, education would refuse today to isolate vocational training on any of its levels from a continuous education in the social, moral, and scientific contexts within which wisely administered callings and professions must function.[5]

As an illustration of a typical misunderstanding, let us consider a direct comment on this position made by Mr. Hutchins:

> A truck driver cannot learn to drive a truck by studying physics, chemistry and mathematics. . . . The truck driver, both as truck driver and as citizen, needs to learn to control himself, to take his place in a democratic organization, to discover the meaning and aim of his existence and of the society of which he is a part. Musing over the laws of thermodynamics as he drives is doubtless better than musing over some other things; but it is not likely to prevent him from wrecking both his truck and his life.[6]

---

[5]*Fortune,* August, 1944, p. 156.
[6]*Christian Century, loc. cit.*

Mr. Hutchins' illustration speaks worlds. There is no vocational curriculum on "How to Drive a Truck" in any reputable institution in the country. I doubt whether there is even a course! There are courses in the physics of gas engines which is something quite different. But aside from what we will find or not find in our congested curriculums, driving a truck is precisely one of the things which it is *not* the business of vocational education to teach because it is learned in the same way that everybody learns how to drive a car or a bicycle. It is even questionable whether piloting or navigating a plane, which requires skills that cannot be safely learned on the job without considerable previous instruction, should by itself constitute the subject matter of a vocational course. Vocational instruction should be given *in the basic principles that govern a whole class of practical skills for which the individual has a bent or interest*. It should not aim at robotlike conditioning of human machines to other machines. Truck driving is as honorable a pursuit as any other but why assume, as Mr. Hutchins apparently does, that whoever begins with it must necessarily remain with it? The function of knowledge of thermodynamics wherever it is pertinent to vocational education is not to be mused over by the driver in the cab of a truck. That would be almost as dangerous as musing over "the meaning and aim of his existence," which Mr. Hutchins would apparently substitute in its stead. The function of such knowledge when it has been given vocationally is to enable the truck driver if he so desires to master other tasks, to make himself eligible for other vocations, perhaps better paid, perhaps more congenial, perhaps more interesting.

That the truck driver needs to learn to fulfill his duties in a democratic community *both* as truck driver and citizen is a welcome admission by Mr. Hutchins. A continuing education in the problems and issues of democratic social life is precisely what Mr. Dewey recommends as part of the curriculum of all vocational education. The difference between them on this point is that for Mr. Hutchins, since these matters are decidable by eternal truths previously imparted by liberal education on its appropriate level, no further instruction is necessary when job training occurs; whereas for Mr. Dewey questions of social policy and direction, which affect the truck driver as citizen and truck driver, demand a continuous and specifically related study.

This is not confusing liberal and vocational education. It is relating them in such a way that no matter how a man earns his living he will not lose sight of the communal traditions to which he owes his knowledge and skills, the communal responsibilities he shares with his fellows, and the communal tasks to which he can make his distinctive contribution. Vocational education which fails to do this is illiberal and had best be abandoned.

The difficulties of giving organizational form to this integrated curriculum are tremendous. But they must be faced. There are certain healthy developments in existing practice which should be encouraged. In many courses in the liberal arts colleges today an attempt is made to provide either some work experience or firsthand contact with practical activities in which general principles are given application. Instead of being done in a haphazard and episodic way, this should be systematized.[7] During the third and fourth years of the typical liberal arts college studies are concentrated around a vocational interest but in isolation from the vocation. Guidance by self or others is hardly likely to be sound unless the student is given an opportunity to savor for himself the quality of his prospective vocational career.

The desirable integration between liberal and vocational education cannot be achieved on a wide scale until the schools and colleges revolutionize their entire attitude towards the vocational future of their students. They must recognize that vocational future as in large part *their* future responsibility, too. Until now the schools have naturally been most interested in what happens to the student while he is studying. And next to that they have been concerned with the problem of his past education not to mention the competitive devices of enrolling him. What happens to the student after he has finished his studies or received his diploma is regarded as completely his own individual concern. In one sense of course it is. He is on his own. In another sense he really is not on his own until he is given the chance to bring his capacities into action in the most appropriate place for them. The school co-operating with all agencies of government and industry should help him find that most appropriate place. It is then that the student is truly on his own.

It is not true that the right man always finds the right place by his own unaided efforts. It is just as true that his right place is found by someone quicker, someone nearer, someone more adroit in the political handling of people than in the capacities demanded by the job. And for many occupations it is even truer that his right place is given to someone else who knows the right people or is born into the right family.

It would be utterly Utopian to expect every man to find his right place. For many more things determine what constitutes "the right place" than the public good or bad that would result from an individual's filling it. But it is not Utopian for educators to accept as a working ideal the general principle of civil service—vocational opportunities should go to those who best merit them. There are many vocational opportunities which are best merited by those who *can* get them, especially when the qualities displayed in the

---

[7]The single example of systematization is the Antioch College co-operative work-study program.

getting are the same as the qualities required in the doing. But there are many more vocational opportunities in which there is no intrinsic connection between the two sets of qualities. It is in respect to these opportunities that the schools must extend their vocational guidance to include voluntary, co-operative placement.

The word to emphasize is voluntary. For industries and government agencies will co-operate with schools only if they discover that students recommended as the most likely prospects for vocational openings actually succeed as a rule much better than those who are not recommended. The co-operation would be a genuine two-way process with mutual benefits. On a small scale in certain corners of highly technical vocational curriculums this is now being done primarily for economic reasons. But it is the social and educational validity of the practice which should be stressed, since there are numerous vocations in which the economic advantage, considered only in terms of dollars and cents, cannot be easily assessed. The extension of this practice depends largely upon its recognition by educators and the leaders of the community as an effective method of meeting the rightful claim of the qualified individual for a chance to make good.

It depends upon more than that. As is the case with every other basic educational insight, although it can be given some institutional force here and now, it cannot be built into the fabric of social life without a profound change in the pattern of our economy. It waits for the time when instead of using individuals as instruments for the production of wealth, the entire economy will be conceived as an instrument for furthering the all-around growth of individuals in a democratic society.   —*Fall* 1945

STANLEY EDGAR HYMAN

The Marxist Criticism of Literature [1]

THE sociological criticism of literature originated, like so much else, with the Greeks. Plato's *Republic* includes an exhaustive application of sociological criteria to literature, in terms of both its genesis and its function. Not only is poetry propaganda, he proclaimed, but the greater the poetic charm, the greater the propaganda danger, and he fittingly banned all but types of art he considered useful or harmless from his ideal state. Aristotle's concept of the social origins and function of art was, like Plato's, based on psychology, but since it was a different psychology, the catharsis of passion versus the stimulation of passion, it resulted in a very different social view. Horace continued Aristotle's functional view, but made it ethical and legal rather than psychological and reduced form to no more than a sugar-coating for functional content, so that it was originally the function of the poet to

> set the bounds of public and private property, and the limits of the
> sacred and the secular, to prohibit promiscuous concubinage, and found
> the rite of marriage; to establish the civic order and record the laws:
> it was in these performances that the honor and renown of the divine
> bards and poems came into being.

In the Renaissance, the Classical view of the social origin and function of poetry was revived. Lodge, in his "Defence of Poetry" against Gosson's "School of Abuse," quotes approvingly the theory of "Donate the grammarian" that tragedy and comedy were invented as ways of praising God for a good harvest or a fruitful year. The Puritans, represented by Gosson, were as eager to establish the social function of poetry, but, like Plato, to establish it as harmful. The Classical view survived as late as Shelley's "Defense of Poetry" in 1824, which not only defines the poet as the "unacknowledged legislator" of mankind, but gives rather dubious anthropological theory for the origin of poetry in savage attempts at social communication.

[1]This essay is the background section from a longer study built around the work of Christopher Caudwell, the brilliant young English critic killed in his twenties fighting on the Loyalist side in Spain. It was later included in *The Armed Vision* by Stanley Edgar Hyman, published by Alfred A. Knopf, Inc. Copyright 1947, 1948, by Alfred A. Knopf, Inc.

Modern sociological criticism of literature more or less begins in the eighteenth century with Vico, who explained authors in terms of their historical conditions in *La Scienza Nuova,* and continues in Herder's view of literature as primarily the product of national and temporal conditions. In England at about the same time, relative social criteria began to be applied to literature, particularly to the "barbarous" work of Shakespeare, by critics like Pope and Dr. Johnson, and Warburton and Bishop Hurd came out for a complete historical relativism, the latter arguing that Gothic architecture must be judged by Gothic standards and no other, and analyzing romance literature in terms of feudal society and chivalric life. The great line of sociological criticism, however, developed in France, from Montesquieu, through Madame de Staël's *Literature in Relation to Social Institutions,* to the historical criticism of Michelet and Renan. In Sainte-Beuve it became an important literary criticism, but with personal and biographical elements emphasized more than the social, and in Sainte-Beuve's disciple, H. A. Taine, finally emerged as full-fledged modern sociological criticism.

Taine's *History of English Literature,* published in 1864, is still the best history of English literature we have, an almost miraculous feat for a foreign critic. It studies English literature as the result of changing English society, the product of race, epoch, and environment. At times it is almost a class analysis, with Robin Hood a poetry of the yeoman class, Burke a literary representative of the "natural landed interests," Addison a spokesman for the new bourgeoisie, etc. The literary judgments are sometimes off, particularly in the sort of English author difficult for foreigners to handle, like Skelton and Donne (the latter "of terrible crudeness"), and Taine doesn't understand Shakespeare very well, vastly underrates Coleridge, and dismisses out of hand the whole English classical tradition. His picture generally, however, is so learned, so sensitive to poetic nuance, and so full of insights and sharp perceptions (he sees Tudor architecture, for example, as the giving-up of fortresses) that it more than outweighs the deficiencies. Taine's *History of English Literature* remains to this day the great triumph of sociological criticism, and he showed in his *Balzac* that the method is just as valuable used intensively on one writer as it is in literary history, reading the *Human Comedy* as the bourgeois heroic epic with a complete sensitivity both to its social implications and its literary values.

The great continuers of Taine's tradition of socio-aesthetic literary history were Francesco de Sanctis, whose *History of Italian Literature* appeared in 1870, and Georg Brandes, the Danish critic, whose monumental *Main Currents in Nineteenth Century Literature* began appearing in 1872. Both, like Taine, were liberal or radical in sympathy, Romantic, class-conscious, rationalistic, deterministic, and enamored of science; and both had, in addition, Taine's deep sensitivity to literature that enabled them to avoid mechanical pigeonholing and evade the rigid determinism of their own concepts. De Sanctis' book (although difficult for anyone substantially ignorant of Italian literature to judge) is a large-scale picture of Italian literature as an expression of the Italian people, and its insistence on the importance of aesthetic form and the relation between form, rather than content, and social conditions, make it a very important work. Brandes' great book is an intensive coverage of the first half of the nineteenth century in French, German, and English literature. Although Brandes' class analysis is sharper than either Taine's or De Sanctis', and he quotes specific texts a good deal less than Taine, his aesthetic and formal perception is fully as deep as that of either. Like Taine, Brandes carried the method into full-length individual studies, including books on Goethe, Shakespeare, Nietzsche, Voltaire, and a number of others, in each case exhaustively relating the man to his society without losing either him or the work as individual and unique values.

Non-Marxist sociological criticism in America has not been a very substantial movement. Its only major work is Parrington's *Main Currents in American Thought*, which drew largely on Taine, Brandes, and the economic determinism of J. Allen Smith, but also made liberal use of Marxist insights (most of them unidentified). Besides Parrington and Van Wyck Brooks and his school, the most important American sociological criticism is probably that of John Macy. Macy's first book, *The Spirit of American Literature,* published as long ago as 1908, is the application of social criteria, including a good deal of direct propaganda for socialism, to the major figures of American literature, but in terms of economic and social debunking (literature is "the expression of outworn states of society") rather than Marxist analysis. Macy made little or no use of Marxist concepts, and his second book, *The Critical Game,* made it clear that he was a Socialist whose critical mentors were Poe, Tolstoy, and Rémy de Gourmont (the latter "the greatest critic that has been born"). His only other book, *The Story of the World's Literature*, is a tasteless and ignorant hack book in the Van Loon tradition, requiring no discussion.

Randolph Bourne continued the Macy tradition of independent radical criticism, drawing on native sources like Veblen, but his work was much more aware of Marx, and *The History of a Literary Radical* and essays in *Untimely Papers* (particularly a class analysis of morals) make it pretty certain that he would have emerged as a Marxist critic had he lived. His revival of the nineteenth-century theory of the book review as "an independent inquiry," in which the reviewer turns up his own information and develops his own views on the subject, restored one of the most fruitful methods possible for sociological criticism (Marx and Engels had used it), but it faded out again as an idea after Bourne's death for the good reason that it demanded more of the critic than almost any of our contemporary sociological or Marxist critics have.

Another American sociological critic who did not live long enough to fulfill his promise was T. K. Whipple, who died in 1939 in his forties. He had lived long enough, however, to progress from a marked indebtedness to Brooks in his first nonacademic book, *Spokesmen,* in 1928, to a clear-headed and independent Marxism in his second, *Study Out the Land,* published posthumously in 1943. *Spokesmen* dealt with contemporary American writers in terms of the Brooks thesis of the artist truncated by society, but the pieces in *Study Out the Land* are a genuine attempt, not to assign truncations *a priori* to writers, but to study calmly and analytically the complex web of relationship between a work of art and society. (Even when using a wholly pejorative term like Michael Gold's "fascist unconscious," Whipple remakes it as a term of objective social description.) With the conversion of Whipple sometime in the '30's, with Bourne and Parrington dead and Macy retired, the last possibility of a non-Marxist American sociological criticism disappeared. From then on, American sociological criticism was either Marxist or it was nothing. In the case of Brooks and his school, it was nothing.

Little contemporay literary criticism has attempted to use any formal sociology other than Marxism. L. C. Knights has drawn heavily on Tawney, as well as on Weber, Sombart, and others, in *Drama and Society in the Age of Jonson.* The contemporary German critic Levin L. Shücking published *The Sociology of Literary Taste* in 1931, apparently influenced by both Mannheim and Weber, but rather than an actual sociology it is only the barest sketch for a proposed science. Although it asks some of the questions about the determinants of literary popularity, it has none of the answers. *Toward a Critique of the Popular* would be a much more apt title, and what warrant the book has to discussion is in connection with I. A. Richards' critical analysis of reader reaction.

II

The Marxist criticism of literature begins, naturally enough, with Karl Marx, although he himself wrote comparatively little specifically on literature.[2] Its theoretical basis is the relationship of literature to society defined by Marx in the Introduction to the *Critique of Political Economy:*

---

[2] All but a few of the writings of Marx and Engels referred to below, as well as much additional material, are now available, in better and smoother translation, in *Literature and Art,* an anthology of selections from the writings of Marx and Engels, published by International Publishers in 1947. Although it contains many of the important documents, the book is much skimpier than such equivalents as Lifschitz' 800-page job in Russian, and the publishers announce an additional volume in preparation.

In the social production of their means of existence men enter into definite, necessary relations which are independent of their will, productive relationships which correspond to a definite stage of development of their material productive forces. The aggregate of these productive relationships constitutes the economic structure of society, the real basis on which a juridical and political superstructure arises, and to which definite forms of social consciousness correspond. The mode of production of the material means of existence conditions the whole process of social, political and intellectual life. It is not the consciousness of men that determines their existence, but, on the contrary, it is their social existence that determines their consciousness.

Literature, then, like the rest of culture, is a superstructure of social consciousness erected on productive relationships. However, as Marx points out elsewhere, like the rest of culture, through dialectical interaction it then modifies and conditions productive relationships.

Little of Marx's writing directly discusses literature. He quotes Sophocles (in Greek), Balzac, Dante, and *Timon of Athens* in *Capital*, but only their attacks on the evils of money. He discusses "literature" in Section III of *The Communist Manifesto*, but it turns out to be the "literature" of socialist pamphleteering. The Introduction to the *Critique of Political Economy* discusses Greek art, literature, and mythology, but in no real detail. Marx's most detailed critical writing is probably *The Holy Family*, a discussion of speculative aesthetics, including a lengthy analysis of Eugène Sue's *The Mysteries of Paris*. In it, Marx defines the worst feature of bourgeois writing as tendentiousness ("Romanticism is always tendentious poetry," he had written in an article) resulting from an Idealistic attitude toward reality, which transforms living characters into automata designed to prove the author's abstract ideas. In an unfinished manuscript, *Political Economy and Philosophy* (written in 1844, when Marx was just on the verge of Communism, not published until 1932, and not yet translated into English), Marx quotes passages from *Timon* and analyzes them at great length and with remarkable subtlety, but again only as insights into the power of money. Marx wrote a number of lengthy book reviews in collaboration with Engels, including a scorching study of Carlyle ("the whip imagines that it has become full of genius") that shows a real sense of literary craft in its comments on his style. It is hard to say how much of these productions is Marx's, however, and except that the sarcasm is more bitter, they very much resemble Engels' independent reviews. Most of Marx's direct references to literature are asides in books or articles on other subjects, or come in personal letters, mostly to Engels. He sent Engels a copy of Diderot's *Rameau's Nephew*, describing it as a "unique masterpiece" (Freud, incidentally, also thought very highly of it); wrote him about "good old Heine," about his furious dislike of Chateaubriand's work, about a Russian writer named Flerowsky he had discovered; advised him to read "two little masterpieces" by Balzac. One of Marx's most detailed criticisms of literary technique occurs in a letter to Ferdinand Lassalle, commenting on the latter's play *Franz von Sickingen*; and one of Marx's most brilliant literary observations, that the French classical dramatists did not so much misunderstand the Aristotelian unities as understand them "in accordance with their own art needs," also occurs in a letter to Lassalle. With the addition of a comment to his daughter on Shelley as a truer revolutionary than Byron, a few brief remarks in his work on the subjects of style, beauty, and literary movements in England and Germany, these constitute just about all of Marx's writing directly concerned with literature.

Marx was tremendously well read (although he and Engels were hardly, as Earl Browder once announced, "the two most cultured men of history"), and his taste was surprisingly good for an active politician. Paul Lafargue, his son-in-law, reports that he considered Aeschylus and Shakespeare "the two greatest dramatic geniuses of all time," that he read Aeschylus every year in the Greek and had studied Shakespeare exhaustively and seen to it that his three daughters knew him by heart, and that he was a great reader of novels.

> He liked above all those of the eighteenth century, and especially Fielding's *Tom Jones*. The modern authors who tempted him most were Paul de Koch, Charles Lever, Alexandre Dumas and Walter Scott. . . . His favorite novelists were Cervantes and Balzac.

Franz Mehring, his biographer, adds: "In his literary judgments he was completely free of all political and social prejudices." He also thought highly of Goethe, Lessing, Homer, and Dante; learned Russian in order to be able to read Russian literature in the original, particularly Pushkin; and learned Spanish in order to be able to read Calderón and other classics. In his youth he had been a Romantic poet (not a very good one), and when he and Engels, who both loved Heine's work, were disturbed by Heine's political foibles, he reminded Engels that we could not demand of poets what we demand of ordinary people.

Nevertheless, in his youth as a disciple of Hegel he had acquired the Hegelian doctrine of the inevitable decadence of art in modern times, as an inferior way of freeing the spirit, better suited to the childhood of mankind. This idea stayed with him, unconsciously transformed into a conception of the inevitable decadence of art under capitalism. "Capitalist production is hostile to certain branches of spiritual production, such as art and poetry," he wrote, and his bitterest fury was reserved for the bourgeois view of art as a commodity. One of the charges against the bourgeoisie in *The Communist Manifesto* is that it has converted poets into "paid wage laborers," and Marx writes in an ironic article: "even the highest forms of spiritual production are recognized and forgiven by the bourgeoisie" because they represent wealth. As bourgeois civilization progresses, Marx felt, art must inevitably decay, and the artist comes to think of his work as a means, or a trade, rather than a sacred end. Nevertheless, in the classless society, with the disparity between social and artistic development removed and the emphasis taken off specialization, art could again flower naturally as it had in the primitive past. "In a Communist organization of society there are no painters," he and Engels write in *The German Ideology*; "at most there are people who, among other things, also paint."

At the same time, Marx carefully avoided the suggestion of a too-simple correspondence between art and social relations. Along with his statement of the relations between the two in the introduction to the *Critique of Political Economy*, he included a number of important demurrers, writing:

> It is well known that certain periods of highest development of art stand in no direct connection with the general development of society, nor with the material basis and the skeleton structure of its organization. Witness the example of the Greeks as compared with the modern nations or even Shakespeare.

And this art then goes beyond its social relations. Marx adds:

> The difficulty is not in grasping the idea that Greek art and epos are bound up with certain forms of social development. It rather lies in understanding why they still constitute with us a source of aesthetic enjoyment and in certain respects prevail as the standard and model beyond attainment.

It was in this sense of great art transcending both the limitations of its social origins and the artist's views that Marx thought so highly of Balzac, who in terms of the decadence of bourgeois art and his own monarchical-Catholic-reactionary beliefs, should have been detestable to Marx. In *Capital* and in his correspondence, enthusiastic references to Balzac are frequent, and Lafargue reports that "he proposed to write a critical work on *La Comédie Humaine* when he had finished his economic work." His economic work was never finished, and this book on Balzac, which might have been the Marxist aesthetic to prevent, if only by authority, nine-tenths of the idiocy of later Marxists, was never written.

Marx's co-worker, Frederick Engels, not only wrote more specifically on the dangers of oversimple sociological analyses, but devoted the most famous of these warnings, the 1888 letter in English to Margaret Harkness, to the topic of Balzac. He wrote:

> Balzac, whom I consider a far greater master of realism than all the Zolas, past, present or future, gives us in his *Comédie Humaine*, a most wonderfully realistic history of French "society," describing, chronicle-fashion, almost year by year from 1816 to 1848, the ever-increasing pressure of the rising bourgeoisie upon the society of nobles that established itself after 1815 and that set up again, as far as it could (*tant bien que mal*), the standard of the *vieille politique française.* He describes how the last remnants of this, to him, model society gradually succumbed before the intrusion of the vulgar money upstart or was corrupted by him. How the *grande dame*, whose conjugal infidelities were but a mode of asserting herself, in perfect accord with the way she had been disposed of in marriage, gave way to the bourgeois, who acquired her husband for cash or costumes; and around this central picture he groups a complete history of French society from which, even in economic details (for instance, the rearrangement of real and private property after the French Revolution) I have learnt more than from all the professional historians, economists and statisticians of the period together. Well, Balzac was politically a legitimist; his great work is a constant elegy on the irreparable decay of good society; his sympathies are with the class that is doomed to extinction. But for all that his satire is never keener, his irony never bitterer, than when he sets in motion the very men and women with whom he sympathizes most deeply—the nobles. And the only men of whom he speaks with undisguised admiration are his bitterest political antagonists, the republican heroes of the Cloitre Saint-Merri, the men who at that time (1830-1836) were indeed the representatives of the popular masses. That Balzac was thus compelled to go against his own class sympathies and political prejudices, that he saw the necessity of the downfall of his favorite nobles and described them as people deserving no better fate; that he saw the real men of the future where, for the time being, they alone were to be found—that I consider one of the greatest triumphs of realism, and one of the greatest features in old Balzac.

As violently as Marx, Engels opposed mechanical tendentiousness in literature. "The more the opinions of a writer remain hidden, the better for the work of art," he wrote in the Harkness letter, and in a letter to Minna Kautsky:

I am by no means an opponent of tendentious poetry as such. The father of tragedy, Aeschylus, and the father of comedy, Aristophanes, were both very clearly poets with a thesis, as were Dante and Cervantes. . . . But I believe that the thesis must inhere in the situation and action, without being explicitly formulated, and it is not the poet's duty to supply the reader in advance with the future historical solution of the conflict he describes.

Most of Engels' writings on literature are attacks against "vulgar sociology," in defense of aesthetic values.[3] His *Anti-Dühring* includes violent sarcastic abuse of Dühring's project for a "people's school of the future" purified of the humanities. He writes:

As for the aesthetic side of education, Herr Dühring will have to fashion it all anew. The poetry of the past is worthless. Where all religion is prohibited, it goes without saying that the "mythological or other religious trimmings" characteristic of poets in the past cannot be tolerated in this school. "Poetic mysticism," too, "such as, for example, Goethe practiced so extensively" is to be condemned. Well, Herr Dühring will have to make up his mind to produce for us those poetic masterpieces which "are in accord with the higher claims of an imagination reconciled to reason," and which represent the pure ideal that "denotes the perfection of the world." Let him lose no time about it! The conquest of the world will be achieved by the economic commune only on that day when the latter, reconciled with reason, comes in at double time on Alexandrines.

His commentary on Goethe's ambivalence, his letter to Paul Ernst on Ibsen, his letter to Schlüter explaining that revolutionary poetry and song do not tend to be lasting art because they reflect "the momentary prejudices of the people," are all warnings against the easy politicalizing of literature. The Ibsen letter, chiding Ernst for his oversimple dismissal of Ibsen as a typical petty-bourgeois writer, is particularly interesting. First Engels warns that "the materialist method is converted into its direct opposite if instead of being used as a guiding thread in historical research it is made to serve as a ready-cut pattern on which to tailor historical facts." He then goes on to define the difference between the Norwegian petty bourgeoisie and the German; to point out that, petty bourgeois or not, the Norwegian literary

---

[3]Engels illustrated this admirably in his own work on such occasions as his acceptance, in *The Origin of the Family,* of Bachofen's brilliant reading of the *Oresteia* of Aeschylus as a conflict between "mother-right" and "father-right." Engels calls it "this new and undoubtedly correct interpretation" and "one of the best and finest passages in the whole book," despite his fundamental quarrel with it and Bachofen's work in general as philosophic Idealism.

renaissance is important; and to conclude with the statement that whatever the weakness of Ibsen, his dramas reflect a real world of human beings "possessed of character and initiative and the capacity for independent action."

Engels proposed to Miss Harkness the depiction of "typical characters in typical circumstances," but it was characteristic of the skeptical and elastic-minded man who had written in the *Theses on Feuerbach* "that which is recognized now as true has also its latent false side which will later manifest itself, just as that which is now regarded as false has also its true side," not to believe that any rigid principle could be imposed on art. His final warning was the letter to J. Bloch in 1890. He wrote:

> According to the materialist conception of history the determining element in history is *ultimately* the production and reproduction in real life. More than this neither Marx nor I have ever asserted. If therefore somebody twists this into the statement that the economic element is the *only* determining one, he transforms it into a meaningless, abstract and absurd phrase. . . . Marx and I are partly to blame for the fact that younger writers sometimes lay more stress on the economic side than is due to it. We had to emphasize this main principle in opposition to our adversaries, who denied it, and we had not always the time, the place or the opportunity to allow the other elements involved in the interaction to come into their rights. But when it was a case of presenting a section of history, that is, of a practical application, the thing was different and there no error was possible. Unfortunately, however, it happens only too often that people think they have fully understood a theory and can apply it without more ado from the moment they have mastered its main principles, and those even not always correctly. And I cannot exempt many of the more recent "Marxists" from this reproach, for the most wonderful rubbish has been produced from this quarter too.

After Marx and Engels, the great theoretician of Marxist criticism is the Russian, George V. Plekhanov. A typical and very influential work is the essay *Art and Society*, written at the end of the last century, in which he attacks the shifting relationship between art and society from the viewpoint of historical relativism. He shows with abundant evidence that art is always conceived of as utilitarian when "a mutual bond of sympathy exists between a considerable section of society and those more or less actively interested in artistic creation." The doctrine of art-for-art's sake, on the other hand, with its consequent obscure and esoteric forms, arises "when a hopeless contradiction exists between the artists and their social environment." The most important feature of this historical relativism, and Plekhanov's major contribution to Marxist criticism, is the basic recognition that artists reflect their class and time, not another class and time Marxists would like them to reflect. He writes:

> I do not say that contemporary artists *must* seek inspiration in the emancipatory movement of the proletariat. Not at all. Just as apple trees must give forth apples and pear trees pears, so must artists who share the bourgeois point of view struggle against this movement. The art of a decadent epoch *must* be decadent. This is inevitable and it would be futile to become indignant about it.

Plekhanov wrote a number of other works on literature and art, including *French Drama and Painting of the Eighteenth Century, Historical Materialism and the Arts,* his brilliant long essay "Ibsen, Petty Bourgeois Revolutionist" in *Die Neue Zeit* (which perfectly illustrates his relativist theories in *Art and Society*) and others. In addition, a number of his political writings deal extensively with the arts, particularly *The Role of the Individual in History.* In all of them, the depth of his historical and aesthetic knowledge, the relativism of his point of view, the unblinking honesty of his observation, and the power and flexibility of his mind, gave Marxist criticism the soundest documentation and extension it had yet had. He was the first Marxist critic to study the relationship between social relations and artistic *form,* as in his discussion of Ibsen's abstract and symbolist forms in relation to the class basis of Scandinavian society. Plekhanov drew enthusiastically on the best of non-Marxist sociological criticism, Taine and Brandes, just as he anticipated the best of later Marxist criticism, particularly Caudwell, in his use of the most advanced scientific knowledge (in his day, chiefly anthropology), in his undogmatic relativism, in his insistence on the importance of the artist's *sense* of social function at any given time, and particularly in his vast love and respect for literature and art.

The other Marxist theoreticians, outside of Soviet Russia, have added little to Plekhanov in the application of Marxism to literature. Franz Mehring, Marx's biographer, has been called "the originator of historical materialist criticism" and of Marxist aesthetics, but the only critical works of his with which I am familiar, *The Lessing Legend,* 1892, an article on Ibsen written in 1900, and "A Note on Taste," 1898, which appeared in *Dialectics* 4, abstracted from a review of an obscure book, seem much more interested in literature as a reflection of political history than in political history as a clue to literature. One of the most important of Mehring's ideas, and one which he shared with Plekhanov, is the concept in "A Note on Taste," that there is an objective basis of taste, and that it lies in historical relativism. Rosa Luxemburg, another great German

Marxist who was deeply sensitive to aesthetic values ("In a novel I don't look for the point of view, but primarily for its value as art") wrote a good deal in her letters and articles about literature (including a wonderful criticism of the style of Marx's *Capital*, "overloaded with rococo ornaments") but as far as I know contributed little of a theoretical nature. Of the Hungarian Georg Lukacs, whom Slochower has called "possibly the keenest and most learned Marxist critic since Franz Mehring," I am familiar with too little work to be able to venture an opinion.

III

"The philosophers have only interpreted the world," Marx wrote in *Theses on Feuerbach*; "our business is to change it." This turned out to be not quite so sound a principle when applied to literature by contemporary Marxist critics (only a few of whom, for lack of space, can be touched on here). In America it led chiefly to the straight political distortion represented by men like V. F. Calverton, Granville Hicks, and Michael Gold. Calverton, the first and worst of the local Marxist literary historians, published in 1932 *The Liberation of American Literature,* which tears through our literature slaughtering Emerson, Thoreau, Melville, and Hawthorne, to announce that Whitman was our first poet and Twain our first important prose writer, and the only important contemporary writers are the "exponents of the proletarian outlook": John Dos Passos, Michael Gold, and Charles Yale Harrison. Granville Hicks's *The Great Tradition,* published a year later, is the same sort of thing, mechanical class-anglings based on the political criteria of the 1930's rather than on those of his subjects' own time, culminating in the same paean to writers like Dos Passos and Gold. If better informed and less nervy than Calverton's book, it is more given to cheap cracks like calling Faulkner "the Sax Rohmer of the sophisticated." Hicks's second book, *Figures of Transition,* a study of British literature at the end of the last century, is more modest and sensible but even less concerned with aesthetic values, and generally no improvement. Michael Gold has never written a book on literature, but the collections of his *Daily Worker* pieces, *Change the World* and *The Hollow Men,* make it clear that not only is he the most ignorant and provincial of all the Marxist critics, a heroic warrior against Gilbert and Sullivan, but probably the least adequate Marxist. He is rather a sentimental and idealistic bourgeois radical of an earlier century, and the picture of Marx's reaction to his passionate love for Rousseau, "the father of Democracy," or Eugène Sue's "epic melodrama to strengthen the heart and hand of the revolutionary workers" (which Marx put across the barrel in *The Holy Family* as cheap bourgeois romanticism) is interesting to contemplate. Other contemporary American Marxist log-rollers and strait-jacketers of literature include Joshua Kunitz and Joseph Freeman, prominent in the '30's, and Samuel Sillen and Samuel Putnam, prominent in the '40's.

A much more important group of American critics, either Marxist or much influenced by Marxism, have combined sociological criteria with an appreciation of aesthetic values. The most distinguished work produced by this group, and probably the best book yet written about American literature, is F. O. Matthiessen's *American Renaissance*. Matthiessen deals with the work of only five writers, Emerson, Thoreau, Melville, Hawthorne, and Whitman, over a period of only five years, from 1850 to 1855. Nevertheless, his book is on so monumental a scale, with so much concern both for ideas in a social context (drawing on Marxist insights) and for detailed formal analysis (drawing on his own great literary learning, sensitivity, and fine taste) as to represent perfectly the amplification of Parrington he visualized. (It is amusing that Matthiessen, an admirer of the dialectic, should come to the method as a synthesis of his thesis—a sociological, Brooksian study of Sarah Orne Jewett—and his antithesis— a relatively pure aesthetic study of T. S. Eliot. Matthiessen's subsequent book, a study of Henry James' last period tending to slight social criteria, would presumably be the new antithesis his new thesis provokes.) Newton Arvin's *Whitman* represents a similar combination of Marxist insights and aesthetic awareness, on a smaller scale, but almost as successful. Conceived frankly as a job of "scanning the . . . past for whatever resources there may be in it on which a socialist culture may draw," Arvin's book studies the political, social, and economic ideas in Whitman's poetry with honesty, literary awareness, and keen sensibility.

Other critics who have at one time or another attempted to combine Marxist insights and concern with literary form include: Harry Slochower in *Three Ways of Modern Man, Thomas Mann's Joseph Story,* and *No Voice Is Wholly Lost . . .*; Edwin Berry Burgum in *The Novel and the World's Dilemma;* Bernard Smith in *Forces in American Criticism*; David Daiches in *New Literary Values, The Novel and the Modern World,* and *Poetry and the Modern World*; Malcolm Cowley in a number of uncollected articles and reviews and a forthcoming book on American literature; Isidor Schneider in a number of uncollected articles and reviews. A very few examples of Marxist or near-Marxist criticism of this sort by other writers can be found in *Science and Society* and *New Masses*.

Except under Communist auspices or influence, not much Marxist literary criticism has been written in America. *Partisan Review,* the chief literary organ of the anti-Stalin left, has printed almost no Marxist or sociological criticism of literature since its first years, although it has printed a good deal of criticism otherwise useful, as well as a good deal of faddism, hobby-horse riding, and simple spite. Meyer Schapiro and Harold Rosenberg have perhaps come closest to traditional Marxist historical criticism, although always on the verge of veering off into philosophy; William Troy has made brilliant use of Marxist insights within a larger integration; William Phillips and Philip Rahv, the principal editors, still retain occasional traces of Marxist analysis, although in recent years their critical work has become largely a kind of ethical nail-biting; and a number of the younger men, among them Delmore Schwartz, Randall Jarrell, and Robert Gorham Davis, have written excellent criticism in the magazine making some use of political criteria (in Davis' case, effectively combined with psychoanalytic). The only *Partisan Review* critic who has so far published a Marxist aesthetic is James T. Farrell, in *A Note on Literary Criticism* in 1936. It begins with the apology that Farrell is an amateur critic and amateur Marxist, and then goes on to demonstrate it at some length, with Farrell demolishing the oversimplifications of critics like Hicks and Gold, to set up his own oversimplifications in their place. His volumes of collected pieces, *The League of Frightened Philistines* (1945) and *Literature and Morality* (1947), make it clear, in pieces like the study of Dreiser, that his deficiencies include an absolute want of ear (explaining his own execrable style) and a sentimentalism and naiveté vast enough to insulate him from most literature almost completely.

IV

The picture of British Marxist criticism, with the exception of Caudwell, is about as bad as that of America. None of the straight political critics is as egregious as Calverton or Gold, and they are all much better read, but, on the other hand, none of the men combining Marxist insights with aesthetic concern have produced books of the calibre of *American Renaissance*. Of the first group, typical examples are John Strachey, Ralph Fox, and T. A. Jackson. Strachey, the first of them, in the "Decay of Capitalist Culture" section of *The Coming Struggle for Power* in 1933, showed instead only the decay of Marxist sensibility, misreading *The Waste Land,* reducing Proust to simple snobbery, and fantastically overestimating Huxley and his "tragic view of life"; and in *Literature and Dialectical Materialism* in 1934, he projected his own sins of distortion and oversimplification onto Granville Hicks as a scapegoat and killed them off (as Hicks was later to do in his turn, with Parrington). Fox, in *The Novel and the People* in 1937, bent the history of English fiction to the slogan of "socialist realism," and as DeVoto does, from another point of view, assigned "epic" and "heroic" subjects for novelists. Like Caudwell, Fox was killed fighting for the Loyalists in Spain in 1937, and *A Writer in Arms,* an anthology of his work published posthumously in 1937, containing tributes, fragments of his books *Genghis Khan, Communism, Lenin,* and *Storming Heaven,* as well as letters and periodical pieces, shows an aesthetic sensibility capable of breaking through the fetters of his straight political criticism, had he lived. Jackson's study of Charles Dickens, subtitled "The Progress of a Radical," is probably the worst of the lot, a ridiculous, ignorant, and sectarian book, mechanically presenting Dickens' development and mood in exact sequence with the development of Chartism, and noting each occasion on which Dickens shows the proletariat in an admirable light or comes close to recognizing the class struggle. Other British critics whose Marxism results in straight political distortion include F. D. Klingender, an authority on English caricature, whose pamphlet *Marxism and Modern Art* in 1944 carried on the worst traditions of Marxist absolutism, ignorance, and parochialism of the '30's; Edward Upward (temporarily) who achieved what is probably the most stupid single piece of Marxist criticism ever written, an argument that the way to become a good writer is to become a good Marxist, in his essay "Sketch for a Marxist Interpretation of Literature" in C. Day Lewis' symposium, *The Mind in Chains;* and Douglas Gorman, a literary hatchet-man equivalent to Samuel Sillen in this country.

Typical of the British critics who have used Marxism, not as a distorting-glass, but as a sociology with which to understand and appreciate literature more deeply, are Alick West, George Thomson, and Philip Henderson. West is far and away the best, similar to Caudwell in everything but scope, and his small book *Crisis and Criticism,* published in 1937, includes probably the most sensitive detailed reading of texts in Marxist criticism. The book surveys contemporary literary criticism from a dynamic and relativistic Marxist viewpoint similar to that of Caudwell, and with a comparable literacy, general soundness, and informed indebtedness to areas of knowledge like aesthetics and linguistics. The book exposes the critical limitations of men like Eliot, Richards, and Read with neatness and dispatch, and concludes, like Caudwell, affirming the relationship of literature to production as its essential formal determinant. To illustrate his prescription for criticism, West makes brilliant incidental readings of *The Waste Land,* a Shakespeare sonnet, and *Paradise Lost,* and concludes with an appendix constituting the toughest test of his method possible, a long and absolutely first-rate analysis of Joyce's *Ulysses.* Thomson, a professor of Greek at the University of Birmingham, admits his direct indebtedness to Caudwell in his chief work, *Aeschylus and Athens,* a study of the social origins of Greek drama utilizing a combination of Marxism and the Cambridge anthropological approach, and avoiding oversimplification from both directions. (His forthcoming book on early Greek society is to deal comparably with Greek epic.) His pamphlet *Marxism and Poetry,* a study in the origin and evolution of poetry, amounts to a popularization of Caudwell, with the addition of Thomson's knowledge of Greek and primitive Irish literatures. Thomson tends to go wrong when he veers from Caudwell, leaving the basic soundness of his theory of the origin of poetry in the collective ritual of primitive food production to fall for Professor Chadwick's elaborate euhemerism and see Homer as the improvisation of the Homeric bards, or finding Elizabethan drama an expression of the rising bourgeoisie, but his work generally is informed, brilliant, and invaluable. Henderson, although extremely literate, as his edition of Skelton and scholarly introductions for Everyman's Library demonstrate, is frequently disappointing, and his books, *Literature and a Changing Civilization, Poetry and Society,* and *The Novel Today,* tend to be somewhat mixed, capable of sensitive analysis and appreciation alongside blind dogmatism like the statement that *since* William Morris was a real Marxian socialist, he was able to write "the only really successful epic of the nineteenth century."

British critics more or less combining Marxist insights with aesthetic awareness include: Jack Lindsay, in *John Bunyan: Maker of Myths* and *The Anatomy of Spirit* (in his case, along with Freudian insights); A. L. Morton in *Language of Men;* Randall Swingler in a number of uncollected periodical pieces; and several members of the *Scrutiny* group, particularly L. C. Knights, in *Drama and Society in the Age of Jonson* and *Explorations.* Two classics professors, Benjamin Farrington (in *The Civilization of Greece and Rome, Science and Politics in the Ancient World,* and *Greek Science*) and C. M. Bowra (in *Sophoclean Tragedy, Tradition and Design in Homer,* and *Greek Lyric Poetry*), have, like Thomson, applied Marxist concepts (Bowra somewhat tentatively) in their scholarly fields. Other British Marxist criticism of value can occasionally be found in *The Modern Quarterly,* both the old and the new series, *The Left Review* (which came to an end in 1938) and *Our Time.*

A special category of English critics affected by Marxism is the group of poets that first came to notice in *New Signatures* in 1932, including W. H. Auden, Stephen Spender, Cecil Day Lewis, John Lehmann, and (a later affiliation) Louis MacNeice. Day Lewis, in *A Hope for Poetry* in 1934 and *The Revolution in Writing* in 1936, combined manifesto-writing, ancestor-chasing, and praise for himself and his friends with incidental sociological literary criticism, some of it quite shrewd. Spender turned out some first-rate Marxist-aesthetic criticism in *The Destructive Element* in 1935, particularly his capture of Henry James for the Left, and has been working very hard since to unwrite it. MacNeice wrote *Modern Poetry* in 1938, largely an account of the genesis of his own taste, with stabs at social analysis, and a tepid study of Yeats' poetry in 1941 (both praised Caudwell but remained unpolluted by his ideas). Lehmann's work of criticism, a pamphlet on *New Writing in England*, is literary journalism of a high order. Auden, the most important poet of the group, has done the least criticism, chiefly fugitive pieces and reviews of a theological nature (he once attacked Joyce Kilmer's "Trees" as heretical), untouched by Marxism and social criteria even when he called himself a radical. (Auden's real criticism appears in his poetry, in works like "The Sea and the Mirror: a Commentary on Shakespeare's *The Tempest*," and it is very good.)

V

Some account of Soviet Marxist literary criticism is essential, although any estimate on the basis of what little of it has been translated into English is bound to be both fragmentary and misleading. To understand it, in addition to its background of Marxist theory, the reader must know something of the work of a group, almost unknown to the English-reading public, that has influenced it tremendously, the nineteenth-century pre-Marxist Russian "enlighteners": Belinsky, Herzen, Chernyshevsky, Dobrolyubov, and Pisarev. Vissarion G. Belinsky, whom Mirsky calls "the father of the Russian intelligentsia," in the 1830's and '40's propagated the concept of literature as a weapon in the social struggle, tracing democratic ideas in contemporary writers like Pushkin and Lermontov, and bitterly attacking reactionary ones in writers like Gogol and Dostoyevsky. Alexander Herzen, an idealistic socialist who spent most of his life in exile, was chiefly influential in the decade following Belinsky's death, calling in his works, particularly *From the Other Shore,* for realistic revolutionary thinking and writing. Nicholas Chernyshevsky, who inherited their influence, published his doctoral thesis, *The Aesthetic Relations of Art to Reality* (reprinted in *International Literature* in 1935 as *Life and Aesthetics*) in 1853, defining art as the reproduction and interpretation of life and its function as the diffusion of knowledge. In *Studies in the Age of Gogol* in 1856, he applied his aesthetic to the valuation of literature in terms of social utility. His disciple, Nicholas Dobrolyubov, in a tremendously precocious literary career that ended with his death at 24, extended the method further and did a very influential series of articles on literary works, using them only as texts for criticism of Russian life (Goncharov's *Oblomov* became "What is Oblomovism?" Turgenev's *On the Eve* became "When Will Real Day Dawn?"). He flatly ignored the literary aspects of the works he was discussing, making his only aesthetic criterion the quality of "being true to life." Dmitri Pisarev, an even more polemic radical journalist who also died in his twenties, pushed the method even further, rejected out of hand all art except that immediately useful for educational purposes, "uncrowning" writers like Pushkin, until ultimately, in the moderate words of Plekhanov, "he carried this concept to the point of caricature." (It should be obvious that the inheritor of this line of progressive hardening of the aesthetic arteries is Tolstoy, who from a different standard, religious morality, continued in his own criticism the narrow social functionalism and aesthetic unconcern of the "enlighteners.")

All these tendencies: the Marxist view of literature, the Russian critical tradition of social utilitarianism in art, even some of Tolstoy's moralism, came to a focus in Vladimir Ilyich Lenin, along with the characteristics of his own mind and the necessities of his life as a revolutionary leader and head of the new socialist state. Lenin's approach to art is vitally important, since so much of later Marxist criticism depends on it, and it is an incredibly complex approach in which at least six separate emphases (at different times and under different circumstances) can be distinguished. One is the attitude of simple functionalism that he takes in his 1905 article, "Party Organization and Party Literature": that art is a weapon in the class struggle and must be recruited to help make a revolution. Lenin believed in an absolute objective truth, as his *Notes on Dialectics* and *Materialism and Empirio-Criticism* make clear, and he believed that he and his party had it, so that a writer could only find truth and freedom within or alongside of the party. Another attitude is the analytic Marxist view that art reflects social reality but in many respects transcends both it and the creator's views, shown in the six tributes to Leo Tolstoy (five of them available in English in *Dialectics* 6, 1938), that Lenin wrote in the years around Tolstoy's death, trying to reconcile the contradiction between Tolstoy's genius and his reactionary views. A third is a Puritanic resistance to the "sinfulness" of art, related to that of the "enlighteners" and Tolstoy and very like St. Augustine's attraction-repulsion to Virgil. It is best shown in a statement Lenin made to Gorky, explaining why he loved the "miracle" of great music but couldn't listen to it very often:

> It acts on my nerves, makes me want to talk amiable stupidities and stroke the heads of these beings who, living in a filthy hell, can create such beauty. But today you can't stroke anybody on the head— they'll bite off your hand. You've got to pound them on the head, and pound them ruthlessly.

A fourth is the tired businessman's philistine conception of art as a soothing relaxation, shown in his generally academic taste (he wept at Bernhardt's Camille, liked Jack London and Upton Sinclair, saved the Great Theatre after the Revolution because "a theatre is necessary . . . to rest hard workers after their daily work," proposed that the Soviet state arrange mass distribution of reproductions of painters like Rubens and Murillo) combined with his strong dislike for the modern (he experienced "no joy" from modernist painting, wanted to know, like any philistine, whether the artist wasn't concealing his inability to draw, admitted that he couldn't understand Mayakovsky and always fell asleep after three lines of his poetry). A fifth is the social utilitarian view that art is a form of wealth, to be made accessible to the masses under socialism like any other form of wealth, typified by his statements to Clara Zetkin that art must belong to the people and be comprehensible to them ("Must one offer cake to an infinitesimal minority at a time when the masses of workers and peasants are crying out for bread?"). A sixth is a number of reservations and hesitancies about the other five, compounded of his own rich personality, personal respect for the creative artist, devotion to tolerance and personal freedom, and sense of humor (typified by his marginal comment on someone's memo, "The creation of a new fundamental *class* culture is the fundamental goal of the Proletcult": "Ha, ha!" and "Bunk"). All six of these attitudes, despite their contradictions, were to be major features of Soviet criticism, marked by Lenin's strong personality, and were to be adopted as part of the inheritance by Marxist critics elsewhere.

Compared with Lenin's views, the criticism of other early Soviet leaders and literary thinkers is a fairly simple matter, merely picking up one or another strand of his thought. Leon Trotsky, in his collection of essays published in 1923 as *Literature and Revolution*, reveals a genuine sensitivity to aesthetic values, but is, nevertheless, chiefly concerned with criticizing Soviet writers in terms of the political needs of the Soviet state. As late as 1935, in the *Atlantic Monthly,* he was using an article ostensibly about Céline for a lengthy discussion of French governmental politics. Joseph Stalin, as far as I know, has never written on art and literature. He has been responsible for a number of slogans: that culture must be "proletarian in content and national in form," that "the writer is the engineer of the human soul," etc., and he is supposed to have named "socialist realism." His taste seems to be about as academic as Lenin's, with a particular interest in music; if newspaper reports can be trusted, he likes classical ballet and Russian opera of the Glinka-Borodin sort, he walked out on Shostakovitch's *Lady Macbeth of Mzensk* with the comment that the music was difficult and unmelodic and that he didn't care for the story, and he directed Soviet composers to produce tunes that people can whistle on their way to work. In one respect at least Stalin has bettered Lenin: he seems to have a very high estimate of Mayakovsky, describing him as "the outstanding poet of the Soviet era" and writing in *Pravda* in 1935: "Indifference to the memory and works of Mayakovsky is a crime." Maxim Gorky, a major influence on Soviet criticism, reveals a tremendous critical sensitivity in brilliant snatches of his *Reminiscences* of Tolstoy, Chekhov, and others, but his formal criticism and literary pamphleteering, published in English in *On Guard for the Soviet Union* in 1933 and *Culture and the People* in 1939, is greatly disappointing; wholly political and unimaginative. Other Soviet criticism by the older generation ranges from the militant leftism of Karl Radek, announcing that Joyce's work is "a heap of dung," to the moderation and good sense of Anatol Lunarcharsky, cutting the Gordian knot of a Soviet controversy over whether Shakespeare was a spokesman for the feudal or the bourgeois class by announcing that he wasn't a spokesman for any class, but a great and conflict-ridden artist living in a great and conflict-ridden time.

For many years, Soviet criticism was largely devoted to battles between Lefts and Rights, Futurists and Formalists, Constructivists and Proletcultists, On-Guardists and At-Your-Postites, Social-Commanders and Anti-Social Commanders, a man announcing that *Eugene Onegin* would have been written without Pushkin and another man countering that anyway no literary works could compare with revolutionary manifestoes, so that it was a rare literary critic who got a piece of criticism written. Within the past decade, however, Soviet criticism seems to have improved somewhat, and the recent controversies by the younger critics have at least been on issues of serious concern to Marxist criticism, definitely transcending Soviet literary politics. The chief of these was the campaign against "vulgar sociology" in 1936 and 1937 which soon turned into a much more fundamental controversy over relative vs. absolute standards in Marxist criticism. It warrants some space.

The critics of "vulgar sociology" defended absolute criteria, under the aegis of Lenin, Chernyshevsky, and Dobrolyubov; proposing the evaluation of works of art in terms of timeless political values: i.e. were they "for" or "against" the "people"? The group was more or less led by Mikhail Lifschitz of the Marx-Engels-Lenin Institute, the compiler of Marx's writings on art and author of a summary, *The Philosophy of Art of Karl Marx,* which, although generally useful, distorts Marx to make him an absolutist and enemy of "vulgar sociology" (neglecting even to mention, say, his views on Balzac). His camp included V. Grib, the author of an equally simplified study "capturing" Balzac; Mark Rosenthal, editor of the monthly *Literary Critic* and sponsor of the deathless syllogism that since great artists were anticapitalist at any time, and Timon's speeches against gold show that Shakespeare was anticapitalist, therefore Shakespeare is a great artist; and I. Satz and V. Kemenov, of similar views.

The "vulgar sociologists" defended relative criteria, under the aegis of Taine, Belinsky, Plekhanov, and Mehring; that is, the evaluation of works of art in terms of the writer's relation to the social forces and issues of his own day. They were more or less led by Professor I. Nusinov of the Institute of Red Professors, compiler of a Soviet edition of Hugo and comparable works, a sound man insisting in his articles on Plekhanov's point that in a decadent period the greatest writers (Proust and Joyce are his examples) are bound to be decadent; that wicked and antisocial ideas can produce great art; that truth is relative and subjective; that "the writer is no photographic camera, a work of art is no snapshot, and literature is no mirror." Despite Nusinov's ideas, his team included some fairly poor critics slanted toward "rejection": D. S. Mirsky, a Czarist prince who had gone back to Russia in the early '30's an enthusiastic Communist, and ran to such critical excesses as finding Joyce's exactitude of description a "class style" showing "an aesthetico-proprietary desire for 'things' " (just as an equally mechanical Freudian would find it "anal"); A. A. Smirnov, whose book on Shakespeare is the low point of Soviet criticism, analyzing *The Tempest* as a treatise on the colonial question, etc.; and Professor M. Kravchenko, whose studies of Gogol are similar, if not quite so extreme.

What muddled the controversy almost unbelievably was, first, that neither side would fly its proper banners; both sides claimed Lenin (and had proper Lenin quotes), disclaimed Plekhanov and Taine, charged each other with the influence of Trotsky, etc. In addition, a political issue was involved, in that the "vulgar sociologists" were "leftists," "sectarian," in a Popular Front period when the aims were "moving-in-on," "broadening." It seems obvious that the "vulgar sociologists" were actually attempting to be Marxists, and their opponents only utilitarian politicians, capturing writers like Shakespeare and Pushkin for the working class. Nevertheless, the use the "vulgar sociologists" made of their social analyses (which were not terribly accurate as a rule) was generally to reject great writers indiscriminately, while their opponents had a framework, of no matter what validity, for accepting them. The solution here seems to be the approach of Feodor Levin, who took a median position between the two camps in the controversy. He slapped down the absolutists for renouncing Marxist analysis in terms of social classes and historical development, simplifying the past to the point where they could not conceive of a ruling class ever standing for anything but parasitism and exploitation, and "catapulting" present politics into the past. At the same time, he slapped down the relativists for their actual vulgarizations and rejections. Quoting Marx on why we still enjoy Greek art and Engels on Balzac (to flavor the ubiquitous Lenin quotations of the controversy) he concluded that both camps were actually vulgar sociologists, and that a serious Marxist criticism would want to know what social reality a great work of literature arose from *and* why it was great. From Levin's articles, it is possible to get a clear view of the controversy, to see both sides picking up aspects of Lenin's thought and using them in a vacuum, to see each side performing half the process of sociological criticism and coming out with absurd results. The hope would seem to lie in a Marxist criticism using the historically relativist standards of critics like Nusinov, applied with the discrimination and appreciation shown for artists by critics like Lifschitz. That is, Marxist analysis *without* consequent rejection; seeing greatness as best expressing class, rather than contradicting it. Such a criticism would also, of course, stop using names, slogans, and Lenin quotations as arguments, discard its pieties, and start looking at literature.

A few examples of Soviet criticism of this sort give cause for hope. One is an essay called "Bacon in Shakespearian Surroundings," by Lunacharsky, part of an unfinished book on Bacon (published posthumously in *International Literature,* 1936, No. 1). It is a brilliant and imaginative study, very much in the tradition of modern criticism, defining two Shakespearian progressions, the "melancholy," Jaques to Hamlet to Prospero, and the "cynical," Richard III to Edmund to Iago, and then interpreting Bacon's mind and character against the pattern of those two movements. A piece even more impressive is J. Kashkeen's "Ernest Hemingway" (*International Literature,* 1935, No. 5). It is a really remarkable study of Hemingway's work, perhaps the best written to date, revealing a thorough knowledge and understanding of American literature (Kashkeen deals with the influence of writers from Thoreau to Gertrude Stein on Hemingway); a brilliant comparative method (he discusses Hemingway in terms of Dostoyevsky, Flaubert, Céline, Eliot, and innumerable others); great sensitivity to style; and a genuine understanding of the nature of Hemingway's power and depth as well as of his limitations.

In the decade since the "vulgar sociology" controversy, almost no Soviet criticism has been published in English. A volume of anniversary tributes to Pushkin published in English in Moscow in 1939, principally the work of Soviet professors, is as uninspired and academic as its equivalent elsewhere. During the war, the few articles by Soviet critics that appeared in *International Literature* were almost entirely concerned with problems of war writing and morale, and of little general literary interest. Since the war, the chief critical manifestation has been the depressing attack by Andrei Zhdanov on two writers named Akhmatova and Zoschenko, as well as on general aspects of Soviet culture. Zhdanov's attack appears to mark a return to the senseless tradition of the politician's laying down a literary "line" that so much inhibited Soviet criticism in the past, and seems an unhappy omen. He announced that the "great historical mission" of Soviet literature is "strengthening the moral and political unity of the people"; resurrected scapegoats dead for a quarter of a century, like the manifesto of the Serapion Brotherhood in 1922; and even revived the old turkey of scorn for the "outwardly beautiful form" of inwardly "rotten" bourgeois culture. Despite this setback, and with no particular evidence to go on, we can only hope that Soviet critics of the type of Levin and Kashkeen, the legitimate successors of Marx, Plekhanov, and Lunacharsky, have somehow continued over the last decade, and are continuing now, to build the truly Marxist Soviet criticism their work promises.

VI

The faults of Marxist literary criticism, the fact that so much of it has been written in the last two decades, and so little of it has come to anything, thus stem from a number of sources. Some of them are implicit in Marx and Engels; that is, in Marxist theory itself: the rosy nineteenth-century teleological evolutionism of Hegel, whereby the world would get progressively better and better, art dropping off somewhere along the line with other imperfect human expressions; the concentration on what men have in common at any given time, tending to slight their differences, which are the seeds of art; the constant confusion between interpreting the world and changing it, between the inevitability of socialism and the necessity of bringing it on by revolutionary action, between understanding the class nature of literature and making writers enlist in your class or party. Many of them come in with Lenin and to a lesser extent with other leaders: the revolutionist's unyielding absolutism, the busy politician's untrained philistine taste, the dedicated man's puritanic resentment of the temptations of art. Some of them are accidental Russian features that have been foolishly adopted by Marxists in other countries: the critical moralism and narrow functionalism of the "enlighteners" and Tolstoy, the special educational necessities of a new socialist country with a largely illiterate population. The principal faults, however, are none of these things, but the personal deficiencies of most of the Marxist critics. These are chiefly three. First, as Arnold said of the Romantics, they do not know enough, either enough history or enough literature. As Plekhanov wrote, noting that Michelangelo said his teaching would procreate a great number of ignoramuses: "Nowadays it is Marx's teaching which is procreating ignoramuses." Second, most of them do not really like literature, or wide areas of it, and use Marxism as a weapon for killing it off. Third, they do not have enough imagination; their categories are too narrow, and their views too simple and mechanical. Examples could be obtained almost everywhere, but perhaps the clearest illustration is V. F. Calverton's *The*

Liberation of American Literature. He didn't know American history, and he hadn't read, let alone understood, much American literature. He didn't much like it, either, particularly its great artists, its Hawthornes, Melvilles, and Thoreaus. Finally, his categories were far too narrow and his thinking childish. He announced that we had no Puritan art and that Franklin was opposed to art, thinking of the Greek arts, whereas Parrington and Constance Rourke, with a broader definition of art, recognized the "drama" in Indian treaties, the "lyric" in sermons, and the "art" of Franklin's fine printing. Finally, he was obsessed, as almost all the bad Marxist critics have been, with the term "escape" and "escapist."

It is about time someone polished off the term "escape" as a critical concept. Used as a Marxist term of abuse by such men as Michael Gold, it tends to mean that any writing about the past is a wicked avoidance of contemporary social reality. As F. O. Matthiessen sensibly pointed out in *The Achievement of T. S. Eliot,* "Only the narrowest conception of realism can hold that an author necessarily acquires any sovereign virtue by recording the surface details of a middle western city instead of those of eighteenth-century Peru." As generally used, however, the charge smuggles in a much more absurd assumption, actually the height of flattery to the reviled author, that it really is possible for him to "escape" the problems of his life and time in his work if he wants to, rather than, as Kenneth Burke has devoted much of his criticism to pointing out, facing them inevitably on another level, in another form, generally one on which they are less capable of realistic solution. In *Permanence and Change,* Burke writes:

> Properly used, the idea of escape should present no difficulties. If a situation is unsatisfactory, it is quite normal and natural that people should want to avoid it and should try any means at their disposal to do so. But the term escape has had a more restricted usage. Whereas it properly applies to *all* men, there was an attempt to restrict its application to *some* men. . . . In the end, the term came to be applied loosely, in literary criticism especially, to designate any writer or reader whose interests or aims did not closely coincide with those of the critic. While apparently defining a *trait of the person referred to,* the term hardly did more than convey the *attitude of the person making the reference.* It looked objective, as though the critic were saying "X is doing so-and-so"; but too often it became merely a strategic way of saying, "I personally don't like what X is doing."

Marxist criticism would discard meaningless battle-cries like "escape," "ivory tower," the pejorative use of "decadent," and the rest, if Marxist critics recognized that their sociological analysis is a tool for the understanding of literature, not the debunking of it, "unmasking its ideology," etc. In a sense, this would violate the whole Marxist tradition, which, as a theory of interpreting society inextricably bound up with overthrowing it, sees all analysis in terms of present struggles and weapons. It would require making the "essence" of Marxism for literary criticism neutral, not polemic. Nevertheless, in a deeper sense, the sense in which the truth is always political, is always a revolutionary weapon, it would violate only shortsighted Marxism, the sacrifice of truth for immediate expediency. It was this that Marx and Engels saw in Balzac, as later Marxists have seen it in writers like Proust: that the *truthfulness* of great art results in a portrayal of social reality, whatever the class or views of the artist, more valuable to Marxism than all the pious slantings of propaganda artists.

Like Freud and psychoanalysis, Marx and Marxism can be of tremendous use to criticism if the critic has a clear delimitation of what the method can and cannot do. Psychoanalysis, Freud admitted, can deal with the personal origins and psycho-symbolic interrelations of the work, but not with its formal artistic techniques and its aesthetic value. Similarly, Marxism can deal with the social origins and socio-symbolic interrelations of the work, but it can, in addition, deal with its formal artistic techniques to some extent in social and historical terms, and in the same terms it can make rather limited statements of aesthetic value. What it *cannot* do is use its social analysis as a technique for debunking, erect reflection-of-social-reality as the major criterion of aesthetic value, or dismiss the author, his psyche, and his personal artistry as factors less important than social and historical factors. It is within these strict limits that the critics who have made the most effective use of Marxism in moderation—Burke, Empson, Matthiessen, Knights, etc.—have operated. The best Marxist critics, from Plekhanov to Christopher Caudwell, have recognized similar limitations.

—*Winter* 1947-48

JIM CORK

John Dewey, Karl Marx, and Democratic Socialism

Marxist criticism, historically a part of the European intellectual tradition, has been singularly opaque in regard to the great and progressive merits of John Dewey's philosophy. (America has no Marxist tradition of any significance. No theoretical works of major importance have been produced by any Marxist or socialist political organization, whether defunct or still in existence. The same can be said for the academicians. Sidney Hook and Lewis Corey practically exhaust the names of those who have produced significant works either critical or original.) The critiques of Dewey's Instrumentalism, which have periodically come from the pens of Marxists of all political persuasions, have been extraordinary documents. Their consistently biased character was an inevitable outgrowth of the unexamined faith the Marxists yielded to the questionable methodological oversimplifications that had become imbedded in the Marxist tradition—the inflexible overdriving of the sociological bent in its analysis, the forced class-angling of cultural phenomena. It has been no uncommon tendency for Marxists to denigrate American cultural products merely on the basis of the bourgeois character of the society which gave them birth (a raw simplicism, incidentally, of which Marx himself was never guilty). An indication of the social setting, or the historical process which supposedly helped to inspire or shape ideas, seemed sufficient reason for these pundits to assign them to limbo, although obviously, the purported social origin of an idea is hardly identical with a judgment of its possible validity. The first is cultural history. The second requires logical analysis and testing.

The worst offenders against decent canons of logical discourse in these matters have, of course, been the Russian Stalinists, whose claims to being the best descendants of Marx have acquired an increasingly strident, propagandistic tone down through the years. What their theoretical cretinism in the realm of analyzing cultural phenomena has led to can be seen in the present Russian denigration of all Western culture,

137

and the barbaric restrictions placed upon the natural development of art, music, literature, philosophy, and even science, in Russia itself.

The periodic respects the Russians have paid to Dewey have presented a fantastic, almost indescribable compound of political bias, cavalier disregard of the written word, outright fabrications, and violent name calling—that unusual blend of ideological discussion (recalling nothing so much as a courtroom atmosphere) so peculiarly characteristic of Russian polemics since the Bolshevik ascendancy. We are treated to the obscene spectacle of the use of the technical jargon of philosophy to squeeze and torture ideas into the pre-formed mold dictated by party and ideological loyalty.

The vices of this tradition, however, have been characteristic not only of the Stalinist "philosophers," Russian or otherwise. They attach in almost equal degree to those movements that were offshoots of Bolshevism (Trotskyism, Brandlerism, and other independent communist sects). They even extend, unfortunately, beyond these to many European socialists who, though never enamored of Bolshevism and able to dispute the findings of the Stalinists on the political and social fields, seem unable to disguise completely an unconscious snobbery towards American culture, *per se,* or to muster the necessary critical acumen to overcome the hypnotic hold that class-angling of cultural phenomena has acquired over them.

The favorite (and foregone) conclusion commonly arrived at by the Bolsheviks and their epigones is that Dewey is the philosopher of western imperialism. August Thalheimer, for instance, a leading theoretician of the split-off Brandler wing of communists, had this to say about Dewey and Pragmatism in his *Introduction to Dialectical Materialism* (Covici-Friede, 1936): "It is therefore not so easy for the uninitiated [!] to recognize that the true character of this philosophy is reactionary and idealistic . . . that [like] all the various schools and sects of bourgeois philosophy after Feuerbach [it] revolves about just one problem, namely, how bourgeois society and the capitalist order can be defended against the socialist . . . it reflects the characteristic spirit of the American bourgeoisie . . . hence the distortion of cause and effect and the tendency towards commerce. Pragmatism is *literally* [my emphasis] the philosophy of commerce. . . . Since it recognizes no reality external to the human mind it can have no touchstone for truth. For Pragmatism there is no objective measure for truth, . . ." etc., etc., etc. (pp. 241, 245 and 248).

This accusation against Pragmatism, that it has no objective touchstone for truth, that truth is what "works," what is useful, what gives inner satisfaction, hence is subjectively measured, represents one of the commonest and most persistent misconceptions of pragmatic logic. (Incidentally, this misconception is notoriously shared by Bertrand Russell.)

The test for truth is objective and is not concerned with ministering to subjective feelings, needs or desires. As Dewey says: "Truth is not verified just by any kind of satisfaction but only by that satisfaction which is born of the fact that a working hypothesis or experimental method applies to the facts which it concerns and effects a better ordering. No misconception concerning the instrumental logic of Pragmatism has been more persistent than that one which would make of it merely a means for a practical end."

Or take one C. P. West, writing some years ago in *New Essays* (an organ of independent anti-Stalinist communists whose moving spirit then was Paul Mattick) in an article whose very title gives the cue to the nature of the forthcoming treatment, "Pragmatism: The Logic of Capitalism." There the author says, "Actually, Dewey does not provide us with a technique or logical method for thinking our way through our problems. We are given, rather, the psychology of a particular class behind the instrumentalist or class logic of Dewey and his fellow pragmatists . . . instrumentalist logic—like the philosophy of Pragmatism itself—is the ally of the class in power today, safeguarding the vested interests of the capitalist preserves" (Vol. 6, No. 4—Winter, 1943).

The Trotskyites, on their part, have not been quite so crude. They have satisfied themselves in the main, in their periodic "notices" of Pragmatism, with the impassioned defense of the mystic mummeries of the dialectic, and an occasional attack on Sidney Hook for the latter's purportedly profane attempt to water down the revolutionary purity of Marxist philosophy by his espousal of Pragmatism.

It was Hook who, after a thorough, objective study of the original sources, made the assertion that the doctrinal positions of Karl Marx and John Dewey are basically similar. He first raised the question forcefully in his *Toward the Understanding of Karl Marx*, published in 1933. In 1935, in his essay, "Experimental Naturalism," in the American Philosophical Series, he claimed that "their fundamental logical and metaphysical positions are the same. . . ." In 1939, in his book, *John Dewey,* he says: "it seems to me that, were realistic Marxists prepared to submit their methods of achieving democratic socialism to serious scientific criticism, and were Dewey prepared to work out a more detailed program of political action with reference to the social and economic relations of the current scene, their positions would converge on a set of common hypotheses leading to common activities."[1]

The persuasiveness of Hook's thesis has more to recommend it than the mere surface resemblances between elements of Marx's and Dewey's

---

[1]Hook's brilliant little book on Dewey, incidentally, provides the best single introduction to the entire span of Dewey's thought.

thought that various commentators have periodically pointed out. That Hook's cogent defense of his position has not been accorded the serious consideration it deserves is due to a combination of prejudice and ignorance prevailing in the ranks of both Marxists and philosophers. Both sides seemed intent on preventing a favored doctrine from being contaminated by another, obviously regarded as foreign. Though the Marxists have by far been the greater sinners in this matter (as already indicated above), Dewey himself, unfortunately, has not been blameless in helping to foster mutual misunderstanding between the two doctrines.

Dewey on Marx

Dewey's conception of Marx represents one of the rare occasions when he has forsaken the usual scientific caution and genial objectivity with which he deals with opponents. He has paid more attention to Marx and Marxism in his *Freedom and Culture* than in any other of his works. Therein he betrays his own lack of first-hand knowledge of Marx's writings; does not distinguish between Marx's own ideas and encrustations upon them of later interpretations; and allows himself to make accusations on the basis of hearsay and current interpretations of Marx that have been frequently refuted by really reputable Marxist scholars, among them most convincingly by Sidney Hook himself. These accusations are:

1) Marx's ideas on the causal factors influencing historical change were a-priori concoctions and not derived from empiric investigations: "This law [i.e. Marx's, on historical causation] was not derived nor supposed to be derived from study of historical events. It was derived from Hegelian dialectical metaphysics."[2] This is an astounding charge in view of the historical parts of *Capital* and Marx's writings on 1848 in France and Germany, on the Paris Commune, Spain, the American Civil War, etc., all of which are concrete analyses of the actual historical events and served as testing ground for his theoretical constructions.

2) Marx denied social efficacy to human values, ideas, efforts: "The denial that values have any influence in the long course of events is also characteristic of the Marxist belief. . . . I shall criticize the type of social theory which reduces the human factor as nearly as possible to zero since it explains events and frames policies *exclusively* [my emphasis] in terms of conditions provided by the environment. Marxism is taken as the typical illustration of [this] . . . absolutism. . . . He [i.e. Marx] also, in the name of science, denied moving power to human valuations."[3] That some

[2]*Freedom and Culture*, p. 79.
[3]*Ibid.* pp. 12, 75-76, 80.

Marxists mistakenly made out of Marx's theory an automatic inevitability that left completely out of consideration the instrumentality of men consciously working toward desired ends is undoubtedly true. But it is as undoubtedly false that Marx was guilty of the same simplicism. He had too much respect for the dynamic creativeness of human thinking for that. Indeed, his theory of social change is inseparable from the social voluntarism (and possible social efficacy of their actions) of individuals: "Men make their own history."

3) The same considerations would serve to refute Dewey's charge that Marx claimed for his laws an inevitable and automatic certainty: "The Marxist has laid down a generalization that is supposed to state the law governing the movement and outcome of all the social changes."[4] Marx was the last man in the world to subscribe to such teleological certainty. He may not have sensed *all* the possibilities of alternative development (his assumption, for instance, that complete *laissez-faire* capitalism and complete collective socialism exhausted the alternatives. He didn't see that mixtures of both were possible, and possibly desirable, and certainly didn't anticipate the dangers of totalitarianism) but he didn't guarantee the inevitable success of socialism. He at least envisaged the possibility of social regression if the forces making for socialism were not successful.

It is difficult to see why Dewey has so signally failed to distinguish between Marx's ideas and morals and those of the Stalinists, for instance. He seems to have been unduly influenced by the latter's raucous claim that they were the only legitimate descendants of Marx. Accepting that, his logical and moral critiques, which certainly hold water against the Stalinists, would seem to him to be imperative, especially when he has seen the supposedly liberating event of the Russian Revolution turn Russia into a ghastly prison house and the purported descendants of Marx violate every precious freedom and trample on all human rights; when, as chairman of the Defense Commission in the Trotsky trial, he saw how the cynical lie and the vicious frameup operated as the essential elements of Soviet morality. When, further, he saw Trotsky, himself the most celebrated victim of the well-known illogicality of Stalinist fanaticism (i.e., the amalgam smear—all anti-Stalinists are against progress, are reactionaries, fascists, etc.), indulging in the same type of fanaticism, condemning all bourgeois democrats, social-democrats, anarchists, humanitarians, (i.e., all anti-Trotskyites), as helping reaction to maintain itself and even acting as brothers in spirit of the Stalinists (". . . the democratic philistine and the Stalinist bureaucrat are, if not twins, brothers in spirit. . . . In the

---

[4]*Ibid*. p. 53.

mechanics of reaction Stalinism occupies many leading positions. All groupings of bourgeois society, including the anarchists, utilize its aid in the struggle against the Proletarian Revolution. . . .");[5] and the same Trotsky, the most brilliant of living revolutionaries, for all his brilliance, unable to break out of a confining circle of faith and fanaticism, insisting on dogmatic assertions, unwilling to re-examine assumptions,[6] then he must have reasoned that there was something incipiently dangerous in the thought processes of the man commonly accepted as ancestor by both brutal victor and brilliant victim, and that that dangerous element had to be uncovered.

Be my highly speculative psychological reconstruction what it may, the assumption, on Dewey's part, of a basic similarity between Marx's thinking and that of the Bolsheviks is a gratuitous one which is itself the product of that type of abstract deduction Dewey himself so correctly decries, rather than the result of painstaking investigation of original sources. In both logic and morals, the Bolsheviks violated rather than followed basic, even decisive, elements in Marx's system of ideas.

Marx and Dewey—The Similarities

My statement of these will, of necessity, have to be in brief, summary fashion, suggestive and assertive, rather than fully elucidated:

1) Both find a common heritage in Hegel, who impressed them with the ideas of continuity and change and the organic nature of a society or epoch which, for all its disparateness, yet showed basic, underlying, unifying characteristics. As Hegel said: "The Constitution adopted by a people makes one substance, one spirit with its religion, its art and its philosophy, or at least with its conceptions and thoughts, its culture generally." Each in his own way emancipated himself from the idealistic heritage of Hegel without sacrificing the great insights of the German philosopher.[7]

2) Both consider philosophy as not "outside" this world and above common human practices, but a very important part of the general culture of any epoch, reflecting its common experiences, problems and needs. As such, philosophical ideas reflect also social divisions and conflicts and may be used for the purpose of buttressing dominant-class views: "The belief

---

[5]Leon Trotsky, *Their Morals and Ours*, New International, June 1938.

[6]Dewey's answer to Trotsky (see note 5 above) in the August issue of the same magazine, where the great philosopher easily convicts the great revolutionary of the most childish illogicality on the means-ends relationship.

[7]For Dewey's original allegiance to Hegelianism, see Morton G. White's *The Origins of Dewey's Instrumentalism*, Columbia University Press, 1943.

that a theory of knowing, which in its origin was inherently a leisure-class theory, has influence in justifying the state of society in which only a few are thus privileged, hence in perpetuating the latter condition, *is* a part of my complete theory."[8]

3) The strong secular, naturalistic note in both philosophies. Both are opposed to all forms of irrationalism, mysticism and supernaturalism. Dewey had nothing to do with James's religious vagaries and rejected F. C. S. Schiller's religious apologetics.

4) Both are in the materialistic strain in philosophic thought, even though Dewey polemicizes against the use of the term "materialism" in favor of the word "naturalism" (see Schilpp, pp. 604 and 605). His argument against certain types of materialism would not hold against Marx who was opposed to both mechanical materialism and reductive materialism. Dewey accepts the reality of the existence of the external world and the emergence of life and mind from physical (inorganic) matter and events: "Yet I cannot refrain from saying that (as Reichenbach's *Experience and Nature* clearly shows) upon his view the existence of the external world is a *problem* for philosophy, whereas according to my view the problem is artificially generated by the kind of premises we call epistemological. When we *act* and find environing things in stubborn opposition to our desires and efforts, the externality of the environment is a direct constituent of direct experience" (Schilpp, p. 542).

5) Both are opposed to atomism, a-priorism, sensationalism, Platonic essences.

6) Both are opposed to the traditional philosophies of dualism (Kant, Descartes, etc.).

7) Both are opposed to absolute truths in favor of relative and provisional truths dependent for verification (and possible further extension) upon future inquiry: "The truth of any present proposition is by definition subject to the outcome of continued inquiries; its truth, if the word must be used, is provisional; as near the truth as inquiry has yet come, a matter determined not by a guess at some future belief but by the care and pains with which inquiry has been conducted up to the present time." (Schilpp, p. 573.)

8) Both have a deep appreciation of the facts of biology and accept the philosophical implications of Darwinism with its central concept of the evolution of the organism (nervous system, brain, mind), developing in physical time, acting in and reacting to a natural environment. Thus the dualism between mind and nature is resolved and human thought

---

[8]Schilpp, *The Philosophy of John Dewey*, Library of Living Philosophers, Vol. I, Northwestern U., p. 529.

appears as continuous with the physical and biological activities of bodies.[9]

9) Both epistemological theories are practically identical. Both stress the unity of theory and practice. Both disagree with the conception of knowing as a passive, contemplative process and stress the knowing process as an active, constructive, practical, transforming proposition. In his essay ("Dewey's New Logic," Schilpp, p. 143), Bertrand Russell, an ideological opponent of both Marx and Dewey on this question, says, "Allowing for a certain difference of phraseology, this doctrine [i.e., Marx's] is essentially indistinguishable from Instrumentalism." How correct this evaluation is can be seen from a comparison of extracts from Marx's *Theses on Feuerbach* with Dewey's statement of his Theory of Inquiry, both of which represent the heart of their respective epistemological positions:

MARX: "The chief defect of all previous materialism is that the object, the reality, the sensibility is only apprehended in the form of the object or of contemplation, but not as sensible activity or practice, not subjectively. Hence it came about that the active side was developed by idealism in opposition to materialism. [Thesis No. 1] . . . The question whether objective truth can be attributed to human thinking is not a question of theory but is a practical question. In practice men must prove the truth, i.e. the reality and power, the 'this-sidedness' of his thinking. [No. 2] . . . The philosophers have only interpreted the world in various ways; the point, however, is to change it" [No. 11].

DEWEY: "Inquiry is concerned with the objective transformation of objective subject matter. . . . All thought contains a practical factor, an activity of doing and making which shapes antecedent, existential material which sets the problem of inquiry. . . . The ultimate ground of every valid proposition and warranted judgment consists in some existential reconstruction ultimately effected" (*Logic*).

These nine items constitute an imposing list of agreements, a solid core substantial enough to warrant investigation as to a possible ideological rapprochement between the two doctrines.

SOME DIFFERENCES

The Problem of History and Historical Causation

The complexities of human history are too great to ever permit a completely successful, scientific account of historical development. It does not follow from this admission, however, that these complexities are too

---

[9]See in this connection the very illuminating essay, "Reconstruction of Logical Theory," by Ernest Nagel, concerning the influence of biological concepts on the logical theory of Dewey, in the volume *The Philosopher of the Common Man, Essays in Honor of John Dewey*, Putnam, 1940.

great to permit of *any* ordered resolution of events, that, consequently, past history can never be "recaptured"; in short, that a scientific approach to human history is impossible. One theory may be a more adequate explanation than another in that it permits the ordering of a greater mass of phenomena. Marx undertook the necessary theoretical investigation of the relative weight to be assigned to the various historical factors (economic, political, cultural, psychological, religious, etc.) with the end in view of determining those relatively dominant and those relatively derivative and subsidiary (else only historical description, static historical "photography" becomes possible). Dewey's charge against Marx that ". . . the isolation of any one factor, no matter how strong its workings at a given time, is fatal to understanding and to intelligent action" (*Freedom and Culture,* p. 23) is rather abstract criticism whose emphasis is entirely unfair to Marx's intentions and the spirit of his investigation. That spirit was to the highest degree empirical. Marx did not "isolate" the so-called economic factor (relations of production); rather did he attempt to assign it its relative specific weight in the entire congeries of factors. He merely viewed "the mode of economic production as the fundamental *conditioning* [my emphasis] factor of only the general and most pervasive characters of a culture" (Hook). He neither denied nor failed to acknowledge the necessarily qualifying effects upon historical development of such factors as the weight of tradition, the unique in the development of specific countries, the accident of personality, the relatively autonomous development, especially in their formal aspects, of special cultural fields (law, science, poetry, say) although he did insist that the degree of independent impact generated by these factors was limited by the boundaries set by the economic base. Above all, both Marx and Engels called attention to the reciprocal interaction of the various social factors.[10]

Whatever else may be said about Marx's theory of Historical Materialism, the above at least makes clear that it was not the narrow monistic theory misguided followers have made out of it, and that it takes cognizance of the factors making for causal pluralism. In the hands of the latterday Russians, the monistic conception has led to its most devastatingly negative results, ending up in a narrow sociological analysis of culture generally and a politicalization of art. It is in the field of culture especially that Marx's flexibility contrasts most sharply with the narrow dogmatism of the latterday epigones. He never thought of literature (or the writer) as subservient to narrow, utilitarian, socio-economic ends:

---

[10]See in this connection Engels' "Four Letters on Historical Materialism," to Schmidt, Bloch, Starkenberg and Mehring, in the Appendix to Hook's book, *Toward the Understanding of Karl Marx.*

The writer in no wise considers his work a means. It is an end in itself, and so little is it a means for him and for others, that he sacrifices *his* existence to *its* existence when necessary (*Debate on Freedom of the Press*—1843).

Marx stressed the historical continuity of art and art forms in spite of the sharply delineated and opposed economic and social wellsprings of the different historical epochs or, in other words, he had a definite feeling for those universal aspects of art that transcended the social epoch which gave them birth. It was in the very book (*Critique of Political Economy*) where he formulated his masterly condensation of his theory of Historical Materialism that Marx penned the famous words on Greek art:

> It is well known that certain periods of highest development of art stand in no direct connection with the general development of society, nor with the material basis and the skeleton structure of its organization. Witness the example of the Greeks as compared with the modern nations or even Shakespeare. . . . The difficulty is not in grasping the idea that Greek art and epos are bound up with certain forms of social development. It rather lies in understanding why they still constitute with us a source of æsthetic enjoyment and in certain respects prevail as the standard and model beyond attainment (Kerr Edition—pp. 309, 310, 311, 312).

Dewey and Politics

Compared to Marx's concrete analysis of capitalist society and his proposed program for social change, Dewey's remarks on politics loom as generalities, mostly value judgments as to what constitutes the good society. These have undoubtedly been excellent in themselves, and for Dewey the "Good Society" is obviously the end purpose of all philosophising: "Is there anything in the whole business of politics, economics, morals, education—indeed in any profession—save the construction of a proper human environment that will serve, by its very existence, to produce sound and whole human beings, who will, in turn, maintain a sound and healthy human environment?"[11]

But this very praiseworthy end has remained an ideal, unimplemented (in very uninstrumentalist fashion) by a concrete program of social engineering. This hiatus in Dewey's thought has been so apparent that even his most sympathetic critics have, perforce, had to refer to it.[12] There is

---

[11]Quoted from Hook's *John Dewey*, p. 126.

[12]John Herman Randall, Jr., for instance, in the Schilpp volume, p. 91. See in this connection also Hu Shih's very instructive essay, "The Political Philosophy of Instrumentalism," in the volume *The Philosopher of the Common Man*, p. 205, for an

point, therefore, in Hook's noting that Dewey's contribution to a desired (if possible) rapprochement between democratic socialism and Dewey's instrumentalism would be "to work out a more detailed program of political action with reference to the social and economic positions of the current scene. . . ."

On Democracy and Means and Ends

If, ever since the derailment of the Russian Revolution, Marxian socialists have become increasingly sensitive to the means-ends relationship, it must be admitted that this was not always the case. True, there were always important voices within the internationalist socialist movement which insisted on the necessary consonance of means and ends (within the different camps and in different connections; Rosa Luxemburg, and Martov and the Russian Mensheviks, for instance). But the realization of the central importance of the problem was not very deep and hardly universal. It needed the last decade's experience with Russian developments to give the necessary jolt, especially to those who, in the earlier, more hopeful days, gave their unalloyed allegiance to the November Revolution. If many socialists have painfully retraced their steps, they have but arrived at a position which Dewey has always occupied: "If there is one conclusion to which human experience unmistakably points it is that democratic ends demand democratic methods for their realization."[13]

Dewey's sense of democracy has been more pervasive than that of the Marxists. Democracy serves as the cement which binds the various aspects of his thoughts together. It underlies all his theoretical constructions. It suffuses his vision of the "Good Society." In short, democracy has been for Dewey a complete way of life. The same cannot be said for Marxists. Too many Marxists have tended to view democracy in too narrow a class sense, both historically and in its present manifestations. They have suffered from a blind, almost teleological faith in the automatic beneficence of the mere act of taking power, failing to realize that the problem of the extension of democratic values merely begins there, and that its successful realization is impossible unless the movement has become thoroughly impregnated with

---

illuminating discussion of Dewey's changing theories about the State, and for his conception of the instrumentality of violence. Hu Shih comes to the conclusion that: "After reading all the political writings of Dewey, I have come to the conclusion that he began to work out a truly instrumental political philosophy early in 1916, but, for some unknown reason, has apparently never taken up nor continued to develop this instrumentalist line of thought during the last quarter of a century." It is worthy of note that Dewey admits the justice of Randall's charge against him of relative neglect of the social engineering aspect in his summary essay answering his critics in the Schilpp volume (p. 592, footnote).

[13] Freedom and Culture, p. 175.

faith in democratic values long before winning political power becomes a practical question on the order of the day. Here too Dewey has had the longer-range viewpoint: "But the idea that the Revolution in its immediate occurrence, as of a given date, 1789 or 1917-18, is anything more than the beginning of a gradual process is a case of Utopian self-delusion. The method of intelligent action has to be applied at every step of that process in which a revolution 'runs its course.' Its final outcome does not depend upon the original abrupt revolutionary occurrence but upon the way intelligent action intervenes at each step of its course—as all history shows in spite of ex-post-facto 'inevitabilities' constructed after choice has manifested its effects."[14]

Marx's Humanism

Marx's humanism is central and integral to his way of thinking. His supreme concern was man himself, and the possibility of man's attaining to full freedom and dignity. It was that concern which generated his explosive anger at the tyranny exercised over man by things (economic and social organization) and set him to search for a formula whereby the chains of oppression could be broken and the whole man be able to realize his potentialities of development. Marx's periodic and eloquent defense of the *necessity* of human freedom forever sets him apart from his Russian pygmy followers and would earn him the cognomen "petty-bourgeois decadent" at the hands of the modern totalitarians who pretend to operate in his name. In Russia today, Marx undoubtedly would be considered a fit subject for liquidation.

Marx never lost his concern for human rights and individual liberties which he inherited from the Enlightenment and the French Revolution. His early works especially are replete with eloquent testimony to this effect. At the very beginning, even in his doctoral thesis on the differences between the Democritean and Epicurean philosophies, he was already taken with the splendid and rebellious figure of Prometheus who, himself the victim of the prejudice of the gods, braved their anger to bring aid to mankind struggling up from the darkness. As early as 1844, when Marx was but 26 years old, he declared in his essay on the "Hegelian Philosophy of Right" that ". . . man is the supreme being for mankind and . . . [it is necessary] . . . to overthrow all conditions in which man is a degraded, servile, neglected, contemptible being. . . ." Soon thereafter, in his polemic against Bruno Bauer in *The Holy Family*, we read: "It is our business to order the empirical world in such a way that man shall have truly human experiences in it, shall experience himself to be

---

[14]Schilpp, p. 593.

a human being . . . if man is formed by circumstances, we must make the circumstances human . . . if man is unfree in the materialist sense (this meaning that he is free, not through the negative power of avoiding this or that, but through the positive power of fulfilling his own true individuality), it behooves us, not to punish individual offences, but to destroy the anti-social foci of crime [Marx's humanism here leads to a thoroughly enlightened treatment of crime and criminals, certainly way ahead of the times] and to give everyone social space for the manifestation of his life activities. . . ." The official journal of the Communist League, of which Marx was the moving spirit, which was published in 1847, reveals this dedication to civil rights and personal liberties: "We are not among those communists who are out to destroy personal liberty, who wish to turn the world into one huge barrack or into a gigantic workhouse. There certainly are some communists who, with an easy conscience, refuse to countenance personal liberty and would like to shuffle it out of the world. . . . But we have no desire to exchange freedom for equality." What a contemporary ring this eloquent statement has! Here, though written a hundred years ago, is the essential critique from a democratic and humanist viewpoint of Stalinist totalitarianism. "The proletariat," Marx declared on another occasion, ". . . regards its courage, self-confidence, independence, and sense of personal dignity as more necessary than its daily bread."

It would be idle to deny a definite ambivalence in Marx's conceptions of democracy brought about in his thought structure by his later formulation of the Dictatorship of the Proletariat principle. But even here it is necessary to make the qualification that Marx's concrete picture of the dictatorship, of how it would take over and work, separates him fundamentally from the Bolshevik epigones. His conception had nothing in common with the concentration of all power in the hands of a small bureaucracy exercising a naked dictatorship over the entire population, which is the Russian experience, but a dictatorship of the majority of the population exercised by organs responsible to the people below. Further, Marx envisaged the free organization of producers and consumers—i.e., all the members of the community—democratically planning the entire productive machinery for the benefit of all. Granted without argument that Marx underestimated the dangers of dictatorship generally, and did not sense the totalitarian potential inherent in a complete collectivism, and other naïvetés and misjudgments, the point to keep in mind is Marx's psychologic motivation. That is definitely his concern for the democratic process.

Marx cannot be classed with the modern totalitarians. That would do violence both to his purpose and spirit, as well as to his written words. He stems from Western liberal, humanitarian, democratic, radical thought and made, in turn, some important contributions to it. In spite of the excrescences which mar his thought, that is where he fundamentally belongs.

SOME DIFFICULTIES AND CONCLUSIONS

After this all-too-inadequate summary of mutual misunderstandings, similarities and differences, we return in a somewhat better position to judge the feasibility of Hook's thesis.

How does Dewey feel about his part of the projected "bargain"? Has he shown any indication of having been convinced by Hook as to not only the desirability but the feasibility of the projected ideological rapprochement? There is a puzzling duality to Dewey's attitudes here. On the one hand, in his *Liberalism and Social Action* (1935) he has formulated as eloquently as one could wish the heart of the democratic socialist ethic: "In short, liberalism must now become radical, meaning by radical, perception of the necessity of thoroughgoing changes in the set-up of institutions and corresponding activity to bring the changes to pass. . . . Organized social planning put into effect for the creation of an order in which industry and finance are socially directed in behalf of institutions that provide the material basis for the cultural liberation and growth of individuals, is now the sole method of social action by which liberalism can realize its professed aims. . . . The cause of liberalism will be lost for a considerable period if it is not prepared to go further and socialize the forces of production now at hand, so that the liberty of individuals will be supported by the very structure of economic organization. . . . Socialized economy is the means of free individual development as the end." On the other hand, there is Dewey's resounding (and in great measure, unjustified) attack against Marx four years later in his *Freedom and Culture*. In addition, there has been on Dewey's part no forthright public espousal, to my knowledge, of democratic socialism.

I had always thought of Dewey as a left-wing Jeffersonian democrat with socialist tendencies. Puzzled by the seeming ambivalence of his attitudes, I wrote a note to him confessing my bewilderment and putting the question directly to him. His answer is significant and, to me at least, decidedly encouraging. For, though mentioning certain reservations he has, and emphasizing the need for more critical and systematic study on the part of professed socialists, and stressing that no "existing brand of socialism has worked out an adequate answer to the question of *how* industry and finance can progressively be conducted in the widest possible human interest and not for the benefit of one class . . .", he makes the following extremely significant admission: "I think that on the basis of *Liberalism and Social Action*, and to some extent *Individualism Old and New*, I can be classed as a democratic socialist. If I were permitted to define 'socialism' and 'socialist' I would so classify myself today. . . ." That "permission" (if I may be allowed to speak for democratic socialists) is definitely granted! It would be highly desirable and would prove in the highest degree salutary if Dr. Dewey allowed himself to do so for, undoubtedly, I do not hesitate to predict, he would redirect the thinking of socialists along the lines of: 1) the necessary integration of socialism with democracy; 2) greater sensitivity on the means-ends relationship; and 3) the need for a more scientific, experimental approach to concrete matters. Dewey ends his letter with: "I think that the issue is not as yet sufficiently definite [i.e., the how] to permit of any answer save that it has to be worked out experimentally. Probably my experimentalism goes deeper than any other 'ism!" Certainly a highly meaningful letter, and one that definitely lifts Hook's rapprochement formula out of the realm of mere utopian wishing.

As far as the proponents of democratic socialism are concerned, there can be no objection to submitting their methods of achieving it to the sharpest scrutiny. In the light of recent experiences with Russian developments, democratic socialists have re-affirmed their rejection of the dictatorship principle, whether in the state or inside the party; have rejected the idea of the domination of the single monolithic party; have rejected the idea of the desirability of the working class being the sole active and directing class; have rejected the narrow Bolshevik conception of the State as the undiluted executive committee of the ruling class; and finally, and most important, have increasingly stressed the desirability of a peaceful transition to socialism. Marx stressed that possibility in the case of countries like England and America where democratic traditions were strong. The conquest by the Bolsheviks was achieved through violence and we have the opposite of socialism there, its ghastly caricature, in fact. In England, the Labor Party came into political control peacefully, and we have at least the possibility of getting socialism—granting the continuance of will, vision and principles. We ought to add democratic to peaceful, for it is possible to gain control peacefully, as in Czechoslovakia (the terror came later) but not democratically, and the result is the same *vis-a-vis* socialism as in Russia.

Regardless of how all these questions are settled, we might be reckoning without our host. For the unfortunate fact remains that the socialist movement is hardly unanimous on all the above questions and, further, has hardly taken Dewey to its heart, for the simple reason that too many of its adherents know too little of his philosophy.

Nevertheless, in spite of Dewey's blind spot concerning Marx and the opacity of the socialists (Marxist or otherwise) in relation to Dewey,

the movement for ideological rapprochement between democratic socialism and Deweyism is decidedly worth pressing. It would be regrettable
intellectual waste to see the respective proponents of both doctrines fighting each other. The rationalistic, naturalistic, humanistic elements common to both are so basic; the concrete agreements are so substantial and
so much weightier than the differences, that it would seem to be elementary wisdom to make the attempt. If the pragmatists would stop
confusing Marx with some Marxists, recognize the hard, ineradicable,
humanist-democratic core of Marx's thinking as akin to their own, and
implement their praiseworthy, general value judgments with concrete
instrumentalities applied to political and social questions; and if the
socialists, on their part, would drop overboard the lugubrious excess baggage of the dialectic, would rid themselves of the remaining shreds of
inevitabilism, more thoroughly overcome their narrow class conception
of democratic values, and conquer the still latent prejudice against Dewey
as a bourgeois (!) philosopher, there would seem to remain no major
obstacles in the way of realizing Hook's hope that ". . . their positions
would converge on a set of common hypotheses leading to common activities." That, of course, is asking a great deal, for it would necessitate
overriding long-existing intellectual habits. And that's about the hardest
thing in the lexicon to achieve!

The ideological rapprochement between democratic socialism and
Deweyism, if it could but be achieved, would confer upon the former
one present of inestimable value. It would make it heir to the deepest,
most consistent and most generous radical-democratic strain in the entire
American tradition. Without having to blunt its internationalist ideals in
the slightest, democratic socialism could feel more at home on American
soil.   —*Winter* 1949-50

JAMES T. FARRELL

Some Observations on Naturalism,
So-Called, in Fiction

Let me begin this essay by telling about a young professor with whom I have had considerable correspondence. He first came to my attention when a mutual friend sent me one of his first articles. In the introductory part of the essay, the young scholar attempted to define naturalism in terms of an equation suggested by symbolic logic. I do not recall the exact letters in this logical equation but at all events, it contained three letters, and ran something like this: $F + D = N$. Let us say that in this equation, F equals fiction, D equals determinism and N equals naturalism. Fiction plus determinism equals naturalism.

The rest of his article, as I recall it, attempted to give some content to his equation. The purpose of the young professor was, in effect, to define naturalism in such a way as to satisfy his own uncertain worries about the "issue" of free will versus determinism. He was strongly attracted to books which he classified as naturalistic, and at the same time he constantly criticized these books for not proving that free will exists in the logical sense. In substance, he was trying to explain why many modern novelists have not been Protestant theologians.

I had a long correspondence with him over the course of several years, and I read a number of his articles. In my letters I attempted, with many citations, to show that there were many differences in style, theme, subject matter and types of characters in the books he called naturalistic. I further tried to show, and I think with good evidence, that there were more differences than there were similarities among the writers whom he was lumping together, and that they all had failed to do what everyone else had failed to do—to give a final and conclusive answer to the question of free will versus determinism. He expressed admiration for some of my books—but then and later he continued constantly and persistently, to chide me for not demonstrating an answer to the age-old riddle of free will and determinism. He seemed very disturbed that I was

153

not able to satisfy him, and, additionally, that I didn't seem to consider it an important question for literary criticism.

Later on I tried to get him to pay some attention to, to read and apply his own attitudes and problems to a truly great novel which deals thematically with this very question: Tolstoy's *War and Peace*. I got nowhere. Rather than that, he kept coming back to contemporary novels, and again and again he discovered, to his own satisfaction, that these novels did not prove the "existence" of free will. Finally, he came to the conclusion that naturalism is a method of writing which can be successful only when the characters are poor, dirty, ugly and no good. In passing, I observed both in his letters and his articles that he used many invidious and disgusting adjectives to describe the characters in novels which he professed to admire. When "naturalism" attempted to deal with "nicer" people, he decided, it failed. Why did it fail? Because, again, it did not prove that free will exists.

Finally, this young man, reviewing one of my novels, summarized the essential points which he had made repeatedly in our long correspondence. Now, in my letters, I had gone to great detail to emphasize that I didn't agree with him, and that I didn't consider the problem he posed as relevant to what I was doing. But he seemed to be under some great need to have me agree with him about free will and determinism and also about the "dirty characters," so-called, whom I had put in my books. His feelings were hurt because I wouldn't agree with him. And one of the remarks I had made seemed, if I might judge from his correspondence, particularly disturbing to him. I observed that he was really attempting to create a category of naturalism, and then, to use the category as a means of judgment. In other words, he was thinking about literature categorically. And his efforts to establish a category were leading him away from his real problem, one we all face when we read a book. It is this—how are we going to handle our emotions? He was confusing judgment with categorization, and in addition, making foolish predictions about writing. For instance, on the basis of the way in which he fitted Theodore Dreiser into his categorical scheme he predicted, in effect, that because Dreiser was a naturalist he couldn't finish any more books. Dreiser was then at work finishing novels which this young man "logically" proved couldn't be completed because of the so-called dilemma which Dreiser allegedly found himself in—an inability to discover a conclusive answer to this question of free will versus determinism.

I could multiply examples of this kind of thinking about naturalism many times. When I recall experiences like these and when I then read some of the statements and attacks on "embattled" naturalists in literature, I begin to wonder who is embattled—the writers or the critics? And I sometimes ask myself this question: Is it possible that some of these novels, so unfairly and insultingly and irrelevantly attacked by critics, menace the feelings of certainty and security in the minds of critics? Might it be that they are afraid of these books?

II

Emile Zola is usually characterized as the father of modern naturalism. And quite frequently Zola's "The Experimental Novel" is cited by critics as the gospel of literary naturalism. More than one critic has judged any number of books to be defective, and even dangerous, on the assumption that these books are illustrations of what Zola said in this particular essay in the year 1878. My own work has been attacked on the basis of Zola's essay although I must confess I did not read it until recently. Likewise, I had written five novels and many short stories before I had ever read a novel of Zola's. I made my first acquaintance with Zola as a novelist through *Germinal* in 1936.

Now, what did Zola really say in "The Experimental Novel"? He relied heavily on the writing of a French physiologist, Claude Bernard.[1] In a time when it was argued that medicine was not a science but an art, Bernard claimed that it could become a science. Zola applied this and many other conceptions of Bernard almost literally to the field of the novel. He equated art and science without making any clear distinction. For instance, Zola did not look upon the questions he raised in terms of the difference between problems in the laboratory and those in the writer's study.

What was paramount with Zola was determinism. Paraphrasing Bernard, he declared: "There is an absolute determinism in the existing conditions of natural phenomena, for the living and for inanimate bodies."

Zola conceived of determinism as "determining the conditions necessary for the manifestation of phenomena." Noting that Claude Bernard had found that there were fixed laws governing the human body, he wrote that it could be proclaimed without fear of being in error that the hour would come when the laws of thought and of passion would be formulated in a like manner. And he asserted that in terms of this determinism, the naturalistic novelist was a scientist, who was analyzing man in both his individual and his social relation. Thus, he declared: ". . . We [novelists] operate on the characters, the passions, on the human and social data, in the same way that the chemist and the physicist operate on living beings. Determinism dominates everything."

---

[1] I must add that I have not read the work of Claude Bernard, but Zola quotes him so copiously in this, as well as in other essays, that one gets a fairly clear idea of the outlines of Bernard's thought.

Here, a longer quotation will give a fuller sense of Zola's view.

Man is not alone: he lives in society, in a social condition: and consequently, for us novelists, the social condition increasingly modifies the phenomenon. Indeed our great study is just there, a reciprocal effect of society upon the individual and the individual on society. . . . We are not yet able to prove that the social condition is . . . physical and chemical. . . . We can act upon the social condition, in acting upon the phenomena of which we have made ourselves masters of men. And this is what constitutes the experimental novel: to possess a knowledge of the mechanism of the phenomena inherent in man, to show the masking of the intellectual and sensory manifestations under the influence of heredity and environment, such as physiology shall give them to us, then finally to exhibit man living in a social condition produced by himself, which modifies daily, and in the heart of which he himself experiences a continual transformation. Thus, then, we lean on physiology: we take man from the hand of the physiologist solely in order to continue the solution of the problem, and to solve scientifically how men behave when they are in society.

Affirming these views, Zola looked forward to the day when the experimental novelist, the naturalist, would bring forth decisive results of a scientific character. He emphasized the word, *experimental,* declaring that the novelist would show by experiments the ways that passion acts in certain given conditions, that these experiments would serve as a means of going from the known to the unknown, and that the experimental novelist would thus act as a scientist who went from the known to the unknown insofar as man was concerned. As such, he was to be contrasted with the "idealistic novelist," who deliberately remained in the unknown, and who clung to all sorts of religious and philosophical prejudices "under the extraordinary pretense that the unknown is nobler and more beautiful than the known."

And then, in answer to the charge that the work of experimental novelists needed justification because it dealt with the ugly, Zola quoted Bernard as follows:

"You will never reach fully fruitful and luminous generalizations on the phenomena of life until you have experimented yourself and stirred up in the hospital, the amphitheatre, the laboratory, the fetid or palpitating source of life. If it were necessary for me to give a comparison which would explain my sentiments on the science of life, I should say that it is a superb salon, flooded with light, which you can only reach by passing through a long and nauseating kitchen."

Zola saw the experimental method as a means whereby scientific authority would be substituted for personal authority. With this, he also asserted that naturalism is not a school; ". . . it is nothing but a vast movement, a march forward in which everyone is a workman according to his genius. All theories are admitted and the theory which carries the most weight is the one which explains the most."

Zola was opposed to the supernatural. He believed that science had already demonstrated that the supernatural was not real or true. He saw in science the intellectual leadership of the nineteenth century, and he insisted that the novelist have a place in this movement. Opposing scientists who would not give writers such a place, he declared:

> I have remarked that a great many of the most intelligent savants, jealous of the scientific authority which they enjoy, would very willingly confine literature to the ideal. They themselves seem to feel the need of taking a little recreation in the world of lies after the fatigue of their exact labor, and they are fond of amusing themselves with the most daring hypotheses, and with fictions which they know perfectly well to be false and ridiculous.

To Zola, romanticism and the ideal were lies, that is, unreal and untrue and undemonstrable. Rather than trade in these "lies," as he styled them, the novelist should have equal place with the scientist, and should work as he does. Zola here established a conception of truth as the ideal, and he held that the artist must adhere to it. He believed that the feeling of the artist must "always be subject to the higher law of truth and nature." And he added that ". . . each time that a truth is established by the savants," the writers should immediately abandon their hypotheses to adopt this truth; otherwise they will remain deliberately in error without benefitting anyone. And in terms of these attitudes he also proclaimed the death of "metaphysical man," and the advent of the "physiological man."

In a lecture, "From Poe to Valéry," delivered at the Library of Congress, T. S. Eliot made an excellent observation which can be applied to Zola's theory of the experimental novel. Speaking of the theory which Valéry held as a poet, Eliot said:

> Here I should like to point out the difference between a theory of poetry propounded by a student of aesthetics, and the same theory as held by a poet. It is one thing when it is simply an account of how the poet writes without knowing it, and another thing when the poet himself writes consciously according to that theory. In affecting writing, the theory becomes a different thing from what it was merely as an explanation of how the poet writes.

Zola wrote consciously in terms of his theory. But at the same time that we recognize this fact, if we wish to understand what has happened and what is still happening in literature, we must not test Zola, and a whole series of novels which have been written since Zola's time, merely by a literal-minded effort to correlate and to judge specific works in terms of this theory. We must keep in mind that, up to the present time, no one has succeeded in creating a perfect theory of aesthetics. There is no aesthetic constitution for the novel in the sense that there is a constitution of the United States of America. To apply Zola's theory in a literal-minded manner to his own works and by it also to damn the work of many later writers, as they have been damned, would be to blind ourselves to understanding and to blind those we might influence.

Zola's attempt to embody scientific methods, procedures and conclusions in the novel, should be seen as an effort to incorporate in literature something of the developing mental climate of his own times. Today it is rather easy to make detailed criticisms of his theory, to formulate a clearer statement of scientific method, and to displace the copy theory of knowledge implied in his ideas with a better theory of epistemology. However, such a task is not now a particularly important one to fulfill. The inadequacies of Zola's theory today concern the critics of naturalism, but few others.

The late V. F. Parrington, in *The Beginnings of Critical Realism in America* (Volume III of his *Main Currents in American Thought*), discussed the influence of science in American thought during the latter part of the nineteenth century. He observed:

> To speak exactly, it is not so much science that has taken possession of the mind, as certain postulates of science, certain philosophies presumably derived from science, and justified by science, which we have felt bound to incorporate in our thinking as a hundred years before the conclusions of the Enlightenment had been incorporated.

Parrington's observations can be applied to Zola. The novelist did set down a series of postulates, "presumably derived from science," which permitted him to widen the boundaries of that which was admissible in modern literature. He contributed to enlarging the area of human conduct which can be described by a novelist: he also changed and expanded the kind of theme which could be embodied in novels. He contributed to greater liberty of expression for the artist. His postulates, drawn from science, also gave him greater confidence, provided him with hypotheses which would help him look anew at the material of life, of characters and events. He risked hypotheses concerning heredity which, he recognized, were not completely established by science in his own time, but which seemed plausible and for which there appeared to be some scientific evidence. Was he scientific or unscientific? We have here an open question which we cannot definitely answer with confidence. In passing, I might suggest that Dr. Herman Muller, Nobel Prize winner, has, in his book *Out of the Night* offered a very plausible and scientifically founded argument which gives credence to a theory of hereditary influence. Dr. Muller's theory is more refined, more scientifically grounded than were the ideas of heredity that Zola held to. But if we attempt to deal with Zola's fiction on strictly scientific grounds, we may flatter ourselves with the conceit that we know more than we do, and we will get away from what we can more fruitfully discuss.

The American philosopher, George Herbert Mead, in *The Philosophy of the Act,* made a pertinent distinction between scientific knowledge and information about science. Mead saw science as an evolving system of knowledge. In this evolving system, he contended that what remained of scientific endeavor was the facts which were discovered. And his theories indicated that, while he was a relativist, he more or less held that a fact had the character of factualness within its proper frame of reference. But Mead pointed out that in this system of science, the generalizations or conclusions change. We know this to be so. Mead further asserted that scientific knowledge was really gained only when you performed the experiments yourself, when you actually experience the gaining of the knowledge, the finding out of the facts. Merely to read about this finding of the fact, as Mead properly noted, only gives us information. Zola, then, when he wrote about science, and when he stated his conclusions and hypotheses, was speaking largely in terms of information, the scientific information of his time. To the contrary, when he went out and gathered facts, and was proceeding with the scientific spirit and method, he then was gaining knowledge. He was, then, trying to write with respect for the spirit of truth. This, it seems to me, is what remains important in his legacy.

Oscar Cargill, in *Intellectual America: Ideas on the March,* dismisses Zola with a patronizing air which borders on contempt. Asserting that his essays, particularly "The Experimental Novel," committed a kind of misdemeanor, Cargill declares that Zola has survived his indiscretions; and he reduces Zola's conceptions merely to a view of "pessimistic determinism." Here Cargill illustrates how easily one can fail to interpret a theory of art or aesthetics or of the novel in terms of its relationship, not to truth in general, but to the artist's own work.

Zola's theory of naturalism is not so important today for its scientific as for its historical relevance. His theory should not be regarded simply as pessimistic determinism applied to literature. Nor has he been responsible for a school of novelists who have written books which only describe man as a "trapped animal," or as the critics of naturalism have declared, of man like a rat in a cage. Zola, in fact, exhibited a boldness and adventurousness of spirit when he attempted to formulate a set of postulates for the novel which would be consistent with science and consistent with the mental climate of his own time. It should be obvious to us, in the year 1950, that scientific advances, both theoretical and practical, have changed not only our mental universe but our way of life. Zola sensed that this was happening in his own day and attempted to deal with it in literature.

III

Just what has the problem of free will versus determinism to do with literature? Discussions of this problem are now usually of a piece with those concerning heredity versus environment, in which both elements appear to be solid forces in absolute conflict. When we deal with such broad and all-inclusive categories, it is more than well for us to recall an observation by Whitehead, who warned against committing the "fallacy of misplaced concreteness." It is important here to observe that usually those who pose this question, pose it in terms of a flat either/or. Is man free or is he not free? Does man have free will, or is he completely determined? To me, this is an unanswerable question. John Dewey has somewhere observed that there are some questions which are not unsolved, they are outlived. My own view is that the problem of free will versus determinism has simply been outlived.[2]

Furthermore, we must decide what type of a question we are posing. Are we asking a logical or an empirical question? Are we going to answer this question by a logical argument, or are we going to answer it with the use of empirical evidence, and are we going to base our answer on facts which we can verify? Now, we are here dealing with an inclusive, over-all problem. Usually, when we deal with it, logical argu-

[2]It is my personal opinion that a number of the literary critics of "naturalism" who base their criticisms on free will do so on grounds of temperament. This is understandable. However, a man's temperamental bent cannot be accepted as a justification for the distortion of facts, the false attribution of views to others, and worse, downright slander. Personally, let me add that I am not a monistic determinist. I do not, however, look on free will as an inherent attribute of man; rather, I believe that free will is an achievement of men, gained individually and collectively, through knowledge and the acquisition of control, both over nature and over self. Let me suggest here, to the interested reader, William James's essay, "The Dilemma of Determinism" in *The Will to Believe* (New York, 1909). I do not agree with it wholly, but consider it, unlike many discussions of this question, to be illuminating and instructive.

ments are asserted, pro or con. This is especially so in the case of those who argue that man has free will.

Keeping this in mind, we then might ask—what has this to do with a novel? How will the assumption that man has free will make someone a better writer? In what way does one or another answer to the question of free will versus determinism really relate to the work of fiction? Here I think it important to note the kind of answer a critic of naturalism will give when he warrants or premises his criticism on the basis of an assumption of free will. If he makes a merely logical argument, all that he is doing is proving his own premises, for you cannot prove that anything exists in the world with pure logic. And, usually, those who criticize naturalism from the viewpoint of free will are doing no more than this, although in a great many instances, their logic happens to be bad rather than good. If the question is put as an empirical question, then, all that these literary critics and professors can do is to build up a case on the basis of information. Their arguments have no more necessary scientific ground than do the assertions about heredity which Zola held and applied in his novels. As literary people, we are either reducing literature to a question of logic, or else we are trying to resolve literary questions by talking in terms of sciences which we do not work in. The empirical answer to this question would demand scientific work in specialized fields, such as physiology and biology, as well as psychiatry. In addition to this, we might add that deterministic hypotheses, whether we call them true or false, have had a value in science. We may further note that Freud used a deterministic hypothesis in his clinical investigations. If we keep this in mind, we can say that usually those who dispute over literary naturalism in terms of free will versus determinism are generally opposing the scientific and antiscientific spirit. Zola's attitude was scientific. The attitude of many of his critics was antiscientific. Thus, while Zola was limited when he opposed the physiological man to the metaphysical, he was observing pertinently when he spoke of the metaphysical man.

What is really involved in some of these attacks and criticisms is a view of human nature. One of the very important points which we must keep in mind is that the artist is attempting to present his view of human nature and also of characters and of events. As you will recall, Zola denied that art was an expression of personal views. He insisted that scientific authority must be established in place of the personal authority of the artist. I think he was mistaken. Today we are inclined to be much less optimistic than Zola was. We know that we can know less, and that the unknown is much more vast than many imagined it to be in the nineteenth century. We cannot proclaim with the same old confidence, as Zola did, that the artist must abandon theories when science has disproved them. Proof is a much more complicated process than he thought it would be. With this, it might be added that some scientific warrant can be given, at least tentatively, to substantiate the possible validity of types of art which Zola might have described as unrealistic, idealistic, metaphysical or romantic—as lies.

We can translate Zola's theories so that they can, with many qualifications, have one significant value at the present time. Zola insisted that the experimental novelist must apply methods of observation and analysis. The sense of what was valid in Zola's theories can be included in the statement that the realistic novelist seeks to explore the nature of experience. Zola attempted to do that. Serious writers make a similar attempt at the present time. In some instances, a writer will start with a metaphysical orientation. In other instances, he may start with attitudes or postulates which have some ground in scientific discovery. Marcel Proust, for instance, organized his books in terms of metaphysical conceptions which had some correspondence with Bergson's theories of time and continuity. Bergson, it is to be noted here, was critical of science. Was or was not Proust a realist? Was or was not Proust a naturalist? Whether we answer these questions yes or no, we will still face the question of what Proust means to us when we read him. The same applies if we ask these questions concerning a writer like Dreiser.

But these questions of realism, of naturalism, of free will versus determinism do not seem to me the most important ones. Let me now ask a simpler question. What is all the shooting about? I suggest that you try to make up your own mind about that question. I also suggest that you attempt to read a book in terms of some of the premises and criticisms of the critics of naturalism, and then to ask yourself—do you get any fresh insight? Do you feel anything? Do you learn anything? Are you excited? What happens to your emotions? I would say that when you read a book, the handling of your own emotions, the resolution of your own feelings is much more important than any kind of judgment you make about whether the book is good or bad, especially if that judgment is made in terms of questions which are pseudo-philosophical and pseudo-scientific.

I V

Words such as *realism* and *naturalism* have been applied to many writers. Various definitions of these words have been given. One is that of Cargill, who says that naturalistic writers have in common a theory of pessimistic determinism. Others, in attempting to establish a common meaning for naturalism, have come forth with definitions which are mutually exclusive. Some hold that naturalism is optimistic.[3] Others believe it pessimistic, and will say that if a book has a hopeful ending, it can't be naturalistic. I do not know all of the definitions of naturalism, but I have come across enough to know that they are many. I am reminded here of the state of psychology fifty or sixty years ago, when a so-called instinct psychology was dominant. Apparently, there was a competition among academic psychologists at that time for finding new phrases for new instincts, real or alleged. I get the impression that the same kind of competition must be going on among those who are attempting to get a definition of naturalism. If you accept someone else's definition, you are not original. We have been getting that kind of a situation insofar as the problem of naturalism in literature is concerned.

I have, personally, been called a naturalist, and I have never denied it. However, my own conception of naturalism is not that which is usually attributed to me. I have always used the words naturalism and materialism as synonymous. Possibly this has been a mistake. I would really prefer the word naturalism, and I would define it in a Deweyan sense. By naturalism, I mean that whatever happens in this world must ultimately be explainable in terms of events in this world. I assume or believe that all events are explainable in terms of natural origins rather than of extranatural or supernatural origins. Although this assumption underlies what I have written, I do not write novels to prove or disprove this assumption. I write novels in order to try to reveal what life seems to me to be like.[4] I write novels as part of an attempt to explore the nature of experience. If we have a conception of naturalism which is tighter than mine, we are in danger of becoming rigid. I think that the remarks already made about Zola suggest the possibility.

V

Another way of looking at these questions is in terms of necessity and of tragedy. Some contemporary criticism bases itself on the Aristotelian conception of tragedy. At its most banal level, this type is not

---

[3]In passing, let me say that despite his determinism, despite the character of many of his novels, Zola was fundamentally an optimist: Zola was a man who probably declared: "The truth is on the march." The man who boldly assumes that the truth is on the march cannot be such a die-hard pessimist.

[4]Recently, a reader asked me why my character Danny O'Neill, of my tetralogy, escaped from his environment, and did not end as did Studs Lonigan. On reflection, the only answer I could give was this one: Danny O'Neill was a character who determined and who chose to change. Frequently, at least, defeat and disintegration, when described, appear as though inevitable, and thus determined: to the contrary, growth and change do not at all seem inevitable, and, in fact, even seem to be so inexplicable as to appear fortuitous or accidental.

criticism or analysis at all. It often amounts merely to a kind of self-evident criticism to the effect that such and such a modern writer is not Goethe or Euripides. When such criticism goes beyond the self-evident, certain points based upon Aristotle's conception of tragedy are applied.

Aristotle held that in order for a character to be a tragic figure, that character must be superior. Of tragedy he said: "A tragedy . . . is the imitation of an action that is serious, and also, as having magnitude, complete in itself." And he added: "Tragedy is essentially an imitation not of persons, but of action and of life, of happiness and misery." The function of the poet was to describe not the thing that had happened, but "a kind of thing that might happen," i.e., what is possible is deemed "probable or necessary." When a play is truly tragic, it induces pity and terror in the audience: "pity is occasioned by undeserved misfortune, and fear [terror] by that of one like ourselves."

The tragic deeds of characters in the Aristotelian conception were necessary either to be done or not to be done, and the action could be undertaken either knowingly or unknowingly. This exhausted all of the possibilities. But for the character to be tragic, he had to be "better than the ordinary man."

There are two points involved here which I want to stress. One is the conception of the hero as a superior person, the other the conception of Fate in the Greek drama. The Greek conception of Fate or of Nemesis, as is well known, involves the actions of a God who controlled human destinies. The tragic hero, superior to the ordinary man, a male rather than a female or a slave (but not necessarily a male) met his fate, suffered, and therein lies the essence of his tragedy. It well may be that writers today are far inferior to the Greek dramatists. However, this inferiority cannot be cured by adopting the attitudes which the Greeks reveal concerning Fate or Nemesis, or the conception of a tragic character as a superior person. In modern life, few people can be superior in the Greek sense. And the ordinary person, today, does not possess the freedom in circumstances necessary to a tragedy after the manner of Greek drama.

Quite frequently, tragedy in our society has a representational and a social character. Involved in modern tragic characters are such factors as the following: powerlessness because of one's economic position; lack of experience because of social and economic position, or because of accidents at birth which are revealed in the type of parents one has; suffering of consequences of an economic and political character which are far beyond a person's individual control. All of this is obvious, and yet the obvious is overlooked when a literal conception of tragedy based upon Aristotle's theory and the example of Greek drama is rigidly held.

Today, we assume, with some warrant, that social forces, social factors, social pressures and tendencies play a role similar to that played by the Gods, by Fate and Nemesis in ancient Greece. And this is not reducible to mere difference in postulates. It involves social and technological changes, and also what Whitehead styled "a mental climate."

We live in a different society and we live in a different mental climate from that of Aristotle. Man does not, today, believe himself to be the center of the world, as he once did. He does not now look upon his life as a drama of salvation in the way and to the extent that he did in the Middle Ages. Even the character and the nature of knowledge is different. This is to be seen in the scientific superseding of the Aristotelian world. Substantially, it is revealed in a conception of the world in terms of relationships rather than of essence. All of these changes have been and will continue to be registered in literature. We must take these developments into account, when we concern ourselves with the reasons why and how naturalism, so-called, has developed. It has been an attempt to meet and to reveal and to explore the nature of experience in the modern world.

VI

Many writers, strikingly different from one another, have been called naturalists; thus the brothers de Goncourt, Flaubert, Zola in France, and in America Frank Norris, Stephen Crane, Theodore Dreiser, John Dos Passos, and others. Those linked together as naturalists in terms of a definition like that of Professor Cargill are too often taken as representatives of a school. General similarities are stressed, while significant differences are neglected. Within the framework of the naturalistic tradition, there is an extraordinary variety of theme, subject matter, attitude, ideas expressed or implied, types of character, and so on. This is apparent on its face. For instance, *Madame Bovary* by Flaubert, *Germinal* by Zola, *The Red Badge of Courage* by Stephen Crane, *Sister Carrie* by Dreiser, *U.S.A.* by Dos Passos, could be cited as naturalistic novels. But what insight do we gain by linking them together in terms of a watered-down generalization?

These and other books, linked together in this tradition, are all part of the effort by writers of the nineteenth and twentieth centuries to come to terms with experience. They have been written in the spirit of truth. If they are part of a tradition, that tradition has had more force and more impact, and has been able to nourish and give more energy to successive generations than any other tradition. This is most especially so in America. The majority of critics of this tradition have been exponents of another, the genteel tradition in America. Speaking of the latter, Parrington aptly observed that its essence was to be found in "a refined aestheticism, that professed to discover the highest virtue in shutting one's eyes to disagreeable fact and the highest law in the law of convention." So-called American realistic writers have grown up in a different American world from that of the nineteenth century, particularly of New England. They have lived different kinds of lives. They have different origins.

But they are attacked in the name of nineteenth-century writers. In the light of this, I should like to quote from a long review, "The De-flowering of New England," by the critic Stanley Edgar Hyman in *The Hudson Review* (Winter, 1950). Mr. Hyman, who shares at least some of the attitudes to which I have alluded in this paper, criticizes a number of biographies of Hawthorne, Henry James, Thoreau, Emerson and Henry Adams and Melville—all of whom, let me say, I admire as writers. He writes as follows:

> . . . there is the embarrassing and confusing question of the private domestic lives of these writers, that is, not to put too fine a point on it, sex. On a scale of healthy and normal domestic life, Thoreau, priggish, terrified of women, dependent on his mother, and frigidly ascetic, would be at the bottom, followed closely by the spinsterish James; and Hawthorne and Adams, both of them fortunate in story-book marriages (until the death of Marian Adams) would be somewhere at the top. And yet, dare we say that the latter lives were fuller, or rounder, or even happier? Wouldn't a scale of tough-mindedness, of living in ecological balance with the world and dying with a minimum of whining be just as apt to run the other way? If Emerson's first marriage was passionate, short-lived, and tragic, and his second cold, long-lived, fecund, contented, which one helped his work? What is the condition of health for the artist, is there any, and how would we know it if we saw it?

And then at the end of the review, in which Hyman has defended these writers, whom he considers the best to have been developed in America, from dull and careless critics—at least those whom he considers to be such—he writes: ". . . we are all simmering, simmering: who will be the new Emerson, or even the exhumer of the old Emerson, to bring us to a boil?"

I see in this quotation, as I see in many of those who have criticized the so-called naturalistic tradition, a feeling of insecurity, a lack of sureness, a timidity, although it is often masked by an authoritative use of the hallowed names of the past, and by an association with these hallowed names. I see here a tendency to cling to stereotypes of what literature and the artist should be, to cling to these in times when literature is slowly being remade and changed in a world that is both changing and dangerous. Of course it is one's privilege to cling to elegant and hallowed stereotypes. Likewise, it is one's privilege to criticize any tendency in writing. As long as this remains a matter of criticism, it is within bounds. However, there is another quality to some of these criticisms.

It is a curious fact that it is the writers of this so-called naturalistic tradition who are the ones who have constantly had to bear the brunt of the struggle for freedom of literary expression. It is the writers of this tradition who have been constantly haled into court, who have had to defend their work at law, who have had to face the application of the police power. It is the writers of this tradition whose books have been constantly excluded from libraries, from colleges, from bookstores, from being transported across the boundaries of even democratic countries. The consequences of the best work in this tradition have been an increase in feeling and a desire for more freedom, more frankness, more understanding in the world.

The consequences of the obscurantist criticism of this tradition have been more or less in the direction of censorship, or narrowness, or tightness of feeling and thought. Today, many of these criticisms seem strangely arrogant. It is, today, the critics of this genteel tradition who are asking somebody to boil them up, who are asking someone to discover something in the past which will help them reach this state of boiling. If ever there were the blind talking about the blind, here it is.

In an article titled "The Republic and Literature" Zola discussed politicians, specifically the various Republican politicians who seemed to hate literature. Speaking to those who should have been his allies [Zola himself was a staunch Republican] he said that the only thing they could give him and the only thing they could give other writers was liberty. As long as liberty is restrained—we have very much of it here—the tradition which has been so condemned is likely to be able to maintain itself as one of the great tendencies in modern writing. It has been nourished by great writers; it has been nourished in the spirit of truth and free expression. It has retained sufficient vitality so that in more than one country it has been constantly, persistently, repeatedly attacked with the same arguments, the same charges, the same type of obscurantism. It has been buried more than any other literary tendency in our time. And yet, it does not stay buried. I believe further that I am not misstating the facts when I insist that it has contributed toward nourishing a feeling of freedom.

I have always maintained that all artistic tendencies should have free play for expression, and that there should be a kind of free competition between them so that each tendency may have its chance to attract those who may gain from it. I have always believed that there should be richness and variety and art in literature, in philosophy and thought. In speaking here of naturalism, the tendency with which I have been associated, I do not in any way want anyone to think that I am attempting to establish this tendency in any authoritative way over any other tendency. Those who don't like so-called naturalistic novels do not have to read them. I do not urge them to. All I would state is that this tendency has been the outstanding one in the last century or so in shaping contemporary literature, and it has an *avant-garde* insofar as all the practical considerations of the freedom of the arts are concerned. It has been the tendency more than any other which has produced writers who have fought for and succeeded to a very considerable degree in maintaining their free rights of expression in all countries where there is a democratic process. And with that, it has encouraged a spirit of truth and free inquiry. The problems which the psychologists, the sociologists, and so many others today show much concern over are the very problems which agitated, concerned and provoked many of these realistic writers and impelled them to the creation of books, some of which became lasting books in world culture. This is sufficient justification. If we accept the idea that the only real answer is to be found in the consequences, the consequences of this tradition have been pretty much the opposite of what many critics have asserted.

Recently I came across a remark on the concluding page of Alfred Kazin's book, *On Native Grounds*. I quote it: "It is only those who have no culture and no belief in culture who resent differences among men and the exploration of the human imagination." The naturalistic tradition, so-called, has been one means of this exploration. It can more than stand on its results if we put it to a fair test.   —*Summer* 1950

SHORT STORIES

HOWARD TROYER

Three Tales

How Uncle Perry came to chew tobacco, and as far back as he could mind

As far back as he could mind, Uncle Perry was living in the village of Mud Corners with old Leazer Sears. *According to Uncle Perry, Leazer was a rollin' stone, and what moss he got, came from marryin' and buryin'.*

Before 1841, however, neither Uncle Perry's memory nor the old records tell us much about him. In that year Leazer had come to Milford township from Onondaga County in New York. He must have been a man of thirty-five or more, for he had already been twice married and had had a family of four children by his second wife, Ezra, Isaac, George, and Betsy.

Uncle Perry couldn't rightly say how old he was when he "come to" as a member of Leazer's household, but the records show that he was born in 1847, and was therefore five years old in 1852, the year his mother died. Perry's father, Jeremiah Johnson, of whom he remembered little more than the name, had died three years earlier, when Perry was two. His mother, Diadamie Tuttle, already a widow with a son and two daughters, had married Johnson the year before Perry was born. And a year and a half after Mr. Johnson's death, she had married Leazer Sears.

It is necessary for a moment to record some of the children from these interlocking marriages. Uncle Perry, for instance, had three half brothers and two half sisters on the paternal side, that is there had been five older children in the family before his father married his mother: Thomas, John, George, Nancy, and Sarah, among whom Nancy alone seems to have been a vivid memory. And his mother had had three children by her first marriage to Alonzo Tuttle: Albert, whom Uncle Perry knew only as a grown man he went to visit in Ohio after the Civil War, and Laurinda and Jane, who later married the two older Sears boys. How many of these, in addition to Leazer's own offspring, set their feet under his table after Leazer married his mother, Uncle Perry couldn't say, though he minded well enough that Old Leazer always claimed it was another fellow's good times that ate him out of house and home.

Old Leazer never did have any more than he could stuff in his pants pockets, and even then they wasn't full.

At any rate about a year after Leazer married Mrs. Johnson, when Perry was four, Leazer left his own three boys, Isaac, Ezra, and George, and two of the older girls on Judge Wescott's farm where they all were living at the time, and moved to the village with his wife and the younger children, where he began keeping store.

Eight years earlier Len Appleman had built the first store in Mud Corners. To secure help for the log rolling he had ridden over to the Indian encampment across the river from the grist mill at Mongoquinong. Len promised the chief a whole keg of whiskey for the day's work and along about sunrise the next morning there were some thirty bucks dismounting in his yard. First thing they wanted, too, was the keg of whiskey. Len set the keg out in the open, so they could see he meant to keep his word, and then he told them the first fellow that would so much as lay a hand on it he'd bash in his head with a handspike. When they were through, Len knocked in the head of the keg with his axe. The Indians nearly killed each other getting up to the keg. Some of them scooped it up with their hands. Some of them stuck their heads right down in the keg and lapped it up like a dog. Before dark every buck man of 'em was rolling in the grass, dead drunk.

Then Len and Stiles Goodsell had gone overland to Toledo, or Vistula as they called it then, with two ox teams to fetch the goods. A hundred and six miles it was one way; and it had taken them twenty-one days.

The log building was still standing when Leazer moved, but it was a blacksmith shop then. Len had built a second store along about 1850, a frame building with rough-sawed oak siding, and that was the one Old Leazer took over.

It was Uncle Perry's job to help out in the store, and the first time he really came to know who he was himself, there he was a-toting in wood for the old cast iron stove, or a-fetching rainwater for the family washing from the old uncovered hogshead standing by the back corner where it caught the water from the eaves spout.

Earlier than that he couldn't mind much, though he recalled that it was the summer they moved that he had cut off the big toe on his right foot, chopping kindling for his mother. It bled a lot, and he screamed some. His mother sent Sarah for a bandage and Old Leazer spit tobacco juice on the wound to stop the blood. Then Leazer took some fresh tobacco, wet it under the pump, and tied it onto the toe for a poultice.

He could remember, too, something of the death of his mother the next autumn, when he was five. He could mind that he felt something was wrong when his mother didn't come to supper one night nor to breakfast the next morning, and later on when Nancy took him in to see her all laid out, it came over him all of a sudden that she was dead. On the day of the funeral all of the children came up from the farm and that with the neighbors pretty well filled the little house.

"Get outside," says Leazer.

And Perry did. No one could find him when they got ready to leave for the cemetery, and it wasn't until that night when it was all over that one of the older boys happened upon him in an old empty tipped-up rain barrel into which he'd crawled and cried himself to sleep.

After his mother's death, his position in Leazer's family was rather more anomalous than before, but he stayed on with Old Leazer, who became his legal guardian, for at least another year. During that year the chore he dreaded most was going down to the farm to fetch the freshly baked bread. His own half sisters Laurinda and Jane were living on the farm then with the Sears boys and their sister, Betsy, and every Monday and Wednesday baked the family bread in the old brick oven back of the house. On those days, late in the afternoon, it was Perry's task to dog trot the two and a half miles to the farm, stuff a dozen or so loaves into a flour sack, and swinging it on his back, walk back to town. The road led down to Turkey Creek, across the bridge, and then south along the bank of the stream for three quarters of a mile, before it swung off sharp to the right for the last mile and a half to the farm.

On days when Uncle Perry got to go early in the afternoon, he didn't mind. Then he would loiter along the creek, roll up his ragged trouser legs and go wading, or if he had had time to sneak a piece of string and a broken fish hook, he might dig himself some bait and go fishing. He came to know every deep pool and spring-fed inlet along the stream, and the bushy growth of sumac and hazel gave him ample place to hide if Leazer or one of the boys might happen along. But when Leazer did find out, he put a stop to that.

"Lazyin' and loafin' I don't allow my own children," Leazer says. "From now on if you ain't back in an hour and a half, I'll warm your butt."

Twice after that Uncle Perry forgot, and was cudgeled with the hickory stove poker. Then Leazer didn't let him go until it was late enough in the afternoon, so that if he loitered at all, it would be dark before he got back. Uncle Perry was six then, and he had heard enough stories about bobcats and wolves from listening to the men in the store, so that he was mortally afraid of being out after dark. After that he didn't need to be warned.

One day late in the summer Leazer was gone, however, and his older half-sister Nancy, the one person in the household who seems to have had any special concern for Perry, allowed him to go early.

"Leazer'll be back about six o'clock," she says. "Just be sure to get back before he does."

That afternoon Perry took his string and hook along, and cutting himself a willow pole, went fishing. In one of the pools along the stream he caught a glimpse of a twelve-inch trout. Over and over he baited the hook, only to have the fish slide off the broken barb. Dusk came upon him. Suddenly before he left, he became aware of what he at first took to be a shaggy gray dog crouching in the brush on the opposite side of the stream, watching him intently. Then it came to him that it was a wolf. Dropping his pole, he crawled out through the brush and raced down the road.

It was almost dark by the time he reached the farm. While Laurinda was putting the loaves into the sack, he sought Ezra, the oldest of Leazer's boys, in the barn.

"So you're late again?" says Ezra.

"I see a wolf," says Perry.

"The old man will warm you up good and plenty tonight," says Ezra.

"I see a wolf," says Perry.

"You're a-lyin'," says Ezra. "Get on home. Ain't no wolves around here anymore."

"I be scared," says Perry.

"Get on home," says Ezra, "or I'll take a gad to you."

Perry picked up his sack and started for home. He ran all the way until he came to where the road turned and followed the creek. Then he walked along slowly, conscious of every sound in the night. He could hear the water where it rippled over the stones, and the steady hum of crickets. Halfway along the stretch he heard something move in the brush, and turning back, he saw the wolf trotting boldly into the road some distance behind him. Afraid to run, Perry stood stock-still in the road and waited. The wolf slowed up, slunk over towards the brush, and then stopped and looked at him. Perry could see the bared teeth and hear a muffled snarl. In a minute or two he started backing away very slowly up the road, and when he thought he had gone far enough, he turned around and ran, screaming for help.

He had dropped the bread, but he was too scared to think of that before he met Judge Prentiss, who came running down from his house towards the road.

"Where you going, Perry?" says Prentiss.

"I be scared," says Perry. "I see a wolf."

With that Judge Prentiss picked him up and carried him back to the house, where Mrs. Prentiss washed his face and offered him supper, which he was too sick to eat. Then Prentiss hitched his horse to the buggy to take him home. When they got ready to go, Uncle Perry remembered the bread.

"Leazer can get the damn bread himself," says Prentiss.

Leazer was right surprised when Judge Prentiss brought him into the house and didn't say a thing. Perry could see Nancy had been crying, but she didn't say anything either and took him quietly off to bed. The next morning he felt right good, he said, for when Leazer came home with the slashed and torn sack, without anything but a few crumbs in it, they knowed it was a wolf, and he didn't get the cudgeling he was expecting. Besides that it got to be quite a story, told all around, and everyone that come into the store said he'd done the right thing, and he felt himself quite a man.

"The only thing he needs now," says Joe Foos one day, a-laughing, "is to learn to chew tobacco." But Perry was ready to take that seriously.

In the interior of the store both walls were lined with wooden shelves, and in front of the shelves along the right side ran a low wooden counter. On the other side of the room wooden boxes and chests were piled one on top of the other shoulder high, leaving an alleyway between them and the wall so you could get to the shelves. In the middle of the room sat the cast iron stove and alongside of it a big wooden box full of sawdust, which Leazer insisted his customers use for a spittoon during the winter, when a too continuous stream into the stove itself might put out the fire. Next to the counter on the right-hand side stood a huge sorghum hogshead with a wooden lid, and just above it on the counter itself lay a dozen whiskey kegs whose spigots Uncle Perry said he used to keep clean by licking them with his tongue when old Leazer wasn't watching. Directly behind the whiskey kegs in a compartment of the wooden counter Leazer kept his long twisted ropes of home-grown and home-cured tobacco. In the bottom of the compartment, waste from the cutting and stray leaves, which became unraveled, accumulated, and when Leazer was over on the other side of the store behind the boxes and chests getting something from the shelves, Uncle Perry would slip in, raise the lid quietly, and snitch some tobacco crumbs for himself. The tobacco burned his tongue some, he said, but when he could grab enough of it for a real chew, he liked to slip out of doors and, dodging around to the back of the store, direct the stream of spittle against the butt end of a log or a niggerhead stone, as he'd seen the older men do.

One day as Perry came sneaking out from behind the counter, Old Leazer happened to hear him.

"Perry!" he bellows from behind the row of boxes, where he was replacing some goods on the shelf.

Uncle Perry said he was that scared he froze to the floor and couldn't either move or answer him. Old Leazer bellowed again and then coming out to the middle of the store, he picked up the old inch-thick hickory cudgel he used as a poker for the stove.

Uncle Perry didn't know whether it was because he was that scared or whether it was because he had taken such a large chew he couldn't think of any other way to get quick rid of it, but when he saw Leazer reach for the whip, he kind of gulped, and before he knew what was happening he'd swallowed the chew.

"Are you chewin' tobacco?" Old Leazer shouts at him.

"No, sir," says Perry, finding his voice.

"Perry, if you're lyin' to me I'll take the hide right off your butt," says Leazer.

"I ain't lyin'," says Perry.

"Open your mouth!" says Leazer. "What's that stuff you been chewin'?"

"Sorghum," says Perry. "I was a-lickin' the sugar off'n that sorghum lid."

"Don't let me catch you doin' that again! You stay away from there," says Leazer. "And don't ever let me catch you chewin' tobacco. It'll make you sicker than the bite of a rattler just to touch your tongue to it."

"Yes," says Perry.

But when he had time to think a minute it worried him. He didn't dare to ask any more about it right then, but a few minutes later when Old Leazer was opening up the stove door to spit in it himself, he got up courage.

"Joe Foos says he always swallows his tobacco. What happens when you swallow it?"

"Kills you," says Leazer without turning around.

That set Perry to thinking, and the more he thought about it, the more scared he became. He knew it would make him sick all right, for his stomach was already burning like a mustard poultice, but he hadn't exactly figured it was going to kill a fellow. He knew Old Leazer would lick him if he told him what he'd done, and he knew Leazer would be sure to catch on if he got sick. So the first moment the old man turned his back, he skipped out of the door, dodged around the house when no one was looking and headed down through the timber for Turkey Creek. He knew a dozen places down by the bridge where they'd never find him.

When he got to the bank, he crawled into a thicket of hazel brush and lay down flat on the ground. He figured if he was going to get sick he'd just as soon be by himself, and if he was going to die, well, by the time they'd find him they couldn't tell whether he had been chewing tobacco or not.

But he didn't get sick. He lay out there for hours waiting for it to come on, but nothing came. Once he thought about Ezra's dog Rover and how after the dog had swallowed some rat poison, he retched and threw up all over the yard, and how Ezra said that was the only thing that had saved the dog's life. So he tried tickling his throat with a piece of weed, but even that didn't do any good. Then he just lay there and pretty soon he fell asleep.

When he woke up, it was after dark and he crawled out to the bank and followed the creek out to the road. When he got back to the house, fortunately Old Leazer wasn't at home, so he edged in the back way and wouldn't say a word to anybody where he had been. He got cudgeled the next morning for having run away, but by that time he didn't mind so much anymore.

He said he knowed by that time he wasn't going to get sick and that a chew of tobacco didn't hurt nobody. From that time on he chewed regularly, so he said, come Sunday, come Monday, every goddam day of his life.

How Minot Goodsell came to be baptized a Whig, and the end of the Mayflower Lodge of Good Templars

Minot Goodsell always felt himself to blame for the whole thing. After all he had helped to organize the Mayflower Lodge of Good Templars. But it wasn't really his fault according to Uncle Perry.

Any damn horse'll take a drink once he gets his nose into the water— leastways he will if he's thirsty.

Minot always was a temperance fellow and Perry never saw him take a drink in his life, save a little now and then around home when he needed it or in the winter when it was cold, except for that one time in Dan Hawk's saloon in Kendalville.

And that was no more than a good joke on Minot if he could have seen it that way—leastways it was if what come of it, did come of it.

The way Uncle Perry remembered the story, was that in the late fall of '55 or '56, he wasn't quite certain which, he and Minot's boy, Gene, and Minot himself drove eighty-five head of hogs to market in Kendalville. Kendalville was sixteen miles away, the road leading down past Mud Corners to South Milford, through the three-mile stretch of Sawyer's Marsh and across the Little Elkhart, and then up over the rise and so into town. It took them three days. On the first night they stayed with the Francis family on the shore of Pretty Lake, herding the pigs in the yard around the old log barn. The next night they were down below South Milford and camped right out in the woods along the side of the road.

The pigs were heavy, many of them weighing over three hundred pounds, and a number of them gave out along the way. When that happened, they would bring up the wagon in which Minot was following the boys, take out the endgate and, rigging up a gangway, load the pig into the wagon. By the second night nine of the pigs had been exhausted and, the wagon being full, Minot decided to drive on to Kendalville that night, unload the pigs, and return to pick up additional stragglers in the morning. During the night it began to rain a fine drizzle which turned to snow in the morning and continued until in the afternoon when they arrived in Kendalville. Having been out all night Minot and Gene were that goddam cold they had icicles in their underwear, and as soon as they got the pigs into the yard Minot told them to come on and he'd get them something to build a fire in their bellies. It was then that they went over to Dan Hawk's saloon and had a round or so of whiskey apiece, Minot standing up to the bar and drinking along with them.

While they were drinking and thawing out around the potbelly stove, Perry saw a fellow look at Minot as if he recognized him and then go outside. Sure enough in a couple of minutes he was back and along with him he had Hoss Rogers, both men laughing and joking as they came in.

"Hello, Minot," says Hoss, calling for a couple of whiskeys and then coming over to the stove. "Hello, boys. How are the Good Templars makin' out, Minot?" he says, laughing at his own joke.

"Fine," says Minot. "When you goin' to join, Hoss?"

"Join, hell," says Hoss. "Not me. That's why I got to come all the way to Kendalville to get my liquor now."

"Kind of hard on old Whiskey Butt, here," says Minot, turning to the fellow that had come in with Hoss. "He ain't ever been empty and he ain't ever been full."

"Well, you fellows get your whiskey when you want it, I see," says Hoss. "I'll lay you a bet, Minot. I'll bet a twenty-gallon keg of whiskey that if Amiziah Hood, here, was to open a saloon in Applemanburg, it wouldn't be three days till some of your lodge members would be his best customers."

"I don't think so," says Minot. But he wouldn't take the bet, and Hoss knew Minot wouldn't allow him to say any more against the Templars. He and Hoss had been friends and neighbors for nigh on twenty years then, and there hadn't been a thing in the world to come between them excepting the questions of liquor and politics. Hoss Rogers was a Whig and he could hold more liquor than any keg you could get a bung into, but a good stout fellow for all that who liked what he liked and did what he pleased. He was the best shot in the county with a muzzle-loading rifle, and, Minot always said, the first fellow up to do what needed to be done for the good of anybody in the neighborhood. And Minot Goodsell was his spit'n' image, except that Minot didn't drink and always voted Democrat.

Uncle Perry said he never understood why Minot was so opposed to liquor. Minot's father, Stiles Goodsell, had been a heavy drinking man and Minot's boys all liked their whiskey, that he knew for a fact. Many a morning he saw Marsh, the oldest one, come crawling out of the hay because he had been too drunk to find his way upstairs the night before.

But Minot was against it, and when Minot was against anything, he was harder to gee or haw than an old ox mired up to his rump. Minot and Hoss had been arguing about it for over fifteen years. Minot's handy name for Hoss was Whiskey Butt, and Hoss himself was always badgering Minot about the time he'd baptized him, as he put it. That was part of the story, too, though it had all happened a good many years before Perry was born or came to live with Minot, and what he knew he had from Hoss himself or from hearsay.

It was back in 1840 when that happened—the year of the "log-cabin and hard-cider" campaign. The Whigs had held a big rally over at Mongoquinong that fall, and even though Minot was a Democrat he had gone along with Hoss to see the fun. Minot was a young fellow then and had just been married to Ellen Dyer that spring. Hoss was only eighteen and was still living at home with his mother.

The Whigs imported a speaker from Washington, a Congressman or Senator, and the rally proved to be the biggest ever held in northern Indiana. All day long there was a steady procession of marching men, led by beating drums and waving banners. A big six-horse wagon from Angola with a canoe rigged up on top carried the brass band, and a second wagon which had come all the way from Fort Wayne—a huge log-cabin drawn by ten horses, with smoke coming out of the chimney and filled with men in hunting shirts and coonskin caps—startled and delighted the crowd. In the afternoon there were songs and speeches, the crowd huzzaing loudly and shouting itself drunk with the chant of "Tippecanoe and Tyler too," "Go it, Tip, and come it, Ty." There were games and shooting matches as well, and all day long the big bonfires roared, roasting the wild turkeys. Sam Burnside from over at Ontario set a record in hop, skip, and jump—forty-six feet, two and three-quarter inches—which hadn't been equalled since by man, fish, or kangaroo. It was Minot's estimate that there must have been close to two thousand men there before the day was over.

Late in the afternoon, when the speaking was nearly over and the

Whigs were feeling hefty what with the parades and shouting, the whiskey and the fun, Ott Shephardson from over near Lima took sick to his head in John Nichols' store. In order to oblige Ott, Nichols began rubbing his head with whiskey. Nichols was a Whig and Ott was a Democrat, and some fellows in the store got to joking about it.

"Be you baptizin' him?"

"What church?"

"The Whigs," says Nichols. "I'm baptizin' Ott, here, a Whig. In the name of Tippecanoe and Tyler, too," he says, pouring on more whiskey.

That started it. In less than two minutes a dozen Whigs had grabbed mugs of whiskey and wrestled down the one or two Democrats inside the store. Then they got more whiskey and running out on the porch, they shouted to those outside: "Baptize the Democrats! Baptize 'em Whigs! Grab the Democrats! We're coming to baptize' em!"

When the crowd outside saw what they were up to, it was like a haymow on fire. Whigs started grabbing the Democrats. Others ran to the store for more whiskey. The Democrats fought to get away and shouted to each other for help. There was lots of wrestling and some black eyes, and Nort Latta got a broken leg, and dozens of other men had their shirts and trousers torn right off their backsides.

Minot was pitching a game of horseshoes when the thing started. Being a young fellow, he didn't think many of them knew whether he was a Whig or a Democrat. He might have gotten by all right, he said later, if it hadn't been for Hoss.

"Hold on!" says Hoss when he saw him. "Here's a Democrat!"

"Shut up!" says Minot.

"Here's one!" says Hoss, making a grab for him.

And there were a dozen fellows right there to help him. Before they could get him though, Minot took to his heels and started running. Even Hoss said they had to run him all over Mongoquinong prairie before they caught him—through an old lady's garden, over a fellow's potato patch, into a cornfield and out on the other side, back along the millrace, till he sprained his ankle clearing a six-foot rail fence in Zopher Case's barnyard.

When they got him down, there wasn't a man but had spilled his whiskey, so they carried him all the way back to Nichols' store and made it a public ceremony. Hoss swore he himself knocked in the head of a twenty-gallon keg and emptied the whole damn thing on Minot's head, and when Minot got to be a temperance fellow later on, Hoss used to say he regretted every goddamn drop of it. But Minot always said it couldn't have been that much because he remembered that all the Whigs stopped to have a drink before they baptized him and Hoss himself could have downed half that much.

It took more whiskey before they were through than the old brewery at Mongoquinong could turn out in six months, and not a man from Milford township got home that night, dead drunk or otherwise. Hoss brought Minot home the next day, and when Ellen saw Hoss helping Minot into the house, she became right scared, but the only thing Hoss would tell her was that Minot had gotten himself drunk and fallen down the steps of Hezekiah Barr's saloon.

Whether it was because of what Ellen said to Minot nobody seemed to know, but from that day on Minot was more and more against liquor. And it wasn't long till there was quite a temperance feeling in the township— though whether it was all due to the rally or not it was hard to tell. Perry could remember how the womenfolks still talked about the rally when he was a boy, about how they saw their menfolks come straggling home the next day with bloodshot eyes and bruised heads, many of them bare-backed without more than a stitch of clothing to cover their privates.

It wasn't more than a couple of years later anyway until Minot and Dr. Spaulding of Applemanburg, and Judge "Stiffshirt" Prentiss, and Jessie Huntsman, and a few others—there were a dozen all told—organized the Mayflower Lodge of Good Templars in order to put down the liquor traffic in the neighborhood. It worked pretty well for a while too when they didn't do much except stay away from the saloons themselves. Then they got a good many more members and built themselves a big Mayflower hall at Applemanburg, and after that they were trying to take liquor away from everybody in the township.

When that happened, there were a good many fellows who joined the lodge for what was in it for themselves, to get elected to township and county offices, and so on, and after a while they had over a hundred and fifty members. In the summer of 1854 they closed up every saloon in Applemanburg. Almost everyone in the neighborhood was a Good Templar then except Hoss and Seth Wallace, and Seth next to Hoss was the heaviest drinking man in the country.

"Better join," says Minot to Hoss over at Applemanburg one day.

"No!" says Hoss. "I won't join the goddamn thing till you can't get a drop of liquor anywhere this side of Fort Wayne. Then I may have to, for from what I hear some of you fellows got more liquor now than you allow to anyone outside."

And that was why Minot felt himself to blame that day down at Kendalville in Dan Hawk's saloon. Though no one ever knew just how much that had to do with what came to follow.

At any rate it wasn't more than a month after Hoss saw Minot in Dan Hawk's saloon till Amiziah Hood came up to Applemanburg with a big four-horse wagon loaded with whiskey and rum, and started in selling it right out in the street. When the Good Templars came down to fetch Minot to see what they could do about it, Minot said just to let Amiziah go on if there was anybody fool enough to buy it. But that didn't suit a good many of the other fellows. Some of them were for hiring a fellow to go around with an auger and bore a hole in the kegs. Others were for confiscating the entire load, saying there was a new law in the state against selling liquor in the street. And that's what they did in the end.

About four o'clock that afternoon, twenty Good Templars came sidling out of Dillie's store to where Amiziah was selling liquor. Surrounding the wagon, four of them grabbed Amiziah and carried him inside. The others climbed on the wagon, drove it up to the Mayflower Hall, and carried the liquor inside. When they brought the team back, they hoisted Amiziah up on the wagon and told him they'd give him five minutes to get across the Turkey Creek bridge or else they'd tar and feather him. Amiziah lashed his horses into a gallop, and half the folks in Applemanburg came out to shout and huzza at him as the big wagon clattered and rumbled out of town.

But the matter didn't end there. The next question was what to do with the liquor now that it was in the possession of the Good Templars, and that wasn't an easy one. Some were for knocking in the heads of the kegs and letting the liquor run out into the street. Others were for holding a public celebration and stacking up the empty kegs for a bonfire. But still others were for saving the liquor. It might come in handy, they said, if Amiziah went to law about it, and anyway it was a shame to throw that much liquor away, and the Mayflower Hall was a good, safe place to store it until they saw what happened.

About a year later the Supreme Court of the State of Indiana held that the law against selling liquor in the streets was unconstitutional, and Amiziah no sooner found it out, than he brought suit against the Mayflower Lodge to recover his liquor. Old Elias McMahon from La Grange was judge then, and Amiziah won his case. The Templars were ordered to give the liquor back to Amiziah or else to pay for it.

But the Good Templars said they couldn't give the liquor back now, and even those that were for running it into the streets and making a bonfire of the kegs when they first got it, were against giving it up. When it came to a vote, they stood ninety-six to twenty-one against giving up the liquor. But when it got that far, Minot and some of the other fellows were so mad they quit the meeting and never went back afterwards.

Till they had time to raise the money to pay for the liquor, some of them were for giving Amiziah a note and mortgaging the hall for security, and, since it had to be paid for right away, that's what they did.

But they still had the liquor and something had to be done about that right away, some fellows said, seeing as how there were fellows who knew it was getting less and less right there in the Good Templar's hall. Finally they agreed to auction it off, allowing only members of the lodge to bid for it. On the day of the auction a big crowd collected to see the fun. But it didn't last long for when they come to find out, every single keg was either empty or half empty except one. Old Sam Buskin, himself a high mogul of the lodge then, bid off that keg and carried it down the street on his shoulder. There was some fancy bidding after that, but many a Good Templar went away mad, because there was none left for him to buy.

After that the fellows that didn't get any of the liquor wouldn't come to lodge meeting because they were mad at the fellows that did, and soon there weren't enough members left to raise the money for the note. Six months later Amiziah foreclosed the mortgage and the Mayflower Hall came to be the biggest and best saloon in Applemanburg.

It was goddamn funny the way it happened.

One thing's dead sure. Whiskey'll make a liar out of any man—least-ways it will if he says he's agin it.

How Hoss Rogers killed a man in Sawyer's Marsh, and how they built the Plank Road from Fort Wayne to Lima

Hoss Rogers *was as fine a man as ever pulled a pair of britches over his backside.*

That was Uncle Perry's statement and by that he stood.

Hoss was a heavy-drinking man, and not a fellow in the country dared cross him when he was drunk, and there was Tom Eccles, who would rather have met the devil any day than to stand up to Rogers even if Hoss was sober.

But he wasn't a bad man, not when you knowed him. He killed a man one time down to Sawyer's Marsh, he did, and it was a long time afore he got over it.

That was in the summer of '54 or '55, when the long trains of wagons loaded with wheat met at Os Gilbert's corner for the five-day trip to the market at Fort Wayne. Eight or ten farmers would assemble there, or sometimes even as many as fifteen or twenty, each with his own load, and make the trip together. At night they would tether the horses to the wheels and roll up in their blankets under the wagons or around a camp-fire. But it wasn't so much that they wanted each other's company or that traveling together they could double up the teams in hard-going stretches of the road—as they would have done earlier—as it was that now they were afraid of blacklegs—the horse thieves and highway robbers along the way.

They all come with the plank road; that's what brung the blacklegs.

Before that, that is before the summer of '48 when the planking was completed, the road from Fort Wayne to Lima was no more than a slow-crawling wagon trail winding through the forest mud, in and around the numerous swamps and peat bogs. Where the road crossed the Little Elkhart, just north of Kendalville, it cut diagonally across three miles of Sawyer's Marsh, a low-lying area of swamp grass and tamarack. Here the early settlers had cut the heavier tamarack poles and laid them crosswise for a roadbed. Uncle Perry himself could remember the corduroy, and more than once, he said, he bore home a blistered backside from the jolting and rumble-tumble of the wagon.

There was many a story about Sawyer's Marsh even then. In the winter the frost would heave the tamarack logs out of the ground and the spring floods would wash them askew. Or the mud would form a slimy and treacherous ooze on top so that the oxen would slip and perhaps break a leg between the logs, or the horses would miss their footing and, bolting sideways, step off of the roadbed and mire themselves in the bog. There was the story, for instance, of Stiles Goodsell, Minot's father, who mired two yoke of oxen there in the spring of '45.

Stiles, so the story ran, was engaged by Len Appleman to haul a load of flour and salt pork to Fort Wayne. On his return he was to bring back a load of goods for the general store. The roads being fairly heavy that spring, Stiles set out early in the morning, but even so he did not reach Sawyer's Marsh until dusk. Then, though he was worried about crossing a hazardous stretch of road he had not traversed since the autumn before, he prodded the oxen forward, determined if possible to arrive at Kendalville before he stopped for the night. Halfway across the marsh he came to the most miry part of the bog. A blue mist had settled upon the tamarack and Stiles found himself enveloped in an impenetrable darkness. Alternately he tried leading the oxen, illuminating the path by the feeble light of a tallow lantern, then falling back and exhorting and prodding them from the rear. Suddenly, Stiles himself did not quite know later how it happened, the oxen veered too near the edge of the roadbed and the right wagon wheels slid off into the mire, sinking at once to the hub. Working carefully, Stiles tried to steer the oxen sharply to the left, prodding them fiercely in a hope born of desperation that the two yoke pulling together might yet right the wagon. But the oxen, fatigued by a long, hard day, slipping and stumbling on the muddy logs, became unruly. Bellowing piteously, they plunged to the left and then, as they began slipping, more sharply to the right. The rear yoke lost its footing. At the same time the wagon slowly sank over on its side, the concerted strain pulling the leading yoke into the bog. In an effort to save them Stiles tried desperately to unyoke the oxen, but their lashing heads and the heavy

floundering of their bodies endangered his own footing. Twice he himself
slipped into the bog up to his waist. Seeing it was hopeless, he started for
help, but there was no one nearer than Kendalville. Nor could he persuade
anyone to venture a team on the Sawyer road after dark. "Wait until
morning," they said, "God himself couldn't do anything out there tonight."

The next morning all four of the oxen were dead, their bodies almost
submerged, the black ooze of the bog in their nostrils. In the end Stiles
secured what sacks of flour and hogsheads of pork were still visible and, selling the wagon and goods to a teamster from Kendalville, returned on foot
to his home.

But that was all changed by the summer of '54 and '55. Now the
fifty-six miles from Fort Wayne to Lima had a solid roadbed of three-inch
planking, laid side by side on ten-inch sills. Twice a week a huge stage
coach thundered by, bringing mail, emigrants, and land speculators. Wagon
loads of wheat and flour now made a trip in five days that had earlier taken
a fortnight. Horse dealers, buying and selling among the early settlers, led
and rode their mounts the length of the thoroughfare.

*But it was a bad deal. That's how hell came riding into Mud Corners
on planks.*

With the stage coach and the horse dealers came the highwaymen and
the counterfeiters. The dense tamarack growth of Sawyer's Marsh proved
an ideal place to conceal the horses stolen from the countryside. Little side
trails led off from the road, through the tall grass, to clearings deep in the
tamarack, where the horses were herded and guarded by desperadoes of
such ferocious description that no one dared for a long time to investigate
the truth of the stories. Tamarack House, a tavern at the northern ex-
tremity of the marsh, became the rendezvous for a gang of swindlers, robbers, and highwaymen. And so where men had once banded together in
crossing the marsh to help each other in traversing its insecure footing, they
now banded together to save themselves from the blacklegs that preyed
upon the traveler.

There were a dozen stories of fellows who had gotten robbed in the
marsh. One of them was a peddler whose entire pack had been taken and
he himself beaten and left bruised and half-dying by the roadside. On another occasion Ed Dyer, driving a spanking team of big bays, had taken a
load of wool to Kendalville. When he came out of Dan Hawk's saloon that
afternoon, he found two strangers admiring his team.

"Mighty fine bays there," says one of them.

"They be," says Ed.

"I reckon you might sell 'em?" says the other fellow.

"No, I reckon not," says Ed.

"No harm in askin'," says the first one.

"No," says Ed, untying his team and climbing on the wagon.

For a moment it left him a little uneasy in his mind; then he figured they were just ordinary horse buyers; so he thought no more about it and started out for home. It got pretty dark before he got through Sawyer's Marsh and about a mile this side of the Tamarack House, he said later, he heard a couple of horsemen coming up from behind. He still didn't think anything about it till they came up close and he saw their faces were covered and that they were carrying pistols.

"Hold on!" says one of them.

"I ben't stopping," says Ed.

"All right, Jim," says the other fellow. "Grab that team. I'll take care of him." And with that he rode up close and held his pistol to Ed's face.

Ed started to shout to his horses, or leastways he said he did—but the fellow called Jim was too quick for him. He grabbed the team by the bridles, unhitched them from the wagon, threw the harness down on the highway, and then remounting his own horse, led the trotting bays off into the night.

"We'll just sit here a spell," says the other blackleg who was holding the pistol up to Ed's face.

Ed said he was hoping someone might come along then, but nobody did, and in about twenty minutes the second blackleg rode off in the opposite direction from that taken by Jim and the bays. When Ed thawed out of his scare, he ran back to the Tamarack House and told his story. But they never found hide nor hair of the horses though a dozen men helped him to cover the countryside that night and the next day.

That's the way it was when Hoss Rogers killed a man down to Sawyer's Marsh.

As Perry remembered it, the men were on their way home from one of the wheat trips to Fort Wayne when it occurred. It was late in October, the weather was chilly, and Hoss, whom the men had elected boss for the trip, was always fond of his liquor. When they got to Kendalville, he pulled up his team. "Boys," he says, "I'm for a little whiskey in at old Dan's. I'm nigh froze stiff."

It was getting on about four o'clock then and it was still sixteen miles to Os Gilbert's corner and home, so some of the men were for going on.

They knew how Hoss was. If he got to drinkin', like as not they wouldn't get home before midnight.

But Hoss was like a mule. "No," he says, "I'm cold and I'm hungry. And a little whiskey is good fer the belly." Then he drove his big gray team up to the hitching post and stopped.

Some of the men still wanted to go on, but others began to agree with Hoss.

They were afeared of displeasurin' Hoss, and anyway a lot of them liked their whiskey as well as him.

Hoss set the drinks up for the crowd. Then they had a round or two more. After that a good many of the men were for going on home, but Hoss swore he was drinking his bellyful.

"You're sleepin' in your own bed tonight," he says, "and the old lady will like you better fer a drop o' whiskey in your belly."

But some of the men were worried. They had been five days away from their families, away from a warm bed and a good meal. Their wagons were loaded with victuals and winter clothing, they had money in their pockets, and their way home lay through Sawyer's Marsh. "Suppose," says one of them, "there's a whole gang of blacklegs a-laying fer us, enough to take everything we got?" But Hoss kept right on drinking.

When the men saw it wasn't of any use to talk to him, they rebelled. One by one they slipped out of the saloon, untied their teams, and got ready to go. When they had lined up all the wagons, Jessie Huntsman sent in a fellow to fetch Hoss, who came to the door with a bottle in his hand. When he saw what was up he was right mad.

"Well, I'll be goddamned," he says.

"It's time to go," says Jessie. "And by God, we're a-goin'. If you don't come now, we'll be a-leavin' you ahind."

"Oh, you will?" says Hoss. "You goddamn polecat. You think Hoss Rogers will come sneakin' along. Go on home!" he says. "Go on home and change your britches. I'm a-comin' when I'm goddamn good and ready."

"But you can't come through Sawyer's Marsh alone," says Lafe Kinsman.

"I can't?" says Hoss. "I'd as lief come through there with the devil a-ridin' my wagon as I would with any of you fellers." And with that he went inside and slammed the door.

Some of the men were for waiting, but most of them were for going on. It will teach him a lesson, they said. And those who were for staying were afraid to, and so by and by they all drove off.

It was about eight o'clock when Hoss came to himself enough to make up his mind to go home. He had been drinking steadily, but he was so angry it kind of held him up, and when he staggered out of the saloon and over to his team, there wasn't any one who dared to stop him. He had quite a time untying the horses, twice falling down—so onlookers said afterwards—but he finally got himself up on the wagon and cursing and swearing he drove off.

No one knew exactly what happened afterwards. The next morning Hoss himself could hardly mind. He said he didn't know whether he was more scared than he was angry or more angry than he was scared.

He knew that he was terribly drunk, that he was goddamn mad at some-body, and that the blacklegs would likely be for robbing him in the marsh. When he came to the marsh, he took his whip—it had a long lash and a handle with a pound and a half of lead in it—and wrapping the lash around his wrist he grasped the stock in his right hand like a club.

As the wagon lumbered on over the planks, halfway through the marsh he caught on there was a fellow crawling out from under some empty sacks on the back of the wagon, where he had been hiding. Drunk as he was, Hoss sat perfectly still while the fellow crept up and reached for him. Then he turned, he said, halfway in his seat and struck the fellow one blow with the handle of the whip.

What he had done to him Hoss was too drunk to know. When the man fell he just chucked to his horses and the wagon went on rumbling over the planks. It was after one o'clock when he got home and the grays turned into their own yard, Hoss still sitting high up on the wagon, but dead to the world for all that. His son, Harry, heard him drive in, and he and his mother got Hoss off of the wagon and into bed, where he at once dropped off into a deep sleep. Then Harry went out to the barn, unhitched the horses, and fed them. By that time Os Gilbert, who lived about a quarter of a mile across the fields, had arrived. Os had sent with Hoss for a keg of whiskey, and, seeing as how he had been out of liquor for nigh on two weeks then and a-dyin' for a drink, when he saw the light in the barn, he got himself a lantern and came right over.

"Did Hoss fetch me somethin'?" says Os.

"I don't know," says Harry. "He's drunk. We put him to bed."

"Likely there's none left," says Os.

"We can see," says Harry. "It'll be in the wagon."

When they came to look for it, of course, they found the blackleg lying dead on top of the sacks where he had fallen, his head bashed in from the base of his nose to the middle of his skull. Os and Harry were that scared they forgot all about the liquor. After a hard tussle with Hoss they woke him up.

"Where'd that dead feller in your wagon come from?" says Os.

"What feller?" says Hoss, raising himself on his arm.

"Don't you know you got a feller in your wagon with his head bashed in?" says Os.

"No," says Hoss. "I hit one was a-tryin' to rob me back in the marsh. Goddamn him, I must a-knocked him right off the wagon."

"You didn't knock him off the wagon," says Os. "He's a-layin' in the back of the wagon now, and he's dead."

"Dead?" says Hoss.

"His head's bashed in," says Os.

"Well," says Hoss, "if he's dead, I killed him. Harry, you get on Dick and ride to La Grange to fetch the sheriff. Os, you'd better lay him out somewhere, out in the barn if Hattie don't want him in here. I'll think about it in the morning." And with that he lay back and went to sleep again.

The sheriff came the next morning to look at the blackleg. He was dead all right. And there wasn't anything they could find that would identify him. The sheriff rode down to Tamarack House and then on to Kendalville to ask about him, but no one seemed to know him or had ever seen him before. So the sheriff told Hoss to go ahead and bury him.

Hoss came over to Goodsell's to ask Minot to help him, and Gene and Uncle Perry went along. They dug a grave out in the apple orchard. Then Minot and Hoss carried the body out of the barn. Before they began to fill up the grave, Minot read a prayer. Then Hoss picked up the shovel, but "I see tears in his eyes," Uncle Perry said.

"Well," says Hoss, "I reckon I had a call to kill you. But I'm god-damn sorry I done it afore I even knowed your name."   —*Spring* 1946

RUTH McCOY HARRIS

Up the Road a Piece

SOMETHING was ailing Grampa. Sis could tell it plain as day, but she did not let on. If she let on, Grampa might sit down again. They had to go on, had to get there before dark.

"Where we goen, I reckon they just now gitten up," Sis said, lifting her eyes to the round red sun just showing over the trees. "Reckon they is got on they fine clothes, sitten down in they fine chairs."

"I smells meat fryen," Grampa said. "I smells coffee." He sniffed the air like a bird dog.

"Sho' do smell good, don't it, Grampa? Smell like more."

"Sho' do. Ummp-mmmm!"

"They at a fine table. They got bacon and aigs for breakfast."

"Aigs!"

"Bacon and aigs. Ever' mornen. Two aigs!"

"Now, Sis," Grampa grinned. "You know good and well ain't no niggahs eat no two aigs ever' day."

"Two aigs. Gits in they fine cars and rides around. Has chicken ever' day. And grapes!" Her eyes opened wide at her own extravagance. "Yes, sir. Chicken and dumplen."

"Ummp-ummmph!"

The dust felt soft as kitten fur under Sis's skinny black feet, and the September sun was warm upon her skinny black face, early in the morning as it was. She looked at Grampa and thought how old he was, older than anybody. She thought how it was that Grampa seemed older, every step he took, putting his feet carefully one in front of the other, like sticks of stove wood. Older and younger at the same time. Sis seemed to herself older than Grampa, responsible for him, after the day and night upon the road.

"I'm thirteen," she said aloud. She liked to say it; thirteen was much older than twelve. "I'm goen on fourteen. How old is you, Grampa?"

"I old," Grampa said. "I older than anybody. I so old, they's no tellen." He slowed his steps, almost stopped. "I tired, Sis. Old and tired. I got to take me a little rest."

Sis started praying again. "Lord Jesus, help Grampa," she prayed inside herself. "Something ailen him. Sweet Jesus, help him; he ain't got much farther to go. Help Grampa to git there. We *got* to git there."

She saw a blue jay like a flash of sky, lighting on the limb of a wild plum tree, scolding and fussing at them as they trudged along.

"Lookayondah that old jaybird, Grampa!" Sis said aloud, without stopping her inward prayer. "Sweet good Jesus, help him to keep putten one foot in front the other. You *knows* we near 'bout there," she could not help adding impatiently. "You *knows* us got to git there." She looked slyly at Grampa. "Look at him. Here how he do." Sis imitated the jaybird's noisy scolding, putting her head on one side and making her eyes sharp and mean.

"Here how he go. He go like this. . . . Here how the sweet mocking bird go. He say . . ." and Sis whistled some of the mocking bird's many songs.

"That last ain't no mocking bird. That last a crow."

"This here a mocking bird mocking a crow." Sis laughed, seeing Grampa laugh. They laughed together, free and careless, and each looking at the other would laugh still more. When Grampa laughed, his black face was wiped clean and new. It was like being back at home, safe and happy with Lady.

When they had left, they had simply shut the door behind them.

The house was still back there, away back down the road, Sis thought with surprise. If they were back in the little one-room shack, it would be as if they had never left, except that Lady was not there.

After the funeral everything had been too quiet. Sis could not bear to be in the house alone. And Grampa would not come in, even with the dark coming on. Sis tiptoed past the narrow white bed without looking, past the scrubbed pine table where the layer cake and the bottled drinks had been spread. The bare boards creaked and Sis felt death and darkness in the room, felt a hand reaching out toward the back of her neck.

"Grampa!" Sis screamed, and ran out the back door to crouch beside Grampa in his old chair. He held his Bible in his hand, and his old pipe. Sis could see dimly the scars the gallberry broom had left in the baked earth.

"I here, Sis," Grampa said patiently. "I setten here."

Nothing could induce either of them to go inside, where the sweet rambling roses smelled of the grave and the odorless zinnias stood prim in bottles and jars.

"Niggah buryen make me lonesome," Grampa said impersonally, as if the funeral had not been Lady's, his own granddaughter and this child's mother. "Niggah make too much noise and laughs. Then it so quiet and lonesome."

"Sister? Oh, Sister! Where you all?" The voice, rich and brown and warm, poured through the house and washed away the breath of death. "I declare. Out here in the dark! You all catch malarium. Come on in out the black." Mis' Mott, big and brown, lighted the kerosene lamp. It made a shadow behind the bed. They never expected to go to sleep, but they lay down, the old man on his sagging couch, the child on her pallet, soothed by Mis' Mott's cheerful managing. The black at the window was graying, the lamplight fading when they awoke.

Grampa did not argue when Sis told him. He turned to stare, groping for his old shoes, but he did not argue.

"Lady say us got to go anyhow? Just us?"

"She say go ahead."

"Sudie, too?"

A curtain dropped over the brightness of Sis's eyes. "Not this time, Grampa. Not now." Not ever. Sudie would never go.

Sis could hear Lady saying it. "Sudie ain't worth a chew tobacco. Sudie a no-count niggah. Ever how Sudie do, you do the different. Don't you never let me catch you take after Sudie."

Sudie and her four little blue-eyed children, with their hair too soft and brown and their skin too light. Sudie could never go, but she did not care. She did not feel the thing that Sis felt, the thing driving her on. Lady had talked to Sudie the way she talked later to Sis, but Sudie always laughed and put on her high-heeled shoes and the thick red lipstick and ran out of the house. And now she lived alone, with the four children, her belly big and heavy again. She was always singing and laughing, laughing at Lady and Sis.

They each took their most valuable possessions, tied in a little bundle. Sis took her red dress and her shoes that were almost new and the little red pocketbook Lady had given her long ago. It was full of pennies, with three nickels like prizes among them. Grampa had his Bible that he could not read.

They passed Mr. Jeff Webb's big white house, sitting back from the road, where Lady had worked. They passed other painted houses behind their dusty evergreen bushes, passed the cotton gin and the planer mill, the courthouse and the stores. After more houses and the filling station came the other edge of town, with its shacks like Lady's, straight up and down boards weathered gray, with cracks between and a chimney made of sticks and mud.

No one was stirring at Sudie's house or at Mis' Mott's. At Aunt Lucy Carter's they had hot corn pone and bacon drippings for breakfast, but ask as she would, Aunt Lucy could get nothing out of them.

"Just a little trip," was all Sis would say. "Just up the road a piece."

"I bet you all going to Hattiesburg," Aunt Lucy said, scandalized, for Lady was not good cold in the ground, but Sis would not say. They left Aunt Lucy standing by the chinaberry tree in her yard. The road stretched like an inviting finger. Sis could hardly stand it, her feet wanted so much to run and skip, but she walked along slowly, the way Grampa had to walk.

"I got to go in the bushes," Grampa said, stopping. Sis crept behind a bush, too, and then waited for Grampa. But when he came back, he sat down. "Got to sit a little," he said. "Old Grampa tired."

They sat down in the shade, for the autumn sun was already merciless. Grampa had drops of perspiration on his forehead, below his kinky white hair. Grampa was a great big tall man, but he was so stooped nobody knew how tall he had once been.

"Time to go now, Grampa?" Sis kept asking, but Grampa would only shake his head drowsily.

It was Mr. Jeff's car that stopped.

"Howdy, Sis. What you waiting here for?"

Sis nodded toward Grampa. "We goen to Hattiesburg. Grampa's tired."

Mr. Jeff laughed. "He got tired mighty quick. You all ain't good started. Get in. I'm going to Hattiesburg."

They got into the back seat of the splendid car and sat on the splendid upholstery. Some folks would spread an old quilt first, but Mr. Jeff would let them get right in. Even if he was the sheriff, Sis was not afraid of him. She sat marvelling at the miles flowing behind them. It was like riding in the golden chariot.

"Where's Lady?" Mr. Jeff asked them, after a while. "Lady never showed up to help Mrs. Webb during court last week."

They could only stare at each other. How could it be that he did not know of the heavy earth and the flowers piled above Lady?

"Mama daid," Sis's lips trembled to say the words.

"Dead! Well, I'll declare!" Then, "Lady was a good worker. I've heard Mrs. Webb say many's the time, she wouldn't have anybody help her but Lady." It was his tribute, his flowers for the grave, and it brought the tears to Sis's eyes.

At the edge of town, Mr. Jeff parked the car and Sis almost fell out for staring at the piles of vegetables in a store window.

"Look out, girl," Mr. Jeff said sharply. "You'll break your neck." He locked the car. "I'll be going back about sundown," he said.

They did not tell him they would not be going back with him. He would never give it another thought, if he did not find them waiting.

Sis held Grampa's arm, partly to steady him, but mostly to comfort herself. There were people everywhere, soldiers talking Yankee talk and ladies in fine clothes and colored folks like themselves. Grampa, bewildered, bumped into a lady.

"Look out, Uncle," she said good-naturedly. "You're in town now."

Luckily they made no turns. The street led straight through the town and became an open highway again. Sis was empty and thirsty, but she had no idea where to get anything.

"I thirsty," Grampa said. It was the beginning of a refrain. Every time Sis felt joyful and light, thinking of the wonders ahead, Grampa would say it again. Say it or sit down by the road, fanning himself with his old hat. Once he went to sleep, and Sis, her eyes darting about the scrub oak and pine saplings, saw a grapevine. It had no grapes, but she saw another and another, and finally climbed a tree, her dress falling away from her bare body, and came down with a handful of the sharp little grapes.

"Ummp, ummph! Foxgrapes," Grampa said, wadding them, stems and all, into his mouth. "They not ripe. I remembers when I was a slave boy, eating foxgrapes in the fall after the frost."

He had never been a slave, Sis knew, and his remembering was mixed up with the stories he had heard. He thought he had come across the water in the dark hold of a ship, and described whippings and travellings and battles, even his own birth. No one believed him, but they listened.

They saw a white cottage ahead. Sis told Grampa they would ask for a drink of water. But then the dog started barking, just inside the picket fence, a big fierce yellow dog. Grampa stopped in the middle of the road.

"Go on and bark," he said to the dog. "I know you. You know better to bite old Grampa, you old barken dog, you." But he went no nearer.

"Prince. You, Prince! Shut up!" The voice was shrill and cross.

"Come on, Grampa," Sis urged. "Le's don't mess with that old dog."

Grampa would not budge. A tired bedraggled white woman came out of the screen door. "Prince!" she screamed. Then she saw them. "What you all standing there for?" she called to them. "Why don't you go on; standing there fretting my dog?"

But she held the dog by the neck and told them where the pump was. "Hurry up, now, and don't put your mouth on the spout. There's a tin cup."

Grampa was so slow Sis could not wait. She pumped hard until the water splashed out fast and cold; then she bent over and put her mouth to the cold wet spout. They heard the woman calling.

"Come on, Grampa," Sis begged. "She might let that old dog loose."

"I ain't scared of no old dog," Grampa said, as he filled the cup again. But when the woman came muttering around the corner of the house, dragging the dog by his neck, Grampa moved with dignity toward the gate.

The sun still burned them when it was halfway down the western sky. Sis could not understand it. She had been watching for the place, expecting it at every turn of the road. Surely it would be at the top of that hill; surely it was down in that low swampy valley. But the road ran on and on, white in the blinding sunlight.

"Boy," Sis said to a Negro child they met, "Boy, where the Piney Wood school?" She called him "Boy" to sound important, to show him she was a person going somewhere on business.

The boy tugged at his faded overalls. "Huh?"

"Where Jackson? Jackson up thisaway?"

He nodded. "I been there. On the bus. It ain't far. Rat on up the road a piece."

Grampa walked slower and slower. He hardly lifted his feet, and his shuffling made a scraping sound on the pavement that scared Sis. She tried to push him with her thoughts, with her own urgency, and forgot to entertain him with chatter.

The sun sank lower, behind the trees, and left the woods black and threatening. Night was coming, not far away; night full of danger, full of things with teeth and claws, and soft cold brushing things out of graves.

"Come on, Grampa," Sis begged. "We got to hurry."

"I old, Sis," he apologized. "I too old. Us better go back."

"Back?" She tried not to scream at him. "We can't go back. It's right up yondah." She peered ahead. "Look like I see it up yondah," she murmured slyly. "I sees it rat up yondah, look like."

"You don't see nothing up yondah," the old man told her. "I got to rest some more."

"You sit down, I goen walk rat on off and leave you. Goen walk rat on."

Grampa smiled. But he glanced up at the sky and saw that the sun was gone. He did not sit down.

They were surprised when the rattly old car stopped. Two stylish young Negro girls sat on the front seat and their father, wearing overalls, was in the back.

"We thought you all old Mr. Plum and Sarah May," said the girl driving, racing the engine, getting ready to drive on.

"Oh, Miss," Sis could not hide her desperation. "Oh, Lady!" She could not let them leave her and Grampa among the wildcats and ha'nts. "Us . . . we . . . we wants to get up towards Jackson."

She wiped away the tears of relief when they were safely in the car. Nothing could discourage her, once out of the threat of darkness, not the sullenness of the girls when they heard the man asking her and Grampa to spend the night, not the hostility of the black woman waiting at a board shack like their own, not the way they invited her and Grampa into the kitchen so reluctantly, ashamed of the food. Sis and Grampa slept on a pallet before the gaping fireplace. Sis was surprised to hear the girls giggling behind her back, before she had stretched out good. She saw them putting on their fine dresses and their bracelets at sunup, leaning over the cracked mirror to put on lipstick until their mouths shone thick and red, like bloody gashes.

"Where you all going, Jackson?"the black woman, already knowing, asked them as they got into the car.

"To the Piney Wood School," Sis said. "To get educated."

"Piney Woods!" They were impressed. "I got a girl friend went there. Runs a typewriter and ever'thing."

"We goen buy us a car." It was the younger girl, not to be outdone. "Cost us eight hundred dollar. A fine car, near'bout new."

"Eight hundred dollar!" It was almost the first time Grampa had spoken, drowsing away in the car as it bumped over the ruts back to the highway.

"Yeah. Eight hundred dollar." She let each silver dollar clank impressively. "We makes good money at the plant."

"You could buy a farm! House too." Grampa stared at her.

"We got a farm. Farm enough to do us." Her bitter voice told them the hours she had bent chopping the cotton and picking it, the weary miles of furrow she had travelled over the meager and begrudging land. "We don't want no more farm."

They waved goodbye at the highway, stood watching the car go back the way they had come.

How different, to be travelling in the brightening morning, with stomach comfortably full. How happy the journey, how light her heart. Sis could have run, yelping like a puppy. It was only that Grampa walked the same as before, dragging his feet.

But nothing could hold down the joy inside Sis and she sang in her sweet thin voice. How could she doubt, in the early new day, that they would get to the school? She kept watching. She expected to see it just ahead, at the top of the next hill, showing beyond the next turning. She would see it, all of a sudden, right there in front of them.

But the road ran on and on. After each turning there would be only more and more highway, stretching endlessly. When they passed through a little town, Sis, remembering, stopped in a store and bought a box of crackers and a bottle of pickles. She saw the redheaded boy grinning as she counted the pennies out of her pocketbook. Sis stuck out her lower lip sullenly and switched the tail of her skirt as she walked out into the sunlight again.

With the crackers and the pickles she felt fortified for anything, and Grampa, too, was encouraged.

On they walked, forever and ever, up hill and down, sometimes through woods of pine and oak, sometimes past fields of cotton just bursting its bolls, showing a little white. The corn was parched and yellow; dust softened the green of tree and bush.

Sis was not tired, even when the angry sun stood high above, burning her head through her hair. But she was watching Grampa. He must not stop. She would never let him stop again until they got there. She opened the bundle and handed some crackers to Grampa.

She watched the way he ate the crackers, writhing his lips about them, waiting for them to be soft enough to swallow. He did not look at Sis, and he did not strain his eyes ahead looking for the place. The way Grampa looked, it did not matter much to him, one way or the other.

Sis could not understand the ebbing of her courage, the fear, round and heavy in the pit of her stomach, every time she looked at Grampa. Something was ailing him. He looked ashy, as Lady had done before she died. They could only go on, but Sis was afraid.

It was then that the blue jay alighted on the plum tree. Sis felt the weight lifted from her when Grampa laughed at her imitation of the jaybird. But his feet still dragged. They were quiet, Sis and Grampa, but inside she began the praying again. She felt ashamed of herself, finally.

"Grampa, you looks tired. You want to rest?"

"I'm all right, child."

Sis was proud of him. The day before, he had been complaining all the way. Now of course it was past the complaining time. Sis saw how he favored one foot a little.

"Your feets hurt you, Grampa?" She wished he were back in his old chair by the back door, and she beside him. What had made her start on a trip so far, to a place so unknown? What good was school to Grampa, older than time itself? She could not think what had driven her to do it.

"My feets all right, child," Grampa said. "I got a little stitch in my side is all. Nothing much."

"Mama said to come. She said not to go off and leave you, you so old."

"Um-humm."

"Said I goen learn to read and write at the school. Said I got to."

"Ummm-ummmph!" Grampa had heard this many times. "A niggah that can read and write, he can do anything, git anywhere." Grampa did not know this for a fact; he was quoting Lady.

Sis could feel the heaviness in the pit of her stomach; sometimes it rose and stuck in her throat. She kept glancing at the sun, hardly started on its downward course. She wished Grampa would complain and fuss; his patience scared her. Maybe the school would be at the next turning. It had to be up there at the next turning of the road.

When Grampa fell down, he did not fall all at once. He leaned forward a little, as if he were listening. He cocked his head to one side, listening, and then his knees buckled under him, and he slid to the ground noiselessly and easily as if he had been practicing all his life. He gave a little grunt, "Ummmfff!" of anger or surprise, and lay still.

Sis watched him. She could not believe what her eyes saw. She stood and looked at him lying still in the road before she screamed.

"Grampa! Grampa!" Her childish screams came out of a mouth that hung open, and the salty tears ran into it. She shook him wildly, taking his arms and tugging and pulling, trying to get him to his feet again. She had known all the time that once he was down he would never get up. He lay at the side of the highway. An automobile whizzed by so close it almost ran over Grampa's foot.

"Git up, Grampa!" she kept begging. "Oh, git up. Oh, git up. Oh, Grampa, git up!"

She managed to pull him a little farther to the side of the road after another car had whizzed by his feet. A car might run right over Grampa, lying in the road, run over him before the driver saw him.

Although she was frenzied, she could not truly believe for a long time that Grampa was dead. It was simply that he was so hard to get started, once he stopped. She needed Grampa to be walking beside her. With him lying still, she was scared, lost.

Finally she began to know that Grampa was dead. He was gone, like Lady. That changed everything. She stopped her wailing and her moaning. Grampa was dead and it was her fault. She had killed him.

At the same time, it was not she, Sis, who had killed Grampa. He had died during the journey, but the journey itself had not been a thing they could take or not. Lady had said they must go; Sis knew they had to go; Grampa had not argued against it at all. The trip had to be made; there was something driving her, stronger than any of them. She could not leave Grampa all by himself in the shack and he had died on the trip.

But she was still terrified. With Grampa not there, she was alone, a child in a far-off land, not knowing where she was going, not daring to turn back. She could not stay. She had to get on up the road.

Sis saw a buzzard in the tip of an old dead tree. Buzzards always knew about death. Even before it happened, they knew.

Sis looked down at Grampa. She moved his bundle nearer his hands; his Bible was in it. She glanced up at the sky again to see where the sun stood and without another look at the old man she walked steadily up the road.

Sis knew what she was doing. She knew the horror of not being properly buried, the greatest concern of Grampa's life. She knew about the burial insurance back home, knew he had expected to be buried where Lady was, among his friends, with God watching.

But she walked on. What else could she do? There was no going back, no bringing Grampa back to life; no physical possibility of looking after his body from which his soul had already gone.

It was completely beyond her power and so out of her hands. Sweet Jesus God would have to take care of Grampa's body.

Sis did not feel like skipping and jumping any more. The sun was dropping in the west; hunger was gnawing at her stomach. Her thoughts seemed light and far away, dancing up above the top of her head.

It might be right ahead. At the school, they would know what to do about Grampa. They would know everything at the school. But of course the school was thousands of miles away; she would keep walking until she, too, fell down like Grampa and never get up again. She kept thinking of herself and Lady and Grampa, standing in the kitchen, eating the good hot cornbread and the hot turnip greens. Cold buttermilk. Side meat fried, and molasses.

She passed a filling station where two or three cars were parked.

Some white boys, nearly grown, stood drinking from enormous bottles. She could taste the cold orange flavor as she watched out of the corner of her eye. It would be sweet and a little acid going down her throat. Cold and sweet and wet. She heard them laughing and talking as she hurried past, a thin little Negro girl with knobby knees.

The dusk came on with surprising suddenness. The sun had appeared to stand quite high in the west, above the treetops. Then all at once it dropped behind the tallest trees. There were long shadows. From the woods the dark was creeping toward the road. Sis gave a little cry of despair and tried to quicken her steps. Night coming and she not there. She would never be there. She shivered. Jesus God had seen how she had done Grampa. Jesus was mad with her.

"Keep rat on walking," the voice said. "It ain't far. Just up the road." It was Lady's voice and Sis felt the warm tears come to her eyes.

"Grampa," she said to Lady. "Grampa."

"I knows. You couldn't help it."

"He ain't buried."

"You can't help it," Lady insisted. "You just a little girl. Us niggahs, we got to do the best we can. Jesus looking after Grampa. You just keep on. You goen git there."

"You said to come."

"You got to. You goen learn a heap at school."

"Reading and writing," Sis said, wiping her eyes.

"Ever'thing. Goen learn ever'thing. Be big and rich. Goen ride in a fine car and have plenty firewood. Plenty quilts. All you wants to eat. Apples and oranges. Meat ever' day. Goen have money to give to them what ain't got nothing to eat. Goen be a schoolteacher and teach the chillun what ain't got nobody to teach them. You got to git there."

"Mama," Sis cried, wiping her eyes again. "Mama, you stay with me."

She did not know whether Lady was really there. She knew about ha'nts, but they were cold and creepy, not warm and comforting like Lady.

The car ground to a stop. Sis turned in surprise. She had not heard it approaching.

"Git in, girl," somebody ordered.

"Aw, Pete, for the love of God," another voice said. "She ain't nothing but a young'un."

"Git in, girl," the first voice said.

They were the boys she had passed at the filling station. Sis was puzzled. She was so relieved to hear human voices that she could not understand the little throb of fear in her.

"Git in, git in," Pete said. "You want to ride or not?"

Sis giggled. "I sho' does. I tired."

She got into the back seat, beside one of the boys. "Aw, for the love of God, Pete," the boy not driving kept saying. "You all make me sick."

"Shut up, Ralph," Pete jeered good-naturedly. "Where'd we put that liquor, Ed? You remember?"

"Sure." Ed spoke from his place beside Sis. "Keep on going. I'll tell you."

Sis shrank back into her corner when the boy reached toward her. She sat rigid as a pole as she felt his hand on her.

"She ain't got nothing on," Ed stated. "Not a damn thing but a dress." Pete laughed raucously, but Ralph kept saying, "Aw, for the love of God. This makes me sick at the stomach."

"Listen to the Christer. Sixteen years old and he acts like he was born yesterday. Where is that liquor, Ed?"

"Hey, stop. Wait a minute. Wait, I think we put it right back there."

Pete stopped, put the car into reverse. Sis pushed hard into her corner. The boys were all staring into the darkness.

"Naw, this ain't it," Ed said. "It must be a little farther on."

"Aw, nuts," Pete muttered. "How come we put it there anyhow?" They drove on slowly, still peering into the blackness.

"Wait a minute," Ralph said quickly. "Here it is. This is the place."

"You sure? I can't see a wink."

When the car stopped the three boys got out. "You stay right there, girl," Pete called back, "if you don't want your brains beat out."

Sis heard them crashing about. She was too paralyzed to move. Much as she feared the boys, she was still more afraid of the dark woods.

A voice spoke softly into her ear, making her jump.

"Beat it, girl," Ralph said. "Here, this way. I got the door open. Go down the road a little ways and hide until we're gone." Sis stood up, felt beside her for the little bundle.

"Ain't you got no sense?" he hissed. "Don't never get in no more cars with white boys if you don't want . . ." and he ended up with a mouth full of obscenity. "Beat it."

Sis stumbled out of the car and ran through the darkness, crashing blindly into bushes. She stumbled over a log and fell and crouched where she had fallen, like a rabbit crazed by hounds.

"Hey, Ralph," said Pete's voice very near. "I don't see no big oak tree. Where in hell is that liquor?"

"Maybe it ain't the place," Ralph admitted.

"Oh, the hell you say. Come on." She heard more crashing, then, "Hey, she's gone!"

"What?"

"That little blackbird is gone."

"Well, let her go. Let's get going. I got 'bout enough of this."

When the car had gone, its lights dipping into a hollow and disappearing, Sis got up again and ran along the side of the road. She was past crying, past any feeling except numbness and a creeping at the back of her neck, where a hand was reaching out toward her. She wanted Lady to come back, but there was nobody, nothing.

She heard and trembled at all the little night noises, the insects and the murmur of the leaves in the dark. She heard the far-off bay of a dog, the lonesome whistle of a distant train. She could not stop, but how could she go on? She was breathing in gasps, and in her side a pain caught her and did not let go. When she saw the lights of a car like a probing finger, she stepped off the road into the woods. It was the boys again; she could hear their voices as the car moved slow and threatening, making long shadows about her. Then, the car gone, she was back at the road again, far more afraid of the black woods than of any people.

Time had no beginning or end. There was only the pain under the bottom of her foot, where a blister had burst, and the ache in her side and the ache in her throat. Black woods and black despair. But she kept on walking. If she stopped a minute the hands would grab her. Even when she saw distant car lights again she stepped only a few feet off the road.

Sis never knew when she sank down. She had either fainted or gone to sleep on her feet. One moment she was walking, fearing the distant car lights; the next she opened her eyes and saw the paling of the eastern sky, the first wash of pink. She felt herself trembling, shivering, for the night had been cool with a touch of fall in the air, and the ground where she lay was wet with dew.

The road was right beside her, stretching away into the distance. Where it rose from the low swampy place, she could see the sun shining on the cement, whitening it with daylight and hope.

"It ain't far now. It just up this old road," Sis said aloud. She stood up carefully, keeping her weight off her blisters. She ached all over, but she picked up her little bundle and walked on, her heart as light as spongecake to see the daylight again.

"Just rat at the top of that hill and there it will be. Spelled out in great big words, like Mama taught me from the letter. A great big old building, maybe, all shining like diamonds. Great big letters so I can read it." Sis could read only three words, "Piney Woods School," because those were all Lady knew to teach her.

It was not at the top of the hill. For the first time, Sis wondered whether possibly she had passed it. The sun had come up and the whole sky was brightening. The trees became green instead of gray. Sis heard a squirrel chattering and turned her head to look.

She stared. She could not believe her eyes. It was an iron arch, with the words spelled out in big iron letters, "Piney Woods School."

Sis could read them plain as day, just as Lady had taught her. To think they were there. She knew, reading the words, that she had actually never in this world expected to see them.

Her mouth stretched into a wide grin. She said the words aloud, stepped inside the arch, turned and looked back to see that she was truly inside, gave a skip. She saw nothing but a little dirt road through the trees, but she never doubted what was ahead.

Well inside the fence, Sis slipped off into the woods grown friendly in the daytime.

When she was hidden, she lifted her old dress over her head and stood skinny and naked. Proud Sis took her red dress out of the bundle and slipped it over her head. She put on the shoes, a size too small, arrogantly ignoring the pain of the blister. She reached back to button her wrinkled dress, then, wadding the old dress carelessly, stuck it deep into a red haw bush.

Proudly Sis took her little pocketbook in her hand, and gingerly walked to the dirt road again. Proudly she marched, stepping firmly upon the burning blister, pinched in her shoes. Her face was radiant and impudent with joy. Her face was ashy with dust, her legs scratched and rusty.

"Piney Wood!" she cried, her face transfigured, her sorrow past and forgot. She saw a cluster of unpretentious brick buildings ahead of her and stood still for a moment, seeing palaces. She began to skip awkwardly, on toward the buildings.   —*Winter* 1946-47

ABRAHAM ROTHBERG

The Walls of Jericho

W HEN public school was over, David Freed came home for his Hebrew
school books and his afternoon milk and crackers. He would rather have
remained to play indoor baseball in the schoolyard, and he sat in the
small dark kitchen dawdling with his milk until his mother hurried him
along. "David! you'll be late again for Talmud Torah! Do you want
Rebi Greenberg to tell Papa that you were late again this week?" Remembering his father's angry face and Mr. Greenberg's pinching, ear-
pulling little fingers, David gulped the rest of his milk and went for
his books. At the door, his mother caught him, picked up his black silk
skullcap, embroidered with the blue Star of David, and quickly brushed
his hair into place. "Now remember," she said, her brown eyes large
and serious, "no fighting. Your father said that if *they* want to fight,
you mind your own business and go to the Talmud Torah." David
nodded hopelessly. What was the use of explaining again that you
couldn't go past them? His parents didn't understand that there was
no use talking to the Forty Thieves because they wanted to fight, not
talk. Their favorite hangout was on the street before the Talmud Torah
so that they could get at all the Jewish boys who had to pass them to go
to Hebrew school. And there were always fights, every day. As he was
leaving the house, his mother called after him from upstairs. "Don't
forget what I said, David. No fighting! And I want you home right
after Talmud Torah. Papa will be hungry, and I don't want to wait with
supper."

David didn't answer. He went outside, closing the door silently behind him so it would seem he had already gone when she had called
to him. Outside, Sonny Richter, eating an apple, was waiting for him.

He and Sonny had just worked out a way of going through the back alleys so that they didn't have to pass D'Aquino's candy store where the Forty Thieves always waited. It was always at D'Aquino's that the fights started. The Jewish kids went in twos usually, because so many of them had been beat up, but even that was no good because the Forty Thieves came in fours and fives now.

"Did you do the homework?" Sonny asked, taking another bite of his apple.

David nodded.

"I didn't get time to do mine," Sonny said. "Wanna bite?" He proffered the apple but David shook his head. "Tell me about the homework, huh?"

"Oh, it's Joshua blowing the trumpets and the walls of Jericho falling down," David said.

"Again?"

"It's one of Greenberg's favorites."

They walked down the street, ducked into the alleyway behind Jiggs's apartment house, through the backyard of D'Aquino's, under the twisted little crabapple trees, past the bocci alley behind the Italian grocery store on the corner, where the little black balls lay on the ground like fallen fruit. Then it was only a dash across the avenue and they were half a block from the Talmud Torah and safely past D'Aquino's. "That's a good way," Sonny said, beginning to eat his apple again. "They didn't even see us. Look, they're in front of D'Aquino's looking the other way."

David turned and in front of the candy store he saw four of the Forty Thieves, Banana Nose, Fonzi, Sal, and Petey. "They'll see us some day and catch us behind D'Aquino's and that'll be worse," David said. "Besides I hate to sneak."

"You wanna fight with them every day? Two against four? Two against five?"

David shrugged. "I don't know."

"You know what your father said about fighting them. And my father too. Boy, he gave it to me last time too, when Fonzi tore my shirt."

"I ain't scared of 'em," David said.

"You ain't scared, huh? You look plenty scared," Sonny said.

"Maybe I am scared," David said after a moment, "but I don't like running away."

"But you can't talk to those guys. You know that. Schloime tried last week, so they tore up his Bible and burned his *yarmelke* with matches, and beat him up anyway."

They walked down the few stairs that led under the synagogue to the Talmud Torah. Mr. Greenberg had already started the lesson when they opened the door of the classroom. "Oho, *trumbenicks*, you're here already? Good evening to you." He made them a mock bow and then picked up the blackboard pointer while they hurried to their seats. David opened his book to the place and hunched over it, but he was still thinking of the Forty Thieves. Some day they were going to get it, all of them, and get it good.

"David?" Mr. Greenberg stood next to him.

"Yes, Rebi Greenberg."

"Where is the place?"

"Here." David pointed and Mr. Greenberg brought the pointer down across his knuckles. "That's for coming late. Now, translate."

His knuckles were like fire and he almost got up to hit back, like Nadie Rosen had done when Mr. Greenberg hit him before Rosh Hashonoh, but he remembered what his father had said. There was to be no more trouble with Mr. Greenberg and the Talmud Torah. If there was, his father had promised that he would get it, and good, so David just looked his hatred at Mr. Greenberg's thin, pale face, with the little silver-rimmed glasses and the wispy mustache and sideburns.

"Translate!" Mr. Greenberg repeated. "Are you deaf on an ear?"

David began to translate.

So the people shouted when the priests blew the trumpets and it came to pass that when the people heard the sound of the trumpet, they shouted a great shout so that the wall fell down flat and the people went into the city without trouble and they took the city.

When David finished, Mr. Greenberg called on Sonny, gave him the same pointer across the knuckles for coming late, and then hurried his translating. David hated Mr. Greenberg's teaching. It wasn't like public school where the teachers got mad and maybe made you stay after school, or do extra homework, or even wear a dunce cap. Mr. Greenberg was always hitting, with the pointer or with his hands, on the knuckles, the back, the legs, pinching an arm, or twisting an ear with his strong, hairy fingers. Now, because Sonny had missed a word, because he hadn't done the homework, Mr. Greenberg twisted his ear, while Sonny tried to pull away and finish his translation at the same time. He was half way out of his seat when the unfinished half of his apple fell out of his pocket and rolled on the floor and the class burst into laughter. "Silence!" Mr. Greenberg roared, and after an extra, final tweak, he let go of Sonny's ear and finished the translation himself.

And Joshua then commanded them, saying, Cursed be the man before God who shall come and rebuild this city of Jericho: the foundation of it shall lay in his firstborn, and on his youngest son shall he set up its gates.

When the lesson was over David left the classroom quickly. It was almost as if he had to rush into the open to breathe again, and he went up the stairs two at a time until he was outside of the synagogue. Evening had come swiftly, as autumn evenings sometimes do, fallen like a haze of darkening snow. The air was clean and cool in his mouth and he swallowed it until Sonny and Nadie Rosen came upstairs, and Nadie said, "You let him hit yuh again, Davie." It was half a question, half an accusation.

David said nothing.

"His old man said he'd give it to him if he started up with Greenberg again," Sonny explained for him.

"He musta been talking to my old man," Nadie said. "I seen them in synagogue together on Shabos. I told my old man that no matter what he said, Greenberg better not lay a hand on me any more. Great! So he gets mad and says that if Greenberg won't, he will. He give me some shellackin too."

"Did you cry?" Sonny asked.

"Whaddyu think I'm a cry baby?" Nadie said. Then, changing the subject, he went on. "That Greenberg. He loves that book of Joshua better than all the rest together because there's war and killin and the Jews conquering the Amorites and the Perizzites and the Jebusites."

"Be a lot better if he could tell us how to conquer the Forty Thieves," David interjected. "Now."

"Oh, that," Sonny laughed. "That's easy. Just get your trumpet and we'll blow 'em down just like Jericho."

"Big joke," Nadie said, disgustedly, "but it ain't funny."

At the corner, Sonny, suddenly confidential, said to Nadie, "Listen, we've got a special way to get past the Forty Thieves. You want us to show you?"

Nadie looked at him for a moment, his shoulders hunching under his brown suede jacket. "I'm not runnin away from them, or from Greenberg, or from anybody," he said, his smooth brown face stiffening, and his jaws working.

Sonny stopped. "Well, I don't care about you, but Davie and I are going our way," he said defensively.

"Okay, who's stoppin' yuh?"

"I'm going past D'Aquino's with Nadie," David said, sorry to see Sonny's face fall and his eyes go wide with fright. He knew that there was no use in ducking through the alley anyway. The Forty Thieves would find out and pretty soon they'd wait there, so what difference did it make? Might as well go the regular way.

"You guys nuts?" Sonny said. "You remember what your father said about fights, Davie. You better go with me."

"Scared cat," Nadie said.

"I ain't scared. It's just dumb to fight."

"Come on, Davie," Nadie said. "Let's go."

They stepped off the curb and began to cross the street. "Okay, okay," Sonny called. "Wait for me. If you guys go, I'll go too." They waited for him in the middle of the street and when he caught up to them, they walked three abreast across the street, and then across the avenue to the side D'Aquino's was on.

"Make believe we're talkin'," Nadie said, "like we don't even notice 'em."

"Sure, but they're waiting. Four of 'em," Sonny said. "Banana Nose, Fonzi, Sal, and Petey."

"Hey Freed, yuh sheeny," Banana Nose said. "Yuh running home to Momma to do yuh homewoik, Davie?"

"Listen, you Banana Nose guinea," Nadie ·said, "you too dumb to do your homework. You can't even read."

"He wasn't talkin' to you," Fonzi said. "He was talkin' to little Davie. You mind your business."

They were at D'Aquino's now and Fonzi and Banana Nose had stepped out on the sidewalk to block their way, and Petey and Sal stood at the side, leaning against the Indian nut and poppy seed machines.

"Look, Fonzi, we're in a hurry. We gotta get home for supper," Sonny said, pleading, but Nadie looked at him and he shut up.

"You gonna let us past, Joe?" David said to Banana Nose, calling him by his school name.

"My name's Banana Nose to you, sheeny, see?" he said, pushing his finger into David's chest, and bringing his face so close that David could feel his own eyes pull together to watch Banana Nose's big nose quivering and his dark eyes brimming with hatred.

"Look, Banana Nose," David said, "we didn't come here to fight, but you better not say sheeny again."

"D'yuh hear that, Petey?" Banana Nose half-turned to the two still leaning and watching. "He ain't come here to fight, and we better not say that doity woid sheeny." He turned to David, pushed his face close again, and yelled, "Sheeny, sheeny, sheeny yella belly," and then slapped David's face with a loud-sounding open palm that was like a paper bag blown up and busted. David felt the same burning pain in his face he had felt in his knuckles when Mr. Greenberg hit him, and he punched Banana Nose's head.

The fight was on. Nadie rushed Fonzi and Petey and Sal jumped on Sonny and began to punch him, while he tried to cover his face. After that, David had eyes only for Banana Nose. Banana Nose hit him in the stomach and David felt sick and breathless together. A fist hit his nose, stinging and painful, and he felt the blood run salty over his lips. He put his hand up to his face and wiped the blood away. The sight of the blood, red and rivuleted on his hand made him crazy mad. He jumped at Banana Nose, hit him on the ear, punched his head again, slammed him in the stomach, and then threw him on the sidewalk. Banana Nose pulled his ankles and David went down on the sidewalk with him, rolling over and over, as they both punched each other's ribs and back.

Above the roar of his anger and the beat of his blood, David heard two voices shouting together and hands pulled him away from Banana Nose, and Banana Nose away from him, while both of them kept trying to punch. "Thick heads," a voice cried in Italian. "Calabrian thick heads! Sicilian bandits! What the hell you do in front of my store! You want to bring police here?" It was Mr. D'Aquino, two hundred and fifty pounds of him, his big belly hanging over his thin belt and baggy pants, pulling Petey and Sal off Sonny. The other voice was yelling in Yiddish, "*Trombeniks!* Gangsters! You are thieves and carriage drivers to fight like this in the street?" And in the midst of Nadie and Fonzi, still fighting, David saw Mr. Greenberg, his black caftan flying and his black felt hat on the ground, knocked off his head by Fonzi, revealing his white embroidered skull cap. In a few minutes, it was all over. Banana Nose, Fonzi, Sal, and Petey were lined up behind Mr. D'Aquino's big bulk, and Sonny, Nadie, and David were behind Mr. Greenberg's caftan. Mr. D'Aquino and Mr. Greenberg were talking simultaneously and their words were mixed in David's ears. "Now, whaddyu wanna fight for, huh? . . . You know what you'll get when your parents hear you fight in the streets like gangsters. . . . Whatsamatta, not enough trouble ina woild fa you? . . . How many times in class I have told you that fighting is bad. . . ." There was a sudden quiet as Mr. D'Aquino and Mr. Greenberg stopped together. "Now, you betta go home, no hang around my store no more, you hear," D'Aquino said. "If I see you fighting again, I give you five pages extra to translate," Mr. Greenberg said, picking his hat up and brushing the dust from the nap with his sleeve, before he set it straight and awkward on his head. "Now, go home."

As they turned to go, Banana Nose yelled, "Whatsamatta, yella bellies, need your sheeny teacher to help yuh fight?"

David turned back, Nadie right behind him, but Mr. Greenberg stepped in front of them. "It is enough," he said in Yiddish. "Go home. You will not make them think better of you or me by hitting them."

"Yuch gekitchmeroubaragovok," Banana Nose mimicked the Yiddish. "Whyn't yuh speak English, yuh forriners?"

"Let be ssshah!" Mr. Greenberg ordered them, his face sterner than David had ever seen it. None of them dared answer Banana Nose.

Then, as a parting shot, Banana Nose shouted, "We'll wait for yuh in the schoolyard tonight to finish this, yella bellies."

"You better be there too," Fonzi added, "or we come and drag you out of the house."

"Gwan with you big mouths," Mr. D'Aquino said, lifting his huge hands. "Gwan, before I make you little mouth."

"You big fat slob," Fonzi said.

"You think you own the whole street cause you gotta stinkin candy store," Petey added.

"Scram out!" Mr. D'Aquino shouted, stamping his foot, and the Forty Thieves fell back.

"Don't forget, sheenies," Banana Nose shouted again. "The handball courts at half past eight." Then the four of them slouched to the corner and were gone.

"Go home already," Mr. Greenberg commanded, and they began to walk towards the other corner, while Mr. Greenberg turned back to Mr. D'Aquino. As they walked away, David heard Mr. D'Aquino say, "Whaddyu gonna do with sucha kids?" and Mr. Greenberg's answering, "When they are men, grown, maybe they are smarter?"

Nadie, Sonny, and David walked up the street in silence, trying to straighten their clothing, wipe their faces clean with their handkerchiefs, and smooth their hair with their pocket combs. David's shirt was covered with blood and dirt, and he knew that unless he could get into the bathroom and get cleaned up without his mother seeing him, the whole thing would start all over again, only this time his father would hit him for fighting because Jewish boys did not fight. They got to David's house before Sonny asked, "You gonna be there tonight?"

"Where?" David asked.

"The schoolyard," Nadie said. "Sure he's gonna be there. And me too. You better be there too."

"Whaddyu mean?"

"Just be there," Nadie repeated. "I'm gonna bring Maxie Jonas along too—he's a good fighter—so it's four to four even."

"All right," David said. He hadn't thought of going but maybe this would settle it once and for all. "Meet you at the schoolyard, our side of the street, about half past eight."

Upstairs, David opened the door quietly, and hearing his mother in the bedroom slipped quietly into the bathroom and locked the door.

"Davie?" his mother called.

"Yeh, Ma, I'm in the toilet."

"Hurry up and get out of there. Papa'll be home any minute."

When he had washed all the blood and dirt away, David took off his bloodied shirt and put it at the bottom of the hamper, covering it over with all the other soiled laundry. Then he opened the door, went into his bedroom, and put on a clean shirt. He heard his father come in, his mother's "Jakob?" and his father's grunted "Yah, Leah." He sat down with his Bible to try to do the translations for the next day's lesson in Talmud Torah but he couldn't concentrate. If he went to the schoolyard and fought, his father would find out and beat him for fighting. If he stayed home and didn't go, the boys would think he was a coward and the Forty Thieves would make it miserable for him every time he passed D'Aquino's, and even in school. And what if he did beat up Banana Nose? What difference would it make? You couldn't talk to the Forty Thieves but you couldn't beat them either. They liked to fight and it would mean fights and more fights, with Banana Nose, with Fonzi, with Sal, and all the rest of them until he got licked. You just couldn't win. He tried not to think of it, to concentrate on Joshua and the Amorites.

> Then Joshua spoke to the Lord on the day when the Lord delivered the Amorites to the children of Israel, and he said before the eyes of Israel, Sun, stand still over Gibeon; and Moon, in the valley of Ajalon.
>
> And the sun stood still, and the moon stood still, until the people had avenged themselves upon their enemies.

But David knew that the Lord would not deliver the Forty Thieves to them, nor would the Sun stand still on their street, or the Moon stand still over the handball courts in the schoolyard. At half past eight they'd all be there waiting, and he would have to go.

"David?" his father called.

"Yes, Pa, I'm in the bedroom."

"Come to the table," his mother said.

"What is he doing in there?" his father said to his mother in Yiddish.

"I'm doing my Talmud homework for tomorrow," David answered in English as he came into the kitchen.

"How is it in Talmud Torah?" his father asked in Yiddish as David sat down at the table. Since his *bar-mitzvah* his father had begun to talk to him in Yiddish, as if he now suddenly, and overnight, understood the language for the first time. "I saw Rebi Greenberg in synagogue tonight, at Maarev, but he did not have time to talk with me." David said that he was doing all right, and wondered what luck had kept his father from talking with Mr. Greenberg. His mother came to the table with hot borscht, quartered potatoes and sliced and hard-boiled eggs swimming in it, and his father began to eat. There was halibut, dipped in egg and fried brown and tender, a salad of red cabbage, strips of orange carrot, light pink tomatoes and cool green lettuce, and finally blintzes, with the soft cheese inside the thin brown dough. When his mother brought the coffee, his father spoke. "Mr. Rosen told me that his son, Nadie, is a big fighter. He is your friend, no?"

David nodded, swallowing a bite of blintze too quickly, so that his throat hurt, and he could not trust himself to speak.

"I do not want to hear you made yourself cheap fighting in the street like a hooligan," his father said slowly.

"But Pa," David protested, "even in the Bible the Jews fought. I just finished Joshua's battle with the Amorites, where the sun and the moon stood still, and tonight in Talmud Torah, we read about the fall of Jericho."

"That was another time, and another country," his father said, his eyes far away looking. "It was different."

"You must fight sometimes," David insisted, "they won't let you alone."

"*They? They* will always let you alone if you let them alone."

His mother glanced at both of them, and then looked down at the slim gold band of her wedding ring. "It's that your father knows you cannot fight and win," she said quietly. "It is only by not fighting that you win."

"I don't understand. How can you win by not fighting?"

"By being living," his father said. "It is sometimes braver to turn away than to fight and be killed."

"But Pa, if they call you sheeny and dirty Jew, and beat you, you can't just turn away. They think you are a coward and treat you like dirt. And you feel dirty too, inside. They'll only do it more, anyway, more and more until you can't stand it any more."

"Let them speak their filthy words," his mother said, twisting her ring on her finger. "They are dirtied by such words, not you."

"But I am dirtied too if I let them speak so of me."

"But you live," his father said. "Is it necessary to care what they think? Do you want them to pay you honor?"

"Yes, I want them to pay me honor," David said stubbornly. "Why shouldn't they? Am I a dog, to be kicked and stoned, and spat on? I am a man!"

His mother smiled at that, but his father's face remained grave, the lines around his eyes cut deep into the skin, the eyes dark in the hollows and tired. "You are a man perhaps but a young one. You do not understand that this honor is their honor and whether you fight or not, they will kick and stone and spit. And if you fight, they will kill you. Not the first time, maybe, or even the second, but they will kill you sometime."

"Why? Why?"

"Because, my son, their honor is a thing decided with blows and ours is—and yours should also be—an honor which has to do with righteousness."

"If they call us names and beat us then are we not righteous to defend ourselves, to return their—"

"—blows? What does a blow prove, David? That you are right? or that you have a stronger fist?"

His mother began to clear away the dishes, and his father sat quietly, almost sadly, David thought, smoking his little brown cigarettes. He didn't know why the talk had made his father so sad and quiet. His father might be right, but he could not live that way. He could not suffer Banana Nose and Fonzi and the others to think him a coward, nor would he suffer them to abuse him. He would fight for their honor, even if it was only the honor of a fist, and an honor not worth believing in or fighting for. He got up from the table and went into the bedroom. He put on his old leather jacket and his oldest pants. If they fought, he might tear his clothes and it would be better to tear old clothes. His mother would not be so angry then. When he came out of the bedroom, he saw his father staring into a cloud of cigarette smoke that hung about his head and over the whole kitchen table. As David went to the door, his father spoke in English for the first time that evening and said, "Where do you go?"

And David, also speaking in English, replied that he was going out to play. His mother wanted to know if he had homework and when he said he had done it, she warned him to be back before ten o'clock, and then let him go. He closed the door behind him and went down into the street. Outside, the street lamps cast pale yellow spots of light that made the darkness around seem darker. Above, a few scattered grey clouds were like rags of smoke in the sky, and as he walked towards the schoolyard, David remembered how when he was little his mother had told him that the stars were the eyes of God in heaven, always watching you no matter where you were or what you did. Somehow, tonight, the stars seemed very far away and like blind eyes staring down without knowing and without caring about what went on beneath them.

Nadie Rosen and Maxie Jonas were waiting at the schoolyard. They said hello and he asked for Sonny. Maxie smiled and Nadie said he didn't think Sonny would come. David suggested that they climb the fence and wait inside, and Nadie agreed, saying that the Forty Thieves would probably come from their street. As they got to the top of the fence and were about to go down into the schoolyard, Sonny arrived. "Hey, wait for me," he said, in a hoarse whisper. "I'm coming."

"It's about time," Maxie said.

"What're you shivering and whispering for," Nadie said irritably. "Fonzi got your tongue?"

Sonny climbed over the iron spiked fence and joined them. They walked silently toward the middle of the handball courts where there was a small yellow night light, the only light in the whole darkened schoolyard. As they came up to it, Banana Nose stepped into the circle of light and said, "I didn't think you guys was gonna show up. You tree minutes late." David was surprised to find himself calm. Or was it calm that he felt? It was like a dead circle of cold air in his chest and stomach, but he did not feel shaky. "Dyu bring your boys?" Banana Nose asked.

"Three of them," David said, "but this is between you and me and I don't want them mixing in."

"Yuh mean this is a grudge fight?" Banana Nose seemed surprised. "And yuh ain't gonna let my boys have some fun beatin your gang up?"

"No, just you and me. Who you got with you?"

"Fonzi, Sal, and Petey, same as before."

"Never mind the talk," Fonzi interrupted, sticking his head into the light. "Yuh gonna fight or ain't yuh?"

"Butt out, Fonzi," Banana Nose answered. "Don't you worry. We gonna fight." He turned to David. "We fight in the light and they watch, your boys and mine."

"Okay," David said. He stepped into the light and put his hands up, crouching in the way that Mr. Kay, the gym teacher, had taught him. Banana Nose's arm reached out of the circle of light into the darkness behind him. There was a glint and then the arm came back into the light and the hand had a knife in it. Banana Nose pressed the spring and the long blade sprang out with a loud click.

"Say, wait a minute," Nadie burst into the light, horrified, "we didn't come for a knife fight."

"Whattsa matta, Nadie, yella?" Fonzi taunted.

"You want Davie to fight Banana Nose bare handed against a knife?" Nadie asked. "He ain't got no knife." He shook his head at David.

"Naw, we give him an even break," Banana Nose said. "Give him your sticker, Petey." There was a moment of fumbling silence and then Petey slid a long pearl-handled knife along the ground into the circle of yellow light. David looked at it, unable to touch it, and Nadie called for time out. He pulled David out of the light, but David couldn't take his eyes off the knife. "You know how to knife fight?" Nadie whispered in his ear. David tried to answer but his throat was dry and tight, and he couldn't, so he shook his head. "Listen," Nadie advised, "keep your left arm up so if he cuts you, he cuts your arm. That's not so bad." David nodded, and began to move back toward the light, his eyes still on the knife. "Don't forget," Nadie hissed his final counsel. "Test the knife to see if it's sharp."

David moved into the circle of light where Banana Nose was waiting. He stopped, picked up the knife, and touched the spring button. The blade leaped out like a live shining thing. He looked around at Fonzi and Sal and Petey whose faces were ghostlike in the shadows behind Banana Nose, and as he did so, he hefted the knife in his open palm, as he had seen them do in the moving pictures. He tried to keep the choking sense of airlessness in him down, but it had spread until he felt his whole body empty except for a dull booming beat in his hands and chest and head that he suddenly knew for the frightened beating of his heart and blood. He looked straight at Banana Nose and the ghostly faces behind him and the words came out of his mouth without his even knowing what he was going to say. "Till one of us is dead."

"Dead?" Banana Nose's voice squeaked.

"Dead," David repeated in a flat voice, and then he said, "Like this," intending to run the knife edge along his thumb to see if it was sharp. But his shaking hand drew the knife deep into the flesh and the blood welled out of the skin and darkened the brightness of the blade. "Like that," he repeated dully, showing them his hand. All of them looked at the bleeding hand and then Fonzi's voice came out of the dark, high-pitched and screechy, "Madonna, he cut himself!" And then Petey's low, scared, "He gonna kill you, Banana Nose. He crazy brave to cut hisself with that knife. It some sharp knife. I know cause I sharpen it myself."

David lifted his bleeding left hand, palm up, in front of him, crouched, and with the knife in his right hand advanced toward Banana Nose. For a moment, Banana Nose stood staring at him, his face recast from disbelief to terror, when there was the sudden sound of feet running and a shout, "I'm gettin outta here!" that was Fonzi's, and Banana Nose, hearing his friends running away, took one more look at David's hand, his face shifting from hope to despair, before he dropped his knife and ran into the darkness. David stood still crouched, the knife clutched in his wet palm, listening to their running and the sounds of their climbing the fence mingling with the dripping of his blood on the concrete handball courts. It was a moment before anyone spoke. Then Nadie came into the light and said admiringly, "Boy, you got some guts, David. We ain't gonna have no trouble with those guys no more." He bent and picked up Banana Nose's knife. David turned, feeling suddenly shaky in the knees, and handed him the other knife. "Don't you want it?" Nadie asked, surprised. "You sure deserve it."

David said nothing. Only he never wanted to see another knife again. "Give it to Sonny or Maxie, whoever wants it," he said, carefully shaping the words to keep them from trembling out of his shaking insides. They walked back and climbed over the fence back on to their street.

There Sonny stopped them and picked up the bleeding hand, and took a clean white handkerchief from his pocket and tied David's hand up with it. For the first time then David felt the pain of the cut. At David's house they all said goodnight, their eyes fixed on the white handkerchief and the slow spreading stain on it. After they had gone, David sat down on the stoop and looked up at the night sky, breathing deeply until he felt the shaking hollowness quiet and fill inside him. He held his hands out in front of him and looked down at Sonny's red-stained handkerchief, feeling his own blood flow out of his flesh and over his palm beneath it.

Then a sudden brightness mounted in his throat and choked him with happiness. He had won! He had fought the Forty Thieves their own way, with the fist and the knife, with *their* honor, and he had won. He wanted to cry out his victory loud and strong, but his voice came out softly and sobbing so that no one would hear him. He would tell them though, his father and his mother and Rebi Greenberg; he was right and they were wrong. He had won! They wouldn't dare to scold him for his cut hand or punish him for fighting now. Like Joshua in the Bible, he had flourished the knife and the Forty Thieves had fallen down before him.

When he came into the house, his mother and father were in the parlor and he could easily have walked into the bedroom without their seeing him, but instead he went into the parlor and stretched out his bloodied hand. For a moment, his parents sat staring at it, not moving. Then his father got up and took him into the bathroom and his mother followed. His father took Sonny's handkerchief off, washed the hand with cold water, and then put iodine on the cut. David felt the sear all the way inside him and the nausea in the pit of his stomach, but he didn't cry out. He would cry out only his victory, not his pain. "It's deep, but it's clean," his father said, as if to himself, while he carefully bandaged the hand, gently, ever so gently, and taped the gauze over. They stood there, the three of them, looking at the bandaged hand, and then his mother picked up Sonny's bloodied handkerchief and wiped the washbasin clean.

"Why don't they say something?" a voice inside him cried. "Why don't they ask me what happened?" David looked at them, standing over him and looking down at the bandaged hand. They thought he had lost! That was it and why they were saying nothing. They believed they were right and he, David, was wrong.

They went back into the kitchen and sat down at the kitchen table in silence, still looking at the hand, until his father lit a cigarette and suggested that they have some tea and jam, and his mother got up to bring it. Well, he would tell them what happened, about the knife and the blood and Banana Nose in the schoolyard. His bloody hand was not a wound, or a defeat: it was a victory! Sitting there, waiting for his mother to bring the tea, David tried to put the battle into words for them, carefully shaping and memorizing them in his mind, as he sometimes did for Rebi Greenberg with his translations of the Bible, but somehow the words would not stay together and make sense, but kept blurring and being washed over with blood.

David looked at his father's face across the table, serious and remote, and tried to smile, but although he could see that his father was trying to answer with a smile, he couldn't quite manage it. Instead, he reached his big hand over and covered David's white bandaged hand with his own, and blew so much smoke from his quivering nostrils that the table was covered with a little cloud of grey. Then, seeing the pain in his father's face, and the little dancing muscles under the skin, David suddenly knew he hadn't won at all, and it seemed like he had known all along that it was a funny cut with a knife that had fooled and frightened the others. Just like the priests blowing their horns and the walls of Jericho falling down. A fluke, a lucky break. He hadn't beaten anybody, and neither had they. The walls had fallen, just as the Forty Thieves had been chased, by luck, by accident.

Then the memory of Banana Nose and the schoolyard and the circle of light came back to him so he could see the shine of the knives and hear the dripping of his blood on the concrete. No, he reminded himself, not by accident. By luck, but not by accident. He had gone out to fight in the schoolyard and taken the knife in his hands just as the priests had gone out before Jericho and taken the trumpets in theirs.

His mother brought the old tea kettle and put it on the table, its spout steaming. David watched her set out the cups and saucers, and then pour each of them a cup, carefully putting a teaspoonful of prune jelly in first. When she sat down, they stirred the jelly in the cups in unison and David looked at their faces and saw their sad eyes and quiet pursed mouths. He realized then that they too had once gone out to fight, and maybe even won a victory, not the same victory he had won, but one of their own, one that had lasted twice as long as he had lived and more. They'd been trying to tell him about it, trying in their own way to explain how it was, so that he would not have to go out to fight Banana Nose and cut himself to find out. And then, for the first time, he knew their silence for what it was, and he was glad.

He reached for his cup and sipped the tea, but it was too hot and burned his lips and the roof of his mouth. "It's too hot," he said, not thinking.

"What did you expect it to be?" his mother said.

"Put the cup down," his father said quietly. "If you wait, it will soon be cool enough to drink."   —*Winter* 1952-53

MORTON FINEMAN

My Father the Magician

The day I found out Carro was a magician was the day Manuel, his best friend and my mother's best friend too, brought him home. My mother began to scream, "Oh, what happened, what happened? Is he drunk, Manuel? Why do you let him drink?" Manuel who is big and fat and solemn, not jolly the way you expect a fat man to be, he just shook his head, making the fat on his cheeks bounce, and he said, "Not drunk, Sarah. I am afraid he is very sick." "Call a doctor, Manuel," Sarah screamed, but not so loud this time because she was deathly afraid, "call a doctor, Manuel." "I already called the doctor," Manuel said, and to me he said, "You go outside, cowboy, and find something to do in the sunshine."

Sarah let me go into the bedroom to see Carro after the doctor left. He looked like they had covered his face with flour, he was so white, and his eyes so dark and round, and he moved his head like it hurt him all over. "You be very quiet," Sarah said, "and you go out very soon too."

I was quiet; I whispered, "What's wrong with you?"

"The old music box," he said. "You don't have to whisper. It's not my ears," and he smiled and looked at what I was twisting in my hands. "What's that thing?"

"The Mystic Rope," I said. "Dominic Serini gave it to me. It was in the Magic Kit his father bought for him at the Sons of Italy carnival in New Jersey last week."

"Can you make it work, Houdini?" he said. I shook my head. "Well, give it here."

I handed Carro The Mystic Rope and he turned it over in his hands, his pale, long, thin hands with the knuckles sticking out like boils; and his hands were shaking, just a little: but I saw it as he turned over The Mystic Rope; turned it round and round, smiling at the Christmas colors, the red and green, and at the little copper end pieces so it wouldn't unravel. Then he held it by the ends and twirled it, and it went round and round again; this time beneath his chin, gleaming some in the lamplight, and his black eyes were steady on me, shining like the dark moonlight.

"You old snake eyes," I said to him. "What are you going to do besides spin it. I can do that much myself." Behind the imitation cloth window shades that were down all the way the windows were up to let in air that slipped past the sides and made the window shades move like mice in the dark, all those quick, papery noises they make and those little scratchings. Only there was Carro laughing too. But he had never laughed like this before: like the running of mice, scratchy and dry. I had heard lots of noises come from him: cowboy laughter and Indian laughter, lion roaring and tiger growling laughter when he told me about gold prospecting in Mexico and Indian fighting in old Kentuck and big game hunting in deepest Africa, making up every single fact: but I had never heard the running of mice kind of laughter coming from him.

"You old snake eyes," I said.

He called me by my favorite Indian name, "You, Little Johnny One Crow. What's the smoke signal say?"

"It says you can't do anything with The Mystic Rope."

So he smiled and knotted The Mystic Rope and passed one hand over the knot, waving the fingers like skinny bird wings. And he winked at me; this time it was not the running of mice sound in his throat, but cowboy laughter, Indian laughter, tiger growling and lion roaring kind of laughter; except that it was all in his eyes, gleaming like dark rain drops. Then he dangled The Mystic Rope and it was smooth and wiggling like a garden snake. Then he crumpled it together in both hands saying, "Amo, amas, amat, amabo, amabis, amabit." And when I asked, "What's all that?" he said, "An old Latin prayer of faith to a better man than I am, Gunga Din, for the present and future, and damn the imperfect though it's always with us and is our present and our future, sure as shooting." Then he snapped The Mystic Rope and it was full of loops and bows. He poked his fingers through the loops and bows and waggled them until I laughed. He said, "I'll bet you and Dominic and all the Sons of Italy can't do that." "Show me," I said. "Can't," he said, "it's against the sacred oath of Merlin." "Please show me," I said again. "Why even Dominic can't do that and he's got a whole book of directions with pictures." And he said, "I'll put you in the castle tower where the bats will drive you loony. Right now I see a smoke signal that says you better leave this wigwam, you pesky paleface." He dropped The Mystic Rope and looked tired, like he hadn't slept for days and days.

"Now I told you not to stay long," Sarah cried and pulled me out of the bedroom. "You just never listen to me; nobody in this house listens to me; and that's why there's always trouble and worry and heartache. You go downstairs. I must see how your father is."

Manuel was in the kitchen drinking beer. He looked at me with his bishop's face. "Hello, you wild western cowboy," he said, "you been drinking your Ovaltine and eating your Ralston like all straight shooters, or you just been looping the loop?"

"Where did you get that funny face, you circus fat man," I yelled, and then gasped with stinging hurt, for there was Sarah tall and redfaced over me while I dodged, beating me with her hand the way she did blankets on the line and yelling, "Oh you! you! Impudent, fresh little brat. Talking so fresh and sassy to Manuel! Go, that's right. Go outside and be fresh somewhere else for a change!"

But I didn't; I stayed. I listened to them talking and then my heart felt pinched with a hurt that was worse than Sarah's flailing hand. She was not very strong; just a plump, round woman, so tall because I was so small, with more tears than anybody ever dreamed there could be, and a middle-aged face all cracked and saggy and pouched. But even if she was very strong with muscles big as the muscles of Hercules holding the world on the cover of my geography book in Miss Mishler's class—even that strong, she would not hurt me as much as this pinching of my heart while I listened, standing there in the hall.

There was Manuel's voice like his bishop's face, all slow and heavy, saying, "We will call in a specialist, Sarah; Dr. Katz is not the end of all medical knowledge in this world. I already told him: Dr. Katz get me the biggest specialist there is. I want the best, absolutely the finest, first class specialist in this line."

"Manuel, Manuel," and Sarah's voice was like a gray winter morning, "all this happens because he is against life. He doesn't want to live the way people live."

"For life, Sarah. All of us against life," Manuel said. "He is the only man I know who is for life.

"Other people get middle aged and settle down. They worry about money in the bank and paying a mortgage and educating their children. But Carro just gets middle aged and looks at me when he is drunk and says, 'What happened to the girl who looked beautiful in silver tights in my mind's eye?' "

Sarah said: "I remember my mother said, 'All right, so he is romantic with his fine clothes and manners and his talk about Europe, but what does he do for a living?' 'He's a magician,' I said. 'Such a man will never make a living,' my mother said. I didn't listen to her; I remember how he said, 'You would look beautiful in silver tights on the stage with me, Sarah' and the hundreds of people in Moose Hall clapping for him and how he stood there holding his high hat and bowing. I didn't listen to good advice. No, I had to think: there isn't a girl in Audubon, New Jersey who ever had a man say a thing like that to her. And when my mother said, 'Well, at least is he a good magician who can make some kind of living?' I said, 'In my eyes he is the greatest magician in the world; he can do anything.' 'Well, I don't like this whole idea,' she said, and I should have listened to her. That's what I should have done, Manuel."

The specialist came with Dr. Katz the next day and said Carro had to go to the hospital. Sarah would not let me go with them in the ambulance; she made me stay with Oliver, who works in Manuel's taproom and plays the accordion for the customers. Oliver gave me shrimp out of the big icebox and let me drink root beer from the bottle. He sat near the electric fan and played all the songs on the accordion I could name.

"Oliver," I said, "you are the best accordion player on land and sea and you are my best older friend. But I am not in the mood for music right now."

"You stop feeling the miseries," Oliver said. "They got specialists in that hospital on Broad Street to fix up Carro."

"Dominic Serini tells me his father was never sick once," I said.

"You just got the deep summer pains in your bones."

"That is more of your tomfoolery," I said, "and that's what my teacher, Miss Mishler, would say if she ever heard you talk like that."

"Never mind your teacher. You're just finding out things move along and change and don't even do so for the better, except once in a long, long while," Oliver said. "When that starts, boy, it's just the deep summer pains. They just got to come and stay until they go."

"Maybe Dominic's father never got sick enough to be put in a hospital, but he is not a magician either, and when I see Dominic I am going to tell him, you can bet your last bottle of beer, Oliver."

Oliver lifted his head and laughed; it was shaped like a watermelon, shiny blue black, like the night after it rains and the moon comes out. Then he put his accordion up against his chest and began to play, "Here We Sit Like Birds in the Wilderness," and said "Now you start to sing." Both of us sang and tapped our feet. But Oliver had to stop and say, "Come on, boy, get into the spirit here."

All of a sudden I had to run out. I had to run away from Oliver;

from everybody. Oliver yelled for me to come back, but I ran all the way home, and I had the feeling the whole world was chasing me, although not a single person even noticed me because they were all too busy keeping cool in the shade. Except, maybe they did think: Now who is that crazy boy running in the sun? When I stopped running my belly hurt and my chest jerked and I felt dizzy, so I sat on the steps because the house was locked and Sarah had not come home from the hospital. Then I saw Dominic Serini come out of his house across the street, eating a cantaloupe with a wooden ice cream spoon.

He walked over to me and said, "Hey, what the hell are you breathing so hard for? Don't you know it's hot as Death Valley around here today?"

"Dominic, I got the deep summer pains."

"You always got something special," Dominic said. "You are the goddamnest showoff in the world. Just because they took your father to the hospital, you got to show off."

"Now I'll tell you something," I said. "Since you got such a big mouth, I'll shut it once and for all."

"It'll have to be pretty good," Dominic said, chewing a mouthful of cantaloupe.

"My father's a magician," I said.

"That ain't the first lie you ever told," Dominic said. He opened his mouth. "You see, it's still open and pretty damn big too."

"It'll close when you find out I'm telling the truth," I said. "You won't be such a hot shot then. You wait'll Carro gets out of the hospital. You just wait."

"You're trying to tell me something when I already know the answer," Dominic said. "Your father works for the La Bella Cigar Company on Arch Street right here in the city of Philadelphia, P.A., and besides he doesn't make one half as much money as my father makes, you dumb coot," Dominic cried, tossing the cantaloupe skin at me and running back into his house.

That night it was very hot, even hotter than the daytime, and queer to be in the house just with Sarah as I lay in bed, awake, listening to the trolley cars go past and thinking about Carro; kicking away the sheets and turning to find a cool spot on the bed. When I fell asleep I dreamed Carro was sawing me in half, and the half of me that had the head was begging him to put me together again, and he was crying and telling me he did not remember how to do it; while Manuel just stood there and said, "You see, I told you all the magicians are gone from this world," and Dominic Serini laughed at me, his mouth very wide, saying when he stopped laughing, "Now you are *two* of the biggest liars in the world," and Oliver patted me on the head and told me I had the deep summer pains now real bad but they would go away. Then Sarah saw what happened and she began to scream and shake and push everybody away from me and I said to her, "I must be bleeding terribly bad, like an oil well." Then Carro tried to put his arm around Sarah and he said, "It was supposed to be an illusion; that's all, Sarah; I never meant this to happen." And I said, "What are you talking about an illusion for when I am bleeding so terribly bad? Stop your tomfoolery this instant," I said just like Miss Mishler would, "and put me back together." Then Sarah began to scream and scream. But it was not Sarah; I was screaming and she was standing over me, asking me what was the matter, was I having a nightmare?

"I can't sleep now," I said, looking at Sarah standing there in a long white cotton nightgown.

"You must go to bed," she said, her voice hot and tired, like a dog with his tongue hanging out. But I kept on looking at her and she said, "What's the matter now?" Sweat was coming down her face like big tears.

"I have got the feeling I do not have a father or a mother, or even a name so anybody will know who I am," I said. "I feel all locked up in an empty house some place."

"Oh my God," she said, "now who teaches you such language and gives you such crazy ideas anyway? All right, go downstairs and drink a glass of milk."

"Don't you want to know why I am the way I am?" I said.

"Please don't upset your mother," she said. "A good boy should always be kind to his mother."

"You just remember that a mother should always be kind to her son too," I yelled. "I'm going to stay awake and think about Carro."

I did. I lay down on the floor because it was not so hot there and I thought about him, squinting at the Boy Scouts of America calendar on the wall. It said July. All my calendars said July. Dominic Serini and I collected calendars. I only had fourteen, all of them pinned on the walls, but Dominic had twenty, and they all said July: July, in big black letters. You just wait, Dominic Serini, I said to myself after a while, you just wait until all those calendars name the day Carro comes out of the hospital, and I'll show you who's a magician around here.

But the calendars had to say September before he came home and I stopped feeling that people always looked at me and thought: There is the boy whose poor father, the cigar maker (because they didn't know he was a magician) is in the hospital, now isn't that a shame?

Manuel came to see Sarah early in the morning and he said to me,

"How would you like to go to a party, cowboy? The biggest party in Philadelphia."

"You mean for Carro?" I said.

And all day Manuel kept bringing things into the Greek's house next door because that's where the surprise party was going to be. The Greek's house was bigger than our house and very convenient for a surprise party, Manuel said.

The Greek kept laughing and saying how honored he was to have the party in his house for his dear friend Carro; and the Greek's wife said, "It is going to be a very elegant party because I am going to arrange the table just the way the picture showed this month in the Ladies' Home Journal." The Greek laughed and said, "That wife of mine is a regular book of etiquette when it comes to parties." The Greek's wife was cooking and baking, and Sarah was helping and the Greek was running in and out and asking questions and calling everybody up on the telephone. And everybody was telling me to stay away from the big, white cake baked special for the party with the chocolate words *Welcome Home* on it and the potato chips, the candy, the pretzel sticks, the bridge mixture, all laid out on the table in cut glass bowls and silver trays; telling me not to touch a thing, until I shouted, "Well, Jesuschrist almighty, what can I do? You might think he wasn't my own father the way you act."

"Now now now," the Greek's wife said, while Sarah said, "Oh I'll wash your mouth with soap and water and not let you come to the party if you talk like that again," and outside Dominic Serini was whistling for me loud and hard between his teeth and hollering when he stopped whistling, "Hey, what's going on in there anyway? Stop acting like I'm a stranger here."

"You go outside to your friend," Sarah said.

"I'm supposed to go to the hospital with Manuel and you."

"I'll call you when it's time," Manuel said.

"If you go without me," I said, "I'll hate you till the day I die, and if you die first I'll laugh at your funeral."

Manuel shook his bishop's face. "My my," he said.

I went out to Dominic with two handfuls of the bridge mixture. "Carro is coming out of the hospital today and we're getting ready to have a party," I said.

"Am I invited to come?" Dominic said. He began to eat some of the bridge mixture I gave him, looking at me. "If we had a party, I'd let you come, and you know that goddamn well as anything in this world."

"The only reason I'm letting you come, Dominic Serini, is so you'll find out my father is a magician," I said. "Because today I'm going to prove it sure as God made little green apples."

Then the Greek's wife called me and said to come back into the house and wash my face and hands because we were going to the hospital soon as the taxi came. I left Dominic standing on the pavement chewing the bridge mixture like a cow. "Please don't give me orders," I said to the Greek's wife, "because today I feel very important."

Carro was so thin; thin as a telephone pole that I didn't believe it after I looked at him good; after I stopped running down the hall of that hospital yelling, "You old snake eyes, you old snake eyes," while doctors and nurses wondered what in the world was going on in their hospital. "What's the matter, didn't those specialists give you anything to eat?" I said.

"Stop that," Sarah said. "Stop that kind of talk here."

"I'll bet they never had a magician in this hospital before," I said. Then I remembered I was going to be mad at him for not telling me all these years about that, so I said, "You never told me and I am your own son, your own flesh and blood too."

"I was going to send you a big smoke signal," Carro said.

"You old snake eyes," I said, much more happy than I was mad; especially when I thought how Dominic Serini's eyes were going to pop out of his dumb head when Carro did tricks when I asked him at the party.

The first thing Dominic said to me at the party was, "All right, now you put your proof where your mouth is."

"What's your hurry? You going to a fire?" I said.

The Greek's house was full of people; even Dominic said if they kept coming we would need a can opener pretty soon. Oliver was playing the accordion and people were laughing and talking and dancing and going up to Carro who sat very straight and smiling in the biggest chair like a king on a throne, saying hello to everybody and joking about all his operations and the pretty nurses and the specialists. And Sarah, one minute she was crying, the next laughing; all the time keeping her hand on Carro's shoulder. And the Greek, he was running up to everybody asking them if they had enough wine, enough beer, did they like the music, did they have a special number they wanted Oliver to play, and wasn't the weather ideal for a surprise party? Everywhere you looked you saw the Greek. I looked at Carro and saw Sarah take away a glass of wine and him take it back, smiling at her. "But you are not supposed to drink any more," she said.

"I'm not supposed to drink, or smoke, or get excited, or run up steps, or roll cigars for the La Bella Cigar Company, or breathe too fast, or bend down, or straighten up, or do anything at all," he said, and just for a second he wasn't smiling at Sarah. "I am just supposed to sit still until I die," he said.

"Please, Carro," Sarah said. "Please please please. Is it my fault? I'm only telling you what the doctors told you." She walked away from Carro.

"Well, when are you going to ask him?" Dominic said.

"Maybe I won't even ask him. Just because you don't believe me; me your old friend who never told you a lie yet," I said.

"Our friendship is ended," Dominic said. "And you are a fifty-seven variety liar."

I just laughed because I was still feeling very important and Dominic knew it and that's what made him so mad at me. He ran one finger across his throat like a knife and made a face. Then he talked to his mother and father. They looked at me and Carro, and they laughed, and that made me mad because I knew what he was telling them. So I walked up to Carro while Mr. and Mrs. Serini laughed very hard and the Greek asked them what was so funny and Mr. Serini said this you got to hear to believe because this is the best thing I have ever heard in my whole life.

"Getting all the smoke signals?" Carro said.

"The time has come," I said.

"That's a fact," he said.

Manuel, who was sitting next to Carro, looked at me. "What's all this, hombre?" he asked, winking at Carro and Carro at him as he poured more wine.

"You go loop the loop," I said. "I'm talking to my father here."

Carro put down his glass of wine and raised his hands until they were on my shoulders and I stood between his long legs. "What's the old smoke signal?" he said in a very soft voice.

"I told Dominic Serini you are a magician and he is sitting over there laughing at me and you, and now you have got to show him that you are a magician. Because if you don't, I will be the biggest liar in the city of Philadelphia, and especially on Pine Street. People will say, That boy says his father is a magician, but we know he works for the La Bella Cigar Company on Arch Street when he's not sick."

"We can't have that," Carro said. "They can't make a liar out of Little Johnny One Crow." His voice was funny; it was still soft, but like a sad whisper too, talking to me as if we were all alone at night not in a crowded room.

"Maybe you better not get that idea," Manuel said to him and Manuel didn't sound so drunk all of a sudden.

"I got it," Carro said. "It's right here."

"Sarah will be upset," Manuel said. "You know that."

Carro stood up. "Tell her not to watch me, Manuel. Tell her this is for Johnny One Crow here." He pushed his fingers through my hair and I could feel them shaking. "You just keep those smoke signals going," he said. "I'll be back in a couple of shakes."

Worry was hanging on Manuel's face like a curtain as Carro went out. "Where is your mother?" he asked me. "I've got to talk to her."

"In the kitchen helping the Greek's wife. What's the matter with you anyway? You look like you been looping the loop too much." Manuel rubbed my head too and shook his bishop's face.

I went past Dominic and said, "I guess you are going to get your hash settled pretty soon," and then I sat down beside Oliver who was playing "Billy Boy" on the accordion. I stamped my foot and sang as loud as I could.

"Oliver, play 'Banjo on My Knee,'" the Greek hollered.

"He is silly drunk," I said to Oliver.

"It's the proper occasion," Oliver said.

Instead of Carro coming in through the front door, I saw Sarah, and she was blazing mad. She grabbed me by the arm and hissed in my ear like a snake, "You come home with me," and she would not say another word until we were in our house, although I kept saying, "What's going on here anyway?"

Manuel was in our living room, and Carro was sitting on the sofa in a top hat like the undertaker always wears in a cowboy picture and a black suit with a coat that had long tails. He was drinking whiskey, pouring it into a big kitchen glass and drinking it like water when you are very thirsty on a hot day.

Manuel said to him, "At least put away the whiskey. Do you want to fight the whiskey too?"

"What's the matter? What's the matter?" I yelled.

Carro put his hands on my lips; they tasted sweaty and hot. Sarah was holding her face in her hands and crying. "We are going back to the party," Carro said to me. "Come on, Sarah . . . Manuel?"

"No," Sarah said. "You go. Make a fool out of yourself so I can't hold up my face in the neighborhood any more."

"Explain to the boy that you are no longer a magician," Manuel said. "Sarah is right."

"A magician," Sarah screamed. "A magician! He could never make a card disappear without getting drunk first. Go ahead. If you are such a magician, why don't you wave your hands and make us rich like Mr. and Mrs. Serini? Why don't you make the money for the hospital bills come out of your sleeve, magician? Pull the rent out of your top hat? Go ahead, my magician! Ask me what happened to the girl in silver tights in your mind's eye and I will slap your face. I will slap you right into your grave where you belong."

Carro didn't say anything to Sarah. He took my hand. "Ready for the big performance?" he said to me.

"I want you to do all the tricks you know," I said when we were outside. My voice was shaking like his hand in mine.

"Not tricks," he said to me. "A magician creates beauty."

Manuel came out and called Carro. "At least don't try the hard ones," he said. "Don't try the one with the sword."

"The complete performance," Carro said. He smiled and rubbed my head, and a long streamer of ribbon came out of my ear. "Well Jesus Christ almighty," I shouted. "How in the world did you ever do that? Oh, that Dominic Serini is going to suffer the bells of hell when he sees you!"

Carro laughed. "Look," he said. I looked and the ribbon was gone. "Maybe you are not as rich as Dominic Serini's father," I said, "but you are certainly smarter."

"Carro," Manuel said, "forget about the sword tonight."

The Greek saw us as soon as we came in. "Hey," he cried, "but what is this? *What is this?* You are dressed for a wedding. Everybody, everybody, look at Carro; just look at him!" Carro smiled and told him, and I stood up straight with my chest out, holding Carro's hand so there would be no mistake who was his son and I looked at Dominic Serini. His mouth was wide open at the sight of Carro. The Greek was laughing so hard he could hardly talk. "Now listen everybody," he said. "Carro is going to entertain the guests." And his wife said, "My oh my, we have a regular floor show. Now please, ladies and gentlemen and children, all sit down and let us see what Carro is going to do. Oliver, play the overture the way they do in a theater." She clapped her hands very loud until everybody was quiet.

Carro stood in the wide doorway between the living room and dining room. It was like a small stage. Everybody laughed and clapped as he bowed and I clapped and laughed louder than anybody while Carro said, "Now dear ladies, dear gentlemen, all my friends. Whatever you wish for can be found. First it is in the mind, then in the eye, then it is large and beautiful in the heart, the place of all illusion and truth."

"He sounds much better than Mr. Cochrane, the principal of my school," I said to Manuel. "That's the Thomas Jefferson Public School in case you didn't know."

"I know," Manuel said, watching Carro.

"Hey you, Dominic Serini," I yelled, "what do you think now?"

"Little man," Carro said, grinning at me and raising his hands. They were so beautiful, they were like birds flying slowly in the air. "Little man there, are you trying to be the magician around here?"

"You cannot be the magician," the Greek cried, rushing up and grabbing me and swinging me around. He was all garlicky, smelling of onions, green peppers, wine, cigars, and sweat. He laughed and laughed as hard as I did. "Only Carro is the magician," he said.

"What do you wish for?" Carro said. His hands were moving in the empty air and his eyes were looking up. There was silk ribbon floating from the ceiling and Carro kept pulling more and more of it down. As he kept pulling it, it kept disappearing, and where the ribbon went colored balls were dancing in the air and a tambourine was playing.

"Look," I cried, "look at the roses growing in the air!"

But there were daggers too with jewels on the handle, and they were flying back and forth in front of Carro, one second in front of him, the next gone. Carro's hands were moving; slowly like clouds on a hot day, making shapes out of the air, sending up cards, golden plates, flags. Then they went faster and faster and faster and for a minute nothing was in front of him in the air, then everything was again: daggers, colored balls, golden plates, ribbons, cards, roses.

All of a sudden Carro stopped and everybody waited. He raised his hands. His face was shining with sweat, but he looked like the tallest man in the world standing there with his eyes big and round and dark, and looking right at me now, his mouth tight together, his legs shivering, until I thought, He looks like he doesn't even recognize me.

"Oh my, oh my, Holy Mother of God," the Greek shouted. "Look at the sword!"

It was the biggest sword I had ever seen, with a blade wide as my arm and a handle like solid gold and a big red stone on top of the handle like something full of blood ready to burst open.

"Where did the sword come from?" I said.

The sword was spinning in the air. Carro's hands were not even near it. But there it was, spinning round and round slowly over his head, the point down and the handle like a bright golden star under the light. I watched the sword come closer and closer to him. Then he waved his hands and stepped back. But the sword kept turning. Then Carro seemed to get taller and taller and his face got ugly with twisted lines and the wild look in his eyes. His hands curved out like claws to the sword, to grab it and start swinging it. But he didn't; he just stood there, watching it turn and move towards his hands, over them and toward his body, straight at his white shirt, his heart, going round and round. Now Carro did not even move his hands or his lips. He stood like a statue of sweating wood, his arms out like sticks, his head back, and the sword went through him. I saw it go through him. Everybody saw it. But the sword was not there.

The Greek rushed up to him, wiping his face with a handkerchief. "How did you do it? Holy Mother of God, I will never see a thing like that again in this world."

I wanted to move and look at Carro. Wasn't he my father, the magician? But I couldn't. He came to me and picked me up. His arms were shaking like leaves and they felt cold as ice around me. I was shivering from head to foot and I couldn't stop.

"Why did you try to kill yourself?" I said.

He cried and hugged me. But I could not look at him.

—Winter 1949-50

HENRY STEINER

Rice

I<small>T WAS</small> a day that should have started softly, mounting into noon and afternoon, and then sloping away into the smoky autumn evening. Instead it was bright and hard like the preceding spring when the rice was green and the bitter Korean winter of 1946-47 just past.

In the jeep, Captain Frazer turned around to Mr. Song and said, "It's just like spring."

Mr. Song, sitting in the back seat, smiled diffidently and answered, "Yes."

Frazer waited. When Mr. Song remained silent, Frazer looked at Sergeant Biancoli who, saying nothing, drove with his eyes fixed on the road. On his face was an expression of brooding discontent, and Frazer stared at him curiously, indifferently, as he might have inspected an animal in a zoo.

He turned again to Mr. Song and asked, "You came down from Seoul yesterday?"

Mr. Song said "Yes" again and smiled again, but the smile was jerked out of existence by a violent shock. He clawed desperately for a handhold as he went up off the seat with his arms outstretched like wings and almost fell between the two Americans in the front seats.

Sergeant Biancoli muttered, "Hang on, for Chrissakes."

Mr. Song's hat had fallen off. As he tried to regain his seat, he stepped on the brim and ground the floor dirt into the soft felt. Picking it up and brushing at it ineffectually he placed it askew on his head and caught hold of the seat back just in time to prevent another flight.

"This is your first job with the Americans, isn't it?" Frazer asked.

"No," Mr. Song answered. "When I was a boy I interpreted for an American missionary." He did not tell them that the present job was his last defense against gradual starvation, nor that he had invested all his remaining funds in what he thought were suitable clothes for the new work. He bounced again and felt a sharp edge cut into one of the new shoes where it was tucked under the Captain's seat. Pulling it out with a grimace, he looked sadly at the long scratch on the toe and the polish covered with dust.

"Well, this is a tough one to start you out on," Frazer said seriously. "God knows, rice collection is always a headache, but the old man we're going to see this morning is a hard customer. Did you hear about it in the village last night?"

"No, I did not," Mr. Song murmured. He had come in on the bus with a charcoal burner on the back and all the windows broken, with his paper suitcase in his hand, with his new suit and new shoes and new hat. He had come all the way from Seoul, away from the University and the old life, broken now like the bridges on the road where the bus had to go down in the dry stream bed and waddle up the other side with everyone pushing and the chickens squawking, and Mr. Song still sitting inside looking dignified as befitted a scholar and University professor.

When he had met Frazer, Mr. Song had spread out his ceremonial manners in front of him like an ancient and fragile tapestry. And it had seemed that Frazer had not even known what Mr. Song was doing. Perhaps the formal words sounded silly in English, but Mr. Underwood, the missionary, would have bowed and said them in return. Of course, Mr. Song had reflected, it was too much to expect that all Americans would be like old Mr. Underwood.

After the brief, impersonal instructions, Mr. Song had found an inexpensive hotel. There in a narrow, cold little room with sliding paper doors and no furniture except the sleeping mat, he had spent the night. His sleep was troubled by dreams of the old life at the University with the new young students, and then somehow of childhood.

Frazer said, "You'll have to find out those things. It's up to you to get the information on what's going on in these places. The old man we're going to see this morning—his name is Han—has hidden his rice crop. Every farmer does that, of course, but not even your police could find out where it is. He wouldn't tell them."

Frazer waited a moment. Then he sighed and said, "I suppose you know it's not usual for Koreans to refuse their police anything."

He waited again, but another bump came and Mr. Song's hat fell off for the second time.

"Well, old Han wouldn't tell them," Frazer continued, "and they didn't do anything but threaten him. I think they must be afraid to touch him. He's the head of a clan. There's also the effect of those riots at Kwanju a few weeks ago over the farmers your police tortured. I suppose you heard about that up in Seoul."

Mr. Song nodded, but at the same time he thought, *They are not my police.*

He had heard a little about it. Some students had held a meeting in protest over the police atrocities against the farmers, but the students were so few. All of them put together were only a fraction of the body that had once attended. No one had any money any more, or clothes, or time to go to the University and listen to the quiet voice of Mr. Song explaining the subjunctive in the English language, and how it might be used to translate Li Po. Everyone spent his hours in attempting to sell what he had gathered over a lifetime, and watching the treasures disappear like winter snow and the rice they bought disappear also. Suddenly Mr. Song thought that everything was disappearing, that even he might —especially he might—disappear.

"Well, I'm glad to hear you've heard of something," Frazer said sarcastically.

Mr. Song kept his face expressionless, except for the discomfort which he was not able to conceal.

Frazer spoke over his shoulder. "The old man has got to sell us the rice at the legal price: one hundred and seventy-five won—providing he'll tell us where it is."

Mr. Song said, "One hundred and seventy-five won." He knew that in Seoul the retail price was now almost one thousand won, except in the government sales where the amount one could purchase was rationed, but the price was only one-fifth as much. "Mr. Han will not want to sell," he said.

"You can bet he won't want to sell," Frazer said wryly. "None of them want to sell at the legal price."

Mr. Song's head bounced up and down in what began as a nod.

"I want to be sure, Mr. Song, you understand the necessity for what we're doing so you'll be able to speak convincingly to Mr. Han. You know what would happen in the city if the government didn't buy and sell at a price people can pay?"

"The city people would starve to death," Mr. Song said like a child reciting a lesson.

"That's right," Frazer continued gravely. "They would starve. But many farmers don't care and don't want to know. I've seen violence before during rice collection."

"I understand," Mr. Song said. "I agree that it is necessary to have rice at a low price."

"You clearly understand there may be trouble? Someone may get hurt? I tell you so you'll be warned."

"I understand," Mr. Song said thinking, *This is a difficult service he performs. He is very serious.*

"I hope you do. I certainly hope you do." Frazer stared at Mr. Song's eyes until Mr. Song looked away in embarrassment.

They stopped in front of the house and the truck with the laborers pulled up behind them. While waiting for the dust to pass away they looked at the four pillars of the house and the Chinese characters written on them, all the white-clothed men lounging on the porch who smoked and watched them. Somewhere inside a child began to cry and they listened to that until it was cut off in mid-breath. It left them hanging there in what was now like silence. Gradually it was filled with bird sounds and the wind-rustle in the trees. All of them waited in the little draw off the river like a hostile audience watching an empty stage.

"Well, let's get going," Frazer said and got out. Mr. Song followed him, and finally Biancoli pulled himself abruptly out of the jeep and leaned on the hood on the side away from the house.

"Find out who Han is, Mr. Song, and let's talk to him and get out of here," Frazer said, suddenly impatient.

Mr. Song approached the porch, feeling the eyes on his hat and suit and shoes, wishing that he too wore the traditional white. It occurred to him that this was all foolishness: the ominous atmosphere, and the hostility between the Koreans and the collection party so strong that it was like a bridge under his feet. *I should be back in my chambers translating, or in the classroom teaching*, he thought angrily. But he kept on walking until he was close in front of the porch. After the preliminary words of politeness—Seoul politeness, Capital politeness—he asked for Mr. Han.

An old man rose, and without speaking to Mr. Song, descended with dignity from the porch, walked past him and stopped in front of Frazer. Mr. Song bowed his head at the insult and turned back to stand behind Frazer.

"Tell him we'll give him the legal price of one hundred and seventy-five won for his rice," Frazer said curtly.

Before Mr. Song could say a word, the old man shook his head.

"Wait until you hear the question before you answer it," Frazer said clearly into the old man's unchanging face and unwavering eyes. Mr. Song told him the legal price.

The old man still did not look at him.

"Tell him he must sell to us at that price. Tell him we must fill our quotas," Frazer insisted.

The old man shook his head again.

"Tell him he's got to listen to the question before he answers it," Frazer added patiently.

"You must sell to the government, Mr. Han," Mr. Song said quietly in Korean. "That is the law."

Abruptly the old man recognized Mr. Song's existence. He spoke in a high, rapid voice and in the dialect of the region. "I do not have to sell to anyone. It is my rice, from my land. I will ask what I please for it. The price you offer is far too low."

"Well, what's he say, Mr. Song?" Frazer asked.

"He says he will not sell."

"Tell him if he doesn't sell, we'll confiscate the rice."

Mr. Song said placatingly in Korean, "The people in the cities are starving. They cannot pay the high prices on the open market. That is why the government sets this low price and makes out a quota."

"The government of thieves! Let those in the cities come back to the land if they wish to eat." Mr. Han's eyes, the color of yellow river-water, became bright and wet with emotion. "Let them depend on the rain as I do and starve when it does not come. Let the river sweep away all they have. For years I have worked the land for the Japanese and saw them take my rice away. Now I have the land and the rice. The government wants to take it away again. It is the same as the Japanese."

"What does he say?" Frazer asked.

"One moment please, Captain Frazer." And then in Korean to the old man, "But this is not for the Japanese. This is for your own people. The Americans are helping us."

"Yes, I know. They will sell the rice to the robbers for five times what they give me. Then the robbers will sell it to the people for ten times. What do these foreigners know!" The speech came shooting out of the old man's mouth.

"You are right," Mr. Song said, "some of the rice may go to thieves, there to be sold again, but is it no comfort to know that you are behaving justly, that you are helping others who would starve without you? At least you will gain merit in the eyes of God no matter what sins others may commit."

The old man ignored him again.

Mr. Song turned to Frazer and said, "He says no."

"You mean you talked that much and all he said was no? You interpreters are all alike. Now. Tell him if he doesn't tell us where it is, we'll send the military police and take him to jail. Not Koreans this time—American police."

When Mr. Song had translated that, the old man said earnestly, almost despairingly, "What can a man do?" And then with force, "Tell him he will never find it. I did not tell the police. I will not tell him. Let him know I will let it rot where it is rather than tell him."

Mr. Song said, "He will not sell. This man is very angry. He feels he is being treated unjustly. I think he will fight soon."

On the porch a young man with a thin face rose to his feet.

"Let him fight," Frazer said. "Maybe he can beat the Korean police and the American Army all by himself. Biancoli!" Biancoli straightened up. "Search the house."

Biancoli said, "Yessir," and unbuttoned the holster flap of his .45. He began to walk toward the porch, toward the seated men, with the sun glinting on the insignia pinned to his fatigue cap.

"Do not enter my house!" the old man shouted at his back. "You have no right to enter my house!"

Mr. Song said, "He asks that you not enter his house."

Captain Frazer said nothing.

Mr. Song looked at him in surprise. "He asks that you not enter his house," Mr. Song repeated.

Frazer shook his head disgustedly. "I have no choice," he said slowly. "We've got to fill our quota. To do that we've got to find Mr. Han's rice, and we'll search since he won't tell us where it is. Try and explain that to him."

Mr. Song began, "Captain Frazer says—"

The old man shouted, "Do not enter my house." He looked once at Frazer's face and then, with his straw sandals scuffing the dust, he ran behind the house.

All the men on the porch were standing now. A murmur rose from them when Mr. Han ran. Biancoli hesitated.

For a moment Mr. Song thought the old man had hidden his face from the indignity about to come to his name. He gasped when the old man returned running with the scythe in his hand, yet for a bright instant Mr. Song was filled with the thought that something was going to happen and he would watch it.

The young man on the porch jumped down. With a shout he ran to intercept Han.

While Biancoli fumbled for his gun, the old man, eyes glaring, leaning forward with the scythe clenched in his two hands, dust spurting from his feet, raced toward him.

Biancoli clawed the gun from its holster with rigid muscles and fear filling his face. From the house, a woman's voice cried out.

Biancoli got the gun out, pulled the hammer back, and fired when the old man was almost on top of him, the scythe upraised.

The sound was loud. For an instant afterward, even before it echoed up the valley, all became suspended: expressions, voices, wind, Biancoli with the pistol thrust out from his hip like a pointing finger, and the old man caught in mid-stride, eyes still glaring, scythe still upraised but without life, like a statue.

Then the instant collapsed. The old man's leading leg crumbled under him. He fell at Biancoli's feet, the scythe jabbing the dust and then it too falling over, soundlessly.

Biancoli swung around a little to face the young man running toward him, and Frazer yelled, "Don't shoot!"

The young man went down on his knees next to Mr. Han and began to turn him over. From the house came flying white skirts, swift rubber sandals and an old woman's face, contorted, tears already streaming from the eyes, mouth open. The white-clothed men tumbled off the porch and the laborers off the truck.

The son turned the old man on his back while Biancoli looked down on them, the pistol held limply on the end of his hanging arm.

Frazer came up and bent over the old man. Looking up, he grated, "Did you have to shoot him in the chest?"

"I almost didn't make it at all, Captain," Biancoli's voice sounded full, as if he were about to weep. His face was mask-like with surprise, sorrow, and bewilderment.

The woman was on her knees beside the old man, her hands covering her face as she rocked back and forth.

To Mr. Song, bending over, staring into the old man's face, it was terrifying to see the eyes open and look into his, and the mouth open and the words breathe out, "Yu Bakka!" and then the eyes close again and the bearded mouth remain open with its yellow teeth.

Mr. Song looked at it for a moment before he realized that it was dead. Then he rose and turned to the son, who had also stood up, with the words of sorrow and regret on his lips. Before he could speak, the young face with its eyes glaring was thrust close against his to shout deafeningly, "Ka! Get out! Ka!" He pulled back shocked, and wiped his mouth with his hand.

The son turned to the laborers in their baggy army fatigues and shouted in each of their faces, "Ka! Ka! Ka!" They turned, shamefaced, and went back to the truck.

Before the son could reach him, Frazer returned to the jeep and yelled back, "Let's get out of here," with a slight waver in his voice.

Mr. Song, who had been standing, staring stunned with the back of his hand still to his face, turned and almost ran to the jeep, and Biancoli, with the old expression of brooding inwardness wiped away, came slowly around to the driver's side.

"Put that thing away!" Frazer ordered angrily.

Biancoli shoved the pistol back in its holster. "I almost didn't make it, Captain," Biancoli muttered thickly. "He was right on top of me. I couldn't do anything else." Biancoli waited until Mr. Song had climbed dazedly into the back seat again and then climbed in himself.

"Come on, let's get out of here! Get us moving, for Christ's sake!" Frazer said.

As they started to back out, Mr. Song suddenly awoke. Holding on to the roof supports, his knuckles white, he leaned over the side and yelled back to the son staring after them, to all the faces staring after them, "Do not ever tell them where the rice is! Never!" He leaned back in and sat down, not even bothering to wipe the spittle from the corners of his mouth, not answering when the Captain looked at him questioningly.

They were on their way back to Inchon when Captain Frazer turned around to Mr. Song and said, "What did he say to you just before he died?"

Mr. Song stared past him through the windshield. "He called me a thief," he said. "In Japanese."

Neither of the men in the front seat said anything. Sergeant Biancoli stared at the road and Captain Frazer looked at Mr. Song.

After a while, Captain Frazer said, "Don't let it get you, Mr. Song. You had nothing to do with it." Then he added quietly, "It was the old man's fault. He shouldn't have tried to kill Biancoli."

Mr. Song said, "The old man is dead. No matter what you say, it is true that the old man is dead." He still stared past the Captain's head.

"Yes, the old man is dead. But remember I told you there might be trouble."

Mr. Song did not answer.

"I told you why we were doing this, didn't I?"

Mr. Song said, "Yes."

"Has anything changed now with the argument?"

"The old man is dead."

"Yes, he's dead. Of course he's dead. We all saw him dead!" Frazer glared at Mr. Song's blank, cold face. "That doesn't change the fact that what we did was right. Biancoli had to protect himself. We had to find the rice!" Then with an effort, Frazer said, "A man can't keep what he has while others starve—not any more."

Mr. Song thought, *The old man is dead. The brave, ignorant old man.*

"He did no good, you know," Frazer continued. "The police'll surely find the rice now. They'll question the wife or the son without fear, now that the old man . . ."

Surprise filtered into Mr. Song. "They will find the rice?" he said.

"The police aren't to blame for what happened, so they're free to do what they want," Frazer said bitterly. "Now let's all just forget about it."

They were almost to Inchon when Mr. Song said, "Please stop the automobile."

Frazer turned and examined him.

Mr. Song's face was calm. "Please stop the automobile," he said again. When Biancoli had braked the jeep to a stop, Mr. Song got out.

"Wait a minute, Biancoli," Frazer said quickly. Then to Mr. Song: "I know how you feel. Think of the ten people who'll starve without Mr. Han's rice. Balance them against Mr. Han back there."

Mr. Song heard only a jumble of foreign words which he did not attempt to understand. Wooden-faced, he waited.

"What can I tell you to convince you? To kill a man is a terrible thing, but to kill ten, even though you don't see them die immediately, is much worse. You've seen them starve at Seoul station in the winter. So have I—"

Mr. Song, still not listening, thought, *Why does he argue with me like this?* He was drawn to a detached contemplation of the Western face with the blue eyes, the bitter expression, the twisting mouth, and the almost passionate jargon. Mr. Song was reminded of someone. Of course! Mr. Han had looked exactly like this when he had argued against taking the rice! Something like a chill overtook Mr. Song as Frazer defended himself. He listened.

In a moment, Mr. Song thought: *Who is right? They argue the same way, with the same face, and yet both would have killed. This man speaks to me as if I am his conscience.* Then Mr. Song remembered the yard and Mr. Han with the great stain on his chest and the blood creeping away in little branched vines from some vast root underneath him.

"Yu bakka!" Mr. Song said, in Japanese as it had been said to him. He spoke suddenly, throwing the words from him.

He saw Frazer's face deepen and recede into a mask of defeat. The face itself sighed at him, and Mr. Song almost said, "No, wait. I did not mean it. I would have said the same to Mr. Han had you not killed him." But he did not speak.

Frazer said in a voice drained of expression, "Let's go, Biancoli. It doesn't do any good to explain." He did not look again at Mr. Song, but turned his face away with the blue eyes dead in it.

The jeep sprang forward and Mr. Song was left with the dust sifting down on him. As the jeep grew smaller in his eyes, Mr. Song opened his mouth, his face alive with emotion, and almost shouted after them. Then he looked down at his dusty shoes with the long scratch on one of the toes.

The dust from the jeep blew away from the road and floated over the squares of the rice paddies—dry now that the harvest was in—to fall in minute rain on the brittle, clustered stalks. Mr. Song looked at the barren land and felt himself an old man, felt the dust like the ashes of the dead on his head, and whispered to himself as the engine sounds died away, "I know nothing."   —*Fall* 1951

SAMUEL YELLEN

The Passionate Shepherd

Hᴀᴠᴇ you ever stopped in the middle of a sentence to see if the person you were talking to was paying any attention? I don't recommend it, unless you brace yourself beforehand for a jolt. That is precisely what I did at a cocktail party last October, seven months ago. I was engaged in conversation with a good-looking young brunette, Rose Matthews, whose husband had just joined our faculty. I even remember (as if I could forget) what I was saying at the time, though I hesitate to repeat it here. It was the sort of thing my friends the psychologists would call verbalizing, a piece of cocktail party prattle which I had lifted from Marlowe: "Come live with me, and be my love, and we will all the pleasures prove. And I assure you this passionate shepherd will——" Some sudden caprice which

I still cannot account for made me break off at that point. To my chagrin, the Passionate Shepherd discovered that his love was simply not listening and Marlowe's poesy was wasted on the smoke-laden air. Her ears, her eyes, her whole being were bent elsewhere. What stood there before me was only the empty shell. And even though the shell itself was, as we say, not at all bad, being endowed, for example, with full and firm breasts, I must confess that Professor Cyrus Richard Gray suffered a sharp pain near the heart. Yes, it was a veritable stab of pain, and I am sure that I grew pale. At that moment, while a needle caught in a groove of my brain kept playing *pleasures prove pleasures prove pleasures prove pleasures prove*, I had my first intimation that I did not exist.

It was the usual faculty cocktail party held in the usual faculty home during the Saturday twilight after a football game. The furniture was all straight lines and angles in chromium plate and blond wood. On the walls hung the ubiquitous Sunflowers of Van Gogh, two studies of ballet girls by Degas, and a number of Cubist abstractions tardily executed in water colors by our hostess. Seen through the pall of cigarette smoke, the fifty men and women standing jammed in the small living room and adjoining dining room were shades clamoring in the mists for a sip of the life-giving blood. Except that *these* shades were drinking Martinis and Manhattans. Perhaps my parallel is too lurid, and the illustrator should be not Doré, but Hogarth or Daumier. However, the scene was pathetic, almost tragic, rather than comic. The climate was one of desperation. But not the *quiet* desperation Thoreau speaks of. Far from it. Shrieks, screams, and squeals rebounded from wall and ceiling. Everyone seemed intent on a most frantic search for *something*, something without substance, without form, without name. Wives in their forties and fifties ogled, winked, grimaced, flirted with a frenzied gaiety, as if to give the lie to wrinkle, crow's foot, wattle, and hairy mole. Husbands with dewlap and sagging paunch embraced waists, only to recoil at flaccid breast or inflexibly ribbed girdle. Our host was busy saving on his liquor bill by going heavy on the vermouth. Our hostess, her face stamped with a bright fixed smile, was worrying about cigarette butts and spilled drinks, and wishing the party were over and done with. It was a motley assemblage, the kind you get when the hostess is wiping out her accumulation of social obligations in order to begin the new season with a clean sheet. Otherwise, how account for the presence of E. Feverell Dobson, Professor of Salesmanship (pause for raucous laughter) in our School of Commerce?

I realize that I must sound the petty academic snob indigenous to our large state universities. But that was not it at all. No, my attitude does not derive from the traditional respectability of my position as Professor of History (actually I took my doctorate at Harvard in American

Civilization). Dobson *qua* Dobson is without significance in my story. True, he was hollow brass, undoubtedly an ignoramus, a hail fellow well met given to off-color limericks and guffaws. Likewise true, his title to local fame lay in a great collection of gaudy shirts and Countess Mara ties. Nevertheless, all of that was only his manner of saying to the world, *Regardez! I exist!* Others of my colleagues took other ways of making the same assertion. Some grew beards, some drove around in flashy yellow or crimson convertibles, some issued statements to the press, some dressed in tartan jackets, some cultivated eccentricities, some were constantly and ostentatiously off to Washington on mysterious topdrawer business, some never wore the same suit twice in a month, some never wore anything but the same suit month after month. And even *my* own unobtrusive behavior and dress, invariably, like my name, a neutral gray which rendered me almost invisible against the academic foliage, may have been, after all, nothing more than the reverse side of the medal. Without getting hopelessly lost in the maze of the ego, who can be sure that Dobson was not right? At least, his brassy loudness was a sign of his *presence*. It indicated *his* existence. And certainly at this party he was the gorgeous prismatic cock around whom the silly hens fluttered.

Let me hasten to add that any bitterness expressed above was really a symptom of inner discontent and pain. In part, I suppose, it was pique at the fact that Rose Matthews was not even conscious of disregarding me. Perhaps mine was the occupational sensitivity of the professor. But I think not. It was something else. When Rose Matthews stood before me, all attention fixed, as if by a tropism, on E. Feverell Dobson, I suddenly was simply not there. She had wiped me out of existence. It happened to be a time when I was particularly vulnerable. I had just turned fifty-six. I was raw, without integument to shield me. No longer could I delude myself that the sixties, hemorrhages of the brain, palsy, and *finis* were not breathing hard down my neck. Of course, the handwriting had always been up there on the wall, but now, myopic as I might be, I had come close enough to read it. Moreover, the season of the year vibrated sympathetically, and each leaf falling desiccated and crumpled to the earth echoed my dismal thoughts. Standing there with the Matthews woman, I was stricken with panic. I looked across the room and observed my wife shrilling to some blurred figure who had an arm around her. During the rest of the party, I moved along, an automaton somehow making the expected response to the anticipated stimulus.

As we were driving home that evening, my wife said, "That Rose Matthews is an extremely attractive woman, don't you think?"

Before answering, I waited a minute as though to consider. "Yes, I suppose some would think she is."

I foresaw not only what Helen would say next, but the valiantly matter-of-fact tone she would employ. "Well, I noticed that the men seemed to be taken with her."

Why we skirmished thus I don't understand. I am sure that she could predict my reply and the inflection of my voice as accurately as I could predict hers. Nevertheless, I pursed my lips and said, "She's a bit flamboyant for *my* taste, but *de gustibus*——" I shrugged my shoulders.

Helen should have known that the problem was not Rose Matthews, nor any of the other women whose sting she tried to neutralize by such epithets as "attractive" or "charming" or "beautiful." And yet, perhaps she did know well enough, and she was herself helpless before the compulsion to beat ineffectually against the ruins of time.

In the quiet streets, the lights of the car caught the leaves drifting down. There was no end to them, falling, falling, falling; and what they whispered as they fluttered in the air and their clatter as they dropped to the ground seemed, for the moment, to drown out the purr of the motor. In alarm I glanced quickly at Helen. She was staring ahead, her sharp chin lifted high to undo the half-a-century folds in her throat, her thin straight hair drawn close to the skull into a tight little knot at the back of her neck. My heart suddenly ached with pity. That face, which once launched a thousand ships each time I looked at it, now would no longer launch a single small vessel. And I remembered the fragrance of her young body when she first undressed for me, shy and yet in her pride wanting me to behold the flower which had bloomed in secret. Even that beauty had fallen victim to physiology and chemical equations. Maybe each commonplace reassurance I gave her helped temper the icy wind of truth. We had reached, I felt, a moment of high silent communion. But perversely that was the very moment Helen chose to turn eagerly to me. "Cy, I heard something interesting this afternoon. Guess who's going to get a divorce." I was not the sentient being, Cyrus Richard Gray. I was merely a patient and capacious ear to pour her post-party gossip into. Again I had the sensation that I did not exist.

That night at home I was unable to fall asleep. I lay in our bed as still as possible in order not to awaken Helen. The bed was spacious and obese, the kind without footboard called, I believe, a "Hollywood bed," which Helen had seen in *House Beautiful*. Had I not known her deficiency in the sense of humor, I might have thought she had got this voluptuous couch meant for an unmatrimonial orgy of fleshly passions as a piece of mockery for the decorous conjugality we had declined into.

Getting up finally, I slipped out and closed the door carefully behind me. I tiptoed past the bedrooms of Joan and Ned, down the stairs, and into my study. There I sat for a time in a cocoon of silence trying to analyze the disturbing sensation which had come on me. But the longer I pondered the more elusive became my identity. At last I went into the bathroom and got a sleeping pill to give myself the relief of temporary oblivion. As I was shutting the medicine cabinet, there in the mirror was my image. I studied it closely. Each separate item in the physiognomy was itself familiar enough—the rumpled and ragged slate-colored hair streaked with gray, the regularity of chin and nose, the pale gray eyes, the liverish skin. (Indeed, so ordinary were the items that I wished for a moment I might have some Dickensian grotesquerie of feature to serve as a handle for my identity, so that I might think of myself as the Man with the Red Bulbous Nose or the Man with the Black Beetling Brow.) And yet the total image was that of a stranger. There was about it a suggestion of distortion, as if the parts had been jarred slightly after being assembled, or as if the mirror had some minute flaws. I could not be sure whether the image represented reality or phantom. But I felt that I was on the verge of discovering the real person. Within that gray outwardness I seemed to remember a younger face and a boyish head. Underneath that cracked and peeling surface I thought I could almost see brighter and fresher colors. With a little more effort—no, it was no use. I kept slipping away from myself. And I could not persuade myself to believe that the stranger in the mirror existed. "Well," I said to him, *"gnothi seauton,* Passionate Shepherd, know thyself! That great Thespian, Cyrus Richard Gray, will now enact a little morality quaintly entitled *Passion Redivivus, or the Shepherd in Search of Himself."*

During the following days, while burning leaves spiced the air, a strange unrest took hold of me. My hands often trembled violently as they lifted a cup of coffee, a semaphore ticked unceasingly in my left eyelid, and fever patches blazed through the liverish skin over my cheekbones. I could not rid myself of the conviction that I had somehow, somewhere lost my inner self, that I was nothing but an empty container moving mechanically on fixed tracks. In my desperation, I crept back into the deepest recesses of the shell which had given me shelter in the past during fits of fluttering uncertainty. Like a neurotic straightening books, pictures, dishes, furniture in an effort to padlock his indefinable anxiety, I sought refuge in the formula of routine. Twenty-four years of treading the same invariable paths had rendered my motions automatic. In the morning I met my freshman class in the Introduction to Western Civilization, my advanced class in The Experimental Society in America, or my graduate seminar in The Brook Farm Group, obediently opening and shutting my mouth to the tintinnabulation of bells. The rest of the morning was taken up with correspondence, reading blue books and term papers, conferring with students, and filling out the official forms that streamed from the robots over in Administration. At noon I lunched in the Faculty Club. After lunch I glanced at the *New York Times* or played a hand of bridge. Then came the period of the day, from one-thirty to four o'clock, which twenty years before I had dedicated to research. The small basement room in the Library where I spent those two and a half hours had become my second home. There every afternoon without fail I added the grain of sand to the slowly but steadily growing mound out of which had already come five monographs and nineteen shorter articles. The hour from four to five was given over to faculty meetings and committees. Dinner at home was followed by an evening concert, a lecture, a movie, a visit, or reading the *Saturday Evening Post* serial.

For how many thousands of days this not unpleasant routine had fitted me comfortably! Yet now I sank unaccountably into absent states, from which I would come to with the blood thundering to my head as after a faint. Fortunately (praise be to William James for Habit!) I always found myself performing the proper task at the customary time and place. Nevertheless, these spells worried me, and presently I realized that the Matthews woman was haunting my thoughts. Not, mind you, in the role of femme fatale, but rather as if she had stolen something I needed desperately to get back. It was this necessity, I suppose, which compelled me now and again to walk slowly past her house in one of the side streets off the campus. To my irrational temper, it seemed that the sight of her might restore whatever it was I had lost, might furnish me with the precious clue. At any moment during the day (even in the period sacrosanct to research), like a somnambulist, I would be driven to take my foolish peripatetic exercise. Of course, I never caught so much as a glimpse of Rose Matthews.

In my increasing agitation, there was no one I could turn to for help. Helen did look anxiously at me for a while. But I easily threw her off the scent by allowing myself to be caught in the kitchen furtively mixing myself a bicarbonate of soda, and my malady was, I am sure, soon diagnosed and dismissed as a bout of indigestion. How long this state of affairs might have gone on I can only guess. For it came to an abrupt end one afternoon as I was seated in my basement cell at the Library (such is the treachery of the familiar) reading the letters of Charles Lamb. Unless my memory fails me, it was a letter to Coleridge. *Unless my memory fails me*—now there's an expression! Vestigium of exquisite academic dishonesty! Not only does my memory not fail me, but the very date of the letter—May 20, 1803—is engraved in red upon my private calendar. The fatal words sprang forward from the page to meet my eye: "He seems to have run the whole scenery of life, and now rests as the formal precisian of non-existence."

Even now, so ingrained are the accustomed academic gestures, I find myself obliged to explain why I was reading Lamb, what I was doing, as we like to say, outside my field. (As though it still matters that one of my colleagues might think I was spreading myself thin.) I must first make clear that my specialty is (or was) early Utopian experiments in America. Indeed, two of my monographs, those on New Harmony and Brook Farm, are, with all due modesty, not entirely unknown to the world of scholarship. At the time, I was following up some leads on the pantisocracy which Coleridge, Southey, and Lovell had planned to establish on the banks of the Susquehanna. Since many of Lamb's letters were written to Coleridge and Southey, I inevitably encountered the passage that was to open my eyes. For a minute, I recall, I took *precisian* to be a misspelling, until I realized that it was the noun not for the quality, but for the person. On the instant, I recognized that I had been brought unto Lamb to see what he would call me, and I had been named. I, *I*, Cyrus Richard Gray, was the formal precisian of non-existence. I was the vacant outline, with the Roman numerals, capital letters, Arabic numerals, and lower case letters all correctly indented and set forth. The *content* had faded out of the realm of being. I felt stagnant, lusterless, inert. My heart began to quiver. But that, I told myself, was only because the creature of habit was fearful at the threat to his smug routine. *Creature* of habit? No, I was simply the habit itself. I was that old coat which William James describes as falling into its habitual folds and wrinkles. And no one was inside.

As I sat with the volume of Lamb's letters open on the table before me, I looked around at the old familiar face of my cloister. *There* was the whole scenery of my life. The walls were painted a dull rough gray, and the surface bulged and billowed to the ridges and whorls of the plaster underneath. My long table, strewn with books, pamphlets, note cards, and pads of paper, stood in the center of the worn pine floor. The two large rickety bookcases were loaded with dusty books, piles of off-prints sent me by colleagues, and thirty or so of those mottled black-and-gray cardboard boxes, each neatly labeled, in which the industrious scholar files his note cards. Ah, those boxes! Those boxes! In them reposed what thousands upon thousands of cards, each one covered with my small precise backward-slanting hand! Cards of two sizes, two colors— three-by-five for bibliographical data, four-by-six for notes on my reading,

white for the factual or objective, yellow for my own comments and sug-
gestions. Over the years it had been my sustaining faith that each card
contributed its mite to the sum total of human knowledge. What a silly
farce—written, staged, played, and directed by Vanity! No, each card
was the measure of a certain number of pulse beats lost and never to be
recaptured. In those mottled black-and-gray caskets were interred the
bones of my youth and enthusiasm. There came to my mind the story of
the Harvard professor who, on his death, left hundreds of boxes and
baskets of notes, choking his shelves and even suspended by pulleys from
the ceiling. For his university they were an embarrassment, and not of
riches. They were the indecent remains of a corpse which finally had to
be disposed of hugger-mugger. I could imagine how, after my departure
from this vale of tears, *my* boxes would perplex the university. What to
do with them? Whom to entrust them to? Certainly my colleagues would
want nothing to do with them: each one was diligently storing up his
own boxes of note cards.

I went over to the window, whose sill was level with the ground, and
looked through the ancient fly specks and grime. The cold November
sun painted the skeleton trees upon the earth, with pen-and-ink punctilio
for the filigree of twig. A host of shriveled brown leaves scuttled like
chipmunks before the wind. Some students came along the campus walk
outside the Library, the bare legs of the coeds smooth, strong, and
shapely. I could almost hear the crunch of the dead leaves being trodden
down by those merciless feet. No one is more aware than the college professor of the hungry generations. No one can have a keener sense of how
quickly and impatiently youth discards age. When it came my turn to
go, who would there be to know the difference? Assuredly not my students. Those young egotists at the most egotistical hour of life hardly
conceded existence to their teachers. Some of the more fatuous among
my colleagues talked fervidly about *reaching* their students. I could not
help remembering the student who had sat through an entire semester of
my course under the impression that I was Professor *Thompson!* No, I
could not flatter myself that I so much as cracked the glaze of those
young egotists. And yet, distant as I was from my students, I was in many
ways closer to them than to my own children. Joan and Ned no longer
needed me. To them, I was an old stick of furniture that got in the way
around the house. The language they spoke might as well have been one
of those African tongues, all clicks and grunts. Joan, a senior at the university, was engaged to an accounting major, and already knew that
callow brash stranger much better than she had ever known me. As for
Ned, he was a sophomore wrapped up in his fraternity's hell week, pajama
parties, and other such foolishness. Whenever I tried to enter their world,

they merely waited with ill-concealed patience for me to make a more or less graceful exit.

Standing there at the window feeling a twinge of pity for old Shepherd Gray, I realized that I was whistling a tune under my breath while my fingers drummed a rhythm on the sill. The tune was very familiar, and yet I could not place it. Yes, a thing might be too familiar to be in focus. Surely, if anyone knew me, it was Helen. And yet I could go through a crisis like this without her being aware of it. While the tune teased me with its elusive familiarity, I let my thoughts play about Helen. She had been, in her way, a good wife and would, no doubt, notice my absence from the scene. But how soon she would get over it, and go on with her household concerns, her clubs, her teas, bridges, and luncheons! I watched the leaves scamper along outside. That tune nagged at me in a most distracting way. I recalled the cases of colleagues who had suddenly and inexplicably thrown overboard family, friends, position in the community, hard-earned academic security and reputation. Of Dewhirst, who had deserted a wife and three children to run off to Mexico with a coed. Of the professor of Latin whose name I had forgotten, who had joined an African safari and never returned. Of Templeton, who had gone berserk and shot two of his colleagues. Of Baker, who had simply disappeared into the ether and left no trace. Somehow they were never the E. Feverell Dobsons, but always the quiet ones, the unobtrusive ones. About each one, the rest of us would shake our heads and ask over a cocktail glass, "What*ever* got into him?" Well, now I knew. Just then, I identified the nagging tune, and at the same moment I realized that the semaphore had stopped ticking in my left eyelid. It was a gay tune, the patter song from *The Mikado*. "He never would be missed," I sang aloud. "I'm sure he'd not be missed."

It is not at all difficult to disappear. Indeed, I believe that I could now write a successful handbook for weary academics on *How to Vanish and Leave Not a Rack Behind*. Of course, having time and place which I did not have to account for was of great help. No one ever questioned what I was doing each afternoon between one-thirty and four, and so seldom did anyone else, even the janitor, enter my basement room at the Library that I could have safely kept a chorus girl there. My preparations took only a few days and carried me into the first week of December. I had never realized that Professor Gray had it in him to be such a man of action. I withdrew five hundred dollars from the bank, knowing that Helen would not miss the money until the beginning of the next month. Then down on the levee (a row of secondhand stores, saloons, greasy-spoon restaurants, and disreputable hotels facing the railroad tracks) I bought an old brown suit, a battered brown hat, two woolen work shirts, a heavy sweater, a worn pair of brown shoes, and a cheap black cardboard suitcase, spreading my purchases over three stores. The chief risk I ran was getting these things into the Library. However, luck accommodated me. A little-used side door leads directly to the basement, and no one happened to see me enter that afternoon. My briefcase served to bring over some underwear, socks, and handkerchiefs, a few pieces each day.

On the appointed morning, as I said goodby to Joan and Ned and kissed Helen, I savored to the full the irony of being as perfunctory as usual. In fact, everything was as usual, even the beating of my heart. I met my classes, answered some letters at the office, had lunch at the Faculty Club, played a hand of bridge, and strolled over to my secluded cloister. There I set about transforming myself. Most of my predecessors in the fine art of fading away into thin air had, I decided, tried too hard to disguise themselves and, since nothing is so unoriginal as efforts at originality, had used the very ham-actor stencils foreseen by the police. My commonplace face and figure, my undistinguished dress and manner, the absence of any oddity of feature were in my favor. I did not resort to artificial scars, dark glasses, moustache, or limp. All I did was to remove my glasses and comb my hair in a pompadour instead of parting it as I ordinarily did. Then I changed to the woolen work shirt and brown suit and hat, and put the clothes I had been wearing into the suitcase. A study of my reflection in the grimy window showed me that the metamorphosis was adequate. I was still unobtrusive enough to be completely overlooked. Nevertheless, I must confess that my heart was thumping when I left the Library by the side door, carrying the suitcase. However, on the walk outside the door one of my colleagues passed by me without so much as a second glance. That restored my confidence.

Of course, I had already picked out my destination, and without hesitating I caught the bus which crosses the railroad tracks over into the West Side. During the 1880's and 1890's, that had been the fashionable section of town, and my interest in nineteenth-century domestic architecture had taken me there on occasional walks to view the dozen or so homes in the General Grant style still standing, though now converted into funeral parlors or rooming houses. One of the latter, need I say, was my *immediate* destination. Again luck was obliging to me, for I found a room at the first house I tried. I gave my name as George Brown and paid a week's rent in advance. The room, up in the square central tower which marks the General Grant house, was shabbily furnished, but clean enough, large, and well-lighted. For two weeks I holed up there, going out to the levee for my meals. Actually I did not stay close to my room, nor otherwise behave furtively. I took long walks through the streets of the West Side, over to the gas works, the cemetery, the furniture factory, or the slaughter house. I felt as if I were a tourist in a foreign town. And in a sense I was. For even a city of only sixty-three thousand is really a cluster of quite separate towns, each with its own economy, culture, social strata, flora and fauna.

My chief occupation was studying the local paper to keep track of my *alter idem*. It did not surprise me that my disappearance was not announced until the third day. I could surmise the quiet and discreet efforts of Helen and the university officials to locate me before deciding that they could no longer put off calling the police in. After the news broke, I read and reread the accounts avidly. I enjoyed observing the skill of our publicity director, who always succeeded in balancing the disgrace to the university of having one of its professors turn into an irresponsible missing person by some reference to the "important" research done by the "noted authority" on early Utopian experiments. I had become a problem in public relations. I also enjoyed following the activities of the police, who broadcast descriptions of me and bustled around the university interviewing my colleagues. And the embarrassment of the officers who "found" me in Chicago, New Orleans, and St. Louis furnished me with a perverse amusement.

However, the irony soon doubled back on me. It was something of a shock, yes, a blow to my self-esteem, to see how quickly all the fuss died down. In four days I passed from the front page to a spot among the advertisements for trusses and rheumatism remedies. In another three days I slipped from the news altogether, except for an occasional brief notice that police had begun to suspect foul play and were about to ask the FBI for assistance. Sometimes, with an understandable reluctance to vanish completely from the scene, I tried to chat about the *affaire Gray* with my landlady or with the waitress at the restaurant, but it was amazing how little interest the aborigines of the West Side had in the university and the mysterious disappearance of one of its distinguished professors. I could guess that the crescendo of chatter at the cocktail parties had passed its peak. Sitting for hours at a time in my room, I found that I thought seldom about Helen, and even less about the children. Joan and Ned were well on the way to taking care of themselves. As for Helen, she would have security enough. The house was paid for, our savings were considerable, and in due time she would draw benefits from our insurance policies and the ample pension fund which I had accumulated. I knew, moreover, that the university always found some clerical or secretarial job for its widows and abandoned wives. No, if anything, my desertion might prove a good thing for her. Occasionally I considered my own destiny, what I would do with myself and how I would go about making a living. But most often, I thought despairingly of my lost identity. Where and when would I recover myself? How many other formal precisians of non-existence had engaged in the same frantic search in that very room? While a phantom troop of forlorn figures paced the threadbare flowered carpet, sat brooding in the horsehair chairs, or lay despondently upon the tarnished brass bed, Descartes' first postulate, slightly altered, twanged in my head: *Credo ergo sum. If* I could believe, I would be.

During recent years I had often wondered how an underground was able to flourish in the very teeth of enemy occupation. Now I could see that it might be managed. Even with the police, so to speak, hot on my trail, establishing myself as an approved member of society took but a few minutes. I applied for a job in one of the limestone quarries south of town, saying that I had come from a farm in the hills of Tennessee near Murfreesboro. Without much ado, I was given a social security card and number, as well as a membership card in the stone workers' union. By signing my name half-a-dozen times, I became George Edward Brown. What surprised me was the ease with which I adapted myself. From the first I got along well with the men, who were soon calling me Tennessee. Somewhere Emerson says that the truck driver and the college professor give themselves away by their speech. The Sage of Concord was mistaken. The secret is not to try to speak unlike yourself. The men I worked with accepted me at face value, and whatever formality there was in my speech or manner they attributed to my supposed Southern origin. The work itself was hard in the beginning. But I liked it, and relished the sense of physical exhaustion each night. I slept soundly, and without benefit of pills. Although the pay was low (I *was* inexperienced labor and at what is called an advanced age), it was sufficient for my simple needs. All in all, the life was good. And I well remember the thrill I felt one morning when, clinging shakily to the iron cables, I took my first ride on a huge block of limestone swung high in the air by the derrick. All around me the sheer limestone walls dazzled my eyes with a brilliant display of color. I had not known that there could be so many tints of brown and yellow and orange and purple in such a variety of stippling and shading. Far below was the engine, crowned with a coiling plume of smoke. And (as though to provide the fitting touch for the Passionate Shepherd), on a nearby hillside, in the cold pastoral landscape surrounding the quarry, huddled a flock of sheep.

January and February brought snow, frost, and ice. My hands and face put forth a leathery weatherbeaten skin, and I became quite tough physically. My days were little else than work and sleep. Sometimes after the whistle blew at four o'clock, I accompanied some of the men to a cafe in the vicinity of the quarries for a glass of beer and a game of checkers or dominoes. Since I was tired at the end of the day and went to bed early, the evening passed quickly and I had little time for speculation. Aside from the *Post* and the local paper, I read almost nothing. Now and then I managed to get hold of the campus newspaper, and through it I kept an eye on my family and my deserted track at the university. Frequently I had heard people say that they would like to visit the earth after their death to see whether they were missed and how they were spoken of. That was the position I was in, a ghost haunting the scenes of his former life. And I can testify that I needed all the comfort I could suck from ironic detachment. For a while, it was entertaining to see who would be put into my slot. From various items in the campus paper, I learned that young Bob Hendricks had taken over my advanced course and graduate seminar, and also my seat on three or four special committees. Except that he had already launched himself in early railroad history, I suppose that he might even have been willing to inherit my thirty caskets of note cards. I had a picture of him, gradually taking on my manner, my dress, my neutral gray coloration. Indeed, I began to feel that it would be no more than proper for him to move in with Helen and take my place in that Hollywood bed.

There was undeniably an element of hurt in seeing how soon my shoes were filled. Nevertheless, watching young Hendricks pour, like raw molten metal, into the channels and molds so long occupied by Professor Gray was to have, in the long run, a wholesome effect upon me. I no longer had a carapace to crawl back into. Young Hendricks had cut off my retreat. George Edward Brown was now absolutely on his own. This realization first struck me just a couple of weeks ago, as the calendar wheeled away from Winter. March came in with a roar of wind and a flurry of soggy snow that soaked into the frozen earth. I could almost hear the iron bonds cracking and falling apart. These presentiments of Spring persuaded me to buy a bright red plaid mackinaw and the kind of scarlet cap worn by deer hunters. And it was only last Saturday that, impelled by some unnamed yearning, instead of having a beer and a game of checkers, I donned my new outfit and loitered on the courthouse square, not the fashionable east side with its expensive shops like Mademoiselle, but the west side where were the five-and-tens, the hardware stores, and the loan sharks. This plebeian side swarmed with farmers and laborers on Saturday afternoon, and I felt safely camouflaged as I lounged against a store front. The yearning which had seized me was, I admitted to myself, for someone to take cognizance of *me*, to fill my void with a sense of being. Had Helen come by then, I might even have revealed myself to her. But that futility was avoided. The thread by which fate hung held firm. It was rare for Helen to come to that side of the square. However, two of my former colleagues *did* pass by and fail to recognize me. And then suddenly my heart began to pound furiously. There, coming along my side of the street, was Rose Matthews. Her figure, I now noticed, was even more abundant, riper, than I had remembered. As she passed, without thinking I gave a low whistle. She halted.

"Pleasures prove," I said. "Pleasures prove."

She turned back uncertainly and looked at me. Then I saw that she was not Rose Matthews at all, but another woman I had never seen before. Without glasses, my eyes had played me a trick. The woman was not even a brunette, but a decided blonde.

"What was that you said?" she demanded.

There was a roughness to her voice which I found exciting. For a full minute we looked at each other, hardly conscious of the crowds passing by. Unlike Rose Matthews at the cocktail party, this woman really knew I was there. Not *credo ergo sum,* I suddenly understood, but *credis ergo sum. You* believe, therefore I am. In that moment the distressing conviction of non-existence dropped away from me like a sloughed skin. I felt alive, as you do on shipboard with a new companion to whom nothing about you is old shoe. I studied the woman's face before replying. It was round and lush, with the blood about to flood into the fair skin. Her nose was a saucy pug, and her full chin was pertly dimpled. A little hat perched on her honey-colored hair, and her blue eyes were examining me with a mixture of interest and puzzlement. No doubt, the bright red mackinaw and the cap were doing their work. I gave her body a bold up-and-down glance. "I said, Treasure trove, treasure trove."

She hesitated for an instant, and then smiled. "Now, Daddy," she said with mock reproach. "Behave yourself, Daddy." She gave my arm a pat and walked on, flipping her tail provocatively. I was sure that I would see her again.   —*Winter* 1951-52

PATTERNS OF LIVING

JOHN T. HOWARD

Democracy in City Planning

THE flurry of current interest in city planning has missed the point—except in some little-read technical magazines. A certain New York parkway-builder screams at the long-haired foreigners and the theorists who dream comprehensive visions of "organic urban living" without regard to American institutions. Their academic defenders reply with "politician," "city-patcher," "Philistine," and charge short-sighted expediency. The public gets the impression that city planning offers either utopias fifty years from now—with no way to get from here to there—or piecemeal-built public works, without any real answer to the human problems of city living.

A useful concept that helps put things in their place has been outlined in *Fortune* articles: city planning needs both "strategy" and "tactics." The strategy is the outlining of broad objectives, long-range goals—the job of the theorists. The tactics is the working out of the step-by-step approach to the goals—the job of the front-line officials who have to act, one way or another, *now*. Sound planning obviously needs both strategy and tactics, and in neither line do we lack *technical* know-how. Saarinen and Moses; Wright and the Metropolitan Life Insurance Company; Mumford and Kaiser—we have plenty of thinkers and plenty of doers in the field of city building.

But still our cities rot and fester. The thinkers think too far ahead; the doers build (the right things and the wrong things indiscriminately)

251

on too small a scale to make much difference. And gradually it is dawning on some of both, that this is a democracy we live in.

The bottleneck in effective city planning is people. Planners make the plans, strategic or tactical; the people build them—or don't—by their votes, and by their individual private decisions. Cities are for people, not the other way round. Cities are also of and by people.

We are gradually coming to realize that, since this is so, people ought to have more to say in the making of city plans. If they can take a real part, the plans are more likely to be good—and far more likely to get built!

It's easy to plan a city. All you need is paper, pencils, certain technical skills, a lot of information, and an ivory tower. You lay out a "pattern of land use and population distribution," and design to fit it a series of overlying "systems of utilities and services"—streets, transit, parks, schools, water lines, fire stations. And there you have it—a "guide to the orderly future development of the community"—good or bad, according to the quality of your skill and information.

It's easy to build a city according to a plan, too. All you need is bulldozers, bricks, dirt, space, manpower, money, and organizing ability. In a dictatorship, that is enough. From Egypt down through history to Soviet Russia, cities have been built this way—good or bad, according to the quality of the planning.

In a democracy, fortunately on the whole, it is harder to get either a good or a bad plan built. Your American planner finds that his scheme, thought out as an integrated whole, must be subcontracted for building to a variety of independent responsible agents—park departments, highway departments, school boards; home builders, speculative subdividers, industries, store builders, public utilities. They fall into two broad groups: public agencies, and private individuals and corporations. The first group can be fairly effectively persuaded or dragooned into following a city plan, under our normal machinery of local government—the planning commission with its mandatory referral power and limited veto, the capital improvement budget, and, most important, the planning-conscious mayor and council which are becoming more and more prevalent. The second group presents the real problem. And this is the basic problem; for the private land and development *is* the city—the public works and facilities are only service auxiliaries.

How can we get private citizens—be they home owners, businessmen, industries, or banks—to go along with our city planning? Their daily decisions—where and when to build, remodel or move, to subdivide land to plant trees, even to cut the grass—these things *are* the growth and development of the city. If they can be guided in the direction of a long-range goal, we may achieve the vision of a Saarinen or a Wright. If they will not be guided, all the parkways of a Moses cannot make a city good to live in.

Three tools have been devised to accomplish this purpose: call them compulsion, education, and participation.

Compulsion is the most direct, and the least successful by itself. This is democratic, self-imposed self-discipline, but compulsion none the less as it affects the individual citizen. Its major city-planning use is zoning, a negative control which prohibits industry in business areas and business in residential areas, limits the height and bulk of buildings and the spaces between them, and sets maximum population densities for different districts. There is no doubt that zoning has done a lot to prevent bad situations from getting much worse, but it has not been effective in promoting positive improvement. Another negative control is subdivision regulation, which sets minimum standards for new allotments. These are both municipal controls; for a number of years, the federal government has also exercised a measure of regulation over new residential construction, through the FHA. This, however, is a lollipop kind of control—your reward for adherence to the standards set being the insurance of your mortgage loan. It has had a remarkable influence toward improved quality of building, which is now far better than what most speculative builders gave us before. But this influence is limited to those builders who choose to ask FHA help.

Compulsion, then, has been a helpful tool in a negative sort of way: it has checked further disorder, set a floor under the standards of certain kinds of development (which has too often become the ceiling), and to some extent channelized development in the right—or planned— direction. But the mild kind of compulsion that is acceptable in a democracy, though it can prohibit the flagrantly wrong things, cannot —and should not—compel private individuals to do whatever a handful of public officials might decree as the only right things.

Education is the second tool on which planners have placed heavy reliance. Since the Wacker Manual of the Chicago Plan was credited with getting Chicago's lakefront built when the schoolboys who studied it reached voting age, planners have been fumbling with the unfamiliar techniques of salesmanship. They are gradually getting more skilful. But results to date are fragmentary and piecemeal.

This approach is an effort on the part of public officials to influence public opinion toward a preconceived objective. Like compulsion, it is fundamentally a procedure from the top down—an attempt to impose by propaganda those features of an ivory-tower plan that cannot be imposed by fiat.

By and large, educational efforts by the planners have not had the results that were expected. Grand plans have been prepared, and lavishly published. Newspapers have said "Oh!" Chambers of Commerce have said "Ah!" Everyone has agreed that the plans were very fine. But somehow they never really belonged to the community; they were too much the private product of the planners. So in cities throughout the country, plans—often good plans—mildew in the files, with only a few popular projects carried out.

But though a generation of propaganda has not caused the building of any complete city plans, it has accomplished something else. The words and some of the concepts of city planning have become familiar to a lot of people. They agree that it is a "good thing"; that it is "much needed"; that it is American and "respectable." The stage is pretty well set for action.

Participation, the third tool, is now appearing—in experimental form, unsure as to technique, but spontaneously being tried out in a dozen cities. It is not a substitute for the first two, but a complement. Fundamentally, it is the attempt to bring democracy into city planning: that the people of a community, adequately informed by technicians as to possible alternatives, may choose their own city planning policies, may decide how far they will submit themselves to the self-imposed discipline of legislative compulsion, and how far they will act as individuals and private groups in accordance with their own plans.

There is an important new element in this approach. Before, the *plan* was decided upon *first*, by the technical planners. Then it was brought to the people. It was modified and compromised, of course, in the process of selling it, of persuading the city council to enact parts of it. But this isn't the same thing as helping make the plan in the first place. The new element is to put the *problems* up to the people, *before* the plan is developed. The designing of the plan on paper can then proceed on the basis of their judgments, with the technician comparatively assured that it will be approved and acted on.

This participation technique was not, of course, suddenly invented this morning. It has been maturing for some time. Its germ is evident in the tradition of assigning the planning job not to a solo full-time public official, but to a commission of citizens. We are now recognizing that one reason this form has failed to produce more results is that the citizen participation was not broad enough. What is new is the giving of first place among the tools of planning to the democratic process.

It's hard to make democracy work. That point needs no laboring. It is particularly hard in big cities, where lie our most acute city-planning problems. They are aggravated by the fact that our metropolitan communities are made up of many independent municipalities, to whose boundaries the planning problems pay no attention.

The greatest difficulty, however, lies in the complexity of the problems, and the fact that plans to meet them must themselves be very complex. They must cover things big and small, property private and public, periods of time from tomorrow to the next century. A City Plan is really a bundle of plans, some in drawings, some in words, some in figures—held together not by a rubber band around the outside, but by a strong cord of related thinking running through them all.

To illustrate: major highways must be planned as a metropolitan network, to handle efficiently great traffic volumes. The system must be keyed to other transportation systems, mass transit, railroads, airports. It must be designed to serve industry, business, residential concentrations —where they are now, and where they will be in the future. The new highways must be straight and broad—freeways, expressways, parkways —veritable auto railways. But they must be so laid out that they don't smash neighborhoods, the vital cells, the subcommunities of the city; so that they don't spread blight, but check it; so that they don't wastefully drain people out of older areas beyond the need to relieve excessive crowding.

Other systems of region-wide facilities and services likewise need a combination of over-all and localized co-ordination. These, the dramatic products of city planning that make the best rotogravure pictures, are public responsibilities, built by public agencies. It takes merely the normal operations of political democracy to get them planned and built. Not that the process is automatic, or always gets good results—but it is a familiar process and needs no elaborate description.

The organic parts of the city that are nourished by these "systems" of public services present entirely different planning problems. These are the industrial areas, the business districts, the residential neighborhoods—made up of thousands of individual properties, each the kingdom of its owner. It is in conforming this chaos to a plan that compulsion has been negatively helpful—that education has been useful in preparing the way—that participation is proving the primary essential.

Here, city planning operates at two "levels": city-wide, and neighborhood. There is the over-all scheme of development, allotting the different sections of the city to the different functions: industries of varying types where they best belong, business in the right spots, houses and apartments in appropriate locations. Then each of these districts, the cells that make up the body of the city, needs its own development-scheme. So the "bundle of plans" consists of comprehensive plans for each neighborhood, co-ordinated by the city-wide plans.

Participation in the planning, then, must also operate at two levels. Both in the city-wide and in the neighborhood planning the planner must pull into the process each of the interests which will have a part in carrying out the plans.

In the city-wide job, the participation has to be through representatives. Public officials—city councilmen, suburban mayors—represent geographical areas throughout the metropolitan unit. They have to be in on the ground floor, in the broad geographical decisions (to be given authority through the zoning laws that they will enact) that such and such an area will be heavy industry, or single-family houses, or apartments. The interests, the pressure groups, that will directly benefit or suffer from such decisions have to be in on them too. Because, properly enough, elected officials pay serious attention to the wishes of those who elect them as well as to those whom they hire to advise them on technical matters.

So representatives of special interests have to be given a share in planning counsels. This has never been easier than today, because never before have so many of these groups been aware of their stake in city planning. Every organization has its planning committee: real estate boards, chambers of commerce, professional societies of architects and engineers, retail merchants, bankers' associations, women's clubs, labor unions, social workers, churches, parent-teacher associations. And to take in those individuals whose interests don't fit into any of these, most big cities have citizen organizations whose sole concern is city planning or housing, as such.

It isn't enough for these groups to hear speeches on planning, to pass resolutions and attend public hearings. It isn't enough for them merely to pass judgment on the work of the planning technicians. They each have a genuine contribution to make. They *know* what they will or will not do to carry out a plan. They may be "wrong" about what "ought" to be done. But a practical plan has to be in terms of what can be done.

If investors won't make loans for new apartments in a slum area under any conditions, under any plan, then there is no point in "planning" to have that area cleared and rebuilt by private enterprise. But if they can be led to say under what conditions they will make loans, and the plan of the slum area can be made to meet those conditions, then that plan becomes practical.

This is an oversimplified—but actual—example of the give-and-take that leads to effective planning. What is "practical" for a given investor in a given small area for the next five years may not be "practical" for the entire community over the next twenty years. Stuyvesant Town (a large-scale private slum-clearance project to be built postwar in New York) is charged with being such a case—good tactics, based on bad (or no) strategy. The answer is not "purer" planning, but a broader give-and-take, on strategy as well as tactics; more democracy, not less.

The method worked out for Cleveland was formally to set up a citizen Advisory Committee, as a working adjunct to the Planning Commission. Its membership is representative. Every civic, business, or professional group named a member. It is not a rubber stamp, hand-picked to endorse the Commission's proposals; it is expected really to advise, and its advice carries weight. Its subcommittees on special subjects are self-constituted, and they really work. Plans are presented to them, studied, torn apart, revised. When a proposal—like the one above for rebuilding a certain slum area—after much revision finally gets the nod from the Advisory Committee, it has been thoroughly aired in the newspapers, thrashed out in meetings of individual organizations, subjected to the widest possible discussion and understanding. It can be adopted by the Planning Commission with some assurance that it is practical and realizable. It doesn't please everyone, but it comes as near as possible to being the community's own answer to one of its own problems.

A city-wide, comprehensive development plan takes a long time to put together this way. In fact, it will never be "finished"; as long as the city is alive, its view of the future will keep changing as yesterday's future becomes tomorrow's present. And it is still just the general framework, the fitting together of the plans for each of the city's neighborhoods. Each of them requires the same kind of democratic operation.

The machinery for neighborhood participation in neighborhood planning is usually not ready to the planner's hand, as it is for city-wide participation. In fact, when he goes looking for it, he runs head on into the conditions—sociological, economic—that have made a mess of our cities. The very things that are wrong with our neighborhoods get in the way of effective planning.

The first difficulty is to find the neighborhoods. It is convenient to theorize about the organic cellular structure of a city, but when you come to try to pin it down on a map it just isn't there. The theoretical neighborhood unit, a social community with distinct physical boundaries and all the local facilities for good living, is a city-planning objective; but not even its extent on a map is clearly defined as a starting point.

Your planner takes all the measures he can find of likeness and difference—ward lines, nationality groupings, economic classifications, school districts; major streets, railroad lines, and other physical boundaries. By juggling these enough, he may arrive at the vague outlines of what may some day be a rational organization of the city area into neighborhoods. But he can't be sure till he's tried. That means getting together with neighborhood people, and working with them on their planning problems.

The trial cannot be approached the same way for all of these potential neighborhoods. In fact, a rough analysis sorts them out into four different types, each requiring a different kind of planning. The four types tend to be arranged in concentric rings around the downtown center. Counting from the outside inward, they can be identified in homely language as coming, arrived, going, and gone.

The "coming" neighborhoods are the suburban territory which is in process of being converted from country to city. If they can be caught in time, before the farms are cut into lots and the houses built, they can be designed in advance as neighborhoods of a modern standard. But participation from the future inhabitants is impossible, because the planning must be done before they move in. The effective responsibility lies with city and village governments, working with the developers.

Except in rare instances, such planning is not being done today. These "coming" areas are usually outside the boundaries of the central city, beyond the reach of the revitalized city planning agencies that have been scared into action by intown blight. We face the sad postwar prospect of a splurge of suburban fringe development, badly planned or unplanned, wasteful of public services and utilities, wasteful of private development funds, insecure of investment values, poor in quality of living conditions. The seeds of blight two decades hence are being built into our "coming" neighborhoods.

The "arrived" neighborhoods are sound according to average standards; they have been built up since the last war, and are still "new"—though far from "modern." It is too late for drastic replanning. Their need is for protection. These are the districts for which zoning has done the most; they are free from scattered industries and stores, fairly uniform in character. Already they are being attacked by demands for lowering zoning standards. But an active vigilance can meet their problems.

These are areas where "neighborhood protective associations" are easily formed, or are already in existence. They are often in small suburbs, where the municipal government is itself not much more than an official neighborhood association. The people are generally awake to what helps or hurts living conditions and property values. It is not too difficult to fit into the city-wide plan the "arrived" neighborhoods and their plans—which are usually plans to stay the way they are.

The "going" and "gone" neighborhoods present our cities' greatest planning problems. What to do about "gone" areas has filled popular and technical magazines with spectacular schemes. Stuyvesant Town in New York is one answer; public housing is another. The common denominator is the clearing of the slums that have deteriorated beyond saving and the building of new housing on a large enough scale to establish a new *neighborhood* pattern. This means big operations, backed up with authority and large amounts of capital.

In this job, neighborhood participation is out. People who live in hopeless slums are at the bottom of the economic ladder. There is no way that they can take, or be given, a direct hand in planning the clearing and rebuilding of their neighborhoods, which has to be done either by big private money or by government, or by a combination of the two. Citizen participation in such action can only be through political action. To the extent that city, state, and federal public action is necessary, all citizens have a responsibility to see that proper political steps are taken; for the economic and social health of the entire city require this job to be done. And it is generally agreed that the people who live in these areas must be helped to provide themselves with decent housing, as a part of the rebuilding plan, whether on the same spot or somewhere else.

The "going" neighborhoods remain—the forgotten areas, not bad enough to warrant clearance, not good enough to keep people living there by merely protecting existing conditions. The going neighborhoods cover most of the area of our American cities and house most of the people. Yet most of the talk and writing on city planning leaves them out entirely.

This is not strange, for they are the toughest problem of all—and the least dramatic.

They are technically tough; the making of the plans is difficult. The task is not designing from scratch, as in "coming" areas, nor redesigning practically from scratch, as in "gone" areas, nor mere maintenance of tolerably adequate conditions, as in "arrived" areas. It is remodeling, on a neighborhood scale—saving most of what is there, houses, stores, pavements, utilities; modernizing and patching in new facilities to bring an obsolete environment up to date.

Added to the sheer difficulty of designing a workable plan to do this, is the fact that it is the most difficult kind of plan to bring to realization. You are not dealing with big suburban developers or intown redevelopers, the best of whom recognize the importance of planning to safeguard their investments, nor with individual owners who know they have something good and want to keep it. You are dealing with many individual owners who think what they have is not so good, whose tradition is to move out to something better when they can afford it; with absentee landlords, milking their property as they see values go down, instead of trying to save their investments. Yet it is in these very areas that the participation of individual owners—in doing as well as in planning—is absolutely essential.

Now picture your planner, going out to find somebody to "participate" in what he is trying to do. He has the neighborhood pattern of the city marked out, and classified into the four pigeonholes. In three of them, his approach to neighborhood planning is fairly clear, even though he may not be succeeding too well in all of them at the moment. But in the fourth, he flounders.

He is looking for neighborhood leaders. He is probably looking for you; if you live in a city, the chances are 4 to 1 you are in a "going" area. He often doesn't find any neighborhood life, any sense of community. People don't know their neighbors. They don't feel any common problem. Home-ownership is rarely as high as fifty per cent. People have no roots; they are ready to move across town or out of town in an instant. Other than a vague dissatisfaction, they don't know what is wrong with their neighborhood. And worst of all, they don't realize that it may be possible to make it better, to make it worth settling into.

This instability is both cause and effect. People don't care, so they let houses run down. They don't care enough to insist that they get good public services like rubbish collection, let alone good public facilities like traffic-safe streets and adequate playgrounds, or proper public protection against blighting invasions through strict zoning. And the cause of their unwillingness to accept community responsibility is the effect of past generations of irresponsibility.

So your planner finds himself turning into a combination YMCA secretary and Chautauqua lecturer. He gropes for any evidence of neighborhood leadership; he experiments, and finds a different handle to grasp in each part of town. In Cleveland, we have been groping for a year, and a few of the matches we have struck have kindled small hopeful fires.

Vague generalities about "neighborhood improvement" get nowhere. If you can get a group to listen, it is easy to rouse a flash of dissatisfaction by pointing out what needs doing—a playground; a bypass to keep trucks off streets of homes; protection from nuisance industries. But to maintain the steady heat that will lead owners to put real money into house repairs, or follow through on a petition to the city council, you have to show some results, quickly. It doesn't matter what, but you have to prove that neighborhood co-operation can really mean neighborhood improvement.

In our furthest advanced experiment, this worked. We picked an area, a few blocks set off by main streets, peopled by a strong nationality group. The local councilman told us with whom to start. We got the Civilian Defense leaders, who had been very active and wanted something to go on with, to call a meeting. The parish priest caught the idea quickly, and has been the spark plug. The people, slow to respond, decided juvenile delinquency was their problem, and a playground the first answer.

A petition to a co-operative city recreation department brought the lease, equipment, and supervision of a vacant industrial site. This was in June. Later, signs were put up warning trucks off their streets. Only now, in November, are we beginning to talk zoning (the area needs drastic changes). But the picture is beginning to unfold; the people are grasping the idea that the future of their district is in their own hands. They are recognizing the help city planners can give, but see too that the plan—their plan—is also theirs to carry out. And they are proud to be our first experiment in neighborhood conservation.

Other areas take different methods. The local priest or minister is a good bet; in some neighborhoods, he can be especially helpful in getting people to listen. Civilian Defense machinery clicks in one district, and is weak in another. A councilman with vision will seize on the whole program as a sure-fire way to perpetuate himself in office through genuine neighborhood service. Another will resent what seems like an intrusion into the political affairs of his private bailiwick. A parent-teachers association may be fruitful ground, or a local businessman's group. Nationality organizations, service clubs, settlement houses—any *local* group may hold the leader who will be the spark plug, the man who will have the time and capacity to develop and sustain effective local activity.

Rarely, there will be an existing community organization that can assume the job as a going concern. We have one, fostered for several years by a branch librarian, whose area includes the five blocks recently devastated by a gas-tank explosion and fire. It is functioning now, as the channel for ideas back and forth between the city planners and the burnt-out families. It is our main assurance that we can make a rebuilding plan that will work.

The material is there. We have found an astonishing capacity to grasp long-range, complex concepts where we least expected it. We have met a vitality and initiative that has made us take neighborhoods out of the "gone" pigeonhole and promote them, with real hope that they can be saved by the people that live there. Local leadership is waiting, to be uncovered, to be shown how. We are at the beginning of a long pull, with not much yet to show; but we are convinced that our "going" areas can come back. It takes education; it takes compulsion; but most of all it takes participation.

The bottlenecks in effective city planning is people. That bottleneck can be broken. But not by splashing superhighways across the newspapers, or dreaming visions of the Ideal City of 1970. The problem of city planning lies where people live. They can be led to the solutions of the problem—in its big aspects and its little aspects—only by making city planning come alive to them, making it literally come home to them.

Most city people live in old houses, in old areas. This will be so, as far ahead as we can see. Be as optimistic as possible about new houses in the suburbs, new homes in cleared slums. At the best building rate conceivable, in 1960 three out of every four families will still be living in houses from 20 to 60 years old and older. City planning stands or falls by its success in making these neighborhoods good places to live. Stable investments, property values, costs of public service, tax rates, efficient business and industry, all hinge in succession on our ability to remodel our cities. Good neighborhoods—good "old" neighborhoods—are the blocks with which we must build.

City planning can be effective. But not with the planner as a prima donna. He is just one of the newer mechanics on the crew that makes the machinery of democratic government produce results. Though some of his tools are still unfamiliar, he is fast learning that democracy works.

—*Winter* 1944-45

RALPH ELLISON

Richard Wright's Blues

> *If anybody ask you*
> *who sing this song*
> *Say it was ole [Black] Boy*
> *done been here and gone.*[1]

As a writer, Richard Wright has outlined for himself a dual role: To discover and depict the meaning of Negro experience; and to reveal to both Negroes and whites those problems of a psychological and emotional nature which arise between them when they strive for mutual understanding.

Now in *Black Boy*, he has used his own life to probe what qualities of will, imagination, and intellect are required of a Southern Negro in order to possess the meaning of his life in the United States. Wright is an important writer, perhaps the most articulate Negro American, and what he has to say is highly perceptive. Imagine Bigger Thomas projecting his own life in lucid prose, guided, say, by the insights of Marx and Freud, and you have an idea of this autobiography.

Published at a time when any sharply critical approach to Negro life had been dropped as a wartime expendable, it should do much to redefine the problem of the Negro and American Democracy. Its power can be observed in the shrill manner with which some professional "friends of the Negro people" have attempted to strangle the work in a noose of newsprint.

What in the tradition of literary autobiography is it like, this work described as a "great American autobiography"? As a nonwhite intellectual's statement of his relationship to western culture, *Black Boy* recalls the conflicting pattern of identification and rejection found in Nehru's *Toward Freedom*. In its use of fictional techniques, its concern with criminality (sin) and the artistic sensibility, and in its author's judgment and rejection of the narrow world of his origin, it recalls Joyce's rejection of

[1] Signature formula used by blues singers at conclusion of song.

Dublin in *A Portrait of the Artist*. And as a psychological document of life under oppressive conditions, it recalls *The House of the Dead,* Dostoievski's profound study of the humanity of Russian criminals.

Such works were perhaps Wright's literary guides, aiding him to endow his life's incidents with communicable significance; providing him with ways of seeing, feeling, and describing his environment. These influences, however, were encountered only after these first years of Wright's life were past and were not part of the immediate folk culture into which he was born. In that culture the specific folk-art form which helped shape the writer's attitude toward his life and which embodied the impulse that contributes much to the quality and tone of his autobiography was the Negro Blues. This would bear a word of explanation:

The Blues is an impulse to keep the painful details and episodes of a brutal experience alive in one's aching consciousness, to finger its jagged grain, and to transcend it, not by the consolation of philosophy, but by squeezing from it a near-tragic, near-comic lyricism. As a form, the Blues is an autobiographical chronicle of personal catastrophe expressed lyrically. And certainly Wright's early childhood was crammed with catastrophic incidents. In a few short years his father deserted his mother, he knew intense hunger, he became a drunkard begging drinks from black stevedores in Memphis saloons; he had to flee Arkansas where an uncle was lynched; he was forced to live with a fanatically religious grandmother in an atmosphere of constant bickering; he was lodged in an orphan asylum; he observed the suffering of his mother who became a permanent invalid, while fighting off the blows of the poverty-stricken relatives with whom he had to live; he was cheated, beaten, and kicked off jobs by white employees who disliked his eagerness to learn a trade; and to these objective circumstances must be added the subjective fact that Wright, with his sensitivity, extreme shyness and intelligence was a problem child who rejected his family and was by them rejected.

Thus along with the themes, equivalent descriptions of milieu and the perspectives to be found in Joyce, Nehru, Dostoievski, George Moore and Rousseau, *Black Boy* is filled with blues-tempered echoes of railroad trains, the names of Southern towns and cities, estrangements, fights and flights, deaths and disappointments, charged with physical and spiritual hungers and pain. And like a blues sung by such an artist as Bessie Smith, its lyrical prose evokes the paradoxical, almost surreal image of a black boy singing lustily as he probes his own grievous wound.

In *Black Boy*, two worlds have fused, two cultures merged, two impulses of western man become coalesced. By discussing some of its cultural sources I hope to answer those critics who would make of the book a miracle and of its author a mystery. And while making no attempt to probe the mystery of the artist (who Hemingway says is "forged in injustice as a sword is forged") I do hold that basically the prerequisites to the writing of *Black Boy* were, on the one hand, the miscroscopic degree of cultural freedom which Wright found in the South's stony injustice, and, on the other, the existence of a personality agitated to a state of almost manic restlessness. There were, of course, other factors, chiefly ideological; but these came later.

Wright speaks of his journey north as,

> . . . taking a part of the South to transplant in alien soil, to see if it could grow differently, if it could drink of new and cool rains, bend in strange winds, respond to the warmth of other suns, and perhaps, to bloom. . . .

And just as Wright, the man, represents the blooming of the delinquent child of the autobiography, just so does *Black Boy* represent the flowering —cross-fertilized by pollen blown by the winds of strange cultures—of the humble blues lyric. There is, as in all acts of creation, a world of mystery in this, but there is also enough that is comprehensible for Americans to create the social atmosphere in which other black boys might freely bloom.

For certainly, in the historical sense, Wright is no exception. Born on a Mississippi plantation, he was subjected to all those blasting pressures which, in a scant eighty years, have sent the Negro people hurtling, without clearly defined trajectory, from slavery to emancipation, from log cabin to city tenement, from the white folks' fields and kitchens to factory assembly lines; and which, between two wars, have shattered the wholeness of its folk consciousness into a thousand writhing pieces.

Black Boy describes this process in the personal terms of *one* Negro childhood. Nevertheless, several critics have complained that it does not "explain" Richard Wright. Which, aside from the notion of art involved, serves to remind us that the prevailing mood of American criticism has so thoroughly excluded the Negro that it fails to recognize some of the most basic tenets of western democratic thought when encountering them in a black skin. They forget that human life possesses an innate dignity and mankind an innate sense of nobility; that all men possess the tendency to dream and the compulsion to make their dreams reality; that the need to be ever dissatisfied and the urge ever to seek satisfaction is implicit in the human organism; and that all men are the victims and the beneficiaries of the goading, tormenting, commanding, and informing activity of that imperious process known as the Mind—the Mind, as Valéry describes it, "armed with its inexhaustible questions."

Perhaps all this (in which lies the very essence of the human, and which Wright takes for granted) has been forgotten because the critics recognize neither Negro humanity nor the full extent to which the Southern community renders the fulfilment of human destiny impossible. And while it is true that *Black Boy* presents an almost unrelieved picture of a personality corrupted by brutal environment, it also presents those fresh, human responses brought to its world by the sensitive child:

> There was the *wonder* I felt when I first saw a brace of mountain-like, spotted, black-and-white horses clopping down a dusty road . . . the *delight* I caught in seeing long straight rows of red and green vegetables stretching away in the sun . . . the faint, cool kiss of *sensuality* when dew came on to my cheeks . . . the vague *sense of the infinite* as I looked down upon the yellow, dreaming waters of the Mississippi . . . the echoes of *nostalgia* I heard in the crying strings of wild geese . . . the *love* I had for the mute regality of tall, moss-clad oaks . . . the hint of *cosmic cruelty* that I *felt* when I saw the curved timbers of a wooden shack that had been warped in the summer sun . . . and there was the *quiet terror* that suffused my senses when vast hazes of gold washed earthward from star-heavy skies on silent nights. . . .[2]

And a bit later, his reactions to religion:

> Many of the religious symbols appealed to my sensibilities and I responded to the dramatic vision of life held by the church, feeling that to live day by day with death as one's sole thought was to be so compassionately sensitive toward all life as to view all men as slowly dying, and the trembling sense of fate that welled up, sweet and melancholy, from the hymns blended with the sense of fate that I had already caught from life.

There was also the influence of his mother—so closely linked to his hysteria and sense of suffering—who (though he only implies it here) taught him, in the words of the dedication prefacing *Native Son*, "to revere the fanciful and the imaginative." There were also those white men—the one who allowed Wright to use his library privileges and the other who advised him to leave the South, and still others whose offers of friendship he was too frightened to accept.

Wright assumed that the nucleus of plastic sensibility is a human heritage—the right and the opportunity to dilate, deepen, and enrich sensibility—democracy. Thus the drama of *Black Boy* lies in its depiction of what occurs when Negro sensibility attempts to fulfill itself in the

---

[2] Italics mine.

undemocratic South. Here it is not the individual that is the immediate focus, as in Joyce's *Stephen Hero*, but that upon which his sensibility was nourished.

Those critics who complain that Wright has omitted the development of his own sensibility hold that the work thus fails as art. Others, because it presents too little of what they consider attractive in Negro life, charge that it distorts reality. Both groups miss a very obvious point: That whatever else the environment contained, it had as little chance of prevailing against the overwhelming weight of the child's unpleasant experiences as Beethoven's Quartets would have of destroying the stench of a Nazi prison.

We come, then, to the question of art. The function, the psychology, of artistic selectivity is to eliminate from art form all those elements of experience which contain no compelling significance. Life is as the sea, art a ship in which man conquers life's crushing formlessness, reducing it to a course, a series of swells, tides, and wind currents inscribed on a chart. Though drawn from the world, "the organized significance of art," writes Malraux, "is stronger than all the multiplicity of the world; . . . that significance alone enables man to conquer chaos and to master destiny."

Wright saw his destiny—that combination of forces before which man feels powerless—in terms of a quick and casual violence inflicted upon him by both family and community. His response was likewise violent, and it has been his need to give that violence significance which has shaped his writings.

II

What were the ways by which other Negroes confronted their destiny?

In the South of Wright's childhood there were three general ways: They could accept the role created for them by the whites and perpetually resolve the resulting conflicts through the hope and emotional catharsis of Negro religion; they could repress their dislike of Jimcrow social relations while striving for a middle way of respectability, becoming—consciously or unconsciously—the accomplices of the whites in oppressing their brothers; or they could reject the situation, adopt a criminal attitude, and carry on an unceasing psychological scrimmage with the whites, which often flared forth into physical violence.

Wright's attitude was nearest the last. Yet, in it there was an all-important qualitative difference: it represented a groping for *individual* values, in a black community whose values were what the young Negro critic, Edward Bland, has defined as "pre-individual." And herein lay the setting for the extreme conflict set off, both within his family and in the community, by Wright's assertion of individuality. The clash was sharpest on the psychological level, for, to quote Bland:

> In the pre-individualistic thinking of the Negro the stress is on the group. Instead of seeing in terms of the individual, the Negro sees in terms of "races," masses of peoples separated from other masses according to color. Hence, an act rarely bears intent against him as a Negro individual. He is singled out not as a person but as a specimen of an ostracized group. He knows that he never exists in his own right but only to the extent that others hope to make the race suffer vicariously through him.

This pre-individual state is induced artificially—like the regression to primitive states noted among cultured inmates of Nazi prisons. The primary technique in its enforcement is to impress the Negro child with the omniscience and omnipotence of the whites to the point that whites appear as ahuman as Jehovah, and as relentless as a Mississippi flood. Socially it is effected through an elaborate scheme of taboos supported by a ruthless physical violence, which strikes not only the offender, but the entire black community. To wander from the paths of behavior laid down for the group is to become the agent of communal disaster.

In such a society the development of individuality depends upon a series of accidents; which often arise, as in Wright's case, from conditions within the Negro family. In Wright's life there was the accident that as a small child he could not distinguish between his fair-skinned grandmother and the white women of the town, thus developing skepticism as to their special status. To this was linked the accident of his having no close contacts with whites until after the child's normal formative period.

But these objective accidents not only link forward to those qualities of rebellion, criminality, and intellectual questioning expressed in Wright's work today. They also link backward into the shadow of infancy where environment and consciousness are so darkly intertwined as to require the skill of a psychoanalyst to define their point of juncture. Nevertheless, at the age of four, Wright set the house afire and was beaten near to death by his frightened mother. This beating, followed soon by his father's desertion of the family, seems to be the initial psychological motivation of his quest for a new identification. While delirious from this beating Wright was haunted "by huge wobbly white bags like the full udders of a cow, suspended from the ceiling above me [and] I was gripped by the fear that they were going to fall and drench me with some horrible liquid. . . ."

It was as though the mother's milk had turned acid, and with it the whole pattern of life that had produced the ignorance, cruelty, and fear that had fused with mother-love and exploded in the beating. It is significant that the bags were of the hostile color white, and the female symbol that of the cow, the most stupid (and, to the small child, the most frightening) of domestic animals. Here in dream symbolism is expressed an attitude worthy of an Orestes. And the significance of the crisis is increased by virtue of the historical fact that the lower-class Negro family is matriarchal; the child turns not to the father to compensate if he feels mother-rejection, but to the grandmother, or to an aunt—and Wright rejected both of these. Such rejection leaves the child open to psychological insecurity, distrust, and all of those hostile environmental forces from which the family functions to protect it.

One of the Southern Negro family's methods of protecting the child is the severe beating—a homeopathic dose of the violence generated by black and white relationships. Such beatings as Wright's were administered for the child's own good; a good which the child resisted, thus giving family relationships an undercurrent of fear and hostility, which differs qualitatively from that found in patriarchal middle-class families, because here the severe beating is administered by the mother, leaving the child no parental sanctuary. He must ever embrace violence along with maternal tenderness, or else reject, in his helpless way, the mother.

The division between the Negro parents of Wright's mother's generation, whose sensibilities were often bound by their proximity to the slave experience, and their children, who historically and through the rapidity of American change, stand emotionally and psychologically much farther away, is quite deep. Indeed, sometimes as deep as the cultural distance between Yeats' *Autobiographies* and a Bessie Smith blues. This is the historical background to those incidents of family strife in *Black Boy* which have caused reviewers to question Wright's judgment of Negro emotional relationships.

We have here a problem in the sociology of sensibility that is obscured by certain psychological attitudes brought to Negro life by whites.

III

The first is the attitude which compels whites to impute to Negroes sentiments, attitudes, and insights which, as a group living under certain definite social conditions, Negroes could not humanly possess. It is the identical mechanism which William Empson identifies in literature as "pastoral." It implies that since Negroes possess the richly human virtues credited to them, then their social position is advantageous and should not be bettered; and, continuing syllogistically, the white individual need feel no guilt over his participation in Negro oppression.

The second attitude is that which leads whites to misjudge Negro passion, looking upon it as they do, out of the turgidity of their own frustrated yearning for emotional warmth, their capacity for sensation having been constricted by the impersonal mechanized relationships typical of bourgeois society. The Negro is idealized into a symbol of sensation, of unhampered social and sexual relationships. And when *Black Boy* questions their illusion they are thwarted much in the manner of the occidental who, after observing the erotic character of a primitive dance, "shacks up" with a native woman—only to discover that far from possessing the hair-trigger sexual responses of a Stork Club "babe," she is relatively phlegmatic.

The point is not that American Negroes are primitives, but that as a group, their social situation does not provide for the type of emotional relationships attributed them. For how could the South, recognized as a major part of the backward third of the nation, flower in the black, most brutalized section of its population, those forms of human relationships achievable only in the most highly developed areas of civilization?

Champions of this "Aren't-Negroes-Wonderful?" school of thinking often bring Paul Robeson and Marian Anderson forward as examples of highly developed sensibility, but actually they are only its *promise*. Both received their development from an extensive personal contact with European culture, free from the influences which shape Southern Negro personality. In the United States, Wright, who is the only Negro literary artist of equal caliber, had to wait years and escape to another environment before discovering the moral and ideological equivalents of his childhood attitudes.

Man cannot express that which does not exist—either in the form of dreams, ideas, or realities—in his environment. Neither his thoughts nor his feelings, his sensibility nor his intellect are fixed, innate qualities. They are processes which arise out of the interpenetration of human instinct with environment, through the process called experience; each changing and being changed by the other. Negroes cannot possess many of the sentiments attributed to them because the same changes in environment which, through experience, enlarge man's intellect (and thus his capacity for still greater change) also modify his feelings; which in turn increase his sensibility, i.e. his sensitivity to refinements of impression and subtleties of emotion. The extent of these changes depends upon the quality of political and cultural freedom in the environment.

Intelligence tests have measured the quick rise in intellect which takes place in Southern Negroes after moving North, but little attention has been paid to the mutations effected in their sensibilities. However, the two go hand in hand. Intellectual complexity is accompanied by emotional complexity; refinement of thought, by refinement of feeling. The movement North affects more than the Negro's wage scale, it affects his entire psychosomatic structure.

The rapidity of Negro intellectual growth in the North is due partially to objective factors present in the environment, to influences of the industrial city, and to a greater political freedom. But there are also changes within the "inner world." In the North energies are released and given *intellectual* channelization—energies which in most Negroes in the South have been forced to take either a *physical* form or, as with potentially intellectual types like Wright, to be expressed as nervous tension, anxiety, and hysteria. Which is nothing mysterious. The human organism responds to environmental stimuli by converting them into either physical and/or intellectual energy. And what is called hysteria is suppressed intellectual energy expressed physically.

The "physical" character of their expression makes for much of the difficulty in understanding American Negroes. Negro music and dances are frenziedly erotic; Negro religious ceremonies violently ecstatic; Negro speech strongly rhythmical and weighted with image and gesture. But there is more in this sensuousness than the unrestraint and insensitivity found in primitive cultures; nor is it simply the relatively spontaneous and undifferentiated responses of a people living in close contact with the soil. For despite Jimcrow, Negro life does not exist in a vacuum, but in the seething vortex of those tensions generated by the most highly industrialized of western nations. The welfare of the most humble black Mississippi sharecropper is affected less by the flow of the seasons and the rhythm of natural events than by the fluctuations of the stock market; even though, as Wright states of his father, the sharecropper's memories, actions, and emotions are shaped by his immediate contact with nature and the crude social relations of the South.

All of this makes the American Negro far different from the "simple" specimen for which he is taken. And the "physical" quality offered as evidence of his primitive simplicity is actually the form of his complexity. The American Negro is a western type whose social condition creates a state which is almost the reverse of the cataleptic trance: Instead of his consciousness being lucid to the reality around it while the body is rigid, here it is the body which is alert, reacting to pressures which the constricting forces of Jimcrow block off from the transforming, concept-creating activity of the brain. The "eroticism" of Negro expression springs from much the same conflict as that displayed in the violent gesturing of a man who attempts to express a complicated concept with a limited vocabulary; thwarted ideational energy is converted into unsatisfactory pantomime, and his words are burdened with meanings they cannot convey. Here lies the source of the basic ambiguity of *Native Son*, wherein in order to translate Bigger's complicated feelings into universal ideas, Wright had to force into Bigger's consciousness concepts and ideas which his intellect could not formulate. Between Wright's skill and knowledge and the potentials of Bigger's mute feelings lay a thousand years of conscious culture.

In the South the sensibilities of both blacks and whites are inhibited by the rigidly defined environment. For the Negro there is relative safety as long as the impulse toward individuality is suppressed. (Lynchings have occurred because Negroes painted their homes.) And it is the task of the Negro family to adjust the child to the Southern milieu; through it the currents, tensions, and impulses generated within the human organism by the flux and flow of events are given their distribution. This also gives the group its distinctive character. Which, because of Negroes' suppressed minority position, is very much in the nature of an elaborate but limited defense mechanism. Its function is dual: to protect the Negro from whirling away from the undifferentiated mass of his people into the unknown, symbolized in its most abstract form by insanity, and most concretely by lynching; and to protect him from those unknown forces *within himself* which might urge him to reach out for that social and human equality which the white South says he cannot have. Rather than throw himself against the charged wires of his prison he annihilates the impulses within him.

The pre-individualistic black community discourages individuality out of self-defense. Having learned through experience that the whole group is punished for the actions of the single member, it has worked out efficient techniques of behavior control. For in many Southern communities everyone knows everyone else and is vulnerable to his opinions. In some communities everyone is "related" regardless of blood-ties. The regard shown by the group for its members, its general communal character and its cohesion are often mentioned. For by comparison with the coldly impersonal relationships of the urban industrial community, its relationships are personal and warm.

Black Boy, however, illustrates that this personal quality, shaped by outer violence and inner fear, is ambivalent. Personal warmth is accompanied by an equally personal coldness, kindliness by cruelty, regard by malice. And these opposites are as quickly set off against the member who gestures toward individuality as a lynch mob forms at the cry of rape. Negro leaders have often been exasperated by this phenomenon, and Booker T. Washington (who demanded far less of Negro humanity than Richard Wright) described the Negro community as a basket of crabs, wherein should one attempt to climb out, the others immediately pull him back.

The member who breaks away is apt to be more impressed by its negative than by its positive character. He becomes a stranger even to his relatives and he interprets gestures of protection as blows of oppression —from which there is no hiding place, because every area of Negro life is affected. Even parental love is given a qualitative balance akin to "sadism." And the extent of beatings and psychological maimings meted out by Southern Negro parents rivals those described by the nineteenth-century Russian writers as characteristic of peasant life under the Czars. The horrible thing is that the cruelty is also an expression of concern, of love.

In discussing the inadequacies for democratic living typical of the education provided Negroes by the South, a Negro educator has coined the term *mis-education*. Within the ambit of the black family this takes the form of training the child away from curiosity and adventure, against reaching out for those activities lying beyond the borders of the black community. And when the child resists, the parent discourages him; first with the formula, "That there's for white folks. Colored can't have it," and finally with a beating.

It is not, then, the family and communal violence described by *Black Boy* that is unusual, but that Wright *recognized* and made no peace with its essential cruelty—even when, like a babe freshly emerged from the womb, he could not discern where his own personality ended and it began. Ordinarily, both parent and child are protected against this cruelty —seeing it as love and finding subjective sanction for it in the spiritual authority of the Fifth Commandment, and on the secular level in the legal and extralegal structure of the Jimcrow system. The child who did not rebel, or who was unsuccessful in his rebellion, learned a masochistic submissiveness and a denial of the impulse toward western culture when it stirred within him.

IV

Why then have Southern whites, who claim to "know" the Negro missed all this? Simply because they too are armored against the horror and the cruelty. Either they deny the Negro's humanity and feel no cause to measure his actions against civilized norms; or they protect themselves from their guilt in the Negro's condition and from their fear that their cooks might poison them, or that their nursemaids might strangle their infant charges, or that their field hands might do them violence, by attributing to them a superhuman capacity for love, kindliness, and forgiveness. Nor does this in any way contradict their stereotyped conviction that all Negroes (meaning those with whom they have no contact) are given to the most animal behavior.

It is only when the individual, whether white or black, *rejects* the pattern that he awakens to the nightmare of his life. Perhaps much of the South's regressive character springs from the fact that many, jarred by some casual crisis into wakefulness, flee hysterically into the sleep of violence or the coma of apathy again. For the penalty of wakefulness is to encounter ever more violence and horror than the sensibilities can sustain unless translated into some form of social action. Perhaps the impassioned character so noticeable among those white Southern liberals so active in the Negro's cause is due to their sense of accumulated horror; their passion—like the violence in Faulkner's novels—is evidence of a profound spiritual vomiting.

This compulsion is even more active in Wright and the increasing number of Negroes who have said an irrevocable "no" to the Southern pattern. Wright learned that it is not enough merely to reject the white South, but that he had also to reject that part of the South which lay within. As a rebel he formulated that rejection negatively, because it was the negative face of the Negro community upon which he looked most often as a child. It is this he is contemplating when he writes:

> Whenever I thought of the essential bleakness of black life in America, I knew that Negroes had never been allowed to catch the full spirit of Western civilization, that they lived somehow in it but not of it. And when I brooded upon the cultural barrenness of black life, I wondered if clean, positive tenderness, love, honor, loyalty, and the capacity to remember were native to man. I asked myself if these human qualities were not fostered, won, struggled and suffered for, preserved in ritual from one generation to another.

But far from implying that Negroes have no capacity for culture, as one critic interprets it, this is the strongest affirmation that they have. Wright is pointing out what should be obvious (especially to his Marxist critics) that Negro sensibility is socially and historically conditioned; that western culture must be won, confronted like the animal in a Spanish bullfight, dominated by the red shawl of codified experience, and brought heaving to its knees.

Wright knows perfectly well that Negro life is a by-product of western civilization, and that in it, if only one possesses the humanity and humility to see, are to be discovered all those impulses, tendencies, life and cultural forms, to be found elsewhere in western society.

The problem arises because the special condition of Negroes in the

United States, including the defensive character of Negro life itself (the "will toward organization" noted in the western capitalist appears in the Negro as a will to camouflage, to dissimulate) so distorts these forms as to render their recognition as difficult as finding a wounded quail against the brown and yellow leaves of a Mississippi thicket—even the spilled blood blends with the background. Having himself been in the position of the quail—to expand the metaphor—Wright's wounds have told him both the question and the answer which every successful hunter must discover for himself: "Where would I hide if *I* were a wounded quail?" But perhaps that requires more sympathy with one's quarry than most hunters possess. Certainly it requires such a sensitivity to the shifting guises of humanity under pressure as to allow them to identify themselves with the human content, whatever its outer form; and even with those Southern Negroes to whom Paul Robeson's name is only a rolling sound in the fear-charged air.

Let us close with one final word about the Blues: Their attraction lies in this, that they at once express both the agony of life and the possibility of conquering it through sheer toughness of spirit. They fall short of tragedy only in that they provide no solution, offer no scapegoat but the self. Nowhere in America today is there social or political action based upon the solid realities of Negro life depicted in *Black Boy*; perhaps that is why, with its refusal to offer solutions, it is like the Blues. Yet, in it thousands of Negroes will for the first time see their destiny in public print. Freed here of fear and the threat of violence, their lives have at last been organized, scaled down to possessable proportions. And in this lies Wright's most important achievement: He has converted the American Negro impulse toward self-annihilation and "going-under-ground" into a will to confront the world, to evaluate his experience honestly and throw his findings unashamedly into the guilty conscience of America.

—Summer 1945

P A U L   M .   G R E G O R Y

The Deformed Thief

"See'st thou not, I say, what a deformed thief this fashion is?"
—Shakespeare, *Much Ado About Nothing.*

Fashion has always elicited much criticism, for its influence touches the whole habitable and habilable globe. Roman philosophers denounced it; Church Fathers thundered against it; social satirists still tilt with the fashion windmill. In fact, the literature of all modern nations disparages fashion, but largely on aesthetic and moral grounds. Some of the literature, both ancient and modern, it is true, censures fashion on economic grounds, but even such criticism has generally been directed against the luxuriousness or costliness of the clothes themselves. Usually overlooked or minimized is the fundamental fact that, by outmoding existing wardrobes, fashion is wasteful by its very nature, regardless of the cost, the beauty or the usefulness of the new clothes. If fashion turns Woman into an artist, it turns Man into a critic. But this essay criticizes the institution of fashion, not Woman, who is often the slave rather than the mistress of her costume.

The term "fashion" has three distinct meanings. First, it may refer to the apparel currently in vogue; a certain dress is "the fashion." Second, fashion as an institution means the process of annual or seasonal change. Third, in psychological or sociological definitions, fashion refers to the collective behavior of imitation, or the tendency of the masses to follow fashion leaders. We are interested chiefly in the second meaning: fashion as an institution, or as the process of perennial change in costume design. Fashion and style are not synonymous, although most writers confuse the two terms. With reference to clothing, style is any distinctive mode of tailoring, while fashion is the style, or the variant of the style, prevailing at any given time. A style evolves slowly and reflects the people's way of life; fashion is a chameleon, ever changing, never in vogue long enough to reflect basic tastes and habits. Frequent fashion changes artificially shorten the period during which a style prevails; thus fashion is a parasite on style.

276

The loose drapery of ancient Greece and Rome, the velvet, gold-trimmed robes of the Renaissance—these are styles, and they call to mind certain periods in history. Togas, hoopskirts, bustles, hourglass figures, form-fitting dresses—all remain distinctive styles; and, like Hattie Carnegie's bustles, they sometimes come back into fashion as revivals or adaptations of old styles with modern touches of detail. Style is concerned with the basic shape or silhouette of clothes. For, as Elizabeth Hawes says in *Fashion Is Spinach*, "style doesn't give a whoop whether your . . . clothes are red or yellow or blue, or whether your bag matches your shoes."

Clothing styles give the social historian some insight into the life of the people who wore them, as Anatole France realized. Two centuries hence historians may infer from the functional design of bathing suits, sports clothes and women's business suits, that ours was an age in which women won for themselves greater physical and social freedom and economic opportunity than our grandmothers had in the nineteenth century. Such a distinct design constitutes a *style*. But the slight shifting of waistlines or necklines from season to season, the popularity of certain colors, the shortening or lengthening of skirts by two inches, will tell nothing of the life of the people. Such trivia are the heart of *fashion*.

In *Recurring Cycles of Fashion, 1760-1937*, Agnes Brooks Young develops an interesting theory of what she terms fashion changes but which should really be called style changes. She points out that in the past two centuries woman's silhouette, characterized chiefly by the shape of the skirt, has moved through a series of recurring cycles lasting about thirty-five years each; within each cycle the annual fashion changes have consisted of minor variations on the major theme; and finally, there have been only three basic styles, or silhouettes, which have succeeded one another in unchanging order: the bell (characterized by the hoopskirt), the back-fullness (characterized by the bustle), and the tubular (which is relatively form-fitting or, in some cases, straight). These skirt types seem to exhaust all the possibilities. Side-fullness of the pannier type is a variant of the back-fullness and the bell types; extreme front-fullness is not only impractical but also undesirable, as it might suggest maternity.

There seems to be a popular antipathy toward reintroducing remembered styles. Women consider the earlier variants of the current tubular style era (for example, the boyish silhouette of 1925) ridiculous or distasteful. Older women retain disagreeable impressions of the bustled dresses their mothers wore in the late nineteenth century. Since these two silhouettes are taboo, and there are only three basic types to choose from, a change to a new style cycle must revive some variant of the bell, or hoopskirt, which, absent from the memory of women now living, takes on a quaint, charming or romantic character. Mrs. Young predicted (in 1937) that, because the tubular cycle had run since the turn of the century, we would soon enter upon another bell cycle.

If this theory of long cycles in silhouette (or style, in the broad sense of the word) is valid, it still remains to explain and evaluate the phenomenon of annual or seasonal changes within each cycle, or fashion as distinct from style. Why do fashions change? The ultimate causes of fashion are the subject of much speculation, some of it fantastic, some of it plausible. Thorstein Veblen emphasized the role of conspicuous consumption and the desire for distinction through dress. Others attribute fashion changes to the desire for decorative dress to enhance sex appeal. "No fashion is ever successful unless it can be used as an instrument of seduction," according to James Laver, costume authority of the Victoria and Albert Museum in England. This may explain decorative dress, but not the incessant *changes*. Nor is dress itself an indication of modesty, for it is our faces which present our ego to the world. "If we really had modesty," says Raymond Mortimer in his *Essay on Clothes*, "it is our faces that we should conceal. By comparison our legs are anonymous, our bellies uneventful."

In explaining *Why Women Wear Clothes*, C. Willett Cunnington develops a fascinating theory of fashion. Women wear clothes chiefly to enhance their sex appeal. Sex appeal is heightened by novelty, and so fashion covers up one part of the body and exposes another part; and the bits selected for concealment or display are constantly changed in order to stimulate man's curiosity. Complete exposure of the whole body is less exciting to man than partial exposure; therefore fashion each season will "feature" one special region, either by exposure or by elaborate concealment of innocuous regions. Once fashion chooses to bare a particular area, women rapidly lose their inhibitions concerning that region, and these taboos are shifted to some other part of the body. "When the naked bosom is freely exposed, the foot may coyly retire into obscurity. Thus does Woman play on Man's feelings a perpetual game of hide-and-seek with bits of her body." The huge crinoline skirt, denying the facts of anatomy, arouses man's exploring instincts. Provocative petticoats inspired the Victorian gentleman with uplifting thoughts. Such armaments, he reasons, surely must protect a rich treasure; and the thief is allured by the illusion of the locked casket. Or part of the dress may be flimsy, fenestrated or transparent, to remind man that "Stone walls do not a prison make, nor iron bars a cage."

Other factors leading to sartorial experimentation are, of course, the restless and unending search for perfect beauty, and curiosity. Some people even believe that vanity and curiosity spring from a subconscious modesty; dissatisfied with our appearance, we seek perfection, an ideal which always eludes us. We try whatever promises improvement, and then embark on a fresh experiment. And we seek the irreconcilable goals of submergence in the crowd and the appearance of individuality. In temperate zones, moreover, seasonal changes may accentuate the desire for fashion changes. Finally, there is the social and economic class structure. The rich, the bored and those lacking in outside interests seek to distinguish themselves from the masses by dress, and succeed in doing so temporarily. The imitativeness of the lower income groups and the desire of the garment industry to capitalize on a novelty lead to imitation and vulgarization of original designs and deprive the "elite" of their distinction. Thus the *haut couture* must constantly evolve new fashions, or revive old styles, in order to continue to supply "exclusive" apparel for its clients.

II

Profits from producing or selling fashion goods may be profits of monopoly, of innovation or of risk-taking. Producers or sellers who can control or influence the trend of fashion—sometimes through fashion magazines which "predict" what they have already decided to sell—and whose "creations" are not imitated, are largely relieved of risk, and they receive monopoly profits; for their "exclusive" apparel sells at monopoly prices. (Around 1929, for example, cotton house dresses, originally $3.95, were sold for $19.50 after Mary Lewis, then of Best and Company, promoted them as fashionable frocks.) Even with imitations, sellers obtain profits of innovation as long as a new fashion remains exclusive. Eventually the "creations" of Hattie Carnegie, Valentina, and others, are copied by the garment manufacturers on Seventh Avenue, New York, and these profits of innovation disappear. But by that time, still other "creations" are developed, and the profits of innovation may be permanent so long as the stream of new ideas does not run dry. Finally, those who can neither influence the fashion trend nor be among the first to introduce new designs must anticipate the future demand. The manufacturer or seller who guesses correctly gains profits which are a "reward for risk-taking," while those who guess wrong may take losses on unsold inventory and markdowns, may also suffer from the wastes which result from hand-to-mouth buying, seasonal production and small-lot production.

Although some manufacturers and sellers may lose, business in general profits from fashion changes. Large-scale producers take added risks, and some lose; but some gain enormous profits in the steady market for replacement sales of clothing. The loss of some producers results, not from fashion itself, but from an incorrect anticipation of future fashion trends; it is analogous to producers' losses from other economic risks. If manufacturers always lost, they would oppose fashion changes! If fashion gyrations were eliminated, one of the risks of business would be gone and there would be less potential loss, but there would also be less profit from heavy repeat sales of clothing and accessories. And fashion editors, designers, fashion magazines that sell patterns, and the large and growing clan of publicity organizations which make toeless shoes smart this summer and iridescent hosiery next winter—all lose or gain from the fashion merry-go-round. Ultimately, the real losers from fashion are consumers.

Frequent fashion changes are stimulated by producers and sellers in order to make people dissatisfied with their present garments and induce them to buy new ones long before the old ones are worn out. Sales volume is based largely on repeat sales. If a garment is durable and well made and will last five years, a fashion change which makes consumers discard it in one year destroys much of its utility. This puts a strain on the consumer's pocketbook; it reduces our scale of living and encourages a tremendous waste of economic resources. But fashion gyrations may have an even more insidious effect; for if clothes are discarded after one season's wear, the customer may come back to the retailer for "new" fashions before she can discover whether her "old" dress was really durable or well made. This may encourage some unscrupulous manufacturers to adulterate their product. They may produce shoddy goods; cut costs by not allowing enough material for shrinkage or alterations; save a few yards of material per hundred dresses by skimping on yardage, causing seams to split; or use fugitive dyes and composition buttons which melt. Producers may try to beat the price of their rivals, not by more efficient production but by diluting quality and durability; and they may succeed in this practice because the public has been taught to pay attention to fashion but not to inquire too closely about the technical composition of materials. Indeed, part of the garment industry opposed the "Truth in Fabrics" bill because they feared that honest labeling would take women's attention from fashion and make them buy more rationally. "Nothing should be done that would take the woman's attention from fashion and direct it toward the technical composition of materials," said an industry witness before a congressional committee in 1938. When fashion does not lead to adulteration and reduced durability, it fosters premature replacement of apparel in order to stimulate sales volume. Truly, "the fashion wears out more apparel than the man."

Lately* there has been a wave of protest against the exaggerated silhouette which the industry is promoting. Some writers have denounced the new fashions. Women have organized short-skirt clubs and "Little Below the Knee Clubs." Some women dislike the expense of acquiring a new wardrobe, and many men prefer short skirts on aesthetic grounds.

---

* 1947.

In Hollywood, women have paraded in bathing suits to prove they need no artificial padding around the hips. And in London, the National Federation of Merchant Tailors has frowned upon the proposed long skirts on economic as well as aesthetic grounds. The effect of such protests has been a slight temporary decline in dress sales, and many retailers have presented full-page advertisements in defense of the new fashions. Copy writers are urged by the industry to describe the current dresses as "new length" or "the new look" instead of "long length." The fullness of the skirt is defended on the ground that it is needed to balance the general effect of longer skirts. And the whole radical change is declared a "natural" reaction of the public against the frozen silhouette under Order L-85. Such apologetics seem to indicate that the industry is determined to have its way.

Although industry leaders loudly deny that the new designs were deliberately chosen in order to outmode existing wardrobes, they have also admitted (sometimes in print) that they intend to get their share of the growing national income, regardless of popular criticism of the new fashions. (And the men's wear industry intends to profit from the cashing of veterans' terminal leave bonds.) Businessmen know that women will eventually accept the new fashion, as they did the Irene Castle hair bob, the hobble skirt and the tubular monstrosities of the '20's. Eventually women will have to wear the new dresses, or wear "outmoded" styles. Significantly, while manufacturers argue that the sharp change in fashion is needed in order to overcome price resistance, retailers are trying to explain the higher prices by pointing to the radical changes in the clothes. In a postwar period, fashion changes are an inflationary influence.

III

Although a particular fashion may possess great utility, the fashion industries are not essentially concerned with utility or with genuine improvement in clothes. Society has usually scorned utilitarian dress reformers —except Mrs. Bloomer, whose simple invention exalted her to the seats of the mighty. It therefore seems appropriate to discuss fashion in the light of utility.

Clothes are semidurable goods which yield "services" of gradually diminishing utility, because of depreciation and obsolescence. (It is possible, of course, to purchase a single service by renting clothes for a single occasion.) As these services decline in utility, the consumer must decide when to discard the garment and replace it. Now, the utility gained by replacing a not-yet-worn-out article is not the total utility of the new article, but the *difference* between the total utility of the new article and the utility (or potential services) remaining in the discarded article. Since the rate of fashion change almost never coincides with the physical life of the goods, fashion induces premature replacement; and this wastes the utility remaining in the discarded garment.

The rate of replacement of clothes is influenced by their price, the consumer's income, and the rate of depreciation and obsolescence. If the garment is priced low, a consumer (with any given income) is warranted in replacing it earlier than if the price is high, for at a low price the utility of the expected added services exceeds the utility anticipated from alternative purchases. The richer the consumer, the less each dollar is worth to him, and the earlier he is likely to discard clothes and replace them. But since a dollar seems large to a poor man, he should (rationally) wear his clothes longer. Finally, wear and tear causes depreciation, while monotony, conspicuous waste and, of course, fashion, all cause obsolescence. Even in the absence of wear and tear, it is usually claimed that long use of the same styles is monotonous, and their utility will decline because people like change and novelty for its own sake. Also, in a pecuniary culture which stresses conspicuous display of wealth, people may lose prestige if they wear the same style for a long time. Except for fashion, these factors are largely outside the control of any individual or business firm. But since fashion changes are influenced by business, they create deliberate or *purposeful* obsolescence of goods, and induce premature replacement and much waste, even in the absence of wear and tear and such monotony and conspicuous consumption as is normal.

Most people dislike tension; satisfaction consists in the relief from tension. Fashion—and suggestive advertising, with which it is allied— makes people dissatisfied with their existing clothing, arouses desires, and if people lack the purchasing power to indulge their newly created wants, sets up tensions which cumulate. Fashion and advertising are a gigantic burlesque show at which millions gape. Seeing new fashions temptingly and teasingly advertised—clothes they can never hope to own, changes they cannot afford to keep up with—must set up a tremendous store of insatiety in the poor and the modest-income groups, an insatiety which probably contributes to the neurotic personality of our time. And fashion may destroy utility, not only for one but for many. Just as becoming apparel is satisfying to all who behold the wearer, so a fashion change makes last year's apparel distasteful not only to the wearer, but also to her friends, who may be ashamed to be seen with her.

If fashion changes reflected changing tastes and habits, then each season's fashions might be an improvement over the last, and might possess more utility by being a closer approximation to our basic needs. But this would be so only if styles changed gradually and were not forced. If fashions changed in order to attain beauty in dress, the result should be a gradual approach to artistic perfection. But this is not the case. As Veblen pointed out in the *Theory of the Leisure Class*, the alleged beauty of the prevailing fashions is spurious, since none of them will bear the test of time. The Chinese and Japanese, the ancient Greeks and Romans and the peasants of many European countries have evolved fairly stable styles which many critics consider more artistic and more satisfying than the fluctuating fashions of modern industrial communities. Indeed, in copying or adapting them, modern designers either admit their intrinsic superiority or else betray their own poverty of creative imagination.

As John Brophy indicated in his delightful book *The Human Face*, there have been fashion revivals in faces, in eyebrows, in foreheads, in hairdressing and hair color and in cosmetics, as well as in clothes. In the 1930's for instance, there was a remarkable metamorphosis of brunettes into the ancient Egyptian queen Nefertiti, while many blondes tried to imitate Botticelli's Venus. Most current fashions, in dress and in other spheres, are revivals of bygone styles, and their promoters are highly conscious of history. Today's artificially swollen habiliments—like the exaggerated use of cosmetics—hark back to Elizabethan times. Elaborately decorative rather than functional, many currently fashionable dresses appear to be designed to impress the casual observer rather than those sufficiently intimate to come to close quarters; and this may indicate that women are supposed to please the general community rather than their husbands or lovers.

Fashion destroys utility, however defined. If utility is considered a physical attribute, then the changed fashion forces consumers to discard still useful garments. For people who are concerned with wearing the "right" things, utility based on social approval is immediately destroyed when the old garment loses social caste. But perhaps the true function of apparel is to attract attention to the wearer. A man may criticize a woman he has seen in a ridiculous hat, but without it he might not have seen her at all. It has served its purpose if it provokes notice, if not admiration. But even if utility is based on novelty, only the new clothes have utility; and every change in fashion destroys the attention-arresting features of the displaced garment.

Whatever the utility of fashion *goods* may be, we must subtract from it the loss of potential services remaining in prematurely discarded garments, the disutility and "care costs" of frequent shopping and concern over "matching" clothes with accessories, and the heightened irrationality of buying which result from fashion *changes*. Thus fashion as an economic institution creates disutility, regardless of the usefulness of the fashionable clothes themselves. In the absence of annual fashion changes, all people would wear the same styles longer, and more people than today would feel appropriately dressed. Industry ought to provide a wide range of styles at any given time, in order to complement the great variety of ages, physical types, and personalities. But stability of styles is not the same thing as standardization; variety can exist without changing designs one jot or tittle from season to season.

I V

Despite intense rivalry in the production and sale of clothing, fashion itself is a monopoly element, for it reduces competition in two ways. First, producers differentiate their goods from all rival "creations" at any one time. A distinctive or "exclusive" fashion has the same economic effect as a brand or trademark: it distinguishes a particular product in the minds of buyers and creates loyalty to a particular producer or seller; it lifts the product out of the market for more standardized goods and creates a specialty which is relatively free from comparative judgment of price, quality or durability. In this sense, fashion is a pure monopoly element, although it results not in monopoly but in "monopolistic competition"; for there is always the possibility of consumers switching to some other producer's designs.

Second, each producer differentiates his own offerings from the model he was selling last season. This differentiation over time, or "temporal differentiation," with its incessant emphasis on newness, makes people dissatisfied with their existing clothing and leads them to buy newer fashions. Their dissatisfaction begot of obsolescence, they do not necessarily forsake their original buying source. In fact, a producer or seller who can offer the "latest" fashions has a selling advantage over his more conservative rivals, once people are induced to think of utility in terms of novelty and get into the habit of frequently replacing their clothes. The garment industry, the millinery, shoe, glove and other industries which depend on fashion for sales volume recognize the importance of temporal differentiation. They employ "adapters," who are not true creators or designers, but whose function is to evolve dresses, hats or other articles of apparel that are "new." These fashions must be definitely earmarked for the current season and must have at least one talking point—if only a new name for an old color—easily recognizable as different from last season's fashions.

In the long run free consumer choice is more seriously restricted by fashion than by ordinary brand differentiation, because merchants do not generally carry "unfashionable" goods, even though people may want them. Many women who buy and wear the clothing in vogue rather than the clothing they want explain it by saying: "It's what everybody is wearing. The stores don't even show anything else." Thus fashion limits the genuine variety available to consumers, and at the same time encourages spurious differentiation which impedes rational choice. And by taking women's minds off price, quality of materials and workmanship, fashion encourages wasteful buying.

In the case of ordinary brand differentiation, moreover, a consumer will insist on his favorite brand—though better or less expensive ones are available—but he can at least buy several units at a time (for example, a carton of Chesterfield cigarets instead of one pack). But under temporal differentiation the high rate of obsolescence of fashion goods makes people reluctant to buy ahead. If styles were more stable and annual fashion changes nonexistent, a prudent buyer could purchase several identical items at once (at a sale, or out of season), thus saving money and the time and energy of shopping, as well as being able to use one garment while letting the others "rest" or be repaired or renovated. In some markets, for example that of automobiles, the loss from annual model changes is to some extent the gain of the used-car buyer, for heavy trade-in sales swell the stock of used cars and facilitate automobile ownership by lower-income groups. But unfashionable clothes do not so readily find their way to poorer people, either through charity or through secondhand clothing markets. The latter are not so highly organized as the used-car market, and, besides, there is some social stigma attached to wearing secondhand clothes. "These honest mean habiliments" are often discarded, or left to hang unused in closets. Thus fashion in clothing may create greater waste than style changes in automobiles, socially as well as personally.

According to M. D. C. Crawford, in *The Ways of Fashion*, the New York market produced 125,000 models in women's dresses in 1939-40; in dresses above $4.75, wholesale, less than 300 dresses per model; below $4.75, less than 1,000 dresses per model. Some of these models were from earlier seasons; some were "new." Fashion as a brand or trademark (ordinary differentiation) accounts for some of the designs; but fashion as a device to stimulate obsolescence and premature replacement (temporal differentiation) must account for the larger part of this multiplicity of models, for there could be great variety at any given time without so many models if a new set were not "created" every season.

Many writers attribute the excessive number of models to design piracy, and urge the passage of legislation similar to that in France to prevent and punish the copying of designs. The merit of such a law is debatable. The two American attempts at legal design protection—the NRA garment industry codes and the Fashion Originators Guild of America (FOGA)—were both thrown out by the Supreme Court. Since standardized models have often led to cutthroat competition, producers and sellers rely on constantly shifting fashions in order to have a specialty which is removed from comparative judgment. Legal design protection would encourage further product differentiation and would make the market less competitive; for imitations, copies, and adaptations of "original creations" blur the sharp differences which are the essence of monopoly power in the area of fashion goods.

Nor does the entire fashion industry object to design piracy. Fabric manufacturers know that copying goes on all the time, and they realize that imitations swell the sale of their fabrics to garment factories and large department stores. The Paris *couturiers*—Chanel, Patou, Vionnet, Molyneux, Schiaparelli—are the display windows for the great French fabric manufacturers—Bianchini, Ducharne, Rodier—and are heavily subsidized by them. The manufacturer sells the material not only through the original designer, but also through the other firms which copy the model. In fact, fashion could not exist without imitations of high styles in lower price ranges.

Design piracy, like trademark infringement, would increase competition if the copy were perfect, for it would prevent monopoly profit from an "exclusive" design and would rapidly dilute the profits of innovation. But in the garment industry the copy is seldom perfect; it is usually a vulgarization of the original, often frankly called a "copy" or an "adaptation" and sold to a different income group. The *haut couture* prepares originals for the rich, while the garment industry capitalizes on the imitative tendency of the lower-income groups and emphasizes price appeal as well as (an often superficial) style appeal. This is not the same as attempted trademark duplication, through which a new firm tries to tap the same market in the same price range and to huddle under the umbrella of good will built up by the original firm through sustained advertising.

Where the customer is a poor judge of quality (for example, where rational buying requires technical knowledge or a highly developed aesthetic sense), producers, by sheer propaganda, can sell inferior goods at high prices. The public is told that each season's fashions are new, different. But they are seldom genuine innovations; if they were, there would be some sense in the public's reliance on the tastes of "fashion leaders." The ignorance of consumers in the area of fashion is fostered by businessmen and copywriters who insist that fashion is a "mystery" which only the elect can understand. Now, there is nothing mysterious or esoteric in designing clothes that are truly attractive, functional, and useful. If businessmen were interested in genuine style and quality, the public would not be so generally bewildered and misled; they would not confuse utility with novelty. Designers and producers rarely create an entirely new style; they simply vary an existing one. They seldom experiment with very low prices; they simply cut prices a little, or not at all, or even raise them, and trust to the forced obsolescence of clothes to stimulate repeat sales in a stable price range. Most sellers are reluctant to compete in price or quality; they prefer to rely on fashion to gain customers.

Fashion is intimately related to waste in production and consumption, to seasonality in production and to excess plant capacity, to the business cycle, to advertising and the maturity of industry; and through all of these, fashion changes impinge directly on consumer welfare. By requiring highly specialized equipment and changes in dies and patterns, fashion obstructs diversified production and reduces the mobility of investment. A sudden fashion change may make valuable equipment such as dress patterns or shoe lasts worthless. Moreover, subsidiary industries are also affected. For example, the trend to soft collars for men (although good in itself) has rendered obsolete much expensive laundry equipment. Even Hollywood is affected; by the time a picture is released, the actresses' clothes may be out of fashion. By requiring hand-to-mouth buying of materials, small-lot production, excessive inventories, markdowns of unfashionable goods, and by causing a host of other production and marketing wastes, fashion keeps prices too high in most cases, and wages and profits too low in many cases. Some of the labor, capital and business ability now used in the garment and accessories industries could well be diverted to other fields; Americans are, for instance, relatively overclothed and underhoused. The quintessence of fashion is waste.

Frequent fashion changes imply the absence of genuine (or workable) competition. If clothing styles were stable, sellers' rivalry might take the form of price cuts or improved quality, or both. Producers could charge less for the same clothes or could sell better or more durable clothes for the same price, and all selling rivalry could be reduced to price competition. Most so-called "quality competition" in the realm of fashion is really an attempt to stimulate sales without reducing prices and without improving the product. "New" fashions seldom change the product; they change the mind of the buyer, they make her dissatisfied with her existing clothes, which therefore become prematurely obsolete. Emphasis on shifting fashions is an attempt to remove the product from comparative judgment of price, quality and durability, and to create a specialty which will not have a host of imitators to share in the profits of monopoly or the profits of innovation. Fashion gyrations are relied on to maintain sales volume by frequent replacements in the same income groups, instead of by price reductions to stimulate sales to lower-income groups. Thus fashion is employed to avoid price competition, and in still other ways it deprives the public of the benefits of a rational market: by playing upon and reinforcing consumer ignorance; by providing the shadow instead of the substance of variety and consumer choice; by taking the buyer's mind off price, materials, workmanship and durability; by encouraging waste in production and marketing; by preventing the independent development of the public taste; by getting the public in the habit of following self-appointed fashion arbiters instead of relying on their own aesthetic values or those of disinterested artists or designers; and by substituting *ars gratia pecuniae* for *ars gratia artis* or *ars gratia populi*.

V

Unequal distribution of income is one of the causes of fashion gyrations, for, if the poor had greater purchasing power, markets would not approach saturation so soon, and there would be less incentive for forced fashion. But here we are interested in the effects of fashion on people of various income levels. Who suffers most from fashion changes? Some writers maintain that the poor, especially working people, do not lose as much from fashion as the middle classes do, because working clothes are functional and the poor do not need to keep up with the latest fashions. This may be true of overalls, uniforms and special attire designed for particular types of work, such as factory employment, farming or domestic service. But the very spirit of most fashions makes functional design difficult, for most fashions are designed in relation to women who lead lives of leisure; few of them are conceived in relation to the everyday lives of the masses. Very little advertising space is devoted to showing clothes designed especially for working girls, and the clothes which are available to them are poorly adapted to office work or most other employments.

The great in-between classes of American women, neither rich nor poor, with some money to spend but none to waste, are said to suffer most from fashion. If this is true, it may be because middle-class women attach more importance to social approval through dress than do poor women. Or, if poor women would like to wear the latest fashions, they simply cannot afford to. Thus the poor may not waste as much money as the middle classes through fashion changes; but if their desire is unrequited, they may, as a result of frustration, lose more from fashion psychologically. Some people, it is true, pay no attention to fashion. They may be too poor, or, leading a Bohemian existence, they may wish to husband their time and energy for more important activities of a creative nature, or—like the late Mrs. George Apley—they may cling to a bygone era. But few people would, like George Fox, stitch for themselves one perennial suit of leather.

It is impossible to prove what class suffers most, but the following generalizations are probably valid. Except for some kinds of working clothes, which are fairly functional, the poor, who can afford it least, may suffer most from fashion changes, especially since emphasis on novelty is often at the expense of quality and durability; the rich, who can afford to discard unfashionable clothes and can have their clothes made to order, certainly suffer least; while the middle-income groups probably suffer in proportion to their desire to emulate the rich and to distinguish themselves from the masses. This may be one index of their middle-class status. In countless advertisements business teasingly dangles "new" fashions before the eyes of people who lack any kind of serviceable clothes. The poor, like Moses, see the Promised Land, but do not enter.

Men suffer less from fashion than women do. Whereas women of all classes seek or accept novelty and incessant change, men demand sartorial conservatism. (Men's clothes may be less comfortable than women's, but here we are interested in fashion *changes*, not in intrinsic suitability of clothes.) We have had our Bucks, Bloods, Macaronis, Incroyables, and Dandies, but since the nineteenth century most men have imitated the common sparrow rather than the peacock. Since the adoption of long trousers over a century ago, there has been no fundamental change in men's silhouette. In the twentieth century men's clothes have changed very slowly, and annual changes are so subtle that only an expert can tell a five-year-old suit from a new one. Not that class distinctions and conspicuous consumption have been absent in men's apparel. Two generations ago paper or celluloid collars, the made-up tie, and the dickey or false shirt front were regarded as signs of poverty and vulgarity. But today the only observable difference between the business suit of a millionaire and that of an office boy is in the quality of the materials used, and most men seek correctness rather than sartorial distinction.

For men, especially those in responsible positions, there is greater social pressure toward conformity and conservatism than for women. The London Stock Exchange recently banned a member who appeared in a plum-colored suit. Agnes Brooks Young tells the story of a bank official who was asked what he thought would be adequate compensation for wearing his wife's hat to the office some morning. "His first reply was fifty thousand dollars, but after a moment's thought he said it would have to be as much as he could expect to earn the rest of his life, since afterward he could never expect to hold a position of financial responsibility again; and in the end he concluded that no price would be enough for the loss of prestige entailed."

Some people believe that men's clothes are more conservative and less variable than women's because men are largely engaged in earning a living and have so little time to indulge in conspicuous consumption that they put the burden on women, who have more leisure. But this theory may be questioned, for working women take at least as much pride in clothes as nonworking women do. In matters of personal appearance, women are probably more analytical than men. It is interesting to note that in men's clothes changes toward greater comfort generally come from the working men and very slowly influence the middle and upper classes; while in the case of women the changes come, more rapidly, from the top of the economic and social hierarchy.

We must also consider the changing age distribution of the American population. From 1930 to 1940 the average age increased two and one-half years, and the trend continues. Will this encourage or discourage the desire for novelty? Are older (wiser?) people less likely to be influenced by fashion and more likely to insist on stability? Certainly, tastes become more settled with age, older persons tend to have a larger percentage of their income taken up with commitments, the mental effort of choice and the physical effort of shopping become more onerous as one ages, and after years of experiment a woman often finds the styles which are most satisfying to her. Young people may welcome frequent fashion changes which give them a chance to experiment and still be like everybody else. Although much fashion advertising is addressed to the young, some fashions are promoted for middle-aged people who seek a more youthful appearance. Moreover, as one grows older, one gets in the habit of expecting and following changing fashions. And some young people, such as college girls, are temporarily able to ignore fashion changes because they can achieve a feeling of security within their group simply by wearing comfortable sweaters, skirts and moccasins, or other clothes approved by their peers and therefore partaking of the nature of a campus uniform. Their independence of fashion is similar to that of the nun, or member of an order, but it is only a group independence, for it imposes on the individual a uniformity as tyrannical as that of fashion.

VI

There is apparently a connection between fashion and the business cycle, but the relationship is not entirely clear. If fashion changes were introduced with the public's welfare in mind, one might expect elaborate and expensive fashions during prosperity, when the national income and purchasing power are high; and simple, inexpensive fashions during depression, when purchasing power is at a low ebb and women must economize. But that is not the case. The long depression of the 1870's was accompanied by a change from simple to more elaborate dresses. During the prosperous 1920's dresses were fairly simple and their short skirts and straight lines required little material. Late in 1929 the short skirt was abruptly discarded, and dresses, hats and shoes became more elaborate. This required more material and, in the face of the general crisis, it brought prosperity to manufacturers of dress trimmings and increased textile sales.

Business always has a vested interest in fashion changes. (When real hoops were worn after 1854, the wire industry profited greatly.) But perhaps in depression there is a special incentive to hasten obsolescence of existing wardrobes and to use more materials and labor, thereby stimulating the clothing and accessories industries. Of course this cannot bring general prosperity; it simply shifts the burden of depression to other industries, which feel the pinch of reduced spending. The problem is further complicated by the possibility that the public may welcome more elaborate dress for psychological reasons, perhaps as an escape mechanism from the demoralizing realities of a major depression.

In the current postwar prosperity, with clothing scarcities and high consumer income, one might suppose that the apparel industries would see little need for radical fashion changes. But it seems that, after several years of war-frozen styles, the industry is anxious to get the public back into the habit of expecting annual fashion changes, and further, that only a radical change can be used as an excuse for greatly increased prices. Besides, the wartime reduction of consumers' wardrobes decreases the possibility of a buyers' strike; the depletion of retailers' inventories prevents markdown losses on former styles; and both of these factors reduce the risk in promoting new fashions. Thus the elaborateness of the current fashions does not conflict with the above hypothesis that business tends to promote elaborate fashions in depression and feels relatively less need for forcing obsolescence and selling much material in prosperity.

Fashion changes more rapidly in a democracy than in a caste society where the masses are restricted in purchasing power and in social position. And fashions change most frequently in time of great social upheaval, such as war or revolution. For instance, in the two years from 1784 to 1786 French fashions in women's hats changed seventeen times; and more styles of headgear were produced in the single decade from 1800 to 1810 than in any fifty years since. The French Revolution inspired many macabre fashions. The Sainte-Amaranthe scarf commemorated victims of the Terror draped in red on the way to the guillotine. In 1792 and 1793 the liberty cap was worn as a political headdress. At the end of the Revolutionary period the *ceinture à la victime* imitated the cords which had bound the condemned, and the *coiffeur à la guillotine* reproduced the victims' short haircut. Miniature guillotines were even worn as earrings. In eighteenth-century England party politics inspired ladies to wear political patches on their faces, to distinguish the Tory dame from the Whig.

But in more modern times fashion has eschewed politics, and in modern American dress one cannot tell a Republican from a Democrat. Fashion now apparently avoids grave political, economic, and social problems; instead it derives fleeting inspiration from romantic and eccentric sources. In *The Soul of Woman*, Gina Lombroso explains that women's clothes acquire stability when social conditions are fast and rigid and it is not possible to pass abruptly from one class to another. "When woman's position is stable her costume becomes almost invariable, as in religious or charitable orders, where her position is not affected by her appearance and where she can assert herself by other means than by her clothes and jewels." But when society is in upheaval, as it was during the French Revolution, her clothes change perpetually. "When woman's position is unstable and there is a possibility for her to pass easily from one class to another, her costumes vary incessantly, as she changes banner and coat of arms."

The influence of war on fashion is two-sided. War, with its insatiable demand for men and materials, creates a condition of universal scarcity and at the same time swells the purchasing power of large groups in society. Moreover, the heavy backlog of deferred demand tends to exceed the supply of clothes in the immediate postwar period. The resulting sellers' market, with no need to stimulate sales volume, ought to minimize the influence of fashion during war and postwar years. In wartime, social pressure and scarcities tend to reduce conspicuous consumption by the wealthy and emulation by the poor and middle classes. Durability, comfort, and simplicity are emphasized, and distinction is sought in direct or indirect social service, or its appearance; in a wartime economy, the pecuniary canons of taste are temporarily weakened.

But in another sense, war strengthens the hand of fashion, which adapts itself to the wartime psychology. Civilian apparel and accessories use the wartime motif; and, except for government restrictions on materials, such as CPA's Order L-85, fashion is stimulated by war. For war brings new ideas, breaks down old customs and is an ally of rapid change. Minor wars, which are picturesque, quaint or colorful, influence fashion directly. In England, for example, the Peninsular Campaign of 1808 introduced many Spanish effects. The Blücher bonnet appeared in 1814, the Bolivar hat in 1825, the burnous in 1856. The cuirass bodice and the dolman were borrowed from the army, along with *soutache* and "frog" trimmings. The Crimean War inspired a vogue for Turkish effects such as tassels and Oriental colorings. Fashionable colors included Navarino Smoke in 1828, Bosphorus green in 1854, Magenta in 1859. After the Egyptian campaign of 1882, fashion adopted the colors of the victorious Household Brigade, and in 1900 the civilian popularity of khaki was inspired in England by the Boer War and in the United States by the Spanish-American War.

During and after most minor wars, military and naval designs have been adapted for feminine use, especially in trimmings and millinery; and war heroes have supplied names for fashionable items of dress. But a major war influences fashion indirectly, by producing profound psychological and economic disturbances in the civilian population. Perhaps, as Cunnington suggests, a major war provokes the sexual instinct. Ordinary, prosaic men suddenly become heroic figures, desirable to women, who quicken their efforts to attract them. This may explain the exhibitionism which appears in women's fashions during and after major wars.

Even during a war, postwar style changes are planned and are hinted at in advertisements. Wartime restrictions cause the public to overemphasize novelty and change when these restrictions are finally lifted. In the depths of the austerity movement following Dunkirk the British government, rationing clothes as strictly as food, dared not ration hats. The couponless hat, says John Brophy, was the outstanding and highly successful bribe to maintain feminine morale. Once the custom has been established, each firm considers frequent fashion changes necessary as an advertising device to maintain its market position. And the wartime development of new fabrics of great durability, to be put on the market after the war, increases the reliance on fashion to stimulate replacement sales. Moreover, by getting people in the *habit* of prematurely discarding clothes, fashion intensifies wartime shortages, thereby delaying conversion of plants to war production, and later, by inducing a buying spree, it fans the flames of postwar inflation.

VII

Wholly aside from aesthetic and moral considerations, fashion is an economic absurdity, and there is little to be said in its favor. Nevertheless, we can appreciate the wisdom in Gina Lombroso's belief that the enormous stress which women lay on everything pertaining to clothes and the art of personal adornment is connected with the tendency to crystallize sentiment into an object. Woman symbolizes every important event in her life by a special dress; and a jewel or a beautiful gown means to a woman what an official decoration means to a man.

> The temptation of dress is the last step in the ceremony to which the novice has to submit before entering the cloister. The memory of the gown which she, too, might have worn, was the strongest temptation that assailed St. Catherine before she took her solemn vows—a gown embroidered with gold and stars like those her sisters had worn, which her grandchildren would have gazed at with eyes filled with wonder and admiration. . . .
>
> If woman's clothes cost the family and society a little time, money and activity, they allow woman, independently of lies and calumnies, to triumph and come to the fore outside of man's world and competition. They allow woman to satisfy her desire to be the first in the most

varied fields by giving her the illusion that she is first, and at the same time enabling her rival to have the same illusion. Clothes absorb some of woman's activity which might otherwise be diverted to more or less worthwhile ends; they give woman real satisfaction, a satisfaction complete in itself and independent of others, and . . . they constitute a safety valve which saves society from much greater and more dangerous evils than those which they cause.

The aptness of these observations lies in their emphasis on clothes which are really beautiful and distinctive. But fashion is not primarily concerned with beauty; and fashion connotes uniformity, not the individuality so cherished in our society and so artfully suggested by the copy writers. Many people who rigorously follow fashions believe they are following their own inclinations; they are unaware of the primitive tribal compulsion; and this is true of fashions in manners, morals and literature, as well as clothes.

Is the desire for novelty and change in clothes rooted in human nature, as most writers assume? If so, businessmen can truly claim that they are simply meeting a deep-seated public need. But this explanation assumes too much. There may be a general desire for novelty and change, but it need not express itself in our apparel. Dress is simply an easy way for otherwise undistinguished people to distinguish themselves, or to have the illusion of distinction. We do not seem to tire of living in the same house, listening to the same great music, enjoying social intercourse with the same old friends. In fact, we grow more attached to certain possessions through long use—for example, houses, pipes, and even some articles of clothing. The so-called monotony of wearing the same styles a long time does not really flow from inadequacies in the clothes themselves. The constant desire for novelty in clothes (never to be confused with beauty or variety) flows from boredom and lack of more genuine goals in life than merely impressing people or courting social approval through externals, such as dress. It may also stem from absence of an integrated personality, from monotony of ideas, and from personal and social frustrations.

Fashion changes are thus a symptom of intellectual, emotional, and cultural immaturity. Perhaps, as Carlyle said in *Sartor Resartus*, the beginning of all wisdom is to look fixedly on clothes till they become transparent. The subtle insinuations of the fashion industries lead people to believe that newer fashions in clothes will solve their problems. But they do not, will not, cannot solve our problems. Whence, change is incessant. Canny businessmen know that people seek an easy escape from personal inadequacies or from the slings and arrows of outrageous fortune. So they build a folklore of fashion, and every milliner hawks his wares as if he were selling Fortunatus' magic wishing hat. They invest goods with subjective qualities which they cannot possess, and prescribe their wares as a panacea, a sedative, an elixir. Failure in the economic arena, love unrequited, confusion in a chaotic world—all these lead people to fashion's balm.

If people were not "infected with the fashions," they would grow accustomed to using their clothes a longer time, and would have more of Carlyle's respect for old clothes as "the ghosts of life." Their desire for change and novelty would express itself in other fields—perhaps in other goods, perhaps in absorbing activities, perhaps even in the world of ideas, which offers an amazing variety to tempt the most jaded tastes. As our culture is now constituted, monotony does appear to lie behind most fashion changes, but this monotony is not natural. Business has a vested interest in promoting new fashions and in thereby intensifying the monotony of existing styles. The public may be ignorant, gullible and vain; but when we hear fashion-mongers say they must adapt their production and advertising to irrational consumer behavior, we seem to hear Aesop's wolf complaining of the lamb.   —*Winter* 1947-48

ROBERT K. MERTON

The Self-Fulfilling Prophecy

In a series of works seldom consulted outside the academic fraternity, W. I. Thomas, the dean of American sociologists, set forth a theorem basic to the social sciences: "If men define situations as real, they are real in their consequences." Were the Thomas theorem and its implications more widely known more men would understand more of the workings of our society. Though it lacks the sweep and precision of a Newtonian theorem, it possesses the same gift of relevance, being instructively applicable to many, if indeed not most, social processes.

"If men define situations as real, they are real in their consequences," wrote Professor Thomas. The suspicion that he was driving at a crucial point becomes all the more insistent when we note that essentially the

Later published as a chapter in *Social Theory and Social Structure* by Robert K. Merton; copyright 1950 by The Free Press, Glencoe, Illinois.

same theorem had been repeatedly set forth by disciplined and observant minds long before Thomas.

When we find such otherwise discrepant minds as the redoubtable Bishop Bossuet in his passionate seventeenth-century defense of Catholic orthodoxy; the ironic Mandeville in his eighteenth-century allegory honey-combed with observations on the paradoxes of human society; the irascible genius Marx in his revision of Hegel's theory of historical change; the seminal Freud in works which have perhaps gone further than any others of his day toward modifying man's outlook on man; and the erudite, dog-matic, and occasionally sound Yale professor, William Graham Sumner, who lives on as the Karl Marx of the middle classes—when we find this mixed company (and I select from a longer if less distinguished list) agree-ing on the truth and the pertinence of what is substantially the Thomas theorem, we may conclude that perhaps it's worth our attention as well.

To what, then, are Thomas and Bossuet, Mandeville, Marx, Freud and Sumner directing our attention?

The first part of the theorem provides an unceasing reminder that men respond not only to the objective features of a situation, but also, and at times primarily, to the meaning this situation has for them. And once they have assigned some meaning to the situation, their consequent behavior and some of the consequences of that behavior are determined by the ascribed meaning. But this is still rather abstract, and abstractions have a way of becoming unintelligible if they are not occasionally tied to concrete data. What is a case in point?

It is the year 1932. The Last National Bank is a flourishing institution. A large part of its resources is liquid without being watered. Cartwright Millingville has ample reason to be proud of the banking institution over which he presides. Until Black Wednesday. As he enters his bank, he notices that business is unusually brisk. A little odd, that, since the men at the A.M.O.K. steel plant and the K.O.M.A. mattress factory are not usually paid until Saturday. Yet here are two dozen men, obviously from the factories, queued up in front of the tellers' cages. As he turns into his private office, the president muses rather compassionately: "Hope they haven't been laid off in midweek. They should be in the shop at this hour."

But speculations of this sort have never made for a thriving bank, and Millingville turns to the pile of documents upon his desk. His precise signature is affixed to fewer than a score of papers when he is disturbed by the absence of something familiar and the intrusion of something alien. The low discreet hum of bank business has given way to a strange and annoying stridency of many voices. A situation has been defined as real. And that is the beginning of what ends as Black Wednesday—the last Wednesday, it might be noted, of the Last National Bank.

Cartwright Millingville had never heard of the Thomas theorem. But he had no difficulty in recognizing its workings. He knew that, despite the comparative liquidity of the bank's assets, a rumor of insolvency, once believed by enough depositors, would result in the insolvency of the bank. And by the close of Black Wednesday—and Blacker Thursday—when the long lines of anxious depositors, each frantically seeking to salvage his own, grew to longer lines of even more anxious depositors, it turned out that he was right.

The stable financial structure of the bank had depended upon one set of definitions of the situation: belief in the validity of the interlocking system of economic promises men live by. Once depositors had defined the situation otherwise, once they questioned the possibility of having these promises fulfilled, the consequences of this unreal definition were real enough.

A familiar type-case, this, and one doesn't need the Thomas theorem to understand how it happened—not, at least, if one is old enough to have voted for Franklin Roosevelt in 1932. But with the aid of the theorem the tragic history of Millingville's bank can perhaps be converted into a sociological parable which may help us understand not only what happened to hundreds of banks in the '30's but also what happens to the relations between Negro and white, between Protestant and Catholic and Jew in these days.

The parable tells us that public definitions of a situation (prophecies or predictions) become an integral part of the situation and thus affect subsequent developments. This is peculiar to human affairs. It is not found in the world of nature. Predictions of the return of Halley's comet do not influence its orbit. But the rumored insolvency of Millingville's bank did affect the actual outcome. The prophecy of collapse led to its own fulfillment.

So common is the pattern of the self-fulfilling prophecy that each of us has his favored specimen. Consider the case of the examination neurosis. Convinced that he is destined to fail, the anxious student devotes more time to worry than to study and then turns in a poor examination. The initially fallacious anxiety is transformed into an entirely justified fear. Or it is believed that war between two nations is "inevitable." Actuated by this conviction, representatives of the two nations become progressively alienated, apprehensively countering each "offensive" move of the other with a "defensive" move of their own. Stockpiles of armaments, raw materials, and armed men grow larger and eventually the anticipation of war helps create the actuality.

The self-fulfilling prophecy is, in the beginning, a *false* definition of the situation evoking a new behavior which makes the originally false conception come *true*. The specious validity of the self-fulfilling prophecy perpetuates a reign of error. For the prophet will cite the actual course of events as proof that he was right from the very beginning. (Yet we know that Millingville's bank was solvent, that it would have survived for many years had not the misleading rumor *created* the very conditions of its own fulfillment.) Such are the perversities of social logic.

It is the self-fulfilling prophecy which goes far toward explaining the dynamics of ethnic and racial conflict in the America of today. That this is the case, at least for relations between Negroes and whites, may be gathered from the fifteen hundred pages which make up Gunnar Myrdal's *An American Dilemma*. That the self-fulfilling prophecy may have even more general bearing upon the relations between ethnic groups than Myrdal has indicated is the thesis of the considerably briefer discussion which follows.[1]

I I

As a result of their failure to comprehend the operation of the self-fulfilling prophecy, many Americans of good will are (sometimes reluctantly) brought to retain enduring ethnic and racial prejudices. They experience these beliefs, not as prejudices, not as prejudgments, but as irresistible products of their own observation. "The facts of the case" permit them no other conclusion.

Thus our fair-minded white citizen strongly supports a policy of excluding Negroes from his labor union. His views are, of course, based not upon prejudice, but upon the cold hard facts. And the facts seem clear enough. Negroes, "lately from the nonindustrial South, are undisciplined in traditions of trade unionism and the art of collective bargaining." The Negro is a strikebreaker. The Negro, with his "low standard of living," rushes in to take jobs at less than prevailing wages. The Negro is, in short, "a traitor to the working class," and should manifestly be excluded from union organizations. So run the facts of the case as seen by our tolerant but hard-headed union member, innocent of any understanding of the self-fulfilling prophecy as a basic process of society.

Our unionist fails to see, of course, that he and his kind have produced the very "facts" which he observes. For by defining the situation as one in which Negroes are held to be incorrigibly at odds with principles of

---

[1]Counterpart of the self-fulfilling prophecy is the "suicidal prophecy" which so alters human behavior from what would have been its course had the prophecy not been made, that it *fails* to be borne out. The prophecy destroys itself. This important type is not considered here. For examples of both types of social prophecy, see R. M. MacIver, *The More Perfect Union* (Macmillan, 1948); for a general statement, see R. K. Merton, "The Unanticipated Consequences of Purposive Social Action," *American Sociological Review*, 1936, I: 894-904.

unionism and by excluding Negroes from unions, he invited a series of consequences which indeed made it difficult if not impossible for many Negroes to avoid the role of scab. Out of work after World War I, and kept out of unions, thousands of Negroes could not resist strikebound employers who held a door invitingly open upon a world of jobs from which they were otherwise excluded.

History creates its own test of the theory of self-fulfilling prophecies. That Negroes were strikebreakers because they were excluded from unions (and from a large range of jobs) rather than excluded because they were strikebreakers can be seen from the virtual disappearance of Negroes as scabs in industries where they have gained admission to unions in the last decades.

The application of the Thomas theorem also suggests how the tragic, often vicious, circle of self-fulfilling prophecies can be broken. The initial definition of the situation which has set the circle in motion must be abandoned. Only when the original assumption is questioned and a new definition of the situation introduced, does the consequent flow of events give the lie to the assumption. Only then does the belief no longer father the reality.

But to question these deep-rooted definitions of the situation is no simple act of the will. The will, or, for that matter, good will, cannot be turned on and off like a faucet. Social intelligence and good will are themselves *products* of distinct social forces. They are not brought into being by mass propaganda and mass education, in the usual sense of these terms so dear to the sociological panaceans. In the social realm, no more than in the psychological realm, do false ideas quietly vanish when confronted with the truth. One does not expect a paranoiac to abandon his hard-won distortions and delusions upon being informed that they are altogether groundless. If psychic ills could be cured merely by the dissemination of truth, the psychiatrists of this country would be suffering from technological unemployment rather than from overwork. Nor will a continuing "educational campaign" itself destroy racial prejudice and discrimination.

This is not a particularly popular position. The appeal to "education" as a cure-all for the most varied social problems is rooted deep in the mores of America. Yet it is nonetheless illusory for all that. For how would this program of racial education proceed? Who is to do the educating? The teachers in our communities? But, in some measure like many other Americans, the teachers share the very prejudices they are being urged to combat. And when they don't, aren't they being asked to serve as conscientious martyrs in the cause of educational utopianism? How long would be the tenure of an elementary school teacher in Alabama or Mississippi or Georgia who attempted meticulously to disabuse his young pupils of the racial beliefs they acquired at home? Education may serve as an operational adjunct but not as the chief basis for any but excruciatingly slow change in the prevailing patterns of race relations.

To understand further why educational campaigns cannot be counted on to eliminate prevailing ethnic hostilities, we must examine the operation of "in-groups" and "out-groups" in our society. Ethnic out-groups, to adopt Sumner's useful bit of sociological jargon, consist of all those who are believed to differ significantly from "ourselves" in terms of nationality, race, or religion. Counterpart of the ethnic out-group is of course the ethnic in-group, constituted by those who "belong." There is nothing fixed or eternal about the lines separating the in-group from out-groups. As situations change, the lines of separation change. For a large number of white Americans, Joe Louis is a member of an out-group—when the situation is defined in racial terms. On another occasion, when Louis defeated the nazified Schmeling, many of these same white Americans acclaimed him as a member of the (national) in-group. National loyalty took precedence over racial separatism. These abrupt shifts in group boundaries sometimes prove embarrassing. Thus, when Negro-Americans ran away with the honors in the Olympic games held in Berlin, the Nazis, pointing to the second-class citizenship assigned Negroes in various regions of this country, denied that the United States had really won the games, since the Negro athletes were by our own admission "not full-fledged" Americans. And what could Bilbo or Rankin say to that?

Under the benevolent guidance of the dominant in-group, ethnic out-groups are continuously subjected to a lively process of prejudice which, I think, goes far toward vitiating mass education and mass propaganda for ethnic tolerance. This is the process whereby "in-group virtues become out-group vices," to paraphrase a remark by the sociologist Donald Young. Or, more colloquially and perhaps more instructively, it may be called the "damned-if-you-do and damned-if-you-don't" process in ethnic and racial relations.

III

To discover that ethnic out-groups are damned if they do embrace the values of white Protestant society and damned if they don't, we have only to turn to one of the in-group culture heroes, examine the qualities with which he is endowed by biographers and popular belief, and thus distill the qualities of mind and action and character which are generally regarded as altogether admirable.

Periodic public opinion polls are not needed to justify the selection of Abe Lincoln as the culture hero who most fully embodies the cardinal American virtues. As the Lynds point out in *Middletown*, the people of that typical small city allow George Washington alone to join Lincoln as the greatest of Americans. He is claimed as their very own by almost as many well-to-do Republicans as by less well-to-do Democrats.

Even the inevitable schoolboy knows that Lincoln was thrifty, hardworking, eager for knowledge, ambitious, devoted to the rights of the average man, and eminently successful in climbing the ladder of opportunity from the lowermost rung of laborer to the respectable heights of merchant and lawyer. (We need follow his dizzying ascent no further.)

If one did not know that these attributes and achievements are numbered high among the values of middle-class America, one would soon discover it by glancing through the Lynds' account of "The Middletown Spirit." For there we find the image of the Great Emancipator fully reflected in the values in which Middletown believes. And since these are their values, it is not surprising to find the Middletowns of America condemning and disparaging those individuals and groups who fail, presumably, to exhibit these virtues. If it appears to the white in-group that Negroes are *not* educated in the same measure as themselves, that they have an "unduly" high proportion of unskilled workers and an "unduly" low proportion of successful business and professional men, that they are thriftless, and so on through the catalogue of middle-class virtue and sin, it is not difficult to understand the charge that the Negro is "inferior" to the white.

Sensitized to the workings of the self-fulfilling prophecy, we should be prepared to find that the anti-Negro charges which are not patently false are only speciously true. The allegations are "true" in the Pickwickian sense that we have found self-fulfilling prophecies in general to be true. Thus, if the dominant in-group believes that Negroes are inferior, and sees to it that funds for education are not "wasted on these incompetents" and then proclaims as final evidence of this inferiority that Negroes have proportionately "only" one-fifth as many college graduates as whites, one can scarcely be amazed by this transparent bit of social legerdemain. Having seen the rabbit carefully though not too adroitly placed in the hat, we can only look askance at the triumphant air with which it is finally produced. (In fact, it is a little embarrassing to note that a larger proportion of Negro than of white high school graduates go on to college; obviously, the Negroes who are hardy enough to scale the high walls of discrimination represent an even more highly selected group than the run-of-the-high-school white population.)

So, too, when the gentleman from Mississippi (a state which spends five times as much on the average white pupil as on the average Negro pupil) proclaims the essential inferiority of the Negro by pointing to the per capita ratio of physicians among Negroes as less than one-fourth that of whites, we are impressed more by his scrambled logic than by his profound prejudices. So plain is the mechanism of the self-fulfilling prophecy in these instances that only those forever devoted to the victory of sentiment over fact can take these specious evidences seriously. Yet the spurious evidence often creates a genuine belief. Self-hypnosis through one's own propaganda is a not infrequent phase of the self-fulfilling prophecy.

So much for out-groups being damned if they don't (apparently) manifest in-group virtues. It is a tasteless bit of ethnocentrism, seasoned with self-interest. But what of the second phase of this process? Can one seriously mean that out-groups are also damned if they *do* possess these virtues? Precisely.

Through a faultlessly bisymmetrical prejudice, ethnic and racial out-groups get it coming and going. The systematic condemnation of the out-grouper continues largely *irrespective of what he does*. More: through a freakish exercise of capricious judicial logic, the victim is punished for the crime. Superficial appearances notwithstanding, prejudice and discrimination aimed at the out-group are not a result of what the out-group does, but are rooted deep in the structure of our society and the social psychology of its members.

To understand how this happens, we must examine the moral alchemy through which the in-group readily transmutes virtue into vice and vice into virtue, as the occasion may demand. Our studies will proceed by the case-method.

We begin with the engagingly simple formula of moral alchemy: the same behavior must be differently evaluated according to the person who exhibits it. For example, the proficient alchemist will at once know that the word "firm" is properly declined as follows:

> I am firm,
> Thou art obstinate,
> He is pigheaded.

There are some, unversed in the skills of this science, who will tell you that one and the same term should be applied to all three instances of identical behavior. Such unalchemical nonsense should simply be ignored.

With this experiment in mind, we are prepared to observe how the very same behavior undergoes a complete change of evaluation in its transition from the in-group Abe Lincoln to the out-group Abe Cohen or Abe Kurokawa. We proceed systematically. Did Lincoln work far into the night? This testifies that he was industrious, resolute, perseverant, and eager to realize his capacities to the full. Do the out-group Jews or Japanese keep these same hours? This only bears witness to their sweatshop mentality, their ruthless undercutting of American standards, their unfair competitive practices. Is the in-group hero frugal, thrifty, and sparing? Then the out-group villain is stingy, miserly and penny-pinching. All honor is due the in-group Abe for his having been smart, shrewd, and intelligent and, by the same token, all contempt is owing the out-group Abes for their being sharp, cunning, crafty, and too clever by far. Did the indomitable Lincoln refuse to remain content with a life of work with the hands? Did he prefer to make use of his brain? Then, all praise for his plucky climb up the shaky ladder of opportunity. But, of course, the eschewing of manual work for brain work among the merchants and lawyers of the out-group deserves nothing but censure for a parasitic way of life. Was Abe Lincoln eager to learn the accumulated wisdom of the ages by unending study? The trouble with the Jew is that he's a greasy grind, with his head always in a book, while decent people are going to a show or a ball game. Was the resolute Lincoln unwilling to limit his standards to those of his provincial community? That is what we should expect of a man of vision. And if the out-groupers criticize the vulnerable areas in our society, then send 'em back where they came from. Did Lincoln, rising high above his origins, never forget the rights of the common man and applaud the right of workers to strike? This testifies only that, like all real Americans, this greatest of Americans was deathlessly devoted to the cause of freedom. But, as you examine the recent statistics on strikes, remember that these un-American practices are the result of out-groupers pursuing their evil agitation among otherwise contented workers.

Once stated, the classical formula of moral alchemy is clear enough. Through the adroit use of these rich vocabularies of encomium and opprobrium, the in-group readily transmutes its own virtues into others' vices. But why do so many in-groupers qualify as moral alchemists? Why are so many in the dominant in-group so fully devoted to this continuing experiment in moral transmutation?

An explanation may be found by putting ourselves at some distance from this country and following the anthropologist Malinowski to the Trobriand Islands. For there we find an instructively similar pattern. Among the Trobrianders, to a degree which Americans, despite Hollywood and the confession magazines, have apparently not yet approximated, success with women confers honor and prestige on a man. Sexual prowess is a positive value, a moral virtue. But if a rank-and-file Trobriander has "too much" sexual success, if he achieves "too many" triumphs of the heart, an achievement which should of course be limited to the elite, the chiefs or men of power, then this glorious record becomes a scandal and an abomination. The chiefs are quick *to resent any personal achievement not warranted by social position*. The moral virtues remain virtues only so long as they are jealously confined to the proper in-group. The right activity by the wrong people becomes a thing of contempt, not of honor. For clearly, only in this way, by holding these virtues exclusively to themselves, can the men of power retain their distinction, their prestige, and their power. No wiser procedure could be devised to hold intact a system of social stratification and social power.

The Trobrianders can teach us more. For it seems clear that the chiefs have not calculatingly devised this program of entrenchment. Their behavior is spontaneous, unthinking, and immediate. Their resentment of "too much" ambition or "too much" success in the ordinary Trobriander is not contrived, it is genuine. It just happens that this prompt emotional response to the "misplaced" manifestation of in-group virtues also serves the useful expedient of reinforcing the chiefs' special claims to the good things of Trobriand life. Nothing could be more remote from the truth and more distorted a reading of the facts than to assume that this conversion of in-group virtues into out-group vices is part of a calculated, deliberate plot of Trobriand chiefs to keep Trobriand commoners in their place. It is merely that the chiefs have been indoctrinated with an appreciation of the proper order of things, and see it as their heavy burden to enforce the mediocrity of others.

Nor, in quick revulsion from the culpabilities of the moral alchemists, need we succumb to the equivalent error of simply upending the moral status of the in-group and the out-groups. It is not that Jews and Negroes are one and all angelic while Gentiles and whites are one and all fiendish. It is not that individual virtue will now be found exclusively on the wrong side of the ethnic-racial tracks and individual viciousness on the right side. It is conceivable even that there are as many corrupt and vicious men and women among Negroes and Jews as among Gentile whites. It is only that the ugly fence which encloses the in-group happens to exclude the people who make up the out-groups from being treated with the decency ordinarily accorded human beings.

IV

We have only to look at the consequences of this peculiar moral alchemy to see that there is no paradox at all in damning out-groupers if they do and if they don't exhibit in-group virtues. Condemnation on these two scores performs one and the same social function. Seeming opposites coalesce. When Negroes are tagged as incorrigibly inferior because they (apparently) don't manifest these virtues, this confirms the natural rightness of their being assigned an inferior status in society. And when Jews or Japanese are tagged as having too many of the in-group values, it becomes plain that they must be securely controlled by the high walls of discrimination. In both cases, the special status assigned the several out-groups can be seen to be eminently reasonable.

Yet this distinctly reasonable arrangement persists in having most unreasonable consequences, both logical and social. Consider only a few of these.

In some contexts, the limitations enforced upon the out-group—say, rationing the number of Jews permitted to enter colleges and professional schools—logically imply a fear of the alleged superiority of the out-group. Were it otherwise, no discrimination need be practiced. The unyielding, impersonal forces of academic competition would soon trim down the number of Jewish (or Japanese or Negro) students to an "appropriate" size.

This implied belief in the superiority of the out-group seems premature. There is simply not enough scientific evidence to demonstrate Jewish or Japanese or Negro superiority. The effort of the in-group discriminator to supplant the myth of Aryan superiority with the myth of non-Aryan superiority is condemned to failure by science. Moreover, such myths are ill-advised. Eventually, life in a world of myth must collide with fact in the world of reality. As a matter of simple self-interest and social therapy, therefore, it might be wise for the in-group to abandon the myth and cling to the reality.

The pattern of being damned-if-you-do and damned-if-you-don't has further consequences—among the out-groups themselves. The response to alleged deficiencies is as clear as it is predictable. If one is repeatedly told that one is inferior, that one lacks any positive accomplishments, it is all too human to seize upon every bit of evidence to the contrary. The in-group definitions force upon the allegedly inferior out-group a defensive tendency to magnify and exalt "race accomplishments." As the distinguished Negro sociologist, Franklin Frazier, has noted, the Negro newspapers are "intensely race conscious and exhibit considerable pride in the achievements of the Negro, most of which are meagre performances as measured by broader standards." Self-glorification, found in some measure among all groups, becomes a frequent counter-response to persistent belittlement from without.

It is the damnation of out-groups for "excessive achievement," however, which gives rise to truly bizarre behavior. For, after a time and often as a matter of self-defense, these out-groups become persuaded that their virtues really are vices. And this provides the final episode in a tragicomedy of inverted values.

Let us try to follow the plot through its intricate maze of self-contradictions. Respectful admiration for the arduous climb from office boy to president is rooted deep in American culture. This long and strenuous ascent carries with it a two-fold testimonial: it testifies that careers are abundantly open to genuine talent in American society and it testifies to the worth of the man who has distinguished himself by his heroic rise. It would be invidious to choose among the many stalwart figures who have fought their way up, against all odds, until they have reached the pinnacle, there to sit at the head of the long conference table in the longer conference room of The Board. Taken at random, the saga of Frederick H. Ecker, chairman of the board of one of the largest privately managed corporations in the world, the Metropolitan Life Insurance Company, will suffice as the prototype. From a menial and poorly paid job, he rose to a position of eminence. Appropriately enough, an unceasing flow of honors has come to this man of large power and large achievement. It so happens, though it is a matter personal to this eminent man of finance, that Mr. Ecker is a Presbyterian. Yet at last report, no elder of the Presbyterian church has risen publicly to announce that Mr. Ecker's successful career should not be taken too seriously, that, after all, relatively few Presbyterians have risen from rags to riches and that Presbyterians do not actually "control" the world of finance—or life insurance, or investment housing. Rather, one would suppose, Presbyterian elders join with other Americans imbued with middle-class standards of success to felicitate the eminently successful Mr. Ecker and to acclaim other sons of the faith who have risen to almost equal heights. Secure with their in-group status, they point the finger of pride rather than the finger of dismay at individual success.

Prompted by the practice of moral alchemy, noteworthy achievements by out-groupers elicit other responses. Patently, if achievement is a vice, the achievement must be disclaimed—or at least, discounted. Under these conditions, what is an occasion for Presbyterian pride must become an occasion for Jewish dismay. If the Jew is condemned for his educational or professional or scientific or economic success, then, understandably enough, many Jews will come to feel that these accomplishments must be minimized in simple self-defense. Thus is the circle of paradox closed by out-groupers busily engaged in assuring the powerful in-group that they have not, in fact, been guilty of inordinate contributions to science, the professions, the arts, the government, and the economy.

In a society which ordinarily looks upon wealth as a warrant of ability, an out-group is compelled by the inverted attitudes of the dominant in-group to deny that many men of wealth are among its members. "Among the 200 largest nonbanking corporations . . . only ten have a Jew as president or chairman of the board." Is this an observation of an anti-Semite, intent on proving the incapacity and inferiority of Jews who have done so little "to build the corporations which have built America"? No; it is a retort of the Anti-Defamation League of B'Nai B'rith to anti-Semitic propaganda.

In a society where, as a recent survey by the National Opinion Research Center has shown, the profession of medicine ranks higher in social prestige than any other of ninety occupations (save that of United State Supreme Court Justice), we find some Jewish spokesmen manoeuvred by the attacking in-group into the fantastic position of announcing their "deep concern" over the number of Jews in medical practice, which is "disproportionate to the number of Jews in other occupations." In a nation suffering from a notorious undersupply of physicians, the Jewish doctor becomes a deplorable occasion for deep concern, rather than receiving applause for his hard-won acquisition of knowledge and skills and for his social utility. Only when the New York Yankees publicly announce deep concern over their eleven World Series titles, so disproportionate to the number of triumphs achieved by other major league teams, will this self-abnegation seem part of the normal order of things.

In a culture which consistently judges the professionals higher in social value than even the most skilled hewers of wood and drawers of water, the out-group finds itself in the anomalous position of pointing with defensive relief to the large number of Jewish painters and paper hangers, plasterers and electricians, plumbers and sheet-metal workers.

But the ultimate reversal of values is yet to be noted. Each succeeding census finds more and more Americans in the city and its suburbs. Americans have travelled the road to urbanization until less than one-fifth of the nation's population live on farms. Plainly, it is high time for the Methodist and the Catholic, the Baptist and the Episcopalian to recognize the iniquity of this trek of their coreligionists to the city. For, as is well known, one of the central accusations levelled against the Jew is his heinous tendency to live in cities. Jewish leaders, therefore, find themselves in the incredible position of defensively urging their people to move into the very farm areas being hastily vacated by city-bound hordes of Christians. Perhaps this is not altogether necessary. As the Jewish crime of urbanism becomes ever more popular among the in-group, it may be reshaped into transcendent virtue. But, admittedly, one can't be certain. For in this daft confusion of inverted values, it soon becomes impossible to determine when virtue is sin and sin, moral perfection.

Amid this confusion, one fact remains unambiguous. The Jews, like other peoples, have made distinguished contributions to world culture. Consider only an abbreviated catalogue. In the field of creative literature (and with acknowledgment of large variations in the calibre of achievement), Jewish authors include Heine, Karl Kraus, Börne, Hofmannsthal, Schnitzler, Kafka. In the realm of musical composition, there are Meyerbeer, Felix Mendelssohn, Offenbach, Mahler, and Schönberg. Among the musical virtuosi, consider only Rosenthal, Schnabel, Godowsky, Pachmann, Kreisler, Hubermann, Milstein, Elman, Heifetz, Joachim, and Menuhin. And among scientists of a stature sufficient to merit the Nobel Prize, examine the familiar list which includes Beranyi, Mayerhof, Ehrlich, Michelson, Lippmann, Haber, Willstätter, and Einstein. Or in the esoteric and imaginative universe of mathematical invention, take note only of Kronecker, the creator of the modern theory of numbers; Hermann Minkowski,[2] who supplied the mathematical foundations of the special theory of relativity; or Jacobi, with his basic work in the theory of elliptical functions. And so through each special province of cultural achievement, we are supplied with a list of pre-eminent men and women who happened to be Jews.

And who is thus busily engaged in singing the praises of the Jews? Who has so assiduously compiled the list of many hundreds of distinguished Jews who contributed so notably to science, literature, and the arts—a list from which these few cases were excerpted? A philo-Semite, eager to demonstrate that his people have contributed their due share to world culture? No, by now we should know better than that. The complete list will be found in the thirty-sixth edition of an anti-Semitic handbook by the racist Fritsch. In accord with the alchemical formula for transmuting in-group virtues into out-group vices, he presents this as a roll call of sinister spirits who have usurped the accomplishments properly owing the Aryan in-group.

Once we comprehend the predominant role of the in-group in defining the situation, the further paradox of the seemingly opposed behavior of the Negro out-group and the Jewish out-group falls away. The behavior of both minority groups is in response to the majority-group allegations.

If the Negroes are accused of inferiority, and their alleged failure to contribute to world culture is cited in support of this accusation, the human urge for self-respect and a concern for security leads them *defensively* often to magnify each and every achievement by members of the race. If Jews are accused of "excessive" achievements and "excessive" ambitions, and lists of pre-eminent Jews are compiled in support of this counter-accusation, then the urge for security leads them *defensively* to minimize the actual achievements of members of the group. Apparently opposed types of behavior have the same psychological and social functions. Self-assertion and self-effacement become the devices for seeking to cope with condemnation for alleged group deficiency and condemnation for alleged group excesses, respectively. And with a fine sense of moral superiority, the secure in-group looks on these curious performances by the out-groups with mingled derision and contempt.

---

[2]Obviously, the forename must be explicitly mentioned here, else Hermann Minkowski, the mathematician, may be confused with Eugen Minkowsky, who contributed so notably to our knowledge of schizophrenia, or with Mieczyslaw Minkowski, high in the ranks of brain anatomists, or even with Oskar Minkowski, discoverer of pancreatic diabetes.

V

Will this desolate tragicomedy run on and on, marked only by minor changes in the cast? Not necessarily.

Were moral scruples and a sense of decency the only bases for bringing the play to an end, one would indeed expect it to continue an indefinitely long run. In and of themselves, moral sentiments are not much more effective in curing social ills than in curing physical ills. Moral sentiments no doubt help to motivate efforts for change, but they are no substitute for hard-headed instrumentalities for achieving the objective, as the thickly populated graveyard of soft-headed utopias bears witness.

There are ample indications that a deliberate and planned halt can be put to the workings of the self-fulfilling prophecy and the vicious circle in society. The sequel to our sociological parable of the Last National Bank provides one clue to the way in which this can be achieved. During the fabulous '20's, when Coolidge undoubtedly caused a Republican era of lush prosperity, an average of 635 banks a year quietly suspended operations. And during the four years immediately before and after The Crash, when Hoover undoubtedly did not cause a Republican era of sluggish depression, this zoomed to the more spectacular average of 2,276 bank suspensions annually. But, interestingly enough, in the twelve years following the establishment of the Federal Deposit Insurance Corporation and the enactment of other banking legislation while Roosevelt presided over Democratic depression and revival, recession and boom, bank suspensions dropped to a niggardly average of 28 a year. Perhaps money panics have not been institutionally exorcized by legislation. Nevertheless, millions of depositors no longer have occasion to give way to panic-motivated runs on banks simply because deliberate institutional change has removed the grounds for panic. Occasions for racial hostility are no more inborn psychological constants than are occasions for panic. Despite the teachings of amateur psychologists, blind panic and racial aggression are not rooted in "human nature." These patterns of human behavior are largely a product of the modifiable structure of society.

For a further clue, return to our instance of widespread hostility of white unionists toward the Negro strikebreakers brought into industry by employers after the close of the very first World War. Once the initial definition of Negroes as not deserving of union membership had largely broken down, the Negro, with a wider range of work opportunities, no longer found it necessary to enter industry through the doors held open by strikebound employers. Again, appropriate institutional change broke through the tragic circle of the self-fulfilling prophecy. Deliberate social change gave the lie to the firm conviction that "it just ain't in the nature of the nigra" to join co-operatively with his white fellows in trade unions.

A final instance is drawn from a study of a biracial housing project which I have been conducting with Patricia J. Salter, under a grant from the Lavanburg Foundation. Located in Pittsburgh, this community of Hilltown is made up of fifty per cent Negro families and fifty per cent white. It is not a twentieth-century utopia. There is some interpersonal friction here, as elsewhere. But in a community made up of equal numbers of the two races, fewer than a fifth of the whites and less than a third of the Negroes report that this friction occurs between members of *different* races. By their own testimony, it is very largely confined to disagreements *within* each racial group. Yet only one in every twenty-five whites initially *expected* relations between the races in this community to run smoothly, whereas five times as many expected serious trouble, the remainder anticipating a tolerable, if not altogether pleasant, situation. So much for expectations. Upon reviewing their actual experience, three of every four of the most apprehensive whites subsequently found that the "races get along fairly well," after all. This is not the place to report the findings of the Lavanburg study in detail, but substantially these demonstrate anew that under *appropriate institutional and administrative conditions*, the experience of interracial amity can supplant the fear of interracial conflict.

These changes, and others of the same kind, do not occur automatically. *The self-fulfilling prophecy, whereby fears are translated into reality, operates only in the absence of deliberate institutional controls.* And it is only with the rejection of social fatalism implied in the notion of unchangeable human nature that the tragic circle of fear, social disaster, reinforced fear can be broken.

Ethnic prejudices do die—but slowly. They can be helped over the threshold of oblivion, not by insisting that it is unreasonable and unworthy of them to survive, but by cutting off their sustenance now provided by certain institutions of our society.

If we find ourselves doubting man's capacity to control man and his society, if we persist in our tendency to find in the patterns of the past the chart of the future, it is perhaps time to take up anew the wisdom of Tocqueville's 112-year-old apothegm: "What we call necessary institutions are often no more than institutions to which we have grown accustomed."

Nor can widespread, even typical, failures in planning human relations between ethnic groups be cited as evidence for pessimism. In the world laboratory of the sociologist, as in the more secluded laboratories of the physicist and chemist, it is the successful experiment which is decisive and not the thousand-and-one failures which preceded it. More is learned from the single success than from the multiple failures. A single success proves it can be done. Thereafter, it is necessary only to learn what made it work. This, at least, is what I take to be the sociological sense of those revealing words of Thomas Love Peacock: "Whatever is, is possible."

—*Summer* 1948

DAVID RIESMAN

Some Observations on Changes in Leisure Attitudes

. . . our sole delight was play; and for this we were punished by those who yet themselves were doing the like. But elder folks' idleness is called "business"; that of boys, being really the same, is punished by those elders; and none commiserates either boys or men. For will any of sound discretion approve of my being beaten as a boy, because, by playing at ball, I made less progress in studies which I was to learn, only that, as a man, I might play more unbeseemingly? and what else did he who beat me? who, if worsted in some trifling discussion with his fellow-tutor, was more embittered and jealous than I when beaten at ball by a playfellow?

—*The Confessions of St. Augustine*

T EN years ago, I sat as a member of an international committee engaged in drawing up a Bill of Rights to be presented to some presumptive postwar agency. Among the rights proposed was one stating that all men and women had a right to "reasonable leisure," and that it was the duty of governments to make this right effective. In the ensuing debate, this was dubbed (by a Harvard professor) "Riesman's freedom from work" amendment, and, though the amendment carried, many of the hard-working delegates regarded it as a concession to the modern cult of effortlessness. Others thought the issue irrelevant, on the ground that, until the right to work was secure, the right to leisure could wait.

This was my first introduction to the discovery that many people are uncomfortable when discussing leisure: as with sex, they want to make a joke of it. And there is no doubt that most of us feel vulnerable in a milieu that increasingly asks us whether we are good players as well as good workers—a problem St. Augustine's serious-minded, self-deceiving elders do not appear to have faced. For us, at any rate, there is nothing easy about effortlessness. I want here to trace some of the sources of vulnerability.

I

In his novel, *The Bostonians*, written about seventy-five years ago, Henry James describes a week that his hero, Basil Ransom, passed at Provincetown on the Cape. He smoked cigars; he wandered footloose to the wharves; perhaps he read an occasional book; it does not appear that he swam. He was, *pro tem*, a "gentleman of leisure." It may be that a few fossils of the species are preserved in the Athenaeum, but I rather doubt if they can be found in Provincetown today. At least my impression is that people who go to such places for the summer appear to lead strenuously artsy and craftsy lives: even if they lie on the beach, they are getting a competitively handsome tan, but most of the time they appear to be playing energetic tennis, taking exhausting walks, entertaining children and guests by that mixture of grit, insects, and tomatoes known as a picnic; and in the evening attending lectures, the experimental theatre, and colloquia in private houses. While they may be less systematically engaged than many students in laying by credits, they are gainfully improving themselves in body and mind; and, perhaps unlike many students, they are subject to the additional strain of having to feel and to claim that they are having a good time, being victims of that new form of Puritanism which Martha Wolfenstein and Nathan Leites in their book *Movies* have termed "fun-morality."

All this in a country in which the average industrial work-week has declined from 64 hours in Henry James' day to around 40 in ours, not including the mid-morning coffee break and the other sociabilities which have crept into the hours which the census registers as working ones. We are in the ambivalent position described by Lynn White, Jr., President of Mills College, commenting on a roundtable on "leisure and human values in industrial civilization" of which he was chairman at the Corning Conference a year ago:

> We said, "Ha, ha, I have no leisure; why am I involved in this?"
> It was a sense of guilt and, at the same time, a sense of pride. In
> other words, we feel leisure is a cultural value. Theoretically we would
> rather like to participate in it, but we are sort of proud that we are

such responsible members of society that we really have no time for leisure.[1]

Our responsibility extends, in fact, to a concern for how other people —our children, our pupils, our union members, the community at large —are spending their leisure. In fact, those of us who are in the education industry and its allies, such as the library industry, have developed quite substantial interests—vested interests—in other people's leisure. We see their loose time, as others see their loose change, as our problem and our responsibility. This is, I suggest, one reason why the "gentleman of leisure," whose portrait Thorstein Veblen drew so sardonically in the '90's, is obsolete today. Instead, we are all of us—that is, almost all— members of the leisure class, and face its problems. As Eric Larrabee pointed out at Corning, the expansion of the leisure "market" has brought "friction" in its wake.

It is, of course, characteristic of American life that our bonanzas, our windfalls, whether treasures of the soil or treasures of the self, have been interpreted by the most sensitive and responsible among us as problems. I'm not sure but that the hue and cry against Puritanism isn't beginning to be overdone, and that we won't come to realize that our moral seriousness—in fact, our fun-morality—is not wholly negative. At the Corning Conference, the Wellesley-educated Hindu author, Miss Santha Rama Rau, scolded us; she commented:

> I am wondering why leisure is a problem at all. Surely, nowhere else in the world do people fuss about what to do with their spare time. I think it is rather sad that some kind of guilt has been built up in this particular society so that people feel that they should be pro- ductive in their spare time. . . . What is wrong with lying on the beach and relaxing?

I suppose one, perhaps unfair, answer to her is to be found in the six- and seven-year-old Indian children standing guard over their families' fields all night long, lest a sacred bull trample the crops down and leave the family to starve. It is Puritanism that, in considerable part, has brought us to the point where leisure is or can become a problem for the vast majority. In fact, so great is the sheer quantity of our available leisure and leisure resources, that I do not think we can find very helpful models in other countries.

Recent reading and reflection, and discussion with Mark Benney

---

[1]For this and later quotations, see *Creating an Industrial Civilization: A Report on the Corning Conference,* Eugene Staley, ed., Harper, 1952. I have drawn on the materials prepared for this conference by Reuel Denney and myself.

of the London School of Economics (now visiting lecturer at the University of Chicago), has convinced me that this is true enough, at any rate, for England, from which we once derived our working model of the gentleman of leisure, and from which, too, I suspect the Hindu aristocrats such as Miss Rama Rau have learned more than they will admit. The English remain torn between the aristocratic leisure pattern, which is rural, sportsmanlike, casual, and on the edge of such quasi-criminal activities as cock-fighting, and the middle-class leisure pattern, dating from the sobersides of the Puritan revolution, which is urban, uplifting, strenuous. (The urban working-class pattern, as represented in the London music hall and a vivid "street culture," is pretty much dying out.) A recent extensive survey by Seebohm Rowntree and G. R. Lavers, entitled *English Life and Leisure*, was evidence to me that the English today on the whole know even less than we how to spend leisure—that there is a sameness and lack of imagination about their pastimes and pursuits. The English aristocrats with their natural allies, the lower class, have won the day in the sense that the Victorian middle-class morality appears to be almost dead in England, and sexual intimacy seems the chief leisure resort after puberty. But while the young people are uninhibited, they are not joyful. They have to watch every penny they spend on liquor, but again seem to take no great pleasure in it. They gamble, but often with desperation. The truth is that they can no longer afford the aristocratic vices which are now, with the decline of religious sanctions, psychologically available to them. And the middle-class values of self-improvement are still strong enough so that many are dissatisfied with the aimlessness of their lives; I recall one young middle-class girl, for instance, who told the interviewer that she slept with young men who asked her to, but wished she could find something better to do.

What, then, do Rowntree and Lavers, who are distinguished students of English social life, recommend? They plug the old middle-class model, only more of it. After touring the Scandinavian countries to study leisure practices there, they urge more folk-dancing, more hobbies, more adult education, better books—and, I need hardly add, fewer Hollywood movies.

In fact, their attitude towards Hollywood may be regarded as symptomatic of the attitude of a great many students of leisure— "recreationists" perhaps we'd better call them—here and abroad. In their view, Hollywood is a source of disruptive leisure patterns, of vulgarity, spendthrift living, and false values generally. You know the indictment, I'm sure—an indictment which includes most of our popular culture, radio, TV, and bestsellers as well. Rowntree and Lavers put themselves up, as many school officials have, as angry competitors with this commercial popular culture, waging a losing fight. If they can offer nothing better, I am afraid that both the old aristocratic pattern, which is too expensive, and the old middle-class pattern, which is too didactic, will evaporate from England, leaving nothing of much quality to take their place.[2]

II

Now it is my opinion that Hollywood movies not only are often shoddy but are often profoundly liberating and creative products of the human imagination. And I am not referring to so-called "message" films, pleas for better race relations or labor relations. I refer rather to such films as *The Asphalt Jungle*, or *All About Eve*, or *An American in Paris*, or *The Marrying Kind*, or *The Great Gatsby*, and many others without any patent social message; some successful, some not; movies which take us out of ourselves or force us back in; movies which open a window on life, and movies which exhibit a nightmarish fantasy. If English leisure is sterile and mean-spirited, I doubt if such movies have made it so. Rather, I think English, and American life also, would be enriched if people learned to understand and appreciate the movies, and could enjoy them in the spirit, at once critical and friendly, with which people at different times and places have enjoyed literature. The thought occurred to me some years ago that our schools and colleges, and particularly our altogether too pious adult education ventures, might begin experimenting with courses on movie appreciation, and popular culture appreciation generally—a movement which would require us to develop something we have not yet got in this country: a corps of gifted movie and radio and TV critics. The beginnings are evident in the work of John Crosby, for instance; what is lacking is any program for developing such critics, operating in the different media and at different levels of irony and sensibility. I argued that such a program might help close the gap which now separates the literary culture of the schools—the culture which such men as Rowntree and Lavers narrowly regard as the only true and genuine culture—from the popular culture of RKO and CBS.

I argued too that such a program might help us get rid once and for all of the current distinction between active and passive recreations —"active" being such things as sports, hobbies, and square dancing, and "passive" such things as movie-going, TV-watching, and other things

---

[2]Mr. Benney believes that English leisure is not quite so dreary as this book indicates: the interviewers seem to concentrate on the activities that shock them and, indeed, to encounter a high proportion of rather sad and isolated people; moreover, nothing appears in the book about such gregarious leisure pursuits as political meetings and dart matches in the pubs.

parents and teachers wish their children wouldn't do.* For I am convinced that this is not a real distinction: much leisure which appears to be active may be merely muscular: its lactic acid content is high, but there may be little other content, or contentment. And conversely, such supposedly passive pursuits as movie-going can obviously be the most intense experience, the most participative. Indeed, Hollywood movies could hardly corrupt England and Europe if they were as passive and as pacifying as is charged! And so I wanted to teach people to enjoy the movies as participants in a fine performance, and not merely as a place to neck, to eat popcorn, or to pass the time out of the old folks' reach. In fact, I was particularly eager to develop courses just for the old folks in the understanding of popular culture, thinking in this way not only to open up to them a wide range of imaginative experience but also of helping to close the gap which separates the young, who have been raised with movies, comics, radio, and now TV, from the old who have come to them late if at all, often without the linguistic and emotional vocabularies necessary for their understanding.

But now I am not so sure that the problem I have in mind can be solved by courses, or possibly by any sort of conscious social program. I vividly recall my experience a few years ago when, asked to talk informally at a men's dormitory at the University of Chicago, I chose the movies as my topic, and started to say some things about the contemporary tendency among educated Americans to regard the movies as "just a show," to be "taken in" when one has nothing better at hand. I was talking to an audience most of whom devoutly believed that Hollywood movies other than Chaplin and the early Griffith are without exception junk, and that only England, France, and Italy make movies seriously worth seeing. I was trying to rebut this prejudice by saying something about the differing film conventions on the Continent and in this country: how, for example, we had had a convention of a happy ending which our more arty directors were now tending to exchange for an equally conventional, though Continental, unhappy ending, and that no necessary superiority lay in one convention rather than another, any more than in one sonnet form rather than another. Likewise, I sought to show how the undoubted inanities of the Production Code often resulted in a movie treatment— the so-called Lubitsch touch, for instance—which was a creative surmounting of the constricting forms. And then suddenly I stopped in the middle of my lecture, and for a while could not continue.

For I had realized, as I looked at the intent faces of the students, that

---

Editor's note: Would Mr. Riesman also include reading here? Though most parents and teachers do not seem to frown on that "activity," there is an underground coldness toward it in many schools, apparently because it is "passive" and solitary.

I might well be engaged in closing off one of the few casual and free escape routes remaining to them; that I might be helping to inaugurate a new convention: namely, that one had not only to attend Hollywood movies but to understand and appreciate them. I might be imposing on a group of students already zealously engaged in self-improvement, in social and intellectual mobility, still another requirement—and this in the very act of seeking to liberate them from a common prejudice against American movies. I could continue my lecture only after I had made some of these misgivings explicit, and had indicated that I came to offer some of them an opportunity, not another extra-curricular curriculum.

I realized the problem here was not so much *mine* of becoming a possible taste-leader, as it was one for the students who were looking for such leadership, if not from me, then from somebody. Contrary to the situation in my own undergraduate days, when we were, at least for external consumption, stoutly individualistic, these students were more malleable, more ready to be told. One reason for this is that the general level of teaching has improved, despite all the attacks currently being made against our educational system. Not only has the teaching improved, but the teachers have changed their pace and style; we try to get close to our students, to be good group leaders rather than platform ham actors, and to concern ourselves with more aspects of student life than simply class-room performance. We are perhaps today less distant from the student than we once were, both in terms of social class position and in terms of intellectual attitude. Involved in these institutional changes are psychological ones, some of which my collaborators and I have sought to describe in *The Lonely Crowd*—changes which have led to the spread of a character type I have termed "other-directed," a type guided by the ever-shifting judgments of significant people within one's purview at any given moment, as against the older type, the "inner-directed," more steadily although not necessarily more nobly guided by the internalized voices of ancestors. The students I was talking to, being in the main other-directed, were ready to shift their leisure behavior at a moment's notice; they had learned to do so in playing the popularity game which starts in kindergarten or shortly thereafter. I could envisage a group of them going to a Sam Goldwyn movie and, coming out, being very self-conscious as to how they ought to respond to it, whereas earlier they would have gone to it with the excuse that they needed to relax a bit before hitting the books again. Since so much of their leisure was already highly self-conscious, I hesitated to add to the burden. All planning for other people's leisure has to face this fundamental ambiguity, a form of the ever-present problem of the unintended consequence.

To be sure, leisure is a burden of the sort I am describing only among the educated, among the great many high school and college graduates who have some aspirations towards culture; men and women who, in the absence of any visible aristocratic model of leisure in American life, look to their fellows for clues, look to the magazines and the press, and the "how to" books. For the working class, there is leisure now too, and often money to spend, but it is not usually a burden, not perhaps a burden enough. Hunting and fishing and bowling; puttering about the house, garden, or car; watching television with and without discrimination; playing the numbers—these are recreations, not so very different from those turned up by Rowntree and Lavers in England, which my students have observed among steelworkers in Hammond and Gary. To be sure, there is considerable aspiration towards improved taste on the part of some of the younger wives, who read the women's service magazines. And the unions make sporadic efforts to give political education to the men; you will hardly be surprised to hear that some of the leaders blame the mass media for seducing the rank and file away from meetings—a charge which Mark Starr, educational director of the Ladies Garment Workers' Union, leveled at David Sarnoff of NBC at the Corning Roundtable. I think the charge is quite unjust, for I see no reason why people should spend their leisure in political activity unless that is their form of sport and they enjoy it, save in those cases where conditions are really so terrible that every good man has to come to the aid of the party—and, contrary to what is so widely urged, I believe such conditions are rare in this country.

One reason why the steel workers have so few problems with their leisure is that their work today is itself often quite leisurely and gregarious. It was not like that even thirty years ago when, as we know, there were ten- and twelve-hour shifts, and when the work was so hot and heavy that many men, on returning home, lay exhausted on the kitchen floor before they could get the energy to eat, and tumble into bed. Now at the big sheet and tube mill in Gary the men often take naps on mattresses they have brought in, and cook meals on burners attached to the fiery furnaces; if a new foreman doesn't like the practice, production is slowed down until he does like it. Think here, too, of the extent to which the schools train young people in this kind of comradely slow-down against the teachers and against the system generally, so that I sometimes think of school teachers as foremen who conspire with their pupils, the workers, to conceal the true state of affairs from top management, the principals, and from the parents who are the absentee stockholders, who grouse now and again about their dividends. At any rate, since work has now become so relatively lacking in strain— though it is not nearly so routinized in feeling as it may seem to be to observers of factory life—the worker leaves the plant with a good deal of energy left, which carries him readily through his leisure hours.

By contrast, the professional and business person is apt to leave his work with a good many tensions created by his reactions to interpersonal situations and as a result his leisure "needs" may have to be satisfied before he can rise above the level of needs—before he can rise from the level of re-creation to the level of creation. But it is just this very person on whom fall most of the demands for participative, active, constructive leisure which we have been examining earlier; and he may move from a job, where he is constantly faced with others and their expectations, to leisure pursuits, again in the company of others, where workmanlike performance is also expected of him. While he may nominally have a short work-week— though in many middle-class occupations such as medicine and teaching, hours are as long or longer than ever—he has not got much time which is not filled with stress. As my colleague, Nelson Foote, likes to put it, he has very little reverie as a balance to his sociability.

III

Let us look at a concrete example. A friend and former colleague, Professor John R. Seeley, is now engaged in directing a large research project on the relations between school and community in a wealthy, upper-middle-class suburb. It is a suburb which has one of the finest public school systems on this continent, one which is often held up as a model to others; in fact, the magnificent new modern high school dominates the com-munity, even physically, as the cathedrals did in the Middle Ages. The very fact that this elaborate research is going on there—it is to take a period of at least five years before any final conclusions are reached—is indicative of the alertness of the school officials, the school board, and the other community leaders. Yet, from my own very limited observation and from what has been reported to me, it is plain that the community, despite all material advantages, is not happy. The parents have neuroses; the children have allergies; and the teachers—well, I don't know. What has gone wrong?

If we follow the life of the children after school, we can perhaps get some clues. They are being prepared now for their later careers and their later rather hypothetical leisure. Their parents want to know how they have fared at school: they are constantly comparing them, judging them in school aptitude, popularity, what part they have in the school play; are the boys sissies? the girls too fat? All the school anxieties are transferred to the home and vice versa, partly because the parents, college graduates mostly, are intelligent and concerned with education. After school there are music lessons, skating lessons, riding lessons, with mother as chauffeur and scheduler. In the evening, the children go to a dance at school for which the parents have groomed them, while the parents go to a PTA meeting for which the children, directly or indirectly, have groomed *them*, where they are addressed by a psychiatrist who advises them to be warm and relaxed in handling their children! They go home and eagerly and warmly ask their returning children to tell them everything that happened at the dance, making it clear by their manner that they are sophisticated and cannot easily be shocked. As Professor Seeley describes matters, the school in this community operates a "gigantic factory for the production of relationships."

Since, moreover, the same interpersonal concerns dominate life within this "plant" and outside it, there is no sharp change of pace between work and play, between school and home activities. The children and their mothers—the fathers who work in the city at least make a geographical shift and also something of an emotional one—are characterized by a pervading anxiety. This is connected, I think, with the fact that the older, clear goals of achievement have been called into question, and these family units must decide not only how to get what they want but also what it is they should want. To answer this question, the community makes much use of professionals—the school principals and teachers themselves, who have a very high standing; child guidance experts and mental hygienists; and the packaged professionalism which can be bought in books or over the radio. The result is a well-known paradox: here is a suburb devoted to the arts of consumption and leisure, where these arts are pursued with such dogged determination that leisureliness as a quality of life is very largely absent. While all the appurtenances of variety are present, life is monotonous in the sense that it is steadily gregarious, focussed on others, and on the self in relation to others. As I have observed among some students, at Harvard and elsewhere, even casualness can be an effortful artifact.

IV

Yet it is all too easy to deride these parents and children and assorted experts, to urge them—as some people are now doing in the anti-progressive education movement—to drop all this new-fangled nonsense and get back to hard work and traditional curricula and nineteenth-century or classical "values" generally. It is perhaps not surprising that both aristocratic and working-class stances towards leisure combine in this derision. When, for example, this suburban community was recently discussed in my seminar on leisure, many people, both faculty and students, took the position that what these suburbanites needed was more direct and uninhibited aggression, more toughness and less talkiness. They compared the community unfavorably to a working-class community where, for reasons I indicated a moment ago, leisure is undoubtedly more casually dealt with. What they admired was aristocratic or artisan insouciance, as against upper-middle-class anxiety and preoccupation. Yet I do not know by what standard of value one prefers a broken nose to asthma, or lumbago or gout to ulcers. There is no doubt that the suburb in question, and others like it, is anxious and vulnerable, individually and collectively; otherwise, it would not be quite so receptive to a team of researchers. But I think that overadmiration for toughness is part of a romance which the middle class, in Europe as well as in America, has been carrying on with the lower class for a good many years now. Like the romance which many anthropologists have been carrying on with preliterate tribes, or many historians and philosophers and literary men with the Middle Ages, it narrows our sympathy for the problems of contemporary life and our awareness of the values which may, underneath anxiety and awkwardness, currently be emerging in it.

Thus, I think we can look at the people of this suburb rather differently from the way I have been doing so far, or from the way my seminar reacted to them. We can see them, for one thing, as explorers. Whereas the explorers of the last century moved to the frontiers of production and opened fisheries, mines, and mills, the explorers of this century seem to me increasingly to be moving to the frontiers of consumption. They are opening up new forms of interpersonal understanding, new ways of using the home as a "plant" for leisure, new ways of using the school as a kind of community center, as the chapel of a secular religion perhaps. But frontier towns are not usually very attractive. And frontier behavior is awkward: people have not yet learned to behave comfortably in the new surroundings. There is formlessness, which takes the shape of lawlessness on the frontier of production and of aimlessness on the frontier of consumption. In both instances, the solid citizens who stayed home are likely to feel superior, both to the formlessness and to whatever may be emerging from it, just as most Europeans of the educated strata have felt superior to most aspects of America throughout most of our history. The move to the suburb, as it occurs in contemporary America, is emotionally, if not geographically, something almost unprecedented historically; and those who move to any new frontier are likely to pay a price, in loneliness and discomfort. When the physical hardships are great, as they were for earlier generations of pioneers, the psychological hardships may be repressed or submerged—though we cannot be too sure even of that, for, as Oscar Handlin makes clear in his book on immigration to America, *The Uprooted*, the most devastating strains on the newcomers were in fact the emotional ones, rough though the physical conditions were.

To carry my analogy further, I do believe that discoveries are being made on the frontiers of consumption. Take the American diet, for instance. Once upon a time, and still in many quarters, this was in charge of the nutritionists, the exponents of a balanced meal, adequate caloric intake and colonic outlet, and plenty of vitamins. These good people bore the same relation to food that recreationists do to leisure: they want it to be uplifting, salubrious, wasteless. But now, among the better income strata at any rate, their work is done: it is incorporated into the formulae of bakers, into the inventories of chainstores, the menus of restaurants and dining cars. We have, as I sometimes like to put it, moved from the wheat bowl to the salad bowl. In consequence, in the suburb I have been describing, and elsewhere throughout the country, there is an emphasis, which was once confined to small sophisticated or expatriate circles, on having the right responses to food, on being a gourmet. Save for a few cranks, the housewives are not concerned with having enough wheat-germ, but with having enough orégano, or the right wine—and more than that, with having the right enjoyment of the wine. In the middle of the shopping center in this suburb is a store which stocks a stupendous array of delicacies, spices, patisseries, delicatessen, and European gadgets for cooking; the casserole replacing the melting pot!

Now, as I have indicated, the residents of this suburb are anxious about food and their attitudes towards it. They want to be knowledgeable about it and also to enjoy it, but they are not yet easygoing in the matter. Among men particularly, the demand that one must enjoy food, and not simply stow it away, is relatively new, and again these pioneers are awkwardly self-conscious. (Let me make clear in passing that I am not talking about old-fashioned conspicuous consumption. I am not talking about the hostess' fear of making a gastronomic *faux pas,* or fear that her children's table manners will disgrace her; no doubt these fears may still exist, although greatly muted, in the group I am describing. No, these parents are afraid that they are missing some taste experience, which in turn reveals the lack of a basic personality attribute.) We are observing these families, it appears, in a time of transition, when they have left old food-conventions behind and are exploring, without settling on, new ones. They are, in effect, paying the society's costs of research and development.

And can there be any doubt but that the result will be—in fact, has already been—an addition to the stock of American leisure bounties and benefits? The self-service supermarket, with its abundance of foods capably displayed, where the shopper's caprice and imagination can roam without interference from officious clerks or sabotage from indifferent ones, seems to me as significant an invention on the side of consumption as the assembly line on the side of production. But the invention would be meaningless without a "labor force," without a group of experimentalist families prepared to develop new casuistries of food, new combinations of color and taste. And here enters still another service industry: the cookbook and recipe industry, which has ransacked the world's cuisines and produced a host of books and newspaper columns, as well as those restaurants which serve as pilot plants. I think there can be no doubt that the children of the children now growing up in our demonstration suburb will be reasonably free of fears, guilts, and awkwardness about food prepared as a matter of course for the pursuit of happiness in this area of existence. In fact, I see only one caveat: the return of the nutritionist ghost in the craze for reducing, which makes not only women but men choose between food and figure, with one eye on mortality tables and the other on the way one appears in the hall of mirrors which is society. Even so, the reduced diets on which these figure-chasers bravely live are, item for item, unquestionably superior to anything known before in the American provender—which a generation ago made our food, like our bootlegging, an international joke. Moreover, the cult of one's figure, as of one's dress and one's coiffure, is certainly not an illegitimate one for one's happiness and aesthetic sense.

I could, if there were space, go through a number of areas of current pioneering in leisure—in the fields of music, painting, and literature; in the whole subtle field of sociability and conversation; in sports; in the changing style of vacations—and show how the pioneers are paying in financial and emotional outlay, and particularly in anxiety, the exploitation costs of their discoveries—without, however, the offset of the depletion allowance which the federal government allows to the wildcatters for oil and gas. I have already raised the question of whether our intellectual and literary culture is not too severe and derisive about the middle-class vice of anxiousness, compared with its benign tolerance for the aristocratic and lower-class vices of brutality and indifference. Such very general questions of value judgment are of great importance in determining contemporary attitudes towards leisure. I think, for example, that we make life and leisure harder for the already anxious person—whose anxiety is in fact thoroughly understandable in the light of our discussion so far—by making him also anxious about his anxiety, so that we heap on him a cumulative burden. Like the college student who came to see me not long ago, worried because she had a few of the sexual inhibitions she would have been worried about not having a generation ago, teachers also feel it compulsory not to be anxious, but to be always easygoing, warm, and relaxed—what a burden this puts on teachers in the better public and private schools!—whereas lack of discipline and firmness would have worried teachers in an earlier day. I am inclined to think we should form a union of the anxious ones, to defend our right to be anxious, our right to be tense, our right to aspirin and to our allergies. I was shocked when one of my colleagues remarked, after our seminar had had a description of life in the suburb I have here used as a case, that children were worse off there than they had been under the *ancien régime*. Historical amnesia had blinded him, as it blinds many now-fashionable critics of progressive education, to the brutalities and savageries in the treatment of children a hundred years or so ago. Then children were harnessed to the engine of society with often little concern for their own development. Many were too frightened or too cowed to be anxious; anxiety is on the whole a luxury and a sign of luxury. I urged my condescending colleague to read some nineteenth-century memoirs, to read *Father and Son*, Edmund Gosse's recollections of his awed and prayer-filled but rarely playful childhood; to read *The Way of All Flesh*, or Dickens, or the reports of health commissioners.[3] I have myself no doubt that the work of such reformers as Ellen Key ("The Century of the Child"), Lucy Sprague Mitchell and of course John Dewey, has been a very great advance.

V

But at the same time, I think one implication of all I have had to say so far is that every social advance is ambivalent in its consequences. I have stressed as much as I have the conflicts in our attitudes towards the proper use of leisure, and the kind of training children should get with their later lives of leisure in mind, because I feel that a recognition of ambiguity at the very heart of our problem is a first step towards perspective and a certain necessary detachment. I can't emphasize enough how rapidly our country is changing, and how hard it is even for the wisest among us to grasp what is going on.

Let me give just two illustrations; I am sure there are others. Recently a friend of mine who works for one of the pocket book companies visited an Ohio Valley city of about 75,000. There is no bookstore in the town, but a few books are kept, along with stationery and oddments, in the main department store. My friend asked at the department store why they didn't put in a real bookstore, and was told, "Well, this is a steel town. People here don't read; they just look at television or go to the taverns." Yet over three-quarters of a million pocket books were sold in this same town in 1951 at restaurants, at newsstands and in drugstores, many of them in the Mentor line of modern classics. This is well over a book a month for those old enough to read. I wish we had some knowledge and understanding of what these citizens made out of all they read: the Faulkner novels, the Conant *On Understanding Science*, the Ruth Benedict *Patterns of Culture*, along with the Mickey Spillane and other mixtures of sadism with sex. But studies of this kind in the field of leisure have not yet been made, as far as I know.

I draw my other illustration of the laggard state of our knowledge even of the basic data from an article by Gian-Carlo Menotti which appeared

---

[3]Stephen Spender's remarkable novel, *The Backward Son,* and George Orwell's account of his schooldays, "Such, Such Were the Joys" (which appeared in *Partisan Review* since the above was written), can remind us that even a generation ago the English public school could still treat the sensitive young with ferocious bullying. Likewise, the fictional hero of Salinger's *Catcher in the Rye* might have profited from some of the humaneness and sensitivity introduced by the now maligned progressivists.

in a recent issue of the New York *Times Sunday Magazine*. As you know, Menotti is a gifted and widely hailed young composer who, after some twenty years residence here, considers himself an American. He was complaining about the precarious position of the creative artist in American life, particularly in the field of music. There, he points out, we bestow all our adulation on the performer: the glamorous conductor or singer, the Menuhin or Serkin or Reginald Kell, who interprets music but does not create it, while the modern composer, unless he writes for the movies or gets some help from a foundation or a rich wife, will starve (as Béla Bartók did)—and is certainly not in any case featured in the billing along with the star performers. And he goes on to say that many parents in America are ashamed if their sons choose an artistic career; not only do they fear they will not make a living—even if they (the parents) could afford to support them—but fear, too, that they will be sissies; fathers try to force their sons to become businessmen or doctors or something else equally reassuring. Now I am sure that Menotti has a very good case about the plight of the composer, who seems so much worse off than the painter or writer, having more impresarios standing between him and his public. However, it seems to me that Menotti does not take account of the rapid and widespread change which has been going on in just the attitudes he is attacking. Through amateur chamber music groups and through the fabulous growth of the long-playing record industry, many thousands of Americans are today discovering modern music with a rush, just as they are discovering wine and other pleasures that were once confined to a small cultivated indigenous group and a somewhat larger group of immigrants who brought this culture with them from the old country. Likewise, it seems to me unlikely that millions of middle-class parents would not in 1952 be pleased if their sons exhibited artistic gifts and interests, even if not commercially promising. Many businessman fathers want their sons to be anything but businessmen, and in some circles it is business that is unduly looked down upon today, not art. When I said as much, however, at the Corning Conference, Miss Rama Rau and others said I was mistaken: parents would only accept art if it was advertised in *Life* magazine. But Millard Sheets, the painter, pointed out that the third highest group of students under the GI bill studied art. I would be greatly interested in comments on this topic, for I feel that here again we simply do not know.[4]

---

[4] In discussion, and in correspondence, it was argued that parents will now often accept art as a glamorous stairway to quick success, but that this makes it even harder than earlier for a youngster whose interest in art cannot be readily commercialized: his parents are impatient with him, not because he is an artist or composer—which would lead to a total break and a relatively good conscience on the artist's part—but because,

VI

So far we have been looking at our culture from inside. We have asked ourselves some questions about what is going on, about what attitudes are prevalent towards it, what models of competent use of leisure exist, what differences there are among different social strata, and so on. But there is another way of going at our problem which is to ask, not what play and leisure are like, or were like, in our culture but what they are like in any culture. Is there, for instance, any natural or biological basis for leisure or is it entirely conventional? *Homo Ludens*, a book by the late Dutch scholar Huizinga, offers some interesting clues to this. Huizinga points out that every language he examined had a word for play which is different from the word for work, and that many cultures have a pattern of sport, of noneconomic serious and yet playful competition. Many if not all cultures, moreover, operate on a periodic or seasonal rhythm between heavy work and heavy play—and I might add that many societies also have feasts even if they do not suffer from famines. That there is a cross-cultural solidarity of play may be indicated by a well-known example. Our Army advised soldiers and aviators to always carry a piece of string with them and when downed in a Pacific jungle to start playing cat's cradle if a suspicious native approached; the native would sometimes start to play, too.

All this must rest on something basic in the biological substratum of man and many animals. We know of course that children play even without instruction, provided certain basic minima of security are met. Thus, while children's play has aspects of artifice which the ever-renewed child's culture elaborates, much of it is simply given. In fact, work and play are not yet, for the child, independently organized; and what he makes of play as he develops depends to a very considerable extent on the society's interpretation of his play—is it regarded as "child's play," as useless, as preparation for life, or is it disregarded?

I think we can say, indeed, that the child's play serves as the principal model for all later efforts to free leisure time from its burdens and to cope with its puzzling ambiguities. We all of us know, if we think about it, that children's play is by no means always free and spontaneous; it is often filled with terror and morbidity; but at its best it is surely one of the unequivocally good things of this earth, and no wonder we try to

---

being in a glamorous field, he has not made his way; since the youngster in part also wants success, he finds it harder to cut himself off from his parents' values and anxieties. For thoughtful discussion of this problem, and a critique of the art schools which cash in on this craving for success, see Lyman Bryson, *The Next America* (Harper, 1952), pp. 126 *et seq.*

recapture it as Paradise Lost. But if we look closely at children's play we can observe something else which may even give us a clue as to how that recapture can, in part, be achieved, namely that the child's greatest satisfaction apears to arise from experiences of mastery and control. As Erik H. Erikson has noted in imaginative detail, the developing body itself provides a graded set of experiences; anyone can observe this who watches children play with their new-found mastery of walking or running or talking or diving. Play seems to reside in a margin, often a narrow one, between tasks which are too demanding, and those which are not demanding enough to require the excited concentration of good play. A child or adult who is simply going through the motions is not engaged in play or leisure as we have been talking about it here, however the society may define it. But without some social forms for leisure and play, forms which have to be broken through, yet have to be there to be broken through, I do not think we will have much play either. For the demand that play be constantly spontaneous, unchanneled by social forms, is too overwhelming; spontaneity, as we have already seen, is lost if we strive too hard for it. Thus, play would seem to consist in part of giving ourselves tasks, useless in any immediate sense, which challenge us but do not overwhelm us—tasks which allow us to practice our skills on the universe when not too much is at stake. Some of us, who lose this ability in our waking lives, retain it (as Erich Fromm points out in *The Forgotten Language*) in our dreams, which can be astonishingly witty, brilliant, and artistic—an indication, perhaps, of the child still buried within us, not so much in Freud's sense of the vicious child but rather of the child natively gifted with the capacity for imaginative play.

I have spoken of mastery of tasks, but I do not want to be understood as implying that this necessarily means physical activity—that is only one example. The child in the front of a subway train who intently watches the motorman, the signals, and the tracks may be quiet, but is undoubtedly playing, and may be playing very well—a point Reuel Denney eloquently voiced at the Corning Conference. When we speak of "role-playing," we should have something of this sort of vicariousness in mind. And this leads me to the complicating point that many of our workaday tasks as adults can be handled with a certain quality of leisure if we are able to regard work as a series of challenging tasks to be mastered, where the net of expectations surrounding us is at the same time not too frightening. On the other hand, we can be playful at work as a way of *evading* demands, sometimes by being one of the boys, pretending to ourselves and others that, if we really worked, we would get to the top. Students often play such games with themselves. But this is not really carrying out in adult life the effort at competence which is our lesson learned from the play of the child. That requires that we work at the top of our bent, while at the same time enjoying the very processes of accomplishment—enjoying our awareness, for example, of all that is going on in a classroom; enjoying our understanding of a technical problem; enjoying ourselves, in other words, as functioning and effective human beings.

We get here, it is apparent, into very deep waters indeed, where the boundaries between work and play become shadowy—as I think, for other reasons, they are tending to become in our society anyway— waters where we are looking for a quality we can only vaguely describe: it is various and rhythmical; it breaks through social forms and as constantly re-creates them; it manifests itself in tension, yet not too much of it; it is at once meaningful, in the sense of giving us intrinsic satisfaction, and meaningless, in the sense of having no pressing utilitarian purpose. It is some such model as this, I suggest, which haunts us when we consider leisure and judge its quality in ourselves and others. It is a model which has been elaborated in our culture, and yet which transcends culture.   —*Winter* 1952-53

FREEMAN CHAMPNEY

Utopia, Ltd.

COMMUNISM and socialism were household words in this country over a hundred years ago. They had simple, uncomplicated meanings then— in contrast to the mishmash of demonology that they evoke today. They stood for small colonies or communities of people in which individual property had been more or less abolished and economic and social life deliberately controlled for the (presumptive) welfare of the entire group. These little utopias set up shop under a great variety of conditions and leading ideas, and they experimented with pretty much the whole range of economic organization and social controls. What they had in common was a drive toward a better way of living and a separation from the larger society. Nearly a hundred of them are recorded in early nineteenth-century America.

In most of these utopian groups, the leaders thought of their own little ventures as spearheads of a movement that was ultimately to reform and revitalize society and bring about a new golden age for all mankind. Sooner or later they all either expired or came to terms with society at large. Some failed spectacularly, some dismally. The amount of energy, consecration, benevolence and righteousness that went down the drain is appalling. The utopias failed because of their own inadequacies of ability, of co-operation, of resources; because, in the long run, even the most successful of them could not offer values and incentives comparable to the big, bad outside world. They failed because most people found godly living and common purpose less exciting and less rewarding than the triumphs of the new mechanical and commercial civilization, and because the vision, the discipline, and the consecration they required did not find lodgment in the germ plasm. Finally they largely failed even to be recurring events because the "scientific" socialism of Marx proscribed the futility of little utopias and siphoned off the energy of the rebels and dreamers to the king-size, once-and-for-all revolution.

But the failure of the utopias was, in a sense, a failure of the larger society from which they seceded. The evils from which they tried to escape are still with us. The securities and the positive values they sought are hardly a drug on today's market. The experience for which they paid with lives and hopes still has an unworked residue of relevance. They were little pilot plants in the possibilities of human life and there are things to be learned from the recordings and the debris.

A study of the utopias is especially relevant because some of the conditions which fostered such experiments in the past are present today in augmented form. War and depression have shaken our traditional American optimism and eaten away much of our faith in both the limitless possibility and the value of material success. Industrial technology has wrought miracles without end but life today seems to involve more insecurities and frustrations than ever. Our activities are becoming increasingly compulsive and segmented. Even the individual family is a less and less satisfactory in-group but has to develop multiple relationships with larger groups if it is to avoid dullness and destruction. There is a spreading hunger for a larger and saner life, for work that makes sense, and for a feeling of brotherhood and common purpose.

At the same time, the Marxist dream has lost its idealistic glamour and become a nightmare of dehumanized power and tyranny. It is no longer easy to believe that overthrow of the "system" will result in anything more beneficent than the rise of a new, and tighter, system. Insofar as the promise of large-scale socialism once tended to drain off energies which have gone into utopian experiments, the new disillusion with class revolution should lead to another wave of utopianism.

The chief ingredients that seem to be lacking are the hope and faith that once expected society to be perfected or the Second Coming achieved in one lifetime. We have utopians of a sort today but many of them seem to be looking for personal escape rather than social regeneration. They would gladly settle for a communal hideout safe from atomic bombs, draft boards, tax collectors, and assembly lines—though the rest of the world went to pot. There is a strong element of total rejection of society at large in many of these people—not from any positive drive toward something better but from hatred, fear, and in retaliation for what society has done to them.

This attitude is especially noticeable among pacifists, many of whom are still suffering shock from their war experience. They dissented then from the purposes of society and they suffered for their dissent. Many of them project onto the government or the dominant social structure the hostilities that their creed forbids them to feel toward individuals. A process of mutual rejection has had the results which might be expected. (Society at large has a heavy responsibility on its shoulders for the wholesale jailing of "nonreligious" pacifists and the farce that "Civilian Public Service" frequently became.) What we find today in the little colonies of decentralists, "folk schools," bohemians, and the like is apt to be an assortment of social abstainers rather than reformers. Many of them are utopians only in the negative sense of getting away from the going world and in their pathetic hope that things will be better (for them) if they get together with enough of their own kind.

The mischief is that the larger job of social reintegration needs the moral earnestness and the value-questionings that these people can give it. These qualities are not limited to seceders or pacifists, of course, but they are never in oversupply and we cannot afford to lose any of them. Most of us would agree on a general objective of peace and abundance plus democracy. A variety of approaches can lead toward such goals. The social idealist, if he stays with us, can do important scout and outrider work.

A close-knit, healthy society performs more or less automatically the function of keeping its individual members successfully oriented to their culture and to each other—in other words, it keeps them sane. Today's urbanization, segmentation of life, and moral drift provides little of that essential social function. The burden falls on totally inadequate, pick-up-the-pieces social work institutions and on a relative handful of overworked psychiatrists. The utopian colony provides what the sociologists call "primary group" contacts and it can often do a therapeutic job for its members that they need desperately and are unlikely to find elsewhere. The danger, of course, is that the social orientation provided will be useful only in the closed circle of the colony (or in others like it) and will further alienate the individual from life in the larger society.

Social experimentation is something we need and can use a lot of. But if it cuts itself off too completely from the going world its relevance is at least questionable. There is no particular sense, moreover, in blandly repeating the mistakes of past experiments. Many of today's utopians are discussing plans and places for new hideouts in appalling ignorance of the clear lessons of what should be their special tradition. New Harmony (both under Father Rapp and under Robert Owen), the Shakers, Fruitlands, Brook Farm, the "Phalanxes" of the Fourierists, Hopedale, the Oneida Community, and their many lesser parallels and imitators furnish a background from which conclusions and generalizations can be drawn with some certainty. A "pilot plant" is of no use unless it is trying something new.

II

No utopia was ever launched under more favorable auspices than Robert Owen's New Harmony. It took over intact the physical plant of the Rappites, with its three thousand acres of cultivated land, eighty brick and frame buildings and one hundred log cabins, and its fully equipped industries. Both Owen and his educational associate William McClure had substantial wealth to put into the working capital of the community. The whole official atmosphere of the group was one of confidence and success. The flavor of defeat, maladjustment, and secession from going society—so often embedded in the grain of utopian groups—was not part of Owen's makeup. There was undoubtedly plenty of it in the individuals who came into New Harmony to partake of the new social order, but the hearty indiscriminateness of Owen's invitation to one and all shows his remarkable innocence of the human complexities of his undertaking.

This innocence is underlined by the way he went kiting back to Scotland a little over a month after the establishment of the community. He left it with a paper organization, nearly a thousand inhabitants (strictly self-selected, with no consideration given to skills, character, or stability of personality) and his blessing and bland confidence that all was well. When he returned the following January, Owen was eager to push on to the ultimate objectives and a new declaration of principles and articles of "union and co-operation" were drawn up. This "permanent" community provided, as Robert Dale Owen (the founder's son) said later: "liberty, equality, and fraternity in downright earnest." All offices were elective and the economic rule was share and share alike.

The first of several splinter groups found obscure fault with the new step and moved a few miles away to a new site. Most of the original members signed on with liberty, equality, and fraternity, but within two weeks the new executive committee was beseeching Robert Owen to take over as an extra-legal dictator. Thereafter the history of New Harmony follows a pattern that has been typical of secular utopias: dissensions, new starts, purges, splinter groups, ill-feeling between the industrious and the lazy, personal conflicts projected into matters of holy principle, and final disintegration. By the spring of 1828 it was apparent even to Robert Owen that the great experiment was over. It had lasted three years and cost him the bulk of his personal fortune. The nineteen Owenite communities which had sprung up independently in the East and the Middle West had somewhat shorter lives—the one at Yellow Springs being washed up in three months.

Many participants and observers have tried to diagnose the causes of New Harmony's failure. Owen himself thought that the false principles and wrong habits of ordinary society have too strong a hold on most people and render them incapable of the moral excellence required for community life. Most commentators agreed that the grab-bag character of the colonists would, by itself, have destroyed any such venture. Owen's successes at New Lanark had been with docile and beaten-down employees who were properly grateful and obedient. The New Harmony colonists have been described (by Horace Greeley) as

> for the most part . . . the selfish, the headstrong, the pugnacious, the unappreciated, the played-out, the idle, and the good-for-nothing generally, who, discovering themselves out of place, and at a discount in the world as it is, rashly conclude that they are exactly fitted for the world as it ought to be.

This comment has a strong invidious flavor and suggests that its author felt strongly about his *not* being "out of place and at a discount in the world as it is," but it underlines a problem that is basic to all reform and utopian movements. One of the most epigrammatic judgments came from one of John Humphrey Noyes' associates at Oneida: "Communism must be ruled either by law or grace. [Owen] abolished law and did not employ grace."

The next rash of utopias came in New England in the 1840's and '50's. Its later stages were tied up with the popularization of the doctrines of Charles Fourier by Albert Brisbane, but some of the best known

of the colonies—Brook Farm, Bronson Alcott's Fruitlands, and Hopedale—started before Fourierism became a fad. Brook Farm and Fruitlands had their spiritual origins in the splendid but noninstrumental
verbalism called Transcendentalism. Hopedale had a somewhat similar
background in the Universalist doctrines of Adin Ballou.

Fruitlands was the comic opera of the group. These solemn souls
in their linen tunics not only abjured all "animal substances . . . flesh,
butter, cheese, eggs, milk," stimulants, and warm water for washing,
but they drew a moral distinction between fruits and vegetables which
"aspired" upward and those wretched varieties which huddled in the
ground. Animal manures were banned as corrupting the soil and introducing disease into the crops. Artificial lighting was to be limited to
bayberry candles (which no one knew how to make) until Mrs. Alcott
staged a successful rebellion for oil for her sewing lamp. The results
of this sublime tomfoolery were as might be expected. The "consocate
family" nearly starved when the New England winter closed in. It
dwindled away until only Mrs. Alcott and her four little girls were left
to cope with Father Alcott—who took to his bed to await the end.

Nearby Brook Farm was a cheerier, if less consecrated, place. It had
more members and more capital and although its economy was no more
self-sustaining in the long run than that of Fruitlands, its people ate
regularly for five years. Brook Farm's fame has outlived that of the
other utopias of its time partly because of the concentrated literary distinction of its sponsors and visitors and partly because—almost alone
of its kind—it achieved a considerable success as a pleasant place to live.
Most of the members were young and the school provided a steady turnover that kept down the growth of ingrown conflicts and splinter groups.
The credo of leader George Ripley had balance as well as idealism and it
sounds pretty good today.

> . . . to insure a more natural union between intellectual and manual
> labor than now exists; to combine the thinker and the worker, as
> far as possible, in the same individual; to guarantee the highest
> mental freedom, by providing all with labor adapted to their tastes
> and talents, and securing to them the fruits of their industry; to do
> away with the necessity of menial services by opening the benefits
> of education and the profits of labor to all; and thus to prepare a
> society of liberal, intelligent, and cultivated persons, whose relations
> with each other would permit a more wholesome and simple life than
> can be led amidst the pressure of our competitive institutions.

Brook Farm was fun. They sang while washing dishes. They did
the chores in lighthearted teams and were always getting up musicals

and plays. They were notorious for their punning—a sure tipoff on a relaxed, if not downright anti-intellectual atmosphere. The priggish and righteous Charles Lane of Fruitlands (whom the little Alcotts cordially disliked) found them "playing away their youth and daytime in a miserably joyous, frivolous manner." Interestingly enough, in spite of youth, informality, and freedom there was never any sexual scandal associated with Brook Farm.

But if it was delightful it was also an economic fool's paradise. In spite of a ten-hour day the crops were nearly always less than the dining room consumed. A horse rake and a seed drill were all the farm machinery. They were poorly located for commerce with the outside world (two men and two wagons were kept busy full time). They piddled with handcraft industries but their lamps, coffeepots, doors, sashes, and blinds were uneconomically produced and ineffectively marketed. Their chief commercial success was in raising a total of $14,500 in first, second, and third mortgages on land originally valued at $10,500. When the new Phalanstery burned in 1846 (sloppy chimney construction and carelessness) the jig was up.

Longer-lived and better fed than these secular experiments, the American religious colonies are a study in themselves. Compared to their secular counterparts they were illiterate, undemocratic theocracies. They were governed by priesthoods, with visions, prophecies, and the revelation of heavenly enactment taking the place of group-process or parliamentary procedure. The typical secular community set up a press and issued a periodical; although the religious groups developed more handcraft and industrial enterprises, the printed word was seldom one of them (with the important exception of the Oneida Perfectionists). Without exception, the religious colonies practiced some form of deviation from the prevailing pattern of marriage and family.

Both the Rappites and colonists of Zoar were German emigrants who seceded from the worldliness of their native church and state. The followers of George Rapp practiced a primitive Christian communism, celibacy, and obedience to Father Rapp and his elders. During most of Rapp's lifetime, the community, in its several locations, was a model of harmony, neatness, and industry although visitors usually commented on the dullness and superstition of the people. Most of the theocratic colonies kept strictly apart from the sinful world and there is little record of fruitful contact with the secular utopias—although the more consecrated members of Fruitlands and Brook Farm sometimes moved on to the Shakers after disappointment with Transcendental society.

For pure social inventiveness and a blending of revolutionary thinking and living, John Humphrey Noyes' Oneida Perfectionists have a unique fascination. For over thirty years this group kept its identity in reasonable harmony, made a solid success of its economic life, and carried its experiments with marriage and the family to a point that has no near parallel in the America of its time (or of any previous or subsequent time).

Like so much of the social thinking of the time, the youthful trial flights of Noyes were set in a theological framework. (Very much the same way, perhaps, that the post-depression generations of college students have expressed their idealistic gropings in a neo-Marxist vocabulary of "social significance.") Theology simply happened to furnish the language and the frame of reference then employed. Noyes himself, in his *History of American Socialisms*, finds a close relationship between the utopian experiments and the great waves of revivalism that swept the country. The revival spirit furnished the zeal for salvation, the social ferment of the time suggested striking out from the *status quo* for a new way of living, and the biblical references to the community of the apostles gave hints for the social and economic pattern (Christian living and holding all things in common).

If any one trait can be said to have characterized Noyes it was the ability to follow his inner light wherever it led him—to follow it in sustained and concentrated fashion and to draw others with him. With this stubborn intensity, of course, went an exceptional quality of mind and a sense of responsibility. What would have been mere eccentricity (or howling madness) in other social deviants, became luminous wisdom where Noyes was the initiator. Under his gentle but implacable shepherding, humble people committed themselves to undreamed-of new patterns of life; and the conflicts, heresies, and psychological impossibilities that any merely smart person could have predicted as inevitable consequences were smoothed away in harmony and faith.

Early in his youth, Noyes became convinced that to accept Christ completely in one's life was to become incapable of sin. This principle became elaborated into the doctrines of Perfectionism. The theology is less important than the supreme self-confidence involved. The kingdom of heaven was here and now for the taking and nothing in the positive stuff of life was to be rejected as unworthy. But there was never any slipshod laxity in Noyes' kingdom. Righteousness had to be constantly striven for—individually and by the combined energies of the group. One of the features of social life in the Oneida colony was the principle of "ascending and descending fellowship." Every member of the community was obligated to seek improvement from those above him in the spiritual hierarchy as well as to dispense it to those below. The problem of how Noyes himself was to participate in ascending fellowship was solved with some ingenuity. One of his children remembers seeing his father alone in his study, leaning back in a big chair with his eyes closed and his forehead wrinkling vigorously. The child was led away with the hushed explanation that his father was communing with the apostle Paul.

Early in the history of the Oneida group, the community more or less accidentally got into the manufacturing business. (One of the original New York State members was an Indian-trader and trapper and had developed a superior steel trap.) This enterprise expanded until Oneida Community traps were standard backwoods equipment all over the United States and Canada. Much of the community prosperity came from this participation in the growing industrial-commercial life of the country. Commercial printing and silverware were developed later and the latter industry is the chief reminder today of the experiment in human perfection. The Shakers, in contrast, built a large trade in handcraft wares, garden seeds, and preserved fruits, but they never ventured into mechanized production. This use of factory production for a national market as a part of its economic base is another unique characteristic of the Oneida colony in contrast to the typically agricultural, and often starveling, status of the other utopias.

Although the Oneida Community was unquestionably Father Noyes' creation and existed in its pure form only during his prime, it had a large measure of internal self-sufficiency—a sort of intuitive democracy. Literacy and knowledge of the outside world were high, at least in comparison with the servile animism of the Rappites. The community library was always stocked with current periodicals and there seems to have been comparatively little of the anti-outside animus that drew the blinds around so many utopian attempts. The community children, it is true, were forbidden to have anything to do with outside children and stood in awe and fear of them. When community disintegration became visibly imminent, the older children went through a stage of near panic and two very ordinary newcomers to their group enjoyed immense prestige because they claimed to know the ropes of life on the outside.

One of the techniques which kept individuals in line with righteousness and group purposes was the institution of "criticisms." It was the custom for everyone to take his turn at being candidly dissected and improvingly admonished by a roomful of his fellows. The process was found to have excellent effects on both group solidarity and individual morale and there were sporadic attempts to apply it to more physical ailments, such as an epidemic of diphtheria. Probably every close-living group develops, consciously or not, some such device. It furnishes a constructive channel for the discharge of hostilities, erodes the sharp corners of individuality, and develops a tradition of acceptable community behavior. Some years ago when Louis Adamic visited the then-new Black Mountain College, he found that something of this kind was one of the most noticeable and educational features of its common life. A younger brother of Margaret Fuller used to liven things up at Brook Farm by his own version of criticisms: he confided his unfavorable opinions of people to his diary and occasionally tore out significant pages and left them lying around in prominent places.

III

All of the utopias have experimented with unorthodox relationships of work and property. Many of them were started primarily for economic reasons. Ever since the Industrial Revolution began to hit its stride, one of the factors which has brought people into utopian colonies has been a revolt against the conditions of life in our modern economy. Life in the going world has meant submergence in a consuming struggle for narrowly materialistic ends. This rat race has done nasty things to wholeness of personality and has often been asocial or antisocial in its larger effects. Life in a utopian colony, on the other hand, promises much in security, fellowship, and co-operation. The day-to-day life seems to offer economic relationships of a more complete and humanly satisfying kind than those of the mill and the marketplace.

Complications arise, however, when a utopian group sets about organizing its community work. A voluntary association seeking to escape the drudgeries and the mean compulsions of life in the big, bad world, has still to confront the compulsions of soil, weather, and season—or of production, price, and delivery. Ever since the self-sufficient economy of farm-handcraft-trade began to fade before the blitz of machinery-finance-specialization, there has been a conflict between human personality needs and the disciplines of the new system. These disciplines center around time, money, standarization, and specialization. If mass production is to work, men must work at specified times, at predetermined speeds, in specialized repetitive operations, and within fixed tolerances of accuracy.

There is little room within these disciplines for individual variation, spontaneity, or creativeness. You don't cut imaginative capers on the assembly line or improve on the blueprints as the fancy strikes you. Practically all the urgencies of individual living have to fit into the haphazard units of time that remain after working hours and their penumbra have been blocked out of the week. This regimen does grim things to human personality and it is not strange that individuals and groups try to escape it. The difficulty is that unless a utopian group is willing to pare down its life to a subsistence level (and thereby submit itself to an equally life-limiting set of compulsions), it has to compete in the general market to sell its goods and services. And then it is subject to the same old slavery of time and cost that it was trying to escape— usually under the extra handicap of inadequate skill and capital equipment.

A process of humanizing industrial disciplines, however, seems to be getting under way—and its impetus is coming, not from back-to-the-soil movements, but from the advance guard of big business management. The work of Elton Mayo and his associates has established the revolutionary discovery that people work best when they work as members of a team. Even in repetitive manual work, low efficiency and obsessive delusions seem to result, not from monotony so much as from social unrelatedness. The axiom of classical economists (and of Karl Marx) that men are primarily motivated by economic self-interest, has been experimentally demolished. Men are far more strongly motivated by a sense of belonging and of functional importance. A great deal of "labor trouble" has been found to arise deviously from frustrations and social malfunctioning which had no economic cause whatever. Often the trouble stems from some slide rule genius doing too expert a job of "eliminating the human element."

It is beginning to be realized that jobs of work (which make up so much of all our lives) can be so organized as to provide for more creative participation and social fulfillment than they usually do. Even that something of the sort is good business. The self-made, hell-roaring executive is a diminishing type and techniques which encourage mature human relationships are in increasing demand in industry and business.

The time has passed, moreover, when social theorizers could discuss The Machine on a maybe-we'll-accept-it-maybe-we-won't basis. The all-around skills of the frontier—and the sparse populations—are gone, along with the game and the deep woods. We couldn't go back to a handcraft-agriculture economy without at least half of us starving—which would be a drastic beginning for a new era of humanized living. Given our bear-by-the-tail relation to industrial technology, the homesteading, extreme-decentralism philosophy becomes an individual eccentricity of no particular significance.

I V

Utopian groups derive much of their sustaining afflatus from the subordination of the individual to the group purpose. This was, and is, variously known as Christian communism, association, or co-operation and it has a curious bipolarity. During the honeymoon stage, the individuals concerned have a feeling of release, freedom, and augmented personality. The individual self seems to have found fulfillment in its relation to the group. The honeymoon comes to an end, however, and as the individual needs for privacy, self-assertion, prestige, and possession are frustrated, the close associations become as annoying as they were previously exciting and liberating. If the reaction runs its full course, individual differences become blown up out of all normal proportion and the happy social oneness disintegrates into a chaos of mutually repellent individuals and cliques.

The utopias show this pattern—which in less extreme form is something of a human universal—so strikingly because the people who join up are, practically by definition, deviants of one kind or another from the larger society. They have rejected the common life—or been rejected by it, or both—and they are, at one and the same time, thorny individualists and people with a deep hunger to belong and to find a home. In the first happy days of a utopia they seem to have found it; they have their new associates for mutual reassurance and they have the outside world as a common target for hostility. But as time goes on and the outside world cares very little what the utopians think of it, it becomes a less and less satisfactory and unifying hostile obsession. At the same time, the utopia itself begins to settle into a pattern of social organization, controls, and pressures not so very different after all from the larger society it was abandoning. This is the point where the associates or co-operators begin to regress into antisocial individualism and community disintegration sets in.

But when all the absurdities, inefficiencies, and conflicts that have beset the utopias are tallied up, there remains an intangible personal balance on the positive side. For all its temporary nature and its instability, the taste of fellowship and wholeness that goes with the typical utopian experiment gives a glow and a promise to human life. It has catalytic effects on personality and it leaves its mark on the participant. Which is probably why the experiments are repeated in every generation in spite of the sorry record of waste and failure.

Of all the utopias in our history, Brook Farm seems to represent the pattern which can be most successfully imitated today. The requirements seem to include a steady turnover in membership, a large proportion of unmarried young people, an outside source of income, and an idealistic group purpose which integrates rather than divides (but doesn't integrate too closely). These prerequisites are oftenest met by some form of educational institution, whether a college with an unusual program (like Black Mountain or Antioch) or a summer work-and-study camp or youth institute. Such educational groups have their most significant effects in

maturing and integrating whole personalities rather than training isolated talents. They are notably lively and spontaneous places. And they
run the same risks of social isolationism and internal explosion as the
utopias. There seems to be a consistent pattern that determines the rise
and growth of such groups. The original drive (what Noyes called the
"afflatus") usually comes from a strong leader with qualities of Father
and Prophet. This pattern of personal leadership sometimes continues
through the lifetime of the founder, in which case, the group usually
takes on some of the characteristics of the theocracies. Sometimes personal
leadership generates an opposition group, with its own Father and Prophet
—and the conflict situation which follows results in a splinter group.

The external relationships of such a group interact with the internal
forces in complex ways. The group may go through cycles in which periods of high internal afflatus and revolutionary separation from the larger
society alternate with periods of institutional inertia and comparative acceptance of the *status quo*. Educational groups seem to derive longer
life-expectancy from their shifting and dynamic character. The coming
and going, constant reappraisals of program, and the ebb and flow of
internal factions supply the new blood, the interrelationship with outside forces, and the institutional dynamics which seem to be necessary
to absorb the "afflatus" constructively and keep it from blowing the
group apart.

Those dissident groups which are more in the nature of permanent
colonies are apt to develop a higher degree of "in-groupism," to have
less constructive give-and-take with the outside, and to either peter out
dismally or live a narrow and rather irrelevant existence. Valuable work
is being done today in such fields as city planning, decentralization, and
community organization. The distinction between this kind of thing
and the utopian seceders is important. It is the difference between idealism working with and through going society and idealism curdled into
an anti-society absolutism. The same diagnoses of what ails today's civilization may be found in each. The difference is in approach and personality pattern.

Another comparatively recent development which has absorbed some
of the utopian tradition is the consumers co-operative movement. The
co-ops are important because they are idealistic without being secession-
ists or abstainers. They aim to bring social direction and democracy into
economic life by operating within the economy. In addition, they often
perform much the same functions as the less evangelical churches. They
provide a common body of idealistic doctrine, a center for social life, and
an enterprise in which all may have a stake. Beyond this, they offer a
way in which today's individual, submerged in bigness and anonymity,

can, along with his neighbors, take a hand in the shaping of his own and the country's economic destiny. Because the co-ops are neither altogether idealism nor altogether bread-and-butter but a combination of the two, they are in a unique strategic position. Their idealism is tested by its survival in the marketplace and their business activities are checked for their content of social betterment.

Other than Brook Farm, our historical utopias contribute little positive experience that we can use directly today. Their principal value has been to demonstrate that a number of things won't work, or will work only under special conditions or extraordinary leadership. In the more somber cultural climate of our time we tend to set our sights considerably short of perfection. Which is not altogether a bad thing. We know better what individuals and society are up against and what is available to work with. Some of these limitations stand out sharply in the utopias. They show pretty clearly that problems of social organization and control are a human constant and are intensified rather than eliminated in a small group of seceded deviants. They show that a common doctrine strong enough to overwhelm self-assertion and family loyalties is apt to lead to a theocratic tyranny.

Probably the most useful and interesting findings from the utopias are in the relationships between social and individual behavior. All of the colonies which took the primitive Christians as their model—and to a lesser extent many of the secular groups—have made the assumption that hostility and conflict can be eliminated from human behavior. We have seen that the groups which were most successful in this direction were also notable for priestly sanctions, illiteracy, and dullness. The groups which prized individual freedom and trusted to Reason rather than to God were more apt to come to explosive endings. Superficially it looks as if a close-living group shows an inverse ratio between harmony and individual freedom. The more freedom the less harmony and vice versa. If the factor of "closeness" is diminished, either the freedom or the harmony (or both) increase, also vice versa.

It would be possible to put these relationships into impressive mathematical notation. But it would still be superficial. Beyond a point, for instance, a lessening of "closeness" (an increase in elbow room puts it more clearly) produces neither harmony nor freedom but social chaos and individual disintegration. Also, there have been utopian groups which had a high degree of closeness and harmony *and* much more freedom than the formula would allow. The Oneida Perfectionists are the best example and they show that an important factor has been left out of the formula. Apparently the social apparatus of "criticism," of ascending and descending fellowship, and the guidance of Father Noyes operated to inhibit the simple working of the ratio. There is also the factor of faith, which defies measurement but was certainly an important element at Oneida.

People who think of themselves as free agents inevitably develop frustrations and hostilities in their relationships with other people. In our culture this is intensified many times (if not largely caused) by the pervading competitive tradition. Some mechanism for the constructive discharge of these hostilities is necessary or some people are going to cease to be free. Democracy is the most hopeful form of social organization the race has developed because, at its best, it combines freedom and harmony in optimum amounts. One way of looking at our troubles today is that technology has increased our closeness—both spatially and by enforcing uniformities—and at the same time weakened our traditional social apparatus for sublimating hostilities. The result is less harmony and less freedom—so much less that some people are ready to chuck one or the other of them out of the formula completely.

V

Every utopian experimenter, whether religious or secular, has found that the individual family is an enemy of the community. There is a conflict between loyalty to one's own flesh and blood and loyalty to the larger group. In religious terms it is a conflict of comfort, worldliness, and sensuality with spirituality and righteousness. In secular terms, selfishness and the competitive greed for possessions are tied to the identification of the individual with his family and are poison to the openhearted co-operation called for by the greatest good of the greatest number. The austere Charles Lane commented:

> The question of association and of marriage are one. If, as we have been popularly led to believe, the individual or separate family is the true order of Providence, then the associative life is a false effort. If the associative life is true, then the separate family is a false arrangement. . . . That the affections can be divided, or bent with equal ardor on two objects so opposed as universal and individual love, may at least be rationally doubted. . . . There is somewhat in the marriage-bond which is found to counteract the universal nature of the affections, to a degree, tending at least to make the considerate pause before they assert that, by any social arrangements whatever, the two can be blended into one harmony.

Robert Owen said that conventional marriage, with its bulwark of private property, was "one of the great trinity of evils which have cursed the world ever since the creation of man." Brook Farm was largely composed of unattached young people and this was probably a big factor in its human success. The summer camp groups, experimental colleges, bohemian clusters, and quasi-utopian colonies we have today are over-whelmingly made up of "youth" and a mixture of the over-age single and the survivors of shipwrecked marriages. A family, in effect, is an "in-group" all by itself, and its existence in a strong and integrated condi-tion precludes participation in larger in-groups—participation, at least, with the all-out loyalty that utopias demand. Saint Paul was aware of this also; if we substitute "the community" for "God" in his discussion of marriage and its effects on a man's "cleaving unto" propensity, we have the conflict stated very much as it looked to the founders of utopias.

One answer was celibacy. The family ceased to exist when there were no sexual relationships and no children to be nurtured. This was the answer of the Shakers and the Rappites and the partial answer of the Zoarites. It was an answer that worked quite well under pioneer conditions, when backed up by strong religious leadership and social pressure. It required, of course, that new converts come in steadily enough to keep the group from dying off—the Shakers also adopted wholesale lots of orphans. But the elders lost their authority in time and the young people were apt to elope (the Kentucky Shakers said they "fleshed-off"). There was a strong economic reason for the celibate an-swer, too. Building a colony in the wilderness required a high percentage of productive workers. A large part of the material prosperity which seemed to arise from the religious colonies was simply the result of having few children, nursing mothers, and old people eating up the common store without adding to it.

The polygamy of the Mormons was partly an attempt to assimilate into the family structure the excess of women that their missionary labors brought them. It extended the family to include several women and their children and, in so doing, it undoubtedly weakened the in-group strength of the family and made it more amenable to social controls. Like the "complex marriage" of the Oneida group, it was essentially a responsible social experiment, socially controlled and probably oftener a matter of duty than pleasure.

Noyes faced this problem with extraordinary forthrightness. He was aware of the family-community conflict and of the economic reasons for limiting births in a pioneer colony. He could not agree with the Shakers and the other celibates, however, that sexual love was either inherently bad or in opposition to spiritual virtue. He solved the problem, in effect, by enlarging the family to make it identical with the community. When he was still a young man (and a virgin) Noyes expressed in a private letter his conviction that exclusive monogamy was an error and that complete sexual freedom was both rational and desirable. Through no intention on the author's part, this letter was published and Noyes became a notorious public figure overnight. But even in this youthful tentative approach to the question, Noyes emphasized a corollary to his belief in freedom: holiness must come first. ("Woe to him who abolishes the law of the apostacy[1] before he stands in the holiness of the resurrection.")

This insistence on holiness (for which read responsibility, respect for individual personality, and conformity to community pressures) was always an essential part of complex marriage. The outside world imagined that Perfectionist life was a round of shameless license, but the near neighbors of the community knew better. One of the few members who ever succeeded in getting into the community with the idea that it would be a happy hunting ground for amorousness left it suddenly one evening when the elders heaved him out of a window into a snow bank. Not that he had been greatly successful in his hunting (he hadn't) but because he was an intolerable nuisance.

A study of Oneida indicates, among other things, how nonexistent a goal absolute freedom really is. The Perfectionists had painfully freed themselves of the restraints of monogamy, of exclusiveness, of jealousy and hypocrisy. But they achieved these freedoms only by accepting the guidance of the community as to their love lives. They might be, and were, under pressures to love or not to love as the elders deemed proper. And they were not free to form exclusive attachments even if both parties wanted it that way. The "idolatrous" individual love affair became as much of a menace to the family-community as its opposite was in the outside world—more of a menace, in fact. Even the children were discouraged from spending too much time with any one friend. The freedoms achieved at Oneida, moreover, were possible only in the isolated protection of the Mansion House. The outside world had to be kept at arm's length or better and it was pressure from society at large which eventually precipitated abandonment of complex marriage and the disintegration of the community.

In the early years of the community it was agreed that children would be a serious economic liability and they were deliberately postponed—by another Noyes discovery which he called "Male Continence," details of which can be left to medical journals but which seemed to work, however incredible it may seem today. As the group became pros-

---

[1]Noyes's word, as quoted in *A Yankee Saint* by Robert Allerton Parker. It seems likely that "apostalcy" was the word he originally used. "Apostacy" makes no great sense in the context. The notion that the Perfectionists, however, were re-establishing the community of the apostles (as a sort of half-way station to the resurrection) was a favorite one in Noyes's doctrine.

perous enough to afford children, a deliberate program of breeding superior quality was undertaken. They called it "stirpiculture" and in many ways it was the culmination of the whole venture toward perfection. There was no science of genetics in their time and they thought, or hoped, that the wisdom, the self-control, and the perfection of their best members could be passed on intact to their offspring. It was a major disappointment when the stirpicultural babies turned out to be only a normal, and unusually healthy, batch of kids. They were excellent young specimens but the perfectionist doctrines had not penetrated to the genes and it was evident that the whole community experiment had to be lived through by each new generation—and without Noyes to guide them they might not find the one true path.

VI

Throughout this discussion we have been assuming that the "larger society" is worth preserving. A great many utopians would disagree. They would maintain that the soullessness and the mechanized mediocrity of our culture (or the coercion and militarism of our national state) are both intolerable and doomed and that some form of secession is the only possible answer for an individual of integrity. This attitude, as we have seen, is especially strong among pacifists—and we have looked into its sources. Similar attitudes can be found in other unhappy groups of social dissidents, and for similar reasons.

But the real question demands an honest answer. If the going concern of modern life *is* hopelessly corrupt and fated to disintegration and collapse, the seceders and the utopiacs may be right after all.

This concept of the "larger society" needs working over. It seems to involve three major elements: first, our social inheritance of mores, customs, values, and incentives—our culture pattern; second, the evolving structure of industry and business and the economic and social pressures it generates; third, the mechanisms of government and law. Obviously these categories are abstractions and are mixed and interacting in practice. The justification for separating them is that conflicts between them are always incipient and become vividly apparent in periods of crisis and transition.

During most of American history, all three elements have worked together well enough to avoid total breakdowns and to steadily augment the physical strength of the nation—with the exception of the Civil War, which split all three of them down the middle. The most persistent source of conflict has been an accelerating divergence between the traditional values of the culture pattern and the drive of the economy. Consequently, liberal reform has usually invoked the traditions of democracy, equality of opportunity, and freedom against the anti-democratic, monopolistic, and restrictive forces attributed to Big Business or Wall Street. The political government has been the battlefield—the area where these conflicts are fought out and the resultant balance is codified. The situation is complicated by the fact that the culture pattern has itself been changed (and violently changed) by the social consequences of the economic drives. The muckraking and reform uprisings of the 1900-1914 period may have represented the last concerted assertion of the traditional culture pattern. The First World War intervened and the following generation was too absorbed in giving its Fords a valves-and-carbon job to notice, or care, what was happening to the country. By the time the great conflict of the '30's was here, the culture pattern had become taut with stresses.

Idealistic dissent in American life has been a revolt against all three elements of the larger society but in varying proportions at different times. The most effective reform efforts have been made by those who accepted the basic premises of the culture pattern and directed their fire against the economic forces and their domination of the political machinery. Some of the most vocal dissenters have been primarily rebels against the culture pattern itself and its restraints on individual freedoms and variations from social norms. On the face of it, it looks as if this kind of rebellion had been extraordinarily successful. But the real damage to the traditional culture has come from the environmental changes wrought by economics and these dissenters have really won both a phony and a frightening victory.

Today's dissenters—of the kind who make pilgrimages to utopian colonies—have frequently rejected all three of the elements of the larger society. They are free spirits who scorn the normative customs of society; they want no part of modern business and industry; and, often enough, they remove themselves as far as they can from any participation in, responsibility for, or allegiance to the forms and usages of government and politics. This social alienation can easily set up a closed circle of motivation, in which an original rebellion (often merely a normal phase of adolescence) becomes reinforced by isolation and in-group ideology until the individual may come to have an overwhelming spiritual stake in the collapse of the larger society. Which is not a healthy state of affairs for either society or its dissenters.

Historically, it is easy to see now that our prophets of social doom have been largely wrong in the past. American society, with all its inequalities, injustices, and inhumanities has deviously achieved a higher standard of living, greater literacy and individual opportunity, and vastly improved public health (life expectancy, at least, is undeniable by those who might argue about "health"). To take a less materialistic field, the civil liberties situation, as of the time of writing, is far better than in 1920. The picture is never simple but it seems safe to say that the processes of integration, freedom, and life in this country have more than held their own over those of chaos, tyranny, and death. America has shown a capacity to meet crises by its own special brand of muddling through which gives little support to prophets of despair.

Our national future has, of course, become inextricably linked with that of the whole world and many people find the problems now thrust upon us beyond hope of solution. Certainly our larger society would preserve only a dubious residue of flexibility or humanity after an atomic war. Conceivably, life on this planet could reach a situation in which all large-scale social organization broke down and the forming of isolated little communities offered the only means of keeping the race and the memory of civilization alive. These would not be utopias, of course, but wretched huddlings-together for survival. (The very concept of utopia seems to require a larger going concern as a takeoff point.)

Fundamentally, allegiance to the larger society is a religious faith. In our culture it is based on the common humanity underlying differences of creed, politics, color, or class; it affirms that life is a serious and responsible business, that every individual is a unique sort of miracle to be respected as such, and that good and evil are real. *It also recognizes that personality is partly a social product, that society both restricts and sustains, and that both functions are essential.* It is this common faith which provides the network of decency and predictability which holds us together. Within it, conflict and diversity can churn around to good evolutionary effect and the keeping off of dull times. But setting out to slice through it to a position of greater freedom or moral purity on the outside is risky business.

Those of us who stay with the larger society can maintain that the problem is a common one—just as a final extermination would be a common one—and that those who reject the inheritance we bring to bear on it are not helping to solve it. It is one life as well as one world. Our inadequate personalities and institutions, our baggage from the past, and the mess we have made to date are what we have to start from and work with. We can't escape from or transcend any of it.   —*Fall* 1948

MEN AND MACHINES

C. E. AYRES

Technology and Progress

Technology is organized skill. As a definition this formula is both inadequate and misleading, but there is no better way to explore and clarify the meaning of technology than by discovering the inadequacies of common-sense conceptions such as this one. All skill is organized, of course, and all behavior skilled in some sense or other. We commonly distinguish between the skill of the artisan and the mastery of the scientist or the "creative" artist, and these distinctions are important. But do they distinguish between skill and non-skill? We do not ordinarily think of the scientist or the artist as "unskilled."

However important they may be, such distinctions are between kinds of skill. An artisan is one who performs operations which a scientist has devised. Much of the same distinction is made between the artist who is a "mere" performer and one who is a "creator." But differences appear even within the field of creation. In one of his later essays Roger Fry retracted his earlier declaration that Sargent was not an artist but repeated his earlier judgment in this form, that Sargent was an "applied" artist. The distinction was more than a slight. What Fry meant was that Sargent had adopted the color chords which the Impressionists had "created" (or discovered, or invented), and had used them in painting portraits of rich

This article later appeared as a chapter in *The Theory of Economic Progress* by Clarence Ayres. Copyright 1944 by The University of North Carolina Press.

sitters. Whereas Sargent, according to Fry, had "learned something" from the Impressionists, later painters stood to learn nothing from his canvases.

A similar distinction is made between pure and applied science. A man who knows no mathematics is only a mechanic, however good a mechanic he may be. If he knows and uses the common branches of mathematics, he is an engineer. If his scientific training is sufficient to enable him to understand and reproduce the experiments of scientists, putting them to use in the fashion in which Sargent used the palette of the Impressionists in painting portraits, he is an applied scientist. If he masters the work of earlier scientists in such a way as to be able to carry it on, putting their discoveries to the same sort of use to which they in turn had put the discoveries of still earlier scientists, then he is a scientist, too, in the same sense as they. Considerations of social prestige enter into these distinctions and give feeling-tone to judgments such as Fry passed upon Sargent, but they are irrelevant to the analysis of technology. The distinctions exist independently of the invidiousness which has been associated with them.

But they are not distinctions between skill and non-skill. What they distinguish is types of skill. The word "technique" is generally employed by musicians and other artists to refer to the finger dexterity of the instrumentalist or the hand-and-brush dexterity with which the painter applies his pigments to the canvas. Such technique is a more or less indispensable part of the equipment of every artist; but it is often mentioned sneeringly, and for this reason. A player may have acquired great finger dexterity and still be musically illiterate. Nearly all the great composers were at one time eminent performers, but most of them let their "techniques" run down as they became increasingly absorbed in composition. Does this mean that playing the piano is a matter of skill but that composing music is not? By no means. At another level of generalization it is customary to speak of "the techniques of the composer," meaning such things as skill in using scores. Many a musician who has acquired great skill in reading music, that is in thinking from printed notes to sounds, would experience the greatest difficulty in writing out the notes even of a quite simple tune which he had just heard for the first time. Mozart's celebrated feat of writing out in full an unpublished and closely guarded "Miserere" after hearing it once in the Sistine Chapel was not only an act of "sheer genius"; it was a technical achievement which was possible at all only because even at the age of fourteen Mozart was master of the techniques of the composer. He was indeed "very good at it"; but what he was good at must not be overlooked.

The conclusion toward which all these reflections lead is that all acts of skill involve the use of tools of one sort or another. Such distinctions as we have been considering are made in terms of the differences between these tools. An artisan is not a person of inferior dexterity. He is a person whose tools, however dextrously they may be used, are commonplace. But the skills of scientists and artists—even pure scientists and creative artists—are no less contingent on the use of tools. A mathematician or a composer may "have an inspiration" when he is wandering in the woods or (as in the case of Henri Poincaré) when he is catching a train. At the moment he has in his hands nothing which could be identified as a tool of his profession. Nevertheless his profession is a tool-using profession, and his "inspiration" could never have occurred to a man who had never used those tools. In the case of the composer they are such things as the diatonic scale, musical notation, existing instruments, and the like; but even more important to the particular inspiration of the individual composer is the literature of music: the works of other composers existing as physical objects in the form of printed scores over which he has pored most of his life. The same is true of the mathematician. At any given moment he may be without paper and pencil and not need them. But mathematics as a science could not have come into existence in the absence of paper and pencils (or any substitutes). Teachers of mathematics try from the beginning to impress upon their pupils that a "point" is not a chalk mark on a blackboard. (In *Mr. Fortune's Maggot* Sylvia Townsend Warner has written a very amusing account of the efforts of a lover of mathematics to convey this distinction to an aborigine.) Mathematicians have been able to define a point as "that which has" neither length nor breadth nor thickness, whatever "that which has" may mean in such a formula; but they could never have done so without using physical objects as tools. More important for present-day mathematics are of course the symbols which have been devised as the notation of complex mathematical operations. Here also the symbols are not themselves the operations; but here also it is still true that the operations could not be conducted without symbols, and that no one could learn to think mathematically without having spent years poring over the printed record of the symbolically denoted operations of earlier mathematicians. The current issues of the mathematical journals are perhaps the most important tools of the trade of the practicing mathematician, and they are physical objects which must be used with skill, no less than wrenches and hammers.

This absolute mutual contingency of skills and tools is of supreme importance for an understanding of technology as a function of human behavior for two reasons. In the first place, technical activity can be identified in no other way than by its uniform, unvarying association with tools. In some cases identification is easy. When a primitive community is fashioning a dugout canoe we observe that two sorts of activity are going on.

While a number of men are engaged in hollowing out the log, one rattles sharks' teeth, and roars what are obviously incantations. We identify the former as technological activity and the latter as something else. But the distinction is not so apparent to the tribesmen, since they recognize all these practitioners as members of the same "holy order" of canoe-builders and know that all are following the sacred liturgy of their order, the "workers" no less than the roarer. To us hollowing out logs is a secular activity, but intoning is something else; and we apply our own distinctions as an a priori classification to the other people.

Other cases are not so easy. We recognize astrology and alchemy as pre-sciences; but the whole activity in which their practitioners engaged was that of necromancy. Furthermore, as we have learned to our sorrow, certain ways of thinking have been carried over from the earlier activity into what we have regarded as the age of reason, so that our own science at least in its early stages has been contaminated by foreign elements. How are these to be distinguished? Categories such as "truth" and "knowledge" are disconcertingly inconclusive. It is precisely the "knowledge" of early modern times that is most dubious. The only reliable distinction is provided by what we call "experimental techniques," that is to say the tools of science. Even the necromancers employed "laboratory" techniques and were scientists insofar as they did so, in spite of the romantic names they gave their instruments and operations.

The case of the fine arts is even more confusing. Like science, all the arts were originally sacerdotal. All design and pictorial representation was at first cabalistic; all rhythm and tone patterns, all the gestures and postures of the dance and drama, were at first the literal enactment of mystic rites. Modern anthropological studies have left no doubt on this score. And in this case we have emerged from the savage state only very incompletely. The arts are still associated with ecclesiastical activities and their contemplation and creation are still generally regarded as "spiritual" experiences in a sense that is not true even of science. The effect of works of art is still generally conceived to be a sort of "seizure," and the creation of "masterworks" is still attributed to "inspiration" of a sort that is not vouchsafed to even the greatest of scientists. People repeat Wagner's hyperbole about "God and Beethoven" as though it were a literal transfiguration— and all this in spite of the constant insistence of practicing artists that their achievements are the result of "taking pains."

In this case also there is only one solution to the enigma: that provided by technical analysis. Popular reputations wax and wane. The "seizures" people feel in the presence of great "masterworks" are of the nature of self-hypnosis induced by expectation. Their subjects are usually awe-struck by such things as "the marvelous colors," although the actual pigments may have been renewed half-a-dozen times by quite mediocre and anonymous restorers. To the annoyance of musicians the enthusiastic public admires Mozart for his "quaintness" and Bach for the intricacy of his counterpoint, although what they call Mozart's quaintness was a characteristic of all eighteenth-century music, while Bach's great distinction was that he added to the contrapuntal intricacies of his day a harmonic richness which music had never known before. The achievements of the great creative artists are genuine achievements, but they are technical achievements which can be understood and genuinely appreciated only by a certain amount of study, a certain amount of knowledge of what is actually, technically going on. This understanding and appreciation is understanding of the tools—color and design, tonal structure and texture, and the like—with which artists actually work. In the tangled web of human life technical activities are almost inextricably blended with activities of another sort. The enthusiasm which they merit is almost indistinguishable from religious ecstasy. Nevertheless all tool-using activities have something in common which can be understood by virtue of the tools.

It is the peculiar character of all technology, from chipped flints to Boulder Dam and Beethoven's quartets, that it is progressive. It is inherently developmental. This circumstance which gives technology its peculiar importance in the analysis of culture—and most of all for economists—also can be understood only in terms of tools. If we limit the conception of technology to "skill," we are at once subject to great risk of conceiving technological development as the growth of skills; and since skill is a "faculty" of "individuals," we are preconditioned to think of the growth of skill as in some sense an increase of this faculty on the part of individuals. But we know nothing of any such increase.

That is what makes it so hard for economists of the traditional way of thinking to understand the technological principle. They understand the crucial importance of the issue. Since Veblen first began to write it has been apparent that some sort of claim was being made for technology as a master principle of economic analysis. This claim was seen to rest on the peculiarly dynamic character of technology as itself inherently progressive and the agent of social change, in particular the agent of industrial revolution. As one of the most thoughtful of contemporary economists has remarked, this whole way of thinking "assumes for technology some kind of inner law of progress of an absolute and inscrutable character," as well as "some equally absolute and inscrutable type of 'causality' by which technology drags behind it and 'determines' other phases of

social change."[1] The whole issue between the old and new ways of thinking in economics comes to focus here. The new way of thinking does indeed rest on some kind of inner law of progress. But there is nothing
absolute or inscrutable about it. What makes it seem inscrutable is the in-
veterate predisposition of orthodox economists to think in terms of a conception of human nature as that of the uniquely individual "spirit." Thinking
so, they think of technology as a skill faculty of the individual spirit; and
thinking so, they find the principle of technological development quite
inscrutable—as indeed they must. For the developmental character of
technology is implicit not in the skill faculty of the human individual but
in the character of tools. The whole analysis must proceed on the level of
generalization of culture rather than of individuality in order for the
principle of technological progress to be understood at all.

On that level it is perfectly obvious. As a result of the rapid advance
of machine technology in recent years the process of invention has attracted general attention and has become the subject of a considerable
literature.[2] These studies have given the *coup de grâce* to the "heroic"
theory of invention—the myth which attributes inventions to the sheer
magnitude of soul of the "Gifted Ones." It is now generally agreed that
all inventions are combinations of previously existing devices. Thus the
airplane is a combination of a kite and an internal combustion engine. An
automobile is a combination of a buggy with an internal combustion engine. The internal combustion engine itself is a combination of the steam
engine with a gaseous fuel which is substituted for the steam and exploded
by the further combination of the electric spark. This is speaking broadly,
of course. In actual practice the combinations are for the most part much
more detailed. What is presented to the public as a "new" invention is
usually itself the end product of a long series of inventions.

In this process materials—what economists have so misleadingly
designated as "natural" resources—function as devices. According to the
principle of indestructibility of matter there is no such thing as a "new"
material. Helium gas must have been present in the earth of the Texas
Panhandle geologic ages before man first invaded the Western Hemisphere
some thousands of years ago. Nevertheless helium was not a "natural
resource" of the republic of Texas, inasmuch as helium was not identified
in the sun for many years after the end of the republic, nor isolated from
the earth's atmosphere for many years after that, nor discovered to be a
component of Texas natural gas until still later, nor treated as a resource

---

[1]Frank H. Knight, "Intellectual Confusion in Morals and Economics," *International
Journal of Ethics,* XLV (1935), 208-209.
[2]Outstanding in this literature for clarity and cogency is a little book by S. C. Gilfillan,
The Sociology of Invention (1935).

until it was used in balloons only a few years ago. The history of every material is the same. It is one of novel combination of existing devices and materials in such a fashion as to constitute a new device or a new material or both. This is what it means to say that natural resources are defined by the prevailing technology, a practice which is now becoming quite general among economists to the further confusion of old ways of thinking (since it involves a complete revision of the concept of "scarcity" which must be regarded as also defined by technology and not by "nature").

Furthermore, as regards the nature of the process there is no difference between "mechanical" invention and "scientific" discovery. Scientific discoveries also result from the combination of previously existing devices and materials, laboratory instruments and techniques. It was by combining a magnet with a Crookes tube, for example, that J. J. Thomson discovered that the stream of incandescence in the tube was in fact a stream of physical particles and was even able to calculate the mass of the electrons. It was by combining a prism with a telescope that astronomers were able to identify elements (such as helium) in the sun. Even in the fine arts "creation" comes about in the same way. Leonardo's great achievement illustrated by the famous Mona Lisa, about which so much nonsense has been talked,[3] was that he applied techniques which the monks had devised for the portrayal of angels to the portraiture of living subjects. Cézanne characterized his achievement as resulting from the application of Pissarro's studio technique to painting from nature. In every innovation analysis reveals the combination of previously existing devices. That is what the achievement is which in different fields we call invention or discovery or creation.

This principle of combination is important by virtue of the light it throws on previous obscurities. One of these is the role of chance in discovery and invention. An extraordinary number of the most significant discoveries have been made by chance. Columbus discovered America by accident. Ostensibly he was sailing toward the Indies. The discovery of the X ray resulted from the exposure of sealed photographic plates by their accidental juxtaposition to a Crookes tube. Ehrlich's "magic bullet" treatment for syphilis eventuated from the accidental relation between the spirochete of that disease and the trypanosome which Ehrlich had much earlier selected for experimental purposes because it was easily identified under the microscope and could be bred in laboratory animals. In the case of mechanical inventions the role of chance is even more notorious. Adam Smith relates the tale of the invention of the automatic valves by which the steam engine operates from the trick of a lazy boy who tied the con-

---

[3]See Rockwell Kent's comments on this work in *World Famous Paintings* (1939).

trol string to a moving part which then opened and closed the valve automatically.

But what do we mean by "chance" or "accident"? These words are of course relational. In a sense nothing occurs by chance, but some events are less relevant than others to any given point of reference. In all these cases the point of reference is the previous activities of some individual. The discovery of America was "accidental" with reference to the intentions of Columbus; but it was not accidental that it should have occurred in 1492. The arts of shipbuilding, seamanship, and navigation being what they were by the end of the fifteenth century, somebody was "bound" to have "discovered America" within a decade or so; and this also is true of inventions and discoveries generally. The lore of science and mechanics is full of simultaneous discoveries, often by several agents and as a result of strikingly similar combinations. The simultaneous development of the infinitesimal calculus out of the same mathematical materials by Newton and Leibnitz is a case in point. So is the simultaneous enunciation of the theory of biological evolution by Darwin and Wallace. In this case the identity of the materials which entered into combination and the extreme separation of the agents of discovery are equally striking. Although Darwin thought out his statement in England and Wallace in Malaysia on the opposite side of the world, both were practicing naturalists concerned with the problem of species, and both received definite stimulation to this particular formula from reading Malthus' *Essay on the Principle of Population*. Instances could be multiplied indefinitely. The Patent Office is engaged in a perpetual struggle with the problem of simultaneity. But what seems utterly mysterious so long as invention is regarded as an act of individual inspiration is easily explained in terms of the principle of combination.

These combinations are physical not less than ideational. To be sure they are achieved by men, usually by men of great ability. But the things they put together are physical objects. The coexistence of these objects constitutes a possibility of combination which transcends the acts of any individual. It is in this sense that inventions seem "bound" to occur. As we look back on the recent history of devices for the transmission of sound it seems most remarkable that the audion tube should have been used for years to amplify long distance telephone currents before being applied to "wireless" technology, which had been struggling along all this time with the now utterly obsolete coherer; or that the phonograph should have languished for years after the introduction of radio before it occurred to someone that audion tubes would amplify pick-up currents too. It is no disparagement of genius to recognize that certain combinations would almost necessarily have occurred in somebody's hands sooner or later.

Individual genius not only places its possessor in the front rank of pioneers; it also determines when a discovery is made. Often this happens "before its time." That is, some inspired Mendel works out a given combination, the laws of inheritance among sweet peas, years before other combinations have occurred in the field of cytology to which those laws are supremely relevant. The over-all determinant which defines the universe of discourse within which genius is at play is an objective actuality—the tool pattern.

Another anomaly of the inventive process which also is resolved by the tool-combination principle is the extraordinary role of tyros and amateurs in science and mechanics and even the fine arts. The number of important discoveries and inventions which have been made by juveniles and by such people as lawyers and clergymen whose professional training is wholly unrelated to the field in question is strikingly large—too large to be attributed to the peculiar talents of the individuals concerned who in many cases have done little or nothing else to attract attention. In mathematical physics, for example, the Nobel Prize has been given to so many men of such extreme youth as to give rise to the saying that in this field a man has passed his peak by twenty-eight. Why is this? Doubtless precocity has something to do with it in certain cases. Children learn languages easily, including the special languages of mathematics and music; but it is notorious that most prodigies peter out, and in any case the prodigy theory does not explain the discoveries of the clergyman, Joseph Priestley, or the paintings of the stockbroker, Paul Gauguin.

The explanation which follows directly from the tool-combination analysis of invention is the one which accounts for the annoying facility with which an intruder often finds a solution almost instantaneously for a jigsaw puzzle with which the player has been struggling for hours. Where the solution is a matter of putting together existing pieces, it may be impeded on the part of the regular player, by fixed ideas, preoccupations, and other behavior "sets" from which the intruder is free. Consequently he sees at once the possible combination which has been hidden from the player by his own intense preoccupation. Innovations are often made by people who are so innocent as not to realize how outrageously novel they are. It is even said that important scientific discoveries have been made as a direct result of ignorance on the part of a discoverer who simply did not "know" that the thing he did "could not be done," and so just went ahead and did it. This is the explanation of the importance of detachment for scientific research and other creative achievement, what Veblen called "idle" curiosity. Obviously (though it has not been obvious to hostile critics, perhaps because they lacked detachment) he means "detached" and not "indolent." Excessive preoccupation of any kind—pious, financial, uxorious, or even professional—is inimical to the "free play" of the imagination in the course of which combinations somehow occur. Discoveries are not made by punching time clocks, and closing laboratories and libraries on Sunday is an excellent way to inhibit creative activity.

These corollaries of the analysis of invention in terms of the combination of existing devices, in which Mr. Gilfillan and his colleagues are interested for their own sake, assume increasingly great theoretical importance as they proceed from the particular to the general. If technological development results from the combination of existing tool-material devices, and if such combinations follow the pattern of existing devices and often do so in the hands of people whose peculiar advantage it is to be free from inhibiting preoccupations, then it would also seem to follow that innovations are likely to occur at any time and in any region in which devices are brought together which have hitherto existed in separate regions. This is an observed fact. The diffusion of culture traits from one culture area to another is quite generally accompanied by innovation. Indeed, so striking is the stimulus which results from culture contacts that it has been called the "cross-fertilization" of cultures. But it is the tools themselves, not the people, that have been hybridized. Such innovations—and they include some of the most important technological advances in history—are not to be explained by any special excitation of the imaginations of the people among whom they occur. As a matter of fact the people most directly concerned are usually quite unaware of the importance of what is going on; and furthermore, once the mutually conditioning devices have been brought together no sublime inspiration is necessary to the recognition of the pattern. The combination occurs almost "of itself," often quite anonymously. That is one reason why the history of mechanical inventions is so difficult to trace. No one has bothered to record the event because no one is aware that an act of "heroism" has been committed. It remains for later historians gradually to become aware of the transcendent importance of these almost surreptitious developments. Regarding them, as it is their habit to regard all history, as the sum of the acts of individual men, they are at a loss for an adequate explanation. But on the cultural level of generalization, regarded as combinations of physically existing devices, these innovations are not only explicable but inevitable. Where cultures meet, cross-fertilization is to be expected. It is a direct result of the physical embodiment of technical behavior patterns in tools and physical materials.

We have here the explanation of the "inscrutable" propensity of all technological devices to proliferate. This propensity is a characteristic not of men but of tools. Granted that tools are always tools of men who have the capacity to use tools and therefore the capacity to use them together, combinations are bound to occur. Furthermore it follows that the more tools there are, the greater is the number of potential combinations. If we knew nothing of history but had somehow come to understand the nature of our tools, we could infer that technological development must have been an accelerating process, almost imperceptibly slow in its earlier stages and vertiginously fast in its most recent phase. This is, of course, the observed fact. Mr. H. G. Wells, with his gift for dramatizing history, has remarked that the entire development of civilization (as distinguished from "savagery") has occurred within roughly one hundred generations, which is perhaps not more than one one-hundredth part of the experience of the race. The machine age occupies not more than one-tenth of this period; the mass-production age, one one-hundredth. The old stone age was of prodigious length; the new stone age much shorter but still many times longer than the whole of subsequent history. Archeologists and historians are well aware of this fact. Indeed, it is one of their persistent puzzles. But it is a puzzle to which the analysis of mechanical invention now provides a key.

For the tool-combination principle is indeed a law of progress. If we suppose that tool combinations occur in the same fashion as that in which digits are combined in the mathematical theory of permutations, then the resulting series is a progressive one in the mathematical sense of a series each member of which is derived from each preceding member by the same operation. In such a case it would be sharply progressive in the sense that the number of combinations would increase very rapidly, that is by squares:

$$x; \; x^2; \; (x^2)^2; \; ((x^2)^2)^2 \ldots \text{or } x; \; x^2; \; x^4; \; x^8 \ldots.$$

Obviously this supposition at once calls for a number of reservations. We do not know that tool combinations occur according to the mathematical law of permutations. Indeed we have no way of knowing for any given set of tools, devices, or materials, how many combinations are possible. We know only those that actually occur, and even these present a problem of enumeration which is perhaps insoluble, as is the initial enumeration of the given set. The mathematical analogy also takes no account of time, although time is of the essence of an actual historical sequence. Does the completion of each stage of the progressive series represent a year or a thousand years? Does the time span increase for successive stages as the magnitude of the sets increases? Clearly the mathematical representation of the actual process of technological combination can be nothing more than illustrative, and illustrative only of one aspect of the process, that of increasing magnitude.

Nevertheless the analogy is highly suggestive. Although no one supposes that history conforms to any simple mathematical series, the idea that the actual technological process is progressive and accelerating has occurred to a number of students in widely separated fields of investigation.[4] This principle is not teleological, any more than the physical principles of gravitation or centrifugence. It need not be supposed that any given invention is "bound" to occur. Certainly it will not occur if the solar system is obliterated by the collision of the sun with a wandering comet, nor will it occur if the human species is suddenly and completely obliterated by disease. It will not occur at any given time in any given community if all technological development, or even that particular strain of technological developments, is inhibited by contrary forces at work in that community at that time. No one supposes that the technological process is the whole of culture, any more than anyone supposes that centrifugence is the only physical force to which inhabitants of the surface of the earth are subject. On the contrary, all students of technology have recognized that it is but one aspect of culture and that culture exhibits another aspect which is inhibitory to the technological process just as gravitation inhibits centrifugence. In some communities, apparently, technological progress has been totally arrested. Stone-age culture is still extant in certain regions. There is no community whose history does not reveal periods in which technology has been virtually stationary for long periods of time. But these facts do not deny the existence of technology nor invalidate the analysis of technological development in terms of a continuous, cumulative, progressive process, any more than the fact that we do not fly off at a tangent to the earth's surface invalidates the principle of centrifugence. It means that other forces also are at work, not that technological progress is an illusion.

Granting all this, some students of the social sciences hesitate to identify technological development with progress for another reason. The concept of progress is in bad odor at the present time, and rightly so. In

---

[4]For example, Alfred (Count) Korzybski, *The Manhood of Humanity* (1922), p. 20: ". . . the spectacle we behold is that of advancement in scientific knowledge and technical power according to the law and at the rate of a rapidly increasing geometric progression or logarithmic function"; R. D. Carmichael, *The Logic of Discovery* (1930), pp. 144-5: "(Man's) law of progress seems to be that of the geometrical ratio. As equal intervals of time are added to his experience he seems to increase his wealth of thought in an approximately fixed ratio. . . . The recent rapid development of mathematical science gives support to the law of geometrical progression as the law of man's growth. This body of doctrine has increased at a rate which itself has an increasing rate so that the total body of it in our day has become larger than anyone two generations ago could have contemplated as possible"; George Sarton, *The Study of the History of Science* (1936), p. 20: ". . . the progress of science is constantly accelerated and hence . . . more and more is accomplished in shorter and shorter periods."

the past, progress has been conceived in terms of the prevailing transcendentalism as movement toward a preconceived end or consummatory state. This consummatory state, as we now realize, has always been a projection, or "collective representation," of prevailing culture. That is, every people has conceived "heaven," or perfection, as the pure essence of its own prevailing institutions or mores, just as Dante pictured paradise and purgatory in terms of his own (community engendered) preferences and prejudices. We know today—it is a ground principle of modern social science—that such conceptions have no general validity, and students of the social sciences are therefore chary of any assumption which embodies them.

But when they insist that any conception of progress must be transcendental, they go beyond scientific caution. Why "must" it? What does "must" mean in this connection? It cannot mean that no other conception is possible, since another actually exists. It has been employed in mathematics since ancient times without demur. It is entirely clear and definite. Why, then, should its employment in the analysis of technology arouse resistance? But social progress, we are told, "must" be movement toward a preconceived end. Why "must" it? There is only one answer to this question. Although modern social studies have convinced us that human behavior exhibits no such "end" and therefore no such movement, we are still sufficiently obsessed by traditional ways of thinking to retain the conviction that if we are to think about social progress at all, we must do so in terms of transcendental "ends." We "must" because that is the traditional way of thinking.

This sense of intellectual compulsion to follow traditional ways of thinking is bound up with our whole conception of value and our emancipation will certainly not be complete until it has included that category. But the analysis of technological process by students of mechanical invention and of the history of science and the arts is already sufficient to indicate the existence in all culture of a dynamic force, a phase of culture which is in itself and of its own character innovational, one in which change is continuous and cumulative and always in the same direction, that of more numerous and more complex technological devices. It may be objected that the very word "direction" implies an "end," but this is not so. Direction is implicit in the nature of a series. The series of cardinal numbers is directional, since the numbers continually grow larger as we count. It would be ridiculous to say that in counting we are striving to approximate infinity, or that counting is meaningless except as infinity is preconceived to be its end, and it is just as ridiculous to insist that no continuous process can be conceived in the realm of culture except in terms of a preconceived end.

Indeed, the restoration of the concept of progress is one of the crying needs of contemporary social science. The truth is, our agnosticism has gone too far. In ridding our minds of the naïve collective representations of the past we have gone so far as to deny the intelligibility of any sort of pattern in cultural development. But the development of culture exhibits pattern. The successive layers of artifacts which are laid bare by the digging of the archeologists are not a sheer hodge-podge conglomeration. Each successive layer is somehow related to those below and those above, and the relationship exhibits some sort of continuous process. Whatever the function be called which differentiates one from another, it is a continuous function and still further differentiates the second layer above from the second layer below.

To economists this problem of pattern is presented in the form of industrialization. It is a real problem. Something or other has been going on continuously. Whether good or bad, purgatorial or paradise-approximating, it is the same process in each generation. What is this process? Traditional economic thinking has attributed this continuous development to the agency of business enterprise, and this attribution has been one of the basic postulates of that way of thinking. But its technological character has been suspected all along by intellectual mavericks. It is now strongly substantiated by all the studies which have contributed to our present understanding of the technological process. Students of economics are therefore confronted by a challenge. In spite of traditional assumptions, the origin and development of the industrial economy remains a mystery. Can the technological principle of explanation resolve this mystery? It is to this challenge that we should address ourselves.   —*Spring* 1943

WILL HERBERG

Bureaucracy and Democracy in Labor Unions

TRADE unionism in this country presents a curious paradox. The ordinary rank-and-file union member frequently enjoys less freedom in relation to his own union leader than he does in relation to his employer. Against the arbitrary power of the "boss" he often has protection considerably more effective than against that of the union official. In the administration of his own organization, he sometimes has less to say than, thanks to collective bargaining, he has in the affairs of his shop or factory.

Members of unions, even progressive unions, are on occasion exposed to severe penalties for exercising rights, such as forming "parties," issuing leaflets, holding meetings, denouncing officials, that are specifically guaranteed under the law of the land. Even in democratic unions, the effective power of top officials is greater, their grip tighter, their tenure more secure, their conduct in office less open to public criticism and control, than is commonly the case in our federal or state governments in normal times. These are all facts of ordinary experience, which only special pleading can deny or attempt to explain away.

And yet the trade-union movement in which these things can and do happen emerged historically as a democratic protest against arbitrary power and oppression. It has always claimed to be the champion of a higher and fuller democracy than prevails in our capitalistic society generally, and to provide an exemplification of such democracy within its own ranks.

It is the purpose of this article to examine this paradox and the problems behind it. The method is one of institutional analysis that looks for determining factors in the underlying features of structure and function, embedded, of course, in a specific social environment, which, for our purposes, need not be more than indicated.

If one examines a modern trade union empirically, i.e., as a going concern, a functioning institution, one is struck by its essentially dual nature. A modern labor union is, at one and the same time: (1) a businesslike service organization, operating a variety of agencies under a complicated system of industrial relations; and (2) an expression and vehicle of the historical movement of the submerged laboring masses for social recognition and democratic self-determination. This irreducible duality necessarily results in a fundamental conflict of purpose and orientation. As a businesslike service organization, the union requires efficient bureaucratic administration, very much like a bank or insurance company. The members of the union are merely clients who are entitled to the best service for their money but who certainly should not presume to interfere in matters of administration, since such matters are properly the function of trained and experienced officials specially selected for the purpose. But as a phase of the democratic self-liberation movement of modern times, the union is an idealistic, quasi-religious collectivity; it is a crusading reform movement of which the members, the masses, and their democratic self-expression are the very essence.

The union, as an institution, is thus in the grip of a very real contradiction. Each side of this contradiction, each functional aspect, generates its own appropriate habits and attitudes, so that the institutional cleavage is reflected not only in a cleavage between leaders and rank and file but in a cleavage within the bureaucratic personnel, and not infrequently in a sort of psychic cleavage in the leaders themselves, who may have to function simultaneously as bureaucratic administrators and leaders of mass movements.

In the early days of unionism, the idealistic, democratic, emancipatory aspect is dominant. Indeed, the movement draws its main strength from the quasi-religious spiritual resources of idealism, sacrifice, and solidarity. But with the growth and entrenchment of unionism, the businesslike service aspect inevitably comes to the fore. Today, by and large, American unions have become thoroughly businesslike service agencies bureaucratically operated, like banks or insurance companies. This is a sweeping generalization that requires a number of qualifications.

In the first place, the old ideology, the old idealistic conceptions and phraseology, still persist as underlying tradition, more or less powerful. Standards of judgment follow the idealistic tradition far more closely than the facts of the case would seem to warrant. The labor official is, in a vague sort of way, expected to live up to norms appropriate not to the business executive he actually is but to a dedicated champion of a cause.

The old idealistic approach, moreover, is commonly found useful in agitation and demagogy. It reappears as a genuinely vital force in the early, militant stages of newly launched organizations (e.g., certain C.I.O unions in 1936-37) as well as at critical moments in old, well established unions when their very existence is challenged in sharp industrial struggle. In these circumstances, the old spirit may still come to play a significant role and it should not be ignored in any realistic institutional analysis.

It is necessary to stress, just because the discussion here must remain so schematic, that the contemporary American labor movement presents no uniform picture. There are organizations at every stage of development and the emphasis is constantly shifting. But the general pattern outlined, though abstract, seems to possess value as an explanatory concept.

A survey of trade-union history will indicate a steady tendency for effective power to concentrate at the top. The process may be summarized in the following terms. The original regime (in British unions, and in American unions modeled after them) was a kind of primitive democracy. The membership meeting, the members in mass, constituted the legislative power. Administrative functions were vested in an executive board, elected by the members from their own midst. This board, consisting of workers employed at their trade, would divide itself into committees, with every member of the board functioning on some committee, for the purpose of handling the administrative affairs of the organization in the hours left after work. For the few specific services that required special clerical skill or full-time attention, one or two people would be hired as agents of the executive board. These full-time employees were, strictly speaking, clerks or agents, not officials at all.

Obviously an institutional setup such as this could not last. As the organization grew and its functions expanded, the bureaucratic potential came to assume formidable proportions. A striking shift in the seat of effective power took place. The legislative power gradually passed from the membership meeting, first to the executive board, and then by a further remove, to the paid officials ("the office"). Simultaneously, the administrative functions of the executive board also passed over to the paid officials. But these paid officials had themselves completely changed in status and character. They were no longer "outside" clerks, serving as functionary agents of the executive board; they were leading members of the union, responsible, authoritative executives. Whatever technical and professional functions had to be performed, and these functions naturally multiplied, were relegated, as in any business house, to hired clerks and specialists without official standing or independent executive power.

The net effect of this evolution is to be seen more or less clearly in the institutional setup of any large union, progressive or conservative. All power—legislative, administrative and executive (the judicial function is generally a phase of the administrative-executive)—is effectively concentrated in the hands of "the office," a group of top paid officials. This group may be relatively broad, or it may consist of one man, but in essentials it is "the office" that rules. The executive board and its committees, once the actual administrative bodies of the union, become agencies of formal endorsement, rubber-stamp agencies in the literal sense of the term; in the best of cases, they also serve a vague and undefined parliamentary function, as an arena of discussion where the union leaders can feel out the sentiment of their immediate subordinates. The membership meeting becomes merely a plebiscitary body, and in the more democratic unions, also a medium through which the directives of the leadership are transmitted to the masses of members and the members aroused and inspired.

The old primitive democratic structure is never formally abolished and usually not even modified officially. It remains in a vestigial or fossilized form without greatly hampering the actual bureaucratic concentration of power. The real process of the redistribution of power takes place behind the time-honored façade of The Constitution. Yet the union constitution and its obsolete democratic arrangements are not to be written off entirely; they may become an effective force again in the comparatively rare case of membership revolt or bitter factional struggle, where the effort to revive and utilize some long-disused democratic procedure may prove of considerable importance.

It is necessary to stress at this point that the tendency toward the upward shift and concentration of power is inherent in the very nature of the organization as it grows, its functions multiply, and its responsibilities increase. Thirst for power, where it does exist (and it naturally exists almost everywhere), is essentially a secondary factor, aggravating, accelerating, but certainly not originating the tendency. The bureaucratic potential has its roots deep in the very nature of organization.

Yet power politics and the struggle for power play an important role in the development outlined. Power has its own logic and imperatives. The most idealistic administration—one composed entirely of sincere, high-minded men, intent only on serving their members and putting into effect a genuinely constructive program—even such an administration, once in office, inevitably turns "practical" and "realistic"; it must. It is immediately confronted with a vast and complex mass of administrative problems that in the nature of the case can only be handled bureaucratically. It is, moreover, sooner or later confronted with an opposition that—unscrupulously, demagogically, of course—exploits moods of dissatisfaction and discontent among the members; and such moods are bound to arise for even the best administration cannot conjure away the effects of adverse economic conditions. Caught in this predicament, the new idealistic administration, in order to beat back the onslaughts of those whom it regards as unscrupulous demagogues, is frequently compelled to resort to dubious devices, which it vehemently denounced while in opposition and which it may still sincerely deplore. It is compelled to build up and operate a political machine feeding on patronage and favors, to strain its democratic conscience a little here and there. It should be emphasized that nothing corrupt or improper in law or custom is here implied; everything may be quite legitimate, but it is somehow not the old idealism, and it becomes less and less so as time goes on.

Beginning with the very best of intentions, desirous of power not for its own sake but in order to implement a constructive program, the idealist in office insensibly passes over to an increasingly exclusive absorption in power as such, explained away and justified by all sorts of rationalizations. This is the inescapable logic of power politics, but without power politics there is no administering or running a union.

The fundamental factors here described, it should be reiterated, arise out of the very nature of large-scale organization. Unscrupulousness, personal ambition, abnormal thirst for power, may, of course, aggravate the situation, but the tendencies indicated arise and exercise their effect in any case. It is very largely an impersonal objective process.

The net result of the process, as has been pointed out, is the emergence of a powerful tendency toward the concentration of effective power in the hands of the top leadership of the organization, with the paid officials forming the kernel of the ruling group. The power of a union administration is frequently quite unlimited, for virtually none of the restraining factors we are familiar with in our political machinery (checks and balances, independence of the judiciary, balance of socio-economic interests) are operative. And the power of a union administration gains immensely with the extension of the union's economic control in the industry. The closed shop is obviously a source of power to union leaders, and the Wagner Act, by giving unionism government protection and a quasi-public status, operates strongly in the same direction.

Another aspect of the process is a sweeping trend toward complete bureaucratic administration—i.e., administration by a distinct group of professional functionaries specially selected and at least partly trained for that purpose, as opposed to the primitive self-administration or rank-and-file administration of earlier days. Bureaucratic administration becomes imperative at a certain stage of development of the organization if there is to be any sort of sustained, efficient, and systematic administration at all. The process is greatly stimulated and extended, however, by the compulsions of power politics, for a bureaucratized administrative machinery is certainly of immense assistance in the effort to retain power, which must be a major concern of every union leadership.

A bureaucratic system has two sets of institutional implications: on the one hand, it makes for better, more efficient, more objective administration; on the other, it makes for the cohesion of the professional administrators into a special group or privileged caste with its special interests, loyalties, and solidarities. From the point of view of our analysis, the latter is the significant trend.

Another side of this general development is the systematic narrowing of democracy within the organization, and this in two senses: the limitation, perhaps virtual extinction, of self-government; and the restriction of the civil liberties of members. It is perhaps worth while to examine this aspect at somewhat greater length.

With the expansion of bureaucratic administration, the activity of the mass of members in the organization is necessarily reduced to a minimum. Everything is done for them by full-time professional officials, first because it can be done better and more efficiently that way, and secondly because doing it that way enhances the power and control of the leadership. By and large, the members are quite satisfied to have it so—as long as things go well and they receive what they regard as the proper service and protection from the union. And most union administrations are naturally quite as content, to say the least. Progressive administrations, with a tradition of "mass activity," do occasionally call upon the members to be "more active" but the words are really meaningless, for in an established union, functioning as a going concern, there is increasingly less and less for the members to be active about, except on the rare occasions when sharp industrial conflict breaks out. The whole matter wears a thoroughly unreal aspect because of the widening gap between the realities of the bureaucratic situation and the "mass" traditions carried over from an earlier day.

Self-government passes into a mere shadow, to be somewhat spasmodically revived on the comparatively infrequent occasions of membership revolt or the disruption of the "official family" through sharp internal conflict, when each faction makes its direct appeal to the masses. Normally, however, the membership meeting, constitutionally the highest legislative body of the organization, exercises merely plebiscitary power, if any at all. The top union leadership is typically surrounded by a somewhat broader group made up of the executive board members, business agents and the like, and these in turn by a still broader circle of "active" members, who in some way feel that the administration is theirs. This hierarchy forms the political machine of the union and those who go to make it up are entitled to, and in fact receive, whatever patronage or favors are available. Programs and policies adopted by the top leadership are customarily canvassed among these people first, to obtain their approval, which in most cases is merely a politic gesture, and to "start the ball rolling," by popularizing the idea. General membership meetings are usually composed of the active members supporting the administration plus the active members supporting any opposition that may exist plus whatever ordinary members can be drawn to the meeting by one or the other machine. Where no opposition exists, the meeting is simply a routine procedure to obtain official approval for the administration's acts and policies as required by the constitution, and to "activize" the membership. If a factional situation does exist, the meeting may turn into a test of strength, with lines drawn tight. In either case, there is little left of actual democratic self-government.

Again it should be noted that this is generally not the fault of the leadership, if fault there be. In a large and well established union it can not be much otherwise. Progressive leaderships are frequently very anxious to have the meetings as large as possible and to stir up some genuine discussion and expression of opinion. But as long as things continue more or less normal in the industry and union, such attempts are bound to remain largely unsuccessful. The ordinary member sees no particular reason for "wasting" his time at meetings. "Let the officials run the union, that's what they're getting paid for," just about expresses his attitude.

In other words, the process of bureaucratization and whittling down of effective democracy is not usually or necessarily a process of violent usurpation carried through against the will of the membership. By and large, it is a gradual affair, proceeding imperceptibly with the approval or at least the passive assent of the rank and file. As long as things go well, the average union member doesn't want self-government, and is annoyed and resentful when an attempt is made to force its responsibilities upon him. What he wants is protection and service, his money's worth for his dues.

The situation becomes somewhat more tense when an administration does not feel quite secure in its seat of power or when it begins to develop habits of authoritarianism. Then, not merely are self-administration and self-government reduced to a minimum, as they necessarily must be in a large functioning organization, but the civil liberties of the members are infringed with virtual impunity. Here, too, the mass of members do not come into question, for the mass of members—so long as things go well —are not interested in exercising civil liberties in the union. But actual and potential oppositionists are hard hit, as well as the few "queer" people who show a concern for "good government" and democratic rights as a matter of principle. Restriction of civil liberties in unions may be relatively mild and negligible, like the prohibition of intra-union groups or parties, or it may be quite severe and altogether irregular, such as outright violence and dishonest elections, but even the mildest forms are such as would hardly be tolerated in our national political life.

The discussion so far has concerned the normal regime of trade unions and very little has been said about such sensational developments as corruption, racketeering, and intra-union violence, not because they are nonexistent or of no importance, but rather because from a sociological point of view they are really secondary aggravating factors. However widespread such abuses may be, they do not constitute the basic problem of this analysis, which is the problem of democracy and bureaucracy in the honest, well conducted union with a sincere, responsible leadership. It is the argument of this article that the emergence and spread of bureaucracy and the decay of democracy in trade unions are not abnormal excesses but are rooted in the very nature of trade-union organization, and of organization in general. The very process of institutionalization, of organizational expansion and stabilization, generates a powerful bureaucratic potential.

Are these tendencies irreversible? Is the bureaucratic potential all-powerful? What can be done to preserve democracy in trade unions?

At this point we pass beyond objective institutional analysis into the realm of moral values and practical action. Democracy, we affirm, is in some sense indispensable and must be preserved. Unionism must not be permitted to complete its development toward businesslike bureaucratization. Something must be done to halt, divert, or at least retard this process. These are the assumptions.

I do not believe that the problem can ever be fully solved. As soon as organization develops beyond a certain point, inevitably those tendencies will emerge which go to make up the bureaucratic potential. It is a problem that transcends our social order, or any social order, and penetrates to the very nature of organization and institutional functioning.

But although the problem may never be entirely solved, certain manifest evils may be mitigated or reduced, and thus, in some sense, a solution approximated. The first condition is realism. Facts must be faced frankly, without evasion or self-deception out of false loyalty. Only then will it become possible to understand the underlying forces at work and to frame a program of reform.

Of the institutional reforms which first come under consideration, the one most discussed is governmental control or administrative regulation of unions. I do not believe that anything really worth while is to be accomplished along this road; the medicine would probably be worse than the disease. Administrative control of unions by the government is essentially a totalitarian measure and would deprive the unions of the independence and freedom of action that is their very reason for existence. Whatever may prove to be necessary in the emergency of war, such a system of over-all governmental control, instituted as part of our normal peacetime regime, would have the most disastrous effect on democracy far beyond the confines of the trade-union movement.

Nor would the conversion of the unions into quasi-governmental bodies necessarily serve to protect the masses of members from abuse of power by union officials. On the contrary, the probabilities are that this process would actually increase their arbitrary power, and union officials would then come to constitute a fused government-union bureaucracy. Such, at least has been the experience hitherto, for every extension of the quasi-public character of unionism under recent New Deal legislation has brought additional authority and power to the trade-union officialdom.

Another favorite panacea in business and journalistic circles is the incorporation of unions; this, we are told, will make them more "responsible." There is a vast literature on the subject, running back several decades, which it would be out of place even to summarize here. But the net conclusion seems to be that while the compulsory incorporation of unions might well prove an impediment to their legitimate functioning, it would have little if any effect in making them more democratic or responsible labor organizations. The whole project seems to be rather pointless in the present context.

Whatever institutional reforms are suggested must be within the trade-union movement itself, although, of course, they may be implemented with public sanctions. Thus, I believe it is futile to talk of any reform of trade-union regimes without some effective guarantee of the elementary civil liberties of members, and as things stand, such a guarantee, to mean anything, must somehow be enforceable at law, perhaps through special tribunals. It seems both absurd and intolerable that a man, who is protected by the federal and state constitutions in his rights to free speech, free press, and free assembly, should be subject to arbitrary punishment by his union officials for exercising precisely these rights—for denouncing what he believes to be official misdeeds, for issuing a leaflet, for organizing opposition meetings. A person who has his "natural rights" thus flagrantly violated should at the very least have the opportunity of appealing to the courts for effective protection and relief.

It should be recognized that the question is by no means merely an academic one to be debated interminably. Unions today exercise quasi-governmental powers under the Wagner Act and similar legislation, and they cannot dodge public responsibility. They cannot welcome and court public protection, and then turn around and claim that the public has no legitimate interest in their internal affairs, which are no longer quite internal. Unions are, in fact, no longer purely voluntary private organizations to which the individual worker may or may not belong as he sees fit. They are semi-public and at least partially compulsory. Some form of public or quasi-public responsibility is inevitable; the only question is: which shall it be—authoritarian control from above by governmental administrative agencies or effective judicial protection of civil rights in harmony with the American democratic tradition?

Along with the guarantee of civil liberties might very well come provisions for opening union finances to public scrutiny through full reports published periodically. Some advanced, democratic labor organizations, such as the International Ladies' Garment Workers' Union, do so today, and it would be well if all unions followed this example of their own volition and in good faith. A legal requirement of such publicity could hardly, in my opinion, be regarded as unjust or oppressive. How effective it would be is another matter, but it might be worth trying since the question is a serious one and not to be ignored.

The other problem, that of devising institutional reforms that will make for increasing self-government in unions, for increasing possibility of genuine membership participation in the affairs of the organization, is an immensely difficult one. Traditional reform measures, such as limited tenure or rotation in office, statutory regularity of meetings, referendum, etc., have proved either altogether futile or positively mischievous in their effects. It should be realized that the problem is often not one of forcing simple, obvious reforms on a recalcitrant union bureaucracy, but rather one of devising practicable reforms for a willing, or at least not unwilling, administration to apply.

By and large, it would seem that the most fruitful approach is along the lines of systematic decentralization of power and devolution of function. The inherent tendency of organization, as I have pointed out, is quite in the other direction, so that persistency, purpose, and planning will be required if anything is to be accomplished in this respect. A network, or hierarchy, of delegate bodies, each with a proper function no matter how limited and a proper authority no matter how circumscribed, might help bridge the gulf that now so often separates the group of all-powerful officials at the top from the great masses of rank-and-file members at the bottom. Meetings organized by smaller units of a more organic character than the ordinary miscellaneous general membership meeting might prove useful. Even if these measures and others like them result in nothing more than drawing a broader section of the membership into active participation in union affairs, it would be something. At bottom, it is a problem of fostering democracy at the "grass roots," of creating expanding possibilities of genuine self-government at the lowest levels of the organizational pyramid.

But fundamentally, institutional changes, no matter how ingenious and well contrived, are bound to remain a dead letter unless there is a new spirit to animate the new and improved institutions. What is most needed is a profound transformation of the moral atmosphere. What is needed is the creation of a labor conscience.

Among the masses, a labor civic morality must come into being. Today there is virtually no such thing. Improper conduct, even corruption, meets with no special resentment or indignation in the labor movement; as long as the union leaders "deliver the goods" in terms of protection and service, wages and hours, anything goes. There is no labor public opinion on the alert to rebuke excesses and check abuses, as there is, for example, in some religious communities. There are no moral sanctions or restraints emanating from the masses of workers operative in the labor movement. This lack is but an aspect of labor's general social immaturity and absence of self-consciousness.

As far as leaders are concerned, what is fundamentally needed is a powerful social idealism capable of mitigating, controlling, and transcending the crudities of personal ambition and power politics. Such a moral dynamic once existed to some degree in socialism, which was the conscience of the labor movement. Today, with the decline of the socialist faith, labor is left without a conscience, without a moral dynamic, and thus without protection against the impersonal mechanism of organization and the human lust for power.   —*Fall* 1943

VALDEMAR CARLSON

How Mature Is the American Economy?

THE desperate plight beyond these shores and the relative prosperity of the United States at the present time is causing some moralists to decry American well-being as inimical to the rest of the world. Whatever belt-tightening is necessary for the immediate future to provide food for the starving, homes for the homeless, and tools for the workmen, it is only the fuzziest kind of economic thinking which would justify a low standard of living in the United States as a means of contributing to long-run prosperity elsewhere. Undoubtedly there is much envy of America in other less prosperous countries, but thinking foreigners who are able to project their problems beyond the pressing needs of the moment do not object to American prosperity. What they are worried about is the imminence of an American depression. Especially is that true for Britain which because of close commercial ties, cemented by the Anglo-American loan, is bound hand and foot to the American economy. Should America suffer a depression we are almost certain to pull the British economy with us. During the war an Englishman expressed himself as follows concerning the postwar policy of the United States:

I don't care what you do in America after the war—high tariffs or low tariffs, much international trade or little—so long as you do one thing. So long as you keep prosperous. If you slide into deep depression, not only will you go down, but you will drag the whole world with you.

The world at any rate has already experienced how an American depression can pull it down to the brink of disaster. For the depression of the 1930's had world-wide repercussions and more than anything else can be held responsible for the resurgence of nationalism in Germany and the weak-kneed behavior of the democracies in the face of the fascist threat. Not that America should be held solely responsible for the unprecedented decline of the 1930's. We live in an interdependent world and America is only one unit in a world economy. But America is probably the kingpin in this world and decisions made here in the 1920's brought on the depression of the '30's which had world-wide repercussions. Hence America cannot shun responsibility for the catastrophe of the fascist and totalitarian regimes and the holocaust which followed.

We all look anxiously to the councils of foreign ministers and the United Nations for some sign that permanent world peace is more than a mirage. However important the right kind of international agreements are, they cannot give us peace unless they operate in an economically stable world. But a stable world cannot be established so long as we have a "boom and bust" economy in the United States.

II

In appraising the probable behavior of Americans in dealing with their postwar economic problems there are two conditioning factors which must be taken into account. One is the depression and subsequent recovery of the 1930's; the other, the full employment of the war effort. We live in the memory of these two experiences. What childhood and youthful experiences are to the adult, these two events will be in the years ahead to the collective whole which is America. It is clear that the recovery which we experienced in the 1930's was a government-sponsored recovery and the phenomenal productive output of the United States during the war was government-planned-and-directed. In spite of the clear evidence of the contribution of the government in achieving recovery from the depression and in directing our mammoth war production, in recent months we have seen an apparently successful resurgence of capitalist apologetics with its accompanying denunciation of government interference in the economic process. Although it is perfectly clear to the discerning observer that our system of "free private enterprise" was put into cold storage during the war, we are now being told by all the agencies of public enlightenment that it was American free private enterprise which won the war. The failure of liberals successfully to combat this propaganda of organized business is due to something more fundamental than a lack of informational outlets.

The experiences of the New Deal recovery and of the government-planned war economy have not given us a theory of economic control in which the postwar policy can orient itself. Under the impact of what is known as Keynesian economics a theoretical formulation is gradually being hammered out but it is hampered by a faulty concept of technology which developed during the early days of the New Deal. This is the concept of the mature economy.

Perhaps this theory developed because the New Deal recovery was such a hit-and-miss, a trial-and-error sort of policy. The men who advised Roosevelt were, of course, not without theoretical preconceptions, but there was no well articulated theory which accounted for the developments which took place. The trial-and-error kind of approach to the economic problems of the depression is clearly evident when we realize that during the campaign of 1932 the New Deal did not signify a spending and deficit-financing program, but a budget-balancing policy. In fact Roosevelt criticized Hoover for failing to balance the budget and promised to turn the trick when he became President. It is fortunate that Roosevelt had a flexible mind and adjusted his policies to the exigencies of the situation.

There was much in the New Deal which we must recognize as a struggle for power on the part of economically disfranchised classes; laborers and farmers did gain something as is most clearly evident in the AAA and the Wagner Labor Relations Act. Politically there was some shift of power. How permanent it will prove to be only time will tell. But in the economic arena expediency determined action and no theory justifying government expenditures or interference in the economic process challenged the faith in the ultimate validity of a market-controlled economy.

The homely concept of pump-priming used to justify government expenditures brings out in bold relief the conservative bias of the early New Deal. According to the spending theory then current, the economic pump, which equated production and consumption through the operation of the price system and market processes, had run dry. To bring it back to full working order government expenditures would have to be undertaken. Then like the old-fashioned pump, which will respond to pouring in of water and will continue yielding water indefinitely, so our economic system would respond to government spending, and when a condition of full employment had been attained it could be expected to continue indefinitely.

The concept of pump-priming not only illustrates the rural tradition in American thought but an extraordinary naïveté about economic relationships. It further shows the degree of intimidation exercised over men's minds by the classical theory of automatic control through market processes if such a weak-kneed theory had to be propounded to justify the spending program of the federal government. At any rate, following the severe decline which the American economy experienced in 1937 and 1938, sometimes referred to by New Deal apologists as a recession, the concept of pump-priming became utterly discredited. In its stead there came into vogue the Keynesian theory of compensatory spending. This theory accepts a chronic deficiency in purchasing power which must be offset by fiscal policy.

Whatever fiscal policy was attempted during the 1930's—deficit spending, taxation of high incomes and estates, or of undistributed corporate earnings—it was justified because of the assumed existence of a mature economy. To the query of the businessman who wanted to know why we could not recover from this depression as we had from all others, the glib answer was made that conditions now are not the same. The term "mature economy" became the shorthand symbol for "things are now different." It should be noted that the use of the term "mature economy" was an afterthought; it was not used in the early days of the New Deal. The principle was fully developed in a little volume entitled *An Economic Program for American Democracy* by seven Harvard and Tufts economists. This book was published in 1938 and written in the context of the "Roosevelt recession" of 1937 and 1938. It was both a defense of fiscal measures already undertaken and a manifesto for bolder government measures in coping with the depression which had engulfed the New Deal in midstream. The authors based their belief in the essential change of the economy upon two facts: (1) the disappearance of the frontier, (2) the decline in the rate of population growth. Because of these two conditions, it was said, American prosperity must rely in the future upon intensive rather than extensive expansion.

The investigations of the Congressional Temporary National Economic Committee, which held hearings and sponsored monographs between 1939 and 1941, followed pretty generally the context of the mature economy in its publications. The hearings indicated that corporations were able to finance themselves without the aid of the capital market. Some of the large corporations testified through their representatives that they had expanded and would be able to expand in the future with little aid from the capital market. For instance, Owen D. Young testified "that from 1921 to 1939, the General Electric Company did not spend as much for plant and equipment as was accumulated in depreciation reserves." Alfred P. Sloan of General Motors testified that "in the eighteen-year period there had been substantially no outside financing." Similar positions were taken by other executives of large corporations. The evidence gave hostage to the inference that only through government action could investment outlets for large savings be made available.

It is, however, in the writings of Alvin Hansen, sometimes called the American Keynes, that the concept of the mature economy is most explicitly presented. Hansen justifies active government intervention in the economic process on the ground that the expansive potentialities of the American economy are now less than they were before 1930. He maintains that the constituent elements in economic progress are (1) inventions, (2) discovery and development of new territory, (3) growth of population. Hansen, like the seven Harvard and Tufts economists, sees the end of an era of extensive expansion through private investment. Private enterprise, according to this fiscal expert, cannot alone provide sufficient outlets for all the available savings; hence the government must enter the investment and spending field if we are to enjoy the blessings of full employment.

The New Deal in effecting social change aroused the opposition of all those who fear any change; in bringing about a shift of power it aroused the antagonism of those whose power had been curtailed. Whether a moral defense of the "sound and tested" or a desire to defend vested interests constituted the basis of New Deal opposition, the reforms of the 1930's certainly did not go unchallenged. Most of the criticisms have been merely emotional verbiage such as the attempt to defend the old gold standard and the alleged rights of the rugged individual in the face of a universal demand for security. But the attack on reforms that were based upon the thesis that we had reached a stage of maturity in our economic development has proved to be a powerful weapon in the hands of conservatives who wish to undermine the theoretical base of the New Deal reforms and to prevent any extension of government participation in economic affairs.

III

It is unfortunate that none of the New Dealers took the time and effort to work out the theoretical preconceptions upon which they worked. A few, such as Raymond Moley, who had earlier sought to express the relationships of government and business, became the syndicated writers for a press which welcomed the fulminations of "converted bureaucrats." Others became the consultants of private business which could afford to pay well for the knowledge and the entrees to Washington which important ex-officials could bring with them. Still others felt that a job had been done and retired to the Olympian aloofness of university teaching or private law practice.

Meanwhile the territory of the stagnationist and mature-economy school of thought has become the happy hunting grounds of the defenders of private enterprise. One of the most able defenders of business, Eric Johnston, has been striking some telling blows at the concept of a stagnationist and mature economy. In his pep talk to American business, a book called *America Unlimited,* Johnston takes issue with the notion of a mature economy. In his chapter on "Frontiers of Expansion" he maintains that the frontier is important in making American character and institutions but insists that it had little bearing on the American economy. There is nothing, according to Johnston, that was found in the frontier of fifty or a hundred years ago which from the economic standpoint is not still there:

> The thing that made the frontier important in its day was the vast stretches of cheap land and undeveloped natural resources beyond the line. But these stretches are still there! The undeveloped resources are still there!

He then paints in glowing colors the frontiers of science and invention, even the promise of atomic energy. These resources are of course to be developed by business and the fruits to be widely scattered among all the population. It is a thesis which has been the tradition of business apologists from the time of J. B. Say to Carl Snyder. According to those who believe in "capitalism the creator" technological developments wait upon the capital and the organizing genius of the businessman.

The active participation of the government in economic and business decisions during the depression of the 1930's and during the war upset the validity of classical orthodoxy that economic development depends upon the contribution of capitalists and the action of private entrepreneurs. But due to the inadequacy of the theoretical defense of government participation in economic affairs the resurgence of capitalist apologetics has had no satisfactory theoretical opposition. Faith in the god of private enterprise has been sustained through exorcising the devil of a stagnating economy.

George Terborgh, economist for the Machinery and Allied Products Institute, carries the exorcism to its logical end in his book, *The Bogey of Economic Maturity*. Terborgh has written a carefully documented book although it has many of the earmarks of a propaganda pamphlet. He at-

tempts to demonstrate that there is no correlation between industrial production, real income per capita, and the growth in population. That is
true, he maintains, for different periods in the United States; it is true
for other countries. Obviously a country with a growing population can
be expected to have an absolute increase in production because there are
more people to house, clothe, and feed. But, says Terborgh, "there is
no evidence that countries with high rates of population growth have
had in general any more rapid rise in their per capita production than
others with slow population growth."

Terborgh argues further that the passing of the frontier can have
had little effect on the economy. For, the physical frontier passed in 1890,
but according to the stagnationist school did not begin having any effect
until 1930. The importance of the frontier, Terborgh asserts, has been
greatly exaggerated. "In the period 1870-90, for example, it is doubtful
if the frontier absorbed more than 10 per cent of the national population
growth. No wonder its 'passing' had so little visible effect on the American economy."

Alain Hansen and other protagonists of the mature-economy theory
postulate their belief in the existence of a new kind of economy on the
dearth of new industries. But there is nothing spectacular about great
new industries, asserts Terborgh, in furnishing an outlet for new investments. Railroads and the electrical industry have not contributed any
disproportionate amount to capital formation. He denies the importance
of any spectacular new industry as an outlet for investment and as a
means of furnishing employment. "There is no evidence that one 'great
new industry' is any more dynamic in its impact on capital formation
than ten small new industries," he concludes from the considerable and
pretty convincing data he has accumulated. He is particularly critical of
the TNEC in finding that corporations now can maintain themselves by
internal financing. The corporations were selected with that in mind, he
asserts. If a broader group of corporations is included the thesis that
internal financing will sustain the expanding needs of corporations is
undermined. Considering all corporations, Terborgh found a "lack of
evidence of any trend toward an *increase* in corporate self-sufficiency."
Further, he points out that only a fraction of the savings of individuals
go to incorporated business anyway; a much larger portion goes to finance
the capital formation of unincorporated business and to finance the purchase of durable consumers goods.

These seem telling blows against the concept of the mature economy.
Undoubtedly Terborgh minimizes the importance of new, large industries in providing investment and employment, but in general he is on

pretty sound ground in his denunciation of the stagnationist position. Let us grant him the victory in this bout. Does he by the same token achieve adequate defense of the system of economic controls and distribution of power known as capitalism? We have been living under conditions of underemployment, with the exception of full-scale wars and their aftermath, for several decades. Furthermore, capitalism as we know it has been highly unstable and has been subjected to periodic booms and depressions. Individual insecurity develops as a consequence and probably accounts for the willingness of people to listen to the blandishments of a Gerald L. K. Smith, of neomedievalism or the chiliastic promises of evangelistic charlatans.

Terborgh, Johnston, and others who have come to the defense of business enterprise have not given us an answer to the universal demand of society at the present time—security. They have heartened the souls of businessmen who, under the impact of a government-sponsored recovery and of wartime controls, had lost faith in their own ability to control and direct the economic system by their individual decisions. In effect, they have been telling the sick patient, capitalism, that by shooting and maiming the doctor he would be cured of his ills. It may be, however, that the doctor (fiscal policy) is prescribing the right treatment for the wrong reasons.

By the term maturity Hansen wished to convey a notion that our economy had reached the end of its dynamic growth. But the connotations of the term seem like a flirtation with Spengler. Inferentially, readers will make comparison with the human organism. Maturity follows youth and senility must inevitably follow maturity. So the outlook for America suffering under an ailment known as a mature economy is gloomy indeed. And with the temper of Americans never to sell the United States short, Johnston has found ready acceptance to his faith in an ever-expanding America.

The notion that our economy has reached a state of maturity is not confined to a group of New Deal economists. It is a widely held theory and probably has its origin in a concept of American history and specifically from Turner's account of the frontier. The concept, however, suffers from some fuzzy thinking. If it is examined against the backdrop of Veblen's distinction between the industrial arts and institutions, the nature of Hansen's error will be clearly seen. Perhaps one can speak of a mature capitalism and by such connote that the institution of a free market and all the other appurtenances of capitalism are no longer virile enough to control our dynamic technology. Hansen and others of the stagnationist school, however, make no such distinction, but lump institutional and technological factors together in their use of the term "mature economy."

IV

C. E. Ayres who has sought to fuse the ideas of John Dewey and Veblen into a valid theory of change has referred to institutions as ceremonial behavior. Ayres accepts the dichotomy of institutions and technology as the outstanding problem of modern society. Technology arises from the tool-using proclivities of man while institutions must adjust themselves to the imperative of the going state of the industrial arts. Capitalism is a form of ceremonial behavior which accompanies modern industry, and as such cannot be the cause of the industrial revolution. True, the ideas of the Western World were permissive to industrial growth in a way which Chinese civilization without an alphabet could not be. But it is a mistake to say that the spirit of capitalism generated modern industry. Obviously, it is highly flattering to the conceit of the businessman for him to think that he and his ilk are the causative influences of the changes effected in the industrial world.

Ayres makes institutions subservient to the demands of technology. The generally recognized realization of the necessity for institutional change arising from the discovery of atomic energy makes a statement about the subservience of institutions to technology trite. It is not trite to emphasize, however, that man as a tool-using animal is the instrument of a technological continuum. Scientific and technological progress takes place because of the application of the tool-combination principle. Our unprecedented industrial achievement during the war was due in no small part to the fact that industrial know-how became the common property of all who produced for the war effort. The sharing of skills, patents, and knowledge, virtually demanded by the government to promote the war effort, robbed particular firms of competitive advantages. The atomic bomb, it is safe to assert, was discovered sooner because scientists of three nations pooled their knowledge to a common end. Had Russia been included in the atomic bomb research, I believe that an even earlier discovery might well have occurred. Technological change taking place because of the combination of tools should increase at a progressive rate. With more men working with more tools a progressive industrial progress can be expected to take place. Ayres suggests that technological progress might well take place on the basis of a geometric ratio. He throws out this idea only as a hypothesis for which no verification is available. But insofar as progressive technological change can take place under the most favorable of environmental conditions, it is slowed down because of the inhibiting influence of ceremonial behavior.

Productivity of American industry has increased in the last fifty years at a rate of between three and four per cent a year. Hansen predicts a slowing down of the rate of growth to about two per cent in the decades ahead, but that will be true only if institutions are permitted to hamper more in the future than they have in the past our utilization of potential technological development. On the basis of the technological theory of progressive change there is no reason to expect any decline in industrial growth. The growth, rather, should be accelerated.

The history of specific industries seems to give countenance to the principle of maturity. It has been typical of industries to experience dynamic change in their younger years and then to level out. So industries seem to go through childhood, maturity, and old age setting a pattern for the behavior of the whole economy on the principle of a mature economy. Does that mean that the tool-combination principle has run its course as an industry becomes older and further room for improvement seems impossible? Or is it due to institutional factors which limit technological development? Let us take the railroad as a typical example. And particularly that of sleeping cars operating on the railroads. Why have no basic improvements been made in Pullman cars in fifty years? Has the apex of development in sleeping arrangements on a moving vehicle been made so that no further changes are conceivable, or can we attribute this static situation to the control of a complacent and profitable monopoly? I am inclined to attribute the lack of improvement largely to the control of monopoly. It may well be that the failure of many an old industry to develop as rapidly as it did in its youth is due to similar restrictions. Whatever the situation in particular industries may be, we should expect no slowing down in the over-all increase of productivity of the whole economic system since new and expanding industries should be more than adequate to replace technologically obsolescent ones.

The discovery of atomic energy has made Veblen's distinction between science and technology on the one hand, and institutions on the other, a clearly realized dichotomy. Scientists have plumped for world government because only through a world state can they see any hope for permanent survival of the human species, with a high civilization, on this planet. It becomes clear that some institutions must change if we are to survive with our technology. No one considers seriously the proposal that science and technology take a vacation and do so retroactively in order to avoid learning how to live with atomic energy.

If our biggest social problem in the future will be adjustment to an ever-expanding technology, it would appear that economists should devote much of their attention to a study of the adequacy of existing institutions to its demands. The neglect and, among many economists, the utter disdain for Veblen would indicate that this aspect of the subject was considered outside the scope of their professional activity. A consideration, however, of the problems with which economists busy themselves will show that implicitly, at any rate, the adequacy of institutions to the expanding technology was receiving some attention. As a concrete example, the subject of unemployment after a hundred years or more of neglect has been taken into the fold of economic orthodoxy, due in the main to the writing and influence of J. M. Keynes.

The failure of our economic system to function at its maximum capacity was the one fact which caused Keynes to develop his heretical ideas. The development of his theory of unemployment was already under way in the 1920's when England was suffering a chronic depression. His economics has emphasized unequal income distribution as the basic cause of unemployment and less than full use of resources. He and his followers have placed main stress on the maintenance of purchasing power as a means of preventing unemployment. The wealthy few, it is obvious, can contribute relatively little to the spending stream and by refusing to invest they may dampen the operation of the whole economic process. The wide distribution of purchasing power, on the other hand, will do much to sustain a full-employment economy. The advocacy of more equal income distribution represents, however, a revolution in economic theory. For under the dispensation of the nineteenth-century classical economics inequality in the distribution of income was not only tolerated but considered positively necessary in order to provide society with the necessary capital for production. As J. S. Mill said, "every increase of capital gives, or is capable of giving, additional employment to industry; and this without assignable limit."

Not that Keynes has achieved a total victory. According to some of the die-hards of the classical tradition, the Keynesian economics is just a flash in the pan. Ludwig von Mises, as well as his fellow Austrian economist, Frederick Hayek, has been cashing in on the American businessman's fear of government. Unfortunately for Herr von Mises' royalties he did not consult an advertising expert before naming his books. If he had known more about the tastes of movie-going and book-reading America he might have subtitled one of his books, *The Road to Hell Is Paved with Incompetent Bureaucrats*. At any rate, von Mises in a pamphlet called *Planning for Freedom* says the assertion of J. M. Keynes that "In the long run we are all dead" is "the only correct declaration of the neo-British Cambridge school." In general, Keynesian economics has found an unwelcome reception among the orthodox economists of the classical tradition.

Marxists and Veblenians, on the other hand, have been able to embrace the Keynesian economics with no difficulty. I mention as prominent Marxists who are more recently Keynesians, A. P. Lerner and John Strachey.

Stuart Chase and C. E. Ayres are outstanding Veblenians who have become partial to the Keynesian approach. Undoubtedly it is easy for followers of Veblen to accept the necessity for a decline in the rate of interest if not the "euthanasia of the *rentier*" because of their disdain for the institutions of capitalism. Marxists can hardly be expected to object to an economic theory which advocates more equal income distribution. With both the regard for the capitalist is slight; hence their common willingness to follow a program which would move in the direction of reducing unequal income distribution.

The Hansen school of Keynesian economics has accepted the historical necessity of unequal income distribution for the nineteenth century when, they assert, we had a dynamic economy, but with the so-called mature economy necessitating less private investment a greatly skewed income distribution makes for unemployment and less than full use of productive equipment. While they are right as to their conclusions about a need for a change in income distribution, resting their demand for reform upon the alleged existence of a mature economy immeasurably weakens their theoretical position. The maintenance and further development of Keynesian economics in the United States will necessitate the abandonment or revision of the concept of the mature economy.   —*Fall* 1946

JOHN P. LEWIS

Our Mixed Economy

THE phrase, "the mixed economy," is not yet a venerable cliché, but it is already a significant one. It has been widely used in this country only since Alvin Hansen and other American Keynesians began popularizing it a dozen years ago. Of all the watchwords now clogging public policy discussion, however, the term probably comes closest to encompassing what there is of a doctrine or conceptual core among moderate, slightly-left-of-center, postwar "liberals." And, by the same token, its fuzziness and lack of charm evidence the terminological doldrums into which "the vital center" has drifted.

The ideological plight of middle-of-the-roaders has been well publicized. Roll the words "mixed economy" around your tongue for a moment, and you have the essence of it. Smacking as they do of mixed vegetables and mixed metaphors, they invite a neither-fish-nor-fowl indictment. And this, of course, they regularly incur from critics, like Professor Hayek, who make the most of middle-of-the-roaders' classic propensity for being put semantically on the defensive. Invariably moderates get trapped into arguing their case in the language of the extremes on either hand. As soon as they do, their credos become constipated with exceptions, qualifications, and apparent inconsistencies.

For another thing, you will notice that the essential savor of a "mixed economy" is hard to define. It appears to be all things to all people. To you it stands for the present British experiment poised somewhere between American "free enterprise" and Russian "communism." To your neighbor it connotes a system under which government regulates utilities but does not engage in any socialistic tomfoolery like TVA. In the old *New Yorker* cartoon, the wizened patrician in the club chair presumably was talking about the mixed economy when he quavered that ". . . it all started when they took over the Post Office."

Can a phrase susceptible of such diverse readings be given any rigorous and, at the same time, widely acceptable meaning? My intent here is to suggest that this one can. The attempt to find a hard, but relatively noncontroversial, core of meaning in the mixed economy idea must be prefaced, however, by a closer look at the intellectual flabbiness which currently besets the concept. And even before this, a charge must be met: the charge that any effort of this kind is a mistake—or, at least, that any attempt to specify in something like systematic detail the area of agreement among contemporary middle-of-the-roaders is a disservice to the moderate-liberal position.

The mists which cloud the ultimate goals and social ideals of moderates are, without doubt, a considerable political asset. Caught in the cross fire of the either/or dialectitians, the moderate is apt to grow impatient with grand designs in general. But, however much he seeks public protection in the garb of the "practical compromiser" who cannot afford to waste time on a lot of highfalutin verbalizations, and however publicly he erects into a life principle "the art of muddling through," privately he still requires some positive directional goals. Even the most sophisticated moderate is likely to get his goals by falling back on a set of simple, unspoiled "common sense" values which he exempts from critical inspection. He deliberately de-intellectualizes his ideology. He is *for* the underdog and free speech and *against* discrimination and grossly unfair income distribution, and that is that.

The only conceptual common denominator which can be detected in the New and Fair Deals era thus far is a kind of pass-the-meat-and-potatoes philosophy of this unsophisticated sort. It has provided a broad, unexacting basis for agreement, enhancing the ability of moderates to hold together working majorities as often as they have. The trouble is that the kind of conceptual core which boils down to a fine, warm feeling has become too expensive a luxury in the postwar world. It contributes a shapelessness to policy harder to tolerate now than during the great improvisations of the '30's when government threw around only a fraction of its present weight. Furthermore, it provides no robust, well-understood criteria for differentiating moderate-liberal views from those of the extreme left. The lack of such standards is proving embarrassing and enervating. Witness, for example, the time and effort which Americans for Democratic Action has felt constrained to spend in rather frantic, negativistic anti-commie name-calling to prove that it isn't tarred with the nasty brush. And ADA, of all moderate-liberal organizations, is probably the one with the greatest leadership potential.

At this stage of the game, then, the middle-of-the-road cause seems likelier to be helped than hurt by an effort to probe beneath its public relations surface in search of a more rigorous set of controlling ideas than commonly is attributed to it. "The mixed economy" is fair game for a laying on of analytical hands; it has academic roots, and it never was very good phrase-making anyway.

II

In the great debates about "social systems," nothing else does quite as much to tie the tongues of middle-of-the-roaders as the sleight-of-hand artistry of their adversaries. An extremist of the "right" or "left" almost never pleads his case without ricocheting back and forth between two distinct levels of discussion. Part of the time he is talking about some extant set of politico-economic arrangements spread out as of this date over some particular portion of the earth's surface. He may, for example, be defending the present set-up in Soviet-occupied Germany or in our automobile industry. But much of the time, while still seeming to speak factually of East Germany and American automobiles, actually he is extolling an ideal system, or—to use the more neutral phrase—an *abstract model*, which bears only theoretical resemblance to his real world subject.

The facility with which extremists hop back and forth between the world as it is and models of what ought to be is a phenomenon of the modern ideological universe of public discourse. It is a kind of polarized universe in which there stands, at each of the poles, a utopian abstraction, wholly self-consistent and timeless. Neither of these ever has been mirrored in the real world, or ever will, because, to put it garishly, each is a popular notion of what heaven should be like.

The polar model technically labelled "classical liberalism" and commonly designated by variations on the "free enterprise" theme has radiated the dominant American ideology for a century and a half. Closely examined, its details are complex and often surprisingly unfamiliar. In its economic aspect alone, as many as fifteen essential conditions must be assumed if the model is to work the way it's supposed to.[1] None of the assumed conditions match the circumstances of our 1950 economy exactly; many are grossly unrealistic. Nevertheless—granting the unfamiliarity of many of us with the intricacies of the classical liberal model—the width of the gap between it and any advanced twentieth-century economy has been dinned into enough heads by enough economics instructors long enough to make it unnecessary to belabor the point here.

The hiatus, for instance, between "perfect competition" and the kind of competition existing among large American corporations is, by now, pretty widely recognized. There is less awareness among Americans of the even wider gap between, let us say, Russian arrangements and the ideal construct at the other ideological pole. In order to avoid the distractions imposed by the usual labels, I shall call this model "pure communalism." Whereas in classical liberalism individuals are the irreducible and insoluble atoms out of and for which the system is made, in its opposite number the individual finds himself by losing himself in the community. The latter is the essential concept, the organism of which the individual is a cell. People, in the one case, work and contribute out of an acquisitive propensity and fare accordingly. In pure communalism they are selfless. Public service is the sole motivation, and incomes are related to need rather than contribution. Under classical liberalism, economic activity is organized and administered in what is taken to be the public interest by the automatic directives of an impersonal market actuated by the quest for profit. Similar market mechanisms can be installed in a purely communal system, but there they lack the automatic motive force; they must be consciously and centrally co-ordinated. Government, in the classical liberal model, polices the market place and performs a few other community-wide functions. But its role is minimal. Its role in pure communalism is ambiguous. From one point of view, it is all-pervasive: a co-ordinator who, from the vantage of a society-wide perspective, can define what, in particular instances, the public interest is. But, by definition, it wields no coercive authority for

---

[1] In his essay, "The Ethics of Competition," published in the volume of the same title (New York: 1935), Professor Frank Knight names twelve assumptions of the classical economic model, and his list permits several amendments.

the simple reason that there is no place for a big stick in a society populated exclusively by Good Samaritans.

Weighed in the scales of our dominant religious traditions, pure communalism is, pretty clearly, the loftier of the two ideals; and, in its utterly visionary reading of human nature, it is even less realistic a model of any predictable industrial society than is classical liberalism. One measure of this unrealism is the amount of elaborately coercive government Russian Marxists have required in their haste to achieve the millennium—government endowed with so much disciplinary authority that it bids fair to forget its expendability. And, under Western eyes, its workings, at any rate, are extremely distasteful.

The ideological predicament of the mixed economy advocate in a situation where our ideas are polarized and our institutions are not is obvious. He denies himself the easy identifications between polar models and Soviet income distribution or the market superintended by the American Medical Association. At the same time, he lacks effective alternative models of his own around which to rally like-minded people. He has some, but they are emotionally and aesthetically inferior. Made explicit, they rouse dissension in the ranks. In part, of course, the predicament is unavoidable; there is a link between religious fervor and unworldly ideals to which the concept of the mixed economy never can aspire. But I think that it is the *kind* of mixed economy model ordinarily lofted to public view which is mainly at fault.

The usual explanation of "what the mixed economy means" contains some statement about the division of productive activity between private and public enterprise. And if the expositor is trying to be precise enough to be meaningful, he gets himself into hot water. It is clear enough that the postal system ought to be public and delicatessens private, but what about the electric power industry? Should it be private and regulated, partly that and partly public, or wholly public? Should we follow Adam Smith's advice and nationalize the insurance business? The meticulous model-builder chooses up sides and makes enemies.

A conventional description of the mixed economy goes on to speak of parallel public and private expenditures; in a mixed economy people do a considerable fraction of their consuming and investing collectively, via government spending. Invariably a proponent of this state of affairs mentions, by way of explaining it, that the relevant expenditure ratio in this country at present is one part public to three or four parts private. But does that mean that this is the "right" ratio? Shouldn't the public share be less? Shouldn't it be more? Whatever magic fraction he chooses, the conscientious advocate sheds sympathizers on either side.

In addition, the usual exposition talks about—and probably this is its most significant phase—controls. It may be said, for example, that the intricate regulation of most commercial activity is best left to the control of competitive markets disciplined and purged by a vigorous government anti-monopoly program; and that in those few markets where competition is unattainable or undesirable—the public utility and "natural monopoly" area—government must do the regulating itself. One sure way to thin the mixed economy ranks, however, is to press this prescription dogmatically. There are many reasonable middle-of-the-roaders who doubt the effectiveness of any achievable anti-trust policy. Few of them will countenance the literal application of such a program to wage bargaining. Some favor partial or full public operation of natural monopolies. Others question, as the Supreme Court has been inclined to do for the last sixteen years, the feasibility of compartmentalizing business into one kind which is somehow "affected with the public interest" and another kind which is not.

Still under the heading of controls, the standard mixed economy prescription almost certainly emphasizes the particular responsibility of government for using its unique fiscal and monetary powers to regulate the amount of total expenditures in the community with an end to promoting high, stable levels of employment. While a fiscal policy so employed comes close to being an essential area of agreement for mixed-economy-ites, sharp and divisive differences arise over the degree of fiscal and monetary flexibility desirable; over the distribution of authority between legislative and administrative agencies; over the subordination of stabilization objectives to other policy purposes; and over the supplementation of fiscal and monetary programs, particularly in periods of inflationary pressure, by more direct and meddlesome government interventions.

The foregoing is not an exhaustive review of the controversial details of politico-economic structure with which the ordinary mixed economy architect is likely to concern himself. But it is enough to indicate why this kind of model-building inspires so little agreement and has no permanence. It tries to ape the polar models in their one supremely unworldly aspect. That is their exclusion of the critical factor of social change. Neither classical liberalism nor pure communalism allows for any reshuffling of institutional patterns once the ideal system is attained. They do permit quantitative growth or decline in population, income, and resources; they even allow for changes in consumer tastes, the composition of the economy's output, and productive methods as long as they don't upset the organization of industry. But *structurally*, the polar models are static. Given the ideological universe, it would be rather silly if they weren't, for they are the limits which real world situations approach. There is no place for reform in heaven.

When the mixed economy designers try to market the same sort of static blueprint—when, in effect, they single out, from the numberless series of possibilities which stretches between the two poles, one particular expenditure, production, and control pattern for the special contemplation of posterity—they instigate bickering among their own people. And, what is worse, they disqualify themselves from answering the one question they are in the best position to handle: namely, how the process of structural change itself should be effected. They are at their strongest here, and not when specifying utopia, or even the next way-stop to it.

It is precisely here, on the dynamics of change, that there is something very close to a consensus among middle-of-the-roaders. They do share beliefs concerning the fact, the general direction, the desirable character, and the desirable rate of structural change in the American economy. Here, not in snapshots of ideal institutional patterns, lie the imperatives of their position.

III

What follows is going to be dogmatic in any case. There is no point in trying to phrase it delicately. There are seven propositions which seem to me fundamental to the area of agreement among proponents of the mixed economy.

1. *Modern democratic government has an unlimited responsibility for protecting and promoting the general welfare.*

This point is not always made explicit by contemporary middle-of-the-roaders, but it always underlies their position. Government is the highest formal authority in our society. It is the one organization responsible to the whole community and the only organization to which we all belong. The Church once claimed this role; later it offered to share it. But today the Church must rely on government to enforce its limited claims—such as freedom of worship—and there is no social problem which government does not have the ultimate responsibility for solving.

It does not always pursue this responsibility overtly, and it is a good, though not conclusive, symptom when it does not. But if a problem does grow really serious in the eyes of a considerable portion of the community, a popular government must do something; it cannot persistently duck the issue and survive. There are, in this country, no significant economic difficulties which lie outside the latent or potential bailiwick of government—although there certainly may be some which lie beyond its competence. Constitutional restraints upon governmental powers do not upset this contention. For actually the "living Constitution" is articulated by the courts, and it represents only a wise and systematic official reluctance to extend government activities to new problem areas precipitously. It offers no permanent block to the doctrine of unlimited responsibility regularly enforced at the polls.

2. *The overwhelming balance of both economic and political power in the American economy is concentrated now and for the foreseeable future in the hands of a relatively small number of well organized producer groups.*

This is not a very attractive proposition to most mixed economy proponents, but they do accept it as an essential fact which cannot be wished away or overlooked in devising a workable procedure of reform. To say "a relatively small number" of groups is designedly inexact. But it conveys the correct impression if the classical liberal model is the standard for comparison. A roster of the institutions which make most of the strategic commercial decisions and which are mainly influential in shaping public policy in the United States would run to several hundred names. But such a list of large corporations, corporate and financial interest groups, trade associations, national business organizations, national unions, labor federations, and farm organizations can be grouped in a few clusters, each of which is fairly homogeneous in its attitudes and actions.

3. *The process of structural economic change is continuous, and its present and proper direction is toward the integrated community in which government plays an increasingly active role in behalf of the public interest.*

Any reasonably literate student of history must subscribe to the notion that, in the real world, patterns of social structure always are shifting and that the intelligent objectives of reform, at any moment, are not so much to arrest social change or to reverse its direction as they are to modify its character and speed it up or slow it down. Some middle-of-the-roaders, however, deny that the prevailing trend continues to be from "right" to "left." Or at least they deny that their own structural objectives lean in that direction. Their disavowal, however, is more a disguise than a defensible position; it is an attempt to conceal from themselves what appear to be the unsavory implications of their posture. If they accept the fact of social change and if they explain, as they always do, the shifts of the last century as responses to deep-rooted technological developments still in progress, then it is a little hard to see how the present can be interpreted as the moment of reversal.

The reluctance of moderate-liberals to accept the present proposition does not stem from any nostalgic preference for the dog-eat-dog aspects of the classical liberal model. Rather, it is the product of a popular persuasion that the farther real world situations are removed from "laissez-faire," the less they can partake of certain political values which Americans rank very high. That this persuasion is thoroughly erroneous is the central hypothesis of the present argument. To understand how the political and the economic objectives of the mixed economy outlook can be reconciled with each other, it is essential to see that the amounts of freedom and of government-by-the-people in a system at any given moment are *not* functions of the structural pattern at the moment. They are functions of the rate at which social change is going on. This is amplified in Proposition 5 below.

4. *It is supremely important that our politico-economic system be modified by a peaceful process; social change should not entail violence.*

This is the unconditional imperative among the postulates which define the mixed economy outlook. It is here that the middle-of-the-roader stands out most starkly as a different kind of animal from either brand of extremist. Of all bad things, he finds civil strife most abhorrent. He is unwilling to see the disintegration of a system in which side-arms, tommy-guns, and concentration camps are not the accepted instruments of persuasion. Convinced, as he is, that social renovations will continue as long as he or his most distant progeny survive, he is mainly concerned that the changing structure remain as livable as possible while alterations are going on.

5. *Since the amount of governmental coercion in a social system is a function of its rate of structural change, a slow rate is essential for the protection of American political values.*

This is the most abstruse proposition in the mixed economy's conceptual framework and the most difficult one to sell. Extremists on the right who insist upon identifying democracy with an atomistic economic order charge the middle-of-the-roader with double talk. And critics on the left, who bow to no one in their public adoration of the political virtues, nevertheless call him a namby-pamby when he persists in the present view.

The view, however, is firmly grounded. American political values break down roughly into two broad persuasions: (1) government is good to the degree that it is directed by the decisions of the rank-and-file members of the community and is responsible to them; (2) the more freedom a political system provides for these rank-and-file members, the better it is. Mixed-economy-ites share these persuasions, but they see, either explicitly or intuitively, that the extent to which we can make high scores in either of these dimensions of democracy depends on the rate at which the scope of governmental activity changes.

On the positive, popular sovereignty, side, there is no absolute limit to the size and complexity of the problems over which the rank-and-file American citizen can, via the groups in which he works and votes, exercise intelligent direction. But he must have time to grow with the job. There is every reason to believe that he is better equipped to cope with, and plays a more active part in solving, the problems of the national government now than he did in 1790. But it is equally evident, if we are to trust those indexes which are available, that he is a good deal less literate and thoughtful about public affairs than, say, his contemporary in Britain. If reformers do not want to leave him by the wayside, they must make haste slowly.

The relationship between freedom and the rate of social change is a double one. First, there is the obvious point: The more time the public has to understand and digest the reasons for new kinds of government participation in economic affairs, the more willingly it accepts them without compulsion. The second point, which the sociologists have been making for some time, is more subtle and may seem even cynical to some. But it is hard to refute. It is that freedom is a relative thing anyway. If you suddenly could transport the nineteenth-century "mountain man" of Guthrie's *The Big Sky* to the free society of mid-twentieth-century metropolitan New York, he would feel most horribly penned up. If you could convey a contemporary New Yorker in the same direction over the same time-space route, he would experience an equal sense of release from the most devastating and primitive restraints.

To say that freedom is relative—to realize, for example, that enforcement of labor's right to bargain collectively in 1950 does not rob employers of as much freedom as it did in 1935—is in no sense to debunk it. Most middle-of-the-roaders place a very high intrinsic value on this feeling of non-penned-up-ness. For that reason, they have no use for structural adjustment so rapid that it produces a claustrophobic community.

6. *As government guides and participates in the structural change of the mixed economy, it must operate essentially as an agent of suasion and advice, not of force.*

This follows from the fact that we live in a group economy, in the sense noted above, and from the demand that reform be achieved by peaceful methods. The differences between the political composition of the present system and that of either polar model go pretty deep. They can be stated either in terms of the power of government or of the relationship between public and private interests.

In all three cases the government, legally, is the highest authority on the scene. But its practical, political power varies. In pure communalism, being coextensive with the community, it is the only power in the system, and, while the government of the classical liberal model may seem puny by our standards, because of the extreme dispersion of private organization, it is the biggest single power-concentration present. In the mixed economy, where large producer organizations constitute the real reservoirs of politico-economic strength, government is in its weakest position. It is the political subordinate of the groups it is supposed to direct.

This would be less disquieting if, in the mixed economy, there were the same identity of private and public interests that is posited in each of the polar models. But such, most patently, is not the case. On the one hand, we are abandoning the myth that, in some sense or other, the algebraic sum of all the private interests in the community—even when they are those of group concentrations—is equivalent to the public interest. The foolishness of this bromide just has been freshly redemonstrated in the spectacle of the price-wage sweepstakes of an inflationary period. On the other hand, however, classical liberalism still packs enough ideological potency in the United States to justify and even encourage group leaders in unrestrained pursuit of private objectives.

The dilemma of government is obvious. Its continuing mission is to sell its political superiors programs they are loath to buy. As a partisan of dispersed power, the mixed economy advocate would not want the situation otherwise. But he does see that the system depends upon a delicate balance of private and public efforts to remain viable. The producer group leaders must show an increasing concern for the general welfare in their decision-making. And government must not only identify and announce those directions in which the public's interest lies; it must use a most effective tactic of persuasion in securing farm, business, and labor compliance; and it must not overreach its hand. A national administration with good ideas that goes around brandishing a papier-mâché club, thereby getting itself tossed out of office and discrediting reform in general, is of no more service to the mixed economy than one which is thoroughly reactionary.

7. *In guiding the structural change of the economy, it is very important that government husband its own resources carefully; in particular, it must make optimum use of unregulated or semi-regulated markets as regulatory devices.*

To the mixed economy advocate there is nothing sacrosanct about the free market. To the extent that it can be made to function tolerably well, however, he esteems it as an enormously useful labor-saving device. He recognizes that government reformers operate perennially and unavoidably on thin ice. Their political elbow-room, their financial resources, the supply of competent personnel upon which they can draw, and their store of workable techniques for economic problem-solving all are sorely limited. There is a staggering welter of detailed day-to-day decisions which must be made to keep an economy going—such determinations as the prices to be charged and the qualities and quantities of outputs to be produced by particular plants. If American government is to do a decent job of economic supervision in the near future, it is unlikely that, in peacetime, it can afford to expand its direct responsibilities for this kind of decision-making appreciably. It badly needs the assistance of markets which do a respectable job of disciplining themselves.

The mixed economy proponent, consequently, is deeply interested in developing whatever forms of "workable competition" can be devised in a group economy. He would commit government to furthering this end— whether by reinforcement of its anti-monopoly program, sponsoring of new forms of intergroup bargaining, or the development of improved techniques for delivering more pertinent and specific intelligence and advice to private decision-makers than it now supplies.

IV

Such are the essentials of the mixed economy position as I see them. This, of course, is a skeletal statement. It leaves much room for debate of its implications and degrees of meaning. It would be callow egoism, moreover, to pretend that all who claim the middle-of-the-road label should come flocking to this particular seven-postulate description of the mixed economy model. I am convinced, however, that this *kind* of definition is on the right track. For a summary of the mixed economy outlook to be intellectually rigorous without losing breadth of appeal, it must confine itself to the process of social change and avoid static structural models. Or, to put it in the language of public law, *"the mixed economy" is much more a procedural than a substantive concept.*

Examined in this light, the weaknesses of the concept stand out pretty starkly. It relies upon the potential reasonableness of every-day people and upon the educability of group leaders. It assumes the development of a citizenry and group constituency able to make discriminating comparisons between the value and cost of public services. It requires that government be positioned to attract and hold personnel not only technically proficient but adept in human relations. It demands a certain sense of balance and flexibility of mind all along the line. It is a scheme for bringing out the best in people. Most certainly, it is a doctrine of optimism. But it also is the most civilized ideology currently available.   —*Fall* 1950

POETRY

HOWARD GRIFFIN

Lines

Suggested by the photograph "Women Weep for the Children of Naples" in Robert Capa's Slightly Out of Focus

If I am to become finished with violence
which is always incomplete I must become
unfinished, half-made, splayed,
spaded by suffering for I must live
cut-off from lust, upheld in air,
upborne on wires intangent to the earth
like that wild sketch of Michelangelo
full of the girdered drawing, done
in an hour, the bitter lines of ink
graven in truth, made up
of architectural chest and pinioned hand
and feet that run (from hurry incomplete)
out of the picture racing toward

the barren land of war. Observe
the shattered hand, the tendoned limbs
truncated by the pen. So war itself
propels itself. He could have finished it
for power is here but then it would have been
perhaps less fair, more perfect now the ruined.
More perfect now the dead.

Out of the past the image of all truth
is the wild sketch through which we gaze
as through the aperture of defeat half through
the ink-slashed skeleton of a man
into a mirror-land. This skull, this
wolverine grasp, this deep contractile
thigh, this dream of arrogant vein runs swift
to war.—But now the dead are framed,
they hide in sweating photographs of black
held up by women dressed in shrieking black
and posed against a wall: the camera eye
caught this carved woman who had lost a son.
The grief is near as dew upon her face
scalpeled of death: she holds
him up for all the world to see
as if contagion of the dual lens
could stir his limbs to breath and bring
the slow sad smile at last. As though
the congress of our eye looking at his
could be some comfort of an After-life
or more perhaps the trophy of a loss:

he looks out, smaller, held in thrall
of ancient studio as if in cage
of doom— but she, she stands right through
the war, slashing the written page to bits—
the ancient woman in the tribal black
to whom all ruin is a personal death
steps through the slender paper to my thought
and sears her asking eyes upon my day.
She is unfinished too: she sends to air
the life she dreamed from naught
as if the air itself infection held
and took these boys back to their home again.

—Fall 1948

DANIEL G. HOFFMAN

Near Independence Square

Junebugs hum against the gleaming panes:
their thrumming drones dirigibles of sound
that shake the catkins down the roaring street.

Beetlebuzzings burst the street apart:
Now idle footsteps gather to a crowd
where children clap & dance &
cry aloud:

(Three spindly fellers with a
pickle-keg drum
& couple a sticks beat to
Kingdom Come,
One to holler, another
to beat,
third one to shuffle with his
flat black feet)!

Two dozen feet are tapping to his time,
their bodies swaying all in equipoise
to the dark limbs of that liquid boy.

They drink him in until their pulses make
involuntary music with his own,
surging underfoot, rising to break

pounding pounding on the inner shores
of flesh to sound on down the deep bloodcourse.

My baby lef' me lonesome,
she is nowhere to be found . . .
"Here's a quarter, niggerboy.
Watch'm pick it off the ground!"
Liquid limbs freeze rigid
stiff out of time
stop for coins that roll around in
guttermuck & grime,

the surging wave is shattered. All
feet that danced before
trample dancing underfoot.

The musicale is over.

—*Winter* 1948-49

PETER VIERECK

A Masque of Tsars

At midnight every hundred years
A yawning earthquake reappears
Across the land of Rus and leers
    With grin so fierce

That from its throat, up hell's steep stairs,
With lumbering lurch and pompous airs,
Gangle the shaggy ghosts of tsars
    Like bears from lairs.

Each plugs back on the head he lost.
Tsar Boris is their slant-eyed host;
"To Terrible Ivan!" is his toast
    While all face East.

"Hurrah," they cry, "a Turkoman:
A khan, a khan from Astrakhan!
Pull out your old wild yataghan,
        Pound us a Mongol tune."

Pounding while elders clap and nod,
He howls a Mongol tune so sad
That all the ghosts of tsars go mad
        And bay at God.

From dung a peasant-clown sprouts forth.
They flog him for so vile a birth.
"Crown me," each pants in maddened mirth,
        "Caesar of earth."

"Sirs, at your service," fawns the clown.
On scalps still tingling for that crown,
He swings his muzhik-sickle down.
        Each begs in vain:

"Not me! Je suis un beau garçon.
I'm quite, quite West in my salon."
The sickle tolls their necks ding-dong.
        Hearing dawn's gong,

They vanish hellward, heads in hand,
Prancing a Georgian saraband
Straight down the earthquake where the land
        Of Rus has yawned.

—Spring 1950

DAVID IGNATOW

Singers of Provence

Was it beauty for one's head
to be hoisted upon a petard,
or to be run through with the sword,
or to be strung up by the wrists
for some slight against your king,
singers of Provence? You made music
to cover your guilt, you were all scared;
and you sang to bring on the ecstasy of lies;
while we with the door wide open
on the scene of the crime face the day
clearly with these words: we were here
and we witnessed it, the deaths and drownings,
the deeds too dark for words;
they would rumble in the belly meaninglessly,
but we speak our minds and the song sticks.
The people sing it, the singer believes it.
The air springs with a new song.

—Summer 1950

SAMUEL YELLEN

As I Was Walking down Fifth Avenue

As I was walking down Fifth Avenue,
I came upon Summer trapped behind plate glass;
The roses were rose red, the sky was sky blue,
And the grass, the grass was green as grass.

And three enchanting women stood, immaculate,
On the green grass that would never need mowing,
Their dresses unruffled, the hem lines straight,
And not one slip was showing.

And two bronzed men sipped amber at a table,
A brand-new rake leaned against the nearby wall;
Off in the corner a child reached for a bauble,
And a little dog played with a colored ball.

And clean straw was there for hayride or barn dance,
All was ready, yes, eager, about to, on the verge;
Yet landscape and attitude were held in a trance—
And no mere window dresser the thaumaturge.

This poem also appeared in *In the House and Out* by Samuel Yellen, published by the
Indiana University Press.

Frowning, I wondered why they had not the strength
To break so benign a spell; and as I paused there guessing,
The scene had depth and width and length,
I saw, but one dimension was missing.

For strangely there was no bark, no cry,
No pulsing at the throat or wrist,
No stir, no flicker on the sky-blue sky:
And Time must have sound and motion to exist.

And then it was, foreknowing Winter,
My heart ached to join that happy scene;
I knocked and called and tried to enter,
But more than plate glass stood between.

—Spring 1951

ALFRED KREYMBORG

Middle-Aged Reactionary

*I have sometimes asked myself whether my country
is the better for my having lived at all.*
—THOMAS JEFFERSON

A youth one used to love in former days,
When he and I were liberal companions,
Has reached a state of middle age where he,
Though younger than myself by twenty years,

Treats me with evasion when it appears
That I might speak to him. His voice is cold,
His manner no longer free but old, old
With the shade or need of that security
He buys by selling himself to some concern
Which has a much more plutocratic frame
Than leaves of grass through which he used to earn
Less than enough to live on. And the flame
That once imbued his romantic energy
With light and courage against the living dead,
Is now the tune of one who plays the game
Of compromise and safer goals instead.
What has happened to him since last we met
Has the military bearing of an ape
Or a crab attending backward schools today
To give himself a more becoming shape
In this dark time that few of us escape.
Although he has no weapon to aim at me
One feels some growing treachery somehow
Trying to stab the past between ourselves.
If I should bare myself with liberties
Which are out of fashion now, I'd be consigned
With other true men who find themselves opposed
By sudden foes whose reactionary stride
May count on leaders to strike us all aside
Or drag us off to dungeons cold and vast
Through whose dark walls no freedom ever passed.
The friend who shunned my path is out of sight
With all the other shadows of the night,

Yet one who walks as nakedly as I
Must learn to reason with all he loved before,
Hateful though that may be, or turn his heart,
A creature often thwarted in its faith,
Against spies and informers who invade
Our native land from within and spread their webs
To catch and poison our democracy
And hang it out to dry under tyranny.
Thus, before I shake hands with another man,
The utmost circumspection forces my tongue
To be silent until his soul reveals
Just what he thinks of me before I speak—
A game that always leaves me rather weak.
And so if another friend should come my way
He must kindly pardon differences I feel
May rise between us, or I myself begin
In self-defense before one gathers ground
And listening first to what he has to say,
Rushes on to the love we shared of old.
For I was ever a creature manifold
With warm affection and enthusiasm
Never spasmodic, hesitant or cold.
Shy though I am by nature, give me the bold
Greeting that crosses any worldly chasm
And takes two men together as the same
Fellows they were and are as they stand here
With friendship clear and pure in trustful eyes,
And in their hands, hearts, heads and future skies.

—Summer 1951

FRANCIS BARRY

To the Knowing

No slave to ritual, be errant.
Sin boldly against the Holy Ghost.
Sponsor nothing unless it's current.
Veer with those who veer the most.

Be deft with epigram, and quick
Where public causes are concerned,
Only don't bother to visit the sick,
Pay workers what their fathers earned.

Enjoy the negative innocence
Of childhood, but make sex as cheap
As food and drink. Write snowy poems
About the lovely whores you keep.

Be able with your reasoning
To prove the earth both round and square.
Drink from a hundred private springs,
Except the healing one, despair.

Acquaint yourself with death when he
Has dug your grave, and not before,
And leave your friends the certainty
Of your dying and no more.

—*Spring* 1952

WILLARD N. MARSH

Rooming House

Past doorways like upended coffin lids
It leads you, to four walls equipped with care
With pitcher, lamp, Retreat from Waterloo,
The stepped-off yards of predigested air.

It fluffs its hennaed hair and sniffs your breath,
Recites the canons of its regimen:
No credit, rebates, nor excessive use
Of radios and women after ten.

And leaves you to unpack above a view
Of plank-faced children in the next-door flat
Preparing for an appendectomy
Upon a neighbor's apathetic cat.

Each time you meet a stranger in the hall
It will be you, alive, dying, or doing
Nothing but getting home in time for death
Who always seems to smell of keys and blueing.

—Summer 1952

PHILIP MURRAY

The Ballad of Charlotte

Charlotte decided on Monday morning
To have sight without glasses;
Charlotte decided on Tuesday at noon
To read better and faster;
Charlotte decided on Wednesday night
To listen with her third ear;
Charlotte decided on Thursday at dawn
To face childbirth without fear;
Charlotte decided on Friday at tea
To be slim without hunger;
Charlotte decided on Saturday evening
To look younger, live longer;
But all day Sunday Charlotte cried—
She couldn't decide, she couldn't decide.

—Winter 1952-53

REVIEWS

GEORGE GEIGER

The Consequences of Some Ideas

THIS is not a review of Richard Weaver's notorious *Ideas Have Consequences*.[1] The reviews have by now been many, and the reviewers have been neatly divided—those who have been baptized on Chicago's Midway and the gentiles. This is not a review, simply a violent reaction to what can only be called a pompous fraud. And if the reaction seems extravagant, Mr. Weaver's pretentious style—combining the most obnoxious features of Milton Mayer and Mortimer Adler—must be held responsible. He is at least successful in provoking violent reactions.

For the innocent reader who may not be familiar with what, despite its air of professional piety, is essentially an evil book (the University of Chicago Press must have a special endowment to promote perversity: Weaver follows Hans Morgenthau who follows Hayek, and, not to mention a number of other links, the chain of reaction begins to get conspicuous), one may itemize some of Mr. Weaver's likes and dislikes. This is really a fairer introduction than an outline of his argument, which is: The Western world is through. The Reason Is Disbelief in Eternal Truth. The Solution Is Belief in Eternal Truth. But the things Mr. Weaver likes (those going in the direction of Eternal Truth) and dislikes (those going the other way) are more suggestive.

A. He dislikes: music since Mozart, but especially jazz; all literature

---

[1] University of Chicago Press, 1948.

since, say, Alexander Pope—except, of course, the neo-Papists; about all postmedieval art; labor unions; semantics; bureaucrats; the French Revolution—oh, all revolutions; the nineteenth and, above all, the twentieth century; feminism; liberal democracy—communism and fascism are to be preferred since they are at least realistic and not sentimental; state universities; science; indoor plumbing. In other words, materialism, relativism, pragmatism, and positivism.

B. He likes: Plato; the Middle Ages; caste, hierarchy, and the Southern Gentleman; Santayana; heroes; hardness; fertile women—good breeders; New England farmers; Dante; Edmund Burke; Aquinas; authority; private property; religious faith; *universalia ante rem;* the rural life—well, at least suburban. Namely, idealism, transcendentalism, and metaphysics.

But a man's likes and dislikes are not in themselves fraudulent. We can be tolerant about taste—not that Mr. Weaver is. Nor do strange bedfellows necessarily indicate fraud. Mr. Weaver finds himself revolving around that strange new axis linking Chicago's Midway with the Chicago *Tribune;* he sounds sometimes like an unholy combination of T. S. Eliot, a pseudo-Plato, and Curly Brooks. Yet an undigested mixture of Southern Agrarianism, reconditioned literary humanism, and the new evangelism of Chancellor Hutchins is more constipating than deceiving.

Finally, there is little of fraud in his strictures on contemporary life, on the barbarism and vulgarity of radio, cinema, and press, on the hideousness of war and misapplied technology. Here Mr. Weaver is just being sophomoric. He wants to make our flesh creep. He recites commonplaces, apparently on the assumption that people can still get a reputation by being against Sin. The only other assumption which can lie behind the chamber of horrors he presents in his opening chapters is that his enemy, i.e., the believer in scientific method, is in favor of barbarism and vulgarity or doesn't recognize them when he sees them. And certainly Mr. Weaver can be neither so flagrantly naive nor dishonest.

Why, then, is the book a pompous fraud? To start on a minor key and with only a small, venial deceit in mind, we can turn to the promised "solution" which the author dangles before our noses. For he writes, apparently in all seriousness, that "the remaining chapters therefore present means of restoration" (p. 129) and "I shall proceed to outline the task of healing" (*ibid.*). Here is the restoration and the healing (no fooling—if you don't believe it, read Chapters VII, VIII, and IX): (a) sanctifying the right of private property, (b) the study of Greek and Latin and "Socratic dialectic," and (c) a piety for the past.

Of course, in a way this is unfair. Since we have not yet mentioned the *cause* of all the ills the West is heir to. That cause is the substitution of nominalism for Platonic realism, i.e., that abstract concepts like Justice and

Man came to be regarded as names rather than as existential entities subsisting in some absolute heaven. Indeed, according to Mr. Weaver, we misunderstand the essentially serious business involved in determining how many angels could stand on the point of a pin; the failure to take it seriously, he insists, was prognostic of the decline of the West.

Thus, if the cause of collapse is so simple, well, the remedy can be just as simple. Perhaps, then, our writer is consistent. Especially since he proposes (p. 123) "that the most promising bid for peace would be for the two great rivals to dispatch, each to the other, their ablest philosophers." (Since "philosophers," by Mr. Weaver's definition, must be absolutists, Platonists, the true-blood metaphysicians, presumably we should dispatch Mr. Weaver himself, or one of his pals down the hall.) But Mr. Weaver admits that this suggestion might seem whimsical. So, maybe the whole book is engaged in pulling our leg, a welcome hoax indicating a sense of humor being restored at Chicago. This would be a salubrious and nonfraudulent explanation of the amazing letdown inspired in his reader by Mr. Weaver's explanation of the rise and fall of the Western world.

But this, I'm afraid, won't do. The author is too precocious a young man to be funny.

In any event, the indications of a fraud which is far from venial are twofold. The first is a patently deliberate refusal to tell us what key terms like Knowledge, Truth, Ideals, and Right are. That they are absolute and transcendental, we are left in no doubt. Perhaps *we* are the ones to blame because no bulb glows red when august terms like these are thrown at us. Modern man is a "moral idiot," we are told, and can never understand what is "truly right." He doesn't even know what values are. Mr. Weaver does. But he is coy. Outside of telling us that knowledge is of universals and that right is absolute and transcendental, he, like Plato, will refuse to write down his esoteric doctrine. He will simply repeat that magic word "metaphysics" which has all the charm of "Mesopotamia." But the esoteric doctrine of Mr. Weaver is being whispered around the Midway by his friends. It goes something like this: Metaphysics, or the absolute truths of philosophy, must be set above science; and theology, the revealed truth of religion, must be set above all. That revealed truth was the property of Thomism. And this is what, perforce, we must teach. Nonsense and obscurantism this may be, but it is not open fraud.

"Fraud" may seem a strong word—even if it is intellectual rather than legal. But when a contemporary writer on ideas, talking of epistemology, shrugs off with not a mention the patient and painstaking efforts of scientists and philosophers to tell us precisely what they mean by knowledge, what tests a "true" idea must meet, what are the possibilities and limitations of scientific knowledge—he is ignorant or intends to deceive. Mr. Weaver would never admit the former. Instead of examining the meaning of a scientific approach to human knowledge, he keeps repeating: The real world is not the one science talks about. It is another. It is Metaphysical. His formula is the old one, well tested in journalism as in philosophy: say a thing three times and it's true.

The second serious deceit may perhaps be pardonable, since it is always effective in polemics, and can only be rebutted by a *tu quoque*. This is to play the martyr. For four hundred years, laments Mr. Weaver, "we" have been in retreat. (You will remember the *cause* of the retreat—no one took universals seriously any more.) No, we cannot permit Mr. Weaver to be a martyr. His ideas are in the saddle now, as they always have been. He has with him all the religions of the world, for example. But that's not really the point. He will understand that the very development of science itself (and, as Mr. Weaver admits, it is *only* four hundred years old, just yesterday in human history, with ages of transcendentalism behind it) has taken place against an ideological background dominated by the Greek and Christian metaphysics which this book celebrates. Even in the four centuries of its spotty growth science has had to fight at every turn the intellectual hang-overs inherited from the millennia of absolutism Mr. Weaver is so eager to restore. Why, science itself has developed a notorious inferiority complex because of its background, so that even now most reputable scientists will concede all he wants, i.e., that science deals only with means and techniques, but that something else, say, philosophy must handle ends and values. This is timid and inconsistent, but a clear sign that the ideas Mr. Weaver cherishes have already produced pathetic consequences.

All of Mr. Weaver's confreres seem to make one assumption: modern culture is indeed ruled by science, by the genuine practice of scientific methods in all fields and by an emotional commitment to them. To recite this assumption is to refute it; yet without it the position of the antinaturalist becomes ludicrous. To act as if scientific humanism has had a long opportunity to practice, and a long record of failure to show for it, and that it must now be supplanted by something else is to misread history disastrously and dishonestly. If any blame is to be laid at the door of human failure to understand the world and to adjust to it, if responsibility is to be fixed for man's inhumanity to man, transcendentalism must be held as guilty as anything else. Certainly it has had a longer period to demonstrate its supposed competence and to practice its exorcisms and exhortations. For it to accuse a scientific naturalism which is barely getting under way for not yet having made man a god is impertinence.

This has nothing to do with the ideas of "progress" which Mr. Weaver so egregiously attributes to his straw men. Man may never solve his problems and he may well blast himself soon into oblivion. But if he is going to solve his problems he is going to solve them by a critical and reflective intelligence that derives far more from scientific method than from Platonic metaphysics. He can run away from his problems by questing for certainty and postulating a fairyland of absolute essences. It is what Mr. Weaver does. Whatever euphemisms may be used, this is surrender and nerve-failure of a peculiarly indefensible kind. Yes, ideas have consequences—that's the hell of it.

—Summer 1948

LEWIS COREY

James Burnham Rides Again

Wᴀʀ with Russia is inevitable and the United States must wage it, predicts James Burnham in a new book, *The Struggle for the World.*[1] So let us make war while Russia is relatively unprepared, which is the only logical policy, Burnham argues, since the war is *inevitable.*

If inevitable, the prospect is horrifying. But one must remember that James Burnham is a master-artist in the use of the word "inevitable"— it is his chief stock in trade. There were quite a number of "inevitables" in Burnham's earlier writings that never came off. From the record it is clear that whatever Burnham, at any particular moment, *thinks* will happen is "inevitable," but if he changes his mind the old "inevitable" disappears and a new "inevitable" replaces it. Here are several items in proof:

Item. For seven or eight years during the 1930's James Burnham was a Trotzkyite-communist. He wrote with all the messianic passion of the doctrinaire that "the Trotzkyite revolution is inevitable."

Item. Then came a change of mind and a new "inevitable." In 1941 Burnham published a book, *The Managerial Revolution,* which argued with all his earlier doctrinaire passion that socialism is impossible and that a new type of revolution, "the managerial revolution," is inevitable. Within that cosmic inevitable, which cannot be discussed in this space, were a number of minor "inevitables"—and not one of them has come off:

---

[1]John Day, 1947.

1. The Axis will win the war, said Burnham, their victory is inevitable. He predicted an inevitable division of the world among three super-states. "The nuclei of these super-states are, whatever may be their future names, the previously existing nations, Japan, Germany and the United States." (*The Managerial Revolution*, p. 178.) Sad for Burnham, but true: it didn't come off his "inevitable" way.

2. Burnham predicted the "inevitable" break-up of Soviet Russia and its swallowing up by a victorious Germany and Japan: "During the course of the next few years Russia will split apart into an eastern and a western section gravitating toward one of the key areas [Germany and Japan] which constitute the strategic bases of the super-states of the future. Indeed, the process has already begun. Siberia is so far away from Moscow and so badly connected that it naturally swings toward the East as it has for some years been conspicuously doing. . . . And similarly, at an increased rate since the Nazi-Soviet Pact, European Russia swings toward the central European area. The Russian boundaries advance toward the West. At the same time, economic and social relations with Germany increase. . . . Infiltration of German managers into Russian industrial enterprises is a large step on the road toward fusion of European Russia with the European center. We may be sure that the completion of the fusion, under whatever nominal auspices it comes, will find Russia subordinated to the European center, not, as the spinners of Bolshevik nightmares tell us, the other way around." And why this "inevitable" subordination of European Russia to Germany in control of Europe? Because Germany is the most efficient "managerial state" (hence it must win the war) while Soviet Russia is a "managerial state" of a lower order. (*The Managerial Revolution*, pp. 224-26.) Russia defies Burnham's "inevitability." It works to bring a "fusion" by forcible and ideological means, but with the European center subordinated to Slav-Communist-Russia domination. Another Burnham "inevitable" that hasn't come off.

3. The United States was undergoing an "inevitable managerial revolution" carried on through the New Deal. Since "managerialism" is anti-democratic, Burnham brought forth another "inevitable"—an early end of free elections. He wrote: "The 1940 presidential election—which may well have been the last presidential election in the history of this country, or, at most, the next to last—was a symbolical landmark, a guarantee of the course of the future." (*The Managerial Revolution*, p. 261.) But there was a presidential election in 1944 and, despite the "inevitability" in Burnham's "at most, the next to last," we are now in the midst of preparations for a presidential election in 1948, with nothing to indicate it will not be held on schedule.

Life exploded in Burnham's face and made mish-mash of his "inevitables." But was Burnham abashed? Not at all—he comes forth, in all his doctrinaire determinism, and unashamedly, with another "prediction"—this time of an "inevitable" war with Russia.

James Burnham is a pathological determinist. His whole mental bent is toward determinism. The bent was confirmed by the vulgar Marxism that he learned while a Trotzkyite-communist. The personal aspect of this is unimportant, of course. What is important is that Burnham's determinism works to give aid-and-comfort to reaction. His *Managerial Revolution* gave aid-and-comfort to the totalitarian elites, for he insisted with what he called "scientific objectivity" that their victory was inevitable. His *Struggle for the World* gives aid-and-comfort to the people and policies that may bring a Russian-American war, a war that Burnham insists is "inevitable." If the war is inevitable, why try to avert it?

Determinism is only a small factor in history and there are few inevitables. War may come, liberal democracy may go, man may destroy his world. Those disasters *may* come, but they are not inevitable. For, in final analysis, man makes his own history. There are alternatives that man may make come true if he works to make them come true.

—Summer 1947

KEITH McGARY

Koestler: Inside and Out

CONTEMPORARY artistic expression reveals the vital relationship between art and other social experiences. Spurts of vicious censorship on the one hand and on the other the moral approbation heaped on "modern" art bear witness to the power we assign to art. The stringent measures taken by totalitarian countries—by Russia especially—to control the type of art produced provide us with case materials for studies of the effects of repression on artistic production. Our attention is increasingly drawn to the task of determining how art really affects the citizen and whether or not it is either desirable or necessary to exercise control over these effects.

The job is complicated by the fact, receiving more recognition than it used to, that art is powerfully influenced by the sort of society in which it grows. In the present society a number of developments work their effects on art. Commercialism of much of our culture, tending to depreciate the individual and his choices, has been particularly troublesome for the artist. The mingling of many different cultures has had the effect of challenging the arts of each, raising questions pertaining to the role of the artist in his own society. Internationalization, with its rootlessness aided and abetted by the marvels of mass communication and transportation, has only served to confound the matter further.

When works on aesthetics are searched for aids in meeting these problems, little more is found in most of them than evasion or obscurity. Perhaps the single most important reason for aesthetic obscurantism is the fact that art is the last major area of human endeavor which has resisted renovation by the scientific spirit. Efforts have been made, of course, to subject art to "scientific" understanding. Far too many of them, however, have been carried on in the framework of rationalistic definitions. John Dewey's *Art as Experience* is, of course, a striking exception to these generalizations. But while Dewey's revolutionary treatment has been enthusiastically received by creative artists, it has been almost wholly neglected by professional students of aesthetics. The fact remains that current thinking about art is confused and troubled: from every side problems obtrude, many of which are susceptible to scientific investigation.

II

Koestler's *Insight and Outlook*[1] promises to be different from ordinary books on aesthetics in that it is, according to its subtitle, "an inquiry into the common foundations of science, art and social ethics." Already Koestler has demonstrated both by his political actions and by his artistic creations an unusual sensitivity to the problems of modern man. As is well known, he has been personally involved with major political events during the past several decades. His reactions to these events have been recorded in such of his earlier books as *Darkness at Noon, Arrival and Departure*, and especially *The Yogi and the Commissar*. He has attempted to make sense out of a world in which brutalizing and freedom-destroying events usurp the authority of humane and liberating ideals. His latest book is a systematic presentation of his beliefs as they relate to art, science, and ethics.

It is to Koestler's credit that in the face of the collapse of the Russian myth—an important event in his experience—his sensitivity to human con-

---

[1]Arthur Koestler, *Insight and Outlook*. The Macmillan Company, 1949.

cerns has not been dulled, nor have his loyalties to some sort of "objective" investigation been abandoned for a murky obscurantism. In spite of the dangers which critics pointed to in *The Yogi and the Commissar*, Koestler has not yet sunk to a mysticism which enervates. In his attempt to make his thinking relevent to human desires and ends as they operate in the world, he has used science to aid him in formulating intelligent, workable proposals.

Although Koestler's statement of his aesthetic theory is not intended to be complete, the theory is completely surveyed. *Insight and Outlook* begins with an analysis of the comic, after which follows examination of biological findings pertinent to some of the points raised in connection with the comic. The last two sections of the book deal with the "neutral arts: science and invention," and the emotive arts. The anticipated second volume is to be a reinforcement of the theory as now stated with psychological, neurological, and biological data.

III

Koestler operates with three principles in seeking a theoretical basis for art, society, and science. The first principle which he accepts is that of the field theory of nervous response. He argues that we respond to stimulation with behavior patterns which are "self-consistent and structurally homogeneous" rather than with isolated neutral patterns. The responses are independent of each other although any one may involve many parts of the body. His second principle is aptly illustrated by the "Eureka!" experience of Archimedes, by which the problem of the metallic content of the king's crown was solved. One of Archimedes' patterns of response, that produced by the king's query, was joined with another, that resulting from his reaction to the overflow as he sat down in his bathtub full of water. This sudden union of two hitherto unrelated fields of response Koestler calls "bisociation." It is an event that can occur in any area of human experience.

His third assumption—not necessarily connected with the other two—is of greater general significance. It is that the body seeks equilibrium, physically and socially. Field responses and bisociation of those responses contribute to the achievement of equilibrium, which is accomplished in two ways: by aggression and by self-transcendence. To illustrate these two mechanisms, Koestler turns to biology. He points to the process involved in the development of a living organism whereby the cells gradually become specialized to perform limited functions. In this process, the potentialities of the individual cell are transcended by the needs of the whole organism to which the cell contributes its energies. Occasionally, however, a cell will go its own way, heedless of the needs of the others. This individually aggressive behavior, which releases some of the inhibited possibilities of the cell, endangers, and may even destroy, the whole. Hence, Koestler concludes, transcendence on the whole produces biologically desirable results, but aggression, while freeing inhibited potentialities on occasion, in the long run yields biologically undesirable results.

Because Koestler believes social organization is a counterpart to biological organization, he maintains that social self-assertiveness, i.e., that which tends away from the control of the group, is disruptive and destructive, hence undesirable. Much more to be desired is the self-transcendence which integrates the individual with his society and ultimately with the cosmos. Such self-transcendence creates the "oceanic feeling" upon which Koestler has placed great value in earlier writings.

Koestler's third principle, by providing a theory of human nature, is at the heart of his system. Accepting an "operational" dualism of "aggression" and "transcendence," Koestler interprets art as producing either one or the other form of behavior. He makes his case against revolution and the man of action in general by denouncing aggression. Thus, he rejects the Commissar and prefers instead the Yogi, who promotes the oceanic feeling. Because of his theory, Koestler is unable to see possibilities for either a common ground or an alternative for these two extremes. His aesthetic, as well as his ethical, theories and their practical consequences stand or fall with the soundness of this part of his analysis.

IV

The inherent weakness of Koestler's position is disclosed in his acceptance of insect social organization as a model for the optimum human social organization in which the oceanic feeling—the feeling of belonging—would be predominant. In insect societies the behavior of the part, as in biological organisms, is determined by the whole. The result is an organization in which the parts are apparently in equilibrium and suffer from no frustration since each does the job for which he is physiologically fitted. The "stable and dynamic equilibrium" of the ant society is not possible with human beings, according to Koestler, because of the "rapid and radical changes of environment" to which man has submitted himself. Furthermore, such desirable forms of organization will not be possible for man until the technical exploitation of nature has reached a saturation point and man's environment, like that of the ants, becomes "reasonably standardized."

This outlook reveals a failure to discern the difference between the social organization of insects and that of man. Insect societies, like the biological organisms to which Koestler pays so much attention, depend for their structure upon great differences of physiology among their members such as are not to be found in human society. Function in the beehive or ant hill depends upon radical differences in body structure, from queen to workers to drones. Such is not the case in human society. People, within wide limits, are physiologically capable of taking each other's roles. It is only at physiological extremes, with idiots for instance, that problems arise because of structural differences. Human social organization, dependent upon its unique form of communication, rather than upon physiology, therefore, presents different types of problems from those of insects. Not only are the problems different, but the beehive does not offer a model solution.

When Koestler idolizes the stable environment of the insect society as a goal for human society, he discloses further the inadequacy of his understanding of human nature. He treats the environment as if it were something "out there" to which people respond, hence disruptive so long as it is not completely exploited and static. At no point is there any recognition by Koestler of the ambiguity of the term "environment," nor of the reciprocal relation between organism and environment. It is not possible to have a stable environment until there is a stable organism, that is, one which can make only a very limited number of responses. When the organism can become sensitive to new and different stimuli from time to time, as is the case with man, it is folly, or worse, to seek a limit to the environment. Koestler, failing to see that man's great variety of responses gives him a changing environment, cannot build positively with the fact of change. Instead he sees this changing environment only as a nuisance, the product of aggression and in turn the stimulant to further aggressiveness. This reasoning may readily lead to a justification of the present Russian restraint on art in their own environment, although Koestler himself would not want it so.

Many of the ills of society against which Koestler cries out, only to fret over "aggression" and "transcendence," are best explained as arising in large part from the tendency of contemporary society to realize his ideal by organizing like an ant hill. When that happens, man, not physiologically determined for one job only, is tortured by his potentialities for many jobs. A society which is organized so as to fail to engage the interests and potentialities of its members produces frustration and alienation. Totalitarian societies approach that form of organization and offer convincing evidence of inadequacy. The current problem of society is to preserve and enlarge the opportunities for a wide development of individual responses and at the same time to establish some ways of acting with wide enough acceptance to prevent the society from falling to pieces.

V

In spite therefore of Koestler's recognition of a relation between art and other social experiences, it is particularly difficult for him to handle the social functions of art. He has no adequate treatment of problems of censorship or governmental control. (The word freedom is not even indexed!) The inadequacy of his theory of human nature is largely responsible for this inability to deal with social relations. About all he can do is to plead for self-transcendence and to deplore aggression, for his man is not a social product: society is a product of the individual parts working together. Consequently, his primary concern is what effect art has on the individual—either toward aggression or toward self-transcendence.

In approaching art in this fashion, Koestler does not attach significance to problems which are raised by such mass art forms as the comics, advertising, magazines, the radio, and the movies. Nor is he able to see any problems, and then to work with them, in the present dualistic phenomenon of folk art and high or fine art. The problems for the artist which are raised in these fields are not even hinted at by Koestler, although they open serious inquiries in the related fields of art and social ethics.

The corruption of subject-matter by advertising—through both words and visual images—has widespread recognition among artists. Even the problem of technique has been complicated by the efficient methods of duplication which soon make a virtual drug of any example. As a consequence a premium has been put on novelty, which at times runs out of bounds without yielding any systematic experimental explorations with any subject-matter or any new medium. In the matter of taste, the artist faces a formidable block because of the ubiquitous opportunities for its corruption made possible by the mass media. Yet Koestler does not, and can not with his present theory, deal with these problems of the contemporary artist.

The limitations are even more apparent when he places all art into two categories: comic and serious. The former produces aggressive tendencies which are luxuriously dissipated in laughter. The latter produces the oceanic feeling of integration with the cosmos. But a cursory survey of the condition of the arts today reveals the deficiency of this analysis. Rubashoff, in *Darkness at Noon*, when he has the oceanic feeling, has a feeling of belongingness in his society which is also shared by the conventional heroes of *True Stories*. Yet there is a gap between these two productions which must baffle Koestler—provided he sticks to his theory. Likewise, the differences between Orwell's *Animal Farm* and Hatlo's "They'll Do It Every Time" are lost if we say they result merely from degree of skill and choice of subject-matter. Both are satirical but Orwell does not merely laugh the matter off—the reader is made angry. Hatlo is indulgent—he does not expect much to happen other than a quiet chuckle. There are significant differences in these examples other than those of aggression and transcendence; differences which result from a diversity of social function. One type of art, whether serious or comic, seeks to satisfy or deepen human longings, while the other exploits human sentiments and interests. Koestler, by placing such a premium on the separateness of the comic and the serious and upon the oceanic feeling opens the door to unlimited exploitation of human sentiments.

VI

The limitations in Koestler's aesthetic and social theory could be avoided by coupling his analysis of field responses and bisociation and his criticisms of society with a more adequate understanding of the social nature of man. An appreciation of the American contributions to the problem of human nature by such men as John Dewey and George Herbert Mead would help to overcome the inadequacies of Koestler's individualistic psychology. Mead's work, because of his interpretation of biological and neurological data to show that individuality develops in a social context, bears directly on Koestler's problems and offers possibilities of meeting the difficulties produced by Koestler's present theoretical limitations.

What has promised much, then, turns out to be both richly suggestive and acutely disappointing. Koestler's book is suggestive because it recognizes a relation between art and the rest of social activities; it is disappointing because the inadequacies of his theory of human nature prevent the author from really dealing with his main concern. He leaves unanswered most of the problems regarding the relations of art and society, but he pushes out the conventional boundaries of aesthetic understanding.

—*Spring* 1950

HERBERT S. BENJAMIN

Criticism in Reverse

Rᴇᴠɪᴇᴡᴇʀꜱ so far have chosen to ignore the Theory in René Wellek's and Austin Warren's *Theory of Literature*,[1] and by inference the "theory" of the New Criticism. The appearance of this book at this time is not to be greeted as an event in the history of aesthetics, literary theory, or literary criticism. The authors' intention is not something new, but something final, a synthesis of and case for the kind of literary criticism actually installed, exclusively, as The Style, and The Approach, in the chief literary magazines and the contemporary intellectual camp. If an event at all, it is an anti-climactic one. The campaigns are over, the authors and those who subscribe to their theory are in full possession of the field, the important professional chairs, and the critical organs; it remained but to clarify the issues, to autoptize the foes.

What began as a revolution twenty-five or thirty years ago has for some time been in evident triumph; this is the Code of the new authority. Some of the weaknesses of this Code are apparent on first reading; certainly there are barbarians outside the gates of literary Rome waiting to fight in through the slats. But Messrs. Wellek and Warren have been gracious enough to defend their regime publicly, tell us why they are here, how they have come, what they mean to do, and, most important, why theirs is the best of all possible administrations.

It needs to be seen how far this *Report on the Condition of the Academy* has been mistaken for literary theory, and what the inferences are for our literary criticism.

Anyone familiar with any of the "little" literary magazines, the important books of criticism, and the critical currents of the last few years is an old acquaintance of the authors. But they speak for many more, for Cleanth Brooks, Yvor Winters, John Crowe Ransom, Allen Tate, William Empson, the "Scrutiny" group, and others. T. S. Eliot, Ezra Pound, I. A. Richards, and Kenneth Burke stand somewhat like paternal uncles. The

[1]Harcourt, Brace and Company, 1949.

424

movement has no single father. Its origins, except as a kind of revolt from earlier, "Victorian," tradition, are inexact; and as will be seen, so are its theoretical principles, except as they resolve by negative definition, by what they are not, that against which they militate.

The fruits of the Wellek-Warren approach have been hard harvesting for the nonprofessional casual reader. He perceives a high seriousness and a special critical apparatus at work, without first learning which, the criticism is sometimes unrewarding, frequently incomprehensible. This book is, a little late, an event for him. But even he will be disappointed. As will be seen, the book is only one part statement and application of a theory, and ninety-nine parts a "good offense" against its slain and buried opponents. But if minuscular as theory, it is strong as an approach, a stance, perhaps as an *hauteur*, by which it sustains itself now against all the "theory" it discounts.

Briefly, the methodological principle is that the proper study of the literary middleman (there seems to be no name for him except possibly theorist, as opposed to critic, historian, and aesthetician) is Literature—his subject and focus are the specific creative work or any particular category of works; and anything else is nonprofessional, nonliterary, illegitimate, no more or less than heresy.

Before it can be discussed, the actual statement of .Theory must be extricated from the book where it lies hidden in one or two paragraphs in the chapter on "The Analysis of the Literary Work of Art." The rest, which is somewhat misleadingly called Theory, is not logically built up like most theories one ordinarily sees expounded. It develops with a curious antiseptic dialectic, exposing other theory until it alone remains. Like the cool heat in the middle of the flame it spares only itself. This we can see by following the authors' development of their case. The preface is something like a book review:

> We have written a book which so far as we know lacks any close parallel.
> It is not a textbook . . . nor a survey of [scholarly] techniques. . . . Some continuity it may claim with. . . . But we have sought to unite . . . It comes nearer to . . . though we take into account other perspectives and methods, have written from a consistent point of view. . . . We are not eclectic like . . . or doctrinaire like. . . .

The first chapter is called "Literature and Literary Study," which states the problem "how intellectually to deal with art and with literary art specifically." This "can be accomplished only . . . on the basis of a literary theory. . . . Literary theory, an *organon* of methods is the great need of literary scholarship today."

Chapter Two isolates the literature concerned as "imaginative literature"—as distinguished from other forms, "oral literature," "scientific literature," and "everyday literature." Chapter Three concerns terminologies used in explaining "The Function of Literature," and Chapter Four distinguishes between "Literary Theory, Criticism, and History" ("We must conclude the possibility of a systematic study of literature"). Chapter Five is about "General, Comparative, and National Literature." By the end of this first section it is apparent that the authors are eminently scrupulous men, that they know their problem is "complex." Terms should be clear. They are and somehow they aren't; general distinctions are brightly made, but *the specific work of art directly treated*, the key concept to the theory, is so far only named.

Section II concerns literary scholarship, questions of editing and authenticity, a forgivable delay. Section III, "The Extrinsic Approach to the Study of Literature," is a coruscating series of beware signs—what literature is not. The case that literature is separate from or something more than biography, psychology, sociology, and/or the other arts, is made facilely. Literature is not autobiographical statement primarily; "psychological truth" is not necessarily an artistic value, nor is "social truth," though they may corroborate such artistic values as "complexity and coherence"; it is not *primarily* "ideas" nor is the history of literature the history of ideas; information from the other arts may not only be spurious evidence for judging or treating literature but falls short of the "complex process of literature."

The picture so far is what literature is not, or not to be confused with. The next, and most important, section is labeled "The Intrinsic Study of Literature," or the type of study used by the authors. The chapter in this section on "The Analysis of the Literary Work of Art" is actually what we have been reading toward. It begins by recognizing a debt to the earlier continental system of *explication de textes*. It denies the meaningfulness of the distinction between content and form, replaces these terms with "structure," and sums up with: "The work of art is, then, considered as a whole system of signs, or structure of signs, serving a specific aesthetic purpose." After clearing up certain misapprehensions it is now possible to "open a way to the proper analysis of a work of literature." These misapprehensions concern a literary work being an "artifact," or a psychological experience. I. A. Richards' definition of a poem as the "experience of the right reader" is dispensed with by reference to "the criticism we have made of the psychological method." So far the "theory" still progresses on the strength of what isn't; ideas within this pivotal chapter are introduced like this: "To the question . . . several traditional answers have been given which must be criticized and eliminated before we can attempt an answer of our own." Until, at the conclusion of the chapter:

The work of art, then, appears as an object of knowledge *sui generis* which has a special ontological status. It is neither real (like a statue) nor mental (like the experience of light or pain) nor ideal (like a triangle). It is a system of norms of ideal concepts which are inter-subjective. They must be assumed to exist in collective ideology, changing with it, accessible only through individual mental experiences based on the sound-structure of its sentences. . . .

The unsound thesis of absolutism and the equally unsound antithesis of relativism must be superseded and harmonized in a new synthesis which makes the scale of values itself dynamic, but does not surrender it as such. "Perspectivism," as we have termed such a conception, does not mean an anarchy of values, a glorification of individual caprice, but a process of getting to know the object from different points of view which may be defined and criticized in their turn. Structure, sign, and value form three aspects of the very same problem and cannot be artificially isolated.

This is, frankly, the theory. It is questionable how much the critic is allowed to "know the object" from any "point of view," lest it be "non-literary"; the purely "literary" point of view is an ideal which is apparently impossible to determine, except as an intersection of other nonliterary lines of sight—against which we have been carefully cautioned. It becomes apparent that the other half of the book's title, which the authors dropped as too ambiguous—"and Methodology of Literary Study"—would be more appropriate, or better, "Theory of the Methodology of Literary Study," with the sub-title. "The Case for the Intrinsic Study of Literature as Opposed to the Extrinsic Study of Literature." Otherwise the execution is nothing like the more ambitious intent that the present title implies.

The rest of the book consists of separate, exceptionally lucid and authoritative dissertations on certain major literary problems, such as "Style and Stylistics," "The Nature and Modes of Narrative Fiction," "Literary Genres," etc. These chapters are just so much more evidence of the authors' extensive knowledge of the problems of literature and literary scholarship. The bibliographies are generous and definitive. But the theory, "Perspectivism," "Formalism" or whatever, does not come off. The title is too ambitious, this kind of literary scrupulosity is too ambitious. The philosopher, psychologist, sociologist, and historian have much to say about literature, and their summary exclusion from the "literary" journals can only mean sterilization, clamor as one may about the specific work of art and specifically literary evaluations. By its ubiquitous stress on methodology and supreme conscientiousness this book reveals the new critics (and, until a dissenting voice is heard, with their tacit consent) as something of prodigious bickerers, paradoxically tenured as Leaders of the Opposition in control of a police state which would collapse without biographers, psychologists, etc., to chastize—as faint hearts who will never win the fair lady art, though they will have what we shall call her respect.

The enormous amount of one particular kind of literary talk in intellectual circles today might lead one to imagine that there were some more ambitious organon of theoretical principles to back it up. But the organon is diminutive, a bit of aestheticology, a kind of limited application of symbolic logic to literature. This formalism has functioned well to exorcise from literary criticism the excesses of the evils here listed (under the Extrinsic Approach), but a total elimination of these evils from the critical apparatus can only mean an intellectual parthenogenesis dangerous to behold as any of the evils at their worst.

A certain amount of corrective emphasis has been accomplished by the "new critics," and if their labor has brought forth only this mouse of theory, its diligence alone has been enough to shame many tawdry critics and reform some of them and their audiences. It has been a victory by default, a much needed reform movement, but the very important question is: can these exorcisms be regarded as more than cautionary notes, can the critical faculty function at all if one takes them literally? Certainly the authors don't, and those who might subscribe fastidiously, purified down to grotesques of specialists, would survive only in a hothouse ivory tower, there to be forgotten.   —*Spring* 1950

GEORGE FISCHER

Russia and the Soviet State

Hanson W. Baldwin, the thoughtful, nonbilious military editor of the *New York Times*, has said[1] that America's major wartime errors were all part and parcel of our political immaturity, but that "they were fertilized, too, by a lack of knowledge or lack of adequate interpretation of that

[1]*Great Mistakes of the War*, Harper, 1950.

knowledge." He added—our italics—that *"this was particularly true of our wartime relationship with Russia."* This view of our wartime policy makes one question particularly pertinent: to what extent has current American understanding of Soviet politics matured? How well has the West kept step with the problems created daily by international tension?

Since the end of World War II, there has been a considerable change in the tone and quality of Western studies of Soviet society. In large measure, the scanty Soviet travelogues and rose-colored scholarship of the 1930's and the war years have given way to a more sober and competent genre. It is indicative that of the current books touched upon in this survey, practically each one represents the most superior up-to-date treatment of its subject.

Yet if the Soviet state's somber and peculiar features have been percolating gradually into the consciousness of its Western students, a sizable number of shortcomings, pitfalls, and fallacies continue to jeopardize its proper understanding. That this should occur on a topic as immensely complicated, "unscientific," and emotionalized as Soviet Communism is only to be expected. There can be no certainty, moreover, that a satisfactory answer regarding the true nature of the Soviet state will be evolved until the outside world is equipped with far more perspective and information on the USSR than it possesses today.

Nevertheless, greater effort needs be made to exact a higher standard from studies on Sovietism. Of those to be covered, the first three concern problems of research, the next three deal with Soviet foreign policy, the next two with Soviet public opinion, and the last with what may be called the rationale of the Soviet state.

One of the banes of American scholarship in general is the uncritical loyalty to documentation of all findings by "primary sources," frequently meaning only official ones. Even when dealing with a society like the American, where the veracity of official statements is ever subject to challenge by outside experts and laymen, such a reliance solely on official sources is apt to lead to a grotesque misrepresentation of reality. And yet Western studies of present-day Russia—where no such internal independent verification is feasible—have done just that. (No better, of course, is the other extreme—neglect of Soviet sources—as exemplified by Max Beloff's massive two-volume *Foreign Policy of Soviet Russia, 1929-1941.*[2]

The most notable recent illustration of the practice of relying on Soviet sources is Julian Towster's *Political Power in the U.S.S.R., 1917-1947.*[3] Although—or because?—this study is studded with references exclusively to official Soviet data, both the lay book reviewers and the scholars have

---

[2]Oxford, Vol. I 1947, Vol. II 1949.
[3]Oxford, 1948.

been dazzled by its "singular objectivity of attitude" (in the words of Professor Quincy Wright).

As is often the case with such books, *Political Power in the U.S.S.R.* does not merely reflect Soviet views, and some of it is quite valuable. But it does not explain the Soviet state and its use of political power, as its title promises; the book's reliance on Soviet sources has inevitably produced a picture reflecting a government's picture of itself—as well as an omission of material on negative features of Sovietism. Thus in a book dealing with "political power," the ubiquitous role of repressive organs and methods is hardly even alluded to.

Another pitfall in American scholarship in general and of Soviet studies in particular is the mechanistic projection of terminology, theories, and other premises based on Western experience. In many ways this is a natural and hardly avoidable failing. But it is a key obstacle when dealing with a subject like the Soviet state. The USSR's uniqueness and still not perceived institutional innovations are in reality probably far more important than the apparent similarities and historical connections.

The essentially rationalistic reliance upon Western experience for analyses of the Soviet state is in one way or another a feature—and therefore a drawback—of practically every book touched upon in this survey. In particular is it true of Towster's study. A political scientist, Towster creates even in the book's most sound and realistic passages an unmistakable impression that, whatever the deviations, the Soviet state can well be described by theories and terms applied to Western governments. This almost exclusive emphasis on formal and constitutional structure, while it may resemble the institutions of the West, certainly mocks those of Soviet society.

Injudicious projection of Western theories is exacerbated when it is confined to only one of the narrow academic "disciplines" currently in fashion. A most extreme—and self-admitted—instance of this is provided by Geoffrey Gorer, the British anthropologist, in *The People of Great Russia*:[4]

> The fact that I do not discuss, except incidentally, such subjects as [the Great Russians'] history, their economics, their contemporary social and political organization and the like should not be interpreted to mean that I do not consider these subjects to be of the greatest importance for a complete picture. I do not discuss them because I do not feel myself competent to discuss them. . . .

The modesty is admirable—but what appalling qualification for offering a "complete picture," as Gorer attempts to do, of Soviet Man!

---

[4]Chanticleer Press, 1950.

Still another methodological pitfall in interpreting Soviet actions is the belief that an expert can avail himself of all the necessary facts, if he is truly objective and scholarly. That this is not so is illustrated by the cited works of Towster and Beloff—both are as elaborately annotated as its authors are "objective" and "scholarly." As the latter writer emphasizes himself, "the first point which must be made, and made as forcibly as possible, is that for very much of the history of Soviet foreign policy we still lack the factual information necessary before one can proceed to an analysis of motives." And nothing is as revealing about General Walter Bedell Smith's mature and sober *My Three Years in Moscow*[5] as its author's enforced isolation from his Soviet environment and official hosts. The result is the Ambassador's striking transformation from a diplomatic analyst to a journalist observer, his difference from a newspaper man being largely that of seeing Soviet leaders occasionally and having a trained staff of assistants, secretaries, and translators.

All this underscores a feature of analyzing the Soviet state which is frequently lost sight of: perhaps more than in any other area of intellectual analysis, unremediable factual gaps are apt to continue plaguing us. Moreover, this feature not only must be acknowledged, but it leads to a greater readiness to draw meaningful conclusions despite imperfect evidence. What happens if an expert either accepts the available evidence as adequate, or refuses to provide the missing links through independent analysis, is again illustrated by Towster's *Political Power in the U.S.S.R.*

To turn now to Soviet foreign policy, one particular interpretation was held widely during World War II. As Edward R. Stettinius, Jr., worded it in *Roosevelt and the Russians*,[6] in a world "where objective conditions exist, people with different backgrounds and training can find a basis of understanding." It is evident from the memoirs of Roosevelt's highest associates and of his wife that the President shared the view, and that during the war he followed this assumption: although the USSR is unquestionably a dictatorship, it is probably working in its own way toward democratic ends, and Soviet policies can be decisively altered by Allied statesmanship.

The painful hindsight of postwar years has thrown much doubt on this, at the time, popular political assumption of the United States government. Yet the brief but widely discussed Quaker report on Russia, *The United States and the Soviet Union*,[7] is permeated with its fervent reaffirmation: "renewed conviction that all men, irrespective of creed or

---

[5]Lippincott, 1950.
[6]Edited by Walter Johnson, Doubleday, 1949.
[7]*The United States and the Soviet Union; Some Quaker Proposals for Peace.* Prepared for the American Friends Service Committee by its Working Party on American-Soviet Relations, headed by President Gilbert F. White, Haverford College. Yale, 1949.

cultural heritage, can come into possession of a new wisdom and a new tolerance, and that the unconquerable reaches of man's spirit can triumph even yet over those things which now divide us." To remain unfailingly hopeful for such universal amity is a laudable act of faith. But to project this hope into specific interpretations and recommendations—as the Quaker study does throughout—means to continue dealing with the world of those hopes, and not with the far less malleable planet of ours.

Furthermore, in analyzing Soviet behavior, how legitimate is the emphasis on statements made by Stalin and other Soviet leaders regarding the desirability and feasibility of coexistence and collaboration between the USSR and the non-Sovietized world? The Quaker report, for example, stresses that "in Stalin's speeches at Communist Party congresses ever since 1925 the first point of Soviet foreign policy has consistently been set forth as the preservation of peace and the strengthening of business relations with all countries." The most extensive studies on this question, however, contain evidence exactly to the contrary. Beloff's *Foreign Policy of Soviet Russia* concludes that "to try to comprehend the Soviet outlook and to dismiss the inevitability of the world proletarian revolution is as idle as to try to comprehend the outlook of medieval man and to dismiss the reality of the Last Judgment." And in the exhaustive *Foreign Affairs* study of "Stalin on Revolution,"[8] Historicus—believed to be George A. Morgan, First Secretary of the United States embassy in Moscow—finds that "the passages in Stalin's various interviews in which he indicates the possibility or desirability of coexistence and cooperation between capitalist and Socialist systems do not really contradict the strategic aim of world revolution because they refer to a temporary tactic."

A related dubious analysis of Soviet policy is the view that, as Max Beloff describes it, "the Soviet Union was a State among States, pursuing clearly defined ends by the conventional methods of *realpolitik*." It is revealing that this view is often supported by those who, like President Roosevelt, have espoused either of the two preceding assumptions—the possibility of universal amity regardless of differences, and the preference of Soviet leaders for peaceful collaboration with the West. But the record prior to and since World War II tends to indicate conclusively that Soviet diplomacy is distinctly not guided by power-politics alone, that among its motive considerations are some that have no affinity whatever to the "conventional methods of *realpolitik*."

The question of Soviet policy cannot be dissociated from the question of public opinion in the USSR. In attempting to analyze the foundation of Soviet actions, an increasing number of writers are falling back upon

---

[8] January, 1949.

the "national character" explanation. This explanation contends that Soviet policies reflect the age-old predilection of the population of Russia for autocracy, and its lack of experience or sympathy regarding Western political institutions. The Quaker report on Russia thus states of the most totalitarian features of Sovietism that "these elements were all part of the tsarist regime and have been characteristic of the Russian state for centuries." And Geoffrey Gorer, in his effort to prove—through swaddling customs!—the authoritarian nature of Soviet Man, writes: "the continuities between Czarist Russia appeared most striking; the contrasts, where they existed, between pre- and post-revolutionary Russia seemed like the contrasts between mirror images. . . ." Isaac Deutscher's *Stalin* tops it all off: "The nation over which Stalin took power might, apart from small groups of educated people and advanced workers, rightly be called a nation of savages."

One of the main attractions of this explanation of the Soviet state is that it contains a half-truth, although in precise historical terms it is certainly no more than that. An even greater attraction is the simplicity of the theory: if the Russian people don't know anything beside totalitarianism, that furnishes a delightfully easy and plausible explanation of why the Soviet state persists. Based as it is on historically unsupportable assumptions, this approach clearly obscures rather than illuminates the functioning of Soviet institutions.

The same is true of the thesis that Soviet rule is accepted peaceably and approvingly by the population, and that no discontent or disaffection can be foreseen. The implication of this thesis—as of the preceding one—is that the Soviet state, in the words of the revised edition of the standard text, *The Government of the Soviet Union*, can "claim to have strong roots in the hearts and the hopes of its people." Towster concludes that "the long emphasis on economic rights, associating welfare arrangements with liberty, has created a new popular conception of freedom, and the Soviet citizens are more eager for realization of these rights than for freedom to criticize or change the Politbureau." This view[9] is seconded by General Smith in *My Three Years in Moscow*: "In fact, the Soviet citizen today believes that he has the fruits of democracy."

It is of course self-evident that the Soviet government enjoys support from a segment of the population. But the most impressive available evidence contradicts much of both the just-quoted views and Geoffrey Gorer's recommendation that "it is useless to try to make friends with, or win the sympathy of, the mass of the Great Russian people, in the hope of producing transformations of policy."

[9]See also George Fischer, *Soviet Opposition to Stalin, a Case Study in World War II*, Harvard, 1952.

Even if one chooses to overlook the constant series of local uprisings—
the 1921 revolt of the Kronstadt sailors is the best known—and the
stubborn peasant resistance to government-imposed "collectivization," there
is most striking evidence of more recent origin about widespread Soviet dissatisfaction. What else would call for the unprecedented and ever growing
Soviet police system, described with an astonishing wealth of detail in
Forced Labor in Soviet Russia by two Russian socialist exiles, David J.
Dallin and Boris I. Nicolaevsky?[10] In what other fashion can one reasonably explain the huge wartime desertions of Soviet soldiers and civilians,
impressively detailed in *Life*[11] recently by Wallace Carroll, wartime European Director of OWI? Professor Merle Fainsod's first-hand descriptions
for Harvard's Russian Research Center of the vast mass of Soviet "non-
returners"—exiles who fled their homeland during or since World War II
—certainly belies the cited opinions that active or passive opposition is
beyond the reach or intention of the Soviet populace.[12]

It is thus particularly indicative and regrettable that not one of the
books discussed here mentions this extraordinary Soviet disaffection which
occurred during and since World War II. Only such misconceptions and
apathy can adequately explain the neglect by the democratic West of the
incalculable political and informational potential of the thousands of recent
Soviet exiles.

Lastly, a shortcoming of Western interpretations of the Soviet state has
come recently from a "Marxist" source. This is Isaac Deutscher's impressive,
broad-canvassed *Stalin*.[13] Though expressing distaste for Soviet authoritarianism, Deutscher finds extenuating reasons for much of it. Particular use
is made of a comparative historical approach, popularized by Professor
Crane Brinton's *Anatomy of Revolution* (1938). In *Stalin* this approach
leads to a seemingly plausible relativism, which in reality is both misleading and amoral. The vast difference in time, place, and techniques of
these revolutions detracts much from the apparent validity of Deutscher's
view that "Stalin belongs to the breed of great revolutionary despots, to
which Cromwell, Robespierre, and Napoleon belonged."

As questionable both historically and morally is another of Deutscher's
propositions. Here he suggests that probably only Stalin's methods could
have so effectively industrialized and vitalized "Socialist" Russia and postwar Eastern Europe, and thus—as he says of Poland and Hungary—fulfilled "perhaps imperfectly, a dream of many generations of peasants and
intellectuals." A positive dynamic—as distinguished from the sphere of in-

[10]Yale, 1947.
[11]December 19, 1949.
[12]*American Political Science Review*, June, 1950.
[13]Oxford, 1949.

stitutionalized repression—is also ascribed to the USSR in *The Government of the Soviet Union*:[14] "This mass move upwards from the very bottom of the Soviet pyramid is, together with the ever-present leadership of the Communist Party, the fundamental fact of Soviet life. It explains much of the crudities, toughness and vigor of the Soviet people, as well as their willingness to endure hardships which to most Westerners would be intolerable. . . ."

There is clearly more truth here than critics will often concede. But the key question remains: to what extent do these interpretations ascribe to the Soviet state an *a priori* rationalistic inner logic, which—however plausible it may appear to Western minds—actually greatly obscures its precise functioning?

An answer to this particular question would bring us much closer to our over-all query: the true nature of the Soviet state. For throughout the preceding discussion of present-day shortcomings in analyzing Sovietism, the main criticism has been one. That is the continuing failure—usually not traceable either to ill intent or Sovietophilia—to deal with the essence of Soviet power.

In the realm of methodology, a satisfactory analysis of the Soviet state has been retarded by two features: highly pedanticized canons of "objectivity," and the inability of scholars and even laymen to detach themselves sufficiently from their personal and theoretical assumptions in dealing with something as vastly different as the USSR.

In the case of both Soviet foreign policy and public opinion, the basic premise of most Western analyses is also *a priori* rationalistic. The assumption—explicit or unstated—tends to be that regardless of deviations and aberrations, man's private and collective conduct is governable by impulses and influences which are fundamentally alike.

The same premise is most frequently operative when Western students approach the complex problem of what the rationale, the inner logic of the Soviet system is. The standard answer—even from many bitter critics—again draws upon policies and methods which are familiar and understandable in the context of past Western experience. Thus even when an expert speaks of the USSR as of an autocratic Leviathan, he usually turns to a rationalistic explanation. It may lie in the autocracy of pre-Soviet Tsarism, or in positive motive forces such as industrialization, "progressive social performance," use of nationalism or even religion, or "economic democracy."

All of these current interpretations contain much that is valid. This is as true of the least impressive studies discussed here, such as Gorer's

---

[14]By Samuel N. Harper and Ronald Thompson. 2d ed. Van Nostrand, 1949.

People of Great Russia, as it is of the more competent ones. But none of them seem to treat adequately the key issue—a key issue particularly in a society where individual as well as social actions are more decidedly affected by it than by any other feature: that is the dynamic of the Soviet state. To the extent that this key issue is not grappled with, a radically different approach will be the only guarantee that the present mixture of misjudgments, half-truths and valid insights will be replaced by sounder analysis.

It is no accident that Western thought was also incapable of providing a satisfactory interpretation of the Nazi system in Germany—and continues to fail in this. Such failure is clearly indicated when scholarship is what it has become in the West, and particularly in the United States. Much of it is highly overcompartmentalized. Too many academicians have also become averse to the straining of insight and fantasy so requisite for a grasp of matters outside the realm of rational intellectual pursuit. And how could conventional analysis deal with either Hitler's Germany or Stalin's Russia, when in both instances—regardless of varying origins and aspirations—the world was presented with an unfathomably dissimilar rearrangement of all known political, psychological, social, and economic structures and interrelationships?

Specifically, understanding of the Soviet state must be grounded on an analysis of those new social constellations which were born of the uniquely twentieth-century coalescence of technology, with all its consequences, and an equally unprecedented form of faith-driven despotism.

The never equalled modern means of communication and armament, as well as the streamlined adumbration of "Machiavellian" politics and psychology, have made something possible that has never been feasible in modern times. This is the continuing functioning of a society which is based exclusively or largely on state repression and never-ceasing personal fear—and the likelihood that only a violent explosion can modify it in the foreseeable future.

There is growing evidence that the Soviet state is among the world's first such societies. This evidence may well not be conclusive, and the current interpretations criticized here might in the long run prove to be more valid. But while political scientists have not studied exhaustively what may be called Political Power in the Ice Age, and sociologists and psychologists do not forego methodological alchemy long enough to probe into the social structure of "Nineteen Eighty-Four," an awesome suspicion must remain: is the West's analysis really that of the Soviet state, or merely of a self-created caricature of it? And still more importantly—are the accumulated intellectual resources of free society incapable of understanding what at present is its major challenge?   —*Summer* 1950

ALBERT A. BLUM

Unions in Court

To HELP a class evaluate Socialist philosophy, I once asked the students how valid was the Marxist claim that in a capitalist society like the United States, the government was a committee of the capitalist class. Nearly all of those who believed that it was valid pointed to the Supreme Court as an agent of the business community. This opinion has been mirrored in the views of the working class. In fact, the Supreme Court and the lower courts have been treated with especial opprobrium by labor, for many have believed that the Constitution safeguarded the interests of the employers while the courts formed the bodyguards for those interests. To the radical unionist, it was completely understandable; to the conservative like Gompers, who himself had to face a jail sentence at the hands of the court, it was a more difficult task to explain, though not to justify, the actions of the courts. This is the task which Elias Lieberman attempts to undertake in his new book *Unions Before the Bar.*[1]

The falsity of the myth of the impartial court and the objective historian is clearly shown in this work. Mr. Lieberman, the historian, is by occupation a labor lawyer and he never forgets his position in his book. He constantly plays the role of labor's defense attorney, sometimes reprimanding it for getting out of hand, but generally defending it against management, government and the judiciary. Yet a good defense attorney was needed, for he had to fight against a court which until 1933 was unfavorably disposed towards trade unions, and which before that time enacted into law, through decisions, its own prejudiced and partial views of labor legislation. It is only with the beginnings of the New Deal that we find the court approaching labor with a more sympathetic air. It is only fitting that Mr. Lieberman should have divided his book so that one-half of it or twelve of the twenty-five chapters deal with the pre-New-Deal era, and that of these twelve cases, only one, *Commonwealth v. Hunt* could be considered anything but a defeat for labor.

---

[1]Harper, 1950.

What Mr. Lieberman attempts to do is to take the readers for a chronological trip from the *Philadelphia Cordwainers'* case in 1806 to the *American Federation of Labor, et al. v. American Sash & Door Company, et al.* in 1949. In each chapter, he usually treats one case which he feels illustrates the court's attitude during that period. With admirable lucidity, he traces the political and economic background of each case, summarizes the briefs of labor and its opponents, and analyzes the decision of the court and its effects on labor relations. All of this is done with the author's eye trained on the nonspecialist, and he succeeds admirably in making each case completely understandable as well as enjoyable reading.

It is important to note also what Mr. Lieberman does not attempt to do. He does not attempt to be all-inclusive in his study. All he does—and it is enough—is describe those cases in which the trade unions themselves are involved. Consequently, many important decisions which are generally found in books dealing with labor law are missing here, e.g. *Lochner v. New York* and *Adkins v. Children's Hospital.* He is not concerned with such matters as wage, hour and other similar social legislation, but only with the rights of unions before the bar. Little attention, moreover, is paid to statutes with the exception of the Taft-Hartley Act. This is a perfectly justifiable division but one must question then the accuracy of the complete title of the book: *Unions Before the Bar: Historic Trials Showing the Evolution of Labor Rights in the United States.* Surely, it is not a sufficiently broad view of labor rights to confine them to questions concerning the rights of organized workers and not with those like minimum wages, maximum hours and social security. Within the more narrow compass with which the author does deal, however, his choice of cases is excellent and only persons concerned with the picayune would suggest that he might have chosen one case instead of another.

The reader of the book who is not concerned with the picayune must concern himself with the basic theme made evident by this work. The court, in the past, generally was to be found on the side of the antilabor forces and is again showing a tendency to return to that position. There are many reasons why this took place and may again take place. Some of the causes, but by no means all, can be expressed by describing an attempt, in one industry, to form a body similar in many respects to a Supreme Court. As a result of the impressive Cloakmakers' strike of the International Ladies' Garment Workers Union in 1910, Louis D. Brandeis, not yet a member of the Supreme Court, was called upon to bring about a settlement. The result was the Protocol of Peace. This Protocol, an important stage in labor history, was visualized by Brandeis in terms of a legal system. If a problem arose, an attempt was made to settle it on the lowest levels. If unsuccessful, it went up to an appeals' court, the Board of Grievances. If not settled there, it went on to the Supreme Court, the Board of Arbitration. By the time it reached the latter point much time had elapsed, which besides causing, not preventing, irritation made the solution often purely a theoretical one. Conditions were steadily changing. The Board of Arbitration used the Protocol of 1910 and decisions of past cases to help solve problems of 1915. These, among other reasons, caused the breakdown of this scheme for industrial peace.

How does this compare with the Supreme Court? It takes a long, long time for any decision to be forthcoming from that body and when it does it often has very little value to the persons involved. If a year after an injunction is served, the courts find that it should not have been served, of what value is the decision to the strikers against whom the injunction was issued? The court also bases its decision too often on a constitution which was written before the existence of labor unions and on past decisions both of which may have a theoretical relevance to the case but little to do with the changed economic and social environment. As far as possible, the solution of the problems arising from labor-management relations should be left to these two groups themselves or to the legislatures. The courts should narrowly limit their jurisdiction over such matters as was suggested by some members of the judiciary. As a result of this, a repetition of the embittered feeling which labor held towards the courts before 1933 can be prevented. Students and workers should never again be able to believe that the courts are an arm of management. Mr. Lieberman's book makes its best contribution in increasing the citizens' understanding of the background of this sentiment.   —*Fall* 1950

PAUL BIXLER

Anti-Intellectualism in California

THERE is an established procedure for dealing with violations of academic freedom in the United States. Since the violations usually involve the dismissal of individual faculty members from their teaching positions, the American Association of University Professors is usually called in to make an on-the-spot investigation and recommendation. The AAUP has, in fact, been called into the so-called oath case at the University of California. But can it be expected to correct or materially affect what has been happening in Berkeley in the past two years? The problem there is not so much a matter of dismissal of individuals (although a hard core of eighteen faculty members at last report had sued in the courts to get their jobs back) as it is a mass phenomenon in group distrust. To say that the University of California oath case is a violation of academic freedom is somewhat like saying that McCarthyism is a violation of civil liberties. How do you indict an atmosphere? How do you fix responsibility upon a climate of opinion?

The case began in a request from the university Board of Regents that the faculty sign a non-Communist oath. About this Sidney Hook has commented that for a non-Communist to sign a non-Communist oath is not quite so serious as for a Communist to sign such an oath or for a non-Nazi to sign a Nazi oath. In other words, to sign something you believe in is milder and could even, under some circumstances, be acceptable; whereas to sign something which you do not believe in is not only false but despicable. It is doubtful that the majority of the faculty at the University of California objected to making clear their own opposition to communism as a system of thought. But however that may be, after more than a year of contention on the part of both regents and faculty, the issue turned out to be not communism but independence and the dignity of having ideas of any kind. Out of the tumult and the shouting it presently became clear that the dissident half of the regents (through most of the dispute the board seems to have been split almost down the middle) were seeking to deprive university teachers and thinkers of prestige. Thus the controversy has become one more item—a major one in that it affects the largest university in the land—in the anti-intellectual drive of our time.

George R. Stewart's *The Year of the Oath*[1] gives considerable attention to the disturbed atmosphere which prevailed throughout much of the dispute. On the issues of the controversy, the book is not so clear. A quickie, it was written before the dispute rose to its greatest climax and before the drive of some of the university regents became fully disclosed. At one point, for example, Stewart emphasizes the dismissal from the university of two people who were not faculty members under circumstances which can only be described as confused; in perspective this event would not seem particularly noteworthy. When, later on, the faculty committee on privileges and tenure recommended the dismissal of six faculty members he is not altogether sure that this procedure was correct. But the fact that at this point, control of academic qualifications and the power of dismissal

---

[1]Doubleday, 1950.

was in the hands of the faculty was exactly the issue upon which the controversy should have been (and later on was) fought. Faculty control of tenure would appear to be a principle behind which any faculty group could unite. Stewart and his collaborators were very close to the controversy, and blinded by charges of communism and their own conventional defense of "academic freedom," they did not clearly foresee the third act in the drama.

Last August the obstreperous faction on the Board of Regents at last exposed its real point of view. Governor Warren, who is himself a member of the board, asked at one point whether it was a regent idea to fire faculty who had not signed their contracts simply because they were recalcitrant. And back came the answer from a member of the dissident faction, "It is not a question of communism but one of discipline." The declaration cleared the air. It gave away the anti-intellectual drive for what it was. And it also laid bare a second issue which had been altogether too much obscured.

II

One of the distinguishing characteristics of the American university and one of its chief strengths has been its formal, organizational relationship to its public constituents.[2] The university teacher is assumed to be independent in thought but he has always operated within an atmosphere of public opinion and public responsibility. The American university is distinguished by its lay board of "control"—sometimes a board of trustees, sometimes of regents. The board has sometimes conceived of itself in the role of employer with faculty as employees. But when its mission has been so misconstrued, trouble has frequently followed. This is what happened at the University of California and it is worthy of special attention.

It is fair to say that faculty opinion carries more weight today with most college and university boards of trustees than it once did, and the long-term tendency has been to institutionalize that opinion in some form of participation in control. At the University of California, for example, the faculty has had self-government since the early 1920's. This made the Board of Regents the aggressor in the case—an aggressor in spite of the fact that its action in that role was obscured at times by division and confusion on the part of the faculty. What happened, since early 1949, to bring about the distrust and the active hostility?

The answer is not clear—although some hot-heads would put the blame upon Regent A. P. Giannini of the Bank of America until he

---

[2]Tenth Yearbook of the John Dewey Society. *Democracy in the Administration of Higher Education.* Edited by Harold Benjamin. Harper, 1950.

resigned in personal defeat, and then upon Regent John F. Neylan, former attorney for the university's big benefactor William Randolph Hearst. In one all too brief chapter Stewart examines the makeup of the Board of Regents and their qualifications for public service. Eight of the twenty-four serve ex officio but with a vote—the governor of the state, the lieutenant governor, the speaker of the assembly, the state superintendent of public instruction, the president of the state board of agriculture, the president of the Mechanics Institute, the president of the alumni association, the president of the university. Stewart concludes that only three of these— the governor, the superintendent, and the university president have enough interest in university affairs to require representation. The lieutenant governor and the speaker of the assembly have no particular educational qualifications and are frequently a political hindrance. The time has passed when state agriculture needed a special and permanent representative. Selecting a representative from the Mechanics Institute is not only anachronistic, but in practice it is also undemocratic. As to the president of the alumni association, Stewart argues that the actual selection is undemocratic, that the term of one year is too short to be effective, and that normally the alumni are represented by other regents.

What of the appointed members of the board? In another chapter called "To the Dissident Minority: a Letter," Stewart points out that the dissident regents are men without degrees and without any other marks of educational background or interest. The trend of this argument is dangerous, for at its end lies intellectual arrogance. A university could well use many of our men of marked accomplishment without asking of them a degree. If degrees are a criterion then obviously certain labor leaders and for that matter others would not be able to make the grade. It is right here that the educational institution meets the public and its responsibilities to the public. Presumably one would ask of a prospective trustee or regent that he be a man of proved accomplishment and good citizenship. Beyond that what should one ask except that he also be educable? (Which, incidentally, might be a requirement, too, for faculty and students.)

More fruitful for examination are the areas from which the appointed members are drawn. Here is the breakdown of 41 such regents from 1920-1949, as given by Stewart:

lawyer	12	clergyman	1
business executive	9	lecturer-author	1
banker	7	civic worker	1
editor-publisher	3	retired admiral	1
physician	3	clubwoman	1
farmer	2		

Concentration in the first three groups takes on special significance in that they seem to be so closely associated as to classify largely in one narrow group—people of importance in the business world. Stewart also points out that the farmers are not the sort who handle pitchforks. The editor-publisher is mentioned in *Who's Who* as a "financier," and one of the doctors could claim the same classification. The clubwoman is a banker's wife. This seems altogether too narrow a group to be considered representative of the public. Since 1920, the period under examination, there has been on the board no engineer, no newspaperman (the one editor-publisher in 29 years was perhaps the most distinguished of all the regents), no labor leader, no grassroots farmer, no small businessman; and the professions outside of medicine and law have been largely ignored.

Furthermore, why should not the board include someone from the University of California faculty (the president is already a member), a man of letters, or even a faculty member or two from another California university? This is not to say that these neglected professions should completely displace the business group. There is no more reason why there should be a half dozen writers or a half dozen engineers than that there should be a dozen businessmen or a dozen politicians. Nor does it mean that membership should be distributed on a basis of social or religious pressure groups. If the job of the Board of Regents is to manage and watch over the business affairs of the university, then perhaps the present group does fit its responsibilities. But the board is supposed to be a buffer between the people of the state and the university. There is no reason why such a board should not include important Californians from all walks of life— not to represent their vocations or special interests but to broaden the knowledge and the cross-fertilization on the board. It is perfectly clear that men of distinction do not arise simply in one vocation or in one segment of the population; if the university and the governor are searching for such men they should look far more widely than they have. The error here is pervasive, fundamental, and unmistakable.

III

What about the faculty? Stewart was one of the "dissident minority" who were seriously and emotionally upset over the controversy. He has tried to remain objective about it but his attention emphasizes the effect upon the minority who felt themselves most deeply involved. The atmosphere during this time was physically and emotionally unhealthy and upsetting. Stewart makes clear that a number of faculty lost their feeling of identity with the community. It was freely said that stool pigeons were running from the faculty to the Board of Regents although no communication between the groups is presumed in the ordinary course of events to take place. Not only was the atmosphere not conducive to thought for many of these teachers but it was not conducive to activity of any kind. The tension which held many of them in its grip during the greater periods of stress disrupted teaching, research, and even extra-curricular activities.

At one point Stewart makes something of the fact that a slogan developed among the faculty—"Stay, sign, and fight!" This was a signal that the teachers would not leave a nasty situation for peace somewhere else. College teachers are not constituted generally for fighting battles. They sometimes enter the teaching profession because they personally like a quiet life undisturbed by the constant wear and tear of worldly affairs. Yet a good, tough dispute may not be so frightening in actuality as in contemplation. To those California teachers who fought, whether they signed or left, the experience must have had its compensations as well as its defeats.

Social courage is a much needed element in the university scholar's kitbag—and there is still another important element, which we have already suggested in the relation between the professor and the public. A major part of the university world was alerted to the California dispute last April. At that time Chancellor Hutchins and the faculty at the University of Chicago sprang to the defense of their California colleagues with pledges of money and words of encouragement. Chancellor Hutchins, in fact, has frequently heartened the entire teaching profession by his plain, vigorous words concerning the scholar's duty to think and to brook no opposition in allowing him to perform his particular job. One may congratulate Chancellor Hutchins and still add a point of warning which to date he has neglected. Freedom to think does not mean freedom to think irresponsibly or in a vacuum.

One remembers the freedom to think in the German university before Hitler and how ineffective it was in the later days of German crisis. Nowhere before or since has such freedom been more celebrated for its purity. Yet in the days of Nazi storm and stress the purity of thought in German universities turned out to be helpless because it was irrelevant. Thought was so free and pure there that it had no connection with German life and German reality. Thus it had no real application and no influence on social developments. And in the ensuing debacle, it sank with scarcely a trace.

There is a missing, unspoken link in Chancellor Hutchins' words about freedom of thought—words which by themselves are heartening in a moment of crisis or defeat but which lack a long-term relevance. The truth is this—that thinking has its public responsibilities. In the end thought must be known by its works, its applications, its uses. It must also have its place within society, not outside it. Without true relationship to social institutions, thinking can become simply an escape mechanism. One of the concrete manifestations of this relationship in higher education is the university lay board of trustees. And to say that the regents of the University of California misued their public responsibility and their relationship to the university faculty is not to deny the need for trustees, as we have already noted, but to indicate the magnitude of a particular failure.

There is still a broader application to this truth. The American intellectual, both inside and outside university walls, has not always accepted his responsibilities for thought and action. True, the atmosphere he has operated in has often seemed hostile; yet it could not be wholly so, or the institutions for thought—such as universities and foundations—would not have attracted so many private gifts and so much public support. It may be better to say that many American intellectuals have been excessively tender, that they have been unwilling to face indifference or unfriendliness, and have rejected not just the skepticism and hostility but all of American culture. Until about the time of the depression, the intellectual was as likely as not to dismiss America entirely and look to Europe.

In the '30's the number of intellectuals, encouraged by the colleges and universities, greatly increased. And under the stimulus of the New Deal, many of them became socially and politically conscious. Many, indeed, actively entered the ranks of the New Deal itself where, whatever their backgrounds, their welcome was warm. To say that they were socially conscious, however, is not to say that they all appreciated American culture or that they had personally experienced the democratic process. There was a hurry about the New Deal (especially in its earlier days), a sense of "let's-do-this-now-before-the-reactionaries-take-over" which by-passed the more solid democratic structure of thorough discussion and a measure of fair play. Distrust arose because of the activities of these men, and the distrust did not come simply from American Bourbons, for among the intellectuals involved was a strong, perhaps a majority element out of American aristocracy.

If there is a social nexus between Senator McCarthy-W. R. Hearst and some of the University of California regents, there is also an atmospheric connection running, however faintly or unfairly, from the Lee Pressmans in Washington and the Alger Hisses in New York to intellectuals everywhere including the University of California faculty. This is unfortunate, but it is a connection which must be faced, lived with, and rubbed out. *The professor-intellectual has to face the dilemma of thinking responsibly* about the world in which he lives at the same time that thinking has been repudiated. This may be wormwood to sensitive natures, but it is perhaps no more bitter than the difficulties all of us face today in a divided world.

In the anti-intellectual drive of our time, and in the failure of communication and understanding between intellectuals and the public, there is great danger to our way of life and to our institutions. The need for relevant, thoughtful solutions to our problems was never more pressing.

—*Winter* 1950-51

ALFRED WERNER

Books in Western Germany

MUNICH, where I spent some time last summer, is an excellent lookout for observing Western Germany's cultural development, particularly if Hugendubel's spacious bookshop on the Salvatorplatz is your headquarters. It is true that the Nazis almost succeeded in giving Munich the reputation of being the *Hauptstadt der Bewegung*, the center where Hitlerism originated. But before 1933 the city was known as the "Isar-Athen," the Athens on the Isar river, and it was a place of painters and museums, writers and publishing houses. In this city the Thomas Manns lived until their emigration. Some of Germany's most distinguished publishing firms had their headquarters in Munich, from the C. H. Becksche Verlagsbuchhandlung, founded in 1763, to the modern Kurt Wolff Verlag. Beck still functions there, yet the Nazis forced Wolff to emigrate to the United States where he organized another firm, Pantheon Books. As a kind of postwar counterpart, several publishers fled from the ruins of Leipzig to those of Munich to escape the censorship and restrictions of the Eastern Zone.

Hugendubel's premises—perhaps as large as those of Brentano's in New York—survived the war unscathed. Other booksellers who were less lucky have set up their shops in flimsy makeshift stalls, where business goes on "as usual." It cannot be said that the book trade is really flourishing in the Bonn Republic; the number of copies of the average printed book is generally below five thousand because of the lack of material and labor, and the fact that for large numbers of people the purchase of a book is a luxury. Moreover, there is no legal trading in the book market between the German Federal Republic in the West and the German Democratic Republic in the East. Still, it is amazing how strongly Western Germany's economic recovery reveals itself in a well-supplied bookshop.

There is, of course, the psychological aspect. Anyone who visited Germany immediately after the war was struck by the *Lesehunger*, the book famine from which many Germans suffered almost as strongly as from physical hunger. Throughout the twelve years of the Nazi regime the Reich was an intellectual desert; an inestimable number of "undesirable" books perished in the bonfires supervised by Dr. Goebbels; then the Nazis decreed what books could or could not be printed, and what books could or could not be imported. In addition, the war losses of private and public libraries have been estimated as high as thirty million volumes.

Depleted of all intellectual substance, the postwar Germans read whatever books they could get. In the first months after the armistice, an emergency supply was provided by Overseas Editions, Inc., the paper-bound, pocket-size volumes produced by our Office of War Information. These books introduced our former enemies to German translations of American authors. Next came an experiment necessitated by Western Germany's economic poverty. To reacquaint his compatriots with the world's great books, Ernst Rowohlt, one of the foremost publishers in pre-Hitler Germany, printed millions of large-sized pamphlets on very cheap paper by means of rotogravure. These "books," which looked like tabloid newspapers, enabled the impoverished Germans to obtain for the equivalent of a dime the greatest works of foreign fiction, from Homer to Hemingway, as well as some native products, including Hjalmar Schacht's concoction, *Settling Accounts with Hitler*.

By now the Overseas Editions volumes, as well as the ungainly Rowohlt Rotations-Romane, have virtually disappeared. Instead, you see superbly printed and bound books, and many lavishly illustrated monographs on art and artists. Far from having abated, the *Lesehunger* seems to be as strong as it was when I first visited Frankfort, Heidelberg, and other cities several years ago. Nor has the demand for foreign authors, especially Americans, come to an end. Even diehard Nazis who refused to revise their *Weltanschauung* after the debacle of 1945, read Yankee books—if only to find out what makes the Americans tick. Out of twelve new titles recently published by one firm, six were foreign (the Americans Hemingway, Thurber, James M. Cain, and Thomas Wolfe, and the French authors, Simone de Beauvoir and Jean-Paul Sartre).

It is, however, of greater importance to learn what German authors are in demand in the Bonn Republic. The classics derided by the Nazis unless (as in the case of Schiller and Heinrich von Kleist) they could be exploited for chauvinistic purposes are in vogue again. Heinrich Heine was verboten while his *Loreley* ("Author Unknown") was still sung, but now several selections from his romantic and satirical poetry and prose have been printed; nobody has as yet attempted to reissue his complete works, most editions of which were destroyed in 1933. Jacob Wassermann, who was one of German's most widely read novelists in pre-Hitler days, still retains his public. Stefan Zweig's highly indirect reaction to Hitlerism, his biography, *The Triumph and Tragedy of Erasmus of Rotterdam*, has only recently been presented to the Germans, seventeen years after its original publication outside Germany. Yet the "old-fashioned" liberalism and humanism of the Wassermanns and Zweigs has no strong appeal to the young Germans of today. Men and women who grew up in the apocalyptic years of 1933-45 cannot listen easily to the voices of reason and equanimity that stem from the halcyonic pre-1914 tradition.

In general, the trend is towards surrealist metaphysics (which has nothing to do with escapism, for the metaphysical realm is hardly a comfortable place to dwell in), or towards its opposite, ruthless realism. As after other great conflagrations (the Thirty Years' War, the Napoleonic Wars, and the First World War), the preference is for metaphysics in a physically unpleasant world. Kafka, who was in vogue in the mid-'20's, and forbidden under Hitler as a Jewish author, is now being reissued. The most recent items have been his *Diaries*, and the Kafka biography by his friend, Max Brod. The German has an inherent knack for *gruebeln*, an almost untranslatable verb that stands for the tendency to ponder endlessly over the mysteries of life. Now he has a fondness for discovered Kafka, the author who coined the phrase, "Writing is a form of prayer," and for whom writing was a way of getting closer to the Truth and to God. At least two current best-sellers are Kafkaesque in nature, Hermann Kasack's *City Beyond the River*, and *Those Who Cannot Be Found* by Ernst Kreuder.

Kasack's novel begins with the death of the hero. After having been transported across the river Lethe, he falls into the clutches of the uncanny Gestapo-like bureaucracy of the City of the Dead where he is mercilessly screened; in this city factories work day and night, some to produce goods, others to destroy them. Eventually the hero returns to life, only after having seen, as in a mirror, all the horror of modern technocracy and bureaucracy. In Kreuder's novel, the hero, hunted by the bloodhounds of the police, flees into an impenetrable forest where he meets a wise fisherman who teaches him that in order to be out of the reach of the "police" one has to live in peace with the powers of nature.

A similar message, but from a Christian viewpoint, is preached in the books of Ernst Wiechert. His novels would have been appreciated by Thoreau, but they have been a failure in twentieth-century America. Written in lyrical prose, they are tales in praise of the contemplative life, with little action and a great deal of metaphysical meditation. Their heroes are foresters, peasants, landowners, pastors, and retired army officers who live in a setting of woods, heaths, and lakes. Once a heathen and a nationalist, Wiechert became a devout Christian and anti-Nazi about the time when the Hitlerites came to power. He made public addresses in which he criticized the Nazi regime until he was shut up, for a while, at the Buchenwald concentration camp. Wiechert lived to see the end of the hated regime, but after the war, disgusted with the Fatherland, moved to Switzerland where he died in August 1950. Curiously, several other German authors, among them the Christian existentialist, Professor Karl Jaspers, have sought a voluntary postwar exile in Switzerland. In commemoration of the first anniversary of Wiechert's death, his publisher released his "inflammatory" speeches, *An die deutsche Jugend*, which were made mainly in Munich. Even in 1935 he had had the audacity to warn Munich university students that a nation which had abandoned the principles of religion and love was doomed to perish.

Just as Wiechert's anti-Nazi addresses were secretly passed from hand to hand in typescript during the '30's, the poems of Reinhold Schneider, advocating such subversive ideas as Christian morality and the brotherhood of man were clandestinely circulated among anti-Nazis. Once, however, the author managed to outwit the Nazi censor by publishing a "historical" novel, *Las Casas vor Karl V*. Las Casas was a 16th century Spanish priest who vainly worked for the abolition of slavery forced upon Latin American Indians by the Conquistadores. The book was a thinly disguised attack on the Nazi persecution of allegedly inferior races. Hardly noticed in this country (where it was published as *Imperial Mission*), it continues to be a bestseller in Germany where the memory of a tyrant far worse than Charles V is still undiminished.

Another Christian metaphysicist was Elisabeth Langgaesser, a poet and novelist who died a year ago. Her best-selling novel, *The Indelible Seal*, is a Catholic confession of faith. The hero is a Jew, who, after having been restless and unhappy all his life, gradually learns that salvation can come to him only through baptism and the abandonment of wealth. While appealing primarily to Catholics, the book has been praised by Protestants as a valid search for solution in a world of uproar and travail.

Included among the authors within the "surrealist" camp are writers who can hardly be called Germans, though they wrote in the German language. Among these are Kafka, the lyrical poet Rainer Maria Rilke, and the Jewish Catholic novelist, Franz Werfel, all of whom were born in Prague, and have been dead for many years. They are now again bestsellers in the Bonn Republic where they appeal to the sensitive and the young. Whenever questionnaires were sent out to German readers in order to learn which authors they preferred, Thomas Mann and Hermann Hesse, both in the "metaphysical" group, would head the lists of favorite writers; yet Mann is now considered by many to be an American author, while the Nobel Prize winner Hesse has been living in Switzerland for such a long time that he is rightly considered a Swiss author.

The opposite camp is that of the "neo-realists" who write in a style reminiscent of Hemingway, or of Norman Mailer. Among them are quite a few young Germans who try to give sincere accounts of the 1933-45 era. Significantly, several of their books have been translated into English, whereas Langgaesser, Kasack, and Kreuder (the "metaphysicists") are still untranslated. In *The Slaveship* Bruno E. Werner tries to cover the whole era from the burning of the Reichstag to the fall of Berlin; his hero, a newspaper editor, is a keen observer who loathes the Nazi regime but lacks courage, and accepts the monsters with resignation. Of particular interest are the books written by men who were in the Wehrmacht. Albert Goes was an army chaplain; in *Unquiet Night* he describes such a chaplain's heroic efforts to pursue his vocation in a war during which atrocities unparalleled in history are committed. Hans W. Richter in *The Vanquished* tells of the last horrible battles in the mountains of Cassino; his hero complains that, when the German soldiers surrender to the Americans, the latter fail to distinguish between Nazis and anti-Nazis, and treat all of the Germans alike in the POW camps. Erhard Kaestner, an ex-member of the Afrika Korps (not related to the famous satirist and author of children's books, Erich Kaestner), in *The Tent Book of Tumilad* proved himself to be capable of deep philosophical insight amidst the turmoil of war. Lighter and less important is Hans Helmut Kirst's *The Lieutenant Must Be Mad*: First Lieutenant Strick fights the Nazis by means of Till Eulenspiegel pranks and, in the last minute, manages to escape to Switzerland. In *Flight in the Winter* by Juergen Thorwald, who was a young German naval officer during the war, truth is stranger than fiction; his book describes factually the Russian invasion of East Prussia toward the end of the war, and the Nazi hierarchy in the days of the *Goetterdaemmerung*. While Thorwald was horrified by what he saw, Erich Kern, a former officer in Hitler's Elite Guards, shows no traces of regret—in *Dance of Death* he merely deplores that the Germans were unable to conquer the hearts of the Russians, and bring freedom and *Kultur* to these primitive people.

One of the greatest losses to postwar German literature was the premature death of Wolfgang Borchardt, another ex-soldier. A sensitive poet, he said "No!" to war, and all the cruelties it implies, and hence was jailed again and again by the Wehrmacht authorities. His drama, *Outside the Door*, which was played in New York on Piscator's Experimental Stage, mirrors the eternal tragedy of the homecoming soldier who is always "outside"; the spokesman of millions of disillusioned ex-Wehrmacht soldiers, he died in 1947, at the age of twenty-six, the day after his drama had its successful premiere at Hamburg. In this group of neo-realist works we might put *The SS State*, by Eugen Kogon, who was a soldier, too—he fought with his pen against the Nazis until they caught up with him. A work of nonfiction, *The SS State* has been selling well for the past five years. An ardent Catholic, Kogon describes in the greatest detail yet attempted, life in the concentration camps. He analyzed these camps as a social and political phenomenon bound to recur unless all Fascist tendencies are eradicated.

Unfortunately, Nazi tendencies are visible again in the book market of the Bonn Republic. In the first years after the war, nobody who was connected with the Nazi regime dared open his mouth. Doctor Schacht, in 1948, was the first to break the silence, attempting, with his memoirs, to do a little whitewashing. Then came *Hier spricht Hans Fritzsche,* published by a Zurich firm which insisted that these excerpts from speeches by the Third Reich's Radio Boss were issued without Fritzsche's knowledge. Next were the memoirs of Weizsaecker, Ribbentrop's Good Man Friday. The most recent publication in this category has the affected Latin title: *Ex Captivitate Salus: Experiences, 1945-1947.* Its author, "Staatsrat" Professor Carl Schmitt, a brilliant jurist, lent his talents to legalize and justify the crimes committed by the Fuehrer. Did "salus" (well-being) come to him through his captivity as a Nazi offender? Judging by the mixture of self-pity and haughtiness in this little book, the answer can only be negative.

More dangerous, because they are confusing, are the concoctions served us by literati who were only part-Nazis. Ernst Juenger's *Radiations* is the diary of a high-minded fascist who, serving in the Wehrmacht in occupied Paris, calmly jots down his witty notes on French culture while only a block away French hostages are shot by the Gestapo. Gottfried Benn, a highly cultured physician and poet, has reissued his autobiography of 1933, with a lengthy postscript purporting to show that what he said in praise of the Third Reich and racialism was written tongue in cheek; his 1949 appendix is not convincing. A much better effort in this direction is the autobiography of his colleague, the physician and poet Hans Carossa, *Dissimilar Worlds.* Though Carossa lacked Wiechert's fortitude, he refused to howl with the wolves as did Dr. Benn.

The apologies by Ernst von Salomon and Hanns Grimm are vicious. Von Salomon who, in 1922, participated in the assassination of Walther Rathenau, the German foreign minister, was not a Nazi insofar as he despised the cruder, plebeian aspects of Hitlerism. His present book, *The Questionnaire,* a current bestseller despite its stiff price and its 800 crowded pages, purports to contain the answers given by a person suspected of former

Nazi activities to all of the 131 questions asked by the Army of Occupation. As in a bad movie, the final outcome is clear from the first page: Von Salomon is innocent, and the only people at fault are the Allies. In *The Archbishop's Letter* Hanns Grimm answers the Archbishop of Canterbury who urged the Germans to atone for their crimes. Grimm who once coined the dangerous nationalistic slogan "Volk ohne Raum" (a nation which, lacking living space, has a moral right to expand its territory) tries in this book to turn the tables: the crimes the Germans are supposed to have committed are insignificant compared to those of the Allies.

At Hugendubel's in Munich there is a constant demand for *The Questionnaire* and *The Archbishop's Letter*. It would be unfair to say, however, that these "literary Remers" dominate the field. Among young Germans there are many, I have been told, who have not the slightest sympathy for a revival of Nazism, literary or otherwise. Throughout Germany, one does not have to walk far to find remnants of concentration camps. The Munich anti-Nazis, in particular, know that there is a Dachau just outside their city.

—*Winter* 1951-52

HEINZ EULAU

Social Science at the Crossroads

Last year's decision of the multimillion dollar Ford Foundation to throw its great financial resources behind the effort "to advance human welfare" through the application of scientific methods and techniques to the study of human behavior was a milestone in the development of modern social science. The decision was the more eventful as, until now, no foundation with means comparable to those of the Ford Foundation has ventured so far as to lay all of its golden eggs into the shapeless basket of social science. One reason for this probably is that the scientific status of social science can be doubted, if not denied altogether, when invidious comparisons are made with the physical and biological sciences. Hence, the Ford Foundation's decision was an act of faith—the faith that, at long last, human behavior too is a proper subject of scientific inquiry, and that social science is ready to contribute to the solution of the manifold problems which vex mankind.

The *Report of the Study for the Ford Foundation on Policy and Program*,[1] prepared by a distinguished committee, is unequivocal in denying the long-held myth that social science can somehow operate in a no-man's land of scholarly disinterestedness, removed from the urgent questions of public policy and social values. It affirms that social science possesses not only theories which promise a more complete understanding of human behavior, but also techniques for their testing. And it candidly criticizes the fact that much of what goes under the name of "social science" has been "polemical, speculative, and pre-scientific." In spelling out criteria for desirable social science research, the Report demands concern with general concepts and their interrelations, refinement and testing of theoretical formulations, superior research design with carefully specified variables, full utilization of concepts, theories and techniques from related disciplines, repetition of studies in order to check the generality of conclusions, and various other research desiderata.

These are exacting expectations, and judged by the multitude of studies in what is called "social science" the Ford Report criteria sound more like a prospectus (which, indeed, was its design) than a description of reality. It is fortunate, therefore, that in the past year at least three major research projects have been published which do not only measure up in varying degree to the Ford Report's high demands, but which also set high standards of achievement for subsequent social science research.

It is especially interesting to note that each of these three research projects was inextricably bound up with a question of public policy. While only one of them can be considered "action-research" proper, however, the other two also originated out of the need for solving urgent social problems. *Culture in Crisis, A Study of the Hopi Indians*[2] reports research which was sponsored by the Office of Indian Affairs for the purpose of discovering, by scientific means, how "the effectiveness of Indian Service long-range policy and program might be increased from the standpoint of improving Indian welfare and developing responsible local autonomy." *The Authoritarian Personality*[3] was made possible by a grant of the American Jewish Committee which was interested in enlisting scientific method in the cause of fighting religious and racial prejudice. The volumes on *The American Soldier*[4] grew out of the work of the Research Branch, Information and Education Division, of the War Department, whose purpose was "to provide the Army command quickly and accurately with facts about the attitudes

---

[1]The Study Committee. Ford Foundation, 1949.
[2]Laura Thompson. Harper, 1950.
[3]T. W. Adorno and others. Harper, 1950.
[4]*Adjustment During Army Life* and *Combat and Aftermath*. Samuel A. Stouffer and others. Princeton, 1949.

of soldiers which, along with other facts and inferences, might be helpful in policy formation."

The action or policy orientation of these studies is important because they contain theoretical and methodological formulations which are richer and more serviceable than much so-called "pure" research. They suggest that the dichotomy which is often made between "pure" and "applied" social science is fallacious. In fact, as Harold D. Lasswell and Abraham Kaplan wisely say in their rich theoretical study, *Power and Society,*[5]

> to rely exclusively on the manipulative approach—thus limiting inquiry to a consideration of ways and means—is to court the danger of interfering with inquiry if it has implications contrary to antecedently fixed policy (ends). The purely contemplative standpoint, on the other hand, fails to maximize the relevance of inquiry to the richest potentialities and most pressing needs of society in the given situation.

Lasswell and Kaplan refer to social scientific inquiry which asks its questions in terms of both "basic" (or contemplative) and "applied" (or manipulative) approaches as "configurative analysis"—a forbidding term, perhaps, but theoretically feasible. And as the Hopi project proves, it is a formulation which finds operational sanction in "action-research."

II

What was the concrete practical problem which occasioned the Hopi inquiry? Beginning in 1929, government policy toward Indians had been changed from one of assimilation to one of fostering Indian cultural autonomy. The initial question asked was, therefore: how did the new policy affect the welfare of the Hopi as individuals and as a cultural group? This practical question had to be translated into a scientific problem. As such it involved "an analysis of the development of Hopi personality in the context of the social system under varying degrees of pressure from the outside world." An experimental design had to be devised which would allow comparison of varying acculturation factors in Hopiland. Otherwise a distorted picture would have emerged. It was necessary to investigate a representative sample of Hopi individuals from a sample of Hopi communities representing differing degrees and kinds of influence from the outside world. And not only scientists, but also members of the communities being studied cooperated in the research. For some operations, such as observation of behavior in school, home and community could be best performed by local residents. When, in the second phase of research, the first findings were interpreted for the use of Indian Service personnel, understanding of the

---

[5]*Power and Society, A Framework for Political Inquiry.* Yale, 1950.

Hopi child on the part of teachers participating in the project was markedly increased.

After two field investigations it became clear that the administrative problems in Hopiland were more complex than first conceived. They revealed a serious and far-reaching crisis which began with the coming of the Spaniards four hundred years ago and the introduction of new values, techniques and means of livelihood. It was aggravated by the conversion efforts of Franciscan missionaries and Navaho encroachments on Hopi lands. Natural erosion, denuding Hopiland of its plant cover during the last century, and contact with Americans added to the stress. The crisis became acute in 1943 when the government insisted on reducing Hopi land-use and livestock, and when about one-third of the tribe moved into the armed forces or war industry. "By 1944," writes Miss Thompson, "the crisis had repercussions in every Hopi community and in nearly every aspect of Hopi life. It has been augmented subsequently by many factors, among them the return, after several years off the reservation, of veterans and defense workers, who have brought new ideas, attitudes, needs, and diseases."

Once more it became necessary to reformulate the practical problem: "What should be the government's long-range policy and program in terms of the Hopi crisis?" Two methodological considerations were introduced in redefining the scientific problem at this point: (1) "the scientist's frame of reference had to be as broad and multidimensional as that in which the administrator operated," i.e., the personality system of the Hopi "had to be placed in full cultural context, in geographic and historical setting, and in acculturation perspective"; and (2) "the biosocial personality needs, trends, and values of the individuals as members of a community in environmental setting and under changing pressures from without and from within" must be the focus of the administrator. In other words, the approach as finally evolved shifted emphasis from economic standards of living to standards of organic life-webs, personality balance, and biopsychological health in the total environment.

As presented in *Culture in Crisis,* the research findings were these: In traditional communities like those of the Hopi we find a balanced and self-regulatory culture structure which is highly integrated with the total environment. New culture elements may be added to culture content, and culture content may change. But under favorable circumstances the ancient culture structure will endure. Culture crisis is created not so much by changes in culture content as by structural disturbances which cause imbalance in one or more essential dimensions of the culture and generate a strain throughout the whole structure. In other words—to be heeded by the administrator, "the Hopi does not resist change at the periphery of his culture—changes such as improved farming methods and new grazing techniques—if he is convinced by actual experience that they may be useful. But he is extremely tenacious of his intangible values and his way of life."

III

Of particular interest from the point of view of an emerging modern social science, however, are less the findings and applications of the Hopi project than its theoretical formulations. Its theory gradually evolved in the course of the empirical research and did not precede it. But its immediate utilization as the research progressed saved the Hopi project scientists from being limited to the kind of *ex post facto* interpretation which still predominates in most social science research. Needless to say, such interpretation, unless it is rigidly controlled by design, is always consistent with the findings because the hypotheses are circular, i.e., they are selected in terms of the findings. Such interpretation is plausible, but it is illustrative rather than tested evidence. Most historical evidence is of this kind.

Lasswell and Kaplan are sensitive to this problem. Their *Power and Society* is the kind of theoretical treatise long needed in political science, a discipline which has been traditionally historical and descriptive. While it does not represent a generalized theoretical system which uses concepts as tools by which data can be collected and specific empirical solutions found, it is a sophisticated attempt to formulate the basic concepts and hypotheses of political science. It consists exclusively of definitions and propositions centering in such key concepts as persons, perspectives, groups, influence, power, symbols, practices, functions, structures, and process. Its presentation does not make for easy reading, but it makes for lucidity and precision. As Lasswell and Kaplan emphasize, their propositions are "regulative hypotheses," intended to serve "the functions of directing the search for significant data, not of predicting what the data will be found to disclose."

Considerations such as these underlie the theoretical formulations of the Hopi project, not accidentally a "field theory" of culture which is proving itself increasingly useful in social science. For it facilitates the simultaneous treatment of interdependent phenomena and of all relevant interacting variables as a dynamic process. In the Hopi project, for instance, this multidimensional "field theory" approach permitted relating the findings of one dimension—such as the ecologic, somatic, sociologic, psychologic and symbolic—to any other and to the culture as a whole. Field theory provides "speculative models" which help to discover and organize not directly observable relationships. But it has nothing in common at all with the "comprehensive, speculative systems prominent in the early history of social science" which the Ford Report justifiably excoriates.

Field theory promises other rewards. It may help to break down the still rigid departmentalization of the various social science disciplines which originally represented an understandable and rational division of labor in regard to *subject-matter*, but which gradually ossified into a sterile specialization in regard to *approach*. Field theory, then, points the way not only to interdisciplinary understanding, but also to the possible theoretical "integration" of social science.

An example of the tendency toward integration is Werner Levi's *Fundamentals of World Organization*.[6] "Peace," writes Levi, "is determined by biological, psychological, political, economic, social, cultural, ideological, metaphysical, military, institutional, technological, and probably many other factors, whose effect is modified by any number of combinations between them and their position in time and space." It follows that the assumption which logically underlies most peace plans, i.e., that the prerequisites for the preservation of peace are known, is of doubtful validity. Most of these plans seek to account for the multiplicity of phenomena involved in the problem of war and peace in terms of a single factor. But from the field-theoretical point of view, peaceful society can only be "the continuum of uneasy equilibria between many different forces which must be constantly adjusted by adequate institutions."

Applied in international relations, therefore, field theory makes for humility rather than grandiosity. The problem of peace is not one of "establishing an immutable international order" such as most peace plans envisage. Knowledge of the factors making for war or peace is so inadequate that explanation can only be general and unsatisfactory. However, Levi does not believe that because of the inadequacy of our knowledge any endeavor to preserve peace should be abandoned. Even though not even a significant fraction of the multitude of possibly relevant factors can be brought under control, Levi emphasizes that "a few so controlled could make a crucial difference." All of which makes good scientific sense.

IV

The trend toward integration is furthered by the need for team work which results from the multidimensional complexity of modern social problems. No one social scientist possesses all the knowledge, skills and experience necessary. In the Hopi project, for instance, anthropologists, psychiatrists, psychologists, political scientists, linguists and ecologists—at one time or another over fifty—collaborated in the field, in the analysis of data, in formulating the findings, or as advisers. Working as a team, they developed the project's methodology experimentally as the research went on.

Similarly, the theory of *The Authoritarian Personality*, involving the

---

[6]University of Minnesota, 1950.

cross-fertilization of different social sciences and psychology, is the product of close co-operation of a team of experts—in the fields of social theory and depth psychology, content analysis, clinical psychology, political sociology and projective testing—who "pooled their experience and findings." The finished work represents "the mobilization of different methods and skills, developed in distinct fields of theory and empirical investigation, for one common research program." Of course, both the Hopi and the authoritarian personality studies relied on earlier theories such as those of Sapir, Mead, Benedict or Kardiner in the former, and of Freud, Samuel or Fenichel in the latter. Indeed, the uses of these earlier formulations are probably indispensable prerequisites for the methodological integration and organization of any large-scale research project.

Again, the 135-odd social scientists who participated in the American soldier project, in spite of the project's theoretical diffidence, operated from theoretical bases which represented "several streams of influence which are converging to develop social psychology and sociology into sciences with conceptual schemes," and from which "empirically verifiable inferences and predictions can eventually be made." As in John Dollard's and Neal E. Miller's *Personality and Psychotherapy*,[7] where these streams of influence have been integrated into a consistent whole, the American soldier project acknowledges the contributions of dynamic psychology, including what proved useful in Freud; modern learning theory; anthropological and sociological theories relating to human behavior; and theories of social control and social change. However, no attempt was made to organize the various studies around "any single conceptual scheme." An open mind was held to be desirable with respect to the potential utility of various conceptual models. However, aware of the need for maximizing the project's utility in the future, "a compromise position with respect to introduction of explicit conceptualization" was adopted; "on the one hand, these reports are not conventional chapters in history. On the other hand, while theory is used both explicitly and implicitly, the data have not been selected merely because of their relevance to some general proposition now current in the psychological or sociological literature."

This position is perfectly understandable, but it really refers to those "conceptual models" needed to verify the validity of techniques, and not to the kind of theory or scientific methodology which must precede empirical investigation. For, sooner or later, conceptual models must be internally consistent enough to fit into some generalized scientific theory which transcends them precisely because it uses concepts as tools rather than as verified generalizations. If the strength of the American soldier studies lies in their

---

[7] McGraw-Hill, 1950.

contribution to cumulative social science technique, then, indeed, they cannot be assessed in terms of incisive theoretical formulation. But as to the former, their contribution is surely magnificent.

V

Above all, however, the American soldier studies contain a mine of data, "perhaps unparalleled in magnitude in the history of any single research enterprise in social psychology or sociology." They are descriptive reports of soldiers' attitudes and adjustment problems, determined by responses to questionnaires. Variations in response are analyzed in terms of both variations in army experience and variations in personal background. *The American Soldier: Adjustment During Army Life* includes a case study of an infantry division which throws light on the problem of the army as an institution, and studies of variations in personal adjustment proper which serve as background for such selected problems as social mobility, job assignment and job satisfaction, attitudes toward leadership and social control, orientation of soldiers toward war and Negro soldiers. *Combat and Aftermath* is chiefly devoted to studies in motivation and attitudes of combat troops, and the aftermath of combat, including neuropsychiatric manifestations, problems of returnees from overseas, initial problems of occupation in Germany (the failure of the nonfraternization policy was predicted), and attitudes toward the civilian future. Such important army policies as the point system for demobilization or the GI Bill of Rights were based on data produced by these studies.

Experiments on Mass Communication[8] contains a number of studies measuring the effectiveness of efforts to impart information and alter opinions and motivations through the use of such mass media as film and radio. Such questions as the differential effects of films on different types of soldiers, or the impact of specific elements of film content are analyzed. Other experiments compare the effectiveness of films and speeches. Radio communications were used to explore the conditions under which the stating and refutation of opposing arguments is more effective than mere affirmation of one's own position. *Measurement and Prediction*[9] combines a series of methodological and technical studies which will be of particular interest to social scientists for a long time to come. It is, by all odds, the most useful volume in the American soldier series, probably unequalled as a reference book in the technical literature of social science.

The great variety of new techniques used in the American soldier, Hopi and authoritarian personality projects is staggering if compared with the tools at the disposal of social scientists even ten years ago. Listing some of

---

[8]Carl S. Hovland and others. Princeton, 1949.
[9]Samuel A. Stouffer and others. Princeton, 1950.

the techniques must suffice here. Scalogram analysis, latent structure analysis and the neuropsychiatric screening adjunct, as well as reliability and prediction tests are described in *Measurement and Prediction*. The Hopi project relied on Rorschach Psychodiagnostic and Thematic Apperception tests, the Arthur Point Performance Scale, the Bavelas Moral Ideology Index and other scales and indices, as well as community interviewing and real-life observation techniques. *The Authoritarian Personality* reports both questionnaire and clinical techniques, including opinion-attitude scales, projective questions, interviews, and TAT.

VI

But *The Authoritarian Personality* is particularly successful in subtly and skillfully combining theory and technique. Nor does the research suffer from the investigators' concern with theory. Actually, empirical presentation predominates in most chapters of the book. But it was theory which made possible the conceptualizing and coding of clinical materials in such a way as to permit statistical treatment and facilitate their correlation with scale data derived from questionnaires. For all scale items, interview questions, projective tests and content analysis codes were structured in accordance with hypotheses concerning the antidemocratic personality.

There are some assumptions about what is "democratic" and "antidemocratic" held by the authors that seem occasionally naïve, or perhaps dogmatic. Is opposition to intermarriage *ipso facto* a symptom of prejudice, and is old-fashioned, purely spiritual religion simply "reactionary"? But these are exceptions which, statistically speaking, are "absorbed" by the cumulative effect of the elaborate quantitative methods used to validate every step in the process of research. In some respects, the explicit statement of value premises, even if they are in part deficient, may be preferable to research which claims to be completely value-free. For it brings to light unsound assumptions. As so empirically-minded a social scientist as Hadley Cantril has pointed out in a little book called *The "Why" of Man's Experience*,[10] "scientific research itself has demonstrated that the scientist's own value judgments are involved in scientific inquiry from beginning to end," including the analysis of the problem, the selection of variables, and the experimental design. Cantril concludes, therefore, that objectivity can refer "only to the use of accepted rules of empirical research *after* the problem, the variables, and the experimental design have been decided upon."

It is impossible here to summarize the multitude of theoretical assumptions, conceptual formulations and empirical findings of *The Authoritarian Personality*. Assertions are constantly qualified, modified and interpreted.

---

[10]Macmillan, 1950.

In general, the study is concerned with that coherent pattern of personality characteristics which makes for ethnic prejudice and susceptibility to fascist propaganda. Two main personality types, with numerous sub-types, are believed to emerge from the empirical findings. On the one hand, "a basically hierarchical, authoritarian, exploitative parent-child relationship is apt to carry over into a power-oriented, exploitatively dependent attitude toward one's sex partner and one's God and may well culminate in a political philosophy and social outlook which has no room for anything but a desperate clinging to what appears to be strong. . . . On the other hand, there is a pattern characterized chiefly by affectionate, basically equalitarian and permissive interpersonal relationships. This pattern encompasses attitudes within the family and toward the opposite sex, as well as an internalization of religious and social values. Greater flexibility and the potentiality for more genuine satisfactions appear as results of this basic attitude."

It must be remembered that these apparently dichotomous and absolute types are not "real," but that they emerge from statistical analysis, i.e., that they are syndromes of correlating and dynamically related factors. Among sub-types the "conventionally prejudiced" and the "psychopathically prejudiced" are important. However, on the basis of statistical results, it was found that prejudiced subjects "are on the whole more alike as a group than are the unprejudiced." Among the latter, no more extreme common variants may exist than the absence of a particular brand of hostility. It would be foolish, therefore, to generalize from the relationships among personality factors discovered about the total population. Yet such generalizations are frequently made.

VII

Studies of the "American character," so fashionable in the last decade, are cases in point. David Riesman's *The Lonely Crowd*[11] is more brilliant, imaginative and exasperating than its predecessors, but like them, in spite of many self-conscious *caveats,* it is not social science. It is a book of persuasive charm which is only made the more deceptive by its apparently scientific paraphernalia.

Riesman constructs three "ideal" character types—not from a cross-sectional study of the population today, but from historical analysis. These types—tradition-, inner-, and other-directed—serve him as models in studying the changing character of the American people. There is nothing objectionable in such "model construction" as such. But as he proceeds, the gnawing feeling arises and persists that Riesman is gradually forgetting his

---

[11]*The Lonely Crowd, A Study of the Changing American Character.* Yale, 1950.

own *caveats*, and that he more and more generalizes on the basis of gross similarities and differences, i.e., that his work resembles more the grandiose three-cornered speculative systems of a Comte or Marx than the patient and tentative formulations of modern social science.

This feeling is accentuated by Riesman's failure, in the book's main part, to follow through on his central hypothesis, namely, that changes in population and technology everywhere are the chief correlates of changes in social character. Could it be that the hypothesis is too far-fetched to permit empirical verification? Why, indeed, is the birth rate selected as a significant correlate of character change? All Riesman says about this is that "it would be very surprising" if variations in the basic conditions of population growth or decline "failed to influence character." It could probably just as well be argued that changing belief-systems or codes of value "influence" sex behavior in different cultures.

According to Riesman's hypothesis, in a "tradition-directed" society the culture controls individual behavior minutely and enforces conformity through careful and rigid etiquette in a tightly-knit social structure. This society is one of "high growth potential." Its population would increase rapidly if the death rate were suddenly lowered. A society where this decrease of the death rate is an actuality is in the stage of "transitional growth." The corresponding "inner-directed" character has its values "implanted early in life by the elders and directed toward generalized but nonetheless inescapably destined goals." Conformity is assured through strong internalization of values which permits individual choice, but within rigid limits that remain relatively unalterable throughout life.

Finally, in the stage of "incipient population decline" the "other-directed" character type emerges. It is above all motivated by a need for approval, sensitized to the expectations and preferences of others. The other-directed person avoids any overt expression of unfriendly attitudes, but anxieties engendered by this behavior make him responsive to a great variety of signals. This hypothesis is supported by a wealth of observations —some empirical, many others intuitive—from wide areas of American culture. For it is this type toward which Riesman sees the American people moving.

If Riesman had simply combined his empirical data with his brilliant insights without bothering about all the irrelevant scientific baggage he carries along, his book would be one of the keenest and most shocking critiques of American culture in the twentieth century. But its scientific presumptions deprive it of a great deal of its potential moral power. This is the more deplorable because social science needs the kind of critical assessment of values explicit in Riesman's essay. As it stands, the Mumbo

Jumbo of *The Lonely Crowd* only confuses the vital issue of the relationship between values and science which stymies social scientists.

VIII

Howard Becker discusses this issue in some of the essays entitled
Through Values to Social Interpretation.[12] He assumes that scientific theories
are "relevant to value," but this "does *not* mean domination by value-
judgment." Hence, Becker argues, the social scientist "is under no compulsion to become a mere technologist who prostitutes the powers of science
to political systems which kill at the source all scientific endeavor that conflicts with the ends of those systems." Yet, such advice is easier given than
practiced. If "values and value systems are indispensable tools of the sociologist," who watches the watchmen? "The only check upon our own exercise
of power," Justice Stone once said, "is our own sense of self-restraint." Can
social scientists be trusted to show such self-restraint? If self-restraint is the
only check on their scientific integrity, is their whole business not a matter
of faith?

Crane Brinton, on surveying the history of Western thought from the
Greeks down to Professor Northrop in *Ideas and Men*,[13] is not sanguine.
He describes by the term "anti-intellectualism" the attempt of modern social
science "to arrive rationally at a just appreciation of the actual roles of
rationality and of nonrationality in human affairs." It is unfortunate (and
it takes historical audacity) that Brinton lumps together under the anti-
intellectual label such diverse thinkers as Dewey, Bergson, Freud, Pavlov,
Pareto, Korzybski, and others. But he creates enough of a doubt to make
one question the value assumptions of social science.

According to Brinton, most anti-intellectuals generally accept the values
of order, happiness, freedom, and so on. But they hold that these goals are
only very slowly attainable through a social science based on cumulative
knowledge and the hope that it will be used to promote the good rather
than the bad. But while they may be in complete agreement on what is
good, they "differ more in their hopes." Pareto, at the time of his death
in 1923, had given up his earlier high expectations. But, continues Brinton
with subtle irony, "contemporary American social scientists influenced by
anti-intellectualism (though they might not like the label of anti-intellectual), among them Clyde Kluckhohn of Harvard and Alexander Leighton
of Cornell, are likely, in the good American tradition, to believe that on
the whole the new knowledge will be put to good ends—that social science

---

[12]Duke, 1950.
[13]*Ideas and Men, The Story of Western Thought*. Prentice-Hall, 1950.

will be used to promote the good working, the health, of society, just as medical science has been used to promote the health of the body."

That Crane Brinton's skepticism is not altogether unwarranted may be substantiated by Karl Mannheim's posthumous *Freedom, Power, and Democratic Planning.*[14] A Brintonian "anti-intellectual" though not mentioned by Brinton, his famous *Ideology and Utopia* had debunked ideas as mental fictions or wish-dreams, depending on whether their holders were in or out of power. But under the impact of Europe's revolutionary crises this German social scientist gradually moved from description to prescription, from analysis of the social role of religion as an ideology to its role as a remedy. Mannheim spent the last years of his life in England where he was deeply impressed by the tolerant pluralism of democracy, but where he was also greatly influenced by a group of Christian thinkers, including T. S. Eliot and J. Middleton Murry.

There is little in this book not to be found in his earlier *Man and Society in an Age of Reconstruction.* The apparent paradoxes of democratic planning, says Mannheim—control *and* freedom, unity *and* disagreement, centralization *and* decentralization—can be overcome by developing personality types which have fully internalized these values, contradictory as they now may appear. In other words, democratic planning can be successful only if we plan for the kind of human beings necessary to make the plan work. It is in creating this democratic type that religion has a role to play. But just here Mannheim's manuscript came to an end because of his death.

Religion as therapy? Social science as therapy? The grim surgeries performed by "scientific socialism" in the Soviet Union should warn against the dangers of an all too therapy-minded social science—even if the values involved are essentially "good." If Mannheim had had the opportunity to read *The Authoritarian Personality,* he might have been more cautious. If the origin of anti-democratic personality traits is in early learning experiences, how can these experiences be controlled? And by whom? Though not altogether pessimistic, the authors of *The Authoritarian Personality* are not optimistic either. Because anti-democratic personalities are typically submissive to authority, a vigorous stand against prejudice and discrimination might at least diminish overt aggressive behavior. Of course, such restraints are concerned with the treatment of symptoms rather than with a cure of the disease itself.

Clearly, social science is at the crossroads. On the one hand, great strides have been made in recent years toward a general science of human behavior. But whatever success it may have had or may have in terms of

---

[14]Oxford, 1950.

"action" or therapy, it must be remembered that, on the other hand, social science deals in probabilities and not in certainties. Only enthusiastic popularizers—who play an important role in our science-minded culture, but for this very reason must be guarded against—tend to exaggerate the modern accomplishments. The social scientists themselves, though they may be justly proud of their achievements, must be more modest and humble. Perhaps it is best to assume that social science in its present phase is where physical science was three hundred years ago. Such an assumption makes for sobriety and perspective.   —*Spring* 1951

ABOUT THE AUTHORS

C. E. AYRES has become known as an "institutionalist" and a "classical Veblenian." He is Professor of Economics at the University of Texas.

FRANCIS BARRY has published poems in a number of little magazines. He lives in Philadelphia.

DANIEL BELL was formerly managing editor of the *New Leader* and of *Common Sense*. He is now Labor Editor of *Fortune* and a lecturer in Sociology at Columbia University.

HERBERT S. BENJAMIN has been living on the Continent, and is now studying for a medical degree in Vienna.

PAUL BIXLER is the Chairman of the Editorial Board of *The Antioch Review*. The librarian of Antioch College, he is now secretary of the Intellectual Freedom Committee of the American Library Association.

ALBERT A. BLUM is working in the Office of the Chief of Military History. Previously he taught labor relations and American History at Long Island University.

VALDEMAR CARLSON is Professor of Economics at Antioch College and was a member of the Editorial Board of *The Antioch Review*, 1943-50.

FREEMAN CHAMPNEY has been a member of the Editorial Board of *The Antioch Review* since its founding and is Manager of the Antioch Press.

LEWIS COREY was a member of the Editorial Board of *The Antioch Review*, 1943-48. He is the author of a number of works on Marxist and economic theory.

JIM CORK, a free-lance writer and old-time Marxist, has been making journalistic studies in Asia and Europe for the past two years.

RALPH ELLISON is the author of *The Invisible Man*, for which he received the National Book Award for the novel for 1952.

HEINZ EULAU is a member of the Editorial Board of *The Antioch Review* and Associate Professor of Government at Antioch College.

JAMES T. FARRELL, author of many novels, including the Danny O'Neill and Studs Lonigan series, has dominated the field of naturalism in American fiction since some time before the death of Theodore Dreiser.

GEORGE FISCHER was the first director of the East European Fund, established to assist former Soviet citizens in the United States. He is now

Lecturer in History at Brandeis University, and is the author of *Soviet Opposition to Stalin: A Case Study in World War II.*

Louis Filler is Book Review Editor of *The Antioch Review* and Associate Professor of American Civilization at Antioch College.

Morton Fineman's long-time avocation has been the writing of high-quality short fiction. He has published in *Harper's Bazaar, Story, Accent, Tomorrow* and other magazines.

George Geiger has been a member of the Editorial Board of *The Antioch Review* since its founding and is Professor of Philosophy at Antioch College.

Paul M. Gregory is Professor of Economics at the University of Alabama. He has published widely in such diverse fields as economic theory, mortgage finance, women's fashions and baseball.

Howard Griffin's poetry has appeared frequently in the little reviews, and he is the author of a volume of poems entitled *Cry Cadence.*

Ruth McCoy Harris is native to the piney woods country of Mississippi. She has published occasional magazine articles and short fiction, and has done editorial work for a number of book publishers in New York.

Will Herberg is well known for his work in two widely different fields— labor research and theology. He is director of research for an AFL union in New York City.

Daniel G. Hoffman has published poetry and the book *Paul Bunyan, Last of the Frontier Demigods.* He teaches American Literature at Columbia University.

Sidney Hook is perhaps best known for his analysis of education and of certain aspects of Marxist thought. He is Professor of Philosophy at New York University.

John T. Howard is a member of a firm of city planning consultants in Boston, and has served as advisor in urban redevelopment in the East and Midwest. He is Associate Professor of City Planning at the Massachusetts Institute of Technology.

Stanley Edgar Hyman is the author of a work of literary criticism, *The Armed Vision.* He is a staff writer for the *New Yorker* and describes himself as a "kind of maverick folklorist and critic."

David Ignatow is an editor of the *Beloit Poetry Journal* and the author of *Poems.*

ALFRED KREYMBORG has published a number of books, of which the most recent is *No More War and Other Poems*.

BEN W. LEWIS has worked with twelve different agencies of the federal government and he has served two terms on the Oberlin City Council. He is Professor of Economics at Oberlin College.

JOHN P. LEWIS has alternated between government work and university teaching, and is now about to shift again, from the staff of the Council of Economic Advisers to the President where he has served since 1950, to teaching at the School of Business, Indiana University.

WALTER LOCKE has been for many years editor of *The Dayton Daily News*. He knew George Norris first as a reporter and then as associate editor on the *Nebraska State Journal*.

WILLARD N. MARSH has been an Air Force radio operator, dance band musician, millworker, waiter, gagwriter. Now living in Mexico, he has published poetry and short fiction in a number of the little reviews.

KEITH MCGARY is Assistant Professor of Philosophy at the University of Wisconsin, and this year is visiting Associate Professor at Antioch College.

ROBERT K. MERTON has been author and editor of a number of books in the field of sociology. He is Associate Director of the Bureau of Applied Social Research and Chairman of the Graduate Department of Sociology at Columbia University.

PHILIP MURRAY has published poetry in a wide variety of magazines. He lives in Philadelphia.

M. C. OTTO is Professor Emeritus of Philosophy at the University of Wisconsin, and is now engaged in writing a book which may be thought of as a deepening and enriching development of material in the present essay.

DAVID RIESMAN is the author of the provocative *The Lonely Crowd* and a number of other books, the most recent of which deals with Thorstein Veblen. He is a member of the Committee on Human Development at the University of Chicago.

JOHN P. ROCHE's long-time interests lie in the nature and development of democratic institutions and in the dynamics of protest. He is Assistant Professor of Government at Haverford College.

ABRAHAM ROTHBERG has been college teacher and editor, and is at present editor of a political magazine for which he also writes monthly feature articles.

DAVID SPITZ is Associate Professor of Political Science at Ohio State University and the author of *Patterns of Anti-Democratic Thought.*

HENRY STEINER lived and worked as a civil engineer in Korea before the war there broke out. He now lives in California.

HOWARD TROYER completed the work of which these tales are a part as a Newberry Fellow in Midwestern Studies, 1947-49. He is Professor of English Literature at Carleton College.

PETER VIERECK is a poet and Professor of History at Mount Holyoke College. He is the author of a number of books including *Terror and Decorum* and the recent *Shame and Glory of the Intellectuals.*

ALFRED WERNER is a literary critic and a student of the fine arts in the European tradition. He was born in Vienna, and traveled widely in Germany before and after World War II.

BERTRAM D. WOLFE has written widely on Russian history, culture and sociology. He is probably best known for his *Three Who Made a Revolution,* a biographical history of the Russian Revolution.

SAMUEL YELLEN is a frequent contributor of poetry and short fiction to the "quality" magazines. He is Associate Professor of English at Indiana University.